5⊀ 5⁵

10⁰⁰

THE ARMED FORCES
OF THE USSR

THIRD EDITION, REVISED AND UPDATED

THE ARMED FORCES OF THE USSR

Harriet Fast Scott
William F. Scott

Westview Press • Boulder

Arms and Armour Press • London

Copyright © 1979, 1981, 1984 by Harriet Fast Scott and William F. Scott

Published in 1984 in the United States of America by Westview Press, Inc., 5500 Central Avenue, Boulder, Colorado 80301; Frederick A. Praeger, Publisher

Published in 1984 in Great Britain by Arms and Armour Press, 2-6 Hampstead High Street, London NW3 1QQ, at 11 Munro Street, Port Melbourne, Victoria 3207, Australia, and at Sanso Centre, 8 Adderley Street, P.O. Box 94, Cape Town 8000, South Africa

Library of Congress Cataloging in Publication Data
Scott, Harriet Fast.
  The armed forces of the USSR.
  Bibliography: p.
  Includes indexes.
  1. Soviet Union—Armed forces. 2. Soviet Union—
Military policy. I. Scott, William Fontaine, 1919–
II. Title. III. Title: Armed forces of the U.S.S.R.
UA770.S35 1984   355′.00947   84-15183
ISBN 0-86531-790-9
ISBN 0-86531-792-5 (pbk.)

British Library Cataloguing in Publication Data
Scott, Harriet Fast
The armed forces of the USSR —3rd ed.
1. Soviet Union—Armed Forces—History
I. Title II. Scott, William F.
355′.00947   UA770
ISBN 0-85368-680-7

Printed and bound in the United States of America

10 9 8 7 6 5 4 3 2

Contents

Tables

Illustrations

Preface

The purpose of this book is to contribute to a better understanding of the Soviet Armed Forces as a whole and of its relationships with the Soviet population, the economy, and the Communist Party. We believe that these relationships have a major bearing on Soviet attitudes toward arms control measures and the use of military force in achieving policy objectives. If we are to negotiate successfully with the Soviets, it is essential that we appreciate their underlying political-military concepts as well as their military force structure.

Since 1979, when the first edition of this book was published, the top Party leadership in the Soviet Union has changed significantly. There have also been a number of major changes in the organization of the Soviet Armed Forces and in its commanders. New writings have appeared on military doctrine and strategy. Both the changes that have taken place in Soviet military affairs, and their continuity, need to be understood by those in non-Communist nations concerned with international security issues.

There is an asymmetry between Soviet knowledge of the military forces of Western nations and Western knowledge about Soviet military forces. Books and pamphlets about the armed forces of probable and potential opponents of the Soviet Union can be found in bookstores throughout the USSR—even in bookstalls in some of the larger railroad stations. These publications, some of which would be classified in the United States, describe in detail the organization and training of NATO forces and their most up-to-date weaponry. The availability of the literature is a deliberate policy; the Soviet Party-military leadership stresses the need to study the "organization, weaponry, political-moral state, military doctrine, and strategy of capitalist states."

In the late 1970s and 1980s a considerable number of articles and books have been published in the West about Soviet weaponry and equipment, in addition to articles about individual segments of the Soviet Armed Forces and certain aspects of its military doctrine and strategy. It would be difficult for anyone interested in the Soviet Armed

Forces, however, to have access to all of the journals in which the articles appear.

For those in the West who do write on Soviet military affairs, accurate information is difficult to find. Certain government agencies appear superbly equipped to use mechanical means to obtain data for determining order of battle information about a possible opponent, especially with respect to the numbers and types of large weapons systems such as submarines and fixed intercontinental ballistic missiles. However, information on Soviet doctrine, strategy, interrelationships within the military power structure, mobilization potential, and the like can be obtained only through long and laborious research. Furthermore, information of this type often cannot even be compared with data about NATO nations, for example, since the military philosophies and force structures of the Soviet Union differ so widely from those of other nations. Too often the data may not be recognized as being important, given the lack of comparable data in the West. In the Soviet Union the military policy of the Communist Party is, by definition, accepted by the state and the Armed Forces as military doctrine. Since NATO nations do not have a military doctrine in the Soviet sense of the term, the very existence of Soviet doctrine is often neither recognized nor understood outside of the Soviet Union.

Even when the need for understanding the Soviet Armed Forces is recognized, the analyst faces the problem of Soviet secrecy. According to Soviet law, "information on the organization of the Armed Forces, their number, location, combat capability, armaments, equipment, combat training and the moral-political state of troops, their material and financial support is a military secret." This even applies to Soviet negotiators at SALT, who are not permitted to do otherwise than follow Soviet law, as stated, concerning military secrets.

Despite this secrecy, the Soviet Party-military leadership must to some degree openly communicate about military matters with the approximately five million men in the Soviet Armed Forces, the millions of youths engaged in premilitary training, the millions of men in the reserves, and the Soviet population as a whole. Everything that is published has meaning, in some way or other. The Soviet military press is under the control of the Main Political Administration of the Soviet Army and Navy, an organ of the Central Committee of the Communist Party. Personal, unofficial, or conflicting views on basic military issues simply are not permitted in the tightly controlled and censored Soviet press, military or otherwise, unless there is a reason.

In researching Soviet material, analysts frequently face problems resulting from poor research or carelessness on the part of Soviet authors. One author may present one set of data or facts, while another writer gives different information. If these mistakes are on relatively unimportant issues—whether Gagarin, the first man in space, was a Navy or an Air Force pilot, for instance—a logical assumption is that the Soviet authors themselves either did not have access to all sources or simply were incompetent.

There is also the problem of reconciling different Soviet points of view expressed at different times. During the early 1960s, Soviet writers blamed Stalin for many of the reverses suffered by Soviet forces during the early days of World War II. By the late 1960s Stalin generally was presented as a very competent military leader. These variances result, understandably, from the absolute necessity for Soviet authors to follow the zigs and zags of Party policies.

Readers of this book are likely to observe gaps in the information presented. For example, information about the organization and structure of the Strategic Rocket Forces is very thin; such information simply is not given in the Soviet press. On the other hand, there are a number of chapters on other areas for which there is sufficient material not included here to warrant further development in another book.

Some readers may object to our literal translations of Soviet material. Our objective has been clarity. An example of the translation problem is the Russian word *doktrina,* literally "doctrine," which some Western analysts of Soviet writings translate "grand strategy," asserting that this is the closest in meaning to the Soviet concept of "doctrine." We believe this approach to be incorrect. The Soviet meaning of "doctrine" must be understood if the Armed Forces are to be comprehended, as further discussed in Chapter 2.

Some readers may also have some difficulty in understanding Soviet general officer ranks. A general major in the Soviet services has one star; a general lieutenant two stars; and a general colonel three stars. The Soviet word order has been maintained so that the reader will not confuse two-star major generals in the United States armed forces with the one-star general majors in the Soviet Armed Forces. (More detailed information on Soviet ranks is given in Appendix B.)

Between 350 and 500 books on military matters are published annually in the Soviet Union. These range from memoirs of World War II to textbooks for use in military schools. In addition, 11 military journals as well as military newspapers, such as *Red Star* and *Soviet Patriot,* contain items of military interest on a timely basis. There is no shortage of Soviet research material; the problem is to extract meaningful data.

Research and analysis of the Soviet Armed Forces should be a continuing undertaking. No analyst can ever be confident that all the facts are available or that what has been found is current. Nevertheless, a time comes when research must cease and data be presented as they appear at that moment.

Readers may properly be concerned whether Soviet military writings available to any Westerner might not be prepared deliberately to deceive. Some Soviet publications are printed primarily for foreign readers, and these certainly should be viewed with caution. Among these are the *Soviet Military Review*, which is published in English, Arabic, French, and now in Russian. However, the very volume of Soviet documents that are available for research—stenographic notes of Party congresses, textbooks for military schools, instruction for premilitary training—provides convincing evidence that they are written for Soviet readers and not designed to deceive Western ones. On the other hand, the Soviet public is deliberately misinformed about many things, such as the size of the defense budget. We have attempted to take such matters into account.

We have presented few data on Soviet weapons systems. A number of publications, such as *Air Force Magazine,* provide information each year about numbers and types of Soviet weaponry. Having seen a number of military parades in Moscow, we appreciate the importance of Soviet weapons and equipment, but to have included them in our study would have complicated needlessly an already complex subject.

We deeply appreciate the assistance provided by the Earhart Foundation, which made this book possible, and we are grateful to Dr. Mose Harvey of the Center for Advanced International Studies, University of Miami, who gave both ideas and encouragement for the task. *Air Force Magazine* has kindly given permission to include charts that previously were included in its special Soviet Aerospace issue. The study has benefited from the critical analysis of those who have read the manuscript, and we are most grateful for the comments of Arthur D. Sorzano, Leon Goure, John J. Dziak, Julius H. Taylor, and William R. Beuch. We are indebted to the lecturers and staff of the Historical and Research Organization (HERO), Trevor N. Dupuy, John A. C. Andrews, Gordon S. Brown, Billie Davis, Grace Hayes, Paul Martell, and John Sloan, for their encouragements and valuable critiques of the various chapters, some of which originated as HERO lectures.

Harriet Fast Scott
William F. Scott

THE ARMED FORCES
OF THE USSR

1
Prologue: The Red Army

In September 1971, illness forced Marshal of the Soviet Union M. V. Zakharov to relinquish his position as chief of the Soviet General Staff. His retirement marked the end of an era; he had been one of that small group of Bolsheviks who, on 7 November 1917 (25 October 1917 by the old calendar), stormed the Winter Palace in Petrograd at the climax of the Russian Revolution. In contrast, N. V. Ogarkov, chief of the General Staff since 1977, was born in October 1917. Ogarkov and other senior officers of the Soviet Armed Forces were trained, indoctrinated, and promoted under the tutelage of officers who were products of the Russian Revolution and who lived under the brief rule of V. I. Lenin and the long regime of Joseph V. Stalin. These Soviet leaders inherited a military organization that by the 1970s had achieved approximate military parity with the United States, the other superpower in the world. The Soviet Armed Forces reached this position of power in approximately fifty years, a period so short that it scarcely spanned the military career of Marshal Zakharov.

The Red Army, as the predecessor of today's Soviet Armed Forces was called, had a turbulent history.

Prelude to Revolution: 1905–1917

The first Communist armed forces organization began with the 1905–1917 revolution, when the Bolsheviks began to attract a following. In December 1905, 8,000 armed workers, called Druzhiniks, led an uprising in Moscow. Dozens of other detachments fought police elsewhere throughout the country. Although this revolution failed, its organizers gained valuable military experience.[1] While the revolution was in progress, the Bolsheviks succeeded in creating illegal organizations in army units and on naval ships, which continued to function in secret after the uprising was put down.

After the February 1917 "bourgeois" revolution, the Bolsheviks began a takeover process by creating volunteer armed detachments at factories

1

and in Party committees throughout the country. By fall of that year, almost every city had detachments of Red Guards, as the armed workers were called. Central staffs of Red Guards, which formulated rules and regulations, were set up in Petrograd, the capital city, and in Moscow.[2]

Red Guards were formed on a territorial factory principle. Primary organizational units—tens—were combined into platoons, platoons into companies or Druzhins, and companies into battalions, which numbered up to six hundred men. As these detachments spread, the Red Guards began military training. In Petrograd, a school was opened to give elementary instruction in military tactics.

At the same time, Bolsheviks in the armed forces worked at winning over soldiers and sailors to their cause. In June 1917, a conference was held to organize dissatisfied soldiers and sailors under Bolshevik military control. By October, there were 20,000 Red Guards, 60,000 Baltic sailors, and 150,000 soldiers of the Petrograd garrison on the Bolshevik side. On 6 November 1917 (26 October 1917, by the Julian calendar, then standard in Russia), the Petrograd Military Revolutionary committee gave the order for an armed uprising in Petrograd. Victory came the next day, culminating in the storming of the Winter Palace. The members of the provisional government were arrested, and the revolution was over.[3] Now civil war was to begin.

Consolidation of Military Power: October 1917–May 1918

The immediate task of the Bolsheviks was to hold on to the power they had grabbed. On 8 November, a Committee on Military and Naval Affairs was formed, made up of members of the Petrograd Military Revolutionary Committee. This committee was given the task of defending Petrograd and directing the Red Guard detachments, which were the cores of the Communist armed forces.[4]

Military units of the former provisional government resisted the Bolshevik takeover in many areas. On 22 November 1917, the commander in chief of the Russian forces, N. N. Dukhonin, was removed from his post after refusing to enter into negotiations with the Germans about a peace agreement. Lenin then ordered all soldiers and sailors to disobey the orders of the Russian Army's General Headquarters, known as Stavka.

During the last months of 1917, thousands of officers were removed from the Russian Army and Navy as the Red Guards and revolutionary soldiers and sailors took control. Subsequently, Lenin ordered his Red Guards, which at the beginning of January 1918 numbered about 150,000 men, to seize Stavka and arrest Dukhonin. By the end of January 1918, Stavka had ceased to exist. Those army units that had not been taken over by the Red Guards were immobilized by the abolition of leaders and the absence of discipline, with the soldiers "voting" on selection of officers and on what orders to follow.[5]

Meetings were held to give direction for the demobilization of the old armies. At the same time, the former War Ministry was undergoing a complete reorganization under Bolshevik guidance. The new leaders realized that certain elements of the old structure had to be preserved, at least temporarily, to provide the beginnings of the new socialist army. While there was great enthusiasm in this Bolshevik military force, few of its members had actual military experience, and there were practically no officers with military training.[6]

Lenin and his followers recognized the danger of this situation and agreed that a disciplined, controlled military force under Bolshevik direction must be formed as quickly as possible. On 23 January 1918, the Third All-Russian Congress of Soviets voted unanimously to create their own military organizations. This resulted in a decree of 28 January 1918, which established a Workers' and Peasants' Red Army, commonly referred to as the Red Army or the RKKA.[7]

Ranks of the Red Army were filled rapidly by Red Guards and former soldiers of the Petrograd Garrison, who were among the first volunteers. The First Corps was formed on 11 February 1918 in Petrograd. Twelve thousand men had volunteered before 22 February and were organized as the First, Second, Third, and Fourth regiments. Almost half of these were sent to the western front, to help hold against a renewed German offensive.

In order to conserve his military resources and consolidate power, Lenin had begun talks intended to conclude a separate peace with Germany, a step he considered essential to save the revolution. However, at the last minute, negotiations were broken off, and early in February 1918 the German command launched a major offensive against Russian units. German forces, penetrating the weak defenses of both the Red Army and the Red Guard detachments, moved deep into the Ukraine, Estonia, and Latvia. On 21 February, Lenin issued a proclamation: "The Socialist Fatherland is in danger." On 23 February 1918—now the day officially recognized by the Soviets as the birthday of the Red Army—mass meetings were held, urging people to join in defending the country against the Germans. Inspired by this call, 60,000 men joined the new army in Petrograd alone; of these, 20,000 were sent straight to the front.[8]

By the beginning of March 1918, Lenin was firmly in control of the heart of Russia. His major danger was external; the German offensive was still threatening the Bolshevik successes. To gain time and to slow the German advance, the Soviet leadership signed the Treaty of Brest-Litovsk on 3 March 1918. However, the Soviets had not the slightest intention of honoring the treaty. Immediate attention was given to training new commanders for the Red Army, which had proven itself ineffective against professionally led troops. Approximately 22,000 officers from the old Imperial Army joined the new army voluntarily or were "persuaded" to join.

To ensure that the former czarist officers would not foment or initiate counterrevolutionary actions, the military commissar system was formed. The military commissars, who in future years evolved into political officers, were trusted Communist Party members who worked with Party cells within the RKKA and controlled the work of the military specialists. Military commissars also started political education classes for the masses of soldiers and reinstated discipline, completely reversing the "democratic" practices of the previous years, which had been used to undermine and destroy the old army.[9]

The Treaty of Brest-Litovsk, which removed Russia from World War I, gave Germany the opportunity to move divisions that had been fighting on the eastern front to oppose the Allied forces in the West.[10] As a result, German forces were able to launch major offensives in France in March and April 1918.

Fearing that Allied military supplies that had been sent to Russia might fall into German hands, British, French, and U.S. troops landed at Murmansk and Archangel early in April 1918. Japanese troops, with an eye on Manchuria, landed in the Far East; later a contingent from the United States was also sent to eastern Siberia, in part to prevent Japan from annexing the area. The Czechoslovak Legion (former Austro-Hungarian soldiers who had been prisoners of war in Russia) wanted to return home and were given permission by Soviet authorities to leave the country via Siberia. In southern Russia and east of the Ural Mountains, the legion clashed with Red Army troops, and a series of battles took place; but eventually the Czechs reached Vladivostok. British troops landed in Baku and Batumi in the Caucasus and French troops in Odessa and Sevastopol. Bands of former Imperial Army soldiers, who chose to reject Soviet rule, and were organized by former officers into a number of "white" armies in opposition to the Bolshevik Red Army, roamed the countryside.[11]

On 12 March 1918, meanwhile, Bolsheviks moved the capital to Moscow, and the Kremlin became the nerve center of the civil war, which was beginning to rage on all sides. At this time, Leon D. Trotskiy was named chairman of the Higher Military Council, and he began to build up the Red Army.

Building Up the Red Army

By May 1918, the Red Army had grown to approximately 300,000 volunteers—but volunteers were not enough. A much larger military force was required to maintain the Soviet regime's authority. Compulsory military service for males ages eighteen to forty was decreed.

Problems of the new government multiplied. Hunger spread throughout the areas under Bolshevik control, causing the Soviet leaders to make forced grain collections. To ensure that the Red Army was completely responsive to the Bolshevik leadership, military commissars were given full powers over the military specialists who previously had served in the Imperial Army. Efforts were made to train new "Soviet" military commanders as quickly as possible. Military commissariats, supported by Party workers, managed to meet mobilization quotas. In contrast to earlier permissiveness, Trotskiy introduced iron "revolutionary" discipline and strict centralization of authority.[12]

Much of the fighting against White Russians was east of the Ural Mountains. On 13 June 1918, a Revolutionary Military Council (RVS) was established in the eastern areas to provide for direction and leadership of the Red Army force that was fighting thousands of kilometers from Moscow. One of its primary tasks was to engage the Czechoslovak Legion. Soon other armies were formed in the east, each with its own Revolutionary Military Council. Each RVS had at least three members, the commander and two military-political commissars. On 2 September 1918, the Revvoyensoviet of the Republic (RVSR) was established, and the Revvoyensoviet system spread to all fronts and armies. As illustrated in Chart 1, the RVSR combined the administrative and operational functions of controlling all fighting units. However, communications between and within armies were so bad that the subordinate RVSs often had to act on their own.

By the end of the summer of 1918, three-fourths of the territory of the former Russian empire was in the hands of White Russians or under foreign occupation. To add to the problem of the new government, an assassin shot and seriously wounded Lenin on 20 August. As a result of these reverses, on 2 September the Bolsheviks declared the territory they controlled to be an armed camp. In October, a Field Staff was created to handle operational functions of the RVSR, while the All-Russian Main Staff, also subordinate to the RVSR, continued to handle administrative and other matters.[13] The Council of Workers' and Peasants' Defense was formed, with Lenin as chairman. The council was given all power to mobilize the country's resources for defense. Under the Council of Defense, direction of the armed forces was concentrated in a single agency—the RVSR.

6

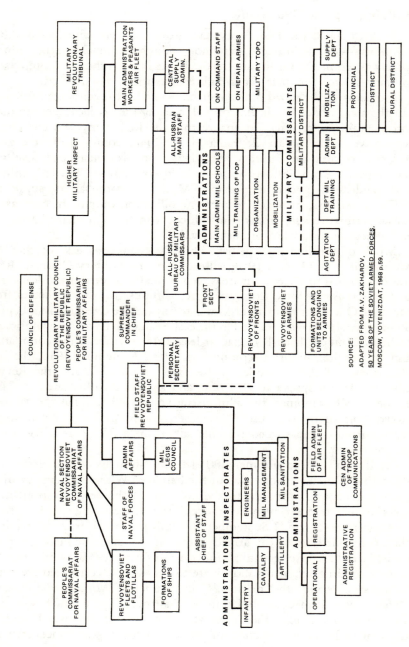

Chart 1
Organization of Military Control in 1918

COUNCIL OF DEFENSE

REVOLUTIONARY MILITARY COUNCIL
OF THE REPUBLIC
(REVVOYENSOVIET REPUBLIC)
PEOPLE'S COMMISSARIAT
FOR MILITARY AFFAIRS

MILITARY
REVOLUTIONARY
TRIBUNAL

HIGHER
MILITARY INSPECT

MAIN ADMINISTRATION
WORKERS & PEASANTS
AIR FLEET

ALL-RUSSIAN
MAIN STAFF

CENTRAL
SUPPLY
ADMIN.

ADMINISTRATIONS

ON COMMAND STAFF

ON REPAIR ARMIES

MILITARY TOPO

MAIN ADMIN MIL SCHOOLS

MIL TRAINING OF POP

ORGANIZATION

MOBILIZATION

MILITARY COMMISSARIATS

MILITARY DISTRICT

MOBILIZA-
TION

SUPPLY
DEPT

ADMIN
DEPT

PROVINCIAL

DISTRICT

RURAL DISTRICT

DEPT MIL
TRAINING

AGITATION
DEPT

ALL-RUSSIAN
BUREAU OF MILITARY
COMMISSARS

SUPREME
COMMANDER
IN CHIEF

FRONT
SECT

REVVOYENSOVIET
OF FRONTS

REVVOYENSOVIET
OF ARMIES

FORMATIONS AND
UNITS BELONGING
TO ARMIES

PERSONAL
SECRETARY

FIELD STAFF
REVVOYENSOVIET
REPUBLIC

ADMIN
AFFAIRS

MIL
LEGIS
COUNCIL

STAFF OF
NAVAL FORCES

NAVAL SECTION
REVVOYENSOVIET
COMMISSARIAT
OF NAVAL AFFAIRS

PEOPLE'S
COMMISSARIAT
FOR NAVAL AFFAIRS

REVVOYENSOVIET
FLEETS AND
FLOTILLAS

FORMATIONS
OF SHIPS

ASSISTANT
CHIEF OF STAFF

INSPECTORATES

INFANTRY

CAVALRY

ARTILLERY

ENGINEERS

MIL MANAGEMENT

MIL SANITATION

ADMINISTRATIONS

OPERATIONAL

REGISTRATION

ADMINISTRATIVE
REGISTRATION

FIELD ADMIN
OF AIR FLEET

CEN ADMIN
OF TROOP
COMMUNICATIONS

SOURCE:
ADAPTED FROM M.V. ZAKHAROV,
50 YEARS OF THE SOVIET ARMED FORCES,
MOSCOW, VOYENIZDAT, 1968 p.59.

With Germany's defeat in November 1918, the Red Army found some relief. While Allied troops, tired of several years of war, gave indications of decreased interest in the Bolshevik seizure of Russia, the Soviet leadership in Moscow was implementing military communism, placing all of the land area controlled by the Communists on a complete war footing. Nationalization of industry was well under way as a result of new edicts. In the field, the Red Army, gaining experience, began to have a few successes.

Mobilization of the Red Army: March 1919–March 1920

Leon Trotskiy, designated commissar of war in March 1918, demonstrated near genius in his military leadership throughout the Civil War. Under his brilliant direction, the Red Army defeated the White Russians led by such capable professional military leaders as A. V. Kolchak, A. I. Denikin, and N. N. Yudenich, who, despite their military experience, failed to develop a coordinated plan for their campaigns against Trotskiy's forces.

Soviet leaders also had problems, however, in coordinating the combat plans of the various fronts. Even as late as the spring of 1919 Russia, the Ukraine, Belorussia, and other regions still were separate entities without a unified military organization. Acting on instructions from the Central Committee of the Communist Party, the Revvoyensoviet met on 28 April 1919 to develop plans for a single military establishment. The decree for the implementation of this plan was approved on 1 June.[14]

As a result of this decree, rapid changes took place within the Red Army structure. By early July the Revvoyensoviet was reduced from fifteen to six members, and the General Headquarters of the High Command was moved from Serpukhov to Moscow. By the end of 1919 the Red Army had increased in size to 3 million men, organized in sixty-one infantry and twelve cavalry divisions and one composite mounted corps. A system of universal military training of workers—*vsevobuch*—was instituted to provide reserves for the Red Army. In 1919 the reserves numbered 800,000.[15] By December 1919, 105 military schools were in operation to produce trained officers, who were urgently needed.

Political cadres for the Red Army were trained in short courses or else received on-the-job training in units. In early November 1919, the Red Army's Teachers Institute was opened in Petrograd, primarily to prepare individuals to teach reading and writing to military personnel, most of whom at that time were illiterate. In addition, graduates assisted with the political indoctrination of the troops.

End of the Civil War: April 1920–November 1920

During World War I, after the seizure of Petrograd by the Bolsheviks, Estonia, Finland, Latvia, Lithuania, and Poland declared their independence of Russia. These nations were recognized as independent powers by the November 1918 armistice. In 1919, the Paris Peace Conference proposed borders between Poland and Russia, known as the Curzon Line, but Poland insisted on its 1772 borders. Fighting began on the western front between Poland and the new Soviet state. The summer offensive brought Soviet troops to the gates of Warsaw. However, the overextended Soviet lines collapsed in mid-August, and the Red Army, after suffering heavy losses, withdrew to the east. Poland acquired most of the disputed area in the Treaty of Riga, 12 October 1920.[16]

At the same time, in southern Ukraine, the Red Army was also fighting the White Guards led by Baron Wrangel. After the peace treaty with Poland was signed, advances were made by the Red Army, and Wrangel's forces withdrew to the Crimea. They were evacuated to Turkey at the end of November 1920. Except for small bands of resisters, the fighting was over.[17]

Between November 1917 and November 1920, the Red Guards had been transformed from a motley crew into a multimillion-man, disciplined, military force. By any standards, this transformation was remarkable. Much of the credit must go to Leon Trotskiy, who welded groups of workers and peasants into an effective combat force. As Lenin's military deputy, he had been sent to negotiate the Treaty of Brest-Litovsk as commissar of foreign affairs, a post he held from December 1917 to March 1918. He had been a major figure in the formation of the Council of Defense, which became the highest agency of the "dictatorship of the proletariat," uniting and directing all departments and organizations—politically, economically, and militarily—toward winning the war. The two top military agencies that had been created, the Revolutionary Military Council (Revvoyensoviet) and the People's Commissariat for Military and Naval Affairs, had somehow accomplished their work.

From volunteers armed with few weapons, poorly clad and fed, Trotskiy developed his army.[18] Compulsory military service, local military agencies to handle inductees, new rules and regulations, harsh discipline, and even the deliberate use of terror had changed illiterate workers and peasants into fighting units. At the end of August 1918 the Red Army had 550,000 men. From September 1918 through November 1920 approximately 5,000,000 more men were mobilized, in addition to nearly 1,000,000 who volunteered. And this immediately followed the heavy losses of World War I!

It is estimated that the Red Army lost as many as 2,200,000 men. Twice as many died from sickness brought on by lack of food, clothing, and medical care as from enemy action. Despite these heavy losses, at the end of 1920, when major military actions had ceased, the last increment of draftees for the year had brought the strength of the Red Army up to 5,500,000 men.[19]

World War I, the revolution, and the Civil War had taken a heavy toll of the civilian population as well. Some estimates show in excess of 12,000,000 civilian deaths in that period. An additional 2,000,000 people fled the country.[20]

First Postwar Stage: 1921–1928

In March 1920, while the Civil War was still in progress, the Council of Defense was redesignated the Council of Labor and Defense and charged with providing soldiers for labor battalions, which were urgently needed to help restore the devastated economy. Despite all efforts, economic conditions deteriorated, and attempts at protest by the civilian populace were ruthlessly suppressed. The best known revolt against the harsh Bolshevik regime was the Kronstadt Uprising of 7–18 March 1921, which was put down by Trotskiy and M. N. Tukhachevskiy. The 14,000 participants who did not die during this attempt to throw off the dictatorship of the proletariat were later shot or imprisoned. Few, if any, survived. Because of economic conditions, Lenin was forced to delay his policy of nationalization of industry at the Tenth Party Congress in March 1921.

Soon after the Tenth Party Congress, demobilization of the Red Army began, with reductions in personnel from a peak of 5,500,000 to 562,000.[21] By October 1924, the total strength was 544,525, allocated as shown on Chart 2.

With no active warfare, a primary defense requirement was to protect the long borders of the Russian Soviet Federated Socialist Republic (RSFSR). Responsibility for this was given to the Cheka, essentially the secret police, who carried out Party politics of terrorization as a means of putting down any opposition. (The Cheka subsequently became the OGPU and finally evolved into the KGB.) A decree of 19 January 1921 transferred some of the best units of the Red Army to the Cheka to act as border guards.

On 29 January 1921, the Revvoyensoviet of the Republic created a single Staff of the RKKA (Red Army), with all central military agencies subordinate to it. The task of organizing the Armed Forces was assigned to this staff and to the RVSR, of which Leon Trotskiy was chairman. At this time, Trotskiy, a very controversial figure within the top Party structure, was a member of the Politburo, where groups were vying for

Chart 2
Soviet Manpower Strengths, 1 October 1924

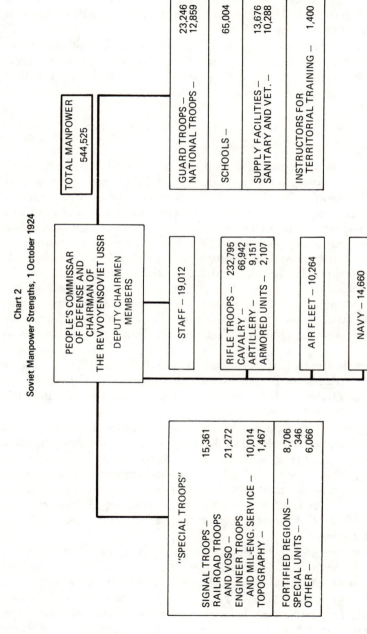

TOTAL MANPOWER
544,525

PEOPLE'S COMMISSAR
OF DEFENSE AND
CHAIRMAN OF
THE REVVOYENSOVIET USSR

DEPUTY CHAIRMEN
MEMBERS

GUARD TROOPS –	23,246
NATIONAL TROOPS –	12,859
SCHOOLS –	65,004
SUPPLY FACILITIES –	13,676
SANITARY AND VET. –	10,288
INSTRUCTORS FOR TERRITORIAL TRAINING –	1,400

STAFF – 19,012

RIFLE TROOPS –	232,795
CAVALRY –	66,942
ARTILLERY –	9,151
ARMORED UNITS –	2,107

AIR FLEET – 10,264

NAVY – 14,660

"SPECIAL TROOPS"

SIGNAL TROOPS –	15,361
RAILROAD TROOPS AND VOSO –	21,272
ENGINEER TROOPS AND MIL-ENG. SERVICE –	10,014
TOPOGRAPHY –	1,467
FORTIFIED REGIONS –	8,706
SPECIAL UNITS –	346
OTHER –	6,066

SOURCE: ADAPTED FROM I.B. BERKHIN, MILITARY REFORMS IN THE USSR (1924-1925) [MOSCOW: VOYENIZDAT, 1958], 179.

power. Sharp quarrels soon arose, within both the RVSR and the Politburo, over the form the postwar Red Army should take.

The Red Army was in need of equipment, technically trained manpower, and professional education for its officers, all almost impossible to obtain in the Soviet Union at that time. These needs could be supplied only by a nation with an advanced technological capability and a modern military establishment. Germany, forbidden by the Treaty of Versailles to rebuild military industry and to provide certain types of training for the officer corps, needed an extraterritorial base for military training and production. Secret talks between military leaders of the two nations took place in 1921, and relations were formalized in 1922 with the Treaty of Rapallo. Junkers constructed an aircraft plant in Moscow, and a flying school for German pilots was established near Lipetsk; some say that Germany may have shipped some modern arms to Soviet forces.[22]

For the Red Army, perhaps the most important contribution made by the Germans was the admission of a number of Soviet officers each year to German staff courses. Among those Soviet officers who received German training was future Marshal of the Soviet Union M. N. Tukhachevskiy, regarded as the most able Soviet officer of that era.[23] In turn, German officers attended maneuvers in the Soviet Union and took part in field exercises, which were forbidden to them on their own soil.

Soviet military matters were directly affected by the struggle that was taking place within the Party hierarchy. In May 1922, Lenin suffered a stroke; a second paralyzed him in December; in May 1923, he lost his power of speech, and on 21 January 1924, he died. The smoldering problem of succession burst into flame. Trotskiy appeared to have been favored by Lenin, with M. V. Frunze the second choice. But Stalin persuaded S. S. Kamenev and G. Ye. Zinoviev to join him in a *troika* to prevent Trotskiy from being selected.[24]

During this period a number of military reforms were being effected that, in great part, were the work of Frunze, who was deputy chairman of the RVS of the USSR. (When the Russian Republic became the Union of Soviet Socialist Republics in 1922, the Revvoyensoviet of the Republic—RVSR—became the Revvoyensoviet of the USSR—RVS of the USSR.) Frunze, who had supported Stalin and his followers in their opposition to Trotskiy, had been one of the outstanding military leaders during the Civil War and later became known even more for his writings on military theory and organization. On 11 March 1924, Frunze became chief of staff of the Red Army, and on 26 January 1925 he replaced Trotskiy as chairman of the RVS of the USSR and as people's commissar for military and naval affairs.

Frunze's tenure of office was brief. Stalin may have considered him a rival, especially since he had stood high in Lenin's favor. In October

1925, Frunze was in a hospital for a checkup, and it is reported that Stalin ordered him to undergo surgery. He died on the operating table, in circumstances that are still murky.[25]

One of the most important of the new military measures introduced by the mid-1920s was the territorial principle of manning the Red Army. Able-bodied men in each administrative region were called up for a limited period of active duty in a territorial unit each year for five years. Almost every male in each region received military training, although only for a short time. The first call-up period was for three months, with one month each year thereafter. In some ways this system was similar to that of the National Guard in the United States. Sixteen to twenty percent of the personnel in each territorial division were regulars who provided the nucleus of the organization.

In 1925, this territorial system of manning encompassed forty-six of seventy-seven infantry and one of eleven cavalry divisions. The rest, along with technical troops, the Navy, and most Border Guard divisions in border districts, were composed of regular officers and enlisted personnel serving two-year enlistments. Officers formed the permanent cadre, training personnel and then discharging them as potential reserves.[26]

A primary advantage of the territorial system was that divisions could be maintained, at a very negligible cost, ready for rapid deployment. By 1930, approximately 58 percent of the infantry units were territorial in principle. Another 10 percent were in national divisions formed in regions that contained ethnic populations, in which few could speak the Russian language. The national division permitted them to serve in divisions whose officer cadre spoke their own language.[27]

Further reforms, including major changes, also were made in the central military apparatus in the mid-1920s. The position of supreme commander was abolished, considered unnecessary in peacetime. The Staff of the Red Army was divided into separate agencies, subordinate to the Revvoyensoviet.

Frunze, during his brief period as chief of staff, developed the pattern of staff work that was followed in future years. He and his two principal deputies, M. N. Tukhachevskiy and B. M. Shaposhnikov, worked on major questions of defense, taking into consideration economic, political, and military factors. The military staff, stated Frunze,

> must not only be the brain of the Red Army, it must become the military brain for all our Soviet state and must supply the material which will lie at the base of the work of the Council of Defense.[28]

The Main Administration (Upravleniye) of the Red Army handled day-to-day matters, such as study, drill, troops services, and repair.

Supplies for the Ground Forces were the responsibility of the Administration of the Chief of Supply. The Air Force and Navy had their own supply organizations. Administration of Naval Forces was headed by E. S. Pantserzhanskiy (November 1921–April 1924), who was directly subordinate to the RVS of the USSR. The Main Administration of the Air Forces, also subordinate to the RVS, at first was under A. P. Rozengol'ts (March 1923–December 1924) and then under P. I. Baranov (December 1924–June 1931).[29] The Political Administration of the Red Army was in the same position as that of the Navy and Air Forces and at the same time had the rights of a department of the Central Committee of the Communist Party.

After some minor reorganizations in 1925–1926, the central apparatus became stable. (See Chart 3.) The concept of unity of command—a principle taken for granted in practically all non-Soviet military forces—was introduced and considered one of the most important of the military reforms. This simply meant that orders no longer had to be countersigned by a military commissar, a practice that had been started in order to control ex-Czarist officers during the Civil War. By 1925 there were sufficient trained Communist officers that the countersigning of all orders could be discontinued.[30]

According to the Law on Compulsory Military Service of 18 September 1925, the Soviet Armed Forces were composed of ground, air, and naval units, the OGPU (predecessor of both the present KGB and MVD), and convoy guards. The Ground Forces included infantry, cavalry, artillery, armored forces, engineer, railroad, chemical, and signal troops. The Air Forces had only a limited number of aircraft, of which approximately ninety of those suitable for military use had been purchased abroad, and its trained pilots were few. The Soviet Navy was very small and had little combat potential, since almost every ship had been damaged during the Civil War. Shipyards were in disrepair.

By 1928 the military reforms initiated by Frunze had been completed. The senior military figure was Klementiy Voroshilov, Stalin's trusted supporter, who became people's commissar for military and naval affairs as well as chairman of the RVS after the death of Frunze. The central military organization was essentially as shown for 1930 in Chart 4.

In 1929, as the Red Army reached a stage of combat competence approaching that of its western neighbors, it received its first test in the Far East.

In the late 1920s, a special Far Eastern Army had been formed, under the command of V. K. Blyukher, a legendary figure who had used the pseudonym Galin. China was having serious internal problems, and its government was unstable. In 1929, Chinese forces seized the Manchurian branch of the Trans-Siberian Railroad, which by treaty ran through

14

Chart 3
Organization of Central Military Control in 1927

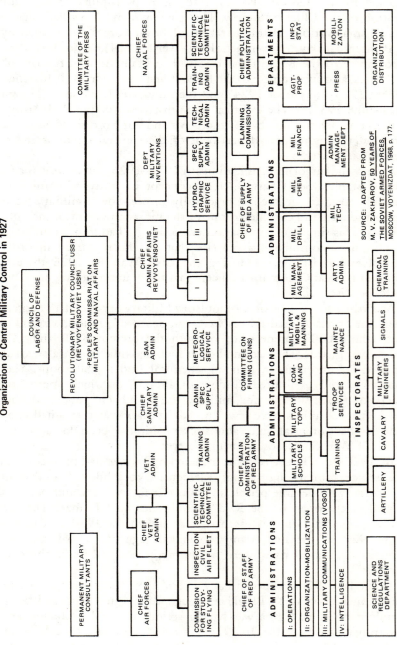

SOURCE: ADAPTED FROM
M. V. ZAKHAROV, 50 YEARS OF
THE SOVIET ARMED FORCES,
MOSCOW, VOYENIZDAT, 1968, p. 177.

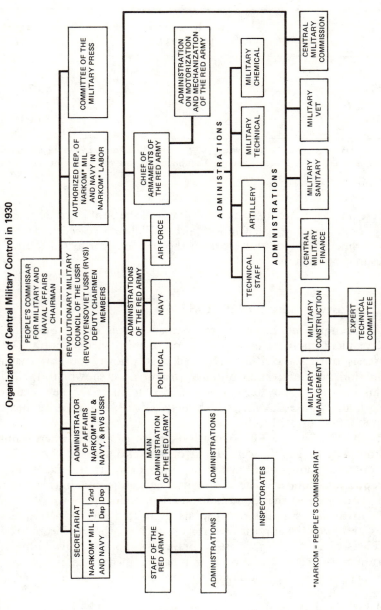

Chart 4

Organization of Central Military Control in 1930

*NARKOM = PEOPLE'S COMMISSARIAT

SOURCE: ADAPTED FROM N. VISHNYAKOV AND F. ARKHIPOV, USTROYSTVO VOORUZHENNYKH SIL SSSR, MOSCOW, STATE PUBLISHING HOUSE, 1930. P. 103.

TABLE 1
Annual Prewar Production Rates of Military Weapons

	Yearly Average 1930-1931	Yearly Average 1935-1937
Aircraft	860	3,578
Artillery	1,911	5,020
Tanks	740	3,319
Rifles	174,000	397,000

Source: Data from A. N. Lagovskiy, *V. I. Lenin ob Ekonomicheskom Obespechenii Oborony Strany* [V. I. Lenin on the Economic Support of the Country's Defenses] (Moscow: Voyenizdat, 1976), pp. 158-159.

Chinese territory. Acting so as not to expand the conflict, the Far Eastern Army took action against Chinese forces. Fighting ceased in December, when Chinese forces withdrew from the area and permitted the railroad to resume operations.[31]

Second Postwar Stage: 1929–1937

The strength and power of the Armed Forces of the Soviet Union are dependent upon the industrialization of the Soviet economy. Defense industries during the 1930s received first priority on raw materials; production rates of certain military weapons are shown in Table 1.

This increase in production was needed to meet the new manpower strength of the Red Army, which between 1933 and 1938 increased from 885,000 to 1,513,400 men.

The buildup in the Red Army took place at a time when hundreds of thousands of people were dying of starvation in the Soviet Union, and millions more were dying of cold, exhaustion, and hunger in concentration camps.[32] The choice between guns and butter has never been a problem to the Communist Party leadership.

The increased supplies of weapons permitted the formation of tank forces and special supporting services, such as the engineers. The Air Force was divided into specialized branches—bomber, dive bomber (the forerunner of frontal aviation), and fighter. Naval vessels entered the inventory in sufficient numbers to form a Pacific Ocean Fleet and a Northern Fleet.

Major organizational changes also occurred. In 1935, the Staff of the Red Army (RKKA) was renamed the General Staff of the Armed Forces of the USSR. When this staff was formed, many of the senior Soviet commanders and staff officers were men who had been trained in German staff and service schools. These military ties with Germany were broken in 1933, when Hitler came to power. To train senior personnel for the Soviet forces, the Academy of the General Staff was opened in 1936.[33]

International problems became a major concern of the Soviet leaders beginning in 1931 when Japanese troops occupied Manchuria, increasing tension along the Soviet eastern borders. Hitler's emphasis on rearming Germany also was carefully watched. Spain, however, was to become the battlefield where Soviet equipment, tactics, and military leadership were actually tested.

The Spanish Civil War started in 1936, with the Loyalist forces (which had considerable popular support in the United States, France, and Great Britain) receiving assistance from the Soviet Union. General Franco's rebel troops were given aid by both Germany and Italy. Among Soviet "volunteers"—who as a rule used pseudonyms—were a number of officers who rose to prominence during World War II and were active in the 1950s and 1960s, among them R. Ya. Malinovskiy, N. N. Voronov, P. I. Batov, and K. A. Meretskov, all of whom reached four-star rank or higher.[34]

Initially, Loyalist military aircraft (mostly of Soviet or American manufacture) were successful in Spain. However, in 1937, Germany introduced the Me-109 fighter into the battle, and air superiority quickly went to General Franco's forces. Other Soviet equipment also proved to be much inferior to that of Hitler's Wehrmacht, and this was an important factor in Franco's ultimate victory.[35]

As a result of their study of the war, Soviet leaders recognized that their own military doctrine, strategy, and tactics were seriously deficient. Major changes were made in the Soviet Armed Forces, based on their Spanish experiences—changes that subsequently, during the Russo-Finnish War and World War II, often proved to be ill-advised.[36]

Between 1935 and 1938 the territorial principle of manning the Red Army was abandoned, and all units were formed on the cadre principle. In essence, this meant that regular officers would provide training for conscripts, who served for specific periods of continuous service. Abandonment of the territorial concept caused a greater degree of centralization of the Ground Forces and major changes in the higher military structure. This brought about a reexamination of the three basic agencies that exercised military control in the mid-1930s.

The first of these was the Defense Commission, headed by V. M. Molotov, and attached to the Council of People's Commissars (roughly the same as the Council of Ministers of the 1980s). This group worked out draft proposals on major questions of defense and presented them to the Council of Labor and Defense (STO). The second was the People's Commissariat for Military and Naval Affairs, headed by K. Ye. Voroshilov, which exercised direct control over the Armed Forces; and the third was the Revvoyensoviet, which Voroshilov also chaired.[37]

The Defense Commission duplicated the work of the Revvoyensoviet, and in 1934 the RVS was abolished. The People's Commissariat for Military and Naval Affairs was renamed the People's Commissariat of Defense. A newly formed Military Council was attached to this commissariat. In 1937 the Defense Commission was changed into the Defense Committee. It still was headed by Molotov, but Stalin and Voroshilov were made members. Concurrently, the Council of Labor and Defense was abolished.[38]

While these changes were taking place, other events were having a profound effect on the Red Army. The Munich Agreement in 1938, by which France and Britain impotently sanctioned Hitler's destruction of Czechoslovakia, demonstrated to the Kremlin the weaknesses of the Western powers at a time when Stalin, like Hitler, was seeking to add to his own power. Stalin's actions were internal. Within the Soviet Union, he began eliminating all enemies and possible rivals by means of "purges" that still are beyond understanding.

Prelude to the Great Patriotic War: 1938–22 June 1941

In 1937 Stalin's purges were directed against the military, and by 1938 they were shaking the very foundations of the Red Army. During these purges, the Soviet military lost a larger proportion of top leaders than were later lost through German action in all the years of World War II. Beginning with S. M. Kirov's death in December 1934, Party and government officials suffered mass executions and imprisonment in concentration camps, where they died by the hundreds of thousands. During Khrushchev's tenure as leader of the Communist Party in the 1960s, the Soviet Pandora's box was opened sufficiently to reveal that

In 1937–1938, and also subsequent to that time, as a result of unfounded mass repressions, the flower of the command and political staff of the Red Army was killed. As "agents of foreign intelligence" and "enemies of the people," three marshals of the Soviet Union (of five at the time)—M. N. Tukhachevskiy, V. K. Blyukher, A. I. Yegorov were condemned and killed; all of the troop commanders of military districts were killed, including I. P. Uborevich and I. E. Yakir, and also the heads of fleets, V. M. Orlov and M. V. Viktorov; outstanding organizers of party-political work in the army were killed, including Ya. B. Gamarnik, A. S. Bulin, G. A. Osepyan, and M. P. Amelin; many outstanding military figures and heroes of the

Civil War were either killed or imprisoned for long periods, among them A. I. Kork, R. P. Eideman, I. S. Unshlicht, Ye. I. Kovtyukh, P. Ye. Dybenko, I. F. Fed'ko, and I. N. Dubovoy. All corps commanders, and almost all division commanders and brigade commanders were eliminated from the Army, also about half of the regimental commanders, members of military councils and chiefs of political administrations of military districts, the majority of corps, division and brigade military commissars and about one-third of those in regiments. In all, during 1937–1938, about one-fifth of the officer cadres underwent repression. But on the eve of war, and in its first months, more than one-fourth the number of those repressed were rehabilitated, returned to the Army, and took an active part in the war.[39]

Human life and suffering aside, the cost of the purges to the Red Army was inestimable. The one-fifth of the officers who "underwent repression" included relatively few of the junior ranks. When the purges ended, less than one-half of the senior Soviet officers remained alive. In the immediate post-purge period there were no regimental commanders who had higher academy educations; few officers had attended military commissioning schools. Most of the division commanders in 1940 had been in their posts less than one year. The 1937–1938 military purges were not the first, nor the last, of the waves of terror that swept the Soviet Union during Stalin's regime and that, to some degree, sweep it today.

Western nations were confused by the purges, and few people at the time grasped their full intensity and scope. Hitler, in particular, reportedly rejoiced to find that the most intelligent and promising of the Soviet military high command were eliminated. The U.S. ambassador to Moscow, Joseph Davies, actually thought there was proof that the Soviet officers accused were guilty of treason.[40] Walter Duranty, correspondent for the *New York Times*, shared Davies' view.[41] British intellectuals were equally mistaken and duped. Professor Harold Laski wrote that Andrey Vyshinsky, the Soviet prosecutor, was "a man whose passion was law reform."[42] Sir John Maynard wrote that "the trials of the leading personages in 1936–1938 were substantially justified by facts."[43]

Despite the purges, the Red Army remained a viable combat force. In July 1938, as the trials were being conducted in Moscow, fighting broke out between Soviet and Japanese troops in the area of Lake Khasan. The commander of the Soviet Far Eastern Front was Marshal of the Soviet Union V. K. Blyukher. The purges had already decimated Blyukher's staff. Then, on 6 August 1938, G. M. Shtern suddenly was given command of the battle. Blyukher's days were numbered. After some fighting, the Japanese forces withdrew. Blyukher was reassigned to Moscow a few days later, then arrested and, on 9 November 1938, he was shot.[44]

A year later, a major battle was fought against the Japanese Kwantung Army at Khal'khan Gol, after the Japanese crossed the ill-defined border of Outer Mongolia, with which the Soviet Union had a mutual assistance pact. The culminating battle, in which Soviet forces were commanded by Georgiy K. Zhukov and G. M. Shtern, took place on 23 August 1939, the very day a nervous Stalin signed his infamous Non-Aggression Pact with Hitler. The defeated Japanese forces again withdrew, as they had a year earlier.[45] Ya. V. Smushkevich, who won a second Hero of the Soviet Union gold star as commander of aviation at Khal'khan Gol and then became head of the Soviet Air Forces, survived until October 1941, when he was shot on orders of Stalin. G. M. Shtern perished with him.[46]

On 1 September 1939, less than two weeks after the Hitler-Stalin Non-Aggression Pact had persuaded the German dictator that the Soviet Union would remain neutral, German forces invaded Poland. On 3 September Great Britain and France honored their treaty obligations to Poland by declaring war on Germany, and World War II officially was under way. No effective French or British assistance was sent to Poland, however, and no effort was made by the French to invade western Germany.

The German forces moved into Poland, and on 17 September the Red Army moved to the west, "liberating" the western portions of Belorussia and the Ukraine, which had been awarded to Poland in 1920. Estonia, Latvia, and Lithuania, and three Baltic republics, were forced to accept Soviet bases in October 1939 and later, in August 1940, were incorporated into the USSR.

To the north, Stalin wanted additional territory to protect the approaches to Leningrad. Accordingly, under the flimsiest of pretexts, the Soviet Union proceeded to attack tiny Finland on 30 November 1939. Fighting against overwhelming odds, the heroic Finns won the admiration of the world for their stand against the Soviet hordes. In February 1940, ice enabled Soviet tanks to sweep around the Mannerheim Line and drive the Finnish forces from their prepared positions.[47] Losses on the Soviet side were high, and the low caliber of Soviet military leadership was carefully noted in Berlin.

Stalin may have watched with some apprehension the German occupation of Denmark on 9 April 1940 and the subsequent invasion of Norway. Hitler then turned to France and on 13 June occupied Paris. France concluded an armistice with Hitler the following week. Britain, protected by the English Channel and by its effective Royal Air Force and Royal Navy, was now opposed by the total weight of the German military forces.

But even as the Non-Aggression Pact was being concluded with Hitler in 1939, the Politburo had been preparing for a possible struggle against

Germany. On 1 September 1939, the Soviet Union adopted a new law on universal military service, providing for a longer period of training (from two to five years). By 1 January 1941, the Soviet forces numbered 4,207,000 men; 80.65 percent were ground troops, 8.65 percent air forces, 7.35 percent navy, and 3.35 percent air defense.[48] The nation was divided into sixteen military districts and the Far Eastern front. Naval forces consisted of four fleets and five flotillas. The central apparatus of the People's Commissariats of Defense and the Navy underwent a complete overhaul in an attempt to implement the lessons of the Spanish and Finnish wars.[49]

On the eve of the German invasion, Marshal of the Soviet Union S. K. Timoshenko was the people's commissar of defense, having been appointed to that position in May 1940. Flagman First Rank N. G. Kuznetsov was the senior naval officer, serving in the capacity of the people's commissar of the Navy. The General Staff was headed by Deputy People's Commissar G. K. Zhukov. Marshal of the Soviet Union S. M. Budennyy, as deputy people's commissar, was in charge of supplies. Deputy people's commissar and chief of the Main Administration of Propaganda of the Red Army was Army Commissar First Rank A. I. Zaporozhets. Marshal of the Soviet Union G. I. Kulik was the deputy people's commissar for artillery. General P. V. Rychagov, also a deputy people's commissar, was chief of the Main Administration of the Air Forces of the Red Army. The Main Military Engineering Administration was headed by Marshal of the Soviet Union B. M. Shaposhnikov, and General K. A. Meretskov was responsible for combat training.[50]

In the first half of 1941, the Red Army was in a period of transition. In both Spain and Finland, Soviet aircraft had proved inferior to their opponents, and a massive program was under way to produce fighter aircraft that would be the equivalent of those in the West. A similar program was begun to produce better equipment for the ground forces. Stalin was attempting at all costs to stay out of the war. On 13 April 1941, he concluded a neutrality treaty with Japan, whose sympathies continued to lie with Germany. He ignored repeated warnings from both Britain and the United States about Hitler's plans for an invasion of the Soviet Union. Accordingly, when the German forces struck on Sunday, 22 June 1941, Soviet forces were completely unprepared.[51]

The Great Patriotic War: 1941–1945

Soviet military historians divide the Great Patriotic war of the USSR against Hitler's Germany into the following periods:[52]

First Period: 22 June 1941–18 November 1942
    Summer campaign (June–November 1941)
    Winter campaign (December 1941–April 1942)
    Summer–fall campaign (May–November 1942)
Second Period: 19 November 1942–end of 1943
    Winter campaign (November 1942–March 1943)
    Summer–fall campaign (April–December 1943)
Third period: January 1944–9 May 1945
    Winter campaign (January–May 1944)
    Summer–fall campaign (June–December 1944)
    Campaign of 1945 (January–May 1945)
    War on Japan (9 August 1945–2 September 1945)

First Period of the Great Patriotic War
(22 June–18 November 1942): Barbarossa

At 3:15 A.M. on 22 June 1941, daylight was approaching when Hitler's forces launched their attack against the Soviet Union. For this attack, Soviet historians claim the Germans had concentrated 152 divisions and 2 brigades opposite the Soviet western frontier, supported by approximately 5,000 aircraft. Nineteen of the divisions were tanks, and another 14 were motorized. There were an additional 29 divisions from Eastern European nations. In total numbers, there were some 5,500,000 men in Hitler's forces. Operation Barbarossa, as the attack plan was called, envisaged three main drives by three German army groups: Army Group North toward Leningrad; Army Group Center toward Moscow; and Army Group South toward Kiev.[53]

Soviet forces altogether consisted of 4,207,000 men, formed in 303 divisions. One hundred twenty-five of these divisions were in the process of being manned and outfitted; few of the remaining divisions were up to full combat strength. The attack caught the Soviet forces almost totally unprepared.

At half after midnight on 22 June, orders went from the Kremlin to place the troops in the west on alert. However, the order was received by the troops too late. First hit were the Border Guards in the western districts, but all other divisions in military districts facing the German advances came under almost immediate attack. Over 1,000 Soviet aircraft were destroyed on the ground in the first German air strikes.

In scattered spots, the Soviets put up a heroic struggle, as at Brest on the Polish border, but in general, Soviet resistance fell apart. In the first three weeks, German troops advanced 500 kilometers on the northern front, 550 kilometers on the central front, and 300 to 350 kilometers on the southern front. Latvia and Lithuania were quickly occupied, as was a large part of the Ukraine, all of Belorussia, and Moldavia. After undergoing years of senseless brutality under Stalin, many of the peoples of the USSR welcomed the Germans as liberators.

Stalin and his followers were saved perhaps by the equally inhumane policies of Hitler. The advancing Germans treated the peoples of the Ukraine and elsewhere as subhuman, killing without mercy and sending back to Germany thousands of Soviet citizens as slaves. These actions stiffened the resistance of the Soviet people against the German invaders.

Unable to stop the advancing Germans, the Soviet command decided to evacuate as much industry as possible to the east. On 24 June 1941— only two days after the attack—the Council of Evacuation was organized and started to work. From July through November 1941, 1,523 industrial enterprises were relocated, of which 1,360 were the largest in the nation. All were engaged in military production of one type or another. Two hundred and twenty-six of these industries were relocated near the Volga River, 667 in the Urals, 244 in western Siberia, 78 in eastern Siberia, and 308 in various parts of Kazakhstan and central Asia. Ten million persons were evacuated with these plants. By the end of 1941 some of the relocated plants already were in production.[54]

As the Soviets were retreating during the first weeks of the war, the system of military commissars was reintroduced to ensure the political reliability of the armed forces. Many senior officers whose forces suffered catastrophic losses were shot on Stalin's orders or committed suicide. Party ranks were opened to the soldiers in an effort to boost morale. One hundred and twenty-six thousand men in uniform were admitted to Party membership in the second half of 1941. However, the appeal by the Russian Orthodox Church to the people to resist Hitler probably was more effective than the call of the Communist Party leadership.

On 30 June 1941, the State Defense Committee (Gosudarstvennyy Komitet Oborony, or GKO) was formed with Stalin as chairman. This was the supreme Soviet agency with political, economic, and military authority throughout the war.[55]

Strategic leadership of the Armed Forces on 23 June 1941 was concentrated in Stavka, the General Headquarters of the High Command (Glavnoye Komandovaniye), headed by Marshal S. K. Timoshenko. On 10 July this leadership passed to a renamed Stavka of the Supreme Command (Verkhovnoye Komandovaniye) with Stalin as chairman, and with V. M. Molotov, S. K. Timoshenko, S. M. Budennyy, K. Ye. Voroshilov, B. M. Shaposhnikov, and G. K. Zhukov as members. On 19 July Stalin became people's commissar of defense and, on 8 August, supreme commander in chief of the Armed Forces. At this time Stavka was renamed Stavka of the Supreme High Command (Verkhovnoye Glavnokomandovaniye) or, as it commonly was called, Stavka of the VGK. In accordance with the principle of strict centralization, Stavka made all the military decisions of the war, sometimes under the direction of the GKO (State Defense Committee) or the Politburo and, for major decisions, with approval of both the GKO and the Politburo.[56]

The General Staff acted as the executive agency for Stavka. At the beginning of the war, this staff was headed by G. K. Zhukov. In July 1941, Zhukov was sent out to command a front and was replaced by B. M. Shaposhnikov, who was regarded as one of the most intelligent of the Soviet military leaders.[57]

Three main commands—Northwest, West, and Southwest—were formed on 10 July 1941, to coordinate the activities of the fronts. The concept of main commands proved unsuccessful.

On the Northwestern Front, the Germans approached the outskirts of Leningrad. The blockade of Leningrad began on 8 September 1941 and was not completely lifted for 900 days.[58]

On the Western Front, the Battle of Smolensk began on 10 July. The Southwestern Front was hard hit. Kiev fell on 19 September. Odessa held out from 5 August until 16 October 1941; then it too fell. The defense of Sevastopol, which lasted from 30 October 1941 to 4 July 1942, slowed the German drive to take the Crimea.

In September 1941, the German command concentrated its efforts on taking Moscow. Three Soviet fronts were deployed to stop the drive: the Western Front, under the command of I. S. Konev; the Bryansk Front, under A. I. Yeremenko; and the Reserve Front, under S. M. Budennyy. Thereafter, as the war proceeded, additional fronts were formed and existing ones realigned or abolished to meet the requirements of combat.

For the offensive to take Moscow, the Germans concentrated 77 divisions with over 1 million men, 1,700 tanks, 950 aircraft, and over 14,000 guns and mortars. Pulling together their shattered forces, the Soviets massed 95 divisions, containing about 800,000 men, 782 tanks, 545 aircraft, and 6,808 guns and mortars.[59] On 10 October, when the fighting became critical, the Western and Reserve fronts were united under Zhukov's command.[60] As German troops penetrated to within 25 kilometers of Moscow, part of the government was evacuated to Kuybyshev. Despite the desperate situation, the traditional military parade was held in Red Square on 7 November 1941.

By this time, the Soviet Union had lost its most important economic regions. Some help was promised on 6 November 1941, when the United States granted $1 billion to the USSR in Lend-Lease credit. After the Japanese attack on Pearl Harbor in December, the United States entered the war against Germany and Italy. Although the Soviet Union would obtain more help soon, the most immediate assistance to the Soviets was provided by the early arrival of one of the most severe winters in years, which the Germans had not anticipated.

Soviet historians consider that the winter campaign of 1941–1942 began with Zhukov's counterattack on 5 December against German positions in the Moscow area and lasted until the following April. Soviet forces not only stopped the German advance, but by March 1942 they had driven back Hitler's troops a few hundred kilometers. Hitler's blitzkreig was halted.

The Soviet summer-fall campaign of 1942 began in May and lasted through November. A Soviet offensive in the Ukraine was unsuccessful. Concentrating most of their efforts in the southern sector, German Army Group B drove toward Stalingrad rather than toward Moscow as expected. By July the Germans had penetrated to Stalingrad, and on 17 July the defense of that city began. On 28 July the people's commissar of defense issued the famous Order No. 227: "Not a step backward."[61]

German Army Group A drove deep toward the Caucasus Mountains, heading for the Baku oilfields. The Battle of the Caucasus began in earnest. All along the coast below Novorossiysk and inland a few dozen kilometers in front of the Caucasus Mountains, the Soviet line held.[62]

Meanwhile, both the United States and Great Britain were willing but hardly able to do much to divert German forces from the Russian front. The initial disasters in the Pacific had made it necessary to take measures to halt the Japanese swarming through the area. But the prewar decision to concentrate first on the defeat of Hitler in a two-theater war still pertained, and on 8 November 1942 United States forces landed in North Africa.

By 9 October 1942, over one year after Hitler's attack had begun, the Soviet command had regained sufficient confidence to abolish military commissars, making those who had held those positions deputies for political affairs, thus restoring "unity of command."[63]

Second Period of the Great Patriotic War
(19 November 1942–end of 1943)

The counterattack at Stalingrad began on 19 November, with troops of the Southwestern and the Don fronts committed. Coordination of the fronts was effected by a Stavka representative, General Colonel A. M. Vasilevskiy. Combined Soviet forces in the Stalingrad area then numbered over 1 million men, 894 tanks, 1,414 aircraft, and 13,500 guns and mortars. Opposing them, according to Soviet figures, were approximately 1 million German troops, 675 tanks, 1,216 combat aircraft, and 10,300 guns and mortars. Using a pincer movement, the two Soviet fronts met on 23 November and completely encircled and destroyed twenty-two German divisions, containing 147,200 men. On 31 January

A memorial to the defenders of Stalingrad.

1943, Field Marshal Paulus was taken prisoner along with 91,000 German troops. The tide had turned.[64]

Other successes followed. On 12 January 1943, the blockade of Leningrad was broken north of the city. In the south, Rostov and the northern Caucasus were freed of German troops by January 1943, except for the Taman peninsula.

After the defeat at Stalingrad, Hitler took drastic measures to try to recapture the strategic initiative. His solution was a major offensive— Citadel—in the area of Kursk in the summer of 1943. The main attack to the south by Army Group Center and the attack to the north by Army Group South were aimed toward Kursk, attempting to encircle the Soviet troops in the Kursk bulge. The Germans, according to Soviet historians, gathered fifty divisions—900,000 men, 10,000 guns, 2,700 tanks, including the new heavy Tiger tank—supported by 2,000 aircraft. Citadel began on 5 July 1943.

Soviet troops of the Central Front under General K. K. Rokossovskiy and the Voronezh Front under General N. F. Vatutin were in the pocket of the bulge. Together they had 1,300,000 men, 20,000 guns and mortars, 3,600 tanks and self-propelled guns, and 2,800 aircraft. Behind them, in reserve east of the bulge, was the Steppe Front commanded by General I. S. Konev.[65]

Initially the German troops penetrated the Soviet lines up to 35 kilometers. On 12 July, near Prokhorovka, one of the largest tank battles in history began. Up to 1,500 tanks and self-propelled assault guns of Army Group South and the Voronezh Front, supported by large numbers of aircraft, took part in the Battle of Kursk. After the Germans lost 350 tanks and 10,000 men the first day, their attack slowed, and they began to go over to the defense. On 16 July they were forced to begin withdrawing.

North of Army Group Center, troops of the Western Front under General V. D. Sokolovskiy and the Bryansk Front under General M. M. Popov began an offensive on 12 July. Driving toward Orel, the troops of the Bryansk Front took Orel on 5 August. In the south, troops of the Steppe Front retook Kharkov on 23 August after severe resistance from German troops there. In the fifty-day Battle of Kursk, the Germans lost half a million men killed and wounded.

The Battle of Kursk was decisive. General air superiority passed to the Soviet side during this battle where it remained, except in isolated areas, for the rest of the war. From this time on, the Red Army retained the strategic initiative.[66]

During August and September 1943, the Soviets went on the offensive along a 2,000-kilometer front. During September and October, the Novorossiysk-Taman operation got under way, with Novorossiysk freed on 16 September and the Taman peninsula on 10 October. Kiev was liberated on 6 November 1943.[67]

In this second period of World War II, the tide of battle definitely had turned. The Red Army drove from 500 to 1,300 kilometers to the west, freeing significant portions of Soviet territory. Italy surrendered to Allied troops in September 1943. The Teheran Conference had been called to plan coordinated Allied war efforts.

Third Period of the Great Patriotic War
(January 1944–9 May 1945)

At the beginning of 1944 German troops still occupied Estonia, Latvia, and Lithuania, plus Karelia, most of Belorussia, part of the Ukraine, Moldavia, and the Crimea. According to Soviet historians, Germany still had 10 million men under arms. Of these, approximately 4,906,000 men constituting 198 divisions and 6 brigades were on the Eastern front. Their armament included 54,570 guns and mortars, 5,400 tanks, and 3,073 aircraft.[68]

Opposing the German forces the Soviet Union had 6,100,000 men, 88,900 guns and mortars, over 2,000 Katyusha multiple rocket launchers,

4,900 tanks, and 8,500 combat aircraft. To this force was given the task of freeing all Soviet territory of German troops.

The winter campaign of 1944 lasted until May.[69] In the Battle of the Right Bank of the Ukraine, which began on 24 December 1943, Soviet troops were successful in reaching their own western border with Rumania. At the same time an offensive in the Leningrad-Novgorod area northwest of Moscow finally succeeded in lifting Leningrad's blockade. The Crimea was retaken during April and May.

In June 1944, the summer–fall campaign opened with the Belorussian Operation.[70] The defenses of German Army Group Center were broken through in six areas, and large numbers of German troops were surrounded. The operation ended with Soviet troops crossing into Poland as far as the Vistula River, on the outskirts of Warsaw.

The Baltic Operation, during July–August 1944, drove German troops from eastern areas of the Baltic states. To the south, a number of campaigns, including the L'vov-Sandomierz Operation of 13 July–29 August, together with the Jassy-Kishinev Operation of August and September, resulted in Soviet troops crossing the western border into Poland, Czechoslovakia, Rumania, and Bulgaria. Rumania surrendered on 24 August, and Bulgaria, which had not been at war with the Soviet Union, surrendered to Soviet forces on 8 September.

The Tallinn, Riga, and Moonsund operations of 1944 cleared German troops from the Baltic republics. Operations in the fall resulted in Soviet troops reaching Hungary and Yugoslavia. They approached Budapest and actually entered Belgrade.

As a result of the 1944 operations, all Soviet territory was cleared of German troops except for a small part of Latvia. Three hundred fourteen German divisions and forty-seven brigades, according to Soviet accounts, were defeated. Of these, ninety-six divisions and thirty-four brigades were destroyed or taken prisoner.

Meanwhile, additional pressure on the Germans was effected by the Allied landing in France in June 1944. Hitler was fighting a two-front war, with both of his opponents rapidly advancing toward his borders.

At the Yalta Conference, 4–11 February 1945, the leaders of the Soviet Union, the United States, and Great Britain planned campaigns for 1945. When the conference opened, major Soviet operations were already under way. The Vistula-Oder Operation, which was launched on 12 January, ended with the German withdrawal from Warsaw as the conferees were assembling at Yalta on 3 February.[71] In East Prussia, Soviet forces had attacked on 13 January in a campaign that would last until 25 April. From 10 February to 4 April, Soviet troops of the First and Second Belorussian fronts carried out the East Pomeranian Operation.

In the Lower Silesian Operation, troops of Konev's First Ukranian Front between 8 and 24 February pushed up even with the troops of Zhukov's First Belorussian Front. After a second offensive from 15 to 31 March, the two fronts were in an advantageous position to launch the Berlin operation.

Farther south, meanwhile, Budapest was taken on 13 February, and Soviet troops pushed on to the area of Lake Balaton from 6 to 15 March.

On 16 April troops of Zhukov's First Belorussian Front and Konev's First Ukrainian Front, followed on 20 April by Rokossovskiy's Second Belorussian Front, began the long awaited attack on Berlin. On 24–25 April Zhukov's and Konev's forces surrounded half a million German troops on the western shore of the Oder-Neisse River, dividing them into two parts. Troops of the Fifth Guards Army of the First Ukrainian Front reached the Elbe, and on 25 April met up with U.S. troops. In Berlin itself, after fierce fighting, Soviet troops stormed the Reichstag on 30 April 1945.[72]

By 1 May, Zhukov's and Konev's forces had defeated 200,000 German troops southeast of Berlin. On 2 May, the remnants of the Berlin garrison surrendered.

During the Berlin operation, Soviet troops engaged 93 German divisions, taking 480,000 prisoners, 1,550 tanks, 8,600 guns, and 4,510 aircraft. On 8 May 1945, Germany formally signed an unconditional surrender. The war in Europe was over.

Soviet participation in the war against Japan was minimal. On 6 August, the first atomic bomb was dropped on Hiroshima. By that time the Japanese Kwantung Army was no longer an effective force in Manchuria, having been dispersed throughout China and the Pacific. On 9 August, troops of the Transbaykal Front, the Second Far Eastern Front, and the First Far Eastern Front—commanded by Marshal R. Ya. Malinovskiy, General M. A. Purkayev, and Marshal K. A. Meretskov, respectively, under the overall commander in chief of Soviet troops in the Far East, Marshal A. M. Vasilevskiy—went on the offensive.[73] The Japanese Kwantung Army was defeated by 20 August, and on 2 September 1945 Japan signed an act of unconditional surrender.

The Workers' and Peasants' Red Army (RKKA), formed in 1918, stood in 1945 as the world's second most powerful military force. Within weeks after the defeat of Japan in August, the United States and other Western powers began a rapid demobilization of their forces. The Red Army was kept at a near wartime footing. As events soon proved, one of its purposes was to keep the nations of Eastern Europe in bondage.

Notes

1. M. V. Zakharov, ed., *50 Let Vooruzhennykh Sil SSSR* [50 Years of the Armed Forces of the USSR] (Moscow: Voyenizdat [Military Publishing House], 1968), p. 15. This book was awarded the Frunze Prize for 1970. The Frunze Prize was inaugurated in 1965 to be awarded to outstanding works in military science. For more information on most points in this book, it is suggested that the reader use the eight-volume *Sovetskaya Voyennaya Entsiklopediya* [Soviet Military Encyclopedia] (*SVE*) (Moscow: Voyenizdat, 1976–1980), bearing in mind that what is presented in these volumes is the Soviet, Party-approved view. For example, on this subject, see "Druzhina" [(Red) Brigade], *SVE*, Vol. 3, p. 265.

2. Ibid., p. 16.

3. G. N. Golikov and M. I. Kuznetsov, "The Great October Socialist Revolution," *Bol'shaya Sovetskaya Entsiklopediya* [The Great Soviet Encyclopedia], 3d ed. (Moscow: Soviet Encyclopedia House, 1971), Vol. 4, p. 347. See also D. M. Kukin, "The Great October Socialist Revolution," *Sovetskaya Voyennaya Entsiklopediya,* Vol. 2, p. 46.

4. Zakharov, *50 Let*, pp. 17–18. See also N. N. Azovtsev, A. K. Selyanichev, "Grazhdanskaya Voyna i Voyennaya Interventsiya v Rossii 1918–1920," *Sovetskaya Voyennaya Entsiklopediya*, Vol. 3, pp. 7–22.

5. Ibid., p. 20.

6. Ibid., p. 21.

7. S. S. Lototskiy, *The Soviet Army* (Moscow: Progress Publishers, 1971), p. 25. See also Zakharov, *50 Let,* p. 25.

8. Zakharov, *50 Let,* p. 29.

9. Yu. P. Petrov, *Stroitel'stvo Politorganov, Partiynykh i Komsomol'skikh Organizatsiy Armii i Flota* [The Structuring of Political Organs, Party and Komsomol Organizations of the Army and Navy] (Moscow: Voyenizdat, 1968), p. 31.

10. Merle Fainsod, *How Russia is Ruled* (Cambridge, Mass.: Harvard University Press, 1967), p. 90.

11. *Bol'shaya Sovetskaya Entsiklopediya*, Vol. 7, p. 233. It is interesting to compare the entries in the third edition of the *Bol'shaya Entsiklopediya*, whose publication began in 1970, with earlier statements in Soviet publications. See also Fainsod, *How Russia is Ruled*, pp. 91–92.

12. Zakharov, *50 Let*, p. 43.

13. Ibid., p. 47.

14. *Bol'shaya Sovetskaya Entsiklopediya*, Vol. 7, p. 228. See also Zakharov, *50 Let,* p. 79.

15. P. N. Dmitriyev, "Vsevobuch" [Universal Military Training], *Sovetskaya Voyennaya Entsiklopediya*, Vol. 2, p. 395.

16. Zakharov, *50 Let*, p. 135.

17. Ibid., pp. 135–148.

18. The many Soviet accounts of the Civil War period scarcely mention Leon D. Trotskiy. Lototskiy, *The Soviet Army,* p. 42, describes Trotskiy as "an opponent of Leninism and a Menshevik," who was "expelled from the Party in 1927, and in 1929 banished from the Soviet Union."

19. Zakharov, *50 Let*, p. 158.

20. Michael T. Florinsky, ed., *Encyclopedia of Russia and the Soviet Union* (New York: McGraw-Hill Book Co., 1961), p. 443.

21. I. B. Berkhin, *Voyennaya Reforma v SSSR—1924–1925* [Military Reforms in the USSR, 1924–1925] (Moscow: Voyenizdat, 1958), p. 181.

22. John Erickson, *The Soviet High Command* (London: St. Martin's Press, 1962), pp. 161–162.

23. Werner Keller, *Are the Russians Ten Feet Tall?* (London: Thames and Hudson, 1961), p. 223.

24. Fainsod, *How Russia is Ruled*, pp. 149–150.

25. Erickson, *The Soviet High Command*, p. 199; see also Roy A. Medvedev, *Let History Judge, the Origins and Consequences of Stalinism* (New York: Alfred A. Knopf, 1972), p. 48.

26. Zakharov, *50 Let*, p. 174; see also Berkhin, *Voyennaya Reforma*, pp. 47–73, for an excellent description of this period.

27. Zakharov, *50 Let*, p. 173; see also Berkhin, *Voyennaya Reforma*, p. 256; S. A. Gladysh, "Territorial'nyy Printsip Komplektovaniya," *Sovetskaya Voyennaya Entsiklopediya*, Vol. 8, p. 29; V. D. Danilov, "Territorial'no-Militsionnaya Sistema," Ibid., Vol. 8, p. 28.

28. M. V. Frunze, *Selected Works* (Moscow: Voyenizdat, 1965), p. 155. This book was the first of the 1960s Officer's Library series.

29. Zakharov, *50 Let*, p. 175.

30. A. Y. Khmel, *Education of the Soviet Soldier: Party-Political Work in the Soviet Armed Forces* (Moscow: Progress Publishers, 1972), p. 23; see also Zakharov, *50 Let*, p. 178.

31. Zakharov, *50 Let*, pp. 189–192; see also V. Dushen'kin, *Ot Soldata Do Marshala* [From Soldier to Marshal] (Moscow: Politizdat, 1966), p. 177.

32. Medvedev, *Let History Judge*, pp. 104–109.

33. V. G. Kulikov, *Akademiya General'novo Shtaba* [Academy of the General Staff] (Moscow: Voyenizdat, 1976), p. 49.

34. See, for example, P. Ya. Yegorov, *Marshal Meretskov* (Moscow: Voyenizdat, 1974). Also see *My—Internatsionalisty* [We Are Internationalists] (Moscow: Politizdat, 1975). This work provides considerable detail about the Soviet "volunteers" in Spain during the Civil War.

35. Alexander Yakovlev, "The Lessons of Spain," in *The Aim of a Lifetime* (Moscow: Progress Publishers, 1972), pp. 75–83.

36. P. G. Grigorenko, "The Concealment of Historical Truth," in *The Grigorenko Papers* (Boulder, Colo.: Westview Press, 1976), p. 30. For more complete details about General Major Petro Grigorenko, the Soviet general exiled in 1977 for dissident activities, read his *Memoirs* (New York & London: W. W. Norton & Co., 1982).

37. Petrov, *Stroitel'stvo*, pp. 229, 237, 240–241.

38. Zakharov, *50 Let*, pp. 198–199.

39. P. N. Pospelov, ed., *Velikaya Otechestvennaya Voyna Sovetskovo Soyuza: Kratkaya Istoriya* [The Great Patriotic War of the Soviet Union: A Short History] (Moscow: Voyenizdat, 1965), pp. 39–40. This work was written while Khrushchev

was in power and published before the "re-Stalinization" period was fully under way. It is highly unlikely that a later description of the purges similar to that contained in this work would have been permitted.

40. Joseph E. Davies, *Mission to Moscow* (New York: Simon & Schuster, 1941), pp. 42–43. Like many men in public service, Mr. Davies "had long experience in law, politics, and international affairs" before being selected as the U.S. ambassador to Moscow, according to the cover on his book.

41. David J. Dallin, *From Purge to Coexistence* (Chicago: Henry Regnery Company, 1964), p. 115. Dallin quotes from one of Walter Duranty's reports, published in the *New York Times* on January 27, 1937, which describes Vyshinskiy as "serious minded and an earnest seeker after truth."

42. Robert Conquest, *The Great Terror* (New York: Macmillan, 1968), p. 506.

43. Ibid., p. 506.

44. Ibid., pp. 459–463. See also "Khasan," *Sovetskaya Voyennaya Entsiklopediya*, Vol. 8, p. 366.

45. Zakharov, *50 Let*, p. 227. See also "Khalkhin-Gol," *Sovetskaya Voyennaya Entsiklopediya*, Vol. 8, pp. 353–354.

46. Even in later years the Soviet political-military hierarchy has had difficulty in explaining these deaths, which took place at the hands not of the Germans but of Stalin and the Party. For example, in 1961, a book about the two-times Heroes of the Soviet Union, *People of Deathless Victory*, failed to mention Smushkevich. The second edition of this book, published in 1965, admitted that "in the period of the personality cult, Ya. V. Smushkevich became a victim of unbased repression. He was killed in February 1942 at the peak of his strength and talent." (p. 324) Another book, *Twice Heros of the Soviet Union*, published in 1973, states only that Smushkevich died in February 1942. A fourth edition, *People of Deathless Victory*, published in 1975, states that he "was a victim of baseless repression and was killed in October 1941. In 1954 Ya. V. Smushkevich was fully rehabilitated." (p. 408) The *Sovetskaya Voyennaya Entsiklopediya* devotes nearly a column to his career (which included his service as commander in chief of Soviet Air Forces in 1939–1940) but only gives his death date, 28 October 1941, without naming the place, a sign of being purged. The *Voyennyy Entsiklopedicheskiy Slovar'* [Military Encyclopedic Dictionary] (*VES*) (Moscow: Voyenizdat, 1983) gives only the year of his death—1941—with no mention of his being killed in the purges. See also Medvedev, *Let History Judge*, p. 248.

47. A. M. Vasilevskiy, *Delo Vsey Zhizni* [A Whole Life's Work], 2d ed. (Moscow: Politizdat, 1975), p. 102. Vasilevskiy, describing the winter war with Finland (1939–1940), tells how B. M. Shaposhnikov, at that time chief of the General Staff, drew up a plan of action that was rejected. K. A. Meretskov, commander of the Leningrad Military District, came up with a second plan, which Stalin accepted. Events proved the plan unsuitable, and enormous efforts were required to conclude the war with tiny Finland. However, Meretskov was promoted to chief of the General Staff in August 1940. Later, according to Vasilevskiy, Stalin admitted the mistake to Shaposhnikov, but said, "The world must know the lessons of the conflict with Finland were taken fully into account.

This is important in order to give our enemies the right impression and cool off hot-headed imperialists." See also P. A. Rotmistrov, *Vremya i Tanki* [Time and the Tank] (Moscow: Voyenizdat, 1972), p. 71.

48. Zakharov, *50 Let*, p. 234. See also S. M. Shtemenko, *Novyy Zakon i Voinskaya Sluzhba* [The New Law and Military Service] (Moscow: Voyenizdat, 1968), p. 16. By the simple lowering of the call-up age from twenty-one to nineteen years of age, the armed forces were able to draft three age categories at once, i.e., nineteen-, twenty-, and twenty-one-year-olds. This immediately increased the armed forces to 4,207,000 men.

49. Zakharov, *50 Let*, p. 234.

50. Ibid., p. 235.

51. A. M. Nekrich, *June 22, 1941*, translated, with analysis by Vladimir Petrov, *"June 22, 1941"—Soviet Historians and the German Invasion* (Columbia, S.C.: University of South Carolina Press, 1968). Nekrich's work was published in Moscow in 1965 and initially attracted favorable reviews. However, as the "re-Stalinization" program gained ground, he was expelled from the Communist Party. Aleksandr M. Nekrich was a senior scholar in the USSR Academy of Sciences' Institute of History until he left the Soviet Union in 1976. Currently (1984), he is working at the Russian Research Center of Harvard University. See also Grigorenko, *The Grigorenko Papers,* pp. 12–51. For a somewhat different view, see I. Kh. Bagramyan, *Tak Nachinalas' Voyna* [How the War Began] (Moscow: Voyenizdat, 1971).

52. P. A. Zhilin, "The Great Patriotic War of the Soviet Union: 1941–1945," *Sovetskaya Voyennaya Entsiklopediya*, Vol. 2, p. 54. Zhilin is the head of the Institute of Military History, Moscow.

53. A. S. Orlov, "Barbarossa," *Sovetskaya Voyennaya Entsiklopediya*, Vol. 1, p. 392. Pierre Accoce and Pierre Quet, in *A Man Called Lucy: 1939–1945* (New York: Coward, McCann, & Geoghegan, 1967), give different figures. A Soviet spy, code-name Lucy, passed to the Kremlin many details of the forthcoming German invasion.

54. Zakharov, *50 Let*, p. 265.

55. *Krasnaya Zvezda*, between 11 February 1973 and 5 May 1975, ran seventy-six articles on the work of GKO during World War II.

56. Vasilevskiy, *Delo Vsey Zhizni*, pp. 127, 535, 538.

57. See, for example, V. G. Kulikov, "The Brain of the Army," *Pravda*, 13 November 1974. For an English translation, see William F. Scott, ed., *Selected Soviet Military Writings, 1970–1975: A Soviet View* (Washington, D.C.: Government Printing Office, 1977), pp. 185–191.

58. N. Ya. Komarov, "Bitva za Leningrad 1941–1944" [Battle for Leningrad 1941–1944], *Sovetskaya Voyennaya Entsiklopediya*, Vol. 1, p. 487.

59. M. V. Zakharov, "The Great Patriotic War of the Soviet Union," *Bol'shaya Sovetskaya Entsiklopediya*, Vol. 4, p. 393.

60. G. K. Zhukov, "Bitva Pod Moskvoy 1941–1942" [Battle near Moscow 1941–1942], *Sovetskaya Voyennaya Entsiklopediya*, Vol. 1, p. 493. Marshal Zhukov was in command of the operation.

61. Yu. V. Plotnikov, "Stalingradskaya Bitva 1942–1943" [Battle of Stalingrad 1942–1943], *Sovetskaya Voyennaya Entsiklopediya*, Vol. 7, p. 517.

62. A. A. Grechko, "Bitva za Kavkaz 1942–1943" [Battle for the Caucasus 1942–1943], *Sovetskaya Voyennaya Entsiklopediya*, Vol. 1, p. 484. Marshal Grechko was in command of the operation.

63. Khmel, *Education*, p. 26.

64. Pospelov, *Istoriya Velikaya*, p. 220.

65. A. M. Vasilevskiy, "Kurskaya Bitva 1943" [Battle of Kursk 1943], *Sovetskaya Voyennaya Entsiklopediya*, Vol. 4, p. 537. Marshal Vasilevskiy was chief of the General Staff.

66. Pospelov, *Istoriya Velikaya*, p. 252.

67. N. I. Shekhovtsov, G. A. Koltunov, "Bitva za Dnepr 1943" [Battle for the Dnepr 1943], *Sovetskaya Voyennaya Entsiklopediya*, Vol. 1, p. 481.

68. Zakharov, *50 Let*, p. 397.

69. B. I. Kuznetsov, "Kiyevskaya Nastupatel'naya Operatsiya 1943" [Kiev Offensive Operation 1943], *Sovetskaya Voyennaya Entsiklopediya*, Vol. 4, p. 157.

70. A. M. Vasilevskiy, "Belorusskaya Operatsiya 1944" [Belorussian Operation 1944], *Sovetskaya Voyennaya Entsiklopediya*, Vol. 1, p. 431. Marshal Vasilevskiy coordinated the operation.

71. Pospelov, *Istoriya Velikaya*, pp. 341–345.

72. G. K. Zhukov, "Berlinskaya Operatsiya 1945" [Berlin Operation 1945], *Sovetskaya Voyennaya Entsiklopediya*, Vol. 1, p. 456. Marshal Zhukov commanded the Berlin Operation.

73. G. K. Plotnikov, "Man'chzhurskaya Operatsiya 1945" [Manchurian Operation 1945], *Sovetskaya Voyennaya Entsiklopediya*, Vol. 5, p. 128.

Part 1

FUNDAMENTALS OF
SOVIET MILITARY DOCTRINE
AND STRATEGY

2
Postwar Development of Soviet Military Doctrine and Strategy

Soviet military strategists identify three specific periods in the post–World War II development of their Armed Forces.[1] The first is from 1945 to March 1953; the second is from April 1953 to 1959; and the third, which began in 1960, continues, with modifications, into the 1980s. Each of these periods has its own characteristics as a specific stage in the development of Soviet military doctrine.

The Soviet meaning of military doctrine is very different from United States military usage. As explained in 1982 by Marshal N. V. Ogarkov, chief of the General Staff, military doctrine *"is a system of views adopted by a given state at a given (certain) time on the goals and nature of a possible future war and the preparation of the armed forces and the country for it, and also the methods of waging it"*[2] (emphasis in original). Soviet sources also declare that

> Military doctrine has two closely connected, interdependent sides—socio-political and military-technical. The socio-political side encompasses questions concerning the methodological, economic, social and legal bases of achieving the goals of a possible future war. It is definitive and has the greatest stability since it reflects the class essence and political goals of the state which are relatively constant for a long period of time. The military-technical side, in conformity with the socio-political goals, includes questions of direct military structuring and technical equipping of the armed forces and their training and the determination of the forms and methods of the conduct by the armed forces of operations and the war as a whole.[3]

Marshal Ogarkov went on to say that the military doctrine of any state answers the following basic questions:

What is the degree of probability of a future war, and with what enemy will one have to deal?

What character might the war take that the country and its armed forces
   might be forced to wage?
What goals and missions can be assigned to the armed forces in anticipation
   (*predvidenii*) of such a war, and what armed forces must the nation
   possess in order to achieve the stated goals?
Proceeding from this, how should the nation carry out military structuring
   to prepare the army and country for war?
Finally, if war breaks out, by what methods should it be fought?[4]

Military doctrine, as demonstrated by these questions, is concerned
with future war. Since it is the military policy of the Communist Party,
it governs the actions of the leadership of the Soviet Armed Forces in
meeting the Party's military requirements.

An understanding of the development of Soviet military doctrine is
an initial requirement in understanding the Soviet Armed Forces.

Last Years of the Stalin Era: 1945–March 1953

The first stage in the postwar development of the Soviet Armed Forces
ended with the death of Stalin. This was a period of significant technological progress. Despite the devastated condition of the Soviet Union
and the millions of soldiers and civilians that had been killed in the
previous decade in Stalin's purges and Hitler's invasion, an immediate
massive effort was made to break the nuclear monopoly of the United
States. Years ahead of most Western projections, the Soviet Union exploded
its first nuclear bomb in 1949. The initial carrier for this new Soviet
weapon was the Tu-4 bomber, a carbon copy of the United States
B-29, called by its designer, Andrei Tupolev, "a locally built Boeing
product." At this time, however, there was very little discussion in the
Soviet press about nuclear weapons.

During this stage, lessons from World War II were closely studied
in military schools. Special faculties were formed at both the General
Staff Academy and the Frunze Military Academy for this purpose. Schools
increased the length of courses to serve peacetime training requirements.
Obtaining qualified faculties was difficult, since Stalin's purges of the
senior Soviet officer corps had not ended in 1938 but had continued
even throughout World War II and into the postwar period. Officers
were not permitted to investigate the possible nature of a future war.

Eight months after Hitler's invasion thrust the Soviet Union into
World War II, Stalin, on 23 February 1942, issued his five "permanent
operating principles," which formed the basis of Soviet military theory
until after his death in 1953. These principles were as follows: (1)
stability of the rear, (2) morale of the army, (3) quantity and quality

of divisions, (4) armament, and (5) organizing ability of command personnel.[5]

In spite of the development of nuclear weapons, no discussion on doctrine was permitted during Stalin's lifetime, and, indeed, he disliked the term. Although senior Soviet officers who served in Berlin and other areas of Europe may have recognized that the nuclear weapon had brought about basic changes in warfare, they had to act as if this weapon did not exist.

Stalin's silence probably was a deliberate tactic. His immense ground forces were digesting their "liberation" of Eastern Europe. He preferred not to call attention to the nuclear weapon as long as the United States maintained either a monopoly or, after 1949, definite superiority both in numbers and in delivery systems.

Stalin also appears to have been making plans for extending Soviet control in the Far East. In the late 1940s he moved a number of his most trusted generals and marshals to the eastern military districts to plan and support a North Korean invasion of South Korea. During this period also, North Korean divisions were sent to the Soviet Union, intensively trained there, and then returned to North Korea. Each was immediately replaced by another division, which would go through the same intensive training course. Marshal R. Ya. Malinovskiy, later to become the minister of defense, was sent to the Far East with a new title: commander in chief of troops of the Far East.[6] General of Aviation I. N. Kozhedub, the leading Soviet fighter ace of World War II, was sent as air commander of the area.

Unexpectedly, the North Korean invasion of South Korea in 1950 involved the United States. The Kremlin's efforts were described as follows:

At the end of 1950, at the request of the government of the Chinese People's Republic, several aviation divisions were transferred to China to cover the northeast provinces of the country from air raid by American aviation. In the event of worsening circumstances, the USSR was prepared to send five divisions to Korea to give the Korean Peoples' Democratic Republic assistance in repulsing U.S. aggression.[7]

Another book stated that "dozens of American aircraft were destroyed in the air by Soviet pilots.[8]

On 5 March 1953, the death of Stalin brought an end to an era of Soviet military affairs. The impact was immediate.

The Revolution in Military Affairs: April 1953–December 1959

Within weeks after Stalin's death, deadlocked talks were reopened with the United Nations toward reaching a truce in the Korean War. The new Soviet leaders—G. M. Malenkov, Party secretary and chairman of the Council of Ministers; N. A. Bulganin, minister of defense; L. P. Beria, head of the MVD; and Nikita Khrushchev—were uncertain as to what might happen within the Soviet Union, now that the long regime of Stalin had ended. More importantly perhaps, they wanted to focus their attention on vying for power in an internal arena without outside distractions.

The vast research and development program started by Stalin was beginning to show returns in military hardware and weapons. In August 1953, Soviet scientists exploded a hydrogen bomb, dropped from an airplane. This was claimed to be the world's first hydrogen bomb, since an earlier hydrogen explosion in the United States had been a "device," exploded on the ground, and not a bomb.[9] New jet bombers, the Tu-16, given the name Badger by NATO, and the M-4 (Bison), entered operational service. By mid-1955 it was estimated by analysts in the United States that Bison production would rise to twenty-five aircraft per month, which would exceed production of the B-52, a somewhat comparable bomber aircraft in the United States.

Soviet successes with development of an atomic and a hydrogen bomb were not the only surprises for the West. By 1955 U.S. intelligence services learned that the Soviets also were achieving major breakthroughs in their missile programs. On 4 October 1957 Soviet scientists put aloft the world's first artificial satellite. In that same year they also tested the world's first intercontinental ballistic missile. In the period between 1955 and 1957 the decision was made by the Soviet Party-military leadership to limit production of aircraft and instead to concentrate on the missile as the primary delivery vehicle for the atomic and hydrogen weapons.[10]

As these breakthroughs were being achieved in research, development, production, and deployment of new weapons systems, major changes also were taking place in Soviet military concepts. In September 1953, *Military Thought,* the classified journal of the Soviet General Staff, carried an article titled "On the Question of the Laws of Military Science."[11] The author was the journal's own editor, General Major N. A. Talenskiy. While not actually challenging Stalin's five permanent operating factors, Talenskiy implied that these principles were not basic.

After discussing the various laws of war and how they might be applied, Talenskiy concluded his article by calling for a critique of existing military concepts. Within the next year *Military Thought* published numerous responses to Talenskiy's article.[12] Despite these responses, and the fact that someone in authority must have given permission for publication of both the article and the letters, Talenskiy apparently had overstepped some undefined bounds. In June 1954 he was removed as editor of *Military Thought* and eventually went to the Institute of History in the Soviet Academy of Sciences.

Questions that Talenskiy had raised in the classified journal were not immediately revealed in the open press. Marshal A. M. Vasilevskiy, who had been minister of defense at the time of Stalin's death, reaffirmed the validity of Stalin's permanent operating principles in *Red Star* in February 1954.[13] Vasilevskiy again declared, in another *Red Star* article in May 1954, that "the outcome of a war is determined not by transitory factors but by the permanently operating factors."[14] This same view was presented in a basic military work, *On Soviet Military Science*, edited by Colonel P. A. Sidorov, which appeared in 1954.

Nevertheless, Stalin's hold on Soviet military thought soon was challenged at high levels. In February 1955, Marshal Zhukov replaced Marshal Bulganin as minister of defense. It has been reported that on the eve of his taking command he gave a secret address to his leading officers, in which he strongly criticized Stalin's permanent operating factors and stressed the need for a new look at military affairs. The following month, the validity of Stalin's concepts was questioned openly by P. A. Rotmistrov, who was marshal of armored forces, doctor of military sciences, and a professor. Specifically, Rotmistrov raised the question of how the permanent operating factors could be valid in the event of a nuclear war beginning with a surprise attack.[15] Within the year Stalin's military views appear to have been rejected by the majority of Soviet military theoreticians.

The Twentieth Party Congress in 1956, at which Khrushchev gave his famed secret speech denouncing Stalin, called for a new examination of questions of military science. (Military science, military art, and military strategy will be discussed in Chapter 3.) In May 1957, a conference was convened to reexamine Soviet military science and scientific research within the Armed Forces. A series of seminars was conducted the following year by the General Staff to examine problems of military art and the nature of future war. These seminars were conducted in secret, with high-ranking Soviet officers participating in the discussions.[16] A general conclusion was reached that the introduction of the nuclear weapon and the missile had brought about radical changes in all aspects of warfare, forcing major revisions in basic concepts.

Khrushchev personally followed these discussions, along with members of both the Politburo and the Secretariat. A number of these Party leaders were qualified to make judgments on both strategy and tactics, having held general officer rank both during World War II and in the postwar years. Senior officers in the Soviet Armed Forces, including "the minister of defense, his deputy, commanders of military districts, senior officers of the General Staff, chiefs of military academies, and the professors and teachers of the higher military education institutions," were directed to prepare studies on the impact of the nuclear rocket weapon on military art. The Party leadership concluded that the nuclear weapon and missile would be decisive factors in any future war. This group of officers produced a series of papers that subsequently were known as the Special Collection and were published by *Military Thought* beginning in January 1960.

According to Colonel Oleg Penkovskiy, a Soviet officer who subsequently transmitted these papers to British and United States intelligence agents, the Special Collection "must become, or perhaps already had become a sort of guide for the Soviet state in preparing its armed forces for war, and it sets forth in detail where and how future military actions should start." Penkovskiy further stated that the new guide asserts that "a future war will begin with a sudden nuclear strike against the enemy. There will be no declaration of war. Quite to the contrary, an effort will be made to avoid a declaration of war." The basic goal was "to try to achieve victory with a short war (by a lightning strike) but be prepared for a prolonged war."[17]

There was no doubt that a revolution had taken place in Soviet military affairs.

The Drive for Nuclear Status: 1960–1968

A new military doctrine was outlined by Khrushchev on 14 January 1960 in a speech before the Fourth Session of the Supreme Soviet of the USSR. Khrushchev, noting, "our Armed Forces have to a considerable degree been switched to the nuclear rocket weapon," outlined general concepts that in his view would determine the nature of a possible war. These concepts were repeated by Soviet military theorists long after Khrushchev had been deposed and become a "nonperson." In summary, he affirmed that:

As stated at the Twentieth and Twenty-first congresses of the CPSU, there is no longer any fatal inevitability of war.

War will begin not as it did in the past by invasions of frontiers, but by rocket strikes deep in the interior, and "not a single capital, no large industrial or administrative center, and no strategic area will remain unattacked in the very first minutes, let alone days, of the war."

Although the Soviet Union should expect a surprise attack, such an attack will not by itself win a war. Duplicate rocket sites have been constructed and there would be sufficient numbers of weapons surviving the initial strike to deal successfully with the aggressor.

Both atomic and hydrogen weapons, together with rockets to carry them, are possessed by the Soviet Union. If attacked, the USSR would "wipe the country or countries attacking us off the face of the earth." If the West starts a war, it would mean the end of capitalism. The USSR would suffer huge losses, but would survive.

The Soviet Union has better rockets than the United States and will seek to maintain that lead until agreement on disarmament is reached.

In modern times a nation's defense capability depends on firepower, not on number of men under arms. Hence, due to possession of nuclear weaponry, the manpower of the Soviet Armed Forces would be reduced.[18]

At the time, Western analysts failed to note the nuclear emphasis of Khrushchev's speech. Instead, they paid great attention to his claim that military manpower would be reduced and that some air and artillery units would be disbanded. Khrushchev noted that "some of the artillerymen and fliers will be used in the newly formed rocket units." He also mentioned the possibility of reverting to a territorial militia system, such as had been used in the 1920s and early 1930s. When speaking of the territorial militia, however, Khrushchev used terms such as "in due course" or "looking ahead."

For anyone studying Soviet demographic trends, Khrushchev's statements about reducing manpower in the Soviet Armed Forces should not have been surprising. The small number of children who were conceived, born, or survived the grim years from 1941 to 1945—and even the period of food shortages and actual starvation in the immediate postwar years—began to have its effect in the 1960s. In 1959 the Soviet Union had 6,915,000 males in the eighteen to twenty-one age bracket. In 1960, the year of Khrushchev's speech, the number was reduced to 6,625,000. By 1964 a low of 3,164,000 was reached, less than one-half the 1959 figure. Even as late as 1967 the figure had climbed back only to 4,625,000.[19] With this manpower shortage, it was necessary for the Soviet Union either to reduce the size of its armed forces or to curtail its industrial growth.

Khrushchev's 1960 speech had an Orwellian title: "Disarmament— For Durable Peace and Friendship." In subsequent years, Soviet publications referenced that speech as signifying the change in Soviet military doctrine. Since Khrushchev's ouster in 1964, writers have simply referred to the person delivering the speech as the "Party's first secretary."[20]

Almost two years later, during the meeting of the Twenty-second Party Congress in October 1961, Khrushchev claimed, "We have achieved indisputable superiority in rocketry and nuclear arms."[21] At the same congress, Minister of Defense Marshal Malinovskiy discussed "the social and political essence of modern wars." He stated that all work in building up the Armed Forces was conducted under the guidance of the decisions of the Central Committee of the Party and the Soviet government.

Referring to Khrushchev's speech of January 1960 to the Supreme Soviet, Malinovskiy stated:

> In that speech, a thorough analysis was given to the nature of modern war, which lies at the base of Soviet military doctrine. One of the important positions of this doctrine is that a world war, if in spite of everything is unleashed by the imperialist aggressors, will inevitably take the form of nuclear rocket war, that is, the kind of war in which the main means of striking will be the nuclear weapon and the basic means of delivering it to the target will be the rocket. In connection with this, war will also begin in a different way from before and will be conducted in a different way. . . .
>
> The use of atomic and thermonuclear weapons, with unlimited possibilities for their delivery to any target in calculated minutes with the aid of rockets, permits the achievement of decisive military results in the shortest period of time at any distance and over enormous territory. The objects of crushing nuclear strikes will be groupings of the enemy armed forces, industrial and vital centers, communications junctions—everything that feeds war.
>
> A future world war, if not prevented, will take on an unprecedentedly destructive character. It will lead to the death of hundreds of millions of people, and whole countries will be turned into lifeless deserts covered with ashes. . . .
>
> In spite of the fact that in a future war the decisive place will belong to the nuclear rocket weapon, we nevertheless come to the conclusion that final victory over the aggressor can be achieved only as a result of the joint actions of all the services of the Armed Forces. This is why we are giving the necessary attention to perfecting all kinds of weapons, teaching the troops to use them skillfully and to achieve decisive victory over the aggressor.
>
> We also consider that, in contemporary circumstances, a future world war will be waged, in spite of enormous losses, by massive, multimillion armed forces.
>
> . . . The importance of the beginning period of a possible war is that in this period the first massive nuclear strikes can, to an enormous degree, predetermine the whole subsequent course of the war, and lead to such losses in the interior and in the troops that the people and the country might be placed in exceptionally serious circumstances.
>
> Evaluating circumstances realistically, it must be taken into account that the imperialists are preparing a surprise nuclear attack against the USSR and other socialist countries. Therefore, Soviet military doctrine

considers the most important, the main and paramount task of the Armed Forces to be in constant readiness for the reliable repulse of a surprise attack of the enemy and to frustrate his criminal plans.

The fact is that in contemporary circumstances, any armed conflict *inevitably* will escalate into general nuclear rocket war if the nuclear powers are involved in it. Thus, *we must prepare our Armed Forces, the country and all the people for struggle with the aggressor, first of all and mainly, in conditions of nuclear war.* (emphasis added)

Our country is big and wide. It is less vulnerable than capitalist countries. But we clearly recognize that this would be for us an exceptionally severe war. We are deeply convinced that in this war, if the imperialists thrust it on us, *the socialist camp will win and capitalism will be destroyed forever.*[22] (emphasis added)

The exact concepts that Marshal Malinovskiy had presented in 1961 before the Twenty-second Party Congress were stressed in 1962 in the third edition of an authoritative Party-military work, *Marxism-Leninism on War and the Army*. The authors of this book were members of the Department of Dialectical and Historical Materialism of the Lenin Military-Political Academy. In some cases they repeated, word for word, the points concerning doctrine that previously had been expressed by both Khrushchev and Malinovskiy:

In its social and political character a future war, if the imperialists succeed in unleashing it, will be an embittered armed clash of two diametrically opposed social systems, a struggle between two coalitions—socialist and imperialist—in which each of the sides will pursue the most decisive goals.

By the nature of the means used, such a war inevitably will be nuclear rocket, and therefore unprecedentedly shattering and destructive. The main role in the war will be played by the Strategic Rocket Troops and also the Troops of PVO (air defense) and PRO (antimissile defense). . . .

Soviet military doctrine proceeds from the fact that the imperialists are preparing a surprise nuclear rocket attack against the USSR and the other socialist countries. Therefore, the main and paramount task of the Armed Forces is to be constantly ready to repulse a surprise enemy attack and to frustrate his criminal plans.[23]

The outpouring of writings describing nuclear war was unprecedented. A major doctrinal decision had been made that would impact upon the very fabric of the Soviet state, and the Party leadership wanted to ensure that this new decision was understood. In December 1962, less than two months after the Cuban confrontation, Marshal Malinovskiy, in a pamphlet entitled *Vigilantly Stand Guard Over the Peace,* once again explained in even greater detail the provisions of the nuclear doctrine.[24]

Military doctrine has two sides, the political and military-technical, Malinovskiy explained. The political side had been worked out at the Twentieth, Twenty-first, and Twenty-second Party Congresses. As agreed at the Twentieth Party Congress, war is no longer a fatal inevitability. Because of the growing strength of the Soviet Armed Forces, he declared, there is a real possibility that world war could be excluded from the world even before the complete victory of socialism. The reason, he went on to assert, is that the Soviet Armed Forces are reaching such a military posture that the imperialists would not dare unleash aggression.

Malinovskiy's statements were clear and concise:

> A future world war, if the imperialists succeed in unleashing it, will be a decisive armed clash of the opposed social systems: . . . it inevitably will be thermonuclear, a war in which the main means of destruction will be the nuclear weapon and the basic means of its delivery to the target, the rocket. . . . Now war might arise without the traditional clearly threatening period, by surprise, as a result of the mass use of long-range rockets armed with powerful nuclear warheads.[25]

Although a surprise attack launched by the imperialists was seen as posing the greatest danger, Marshal Malinovskiy warned that world war might grow out of a local conflict. The West, led by the United States, is trying "to achieve its aggressive goals by way of waging local 'little' wars with the use of conventional and, as the American generals say, tactical nuclear weapons."

The Soviet minister of defense also discussed the "imperialists'" intentions of initiating "preventive war." Because of the possibility of such a war, the Soviet Union must "be constantly ready for the reliable repulse of a surprise attack of the enemy and for frustrating his criminal plans."

As for the duration of a possible future war, Malinovskiy stated that "now no one can reject the possibility of a swift war." At the same time, "it might not be limited only to strikes with the nuclear weapon. A future war might be protracted."

Malinovskiy went on to repeat the basic points of the new doctrine that he had presented the previous year before the Twenty-second Party Congress. For example: "Final victory over the aggressor can be achieved only as a result of the combined actions of all services of the armed forces, of all kinds of weapons." Further, a future war will require mass multimillion men armies. And also:

> Since any military conflict, when the major powers are drawn into it, threatens inevitably to escalate into all-inclusive nuclear war, then we must

prepare our Armed Forces, the country and all the people first of all and primarily to struggle with the aggressors in conditions of nuclear war.[26]

The decision to "prepare our Armed Forces, the country and all the people first of all and primarily to struggle with the aggressors in conditions of nuclear war" established the guidelines. The next step was to ensure that the doctrine would be disseminated and studied throughout the Soviet Union.

Publicizing the Revolution in Military Affairs

It was not enough that the new military doctrine be understood by all members of the Soviet Armed Forces; the implications of the new doctrine must be part of the ideological conditioning of each individual. But the subject of doctrine had to be introduced carefully. Virtually all of the great Soviet strategists and tacticians of the 1920s and 1930s— A. A. Svechin, A. N. Lapchinskiy, M. N. Tukhachevskiy, and others— had died in Stalin's military purges of 1937–1938. Their works had been destroyed, or in many cases only a single copy remained.[27] As late as 1961 there was no reason for the average Soviet officer even to doubt the validity of Stalin's five permanent operating factors. Stalin was at Lenin's side in the mausoleum on Red Square, and Leninism-Stalinism was the official Soviet ideology.

The outlook of the Soviet officer corps required complete reorientation. Most of the officers at this time still were products of World War II. A number of the Soviet leaders of the early 1960s had fought in the Civil War, and a few, including Marshal Malinovskiy, had been in World War I. In the immediate postwar years, 1945–1953, the existence of the nuclear weapon was seldom mentioned in the public press. In 1946, over 1 million horses still were found in the Soviet Armed Forces.[28] The change from mounted cavalry and horse-drawn vehicles to nuclear weapons and intercontinental ballistic missiles in such a few years had to be assimilated.

In the Soviet Union, the Party leaders traditionally use slogans to emphasize to the "masses" changes in directions that have been made by the Party or as guidelines for personal conduct. To make the Soviet Armed Forces, and the population as a whole, fully aware that a major transformation had taken place both in the conduct of war and in its consequences, a slogan was needed that would signify the change. To be effective a slogan must have emotional appeal. The purpose of the Armed Forces, as Soviet ideologists constantly affirm, is to protect the "gains of the revolution." In the Soviet Union, "revolution" is good and associated with the Party, which itself came to power through the "glorious revolution."

"The revolution in military affairs" was selected as the slogan that was to explain the changes in warfare and in the Soviet Armed Forces that had resulted from the breakthrough in nuclear weapons and ballistic missiles.[29] Throughout the 1960s and into the 1980s almost everything written in the Soviet Union on military doctrine made reference to this revolution. An entire series of pamphlets was issued to explain the revolution in military affairs to Soviet noncommissioned personnel.[30]

In November 1963, Marshal Malinovskiy outlined the tasks of the military press in explaining this transformation of the Soviet Armed Forces:

> Military newspapers and magazines, and Voyenizdat, our military publishing house, can and must do a great deal for the thorough explanation of the nature of the revolution in military affairs and the resulting demands produced in the training and education of personnel of different branches and services of the Armed Forces.[31]

Malinovskiy's orders were carried out by military publicists at all levels. Changes were far-reaching and affected every facet of the Soviet Armed Forces. For the revolution

> encompassed all areas of military affairs (this is the content of the revolution): the military-technical base of war which led to the rearming of the troops with new weapons and military equipment; the methods and forms of waging war and military operations, military art; the structure of the armed forces which evoked changes in the organizational structure, in the correlation of the services of the armed forces and branches of the services (the appearance of a qualitatively new service of the armed forces); operational, and combat training, the whole system of training and educating the troops. It evoked a revolution in military theory, in the views of the nature of waging contemporary war. Military-theoretical thought revealed new phenomena born of the revolution, explained their nature, their interrelationships, and practical meaning.[32]

As a result of the revolution in military affairs, military power took on a new dimension:

> Today, the military might of a country is determined by the nuclear rocket weapon, the combat qualities of its nuclear charges and strategic rockets, the level of development of its nuclear and rocket industry, the power of its strategic rocket troops, and the nuclear rocket weapons of all other services of the Armed Forces.[33]

In Marxist-Leninist dialectical terminology, a qualitative jump took place in military affairs when the nuclear weapon, the missile, and the necessary guidance and control were integrated into a new weapons system. According to the Soviets, this was not simply a quantitative change, which takes place in weaponry and in warfare on a continuous basis. The longbow in the hands of English archers produced a quantitative change in warfare. The introduction of gunpowder, however, produced a qualitative jump, bringing about revolutionary changes. Quantitative changes then occurred over a time span of several hundred years, as the musket was replaced by the breechloader and finally automatic weapons came into being. But these, and even the V-1 and V-2 rockets of World War II, as well as the tanks and heavy artillery, still were based on the continuation of the revolution that began with gunpowder.

When—in the view of Soviet political-military theorists—there are sufficient changes in quantity, a qualitative jump occurs. The nuclear bomb, the missile, and cybernetics, making possible the guidance and control systems for the missile, resulted in this qualitative jump, which they call the current revolution in military affairs. According to Marxist-Leninist theory, the old does not disappear all at once; its usable parts remain. However, the only "old" that continues to exist is that which finds a useful place in the environment created by the new.

The Continuity of Soviet Military Doctrine After Khrushchev

In October 1964, the ouster of Nikita Khrushchev caught the Western world by surprise. There was a great deal of speculation in the United States that the military leadership might have had a hand in his removal from power, because of a belief among some "Sovietologists" that Khrushchev had forced unpopular policies upon the Soviet Armed Forces. As a result of Khrushchev's disappearance, many foreign analysts thought there would be significant changes in Soviet military policies.

This did not prove to be the case. Khrushchev's downfall did not have any apparent influence on the new military doctrine, nor did it lessen in any way the significance of the revolution in military affairs. One of the first indications of continuity in these areas was the appearance in early 1965 of a short book, *Problems of the Revolution in Military Affairs.*[34] This book, by P. M. Derevyanko, issued by Voyenizdat, the publishing house of the Ministry of Defense, had been sent to the publishers in June 1964. It was assigned for final typesetting on 21 October 1964, scarcely a week after Brezhnev assumed power. The work consists of articles that had appeared in the Soviet military press in 1963 and in the first half of 1964. In the original text a number of the articles had referred to Khrushchev by name. In the week between Khrushchev's ouster and final typesetting, the articles were edited so as to remove all references by name to the former ruler. Otherwise, the content was unchanged. The first article is a reprint of an article by Marshal Malinovskiy, "The Revolution in Military Affairs and the Task of the Military Press."[35] All of the subsequent articles deal with some aspect of the new doctrine. There is no indication that the military policy of the Communist Party, established under Khrushchev, had been changed in the slightest.

In December 1964, less than two months after the new regime had been installed, *Red Star* announced that a new series of military writings called the Officer's Library would be published. Its purpose would be "to arm the reader with a knowledge of the fundamental changes which have taken place in recent years in military affairs." Readers were told that "in the 'library' there will be works on strategy, tactics, military doctrine, military pedagogics and psychology, and reference books necessary for officers."[36]

The first three books in the series constitute the collected works of V. I. Lenin, M. I. Kalinin, and M. V. Frunze, all dating back to the early 1920s. Stalin, wanting no competition in the military sphere, had stopped their publication. The fourth book of the series, published in 1965, was the fourth edition of *Marxism-Leninism on War and the Army*, written by a group of authors of the Department of Marxist-Leninist Philosophy at the Lenin Military-Political Academy. It continued the same theme that had been expressed in the third edition, which appeared in 1962. For example,

> According to its size, a nuclear war will be an intercontinental war. This is conditioned both by its sociopolitical content and by the presence on both sides of rockets of any radius of action, atomic rocket-carrying submarines and also strategic bombers. War will actually encompass the whole of our planet.
>
> It will be waged by absolutely different methods. Formerly, the direct goal of military operations was the complete and utter defeat of the enemy's armed forces, without which it was impossible to reach the most important strategic centers of the enemy. Now the situation is different. The use of the nuclear rocket weapon will permit the achieving of decisive military results at any distance and over enormous territory in the shortest period of time.[37]

Throughout 1965, articles in military journals and newspapers continued to explain the new military doctrine and the requirement that the Armed Forces, the populace, and the economy should all be prepared for the eventuality of a nuclear rocket war. "On the Nature of World Nuclear-Rocket War,"[38] which appeared in *Communist of the Armed Forces*, the journal of the Main Political Administration of the Army and Navy, astounded many Western readers by its advocacy of the use of nuclear weapons. In November 1965, the same journal issued instructions to political officers on how to explain the new doctrine to members of the Armed Forces. An article for political officers entitled "The Character and Features of Nuclear-Rocket War" specified how lecturers were to discuss: (1) nuclear rocket weapons—the main means of carrying out combat actions in contemporary war, (2) the role and place of different services and branches in nuclear rocket war, and (3) the features of combat actions of units under conditions using nuclear rocket weapons.[39]

In the years following, book after book and article after article continued the emphasis on nuclear rocket war. *The History of Military Art*, published in 1966 as the sixth book of the Officer's Library series, included the following paragraphs.

> The Communist Party and its Central Committee, concentrating their activity on solving the problem of the reconstruction of all military affairs, worked out Soviet military doctrine. What are the basic positions which make up the content of Soviet military doctrine on the question of the nature of waging war?
>
> A future war, if the imperialists unleash it against the socialist countries, will become a world war; the main forces of the world will be drawn into it, and it will be a war of the two coalitions with opposing sociopolitical systems. It will be a decisive clash of two opposing sociopolitical systems. The basic contradiction of the modern world will be decided in it, the contradiction between socialism and imperialism. War is a continuation of politics. It is "politics through and through," as V. I. Lenin wrote. . . .
>
> World war will inevitably assume the nature of a nuclear rocket war with the main means of destruction in the war being the nuclear rocket weapon and the basic manner of delivering it to the target being rockets of various types.[40]

The History of Military Art was a joint effort by faculty members of the Frunze Military Academy and the Lenin Military-Political Academy. A 1967 book, *V. I. Lenin and the Soviet Armed Forces*, written by professors at the Lenin Military-Political Academy, expressed the same thoughts.

> The Communist Party has worked out a military doctrine answering to the demands of modern war and the modern stage of organization of the Armed Forces. What are the basic positions on the nature of future war if the imperialists unleash it?
>
> War will inevitably become a world nuclear rocket war and will draw into the armed struggle the main countries of the world. The bloc of

aggressive imperialist states will face the countries of the socialist community. The main striking force will be the nuclear weapon and the basic means of delivering it to the target will be the rockets of various types.[41]

In 1968 this book was awarded the Frunze Prize, clear evidence of the full acceptance of its contents by the Party-military hierarchy.

The fiftieth anniversary of the Armed Forces of the USSR was celebrated in 1968. *Fifty Years of the Armed Forces of the USSR* was the title of one of the major books, published that year, which two years later was also to win the Frunze Prize. Marshal of the Soviet Union Zakharov, chief of the General Staff, was senior editor of the work, with the chief of the Main Political Administration of the Soviet Army and Navy, General of the Army Yepishev, as vice chairman of the editorial board. Members of the Soviet Armed Forces again were reminded:

> Our military doctrine holds that a new world war, if the imperialists unleash it, will be a decisive clash of the two social systems and it will draw into its orbit the majority of the countries of the world. The powerful coalition of the socialist countries, united by unanimity of political and military goals, will oppose the aggressive imperialist bloc.
>
> It will be a thermonuclear war according to the nature of the means of armed conflict used in the war. The nuclear weapon will be the main and decisive means of waging world war, and the rocket will be the main means of delivering it on target. At the same time, all other kinds of weapons and combat equipment will find broad application in the war.[42]

The views expressed in *Fifty Years of the Armed Forces of the Soviet Union* differed little from what Marshal Malinovskiy had stated in 1961. However, other military writings were indicating that a modification to doctrine was quietly taking place.

Development of a Controlled Conflict Capability: 1969–1973

In a 1968 article carried in the restricted journal, *Military Thought*, Marshal of the Soviet Union V. D. Sokolovskiy and his frequent collaborator, General Lieutenant M. I. Cherednichenko, discerned a regularity in the development of military art, which they set at six to eight years. At the time the article was written, seven years had passed since Nikita Khrushchev had announced a new military doctrine. The two authors went on to state that "at present, military affairs are entering or have already entered the next stage in their development and, apparently, it is necessary once again to introduce essential changes into military art."[43]

The authors failed to inform readers as to what might be the next stage of military affairs, or as to changes in military art. One new theme, however, had started to appear in military writings. The Soviet Armed Forces must be prepared to fight *with or without* the use of nuclear weapons.

The fourth edition of *Marxism-Leninism on War and the Army*, published in 1965, contained the statement:

> Our military doctrine gives the main role in defeating an aggressor to the nuclear rocket weapon. At the same time it does not deny the important significance of other kinds of weapons and means of fighting.[44]

Three years later, in 1968, the fifth edition of the same book contained the identical statement but with an added clause:

> and the possibility in certain circumstances of conducting combat actions *without the use of the nuclear weapon.*[45] (emphasis added)

In the introduction to the fifth edition, Lieutenant Colonel V. M. Bondarenko was specifically credited with having "made more precise" parts of the seventh chapter, in which the above statement was found. At the same time, the addition seemed minor and was not interpreted by Western analysts as denoting an actual modification of basic Soviet military doctrine.

An article by Bondarenko, entitled "The Modern Revolution in Military Affairs and the Combat Readiness of the Armed Forces," appeared in the December 1968 issue of *Communist of the Armed Forces*, one of the most authoritative of the Soviet military journals. A new thesis, different from anything previously written, was presented.

> In our times conditions may arise when in individual instances combat operations may be carried out using conventional weapons. *Under these conditions, the role of conventional means and the traditional services of the armed forces are greatly increased.* It becomes necessary to train troops for various kinds of warfare. This circumstance is sometimes interpreted as a negation of the contemporary revolution in military affairs, as its conclusion. (emphasis added)
>
> One cannot agree with this opinion. The point is that *the new possibilities of waging armed struggle have arisen not in spite of, but because of, the nuclear missile weapons.* They do not diminish their combat effectiveness, and the main thing, they do not preclude the possible use of such weapons. All this forces the conclusion that the present situation is one of the moments in the revolution in military affairs. It flows out of this revolution, continuing it, instead of contradicting it. (emphasis added)
>
> On the basis of this, we are able to define *the contemporary revolution in military affairs as a radical upheaval in its development, which is characterized*

by new capabilities of attaining political goals in war, resulting from the availability of nuclear missile weapons to the troops.[46] (emphasis added in original)

The Soviet minister of defense, Marshal of the Soviet Union A. A. Grechko, picked up the theme the following year. In November 1969, in a speech to the All-Army Conference of Young Officers, Grechko also touched upon the need to be ready to fight with nonnuclear means.

Much attention is being devoted to the reasonable combination of nuclear rocket weapons with perfected conventional classic armaments, *to the capability of units and subunits* (chasti i podrazdeleniya*) *to conduct combat actions under nuclear as well as nonnuclear conditions.* Such an approach ensures the high combat capabilities of the troops and their constant readiness for action under conditions of variously shaped circumstances.[47] (emphasis added)

In a February 1970 article that appeared in *Kommunist*, the theoretical and political journal of the Central Committee of the Communist Party, the minister of defense made the same point in discussing the nature of a possible future war: "The main and decisive means of waging the conflict will be the nuclear rocket weapon. In it, *'classical' types of armaments will also find use. In certain circumstances, the possibility is admitted of conducting combat actions with conventional weapons.*"[48] (emphasis added)

The following month Colonel I. A. Seleznev, in an article entitled "V. I. Lenin—the Founder of Soviet Military Science," published in *Communist of the Armed Forces*, also discussed a future war in virtually identical terms. "The main and decisive means of waging the conflict will be the nuclear rocket weapon. In it, 'classical' types of armaments will also find use. In certain circumstances, the possibility is admitted of conducting combat actions by units and subunits with conventional weapons."[49]

Practically every article and book subsequently published on military doctrine or strategy has used virtually the identical expression. It is apparent that a doctrinal position is being stated as a settled issue.

According to Soviet theorists, the doctrinal modification resulted from the adoption by NATO in 1967 of the policy of flexible response. Prior to that time Soviet doctrine had considered that any conflict between NATO and the Warsaw Pact forces would begin with nuclear strikes.

Chasti generally refers to a regiment or its equivalent; *podrazdeleniya* to a subordinate battalion, company, or battery.

NATO's policy of flexible response took into account the possibility that war might start with the employment of conventional weapons only. The Soviet response, that "units and subunits must be prepared to fight with or without the use of the nuclear weapon," acknowledged the possible use of conventional weapons in the initial phases of a conflict, as well as the need to employ conventional weapons during or between nuclear exchanges. Soviet doctrine continued to make it clear, however, that nuclear weapons would probably be employed and would remain the decisive factor in any war.

In 1971, as the United States–Soviet negotiations on strategic arms limitations were entering the final phase, the *Officer's Handbook*, published as the fifteenth book in the Officer's Library series, continued the nuclear and conventional theme. For example,

> Of all wars possible in the modern era, world nuclear war, which the imperialist aggressors, and in first place the United States, are preparing against the socialist community, and first of all against the Soviet Union as the most powerful of the socialist states, presents the greatest danger. Therefore, in the content of Soviet military doctrine first place is occupied by positions pertaining to problems of preparation and conduct of world nuclear rocket war. At the same time consideration is given to the conduct of military actions of units and subunits without the use of nuclear weapons, that is, with conventional means.[50]

Explanations of Soviet military doctrine were not confined to writings published by Voyenizdat. Also in 1971, Nauka, publishing house of the Soviet Academy of Sciences, issued a paperback entitled *V. I. Lenin on War and Military Art*. The author, one of the outstanding Soviet military theorists of the Lenin Military-Political Academy, was identified as A. A. Strokov, general major and professor. In this work, directed primarily at the nonmilitary reader, the author states:

> A future war will inevitably become a world war and will draw the main countries of the world into armed conflict. The bloc of aggressive imperialist states will face the countries of the socialist community. The main means of destruction in war will be the nuclear weapon and the basic means of delivering it to the target will be rockets of different types. . . .
>
> World war might break out by growing out of a local conflict—a local war. The use of conventional weapons along with the nuclear rocket is a characteristic of modern military doctrines.
>
> The unlimited application of the nuclear rocket weapon and its maximum use for the first crushing strike will encompass the whole of the territory of the country undergoing nuclear rocket attack, annihilating and destroying the most important political, economic, and military targets.[51]

The Soviet leadership seemingly wanted English-speaking readers also to understand its basic doctrinal premises. For example, Progress Publishers in Moscow, which issues books and pamphlets in a number of foreign languages, in 1971 published in English *The Soviet Army*, a work that originally had appeared in 1969 in a Russian language edition, *Armiya Sovetskaya,* published by Politizdat, the political publishing house. For some reason, neither the Russian language edition nor the later English language edition identified its editor, S. S. Lototskiy, as being a general lieutenant (two stars) and head of the Department of History of War and Military Art of the Frunze Military Academy. *Red Star*, on 22 February 1973, well after the signing of SALT I, announced that *Armiya Sovetskaya* was one of five books nominated for the Frunze Prize. English readers are told, as Russians readers were earlier, that

> Placed in a nutshell, the Soviet military doctrine, as Marshal R. Ya. Malinovskiy wrote, states that "the next war, if the imperialists manage to unleash it, will be a decisive armed conflict between two opposing social systems; according to the character of the weapons used, it will inevitably be a thermonuclear war, a war in which nuclear weapons will be the principal means of destruction and missiles will be the principal means of delivering weapons on target. This war will be characterized by an armed struggle of unprecedented ferocity, dynamic, highly mobile combat operations, the absence of continuous stable front lines or distinction between front and rear, greater opportunities for dealing surprise strikes of great strength against both troops and the deep rear areas of the belligerent countries. . . ."
>
> The Soviet military doctrine requires that the Armed Forces, the country, the whole Soviet people be prepared for the eventuality of nuclear war.[52]

The following year (1972), Progress Publishers put out another equally instructive English edition of *Marxism-Leninism on War and the Army*.[53] Essentially, this is a translation of the fifth edition of this famed work that had appeared in 1968, published in 150,000 copies. Military ranks of the authors are given, and they are identified as "philosophers, historians, and teachers at military educational institutions."

Although the work is dated 1972, it did not appear in Moscow bookstores until after August of that year, well after the signing of SALT I. In this book Soviet spokesmen once again reaffirmed that "a future war, should the imperialists succeed in unleashing it, will be a bitter armed clash between two diametrically opposed social systems" and "as regards to the means used, this war may be a nuclear one." With respect to its type, "the nuclear war will be a world war and an intercontinental one. This is determined both by its sociopolitical content and by the fact that both sides possess missiles of practically unlimited range, atomic missile-carrying submarines and strategic bombers."[54] The signing of SALT I had very little effect, if any, on basic premises of Soviet military doctrine.

When the Officer's Library was first announced in 1965, prospective readers were informed that one book in the series would be *Soviet Military Doctrine* by General Colonel N. A. Lomov.[55] For reasons still unknown, this book never appeared. However, General Lomov was the senior editor of the final book in the series, *Scientific-Technical Progress and the Revolution in Military Affairs*, published in 1973. General Lomov had headed the department of strategy at the Academy of the General Staff from 1958 to 1969. Subsequently he was a consultant to the Institute of the USA and Canada. Contributors to the book were outstanding military and political-military theorists from both the General Staff Academy and the Lenin Military-Political Academy.

This final volume did not discuss doctrine specifically. However, the continuity was clear. For example:

> The basic provisions (principles) of strategy are based on the conclusions of Soviet military doctrine and at the same time develop and concretize these conclusions, giving them the character of theoretical and practical rules for solving various problems involved in the preparations for and conduct of armed combat.
>
> Soviet military strategy views and examines a world war under modern conditions, if the imperialists start it, as the decisive clash between two opposing world socioeconomic systems, in which both warring sides will pursue decisive political goals. Such a war can be a nuclear one involving the use of the entire might of the existing nuclear missile weapons by both sides. At the same time, in such a war conventional weapons can also be employed. Under certain conditions, the units and subunits will fight only with conventional means. The development of the war is possible by various means, including the surprise use of nuclear weapons or conventional means of destruction.[56]

These same fundamental tenets of Soviet military doctrine are reflected in writings that have continued into the 1980s. Soviet spokesmen make clear that the new doctrine announced by the "Party's first secretary" remains valid with respect to its basic principles, despite changes in leadership. However, as Soviet military theory teaches, doctrinal modifications and changes in military art are inevitable.

Opening Era of Power Projection: 1974–1982

If Sokolovskiy and Cherednichenko were right in their prognostication of six to eight year cycles in military affairs, there should have been signs of a new phase in the mid-1970s.

The first hint of a change was given by Party Secretary L. I. Brezhnev in March 1971, during his address to the Twenty-fourth Party Congress. He identified a new situation in a cautious manner.

> The Soviet people can be sure that at any time in the day or night our glorious armed forces are ready to repel an enemy attack *no matter from where it comes.* Any possible aggressor is fully aware that in the event of an attempt of a nuclear missile strike on our country, he will receive a devastating retaliatory strike.[57] (emphasis added)

A number of foreign analysts thought at the time that Brezhnev probably was referring to the Chinese and their growing nuclear capability. Soviet spokesmen over the years had asserted that only the "imperialists," headed by the United States, would start a world nuclear war against the peace-loving "socialist camp." Now China, another communist power, not only had nuclear weapons of its own but also had declared that the Soviet Union was a major enemy.

A partial explanation of Brezhnev's meaning was given in 1972, in a book published by the Institute of World Economy and International Relations, a leading research institute under the Soviet Academy of Sciences. *Military Force and International Relations*, edited by Dr. V. M. Kulish, a former colonel and a recognized military strategist, presented a new admission of Soviet theoretical Party-military thought. Kulish's theme was that the Soviet Union needed a capability to project both military power and presence. For example,

> Greater importance is being attached to Soviet military presence in various regions throughout the world, reinforced by an adequate level of strategic mobility of its armed forces.
>
> In connection with the task of preventing local wars and also in those cases wherein military support must be furnished to those nations fighting for their freedom and independence against the forces of international reaction and imperialist interventions, the Soviet Union may require mobile and well-trained and well-equipped forces. . . .
>
> Expanding the scale of Soviet military presence and military assistance furnished by other socialist states is being viewed today as a very important factor in international relations.[58]

The importance of Colonel Kulish's work was borne out in 1974 when Marshal A. A. Grechko, then minister of defense, outlined a significant addition to Soviet military doctrine. Writing in a leading Party theoretical journal, *Problems of History of the CPSU*, Grechko said:

At the present stage the historic function of the Soviet Armed Forces is not restricted to their function in defending our Motherland and the other socialist countries. In its foreign policy activity the Soviet state purposefully opposes the export of counterrevolution and the policy of oppression, supports the national liberation struggle, and resolutely resists imperialists' aggression in *whatever distant region of our planet* it may appear.[59] (emphasis added)

This statement was unprecedented. As a member of the Politiburo and minister of defense, Grechko apparently had been charged with informing leading Party members throughout the nation that the responsibilities of the Soviet Armed Forces had been extended into entirely new areas. Only three years earlier, in 1971, Grechko merely had said that the Soviet Armed Forces are international, "since they serve the noble cause of defending the entire socialist community and the worldwide historical victories of communism."[60] In this doctrinal modification, he asserted that the Soviet Armed Forces are "not restricted" simply to the defense of the Soviet Union and "the other socialist countries." They may operate in any region of the world where the Kremlin might see Party or Soviet interests at stake.

After Marshal Grechko's May 1974 article, the writings of Admiral of the Fleet of the Soviet Union S. G. Gorshkov, commander in chief of the Soviet Navy, took on new meaning. In the late 1960s and the first half of the 1970s, Admiral Gorshkov had written a series of articles that attracted considerable attention outside the Soviet Union. They stressed the role of sea power and the justification for the expansion of the Soviet Navy that was taking place.

A number of Western analysts considered that the Soviet admiral's views represented one side of an ongoing debate within the Soviet defense structure and were not necessarily statements of approved Soviet policy. Other analysts, however, believed that Gorshkov, as a deputy minister of defense and a full member of the Central Committee of the Communist Party (the two hats worn by the very top of the Soviet military hierarchy), would not be permitted to express views that might be opposed by the Party-military leadership. It is highly improbable that the "ongoing debate" theory has any validity; Gorshkov's writings are expressions of top Party policies, which the Soviet leadership wish to be made known.

In early 1976 a new book by Admiral Gorshkov, *The Sea Power of a State*, outlined some of the implications of Marshal Grechko's doctrinal modification. The admiral reaffirmed his previous thesis of the expanded role of the Soviet Navy in international affairs. Naval forces have multiple uses, he pointed out. Primarily, a navy must be capable of fighting naval actions at sea. But also,

> demonstrative actions of the fleet in many cases *make it possible to achieve political goals* without resorting to armed conflict by just *indicating pressure by their potential might* and *the threat of beginning military actions.*

And even further,

> the neutral waters of the world ocean permit accomplishing the *transfer and concentration of forces of the fleet without breaking the positions of international law,* without giving the opposing side *formal ground for protests or other forms of counteractions.*[61] (emphasis added)

Nuclear weapons are both unsuitable and unnecessary in the projection of military power. If Soviet troops were engaged in combat, it would be in local wars, using conventional weapons. Possible opponents would be much different from NATO forces facing the Warsaw Pact in the central regions of Western Europe.

By the mid-1970s Soviet military writings were giving increasing attention to local wars. Such wars are dangerous, Soviet military theorists warned, since they might escalate to world nuclear war. Soviet participation in local wars might be necessary to prevent their spreading to other areas.

The Invasion of Afghanistan

The Soviet move into Afghanistan took most Westerners by surprise. A debate in the United States about Soviet purpose followed. Was the Afghanistan invasion a complete reversal of Soviet foreign policy? Was it a defensive measure, resulting from the Kremlin's concern about instability along its borders? Might it have been due to the Soviet leadership's concern over a possible resurgence of the Moslem religion, which could bring about problems in the large Moslem population of the USSR? Or was the invasion the initial move in a Soviet plan to use Afghanistan as a springboard to move against either Iran or Pakistan?

The invasion of Afghanistan is an example of Soviet military theory in action. For the first time since the 1940s, the Soviet Union used its own military forces to occupy a nation other than one that had been "liberated"—to use a popular Soviet expression—during World War II. Soviet military actions in Berlin in 1953, Hungary in 1956, and Czechoslovakia in 1968 took place in territories that Soviet troops had controlled in their sweep toward Berlin in 1945.

The new trend in Soviet military affairs was made particularly clear in the writings of faculty members of the leading Soviet military academies, such as the General Staff Academy, the Frunze Military Academy, and the Lenin Military-Political Academy. A major work, *War and Army,* published in 1977 and written by faculties of these academies, discussed in detail the new "external function" of the Soviet Armed Forces, declaring it "the basic, main one." They stated that "in terms of internal conditions the Soviet Union needs no army." They also added, however, the following: "In contemporary circumstances the external function of the socialist army naturally is becoming broader and deeper. This is explained by the enormous social and political improvements in the international arena."[62]

The Soviet leadership attempted to justify its invasion of Afghanistan by declaring that the United States and China were seeking to bring about a counterrevolution to oust the Moscow-installed government. When describing attempts by the "imperialists" to hinder "the development of liberated countries," the authors of *War and Army* previously had explained that "in these circumstances the international obligation of socialist states is to give support and aid to liberated countries in suppressing the imperialist export of armed counter-revolution."[63]

As shown in the first edition of *The Armed Forces of the USSR*, only in 1974 did Marshal Grechko declare that "at the present state the function of the Soviet Armed Forces is *not* restricted merely to their historic function in defending our Motherland and the other socialist countries." The new, external function of these forces may take many forms. For example,

> The external function of the socialist army has a number of directions. In contemporary conditions, it is designated to: defend its own state from attack by aggressors; to defend along with other fraternal armies the whole socialist system and each country in the system; help peoples struggling for their freedom and independence; and defend the peace of the whole world.[64]

The external function of the Soviet Armed Forces is characterized by the projection of military power, which includes waging local war. Throughout the 1960s and early 1970s little attention was given by the military leadership to the possibility of Soviet forces waging anything other than general nuclear war or war in a theater of military action. In 1977, Soviet spokesmen were concerned also with the "imperialists" interfering with Soviet-sponsored wars of national liberation, and declared, "All of this obliges our military cadres to study thoroughly problems connected with local wars of today, and make practical conclusions and carefully take them into account in all daily activities in training and educating personnel of subunits, units, and ships."[65]

Just as the Soviet population has been conditioned for the possibility of a nuclear war, in the 1970s and 1980s they were prepared psychologically as well for the possibility of Soviet troops engaging in local wars. Numerous books appeared glorifying Soviet actions in the Spanish Civil War of the 1930s. Soviet pilots who had fought with the Chinese against the Japanese during the same period were called "knights of the fifth ocean." Soviet participation in the Korean War of the early 1950s became an example of how the "international duties" of the Soviet state had been fulfilled.

The shift toward greater emphasis on local war was reflected also in the production and deployment of weapons systems and equipment suitable for power projection purposes. New landing craft, aircraft carriers with VSTOL aircraft, and increased airlift capabilities were among the indications that the Soviet leadership was developing forces that could operate in areas noncontiguous to the USSR land mass.

By 1980 Soviet military personnel were not only in Outer Mongolia and the Warsaw Pact nations of Eastern Europe, but they were also in Afghanistan, Angola, Cuba, Ethiopia, Iraq, Kampuchea, Libya, Mali, Mauritania, Mozambique, Seychelles, Vietnam, Syria, North Yemen, and South Yemen.[66] The external function of the Soviet Armed Forces had taken on new meaning.

However, in a scholarly military book, written primarily for officers, the basic premises of Soviet military doctrine remained unchanged— the nuclear rocket weapon would be the decisive factor in any future war. As explained in a 1980 book, *The Armed Forces of a Developed Socialist Society*:

> The principle of harmonious development does not exclude the more rapid development in certain conditions of one or another service of the armed forces. At the present time, for example, we are giving greater attention to improving the Strategic Rocket Forces—the basis of the nuclear rocket might of our country, the main means of containment of the aggressive aspirations of imperialism. At the same time, other services of the Armed Forces also are being improved.[67]

The Soviet doctrinal shift that encompassed the projection of military power was based first on Soviet strategic nuclear capabilities and, second, on the buildup of the surface fleet of the Soviet Navy. In the late 1960s the growing strategic nuclear forces made possible a nonnuclear option, if needed by the Soviet leadership. In the 1970s this nuclear umbrella also helped to make possible the projection of Soviet military power, with little risk of interference by Western nations.

The Post-Brezhnev Era: 1982–?

In the early 1980s a series of changes took place in the Soviet Armed Forces. Many were organizational: Air Defense Troops were revamped, the Ground Forces underwent a significant reorganization, and long-range aviation lost its identity.

At the same time, vastly improved weapons systems were in the hands of the military services. The Soviet Navy possessed some of the most modern ships afloat, as well as the world's largest submarines. New weapons of the Ground Forces had both nuclear and conventional capabilities. Soviet fighter-bombers now had sufficient range to cover almost all of the NATO territory from Soviet bases. New Soviet missiles, which many in the West considered a violation of arms control agreements, were deployed. (See subsequent chapters for further discussion of these changes.)

Despite these changes, Soviet military theorists continued to elaborate on the same general doctrinal premises formulated in the late 1950s and early 1960s. A 1981 book, *V. I. Lenin and Soviet Military Science*, issued by Nauka, the publishing house of the Soviet Academy of Sciences, contained the following:

> A powerful coalition of countries of the socialist commonwealth will oppose the aggressive imperialist bloc. . . . In scale, the war will assume an international character. . . . By the nature of the means used, it will be, most likely, a thermonuclear war. The main and decisive means of waging world war will be nuclear weapons and the basic means of delivery to the target—rockets of various types.
>
> The beginning period of war will assume exceptional importance in a possible world war. Its significance is determined by the fact that the imperialists are planning a surprise nuclear attack against the USSR and other socialist countries, the result of which might be unbelievably severe.[68]

Military-Technical Progress and the Armed Forces of the USSR was the title of a 1982 book issued by Moscow's Institute of Military History. The authors continued on the basic theme:

> With the adoption of the nuclear weapon into armaments, fundamental changes took place in the views on the nature of war and methods of waging it. This was caused by the fact that now both the economy and the whole system of state control has come within range of strikes of nuclear rocket weapons and could be destroyed at any point on the globe. At the same time it must be stressed that military science recognizes the possibility of conducting military actions both with the use of nuclear weapons, and also without their use. . . .[69]

Strategic Rocket Forces are troops of constant combat readiness. . . . This puts them in first place among the other services of the Armed Forces and demands unremitting attention to their development.

One of the main positions of *Soviet military doctrine* states that for the achievement of *victory* over the aggressor, the combined efforts of all services of the Armed Forces are necessary. Quite naturally, the Central Committee of the CPSU and the Soviet government are giving necessary attention to other services of the Armed Forces as well.[70] (emphasis added)

At the beginning of the 1980s the most authoritative pronouncements on military doctrine were given by Marshal N. V. Ogarkov, as stated in his pamphlet, *Always Ready to Protect the Fatherland*. Ogarkov restates the concept of doctrine:

Soviet military doctrine is a system of guiding principles and scientifically substantiated views of the CPSU and the Soviet government on the essence, character and methods of waging a war which might be forced on the Soviet Union by imperialists, as well as the military organizational development and preparation of the Armed Forces and the country to crush the aggressor.[71]

Ogarkov spoke only in generalities, avoiding specific details. He took care to present the Soviet Union as a peace-loving nation:

The content of Soviet military doctrine in its most general form reduces to this: Predatory wars are alien to the Soviet Union as a socialist state; it has never attacked and does not intend to attack any state either in the West nor in the East, in the North or South to impose its rule or to change the existing social structure in them. The Soviet Union does not need to expand its borders. But that which belongs to the Soviet people and has been created by their labor, it will defend with complete decisiveness, actively and without compromise. And therefore the peaceloving nature of the foreign policy of the Soviet state and its constant readiness to deal a crushing repulse to any aggressor are blended together in Soviet military doctrine.[72]

Both sides of military doctrine, the sociopolitical and the military-technical, were discussed by Ogarkov, but in general terms. With respect to the latter, he wrote:

The most important position of the military-technical content of Soviet military doctrine, dictated by the rapid development of the nuclear rocket weapon and the possibility of its surprise use by the enemy, is the demand to maintain the Armed Forces of the USSR in high combat readiness guaranteeing their timely deployment for repulsing a surprise enemy attack, carrying out powerful retaliatory strikes on him and successfully fulfilling the set tasks in defense of the socialist fatherland. The point here is to be able not just to defend oneself, to oppose the aggressor with corresponding passive ways and means of protection, but also to deliver crushing retaliatory strikes on him and destroy the enemy under any conditions of a situation which may occur.[73]

As indicated by these statements from Soviet doctrinal writings, the Soviet emphasis on nuclear weaponry continued throughout the first half of the 1980s. Deployments of new and improved ballistic missiles, both for theater and intercontinental use, demonstrated the degree to which the doctrine was followed.

The Soviet concept of military doctrine, which demands a never-ending military buildup, is inexplicable to many Westerners. This concept stems from the political side of military doctrine, which is based on a Marxist-Leninist interpretation of the world and of human relationships.

The Political Side of Soviet Military Doctrine

In his 1982 pamphlet Marshal Ogarkov emphasized that military doctrine has two sides: the sociopolitical and the military-technical. Both are carried out "in strict conformity with the policies of the CPSU in the military arena." The political content of military doctrine is the more important and "fully takes into account the fundamental changes in the relationship of forces in the world arena."[74] Western analysts tend to devote greater attention to what the Soviets consider the military-technical side of doctrine and ignore the political side. However, it is the latter that best explains Soviet moves in the international field.

Although Soviet military doctrine is concerned primarily with nuclear rocket war, the Communist Party of the Soviet Union and its Armed Forces support wars of many types, both directly and indirectly. Such support is discussed and rationalized in terms of Marxism-Leninism, whose "teaching on war and the army is closely connected with Soviet military doctrine." The methodological function of this teaching "is directly linked with the class struggle in the international arena and reflects the antagonisms of the contemporary epoch."[75]

Soviet writers assert that "the most important concepts of the Marxist-Leninist teaching on war and the army, reflecting the essence and content of war, are an instrument in the ideological struggle." They acknowledge that "a sharp controversy rages around such concepts as 'war,' 'peace,' 'aggression,' 'military conflict,' and 'military power.' " They also acknowledge, in an indirect manner, that the same words will have different meanings in the Soviet Union and the West:

John F. Kennedy, former U.S. president, said in one of his addresses to the nation that "the Soviets and ourselves give wholly different meanings to the same words: war, peace, democracy, and popular will. We have wholly different views of right and wrong, of what is an internal affair and what is aggression. And above all we have wholly different concepts of where the world is and where it is going."[76]

Some appreciation of these differences may be gained by looking at the way in which the Soviets classify wars: (1) according to political nature, (2) according to the class makeup of the belligerent sides, (3) according to the size of the military conflict, and (4) depending on the means of armed struggle used.

Political Nature. For Soviet theorists there are only two possible categories of war: just wars and unjust wars. Just wars are "progressive," and Soviet military doctrine is "built on the idea of supporting just wars." The Soviet Union *"opposes all and any predatory [unjust] wars, including wars between capitalist states, local wars directed at suppression of people's liberation movements, and considers it its duty to support the sacred struggle of oppressed peoples in their just, liberating wars against imperialism."*[77]

Class Makeup of the Belligerent Sides. For the Soviets there are four types of war: (1) wars between states with opposed social systems, (2) national liberation wars, (3) civil wars, and (4) wars between bourgeois states.

Soviet spokesmen consider the fiercest type of wars to be those between states with opposed social systems. Of these, "war in defense of the socialist fatherland, the gains of socialism, is a special kind of war." It would be "a forced war using extreme means."[78] Such a war "would not recognize political compromises and would be waged with the maximum use of all available forces and means at the disposal of the states."[79]

Soviet theorists claim there cannot be wars between socialist states. The Chinese attack on Vietnam in 1979 and Chinese foreign policy "which calls the USSR enemy number one are being used by bourgeois ideologists as proof socialism causes wars also. This was done by the ruling clique of China, led by Maoism, which turned the ideals of socialism into a policy of chauvinism and hegemonism."[80]

National liberation wars are defined by the Soviets as just wars in which peoples of colonies and underdeveloped countries are fighting against colonial dependence. Some Soviet theoreticians have considered these wars to be difficult to classify as either just or unjust, given that "the national bourgeoisie might actively support the side of the working masses."[81] Marxism-Leninism generally views civil wars as internal wars "between the proletariat and the bourgeoisie, between peoples and monopoly." Imperialist forces, flying the flag of "pacification" in protection of supposedly democratic freedoms, have often intervened in civil wars. The major limitation on such "imperialist intervention" is the presence of the powerful socialist camp. It may even become necessary "for the most decisive repulsion of the intervention in such countries" to be undertaken by the Soviet Union. Accordingly, the political side of Soviet military doctrine provides for the active support of the proletariat in civil wars, in order to "turn the democratic revolution into a socialist one."[82]

In wars between imperialist states, there is no class antagonism between the two sides. Because these wars are not fought for the purpose of changing the existing social order, various compromises are possible. Soviet spokesmen state that "the leaders of the proletariat always condemn wars, calling the people to unite in a revolutionary struggle against governments, to turn the predatory, mutually plundering war into a civil war."[83] Once the war turns to civil war, it can become a just war on the side of the proletariat, who can anticipate help from the Soviet Union.

Scale of the Military Conflict. Modern wars may be classified according to scope: world or local. They also may be classified according to length: short and swift-moving or protracted.[84] The scale may further be determined by the participants, constituting either two states or two coalitions.

Local wars "are defined on one side as the continuation by means of arms of the aggressive policy of imperialist governments and on the other, as a way of struggle for freedom and independence of states who have become victims of imperialist aggression."[85] Imperialists have often used "local wars for carrying out their antinational plans."

World war is the primary concern of the Party leadership. Soviet leaders claim that any war, even a local war, might quickly spread to all parts of the world. A third world war would be different from world wars of the past, since it would be a struggle between coalitions—an acute struggle between classes. In all probability, nuclear weapons would be used. Because of the destruction such a war would cause, "the Communist Party considers as its sacred duty doing everything possible to prevent such a war from taking place." At the same time, Soviet leaders assert that if war does occur, the Soviet Union would be the victor and capitalism would cease to exist.

Means Used. In the early 1960s, wars were divided into two kinds: nuclear (*yaderniye*) and nonnuclear (*bezyaderniye*). Since the late 1960s, Soviet writers have noted that both nuclear and conventional weapons may be used in the same theater. However, as asserted in writings on

Soviet military doctrine, primary attention must be given to the preparation of the country and the Armed Forces for world nuclear war.

With respect to the United States, "the system of wars adopted by the Pentagon divides wars into strategic, that is, world nuclear rocket, and nuclear in a theater of war (TV), say, in Europe, and conventional in a theater of military action (TVD), that is, local war. . . . This is the result of using unscientific methods."[86]

The political side of Soviet military doctrine has changed little since its basic provisions were established by V. I. Lenin at the time of the Russian Revolution. For those in the West concerned with national security affairs, and with arms control in particular, an analysis of Soviet military doctrine may portray the most realistic indication available of Soviet goals.

*   *   *

In the United States, as a general rule, weapons systems are developed first, and later, if production funds are approved, rationalization is given for their deployment into operational units. A different pattern is followed in the Soviet Union. If the state of the art permits a radically new weapons system, a doctrinal modification first may take place, with production and deployment of the new weapon at a much later date.

Once Soviet testing proved the feasibility of the nuclear rocket weapon, a completely new military doctrine was formulated and announced in 1960. A tenet of this doctrine was that any future world war between nuclear powers would begin with nuclear strikes. Since at that time the Soviet Union did not have the military capability to match the doctrinal pronouncements of its leaders, the new doctrine generally was ignored in the United States.

This doctrine was modified in 1967 to take into account NATO's announced military strategy of flexible response. The Soviet response was to consider the possibility of a nonnuclear phase in the event of a conflict between the Warsaw Pact and NATO forces. With this modification, Soviet spokesmen stressed that "units and subunits must be prepared to fight with or without the use of the nuclear rocket weapon."

Another modification to Soviet military doctrine was announced in 1974 when Marshal Grechko declared that the mission of the Soviet Armed Forces was no longer restricted to defending "our motherland and the other socialist countries." This appears to mean that the Soviets intend to project military power and presence into any place in the world where Soviet interests might be perceived. This doctrinal addition was reflected in the commissioning of the cruiser carrier Kiev in 1976. It was demonstrated again that same year by airlift and sealift of weapons and military equipment to Angola and by the employment of Cuban surrogates. In 1978 similar Soviet support was given to other African nations. Soviet troops invaded Afghanistan in December 1979. In 1983, as the Lebanon crisis developed, 7,000 Soviet advisers could be found in Syria. Not unnaturally, Western leaders must be concerned about the extent to which this doctrinal pronouncement will result in major changes in the military posture of the Soviet Union, with concentration on the buildup of forces capable of power projection to distant areas.

Notes

1. A. A. Strokov, *Istoriya Voyennovo Iskusstva* [The History of Military Art] (Moscow: Voyenizdat, 1966), p. 590. See also A. A. Grechko, *Yadernyy Vek i Voyna* [The Nuclear Age and War] (Moscow: Izvestia Publishing House, 1964), pp. 5–10.

2. N. V. Ogarkov, *Vsegda v Gotovnosti k Zashchite Otechestva* [Always in Readiness to Protect the Fatherland] (Moscow: Voyenizdat, 1982), p. 53.

3. "Doktrina Voyennaya" [Military Doctrine], *Voyennyy Entsiklopedicheskiy Slovar'* [Military Encyclopedic Dictionary] (Moscow: Voyenizdat, 1983), p. 240.

4. Ogarkov, *Vsegda v Gotovnosti*, p. 53.

5. I. V. Stalin, *O Velikoy Otechestvennoy Voyne Sovetskogo Soyuze* [On the Great Patriotic War of the Soviet Union], 5th ed. (Moscow: Gospolitizadat, 1952), pp. 43–44.

6. "Glavnoye Komandovaniye Voysk Dal'nego Vostoka," [High Command of Troops of the Far East], *Voyennyy Entsiklopedicheskiy Slovar'*, p. 194.

7. S. A. Tyushkevich, *Sovetskiye Vooruzhennyye Sily* [Soviet Armed Forces] (Moscow: Voyenizdat, 1978), p. 378.

8. B. N. Ponomarev, ed., *Istoriya Vneshney Politiki SSSR, 1945–1970* [History of the Foreign Policies of the USSR, 1945–1970] (Moscow: Nauka Publishing House, 1971), Vol. 2, p. 167.

9. M. V. Zakharov, ed., *50 Let Vooruzhennykh Sil SSSR* [50 Years of the Armed Forces of the USSR] (Moscow: Voyenizdat, 1968), p. 482.

10. V. M. Bondarenko, "Military-Technical Superiority: The Most Important Factor in the Reliable Defense of the Country," *Kommunist Vooruzhennykh Sil* [Communist of the Armed Forces], September 1966. For an English translation, see W. R. Kintner and Harriet Fast Scott, *The Nuclear Revolution in Soviet Military Affairs* (Norman, Okla.: University of Oklahoma Press, 1968), p. 361.

11. H. S. Dinerstein, *War and the Soviet Union* (New York: Praeger, 1962), p. 37. The author quotes at length General N. Talenskiy's article in the September 1953 issue of *Voyennaya Mysl'* [Military Thought]. For a somewhat different view, see S. N. Kozlov, *O Sovetskoy Voyennoy Nauke* [On Soviet Military Science] (Moscow: Voyenizdat, 1964). This Soviet publication asserts that the discussion that took place in 1953, after the publication of Talenskiy's article, was of an abstract character and had no influence on military science.

12. Dinerstein, *War and the Soviet Union*, pp. 37–63.

13. A. Vasilevskiy, "On Guard over the Security of our Soviet Motherland," *Krasnaya Zvezda*, 24 February 1954.

14. A. Vasilevskiy, "The Great Lesson of History," *Krasnaya Zvezda*, 7 May 1954.

15. Dinerstein, *War and the Soviet Union*, p. 51.

16. See, for example, Zakharov, *50 Let*, p. 521. See also Oleg Penkovskiy, *The Penkovskiy Papers* (New York: Doubleday & Co., 1965), p. 251.

17. Penkovskiy, *The Penkovskiy Papers*, p. 258.

18. N. S. Khrushchev, "Disarmament for Durable Peace and Friendship." Address delivered at the Fourth Session of the Supreme Soviet, USSR, 14 January 1960; contained in *On Peaceful Coexistence* (Moscow: Foreign Languages Publishing House, 1961), p. 146. See also Harriet Fast Scott, *Soviet Military Doctrine: Its Continuity—1960–1970* (Menlo Park, Calif.: Stanford Research Institute, Strategic Studies Center, June 1971), pp. 7–8, for a summary of Khrushchev's remarks concerning the new military doctrine and force posture.

19. Murray Feshbach, "Population," in *Economic Performance and the Military Burden of the Soviet Union* (Washington, D.C.: Government Printing Office, 1970), p. 68.

20. Zakharov, *50 Let*, p. 502.

21. N. S. Khrushchev, "Concluding Speech Before the Twenty-second Congress of the Communist Party," 27 October 1961, republished in *Communism—Peace and Happiness for the Peoples* (Moscow: Foreign Languages Publishing House, 1963), p. 319.

22. R. Ya. Malinovskiy, "Report to the Twenty-second Congress of the CPSU." For an English translation, see Scott, *Soviet Military Doctrine*, p. 87.

23. G. A. Fedorov, *Marksizm-Leninizm o Voyne i Armii* [Marxism-Leninism on War and the Army], 3d ed. (Moscow: Voyenizdat, 1962), p. 357.

24. R. Ya. Malinovskiy, *Bditel'no Stoyat' Na Strazhe Mira* [Vigilantly Stand Guard over the Peace] (Moscow: Voyenizdat, 1962), pp. 24–27.

25. Ibid.

26. Ibid.

27. For example, see A. B. Kadishev, *Voprosy Strategii i Operativnovo Iskusstva v Sovetskikh Voyennykh Trudakh* [Problems of Strategy and Operational Art in Soviet Works, 1917–1940] (Moscow: Voyenizdat, 1965). This book consists of a collection of writings by Soviet military theoreticians in the pre–World War II period. Approximately one-half of the authors whose works are listed died in Stalin's 1937–1938 military purges. Marshal of the Soviet Union V. M. Zakharov's introduction to the work discusses the fact that most of the pre–World War II writings on military doctrine and strategy have been destroyed.

28. Zakharov, *50 Let*, p. 476.

29. For a discussion of the revolution in military affairs, see Kintner and Scott, *The Nuclear Revolution*, p. 4.

30. This series of pamphlets was published in identical formats, with this notation on the cover: "Soldatu i Matrosu o Revolyutsii v Voyennom Dele" [To Soldiers and Sailors About the Revolution in Military Affairs]. Typical titles are: *Revolyutsiya v Voyennom Dele: V Chem Yeye Sushchnost?* [The Revolution in Military Affairs: What Is Its Essence?] and *Faktor Vremeni v Sovremennom Boyu* [The Factor of Time in Contemporary Combat]. It is not known how many pamphlets in this series were published.

31. R. Ya. Malinovskiy, "The Revolution in Military Affairs and the Task of the Military Press," *Kommunist Vooruzhennykh Sil* 21, November 1963, p. 9. For an English translation, see Kintner and Scott, *The Nuclear Revolution*, p. 4.

32. Strokov, *Istoriya*, p. 597.

33. Ibid., p. 402.

34. P. M. Derevyanko, ed., *Problemy Revolyutsii v Voyennom Dele* [Problems of the Revolution in Military Affairs] (Moscow: Voyenizdat, 1965).

35. Marshal Malinovskiy's article first appeared in *Kommunist Vooruzhennykh Sil* in November 1963.

36. For a discussion of the Officer's Library, see Harriet Fast Scott, *Soviet Military Doctrine: Its Formulation and Dissemination* (Menlo Park, Calif.: Stanford Research Institute, Strategic Studies Center, June 1971), pp. 81–93.

37. For a comparison of the 1962 and 1965 editions of *Marxism-Leninism on War and the Army*, see Scott, *Soviet Military Doctrine: Its Continuity*, pp. 24–26.

38. Ye. I. Rybkin, "On the Nature of World Nuclear Rocket War," *Kommunist Vooruzhennykh Sil*, September 1965. A number of analysts in the West appeared surprised by the tone of this article and considered that Rybkin was a "hawk," out of line with the policy of the Kremlin's top leadership.

39. S. V. Malyanchikov, "The Character and Features of Nuclear-Rocket War," *Kommunist Vooruzhennykh Sil*, November 1965. For an English translation, see Kintner and Scott, *The Nuclear Revolution*, pp. 171–184.

40. Strokov, *Istoriya*, p. 608.

41. A. S. Zheltov, ed., *V. I. Lenin i Sovetskiye Vooruzhennyye Sily* [V. I. Lenin and the Soviet Armed Forces] (Moscow: Voyenizdat, 1967), p. 226.

42. Zakharov, *50 Let*, p. 522.

43. V. D. Sokolovskiy and M. I. Cherednichenko, "Military Strategy and Its Problems," *Military Thought* 10, October 1968, in Joseph D. Douglass, Jr., and Amoretta M. Hoeber, *Selected Readings from Military Thought 1963–1973*, Vol. 5, Part II (Washington, D.C.: Government Printing Office, 1982), p. 13.

44. N. Ya. Sushko and S. A. Tyushkevich, eds., *Marksizm-Leninizm o Voyne i Armii*, 4th ed. [Marxism-Leninism on War and the Army] (Moscow: Voyenizdat, 1965), p. 244.

45. S. A. Tyushkevich, ed., *Marksizm-Leninizm o Voyne i Armii*, 5th ed. [Marxism-Leninism on War and the Army] (Moscow: Voyenizdat, 1968), p. 292. For a comparison of the 1965 and 1968 editions, see Scott, *Soviet Military Doctrine: Its Continuity*, p. 59.

46. V. M. Bondarenko, "The Modern Revolution in Military Affairs and the Combat Readiness of the Armed Forces," *Kommunist Vooruzhennykh Sil*, December 1968, p. 29.

47. A. A. Grechko, "The Growing Role, Tasks, and Obligations of Young Officers at the Contemporary Stage of the Development of the Soviet Armed Forces, *Krasnaya Zvezda*, 27 November 1969.

48. A. A. Grechko, "On Guard Over Peace and Socialism," *Kommunist*, February 1970.

49. I. A. Seleznev, "V. I. Lenin—The Founder of Soviet Military Science," *Kommunist Vooruzhennykh Sil* 6, March 1970.

50. S. N. Kozlov, ed., *Spravochnik Ofitsera* [Officer's Handbook] (Moscow: Voyenizdat, 1971), p. 74.

51. A. A. Strokov, *V. I. Lenin o Voyne i Voyennom Iskusstve* [V. I. Lenin on War and Military Art] (Moscow: Nauka Publishing House, 1971), pp. 175–176. Note that this is the same Soviet officer who, in 1966, wrote *Istoriya Voyennovo Iskusstva*.

52. S. S. Lototskiy, *The Soviet Army* (Moscow: Progress Publishers, 1971), p. 332.

53. *Marxism-Leninism on War and the Army* (Moscow: Progress Publishers, 1972). For the 1968 fifth edition of this work, see S. A. Tyushkevich, ed., *Marksizm-Leninizm o Voyne i Armii* [Marxism-Leninism on War and the Army] (Moscow: Voyenizdat, 1968).

54. Ibid., p. 392.

55. Harriet Fast Scott, "Soviet Military Literature for 1966," *Military Review,* July 1966, p. 88.

56. N. A. Lomov, ed., *Nauchno-Teknicheskiy Progress i Revolyutsiya v Voyennom Dele* [Scientific-Technical Progress and the Revolution in Military Affairs] (Moscow: Voyenizdat, 1973), p. 136. This work was translated in 1974 under the auspices of the United States Air Force and is available from the Government Printing Office.

57. L. I. Brezhnev, "Address to the Twenty-fourth Congress of the CPSU," *XXIV S'yezd Kommunisticheskoy Partii Sovetskogo Soyuza: 30 Marta-9 Aprelya 1971: Stenograficheskiy Otchet* [Twenty-fourth Congress of the Communist Party of the Soviet Union: 30 March–9 April 1971: Stenographic Notes] (Moscow: Politizdat, 1971), Vol. 1, p. 196.

58. V. M. Kulish, ed., *Voyennaya Sila i Mezhdunarodnyye Otnosheniya* [Military Force and International Relations] (Moscow: International Relations Publishing House, 1972), p. 137.

59. A. A. Grechko, "The Leading Role of the CPSU in Building the Army of a Developed Socialist Society," *Problems of History of the CPSU*, May 1974. Translated by FBIS, May 1974.

60. A. A. Grechko, *Na Strazhe Mira i Stroitel'stva Kommunizma* [On Guard Over the Peace and the Building of Communism] (Moscow: Voyenizdat, 1971), p. 90.

61. S. G. Gorshkov, *Morskaya Moshch Gosudarstva* [The Sea Power of a State] (Moscow: Voyenizdat, 1976), p. 403. The authors believe that Gorshkov's views reflect approved Soviet Party-military policy. It should be noted also that the authors in Dr. Kulish's Book, *Military Force and International Relations*, refer to Admiral Gorshkov as an authority on Soviet naval policies.

62. D. A. Volkogonov, A. S. Milovidov, and S. A. Tyushkevich, *Voyna i Armiya* [War and Army] (Moscow: Voyenizdat, 1977), p. 354.

63. Ibid., p. 354.

64. Ibid., p. 355.

65. Ibid., p. 259.

66. "The Military Balance: 1981/82," as compiled by The International Institute for Strategic Studies, London, printed in *Air Force Magazine*, December 1981, p. 60.

67. K. A. Vorob'yev, *Vooruzhennyye Sily Razvitogo Sotsialisticheskogo Obshchestva.* [The Armed Forces of a Developed Socialist Society] (Moscow: Voyenizdat, 1980), p. 92.

68. N. N. Azovtsev, *V. I. Lenin i Sovetskaya Voyennaya Nauka* [V. I. Lenin and Soviet Military Science] (Moscow: Nauka, 1981), p. 290.

69. M. M. Kir'yan, *Voyenno-Tekhnicheskiy Progress i Vooruzhennyye Sily SSSR* [Military-Technical Progress and the Armed Forces of the USSR] (Moscow: Voyenizdat, 1982), p. 333.

70. Ibid., p. 296.

71. Ogarkov, *Vsegda v Gotovnosti*, p. 55.

72. Ibid., p. 58.

73. Ibid., p. 57.

74. Ibid., p. 56.

75. *Marxism-Leninism on War and the Army*, p. 392.

76. Ibid., p. 388.

77. V. V. Larionov, "The Political Side of Military Doctrine," *Kommunist Vooruzhennykh Sil 22*, November 1968, p. 13. At the time of this article Colonel Larionov probably was assigned to the Military Science Administration of the General Staff. By 1970 he was a section head at the Institute of the USA and Canada. About 1974, having been awarded the degree of doctor of historical sciences, he was reassigned to the General Staff Academy. In December 1976 he was promoted to the rank of general major.

78. N. D. Tabunov and V. A. Bokarev, *Marksistsko-Leninskaya Filosofiya i Metodologicheskiye Problemy Voyennoy Teorii i Praktiki* [Marxist-Leninist Philosophy and Methodological Problems of Military Theory and Practice] (Moscow: Voyenizdat, 1982), p. 282. This book is a textbook, intended for use in military academies.

79. Larionov, "Political Side," p. 14.

80. Tabunov and Bokarev, *Marksistsko-Leninskaya Filosofiya*, p. 278.

81. Larionov, "Political Side," p. 14.

82. Tabunov and Bokarev, *Marksistsko-Leninskaya Filosofiya*, p. 275.

83. Larionov, "Political Side," p. 15.

84. Tabunov and Bokarev, *Marksistsko-Leninskaya Filosofiya*, p. 272.

85. Larionov, "Political Side," p. 15.

86. Tabunov and Bokarev, *Marksistsko-Leninskaya Filosofiya*, p. 279.

3
Military Science

The Vocabulary of the Soviet Military Theorists

In the United States and other NATO nations, such expressions as doctrine, strategy, tactics, military science, and military art (or the art of war) may have very general meanings. In the Soviet Union these expressions have precise definitions. If the Soviet meanings of these terms are not understood, the reader of Soviet military writings may arrive at entirely erroneous conclusions.

The Soviet concept of military doctrine, representing the official policy of the Communist Party of the Soviet Union, already has been presented. "It is a unified system of views and aims, free from private views and estimates."[1] Since military doctrine is official Party policy, there can be no public disagreement with its premises in Soviet military writings.

In contrast to military doctrine, Soviet military science is "a system of knowledge on the nature and laws of war, the preparation of the armed forces and the country for war and the methods of its conduct."[2] In certain components of military science, differences of opinion may be expressed. At times such differences may even be officially encouraged. Military science encompasses the theory of military art; the theory of military structuring; the theory of troop training and education; and the theory of military economics and the rear services of the Armed Forces. It also studies and researches problems of command of the Armed Forces and of troop control on strategic, operational, and tactical scales.[3]

In the Soviet Union, military science is a major field of study. Several thousand Soviet officers possess the advanced degree of Candidate of Military Sciences, a degree only slightly less advanced than the Ph.D. in the United States. A few hundred also hold the degree of doctor of military sciences—the doctorate being awarded by the state only after the individual has completed a prescribed course of study, defended a dissertation, and become a recognized authority in the field.[4] (Degrees of candidate of naval sciences and doctor of naval sciences were discontinued in April 1979.)

Military science has a meaning and significance in the Soviet Union completely unknown in the United States. Its relationships with Marxism-Leninism and Soviet military doctrine are indicated in Chart 5.

Military art is the most important component of military science. Each of its three main elements—strategy, operational art, and tactics—is considered to represent an integral field of scientific knowledge. At the same time, they are "interconnected, interdependent. They supplement each other."[5]

Strategy, the major element of military art, is defined as "the part of military art that studies the foundations of the preparation and conduct of war and its campaigns as a whole. In practice it is policy's direct weapon. With respect to strategy, policy plays the leading and directing role." Further, strategy is "general and common for all the services of the armed forces of the country." Soviet theorists stress that war is conducted by the combined actions of all the services of the Armed Forces and their combined arms, and that the coordination of all actions of the services in war is possible only within a framework of a single strategy.

There are two aspects of strategy: theoretical and applied. The theoretical part encompasses the principles of strategy and the theoretical basis for the development of war plans. Applied strategy addresses more specific questions, such as "the immediate preparation and conduct of the strategic offensive, strategic defense, and other forms of military actions on a strategic scale."[6]

Operational art, the second element of military art, is concerned with "the theory and practice of preparing for and conducting combined and independent operations by major field forces or major formations of services." It involves front and army operations. Each of the five Soviet services—Strategic Rocket Forces, Ground Forces, Troops of Air Defense, Air Forces, and Navy—has its own operational art. As an integral part of military art, operational art "determines methods of preparing for and conducting operations to achieve strategic goals."[7]

Tactics has roughly the same meaning in the United States as in the Soviet military vocabulary, except that it applies in the USSR to operations of divisions and smaller formations. As defined in Soviet military texts, tactics is "the part of military art directly studying the basis for the preparation and conduct of combat actions of small units, medium-sized units and large units of all combat arms and services of the armed forces." Each Soviet service develops its own tactics. Also, within each service there may be a further breakdown of tactics for the various branches and arms. Officers within the Soviet Air Forces, for example, might be concerned with fighter tactics, bomber tactics, tactics of frontal aviation, and so on.[8]

Chart 5

Structure of System of Knowledge on War and Army

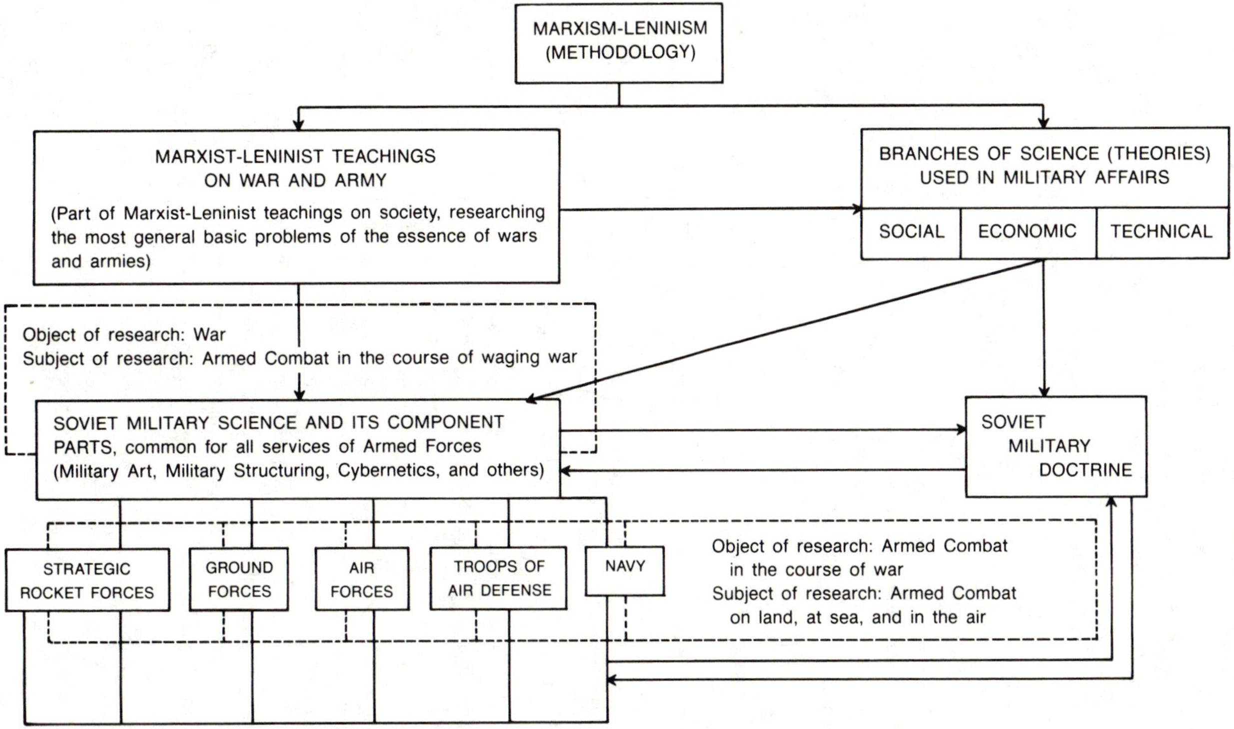

MARXISM-LENINISM (METHODOLOGY)

BRANCHES OF SCIENCE (THEORIES) USED IN MILITARY AFFAIRS

SOCIAL | ECONOMIC | TECHNICAL

SOVIET MILITARY DOCTRINE

MARXIST-LENINIST TEACHINGS ON WAR AND ARMY

(Part of Marxist-Leninist teachings on society, researching the most general basic problems of the essence of wars and armies)

Object of research: War
Subject of research: Armed Combat in the course of waging war

SOVIET MILITARY SCIENCE AND ITS COMPONENT PARTS, common for all services of Armed Forces
(Military Art, Military Structuring, Cybernetics, and others)

Object of research: Armed Combat in the course of war
Subject of research: Armed Combat on land, at sea, and in the air

STRATEGIC ROCKET FORCES | GROUND FORCES | AIR FORCES | TROOPS OF AIR DEFENSE | NAVY

THEORIES OF SERVICES OF ARMED FORCES

ADAPTED FROM G. KOSTEV, "ON THE FUNDAMENTALS OF THEORIES OF THE NAVY," MORSKOY SBORNIK 11, 1981, P. 26.

Pre–World War II Development of Soviet Military Science

In the 1920s and into the early 1930s, Soviet military theorists made detailed studies of war in its various forms. The subject was of major interest to the Party hierarchy; they had achieved their ruling positions by force of arms, and most members had taken part in actual fighting during the revolution and Civil War. The Red Army was the mainstay of the Party, for without it the leaders would have been back in the coffee houses of Western Europe. Many of the most intelligent and ambitious members of the Party remained in uniform.

M. V. Frunze, successor to Leon Trotskiy as head of the Red Army, had stood sufficiently high in Party circles to be regarded by Lenin as the possible Party leader. Frunze's primary interests were the nature of future war and the direction of development of the services and their branches and arms.[9] He also was most concerned with improving the training and education of Red Army personnel. During the year he was head of the Red Army, he introduced a series of major military reforms. His writings were revived in the 1960s, notably in 1965 in the publication *M. V. Frunze: Selected Works,* the first book of the Officer's Library series.

One of the most famous of the pre–World War II Soviet writings is *Strategy,* published in 1926. The author of this work was a former czarist officer, A. A. Svechin, and even in the 1980s his book is still discussed and frequently cited by Soviet theoreticians. Svechin followed his book with *Evolution of Military Art* in 1927 and *Strategy of the 20th Century at its First Stage* in 1937.[10]

Development of the Soviet General Staff, even through the 1970s, reflects the early theories of B. M. Shaposhnikov, also a former czarist officer, who graduated from the Imperial Academy of the General Staff in 1910. His three-volume series, *The Army's Brain,* published between 1927 and 1929, deals with the roles and functions of a staff and the process of war planning.[11]

The Character of Operations of Modern Armies, written in 1929 by V. K. Triandafillov, attempted to analyze the stage of development of various world armies of that period, especially with respect to their equipment and organization. Triandafillov called attention to the importance of the tank and considered it one of the most powerful offensive weapons for any future war. He was concerned with the duration and depth of operations and the changes that tanks and other mobile weapons might bring to the battlefield. In view of this new mobility, he predicted that the static trench warfare of World War I would not be a factor in any future war.[12]

M. N. Tukhachevskiy is generally considered the outstanding Soviet military commander and strategist of the 1930s. Among his major interests were the possibilities of highly mobile forces, which he visualized as a combined tank-air team, supplemented by parachutists and backed up by infantry and artillery. He stressed deep offensive operations, concentration of forces at the decisive point, and combined-arms operations.[13]

This initial, pre–World War II development of Soviet military science, as demonstrated in the writings of early theorists, came to a halt in 1937 with Stalin's purges of the military. Within two years practically all of the Soviet theorists who had written on military science—Svechin, Tukhachevskiy, and scores of others—were executed or had died in labor camps. Generally, their works were withdrawn from libraries and often were preserved in only a single copy.[14]

By 1941 Soviet military theory was in confusion and contributed little, if anything, to the preparations of the Soviet Armed Forces for the coming war with Hitler. Stalin's purges had eliminated many of the senior officers who had taken part in the Spanish Civil War and in the fighting in Outer Mongolia and China. The war with tiny Finland displayed major Soviet weaknesses in almost all aspects of warfare, from leadership to equipment.[15] The situation is well described in the book *June 22, 1941,* written by A. M. Nekrich, a famous Soviet historian, now living in the United States.

> Among the defects of Soviet military theory, one should name the insufficient elaboration of the character and contents of the initial period of the war under the conditions of surprise mass attack. As a result of this, the training of the troops did not always correspond to the type of military operations characteristic of the first period of the Second World War.
>
> It is completely clear that the danger of war with Germany in 1941 was underestimated. Working out the war plan in case of Hitlerite aggression, our command considered that, at the beginning of the attack, military operations would be carried on by limited covering forces, and that after the mobilization and deployment of the main forces, we could smash the aggressor in the frontier zone and pass on to a general offensive, transferring operations to the enemy's territory. . . .
>
> Little attention was directed to the question of strategic defense. Regarding offense as the main means of battle, our theory did not sufficiently work out the organization and implementation of defense, which was considered subordinate in relation to offense.[16]

Nekrich went on to describe the serious deficiencies in the training of the Soviet officer corps. The infantry was understaffed in officers by 20 percent; the number of military school graduates was insufficient to train reserves. Sixty-eight percent of the platoon and company commanders had the benefit of only a short five-month course of instruction for junior lieutenants.[17]

During the brief de-Stalinization period under Nikita Khrushchev, most of the blame for Soviet unpreparedness was placed on the actions of Stalin. Marshal of the Soviet Union I. Kh. Bagramyan stated that "the destruction of prominent Soviet military leaders as 'enemies of the people' on the eve of the war was actually one of the reasons for the great failures in the first period of the war."[18] In Nekrich's own words, "In Germany the news of the massacre of the Red Army Commanders evoked rejoicing. The Red Army lost its best commanders exactly at the moment when the clouds of war were gathering ever more thickly on the horizon."[19]

After the death of Stalin in 1953 and his denunciation by Khrushchev during the Twentieth Party Congress in 1956, military science once again came under close study in the Soviet Union. However, Soviet strategists and military historians were permitted only for a very short period to examine the degradation of military science after 1937. By 1967 re-Stalinization was in full swing, and Soviet writers so twisted history in the following years that actual events during the last sixteen years of Stalin's regime are difficult to identify in contemporary Soviet writings.

The development of Soviet military science in the post–World War II period brought about major changes in military doctrine. Military strategy, as a component of military science, also underwent a complete transformation.

Military Strategy

Military strategy, as carefully explained by Soviet spokesmen, occupies a subordinate position in relation to doctrine. More specifically:

A relationship does exist between military doctrine and strategy. Strategy, as a scientific theory, develops the basic methods and forms of armed conflict on a strategic scale and, at the same time, carries out the military leadership of the war. Theoretical positions of strategy influence military doctrine and its scientific development. At the same time, strategy directly executes doctrine and is its instrument in working out plans for war and preparation of the country for it. *During time of war military doctrine recedes somewhat into the background, since armed combat is guided primarily by military-political and military-strategic* ideas, conclusions and generalizations, which flow from actual conditions. Consequently, war and armed combat are directed *not by doctrine, but by strategy.*[20] (emphasis added)

The new doctrine announced by Khrushchev in January 1960 required a new military strategy. It probably is no accident that the very month in which Khrushchev made his doctrinal address, a highly classified version of *Military Thought* began publication of the Special Collection. The first paper to appear was "The Theory of Military Art Needs Review" by General Lieutenant A. I. Gastilovich. This opening article of the Special Collection series, according to Colonel Oleg Penkovskiy, set the theme that other officers were to develop.[21] Since military strategy is the primary component of military art, it appears that a major purpose of the Special Collection was to establish guidelines for a new strategy, as well as operational art and tactics.

In the summer of 1962, only a few weeks before the Cuban missile crisis, Western attaches in Moscow found a new book in Soviet military bookstores—*Military Strategy*—the first book on this subject to have been written by Soviet authors in thirty-six years.[22]

Military Strategy was prepared by a group of Soviet officers under the general direction of Marshal of the Soviet Union V. D. Sokolovskiy. His introduction to the book clearly stated the need for it.

> In the open Soviet military literature there is a lack of publications dealing with general concepts of military strategy, and the vast variety of the problems concerned. Actually, since the publication of *Strategy* by A. Svechin in 1926 . . . there have been no other publications in the Soviet Union devoted to the problems of military strategy as a whole.[23]

Sokolovskiy added that many of the views on strategy expressed in the Soviet press "have been influenced strongly by the cult of personality of J. V. Stalin, who, in order to justify miscalculations and errors committed by him in the course of the Great Patriotic War, intentionally distorted the concepts of a whole series of questions of military strategy."[24]

Sokolovskiy also affirmed in his introduction that "the appearance of weapons of mass destruction in the armament of modern armies and in particular the development and perfection of missiles with nuclear warheads have necessitated a fundamental review of many tenets of military strategy." A new book on strategy therefore was needed "for a wide circle of Soviet readers and the military and theoretical training of young officers." Sokolovskiy felt the subject should be so presented as to give "the general concepts of military strategy, clarifying the nature and conduct of modern warfare, the preparation of the country and the armed forces of war, and the direction and development of the armed forces."[25]

Marshal Sokolovskiy had been chief of the General Staff from 1952 to 1961. It is not known whether he was removed from this position because of his objection to Khrushchev's program of troop reductions or because of a heart attack, as was reported in Moscow at the time. In any event, he was not removed from his position in disgrace, but was designated a general inspector—a position that permitted him to take an active part in military and political affairs. He continued to be one of the foremost Soviet military spokesen until his death in 1968.

The other fourteen contributors also were Soviet military spokesmen of note, a number of whom remained prominent through the mid-1970s, including General Major I. G. Zavyalov, General Lieutenant M. I. Cherednichenko,[26] and General Major V. V. Larionov.

In the entire book only one contributor, General Colonel A. I. Gastilovich, is identified as having written a specific chapter. This chapter, "Preparing a Country to Repulse Aggression,"[27] provided guidelines for the Armed Forces, the population, and the economy to follow in preparation for a possible nuclear war. (As already noted, Penkovskiy said that the article by Gastilovich in the Special Collection had set the theme for the other articles that followed.)

Military Strategy reflects the views expressed by Nikita Khrushchev in his speeches delivered in January 1960 and before the Twenty-second Party Congress in 1961. It also reflects the speeches of Marshal Malinovskiy, delivered in the same period. One also can find in *Military Strategy* the identical concepts Penkovskiy attributed to the Special Collection—which he gave to Western intelligence agents prior to the publication of *Military Strategy*.

Marshal Sokolovskiy and his contributors outlined the scope of military strategy and discussed each of the specific subject areas in detail.[28] These include: (1) the laws governing armed conflict, which are inherent in strategy; (2) the conditions and nature of a future war; (3) the theoretical foundation of preparing the country and the armed forces and the principles of military planning; (4) fundamentals of civil defense; (5) methods of conducting armed conflict; (6) the basis of the material and technical support for armed conflict; (7) bases of leadership of military forces and of war in general; and (8) strategic attitudes of the probable opponents.

Military Strategy is a book about nuclear war. To ensure that the reader understands the doctrine upon which the strategy is based, the book repeats doctrinal concepts. If a war is "unleashed" by the "imperialist bloc" against the USSR or any other socialist country, such a war might take on the nature of a world war. It will be "a decisive armed clash between two opposed world social systems." Such a war "naturally will end in victory for the progressive Communist social-economic system over the reactionary capitalist social-economic system, which is historically doomed to destruction."[29]

With respect to the means of armed combat, "a third world war will be first of all a nuclear rocket war," with the major role played by the Strategic Rocket Troops. Final victory, however, can be attained only with the efforts of all services of the Armed Forces. "The initial period of the war will be of decisive importance for the outcome of the entire war." Therefore, the primary task of Soviet strategy is to develop the means for reliably "repelling a surprise nuclear attack of an aggressor."

In compliance with the premises of military doctrine, the editors of *Military Strategy* assert that forces should be developed and structured for the attainment of victory over an aggressor within the shortest possible time, with the least possible losses. The Armed Forces must be built to maximum strength in order to inflict a shattering retaliatory nuclear strike during the initial period of the war. It is recognized that in certain cases a quick victory may not be possible. Therefore, strategy must also prepare for the possibility of a protracted war. Attainment of superiority over the enemy in modern weapons, especially in nuclear weapons, is the task of the economy.

In time of peace the Soviet Union must prepare for the "repulsion of aggression." According to General Gastilovich, to whom this discussion is attributed, actions must be taken for "the preparation of the population" to ensure survival in nuclear war conditions.[30]

Initially, 20,000 copies of *Military Strategy* were published. Within a few weeks almost all copies had been sold, and a number of bookstores in leading cities reported that they had unfilled orders for the book.

The following year, in June 1963, a second edition of *Military Strategy* was published, with the same contributors as the first edition. The foreword to the second edition stated that the first edition "was discussed in the General Staff Academy, the military science societies of the Main Staff of the Ground Forces, the Central Club of the Soviet Army and a number of other institutions." Despite all this review, most of the changes in the second edition were cosmetic. Although the Cuban missile crisis had occurred since the first edition, and a nuclear test-ban treaty had been signed, there were no essential differences between the two editions.

Another book, *On Soviet Military Science,* published in 1964, startled Western readers with its nuclear emphasis. This work supplemented *Military Strategy* and presented essentially the same point of view. An earlier edition of *On Soviet Military Science* had appeared in 1960. While critical of Stalin and briefly noting the appearance of the nuclear weapon, the first edition, on the whole, was concerned with conventional weaponry. In contrast, the second edition was about nuclear warfare. After reading the first and second editions of this book, almost any analyst would have recognized that a major upheaval had taken place in Soviet military science during the four years between the two editions.[31]

The ouster of Khrushchev in 1964 did not alter in the slightest the emphasis given to nuclear weaponry in the new military strategy. Close analyses of Soviet military writings have failed to turn up any indication of a change in the nuclear policies outlined in the early 1960s by both Khrushchev and his Minister of Defense, Marshal Malinovskiy. *The History of Military Art,* edited by A. A. Strokov, appeared in 1966, well after Brezhnev had assumed leadership of the Soviet state. This work was specific about the impact of the nuclear weapon on military strategy and the importance of the revolution in military affairs.[32] "On Contemporary Military Strategy," a major policy article by Marshal V. D. Sokolovskiy and General Major M. I Cherednichenko, published in 1966, explained that in past wars changes brought about by new military equipment "appeared first in battle and in tactics and then in strategy." However, in their view, the nuclear rocket weapon changed this pattern, appearing first "as a means of strategy."[33] Writings stressing the decisive nature of the nuclear rocket weapon, published in 1966 with the Brezhnev regime firmly in power, were identical in concept to those written in 1962, even before the Cuban missile confrontation.

The Twenty-third Party Congress met in April 1966, the very month that the Sokolovskiy-Cherednichenko article appeared. This timing suggests high-level Party interest and approval. The two authors restated in italics the scope and tasks of Soviet military strategy.

> *The range of problems of military strategy includes the determination of the bases of the building of the armed forces, its structure, the equipping of it with combat equipment and armaments and with materiel, the principles of using the armed forces as a whole and each service of the armed forces separately.*[34]

And further:

> *The determination of the composition of the armed forces for peacetime and especially for time of war, the making of a reserve of arms, military equipment and, primarily, nuclear rocket weapons as the main means of war, as well as material reserves, deploying strategic groups and organizing the all-round security of the armed forces in time of war—this is the crucial task of military strategy.*[35]

Sokolovskiy and Cherednichenko discussed the "great possibilities for surprise attack" through the launching of nuclear rocket weapons. Such an attack could predetermine the course and outcome of the entire war. However, "the possibilities are growing for the timely detection not only of the beginning of an [surprise] attack, but also for the beginning of the direct preparations by the enemy of any attack, that is, *there are possibilities of preventing a surprise attack.*"[36] (emphasis added)

The exact meaning of these and other Soviet statements about "preventing a surprise attack" or "frustrating a nuclear attack" is never made clear. One might infer that Soviet strategists plan to "launch on warning"— to use a Western expression—which means that if it is believed by the Soviet leadership that an opponent is preparing and starts to launch a nuclear strike the Soviet forces would preempt, seeking to destroy the remainder of those forces before they leave their launch pads. This signifies that during a period of tension each side would be watching the other intently for indications of preparations for and detection of a launch.

Regardless of problems of determining exact meanings of Soviet expressions, the emphasis given by Sokolovskiy and Cherednichenko is clear: *"The most acute problem of strategy in contemporary circumstances is the working out of methods of waging nuclear rocket war."*[37] (emphasis in original)

In the spring of 1968, in the fourth year of the Brezhnev era, a third edition of Marshal Sokolovskiy's *Military Strategy* appeared. There was no change in the list of contributors from the earlier two editions, except for one who had died, and, even more significant, there was no change with respect to the attention given to nuclear weaponry.

Publication of this book surprised most Western Sovietologists, particularly those who thought that in 1968 the Soviets were placing less emphasis on nuclear weaponry than had been given while Khrushchev was in power. Equally surprised were those who had believed that the first edition, published in 1962, represented an ongoing debate between one group of contributors, who favored concentration on nuclear weapons, and the remainder of the contributors, who believed that more attention should be given to conventional military armaments. Other Western readers, however, thought that the views presented in *Military Strategy* were consistent, derived from Soviet doctrinal concepts. Proponents of this school asserted that if the first edition had in actual fact represented two opposing Soviet points of view—which was a very subjective opinion to start with—it is highly improbable that the same debate would have been permitted by the Party leadership to continue among the same contributors for six years, four of them after Khrushchev's ouster.

A line-by-line comparison of the 1968 edition with the 1962 and 1963 editions provides evidence of only a few minor modifications to strategy. Omissions in the third edition are as revealing as the additions. Since Brezhnev's re-Stalinization program was well under way in 1968, Soviet readers were not reminded of Stalin's errors in the conduct of

World War II. Authors of the first two editions of *Military Strategy* had been blunt in that respect.

The greatest changes in the book were in the chapter entitled "Military Strategy of Imperialist Countries." In it Soviet readers were made familiar with Western, and primarily United States, concepts of warfare. The discussion on limited war suggests a high degree of understanding of Western views. The Soviet authors assert that "the military leadership of the West" defines limited war as

> that type of armed conflict in which on the one hand the USA participates, directly or indirectly (usually through their allies) and on the other hand, the USSR. The characteristic feature of such a war is that during its course the strategic bombing of objectives on the territories of the USA and the USSR is supposedly not resorted to.[38]

In the same chapter the Soviet authors also assert that United States theorists consider that "limited warfare includes all types of wars using both conventional and tactical nuclear weapons, as well as local wars." The use of tactical nuclear weapons is of particular concern. Henry Kissinger is quoted: "Limited war will automatically escalate into general war because the losing side will continually commit new resources in order to restore the situation."[39]

In another chapter of the third edition, a new paragraph is added on "methods of unleashing and the scale of the war." For war may be world or limited, local, civil, or national liberation; it may be unleashed by a surprise attack or by the gradual involvement in the war of separate countries; the aggressor may use nuclear weapons in the very beginning or in the course of its development.[40] Military strategy must take all of these possibilities into account.

This third edition of *Military Strategy* was published as one of the Soviet Officer's Library series. It was nominated for the 1969 Frunze Prize and is listed as a basic reference on strategy in scores of Soviet publications, including the *Soviet Military Encyclopedia,* the first volume of which appeared in 1976.

Subsequent Soviet writings on military strategy have been responsive to the modifications that took place in military doctrine during the latter part of the 1960s and early 1970s. Specifically, strategy now takes into account that "units and subunits must be prepared to fight with or without the use of the nuclear rocket weapon" and that the country must be prepared to "resist aggression" no matter "from where and from whom" it comes.

Soviet spokesmen in 1973 reaffirmed that

military strategy depends upon political policy. . . . The dependency of
military strategy upon political policy and its subordinate position vis-a-
vis political policy are emphasized in the Marxist-Leninist definition of
war as the continuation of the political policy of states and classes by
other, namely violent, means.[41]

Even after the signing of the SALT I agreement Soviet statements
outlining the basic tenets of Soviet strategy remained unchanged from
the concepts of the early 1960s. "The possibility of using nuclear
missile weapons has required the development of active and decisive
forms and methods for strategic as well as tactical operations without
any delay from the very outset of the war."[42] And in the period of
relaxation of tensions:

> Also among the important theses of strategy is the necessity for complete
> preparations for and execution of a whole series of measures in peacetime
> providing for the organized conduct of military operations by all the
> services of the armed forces.
>   Military strategy proceeds from the necessity of creating the state and
> strategic manpower and material-technical reserves even in peacetime, with
> the use of them from the beginning of armed combat and the maintaining
> of them on the proper level in the course of the war. The significance of
> these reserves under the conditions of modern war grows decisively.[43]

Emphasis on the importance in time of peace of the need for combat
readiness and preparation of trained reserves for rapid mobilization
continues as a basic requirement for strategic planning:

> An important strategic principle is the necessity of providing firm and
> continuous strategic leadership over the armed forces and their groupings
> in the theaters of military operations *even in peacetime* and particularly
> with the start of military actions. The probability of using enormously
> powerful weapons over great distances and within a short period of time
> requires high mobility and *exceptionally centralized leadership*.[44] (emphasis
> added)

In the 1970s United States intelligence agencies released translations
of the restricted journal of the Soviet General Staff, *Military Thought*.
Scholars who did not have access to classified data found that the contents
of articles in *Military Thought* differed little from what was found in
open source publications.[45] If anything, they noted, the emphasis on
nuclear weaponry was as great, or even greater, than in the Soviet open
press.

During the buildup of the Soviet Navy in the late 1960s and throughout the 1970s, the nature of articles in the Soviet Navy journal, *Naval Selections,* in combination with the 1976 publication of Admiral S. G. Gorshkov's book, *The Sea Power of a State,* led a number of analysts in the West to believe that the Soviet Navy had a strategy distinct and separate from the other four services. There was some surprise in 1979 when a second edition of Admiral Gorshkov's work appeared. The primary difference between this edition and the first was the addition of about fourteen pages, which emphasized that one unified strategy applied to the Soviet Armed Forces. Admiral Gorshkov explained:

> The single Soviet military strategy, reflecting the policies of the Communist Party, directs all services of the Armed Forces to solve one task or another in correspondence with circumstances. Being common for all services of the Armed Forces, Soviet military strategy envisages strategic use of them both together and of each of them separately, taking into account their specific possibilities.[46]

In the early 1980s Soviet naval theorists were permitted to discuss naval operational art and naval tactics. Soviet military strategy, however, had to be expressed in terms of all the services and service arms.

A Restatement of Soviet Military Strategy

In September 1979, Volume 7 of the *Soviet Military Encyclopedia* carried an entry, "Military Strategy,"[47] signed by Marshal Ogarkov. It is the most authoritative statement on Soviet military strategy to appear since the mid-1970s. One of its most significant points is that the chief of the General Staff in 1979 gave essentially the same view on military strategy as that found in Marshal Sokolovskiy's *Military Strategy,* which appeared in three editions during the 1960s.[48] The doctrinal shift that encompassed the projections of military power under the umbrella afforded by strategic nuclear forces and theater forces is covered by reference to local wars.

As other Soviet spokesmen have done, Ogarkov emphasized that strategy is subordinate to politics. He paraphrased Clausewitz's formula that war is a continuation of politics, adding Lenin's modification that it is carried out by violent means. Politics determines the goals of war and the methods of its waging, and it assigns specific tasks to strategy while mobilizing the necessary resources and manpower for the needs of war. Strategy also influences politics in that the theoretical conclusions of military strategy are studied by the political leadership in determining the goals of war and the methods of achieving them. In addition, it influences decisions necessary for military structuring, as well as preparations for and waging of war. Strategic actions are the fundamental means of achieving the political goals of war. This is reflected in wartime by the creation of a single political-military strategic leadership structure. The subordination of military strategy to politics predetermines its class essence.

Ogarkov stressed that the economic and sociopolitical structure of the state influences the character and content of military strategy, which in turn depend on the level of industrial development of the state and the nature of production relationships within the state or coalition. The development of production and the level of science and technology determine the level of weapons technology. This, along with the size and type of population, has a direct influence on the manning and organization of the armed forces and on methods of preparing for and waging war on any scale, including strategic. In peacetime, the economy prepares the necessary military-technical base for waging a possible war in the future. It determines the level of equipment of the armed forces and thereby influences their fighting power. In wartime, economic capabilities determine the nature and scale of tasks that can be given the armed forces and also the scale and intensity of military operations.

Like other Soviet spokesmen, Ogarkov emphasized the close interconnection between military doctrine and strategy. In assigning specific tasks, military strategy is guided by the positions of military doctrine. At the same time, in formulating military doctrine the higher political and military leadership of the nation must take into account the conclusions and recommendations of military strategy and military science.

Soviet military strategy, Ogarkov asserted, reflects the policies of the Communist Party of the CPSU and the Soviet government in the realm of national defense. It proceeds from the tasks set by the Constitution of the USSR on the armed defense of the gains of socialism and serves the most advanced social structure. Its positions are worked out on the theoretical basis of Marxism-Leninism, primarily through Marxist-Leninist teachings on war and army.

Bourgeois military strategy, according to Ogarkov, reflects the policies of the ruling imperialist circles and is aimed at preparing for and waging aggressive wars. Contemporary U.S. and NATO military strategy proceeds chiefly from the concept of waging general nuclear war, in which strategic nuclear weapons have the decisive role. Ogarkov asserted that NATO forces are planning for the possibility of conducting protracted military operations with the use only of conventional weapons and, in isolated theaters of war, with the limited use of nuclear weapons. He accused the United States and other NATO nations of unleashing an unprecedented arms race, with large-scale plans for modernization of their armed forces that go far beyond what is necessary for defense.

In contrast, Ogarkov stated that both Soviet military strategy and doctrine have a purely defensive character and contain no plans for any kind of preemptive strike or premeditated attack. While imperialist military strategy fosters the arms race and seeks the achievement of military-technical superiority, Soviet military strategy proceeds from the necessity of providing the nation's Armed Forces with everything necessary for defense of the country. Soviet military strategy does not permit any probable enemy to achieve military-technical superiority, but it also does not make as its own aim the achievement of military-technical superiority over other countries.

Some of Marshal Ogarkov's statements are almost word-for-word those expressed by Marshal R. Ya. Malinovskiy and other Soviet military spokesmen in the early 1960s. Like them, Ogarkov repeated the thesis that

> Soviet military strategy views a future world war, if the imperialists manage to unleash it, as a decisive clash between two opposed world socio-economic systems—socialism and capitalism. In such a war, simultaneously or consecutively, the majority of the states of the world may become involved. Future war will be a global opposition of multimillion coalitional armed forces unprecedented in scale and violence and will be waged without compromise, for the most decisive political and strategic goals.[49]

In the late 1960s Soviet military doctrine and strategy were modified to include the possibility that world war might begin with the initial use of only conventional weapons. Ogarkov paraphrased earlier statements made by Marshal A. A. Grechko regarding this shift, noting that widening military actions could escalate into a general nuclear war in which nuclear weapons, primarily of strategic designation, would be the main means of waging it. At the base of Soviet military strategy lies the position that the Soviet Union, proceeding from the principles of its politics, will not use this weapon first. In principle, the Soviet Union is against the use of weapons of mass destruction. But Ogarkov warned that any possible aggressor must clearly recognize that in the event of a nuclear rocket attack on the Soviet Union or on other countries of the socialist community, there will be a crushing retaliatory blow from the USSR.

Repeating the basic tenets of Soviet military strategy, Ogarkov asserted that if nuclear weapons are used, a world war might be comparatively short. However, in view of the great military and economic potentials of possible coalitions among belligerent states, he did not exclude the possibility that such a war might be protracted. Therefore, Soviet military strategy proceeds from the fact that if nuclear war is "forced" on the Soviet Union, the Soviet people and their armed forces must be ready for the most severe and long ordeals. Because of the "advanced" character of the Soviet Union and other socialist states, they have "objective possibilities for achieving victory." For this to be realized, the country and the armed forces must be prepared in advance for such a war.

Soviet military strategy, Ogarkov stated, must take into account the possibility of local wars arising, "the political nature of which will be determined according to the classic positions and Leninist thesis on just and unjust wars."[50] The Soviet Union supports national-liberation wars but opposes the imperialists' "unleashing" of local wars, since they not only are of a reactionary nature but also might escalate into world war.

In the 1960s Marshal Sokolovskiy had written about operations in theaters of military operations. In 1979 Ogarkov was more specific:

> In evaluating the strategic content of war, Soviet military strategy considers war to be a complicated system of interrelated major simultaneous and consecutive strategic operations, including operations in continental TVDs. The common goal of each such operation will be one particular military-political goal of the war, connected with assuring the defense and retention of important regions of its territory and, if necessary, also with destroying actual enemy strategic groupings. Characteristic indicators of the scale for each operation will be conditioned by the possibilities of the sides, the range of the means of destruction, the ability to support troops (forces) materially, and also the actual conditions of the TVD.
>
> In the framework of strategic operations in continental TVDs might be conducted: initial and subsequent operations of fronts and in coastal areas, also initial and subsequent operations of fleets; air, antiair, airborne, sea-landing, combined landing and other operations; and also the delivery of nuclear rocket and aviation strikes. Other kinds of contemporary operations might also be conducted. Contemporary operations will be characterized by growing size, a fierce struggle to seize and hold the strategic initiative, highly maneuverable actions of groups of armed forces in separate directions in conditions of a lack of a solid front, deep mutual penetration of the sides, and rapid and acute changes in operational-strategic circumstances. The achievement of the goal of all these operations, just as also the achievement of victory in war as a whole, is possible only with the combined efforts of all services of the armed forces and service branches.[51]

Following the lead of earlier Soviet military spokesmen, Ogarkov stated that modern war will demand multimillion mass armies. Since maintaining such a force in peacetime is impossible in practical terms, great attention must be given to rapid mobilization.[52] This expression by the chief of the General Staff is in full accordance with the law on universal military service in the Soviet Union and with placing nearly all males in the reserves.

While the offensive is the basic kind of strategic action, Ogarkov wrote of the necessity for defensive actions, which should be active and directed toward creating conditions for a counteroffensive. Victory in war, emphasized Ogarkov, requires firm, centralized control over all forces. The Soviet leadership has extensive experience in strategic matters, which should be of great significance in the event of a future war. Troop control is becoming more and more complicated, the volume of work to be done by the strategic leadership is constantly growing, and time demands will be critical. The concealment of troop control in conditions of active enemy radioelectronic countermeasures is becoming more critical.

Marshal Ogarkov's 1979 statement on Soviet military strategy demonstrates the consistency of Soviet aims. The Soviet Party–military leadership's perceptions of the USSR's military needs did not change significantly during the period referred to as détente or as a result of SALT negotiations and agreements. Military strategies and policies expressed by Soviet planners in the 1980s do not differ fundamentally from those given in 1961 and early 1962, before the Cuban missile confrontation.

Military Strategy as a Social Science

In their 1966 article, "On Contemporary Military Science," Sokolovskiy and Cherednichenko commented that RAND and the Hudson Institute in the United States are at work solving "many military problems." They also stated that the British Institute of Strategic Studies, as well as a "technical center" under the NATO Supreme Command, is involved in strategic planning. Work at such institutes, the Soviet writers said, is accomplished by bringing together highly qualified specialists—a "huge army of scientific, military and political figures" who are formulating plans for "an openly aggressive strategy."[53]

Since the "intentions of the imperialists" must be opposed by "the strategy of the socialist countries," the two authors called attention to the need "to work out the contemporary problems of strategy, both on the theoretical and practical plane."[54] The implication clearly was made that the Soviet Union needed research institutes similar to the Hudson Institute and the British Institute of Strategic Studies, where specialists in many fields could work together on problems of military strategy.

As this article was published, Party Secretary Brezhnev, addressing the Twenty-third Party Congress, made specific references to deficiencies in Soviet study of the social sciences.[55] Since military strategy in the Soviet Union is regarded as one of the social sciences, the Sokolovskiy-Cherednichenko article appeared to buttress Brezhnev's charges, saying:

Military strategy and its theory are component parts of military science. The working out of the theory of military strategy, in essence, represents specific social research.

As in other social sciences, the theory of military strategy is called on to expose pressing problems and tasks and to indicate the valid path to their solution, to serve as a scientific basis of party policy in questions of protecting the country. *It is fully understood that the deficiencies of social sciences, being published in our periodical press, are inherent in military strategy as well.*[56] (emphasis added)

In response to a directive of the Party congress, the Central Committee in August 1967 adopted a resolution "On Measures for Further Developing the Social Sciences and Heightening Their Role in Communist Construction." Action on the resolution was taken, among others, by the Social Sciences Section of the Academy of Sciences. Explaining the purpose of that action, V. V. Zagladin, deputy head of the International Department of the Central Committee, writing in *Kommunist* five years after the resolution was adopted, asserted

that these problems need to be elaborated not only for purely scientific purposes but also for Party practical activity and for determining the most effective ways and means to *insure socialism's victory over capitalism.*[57] (emphasis added)

The Central Committee, in its resolution, noted that at present in "the era of transition from capitalism to socialism both Marxist-Leninist theory and the role of the social sciences have become increasingly important." Therefore,

intensification of creative work in the sphere of theory is imperative to strengthen the political, economic and cultural cooperation of the socialist countries and to determine the most effective ways and means *to ensure the victory of socialism over capitalism.*[58] (emphasis added)

Brezhnev's statement during the Twenty-third Party Congress, the resolution of the Central Committee the following year, and subsequent writings, such as the article by V. V. Zagladin, make it appear that Sokolovskiy's 1966 article had been part of the campaign to improve the social sciences as well as to correct the deficiencies "inherent in military strategy."

An initial response to the Central Committee's resolution, as well as to the Sokolovskiy-Cherednichenko article "On Contemporary Military Strategy," was the establishment in 1967 of the Institute of the USA. It is no accident, as the Russians so often say, that the new institute was located immediately across the street from the apartment building where Marshal Sokolovskiy and other senior Soviet officers were living at the time.

As the Institute of the USA was being formed, other institutes were revitalized to help "ensure the victory of socialism over capitalism." Among these were the Institute of World Economy and International Relations (IMEMO), Institute of the Far East (IDV), Institute of Oriental Studies (IVAN), Institute of Africa (IA), and the Institute of Latin America (ILA). Members of these institutes, as their names indicate, study either specific fields or specific geographical areas.[59]

A number of Soviet officers moved from the General Staff or from one of the military academies to join these institutes or to become consultants. Among these were General Major V. V. Larionov, composing editor of all three editions of *Military Strategy*; General Colonel N. A. Lomov, editor of *Scientific-Technical Progress and the Revolution in Military Affairs*; Colonel Lev Semeyko, author of *Foresight of a Commander in Battle*; Colonel V. M. Kulish, author of *The Second Front*; General Major A. K. Slobodenko, on the editorial board of *The Foreign Military Observer*; and General Lt. M. A. Milshtein, a specialist on the military forces of the United States.

Marshal Sokolovskiy's *Military Strategy* notes that strategic intelligence is considered to be one of the components of military strategy. Therefore, since strategy is within the area of study of the social science institutes, it logically follows that institute members also have an interest in strategic intelligence. The mission of strategic intelligence, in both peacetime and wartime, is "systematically to procure political, military, economic, scientific, and technical data concerning possible enemies and to study their military capabilities."[60] When this mission is related to the work of the social science institutes under the Soviet Academy of Sciences, it appears that the Soviet leaders have developed one of the most sophisticated programs for openly gathering strategic intelligence yet devised.

Institute members study the political, economic, technological, and military capabilities of the non-Communist world not only through their own scholarly research from foreign publications, but also from their travels throughout western Europe, Japan, and the western hemisphere. Generally, in their travels outside the Soviet Union they are accepted as scholars, which in fact they are, and frequently they have easy access to the highest professional and government levels within the nations they visit. In addition, the social science institutes, particularly the Institute of the USA and Canada and the Institute of World Economy and International Relations, act as hosts to visiting Western political leaders and scholars. Meetings with such knowledgeable individuals are a great help in providing insights and assessments of the non-Communist world.

Laws of War and Laws of Armed Combat

Soviet military theorists say that their strategy "is guided by the advanced theory of Marxism-Leninism which allows the discerning and correct use of objective laws which determine victory in modern war."[61] These "objective" laws are categorized in a number of ways, such as "laws of war," "laws of armed combat," and "laws of military science." Certain laws deal with *basic* principles of strategy, operational art, and tactics, which are the same for all three of these components of military art. In addition, there are *particular* principles that apply individually to tactics, operational art, and strategy. Also included are principles that apply both to operational art and to tactics, but not to strategy.

The laws of war are of the highest level, followed by laws of armed combat. Below these are laws of military operations on strategic, operational, and tactical scales. Distinctions among these laws often are blurred. As one writer explained, "Each law of war is more or less a law of armed combat, and each law of armed combat is more or less a law of war as a whole. Still, there is a difference between the two."[62]

In conformity with Marxist beliefs, the content and form of these laws change in accordance with concrete historical conditions. Since laws are objective, they cannot be arbitrarily canceled or abolished; however, being objective, they are subject to differing interpretations. Understanding the objective laws of war is an extremely involved matter, particularly so now given the absence of practical experience in waging war with the use of nuclear weapons. This difficulty is admitted in Soviet military writings.

Soviet theorists are permitted to express different views on the order and importance of these laws. One Soviet author, writing on the laws of war, expressed the following view:

> We have not yet succeeded in achieving a unity of opinions on a number of questions examined in this work and in the materials published in our military literature. Some authors express controversial, imprecise and even erroneous theses. Some urgent problems are still awaiting solution, or even have yet to be posed. It is the urgent task of Soviet military science to fill this gap.[63]

The above statement was written in 1972. Despite the uncertainty in identifying the laws, another author in 1977 made it appear as if there were agreement and the laws were firm. For example:

> The known laws of war are taken into account by the military policy of the Party, they are expressed in the military doctrine of the socialist

state, serve as the basis of military science and lie at the base of the principles of waging war, the activities of the command staff and of all personnel of socialist armies. Without such a foundation, military work would be limited to empty hopes of favorable coincidences of circumstances, to hopes on chance.[64]

Specific Laws of War

A study of the laws of war, as given by various Soviet theoreticians over a period of time, may reflect changes in emphasis of military doctrine and strategy. In 1972 one Soviet book listed the laws of war as follows:[65]

- *The first law of war* is that "the course and outcome of war waged with unlimited employment of all means of conflict depend primarily on the correlation of available, strictly military forces of the combatants at the beginning of war, especially in nuclear weapons and means of delivery."
- *The second law of war* is that "the course and outcome of war depend on the correlation of the military potentials of the combatants."[66]
- *The third law of war* is that "its course and outcome depend on its political content."[67]
- *The fourth law of war* is that "the course and outcome of war depend on the correlation of moral-political and psychological capabilities of the people and armies of the combatants."[68]

A 1982 work, in contrast, gave the following general laws of war:[69]

- The course and outcome of war are dependent upon the correlation of the economic potentials of the belligerent states (coalitions).
- The course and outcome of war are dependent upon the correlation of the scientific-technical potentials of the belligerents.
- The course and outcome of the war are dependent upon the correlation of the moral potentials of the belligerents.
- The course and outcome of war are dependent upon the correlation of military potentials of the belligerents.

In discussing the military potentials of the warring sides, the author just quoted indicated that "nuclear missile weapons have shattered the notions which developed on troop strength, and nuclear weapons have become the main indicator and element in the military potentials of the great powers."[70]

Laws of Armed Combat and Their Application

The laws of armed combat differ only slightly from the laws of war. There does not appear to be any agreement concerning their number or content. They "are examined predominantly within military science and are a subject of the general theory of military art."[71]

A 1982 Soviet text, intended for officers studying at military academies, stated that the basic generality of armed combat is *"the dependence of victory or defeat on the relationship of the combat might of the opposing armed forces"* (emphasis in original). The authors went on to state that this generality of armed combat is disclosed through a number of laws. "Specialists in military science consider them to be the following:

- the law of dependence of methods of armed combat on the means of its waging (included in the category of 'means' are not only equipment but also people);
- the law of the cooperation of troops according to place, time, and goal;
- the law of the dependence of combat actions on conformity of the character of control to the aims and means of armed combat;
- the law of dependence of victory in armed combat on concentrating basic forces on the decisive direction."[72]

Laws of armed combat apply to small skirmishes and to front-level operations, as well as to the types of combat actions, whether offensive or defensive. Soviet theorists claim that since the laws of war are objective, based on statistical laws, predictions based on the statistical laws themselves also become laws. Based on this assumption, Soviet military operational research is considered by some analysts to be as sophisticated as anything found in the United States.

Before laws of armed combat can be applied, they first must be determined. The initial step in this process is the study of military history. Skirmishes, battles, and campaigns must be analyzed in great detail. The next step is to *generalize the experience* of past military actions. From this generalization statistical norms are developed that will apply to similar types of combat in future actions. Thus, from detailed analyses of air battles in World War II, Korea, Vietnam, and the Middle East, Soviet analysts engaged in operational research seek to find common characteristics that apply to all similar types of air battles. This process establishes the norm that determines the number and types of aircraft needed in a given situation, and what action each pilot should take. A potential problem for the pilot, or in some cases the ground controller, is to correctly identify the type of situation in which the aircraft might be placed. Operational research also identifies the type of aircraft and armament that should be developed, as well as the numbers of aircraft that are to be produced.

It appears that one goal of Soviet operational research is the ability to enter into computers various norms derived from analyses of past battles, with as many additional facts on weapons, order of battle, and other data as possible. A given Soviet commander might then have access to data much more complete than, and far different from, the data available to an opposing commander.

When the Marxist-Leninist coating is stripped away, many of the Soviet concepts of laws of armed conflict are worth studying. These laws are basic fundamentals, applicable to any military situation. The Soviet approach to military operations research is unique, although the Soviet methodology may have pitfalls.

With respect to Soviet military science, the laws of war and laws of armed combat are still being interpreted. What previously had been referred to as factors or principles now, in some cases, are given as laws. One author has even suggested that there are "permanently operating factors" reminiscent of the permanently operating factors established by Stalin.[73] An apparent move toward codification of certain of the laws is occurring now in the Soviet Union, a move that will take them beyond the stage of discussion and place them in a category somewhat similar to that of military doctrine.

*   *   *

Soviet military science should warrant careful study in the non-Communist world and also in China. Basic Soviet strategy, stemming from the military doctrine formulated in the late 1950s, has changed but little since it was first presented in the 1962 edition of Marshal Sokolovskiy's *Military Strategy*. It is commonly believed in the United States that the Soviet decision to seek strategic nuclear superiority was made as a result of the Cuban missile confrontation. In fact, the nuclear decision was made in the late 1950s, as revealed both by *The Penkovskiy Papers* and by Sokolovskiy's famed work.

Many in the West believed that the Soviet emphasis on nuclear weaponry would change after Khrushchev was ousted and that the new Soviet leadership would follow more conventional military policies. This did not prove to be the case. Soviet military publications, as well as the evident deployment of strategic nuclear missiles, attest that there was no apparent change in either Soviet military doctrine or strategy after Brezhnev came to power.

Since the early 1970s there have been great expectations in most of the non-Communist world that negotiations on arms limitations and mutual force reduction in Europe would curtail the growth of armed forces in both the NATO and Warsaw Pact countries. Judging from the writings of Soviet military-political spokesmen up through the mid-1980s, arms control negotiations and agreements have not had any impact on either Soviet military goals or the buildup of the armed forces of Warsaw Pact nations.

One conclusion that can be drawn is that Soviet military strategy has an integrity of its own and is not a belated reflection of United States strategic concepts. Hence, "mutual assured destruction" is irrelevant in the Soviet context and is not viewed as a realistic or desirable conceptual underpinning for their forces.

Another conclusion is that, even with the revolution in military affairs, Soviet military doctrine is still "classical" in that war remains an extension of politics and that deterrence is not an end in itself.

Notes

1. A. S. Zheltov, *Metodologicheskiye Problemy Voyennoy Teorii i Praktiki* [Methodological Problems of Military Theory and Practice] (Moscow: Voyenizdat, 1968), p. 294.

2. "Voyennaya Nauka" [Military Science], *Voyennyy Entsiklopedicheskiy Slovar'* [Military Encyclopedic Dictionary] (Moscow: Voyenizdat, 1983), p. 136.

3. Ibid.

4. It is estimated that between 350 and 500 Soviet officers hold the degree of doctor of military sciences or doctor of naval sciences. For naval sciences degrees, see *Voyennyy Entsiklopedicheskiy Slovar'*, pp. 315, 240.

5. S. P. Ivanov and A. I. Yeseyev, "Voyennoye Iskusstvo" [Military Art], *Sovetskaya Voyennaya Entsiklopediya* [Soviet Military Encyclopedia] (Moscow: Voyenizdat, 1976–1980), Vol. 2, p. 211.

6. N. V. Ogarkov, "Strategiya Voyennaya" [Military Strategy], *Sovetskaya Voyennaya Entsiklopediya*, Vol. 7, pp. 555–565.

7. V. G. Kulikov, "Operativnoye Iskusstvo" [Operational Art], *Sovetskaya Voyennaya Entsiklopediya*, Vol. 6, pp. 53–57.

8. I. G. Pavlovskiy, P. S. Kutakhov, S. G. Gorshkov, V. D. Sozinov, and I. G. Borets, "Taktika" [Tactics], *Sovetskaya Voyennaya Entsiklopediya,* Vol. 7, pp. 628–634.

9. P. A. Zhilin, *Ocherki Sovetskoy Voyennoy Istoriografii* [Essays on Soviet Military Historiography] (Moscow: Voyenizdat, 1974), p. 192. See also Harriet Fast Scott and William F. Scott, eds., *The Soviet Art of War* (Boulder, Colo.: Westview Press, 1982), p. 27.

10. Scott and Scott, *The Soviet Art of War,* p. 35.

11. For excerpts of Shaposhnikov's writings, see Scott and Scott, *The Soviet Art of War,* p. 46. See also V. G. Kulikov, "The Brain of the Army," *Pravda,* 13 November 1974. For an English translation, see W. F. Scott, ed., *Selected*

Soviet Military Writings, 1970–1975 (Washington, D.C.: Government Printing Office, 1977), pp. 185–191.

12. For an example of Triandafillov's work, see A. B. Kadishev, *Voprosy Strategii i Operativnovo Iskusstva v Sovetskikh Voyennykh Trudakh* [Problems of Strategy and Operational Art in Soviet Works, 1917–1940] (Moscow: Voyenizdat, 1965), pp. 291–346.

13. Tukhachevskiy was a Marshal of the Soviet Union at the time of his execution by orders of Stalin. Excerpts of his writings are found in Scott and Scott, *The Soviet Art of War,* pp. 44, 56.

14. The introduction to Kadishev, *Problems of Strategy,* was written by Marshal of the Soviet Union M. V. Zakharov, while chief of the General Staff. Zakharov states that of many of the pre–World War II Soviet military writings, such as those by Tukhachevskiy and Svechin, all but one copy were destroyed, by orders of Stalin.

15. See, for example, A. M. Vasilevskiy, *Delo Vsey Zhizni* [A Whole Life's Work], 2d ed. (Moscow: Politizdat, 1975), p. 102.

16. A. M. Nekrich, *June 22, 1941,* translated, with analysis by Vladimir Petrov, *"June 22, 1941"—Soviet Historians and the German Invasion* (Columbia, S.C.: University of South Carolina Press, 1968), p. 12. See also Scott and Scott, *The Soviet Art of War,* p. 99.

17. Ibid., p. 131.

18. Ibid., p. 135. According to Nekrich, Marshal Bagramyan made this statement in an interview with a *Literaturnaya Gazeta* correspondent, published in that journal on 17 April 1965.

19. Nekrich, *June 22, 1941,* p. 135.

20. S. N. Kozlov, ed., *Spravochnik Ofitsera,* [Officer's Handbook] (Moscow: Voyenizdat, 1971), p. 78.

21. Oleg Penkovskiy, *The Penkovskiy Papers* (New York: Doubleday & Co., 1965), p. 251.

22. V. D. Sokolovskiy, ed., *Voyennaya Strategiya* [Military Strategy] (Moscow: Voyenizdat, 1962). In September 1962, William F. Scott, then U.S. air attache in Moscow, sent a number of copies of this book to the United States. At least two English translations were commercially published. The third edition of V. D. Sokolovskiy's *Military Strategy* appeared in 1968. This edition, edited with an analysis and commentary by Harriet Fast Scott, was published in 1975 in the United States as V. D. Sokolovskiy, *Soviet Military Strategy,* 3d ed. It includes the material contained in all three editions and will be the edition referenced.

23. Ibid., p. 4.

24. Ibid., p. 5.

25. Ibid., p. 387.

26. For examples of articles by General Major I. G. Zavyalov and General Lieutenant M. E. Cherednichenko, see Scott, *Selected Soviet Military Writings: 1970–1975.*

27. Sokolovskiy, *Soviet Military Strategy,* 3d ed., p. 304.

28. Ibid., pp. 8–9ff.

29. Ibid., p. 210.

30. Ibid., p. 306.

31. M. V. Smirnov, I. S. Baz', et al., *O Sovetskoy Voyennoy Nauke* [On Soviet Military Science] (Moscow: Voyenizdat, 1960) and S. N. Kozlov, I. S. Baz' et al., *O Sovetskoy Voyennoy Nauke* (Moscow: Voyenizdat, 1964). The 1960 edition of this work indicated that all questions of military science are not settled. Printed shortly after Khrushchev's speech of 14 January 1960, the text noted that rocket troops now "appear as the main service of the Armed Forces." The 1964 book, which, looking backward, appears to have explained well the strategy the Soviet leadership was following, generally was ignored in the United States. Most Western analysts thought that Khrushchev's ouster would bring about major changes in Soviet military doctrine and strategy, and therefore that it would be a waste of time to read what was written during the Khrushchev period.

32. A. A. Strokov, ed., *The History of Military Art.* For an English translation, see W. R. Kintner and Harriet Fast Scott, *The Nuclear Revolution in Soviet Military Affairs* (Norman, Okla.: University of Oklahoma Press, 1968), p. 225.

33. V. D. Sokolovskiy and I. M. Cherednichenko, "On Contemporary Military Strategy," *Kommunist Vooruzhennykh Sil,* April 1966. The quotation is from the English translation by Kintner and Scott in *The Nuclear Revolution.*

34. Ibid., p. 269.

35. Ibid., p. 271.

36. Ibid., p. 274.

37. Ibid., p. 272.

38. Sokolovskiy, *Soviet Military Strategy,* 3d ed., p. 65.

39. Ibid., p. 68.

40. Ibid., p. 261.

41. N. A. Lomov, ed., *Nauchno-Teknicheskiy Progress i Revolyutsiya v Voyennom Dele* [Scientific-Technical Progress and the Revolution in Military Affairs] (Moscow: Voyenizdat, 1973), p. 135. Translated by United States Air Force (Washington, D.C.: Government Printing Office, 1974).

42. Ibid., p. 139.

43. Ibid., pp. 139–140.

44. Ibid., p. 140.

45. See Joseph D. Douglass, Jr., and Amoretta M. Hoeber, *Selected Readings from* Military Thought *1963–1973* (Washington, D.C.: Government Printing Office, 1982), Vol. 5, Parts I and II (two volumes). Contained therein are extensive excerpts from the best articles of those issues of *Military Thought* that have been declassified.

46. S. G. Gorshkov, *Morskaya Moshch Gosudarstva* [The Sea Power of the State], 2d ed. (Moscow: Voyenizdat, 1979), p. 316.

47. Ogarkov, "Strategiya Voyennaya," pp. 555–565.

48. Note that in Chapter 3 ("Military Science") all three editions of *Military Strategy* are discussed in detail.

49. This 1979 statement does not differ in substance from statements found in Chapter 2, "Postwar Development of Soviet Military Doctrine and Strategy."

50. Ogarkov, "Strategiya Voyennaya," p. 564.

51. Ibid., p. 564.

52. Ibid.

53. Sokolovskiy and Cherednichenko, "On Contemporary Military Strategy," p. 276 in Kintner and Scott, *The Nuclear Revolution.*

54. Ibid., p. 277.

55. L. I. Brezhnev, "Report of the Central Committee of the CPSU to the Twenty-third Congress of the CPSU," 29 March 1966, published in *Twenty-third Congress of the Communist Party of the Soviet Union* (Moscow: Novosti Press, 1966), p. 109.

56. Sokolovskiy and Cherednichenko, "On Contemporary Military Strategy," in Kintner and Scott, *The Nuclear Revolution,* p. 277.

57. V. V. Zagladin, "The Revolutionary Process and the International Policy of the USSR," *Kommunist* 13, September 1972, p. 15.

58. *Pravda,* 22 August 1967, p. 1.

59. For an account of these institutes, see Harriet Fast Scott, *Soviet "Think Tanks"—IMEMO, IUSA—and Strategy* (Menlo Park, Calif.: Stanford Research Institute, Strategic Studies Center, May 1974).

60. Sokolovskiy, *Soviet Military Strategy,* 3d ed., p. 318.

61. Zheltov, *Metodologicheskiye Problemy,* p. 319.

62. M. P. Popov, "The Laws of Armed Conflict Are the Objective Basis of Leadership of Combat Operations," *Voyennaya Mysl'* [Military Thought], October 1964. Translated by FBIS.

63. V. Ye. Savkin, *Osnovnyye Printsipy Operativnovo Iskusstva i Taktiki* [Basic Principles of Operational Art and Tactics] (Moscow, Voyenizdat, 1972), p. 5.

64. D. A. Volkogonov, ed., *Voyna i Armiya* [War and Army] (Moscow: Voyenizdat, 1977), p. 146.

65. Savkin, *Osnovnyye Printsipy,* p. 89.

66. Ibid., p. 92.

67. Ibid.

68. Ibid.

69. V. V. Serebryannikov, *Osnovy Marksistsko-Leninskovo Ucheniya o Voyne i Armii* [Basis of Marxist-Leninist Teachings on War and Army] (Moscow: Voyenizdat, 1982), p. 155. This work is a textbook for higher military schools.

70. Ibid., p. 165.

71. Ibid., p. 155.

72. N. D. Tabunov and V. A. Bokarev, eds., *Marksistsko-Leninskaya Filosofiya i Metodologicheskiye Problemy Voyennoy Teorii i Praktika* [Marxist-Leninist Philosophy and Methodological Problems of Military Theory and Practice] (Moscow: Voyenizdat, 1982), pp. 304–305.

73. N. N. Azovtsev, *V. I. Lenin i Sovetskaya Voyennaya Nauka* [V. I. Lenin and Soviet Military Science] (Moscow: Nauka, 1981), p. 321.

Part 2

A MILITARY FORCE FOR THE NUCLEAR AGE

4

The Soviet High Command

Much is published in the Western world about Soviet weapons systems and their capabilities. Many Soviet writings on military doctrine and strategy now are available, in various translations, for interested readers. Relatively little information can be found, however, on the organization of the Soviet high command and the men who occupy its key positions.

There appear to be three major bodies in the top Soviet command structure: (1) the Council of Defense of the USSR, (2) the Main Military Council—the *Kollegiya* of the Ministry of Defense, and (3) the General Staff. Closely linked to these organizations are a number of important bodies, such as the Command and Staff of the Warsaw Pact Forces. These staffs and agencies function quite differently from any military or military-political body in the United States. They are not constrained by a division of powers, such as exists among the U.S. executive, legislative, and judicial branches of government. As a group, these bodies, especially the Council of Defense, have virtually complete control over the military-economic direction of the Soviet Union.

Confirmation of the existence of the Council of Defense, its incorporation into the Constitution adopted in 1977, and a number of writings about the operation of Stavka and the Soviet General Staff have made it possible to compose a picture of the Soviet high command and its probable membership both in peace and in war. Its actual membership has not been announced.

The Council of Defense of the USSR (Sovyet Oborony SSSR)

On 7 May 1976, Leonid Il'ich Brezhnev, then general secretary of the Communist Party of the Soviet Union (CPSU) was promoted to Marshal of the Soviet Union. The announcement of his promotion referred to him as chairman of the Council of Defense.[1] Information about this body, or even of its existence, previously had been kept secret. However, biographies published after Brezhnev's death stated that he became chairman of the Council of Defense in 1964, presumably as soon as he replaced Khrushchev as first secretary of the Communist Party.[2]

The predecessor of today's Council of Defense was a World War II organization, the State Committee of Defense, known as GKO (Gosudarstvennyy Komitet Oborony). In time of war the Council of Defense might be given extraordinary authority such as GKO had, as explained in Marshal Sokolovskiy's *Military Strategy:*

> All leadership of the country and the Armed Forces during wartime will be accomplished by the Central Committee of the Communist Party of the Soviet Union with the possible organization of a higher agency of leadership of the country and the Armed Forces. This higher agency of leadership may be given the same powers as the State Committee of Defense during the Great Patriotic War.[3]

The origin of the Council of Defense, and of GKO, can be traced to Lenin's Civil War Council of Workers' and Peasants' Defense. Later, during a lull in the Civil War fighting, soldiers were put to work, and the organization took the name Council of Labor and Defense (Sovyet Truda i Oborony), often called by its initials STO.[4] It continued to be the nation's highest military-economic planning agency even after the Civil War and was concerned with matters affecting the country's defense, economic plans, and government branches. Its decrees were law. By 1932, as industrialization was proceeding, a Defense Commission was given the task of examining matters to be brought to STO's attention, and STO soon became only a rubber stamp. In 1937 STO was abolished, and the Defense Commission was made a full-fledged Committee of Defense.[5]

The German attack on 22 June 1941 found the Soviet defense structure unprepared. Within a week after the attack the State Committee of Defense was formed, with Stalin as chairman.[6] The new committee fashioned itself on the model of the Council of Labor and Defense that Lenin had headed during the Civil War. Having no administrative machinery itself, it used the existing government agencies, coordinating all efforts to stem the German invasion.

First members of GKO were Stalin, Molotov, Voroshilov, Beria, and Malenkov. Later a few more names were added: N. A. Bulganin, N. A. Voznesenskiy, L. M. Kaganovich, and A. I. Mikoyan.[7] This small group of men formed the war cabinet that ran the nation. Each member had a special sphere of activities within his competence. GKO settled political and diplomatic questions, handled the whole complex of the war economy, and made all major decisions on the conduct of the war.

In February 1973 *Red Star* began publishing a series of articles about the work of GKO during the time of the Soviet Union's participation in World War II.[8] Seldom does anything appear in the Soviet press without a reason. The series ran until May 1975, apparently paving the way for disclosing the existence of the Council of Defense the following year.

The situation was regularized by incorporating the Council of Defense into the Constitution and adding "of the USSR." In 1977, Article 121, section 14 of the new Constitution of the USSR stated: "The Presidium of the Supreme Soviet of the USSR shall . . . form the Council of Defense *of the USSR* and confirm its composition. . . ."[9] (emphasis added)

On 9 May 1983—Victory Day in the Soviet Union—Minister of Defense D. F. Ustinov referred to "General Secretary of the Central Committee CPSU, Chairman of the Council of Defense USSR, Comrade Yu. V. Andropov,"[10] indicating his succession to the post of chairman of the Council of Defense even before he became chairman of the Presidium of the Supreme Soviet USSR on 16 June 1983. The Presidium of the Supreme Soviet, as stated in the Constitution, confirmed Andropov as chairman of the Council of Defense of the USSR at an earlier date, presumably as soon as he became the General Secretary.

With the death of Yuri Andropov in February 1984, Konstantin U. Chernenko became the new General Secretary of the CPSU. In April, he also became Chairman of the Presidium of the Supreme Soviet— "president" of the Soviet Union. The members of the Council of Defense of the USSR probably are K. U. Chernenko, chairman, M. S. Gorbachev, G. V. Romanov, N. A. Tikhonov, and D. F. Ustinov—all of whom are Politburo members. Other party and military heads may be called upon to attend meetings, depending upon the matters to be discussed. Among these might be Foreign Minister A. A. Gromyko, General of the Army V. M. Chebrikov, Chairman of the KGB USSR, and General of the Army V. V. Fedorchuk, minister of Internal Affairs (MVD). It is believed that Marshal N. V. Ogarkov, as chief of the General Staff, heads the secretariat of the Council of Defense.

The Council of Defense of the USSR, as the successor to STO and GKO, oversees the preparation of the country, the economy, and the people for war. It ensures that there are standby plans for mobilizing industry, transport, and manpower to meet the requirements for possible war at various levels of intensity. It has the power to form new staffs, create new military districts, or change the entire structure of the Soviet Armed Forces. The council examines proposals, makes its judgment, and issues decrees.

In 1938 a Military Industrial Commission was attached to the Committee of Defense.[11] There is no indication that this commission was ever abolished, and currently it appears to be a working agency attached to the Council of Defense. Its task is probably to ensure the fulfillment—by both defense and nondefense industrial ministries—of Council of Defense plans for production and delivery of arms. Since the size of the defense budget is largely responsible for holding down production of consumer goods in the Soviet Union, the work of the Military Industrial Commission is of major importance to the Committee of Defense and has a significant impact upon the entire Soviet economy.

The Main Military Council—the *Kollegiya* of the Ministry of Defense (Glavnyy Voyennyy Sovyet— Kollegiya Ministerstva Oborony)

The Main Military Council, which is the collegium of the Ministry of Defense, is concerned with problems of the strategic direction and leadership of the Soviet Armed Forces in time of peace.[12] As of 1984, this deliberative body is chaired by the minister of defense, Marshal Ustinov. The chairman of the Council of Defense is assumed to be a member, as are the three "first deputy" ministers of defense—Marshal Ogarkov, chief of the General Staff; Marshal Kulikov, commander in chief of the Warsaw Pact Forces; and Marshal Sokolov, who has responsibilities for general affairs. The council membership also includes General Yepishev, chief of the Main Political Administration and eleven deputy ministers of defense: the commanders in chief of the Strategic Rocket Forces, Ground Forces, Troops of Air Defense, Air Forces and Navy; the deputy ministers of defense for cadres and for armaments; the inspector general, the chiefs of civil defense, billeting and construction, and rear services.

In time of war the Main Military Council would be replaced by Stavka (Headquarters of the Supreme High Command), the equivalent of the senior military command during World War II. According to both *Military Strategy* and the *Officer's Handbook*,[13] Stavka would operate in any future war much as it did in the last, with a degree of centralization of command and control that would be impossible in the West. Since current references both to the Main Military Council and to Stavka are extremely rare, the best way to understand the work of this council is to examine its origins and past functions.

A Higher Military Council (Vysshiy Voyennyy Sovyet) was established and chaired by Leon Trotskiy in 1918. As the Civil War increased in intensity the military councils in the field began to call themselves revolutionary military councils. By the end of the summer of 1918 the Higher Military Council was replaced as the Red Army's highest level of control by the Revvoyensoviet (Revolutionary Military Council) of the Republic. Trotskiy, commissar of military and naval affairs, chaired the Revvoyensoviet, which was directly subordinate to the Council of Defense. As in the case of the Council of Defense, the Revvoyensoviet continued to exercise considerable power even after the end of the Civil War. Frunze succeeded Trotskiy as chairman of the Revvoyensoviet and in turn was succeeded by Voroshilov.[14]

By 1934 the Revvoyensoviet, which was the *kollegiya* of the Commissariat of Defense, was abolished when the Seventeenth Party Congress did away with *kollegialsnost'* (collective leadership) as a principle.[15] At that time a Military Council was formed. This council consisted of eighty members and acted in an advisory role. In 1938, as a result of a kind of bureaucratic schizophrenia that hits the Soviet Union from time to time, the Commissariat of Defense split into two new commissariats, one for the Red Navy and another for the Red Army, each with its own Main Military Council.[16] These Main Military Councils, established at the time the purges were in full swing, were to devote their energies to preparing for a war that the Soviet leadership recognized as drawing ever close. The council made recommendations for dropping obsolete equipment and for doing research and development of new weapons, especially tanks and aircraft. In the case of the Red Army's council, this was of the utmost importance, since Soviet participation in the Spanish Civil War had proved their equipment to be no match for that of Western European nations.

Before the German invasion, Soviet planning had called for the commissar of defense to direct the front commanders through the Main Military Council. There also were untested plans for the creation of a Stavka, or headquarters of the high command, the highest body of Soviet military control, to replace the Main Military Council. The Stavka was formed the day after Hitler's attack, with Marshal Timoshenko, defense commissar, as its head, and Stalin, Molotov, Voroshilov, Zhukov, Budennyy, and Kuznetsov as members. In less than a month, on 10 July, Stalin took over the chairmanship of Stavka. He was designated defense commissar, replacing Timoshenko, and on 8 August became supreme commander in chief of the Armed Forces.[17] Stavka then was renamed Stavka of the Supreme High Command. Shortly thereafter, Marshal Shaposhnikov, who succeeded Zhukov as chief of the General Staff, was added to the membership.

In the first months of war the rapidly changing strategic situation and "frequent disruption of communications" between Moscow and the fronts* made it impossible for Stavka to exercise direct control over the troops.[18] By a decree of GKO on 10 July 1941 three intermediate main commands, northwestern, western, and southwestern were formed between Stavka and the fronts to direct the fighting.[19] After the fronts stabilized, Stavka "was again entrusted with the direct leadership of all active fronts and individual armies,"[20] and the three intermediate commands were abolished.

It was Stavka's job to determine the operational tasks of the fronts and to monitor the accomplishment of these tasks. This made it possible for Stavka "to follow operationally and continuously the development of military actions, to reinforce the front units with its reserves at an opportune time, and to restore their cooperation in case of disruption, and also to direct the main forces of the front or fronts and to lay down additional or new tasks."[21] Thus, Stavka directly ran the field forces of the fighting fronts. From the very first day of the war, Stavka sent representatives into the field to coordinate activities affecting one front and to coordinate operations of two or more fronts. For example, should it be necessary to switch air armies from one front to another, a Stavka representative would order the transfer and ensure coordination. Individuals assigned as Stavka representatives were very senior officers. Zhukov was sent from Moscow to the field in this capacity no fewer than fifteen times.[22] On air matters the Stavka representative often was the commander in chief of the Air Forces, Marshal A. A. Novikov, or his deputy.

In the last days of World War II, after Germany was defeated, GKO created a High Command of Soviet Troops in the Far East to coordinate ground, air, and naval attacks against Japan. Its establishment "was explained by the remoteness of the theater of operations and by the fact that it had a completely independent strategic importance."[23] Direct liaison was maintained with Stavka.

Stavka was abolished in January 1946 just a few months after the war's end, and the Higher Military Council was reestablished.[24] In 1950 the Soviet military structure once again was divided into two ministries: a Main Military Council of the War Ministry and a Main Military Council of the Naval Ministry.[25] In March 1953, within days after Stalin's death, the two councils were recombined into the Main Military Council.

When discussing Stavka, Soviet theorists point out the difference between control during World War II and in the Civil War two decades earlier. In the Civil War Lenin had chaired STO and Trotskiy the

---

*A Soviet front is a higher operational command composed of armies, divisions, and regiments of the Armed Forces.

Revolutionary Military Council. Another person—a military officer—was commander in chief of the Red Army. However, during the Great Patriotic War, Stalin himself as commissar of defense headed both equivalent organizations—GKO and Stavka—and he was the supreme commander in chief as well.[26] In addition, Stalin remained general secretary of the Communist Party and head of the government. This provided unity of leadership of the Armed Forces to the highest degree in every respect—politically, economically, and militarily. The combining of positions in the person of Stalin "meant a further centralization of leadership and a merger of the overall leadership of the country with the strategic leadership of the Armed Forces. In this centralization of political, economic, and military leadership, the unity of policy and strategy . . . found its even more perfected expression."[27]

Soviet writings about the work of Stavka during World War II suggest how a similar organization would operate during any future conflict. For example, as Marshal Sokolovskiy notes:

> The direct leadership of the Armed Forces during a war will obviously be accomplished, as before, by the Stavka of the Supreme High Command. The Stavka will be a collegial agency of leadership under the chairmanship of the supreme commander in chief.[28]

The *Officer's Handbook*, published in 1971, is equally clear:

> Each service of the Armed Forces is designated for waging military actions primarily in one definite sphere—on land, at sea, and in the air—and carries out the fulfillment of the tasks under the leadership of the CINC of these services of the Armed Forces or directly of Stavka of the Supreme High Command.[29]

The General Staff

There were less than a dozen members of Stavka at any one time throughout World War II. Specialists were called in to advise on specific subjects, as needed. Stavka was able to remain small because it had the services of the full resources of the General Staff. Marshal Sokolovskiy's *Military Strategy* specifies that in the event of a future war, "just as during the years of the Great Patriotic War, *the General Staff will be the main agency of the Stavka of the Supreme High Command*"[30] (emphasis added).

There is no equivalent of the Soviet General Staff in the U.S. armed forces. The Soviet staff concept is so radically different from anything found in the Pentagon that its impact upon the Soviet Armed Forces is difficult for Americans to grasp. Soviet writers rarely reveal anything of consequence about the organization of the General Staff or its personnel and functions. Only in the last decade have its activities during World War II been described.[31] Years of painstaking research have been required to determine even the general nature of its activity.

The Soviet General Staff is immediately subordinate to the Main Military Council (which in wartime would be replaced by Stavka) and is the largest of the three primary bodies of the Soviet High Command (Council of Defense, Main Military Council, and General Staff). It is a major link in the extreme centralization of authority that is characteristic of all activity in the Soviet Union.

Origins of the General Staff

The nearest equivalent of the Soviet General Staff was the pre–World War I German Army General Staff, which had been a model for the Imperial Russian General Staff of the early 1900s. The similarity to the German Army General Staff is not surprising, since many of the Soviet officers who were the senior military leaders in the 1930s attended German staff courses in the 1920s.

Like the Council of Defense and the Main Military Council, the General Staff had its origins in the early days of Bolshevik rule. At first, in 1918, there was an All-Russian Main Staff, which combined in itself several directorates: Organization, Operations, Military Transport, and Command Personnel.[32] Later, when the Revvoyensoviet of the Republic was formed, a Field Staff was formed under it to make and execute operational plans. In 1921, the two staffs were combined into the Staff of the Red Army, which, however, proved to be large and unwieldy. Mikhail Frunze, the Civil War leader who replaced Trotskiy in 1924, instigated reforms that took out of the staff all but the most essential directorates. As a result of Frunze's reforms, the Staff of the Red Army developed into the structure[33] shown in Chart 6.

In September 1935, the Staff of the Red Army was renamed the General Staff,[34] and the following year the Soviets opened their Military Academy of the General Staff. The General Staff Academy trains staff officers and future commanders and is closely supervised by the General Staff. The chief of the General Staff personally supervises the General Staff Academy and the Frunze Military Academy.[35]

In 1937, as already noted, the Navy was separated from the Red Army. Thus, in 1939, on the eve of World War II, the Soviet High Command had the organization shown in Chart 7.

After some initial shaking down following the German invasion of the Soviet Union on 22 June 1941, the High Command was reorganized as shown in Chart 8.

Chart 6
Organization of the Central Apparatus, 1924-1930

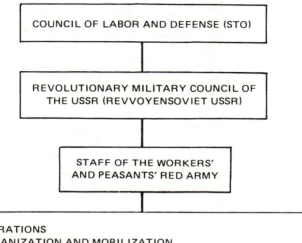

```
┌─────────────────────────────────────────┐
│   COUNCIL OF LABOR AND DEFENSE (STO)     │
└─────────────────────────────────────────┘
                     │
┌─────────────────────────────────────────┐
│   REVOLUTIONARY MILITARY COUNCIL OF       │
│   THE USSR (REVVOYENSOVIET USSR)          │
└─────────────────────────────────────────┘
                     │
        ┌────────────────────────────┐
        │   STAFF OF THE WORKERS'      │
        │   AND PEASANTS' RED ARMY     │
        └────────────────────────────┘
                     │
┌─────────────────────────────────────────────────┐
│  I.   OPERATIONS                                   │
│  II.  ORGANIZATION AND MOBILIZATION                │
│  III. MILITARY TRANSPORTATION (VOSO)               │
│  IV.  INTELLIGENCE                                  │
│  V.   COMBAT TRAINING AND COMPOSITION OF COMBAT REGULATIONS │
└─────────────────────────────────────────────────┘
```

SOURCE: INFORMATION FROM N. VISHNYAKOV AND F. ARKHIPOV, *US-TROYSTRO VOORUZHENNYKH SIL SSSR* [ORGANIZATION OF THE ARMED FORCES OF THE USSR] (MOSCOW: STATE PUBLISHING HOUSE, 1930), P. 102.

Soon after the outbreak of the war, the General Staff began to function as the executive agency for the newly created Stavka. Stalin, as the supreme commander in chief, was chairman of Stavka, which he completely dominated. Even Stalin's first deputy could not give orders to the General Staff.[36]

In view of the attention given in the Soviet press in the 1970s and early 1980s to the wartime organization of the General Staff and its responsibilities, it is reasonable to assume that a similar structure and lines of authority would be used in any future war. Of primary interest are the centralization of authority at the very top and the control from Moscow over the various fronts.

The General Staff was connected to each front by telegraph or telephone. Stalin personally exercised control, which was passed through the General Staff. The supreme commander set the General Staff's schedule, requiring

Chart 7
Organization of the Central Apparatus in 1939

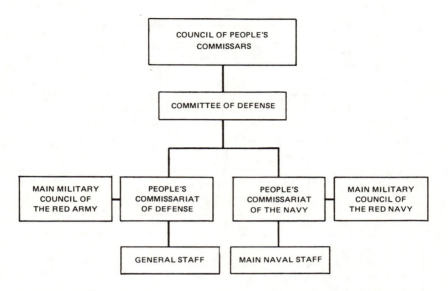

SOURCE: ADAPTED FROM M. V. ZAKHAROV, ED., *50 LET VOORUZHENNYKH SIL USSR* [50 YEARS OF THE ARMED FORCES OF THE USSR] (MOSCOW: VOYENIZDAT, 1973), P. 88.

reports three times daily. The first report at 1000 or 1100 hours generally was made by telephone. Between 1600 and 1700 hours in the afternoon, the deputy chief of the General Staff, or his deputy, reported once again to Stalin. Then at about midnight selected General Staff personnel would go to Stavka to report to Stalin directly on the results of the day's fighting.[37]

At the time of the German invasion, Zhukov was chief of the General Staff. However, from the beginning of the war, he frequently was sent out as a Stavka representative or as a front commander. He was replaced in the General Staff by Marshal Shaposhnikov, who soon had to be relieved because of illness. For the greater part of the war the General Staff was headed by Marshal A. M. Vasilevskiy, who, like Zhukov, spent much of his time at a front as a Stavka representative. Day-to-day direction of the staff generally was provided by the first deputy chief of the General Staff, General Antonov.

At the midnight briefings General Staff officers used maps with a scale of 1:200,000, prepared for each front to show the current situation down to division level. At times there were as many as fourteen fronts,

Chart 8
The Apparatus of the High Command During the War (1941-1945)

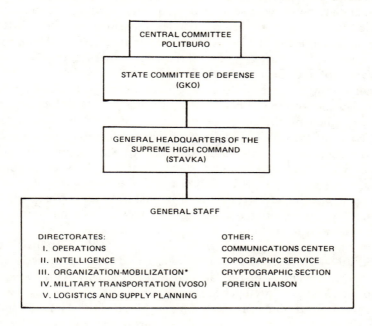

SOURCE: INFORMATION FROM S. M. SHTEMENKO, *GENERAL'NYY SHTAB V GODY VOYNY* [THE GENERAL STAFF IN THE YEARS OF THE WAR] (MOSCOW: VOYENIZDAT, 1968-73), VOL. 1, PP. 126-129.

each composed of three to six armies, in a sector approximately 300 to 400 kilometers wide and up to 150 kilometers in depth. In preparation for the meeting, General Staff officers might spend two to three hours checking by telephone with each front commander directly to determine exactly what had taken place during the day and what was planned for the following day. Requests from the various fronts for additional equipment, ammunition, and manpower replacements were examined, and directives were drafted to be signed during the midnight meetings with Stavka.[38]

Stavka meetings were held either in the Kremlin or at Stalin's *dacha*. In addition to Stavka members, various members of the Politburo might be present and, depending upon the matters to be discussed, the commanders of artillery, tank troops, mechanized troops, or air forces, chiefs of engineer troops, the Main Artillery Administration, the rear services, and others. The situation in the various combat areas would be described in detail, starting with the most active. All briefings were from memory; notes were seldom used. Fronts, armies, and corps were identified by the name of the commander. Divisions, numbering 488 at their peak, were identified by numbers. After the briefing, Stalin might dictate orders to General S. M. Shtemenko, chief of the Operations Directorate of the General Staff, for direct transmission to the front commanders by telegraph. Other directives were signed both by Stalin and by the chief of the General Staff or his first deputy. Minor directives could be signed by the chief of the General Staff or the first deputy.

In the Pentagon the U.S. Joint Staff uses different colored paper to show the particular stage of a Joint Chiefs of Staff action. The Soviet General Staff also used colored sheets, but for somewhat different purposes. Papers prepared for Stavka's approval were color coded: red had highest priority and were checked by Stalin; blue received only brief attention but were acted on during the day; green papers contained honors and awards and might go unread for days.

Most of the preparation for these briefings was the responsibility of the General Staff's Operations Directorate. This directorate worked closely with all other agencies of the General Staff, especially with the second directorate, Military Intelligence.

The third directorate, Organization and Mobilization, was responsible for planning the buildup of fronts and ensuring the readiness of reserves and trained replacements.[39] On 29 July 1941 the Main Directorate for the Formation and Staffing of the Troops of the Red Army (Glavupraform) was created outside the General Staff. This new "main" directorate took the Organization and Mobilization Directorate from the General Staff, an arrangement that proved to be unworkable. In April 1942 the Organizational Directorate was reestablished in the General Staff to keep track of the distribution of troops in military districts and fronts and the casualties suffered and to supervise the training of hundreds of thousands of officers in the school system established in the interior of the country.

Other directorates of the General Staff had to perform a variety of tasks, some of which had been completely unanticipated. Plans made before the war had assumed that all conflict would be on enemy territory. Detailed maps, insofar as the Soviet Union was concerned, were available only for the border area; there were no large scale maps available for the interior. When forced to fall back toward Moscow, Soviet troops urgently needed maps of their own country. In the first six months of the war, 1.5 million square kilometers had to be resurveyed to provide the required maps.[40]

The Soviet General Staff of the 1980s

Although shortcomings of the Soviet General Staff during World War II have been pointed out, contemporary Soviet writings claim that on balance it was a superior organization headed by capable officers. In view of the praise that current Soviet military writers give to the accomplishments of the General Staff during the Great Patriotic War, it is probable that the concept of the General Staff in the 1980s remains essentially as it was during World War II. Some new departments have been added as a result of new weapons systems and new conditions.

The Soviet General Staff is charged with the basic strategic planning for the Soviet Armed Forces and determines what each service shall be assigned to accomplish.[41] Although its members are officers from various services and branches, they are not partisan supporters of individual interests. Once they are assigned to the General Staff, their future promotions are dependent upon effectiveness in that organization and attention to Party duties. Some men in senior staff positions have served a decade or more in their assignments.[42]

The five Soviet military services—Strategic Rocket Troops, Ground Troops, Troops of Air Defense, Air Forces, and Navy—are subordinate to the Ministry of Defense through the General Staff. Commanders of military districts and groups of forces abroad have the same chain of command, since their commands include air, air defense, and ground forces and are capable of combined arms warfare. Commanders of the four fleets are subordinate to the commander in chief of the Navy.[43] In general, orders from the General Staff to the fleets would be sent through the service headquarters. Submarines carrying ballistic missiles probably would receive orders directly from the General Staff, or from the agency in control of Soviet strategic nuclear forces.

Most slots on the General Staff are *nomenklatura* positions, that is, to be filled only by graduates of military academies.[44] Key positions are held only by men who have completed the two-year course at the General Staff Academy, the highest professional school in the nation.

The Soviets have not published an organization chart of their General Staff as it exists today any more than they have disclosed their actual defense expenditures or the size of their Armed Forces. Chart 9, however, is believed to cover current General Staff functions.

The three key General Staff directorates are operations, intelligence, and organization-mobilization. Their primary functions are briefly described in Table 2.

A major task of the General Staff is to ensure "the coordinated actions of the main staffs of the services of the Armed Forces, the staff of the Rear Services, the staff of Civil Defense USSR, the main and central

Chart 9
Soviet General Staff in the 1980s

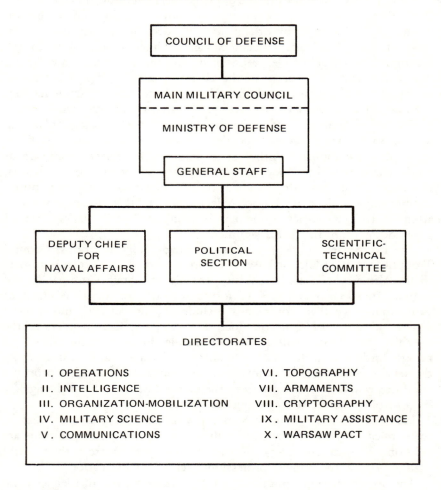

administrations of the Ministry of Defense, the staffs of military districts, groups abroad, and fleets."[45]

It is apparent from the above that the Soviet General Staff in peacetime has functions that are much broader than those assigned to the Pentagon's Joint Staff, with which the General Staff is sometimes compared. And these responsibilities are not all.

The General Staff thoroughly analyzes and evaluates military-political conditions which are taking shape, determines the trends of developments

TABLE 2

Functions of the General Staff Directorates

Intelligence	Organization-Mobilization	Operations
Regarding the enemy	Troop structure	Determination of goal
Regarding own forces	Subordination	Distribution of forces and means
Regarding adjacent units	Personnel	Methods of combat operations
Regarding combat conditions	Distribution of function	Coordination
Estimate and prediction	Interrelations	Assignment of missions to troops

Source: Based on Fig. 4, p. 50, of the English translation of V. V. Druzhinin and D. S. Kontorov, *Ideya, Algoritm, Resheniye* [Concept, Algorithm, Decision] (Moscow: Voyenizdat, 1972); the English translation is in the Soviet Military Thought Series (Washington, D.C.: U.S. Government Printing Office).

of the means of waging war, the methods of their use, organizes the training of the Armed Forces and carries out the necessary measures for assuring their high degree of combat readiness to repulse any aggression. . . . The further development of military theory occupies an important place in the activity of the General Staff. It directs military scientific work, produces the most important regulations, researches actual problems of Soviet military science, introduces its achievements into the practice of operational and combat training of troops and staff.[46]

In the United States these tasks would encompass the work of most of the entire Department of Defense in the Pentagon, some of the work of the National Security Council, plus a great many of the activities of the departments of the army, navy, and air force.

"The further development of military theory" is the responsibility of the Military Science Directorate. In view of the General Staff's responsibilities in this area, it was logical that a former chief of the General Staff, the late Marshal Sokolovskiy, was charged with producing the book, *Military Strategy.* To ensure that day-to-day questions of military theory are understood by all officers, the General Staff publishes its own monthly journal, *Military Thought.*[47]

There is yet another function of the General Staff that demands close study.

Increasing centralization of leadership combined with due regard for the initiative of subordinate direction agencies, a high degree of readiness, if necessary, rapidly to switch over to carrying out wartime functions, and scientific substantiation of proposals and decisions being prepared are characteristic of the work of the General Staff. The broad introduction into the work of the General Staff of scientific organization of work, mathematical methods, and the creation of automatic systems of direction of weapons and troops permits the more operational solution of the complicated tasks of directing the Armed Forces in peacetime and in war.[48]

What will automation mean in the Soviet Armed Forces, and why is so much stress given to its use? As previously discussed, the introduction of nuclear weapons into the armaments of world powers brought about a revolution in military affairs. First was the bomb, then the long-range rocket carrier, and finally the guidance mechanism. The last stage of the revolution in military affairs, sometimes called the cybernetics revolution, continues today. Cybernetics, the science of controlling complex processes and operations in machines, living organisms, and society as a whole is being used by the Soviets in their efforts to perfect the work of the General Staff.

Cybernetics, according to its proponents, will make it possible to automate information processing and accounting and staff and command planning. With the help of cybernetics it is theoretically possible to set up a single automated system able to control all links from individual aircraft, tanks, submarines, launching sites, and combined arms subunits to the General Staff. This would be a quantum jump in achieving the "rigid centralization of control" by the Soviet High Command, identified by Soviet spokesmen as a major reason for their successes in World War II. Operationally, it would allow the actual direct exercise of operational control of both strategic and theater forces by the Soviet High Command.

Much of the impetus to the stress on cybernetics by the Soviet military-political leadership was given by Admiral-Engineer Aksel Ivanovich Berg (1893–1979), one of the Soviet Union's leading experts in this field. From 1950 to 1960 Berg was chairman of the All-Union Scientific Council on Radio Physics and Radio Technology of the Academy of Sciences, and since 1959 he has been chairman of the Scientific Council on the Complex Problem of Cybernetics, under the Presidium of the Academy of Sciences. From September 1953 to November 1957 Berg was also deputy minister of defense for radio electronics. Since 1964, as chairman of the Scientific Council on Programmed Learning, he has worked on introducing programmed learning. In 1970, at the age of 77, Berg was listed as the editor of *Methodological Problems of Cybernetics*, published by the Academy of Sciences.[49]

Berg's successor as deputy minister of defense for radio electronics, from February 1957 to April 1964, was General Colonel of Artillery A. V. Gerasimov, previously chief of Radiotechnical Troops of National Air Defense, who was deeply involved in computer technology. Gerasimov was reassigned as deputy chief of the General Staff for Armaments, and in 1970 he was replaced by General Colonel V. V. Druzhinin, who had succeeded him as chief of Radiotechnical Troops of National Air Defense.

Within recent years the Soviet military press has published dozens of books and articles on the use of computers in military decisionmaking. A 1972 book, included in the Officer's Library series and entitled *Concept, Algorithm, Decision*,[50] presents an analysis of the use of computers in military decisionmaking and control of troops. Had this book been written by unknown authors it would have been of great significance. The fact that it was written jointly by General V. V. Druzhinin and D. S. Kontorov, of the Radiotechnical Institute of the Academy of Sciences, makes this work of unusual importance. General of the Army Shtemenko, then chief of staff of the Warsaw Pact Forces and first deputy chief of the General Staff, wrote the introduction, in which he noted "the time has arrived for extensive adoption of automation in the entire chain of command."[51]

Marshal Ogarkov, appointed chief of the General Staff in January 1977, also appears to be interested in cybernetics. When commanding the Volga Military District in 1966, Ogarkov spoke of "the growing role of scientific troop control in nuclear war."[52] In his 1982 booklet, *Always in Readiness to Defend the Fatherland*, Ogarkov demonstrated his continued support for automation of staffs. He wrote:

> In recent years automation of troop (forces) control has been increasingly more extensively applied to the activities of command cadres and staffs. The principal purpose of automation is to improve efficiency of command and control of subordinate troops (forces), the effectiveness of employment of weapons and military equipment, and troop (forces) combat readiness as a whole, as well as sharply to reduce expenditure of the time and resources of commanders and staff officers on technical tasks.[53]

The attention given by the General Staff to cybernetics suggests the probability of an even greater degree of centralized control in the future. Soviet writers in the last decade have stressed the roles of GKO, Stavka, and the General Staff during World War II as examples of praiseworthy rigid centralization of command, which is becoming ever more important. In the words of one of them,

> A high degree of centralization in the direction of all the services and branches of the Armed Forces has become essential. Victory over a powerful

adversary in a nuclear missile war can be won only if all the services and branches of the Armed Forces are put into action at the very outset. War will require the collection, analysis, and synthesis of combat situation data extremely rapidly, for without this it would be impossible to make well-substantiated decisions. And decisions, in turn, should be immediately communicated to the forces and implemented by them without delay.[54]

GKO (or the Council of Defense), the highest political-military body of the nation, would thus have even greater importance than in World War II. As Soviet spokesmen so clearly state:

The answer to the most critical question of our day depends in large part on the political leadership: Is there or is there not to be a thermonuclear world war?

And if war does begin,

the decision to employ such devastating weapons as nuclear weapons has become the exclusive prerogative of the political leadership. It is primarily the political, not the military leaders, who determine the necessity of employing weapons of mass destruction, who specify the principal targets, and when they are to be hit.[55] (emphasis added)

Party-Military Relationships

The Communist Party of the Soviet Union directs the development of the Soviet Armed Forces. Again and again Soviet spokesmen repeat Lenin's formula: "War is the continuation of politics by other (that is, violent) means, carried out by the ruling class of [a] country." The Communist Party and its Central Committee are directly involved in the day-to-day control of Soviet military affairs.

At the very top of the Party structure, the minister of defense and twelve of his fourteen deputies are full members of the Central Committee, as are the chief of the Main Political Administration and the commanders of a few key military districts. Names and positions as of 1 May 1984 are listed in order of precedence or importance of position. (Since the meeting of the Twenty-sixth Party Congress in 1981, Marshals I. Kh. Bagramyan, P. F. Batitskiy, and V. I. Chuykov have died.)

Full Members of the Central Committee

Minister of Defense: Marshal of the Soviet Union D. F. Ustinov
First Deputy Minister of Defense and Chief of the General Staff: Marshal of the Soviet Union N. V. Ogarkov

First Deputy Minister of Defense and Commander in Chief (CINC) Warsaw
Pact Forces: Marshal of the Soviet Union V. G. Kulikov

First Deputy Minister of Defense: Marshal of the Soviet Union S. L. Sokolov

Chief, Main Political Administration: General of the Army A. A. Yepishev

Deputy Minister of Defense, CINC, Strategic Rocket Forces: Chief Marshal
of Artillery V. F. Tolubko

Deputy Minister of Defense, CINC, Ground Forces: Marshal of the Soviet
Union V. I. Petrov

Deputy Minister of Defense, CINC, Troops of Air Defense: Marshal of
Aviation A. I. Koldunov

Deputy Minister of Defense, CINC, Air Forces: Chief Marshal of Aviation
P. S. Kutakhov

Deputy Minister of Defense, CINC, Navy: Admiral of the Fleet of the Soviet
Union S. G. Gorshkov

Deputy Minister of Defense, Inspector General: Marshal of the Soviet Union
K. S. Moskalenko

Deputy Minister of Defense, Chief of the Rear: Marshal of the Soviet Union
S. K. Kurkotkin

Deputy Minister of Defense for Armaments: General of the Army V. M.
Shabanov (since June 1983)

Deputy Minister of Defense, Chief of Civil Defense: General of the Army
A. T. Altunin

CINC, Soviet Forces Germany: General of the Army M. M. Zaytsev

CINC, Troops of the Far East: General of the Army V. L. Govorov

Commander, Belorussian Military District: General of the Army Ye. F. Ivanovskiy

Commander, Far Eastern Military District: General of the Army I. M. Tret'yak

Commander, Moscow Military District: General of the Army P. G. Lushev

Position unknown: General of the Army G. I. Salmanov

First Deputy Chief of the General Staff: Marshal of the Soviet Union S. F.
Akhromeyev (since June 1983)

First Deputy Chief of the General Staff, Chief of Staff of Warsaw Pact Forces:
General of the Army A. I. Gribkov

Candidate Members of the Central Committee

Adviser to General Inspectors Group: Marshal of Aviation A. I. Pokryshkin

Commander, Kiev Military District: General of the Army I. A. Gerasimov

Commander, Turkestan Military District: General of the Army Yu. P. Maksimov

Commander, Central Asian Military District: General Colonel D. T. Yazov

First Deputy CINC, Navy and Chief of the Main Naval Staff: Admiral of the
Fleet V. N. Chernavin

Commander, Pacific Fleet: Admiral V. V. Sidorov

Chief, Political Administration, Strategic Rocket Forces: General Colonel P.
A. Gorchakov

Chief, Political Administration, Ground Forces: General Colonel M. D. Popkov

Chief, Political Administration, Troops of the Far East: General Colonel M. I. Druzhinin

Position unknown: General of the Army M. I. Sorokin

Members of the Central Auditing Commission

Commander, Transbaykal Military District: General Colonel S. I. Postnikov

Commander, Moscow Air Defense District: General Colonel Aviation A. U. Konstantinov

Head "Vystrel" Higher Officers' Courses: General Colonel Tanks D. A. Dragunskiy

The Central Committee holds plenums two or three times a year. Major decisions are made by the Politburo of the Central Committee, and daily work is handled by the Secretariat. In 1973 Marshal Grechko (then minister of defense) became a member of the Politburo, the first military officer to sit in that body since Marshal Zhukov's ouster in 1957. Marshal Ustinov, a candidate member of the Politburo since 1965, was elevated to full membership at the Twenty-fifth Party Congress in March 1976, only weeks before the death of Grechko in April. Therefore, following upon his appointment as minister of defense in April 1976, Ustinov's Politburo membership was not in question.

Political-military status also comes, to a lesser degree, from selection as a delegate to the Party congresses, held about every five years. Before each congress each Party organization holds a conference and selects delegates to represent it in Moscow. Such delegates usually include the commanders of military districts and fleets, the chiefs of political administrations in these headquarters, and at times the first deputy commander or the commander of aviation. The Moscow City organization, for example, had twenty-nine military delegates at the Twenty-sixth Party Congress. In addition, there were nineteen delegates from the Moscow Oblast Party organization. Many delegates also are selected from the central military apparatus, the five services, and the Main Political Administration. Another prominent group in Party affairs are the so-called retired marshals, generals, and admirals, placed in a group called general inspectors.

The military delegates form a substantial bloc at the congresses. When gathered in Moscow for the meetings in the Kremlin's Palace of Congresses, military delegates are given time to meet separately, by service, to take up matters of Party-service policy.

Each delegate to the Party congress represents a specific number of Party members. Using the number of military delegates and the percentage of personnel in the Soviet Armed Forces that are Party members, one may arrive at a rough approximation of Soviet military manpower strengths. For example, Marshal Grechko stated in 1967 that 22 percent of the Soviet Armed Forces are Party members.[56] In 1983, it was stated that "the number of Communist Party and Komsomol members is constantly growing and now they compose about 90 percent of personnel."[57] Assuming that Party membership is between 20 and 22 percent of military personnel, the size of the Soviet Armed Forces would be approximately as shown in Table 3.

Intermarriage of the civil and military sides of the Party may begin at the level of republics and military districts. For example, General Colonel S. I. Postnikov, as commander of the Baltic Military District, was on the Bureau of the Central Committee of Latvia's Communist Party, the equivalent of the Politburo of the Central Committee of the CPSU at the level of the Union Republic. In Belorussia, General of the Army Ye. F. Ivanovskiy, commander of the Belorussian Military District, is a member of the Bureau of the Central Committee of the Belorussian Communist Party. General Colonel D. T. Yazov, as commander of the Central Asian Military District, is a member of the Bureau of the Central Committee of the Kazakhstan Communist Party, and General of the Army I. A. Gerasimov, as commander of the Kiev Military District, is a member of the Bureau of the Central Committee of the Ukrainian Communist Party. General Colonel O. F. Kulishev, while commander of the Transcaucasian Military District, was a member of the Bureau of the Central Committee of the Georgian Communist Party. And the commander of the Turkestan Military District, General of the Army Yu. P. Maksimov, sits on the Bureau of the Central Committee of the Communist Party of Uzbekistan. Hundreds of top district officers, such as first deputies, chiefs of staff, and chiefs of political administrations, are members of republic central committees.

Senior military officers are often members of city and oblast Party committees, as, for instance, in Moscow and Leningrad. Fleet officers of the Black Sea Fleet sit on the central committee of the Ukrainian Communist Party.

In reverse, the local Party secretary is a member of the military council of the military district of his area. This membership is required by Soviet law.[58] Ties are forged between civil and uniformed Party officials and military commanders at local levels, and each may support the other in obtaining further promotions.

The Military and the Supreme Soviet

In theory the Supreme Soviet is the legislative branch of the Soviet government. In practice this body is ornamental and serves as a facade to present the appearance of democracy. However, membership in this

TABLE 3
Military Delegates to Party Congresses and Size of the Soviet Armed Forces

Congress	Date	Number of Military Delegates	Official Representation	Party Members in Military	Estimated Size of Armed Forces
22nd	Oct 1961	305	1:2000	610,000	@22% = 2,773,000 @20% = 3,050,000
23rd	Mar 1966	352	1:2500	880,000	@22% = 4,000,000 @20% = 4,400,000
24th	Mar 1971	not given	1:2900	—	—
25th	Feb 1976	314	1:3000	942,000	@22% = 4,280,000 @20% = 4,710,000
26th	Feb 1981	not given (about 300)	1:3350	(1,000,000) est.	(@22% = 4,545,000) (@20% = 5,000,000)

group does carry certain prestige and helps to establish position. Deputies to the Supreme Soviet are "elected" every five years. About 55 percent are elected for the first time at each election, including milkmaids, tractor drivers, and other "representatives" of Soviet labor. Most of the remainder are elected or reelected because of their position.

The minister of defense, his deputies and commanders of forces abroad, military districts, and fleets are automatically "elected" to the Supreme Soviet. Also included as deputies are the chief of the Main Political Administration, his first deputy, and the chiefs of the political administrations of Soviet Forces Germany, the Strategic Rocket Forces, and the Ground Forces. First deputy chiefs of the General Staff, the chief of Military Intelligence (GRU), and the commander in chief of Troops of the Far East are deputies. The first deputy commanders in chief of the Soviet services, the chairman of DOSAAF (the Volunteer Society for Cooperation with the Army, Aviation, and Fleet), and a few cosmonauts also can be assured of election. Numbers of representatives to the Supreme Soviet from the Soviet Armed Forces are shown in Table 4.

In addition to the Supreme Soviet of the USSR there are Supreme Soviets of the several republics and autonomous republics. Several thousand military personnel serve as deputies in local soviets throughout the nation.[59] This participation in government affairs at all levels may foster a feeling of pseudodemocracy in servicemen. At the very least, meetings of the Supreme Soviet reflect a holiday spirit and represent a departure from daily routines.

The Soviet High Command

The Soviet High Command represents one of the most experienced bodies of political-military leadership the world has ever seen. All of its members have proved themselves over the course of many years in positions of great responsibility.

In peacetime the names of the senior military leaders of the United States armed forces are not widely known, and few could be identified by the public. Only the United States secretary of defense approaches national stature. Many of the military leaders in the United States have quietly served tours in the highest military positions and then departed. A few have made headlines, but only briefly.

In contrast, many of the senior members of the Soviet high command have been popularized as military leaders. Some remain in one position for a decade or two, sufficiently long to become known. The top Soviet military leadership is much more visible than its counterpart in the United States or elsewhere in the West. As already shown, they are

TABLE 4
Military Deputies of the Supreme Soviet

	7th Convocation[a] (June 12, 1966)	8th Convocation[b] (June 14, 1970)	9th Convocation[c] (June 16, 1974)	10th Convocation[d] (March 4, 1979)	11th Convocation[e] (March 4, 1984)
Military deputies in Council of the Union	30	30	34	33	30
Military deputies in Council Nationalities	26	27	22	23	26
Total military deputies	56	57	56	56	56
Total deputies	1517	1517	1517	1500	1500

Source: [a]*Yezhegodnik, 1966, Bol'shoy Sovetskoy Entsiklopedii* [Yearbook, 1966, of the Great Soviet Encyclopedia] (Moscow: Soviet Encyclopedia Publishing House, 1966), pp. 21-22.

[b]*Yezhegodnik, 1971, Bol'shoy Sovetskoy Entsiklopedii*, p. 30.

[c]Compiled from *Deputaty Verkhovnovo Soveta SSSR* [Deputies to the Supreme Soviet, USSR] (Moscow: Political Literature Publishing House, 1974).

[d]Compiled from *Deputaty Verkhovnovo Soveta SSSR* [Deputies to the Supreme Soviet, USSR] (Moscow: Presidium of the Supreme Soviet Publishers, 1979).

[e]Compiled from *Pravda*, 7 March 1984.

Top Party and military leaders assembled on Lenin's tomb to review a May Day parade.

closely integrated with the rest of the Party, with those at the top wearing two hats: one representing the military position and the other, their membership on the Central Committee.

The road to promotion, prestige, and power in the Soviet Armed Forces is varied.

1. Marshal of the Soviet Union Dmitriy Fedorovich Ustinov, Soviet minister of defense and Politburo member, was born in 1908. His appointment as minister of defense in April 1976 was heralded in the West as a rejection of the Soviet military and a reaffirmation of civilian control by the Party, concepts that represent Western mirror-imaging and are without any factual basis. Ustinov is extremely well qualified professionally for the assignment. In 1934 he finished at the Leningrad Military-Mechanical Institute, and in 1941, at the age of thirty-two, was made people's commissar of armaments. On 19 November 1944, *Red Star* noted his promotion to general colonel of engineering artillery service. At the conclusion of World War II he served as minister of armaments until 1953 and as minister of defense industry until 1957. From 1957 to 1963 he was deputy chairman of the Council of Ministers and from 1963 to 1965 chairman of the Supreme Economic Council. In 1965 he became a member of the Secretariat of the Communist Party

and a candidate member of the Politburo. When designated as minister of defense, he was promoted to general of the army and exactly ninety days later to Marshal of the Soviet Union; but he lost his seat in the Secretariat.

Ustinov played a major role in changing the Soviet Armed Forces from horse-drawn artillery, which it possessed in vast quantities at the end of World War II, to a military force armed with the most modern and sophisticated weaponry of the twentieth century. Like their counterparts in forces of other nations, Soviet field commanders tend to resist innovation and new weaponry, such as satellite reconnaissance, nuclear armed missiles, and the military application of computers. Ustinov, the industrial genius and arms czar, worked behind the scenes to take the Soviet Union into the space age. For example, in 1957, Ustinov, Leonid I. Brezhnev (a Party secretary and Presidium member), M. V. Keldysh, head of the Academy of Sciences, and three other leading Party members were assigned by the Central Committee to ensure Soviet successes in missile production and in space. In 1961 *Red Star* announced the award of Hero of Socialist Labor to this group, "for outstanding service in the development of rocket equipment and guaranteeing the successful flight of Soviet man in space on the spaceship Vostok."[60]

On 30 October 1983, Ustinov turned 75 and was given his eleventh Order of Lenin. He is twice a Hero of Socialist Labor (1942 and 1961) and a Hero of the Soviet Union (1978). In 1982, Ustinov became a Lenin Prize winner, thus adding to the government prize he was awarded in 1953. His latest biography notes that he volunteered for military service in 1922, the year he turned 16, and was demobilized the next year. The others at the top, all full members of the Central Committee, are as follows:

2. *Nikolay Vasil'yevich Ogarkov.* Born 1917. Russian. First deputy minister of defense and chief of the General Staff (since January 1977). Career: Graduated from Kuybyshev Military Engineering Academy (1941), Academy of the General Staff (1959); with field engineer troops (1941–1945); in Staff of Engineer Troops, Carpathian Military District (1946–1948); chief of section of Operational Directorate of the staff of the commander in chief of Troops of the Far East (1948–1953); deputy chief, then chief, of a staff directorate and deputy chief of staff of the Far Eastern Military District (1953–1957); division commander of Soviet Forces Germany (1959–1961); chief of staff and first deputy commander of the Belorussian Military District (1961–1965); commander of Volga Military District (1965–1968); first deputy chief of the General Staff (1968–1974); chief military delegate to SALT (1969–1971). Deputy minister of defense (1974–1977). Marshal of the Soviet Union (1977). Candidate member of Central Committee (1966–1971), member of

Central Committee (since 1971). Hero of the Soviet Union (1977). Lenin Prize (1981).

3. *Viktor Georgiyevich Kulikov.* Born 1921. Russian. First deputy minister of defense and commander in chief of Combined Armed Forces of the Warsaw Pact. Career: Graduated from Frunze Military Academy (1953) and Academy of the General Staff (1959); command and staff work in tank units (1941–1945); command positions in tank troops (1947–1950); chief of staff and commander of a division (1953–1957); first deputy commander of army (1959–1964), then commander of army (1964–1967); commander of Kiev Military District (1967–1969); commander in chief of Soviet Forces Germany (1969–1971); first deputy minister of defense and chief of the General Staff (1971–1977). Marshal of the Soviet Union (1977). Member of Central Committee (since 1971). Hero of the Soviet Union (1981).

4. *Sergey Leonidovich Sokolov.* Born 1911. Russian. First deputy minister of defense [for general affairs] (since 1967). Career: Graduated from Military Academy of Armored and Mechanized Troops (1947) and Academy of the General Staff (1951); with tank troops in the Far East (from 1934); command and staff positions with tank troops (1941–1945); commander of regiment, division, army (1947–1959); chief of staff and First Deputy Commander, Moscow Military District (1960–1964); first deputy commander of Leningrad Military District (1964–1965), then commander (1965–1967). Marshal of the Soviet Union (1978). Candidate member of Central Committee (1966–1968). Member of Central Committee (since 1968). Hero of the Soviet Union (1980).

5. *Aleksey Alekseyevich Yepishev.* Born 1908. Russian. Chief of the Main Political Administration of the Soviet Army and Navy (since 1962). Career: Graduated from Military Academy of Mechanization and Motorization of Soviet Army (1938) and Higher Courses of the Academy of Social Sciences of the Central Committee CPSU (1950); in Soviet Army (since 1930); remained in army while party organizer in factory in Kharkov (1938–1940); first secretary of Kharkov oblast and city Communist Party, Ukraine, military council member during Stalingrad battle, deputy minister of medium machinebuilding (1940–1943); member, military council of Thirty-eighth Army (1943–1946); secretary, Ukrainian Central Committee (1946–1949); first secretary, Odessa oblast and city Communist Party, Ukraine (1950–1951); deputy minister of state security (MGB, predecessor to KGB); first secretary, Odessa oblast CP, Ukraine (1953–1955); ambassador to Rumania (1955–1961) and to Yugoslavia (1961–1962). General of the army (since 1962). Candidate member of Central Committee (1952–1964); member (since 1964). Hero of the Soviet Union (1978).

6. *Vladimir Fedorovich Tolubko.* Born 1914. Ukrainian. Deputy minister of defense and commander in chief of Strategic Rocket Forces (since 1972). Career: Graduated from Military Academy of Armored and Mechanized Troops (1941) and Academy of the General Staff (1950); in Soviet Army (since 1932); command and staff positions with tank troops (1941–1945); command posts, assistant commander in chief of Soviet Forces Germany (to 1960); first deputy commander in chief of Strategic Rocket Forces (1960–1968); commander of Siberian Military District (1968–1969); commander of Far Eastern Military District (1969–1972). Chief Marshal of Artillery (1983). Candidate member of Central Committee (1971–1976). Member of Central Committee (since 1976). Hero of Socialist Labor (1976).

7. *Vasiliy Ivanovich Petrov.* Born 1917. Russian. Deputy minister of defense and commander in chief of Ground Forces (since 1980). Career: Graduated from Frunze Military Academy (1948) and Higher Academic Courses at General Staff Academy (1969); commander of battalion, chief of section, of division (1941–1945); operations section of staff deputy chief and then chief of section of an army staff, commander of a regiment, chief of staff of a division (1948–1957); commander of the Pacific Ocean Motorized Rifle Division (1957–1961); chief of staff (1961) then commander of an army (1964–1966); chief of staff and first deputy commander of the Far Eastern Military District, then commander (1972–1976); first deputy commander in chief of Ground Forces (1976–1978); commander in chief, Troops of the Far East (1979–1980). Marshal of the Soviet Union (1983). Member of the Central Committee (since 1976). Hero of the Soviet Union (1982).

8. *Aleksandr Ivanovich Koldunov.* Born 1923. Russian. Deputy minister of defense and commander in chief of Troops of Air Defense (since 1978). Career: Graduated from the Military Air Academy (1952) and the Academy of the General Staff (1960); fighter pilot, flying 358 combat sorties, in 96 air battles downing 46 enemy aircraft; commander of aviation regiment; division; deputy commander, and commander of aviation of Baku Air Defense District, then first deputy commander of Baku Air Defense District (to 1970); commander of Moscow Air Defense District (1970–1975); first deputy commander in chief Troops of National Air Defense (1975–1978). Marshal of Aviation (1977). Candidate member of the Central Committee (1971–1976). Member of Central Committee (since 1981). Twice Hero of the Soviet Union (1944, 1948).

9. *Pavel Stepanovich Kutakhov.* Born 1914. Russian. Deputy minister of defense and commander in chief of Air Forces (since 1969). Career: Graduated from Military School of Pilots (1938) and Academy of the General Staff (1957); flew 131 combat sorties in Finnish War; squadron commander, commander of fighter air regiment (1941–1945); flew 367

combat sorties, took part in 79 air battles shooting down 42 enemy aircraft, 28 of them in group combat; commanded large aviation units and formation (1945–1967); first deputy commander in chief of Air Forces (1967–1969). Chief Marshal of Aviation (1972). Member of Central Committee (since 1971). Hero of the Soviet Union (1943).

10. *Sergey Georgiyevich Gorshkov.* Born 1910. Russian. Deputy minister of defense and commander in chief of the Navy (since 1956). Career: Graduated from Frunze Naval School (1931) and refresher courses for higher command staff at the Naval Academy (1941); commanded a brigade of cruisers of the Black Sea Fleet, commander of the Azov, then the Danube Flotillas (1941–1945); commander of ship formation of Black Sea Fleet (1945–1948); chief of staff of the Black Sea Fleet (1948–1951); commander of Black Sea Fleet (1951–1955). Admiral of the Fleet of the Soviet Union (1967). Candidate member of Central Committee (1956–1961); member of Central Committee (since 1961). Twice a Hero of the Soviet Union (1965, 1982). Frunze Prize winner (1980).

11. *Kirill Semenovich Moskalenko.* Born 1902. Ukrainian. Deputy minister of defense and inspector general (since 1962). Career: Graduated from Dzerzhinskiy Artillery Academy (1939); deputy commander of Sixth Army (to 1942); commander of Thirty-eighth, First tank, First guards, Fortieth armies (1942–1943) and from October 1943, the Thirty-eighth Army; commander Moscow Air Defense Region (1948–1953); commander of Moscow Military District (1953–1960); commander in chief of Strategic Rocket Forces (1960–1962). Marshal of the Soviet Union (1955). Member of Central Committee (since 1956). Twice a Hero of the Soviet Union (1943, 1978).

12. *Semen Konstantinovich Kurkotkin.* Born 1917. Russian. Deputy minister of defense and chief of Rear Services of Armed Forces (since 1972). Career: Graduated from Orlov Armored School (1930), Military-Political School (1941), Military Academy of Armored and Mechanized Troops (1951), and Academy of the General Staff (1958); commissar, then commander of detached tank battalion, commander of detached tank regiment, commander of tank brigade (1941–1945); commander of division, corps, army (1945–1966); first deputy commander in chief Soviet Forces Germany (1966–1968); commander of Transcaucasus Military District (1968–1971); commander in chief of Soviet Forces Germany (1971–1972). Marshal of the Soviet Union (1983). Candidate member of Central Committee (1971–1976); member of Central Committee (since 1976).

13. *Vitaliy Mikhaylovich Shabanov.* Born 1923. Russian. Deputy minister of defense (since 1978), for armaments (since 1980). Career: Graduated from the Leningrad Military Air Academy (1945); test engineer and assistant head engineer for testing aviation equipment in an Air

Forces scientific research plant (1945–1949); lead engineer, deputy chief of a laboratory, lead and chief designer, chief of a design bureau and then deputy general designer (1949–1972); general director of a scientific production combine (1972–1974); deputy minister of radio industry, USSR (1974–1978). General of the Army (1981). Candidate member of Central Committee (1981–1983). Member of Central Committee (since 1983). Hero of Socialist Labor (1981). Lenin prize winner (1963); government prize winner (1953).

14. *Aleksandr Terent'yevich Altunin.* Born 1921. Russian. Deputy minister of defense 'and chief of Civil Defense USSR (since 1972). Career: Graduated from Frunze Military Academy (1948) and Academy of the General Staff (1957); commander of company, battalion (1941–1945); various command posts, two years in General Staff (1945–1968); commander of North Caucasus Military District (1968–1970); chief of cadres (1970–1972); general of the Army (1977). Member of Central Committee (since 1976). Hero of the Soviet Union (1944).

15. *Mikhail Mitrofanovich Zaytsev.* Born 1923. Russian. Commander in chief of Soviet Forces Germany (since 1980). Career: Graduated from the Military Academy of Armored Forces (1954) and Academy of the General Staff (1965). In the Great Patriotic War in staff positions of tank units; chief of staff and deputy commander of a division, commander of Rogachev Motorized Rifle Division (1965–1968); chief of staff of an army (1968–1969) and commander (1969–1972); first deputy commander of Belorussian Military District (1972–1976); commander of Belorussian Military District (1976–1980). General of the Army (1980). Member of Central Committee (since 1981).

16. *Vladimir Leonidovich Govorov.* Born 1924. Russian. Commander in chief of Troops of the Far East (since 1980). Career: Graduated from Frunze Military Academy (1949) and Academy of the General Staff (1963). In Great Patriotic War; deputy commander of a regiment, commander of a regiment, chief of staff of a division (1946–1958); in command positions (1958–1969); first deputy commander in chief of Soviet Forces Germany (1969–1971); commander of Baltic Military District (1971–1972); commander of Moscow Military District (1972–1980). Candidate member of Central Committee (1976–1981). General of the Army (1977). Member of Central Committee (since 1981).

17. *Yevgeniy Filippovich Ivanovskiy.* Born 1918. Belorussian. Commander of the Belorussian Military District (since 1980). Career: Graduated from Military Academy of Mechanization and Motorization (1941) and Academy of the General Staff (1958); command and staff positions with tank troops (1941–1945); chief of section of army staff (1946–1952); deputy commander of armored and mechanized troops for self-propelled artillery, Belorussian Military District (1952–1953); chief of

staff, then commander of tank division (1953–1956); first deputy chief of staff of Far Eastern Military District (1958–1961); commander of large formation (1961–1965); first deputy commander (1965–1968), then commander of Moscow Military District (1968–1972). General of the Army (1972). Member of Central Committee (since 1971).

18. *Ivan Moiseyevich Tret'yak.* Born 1923. Ukrainian. Commander of the Far Eastern Military District (since 1976). Career: Graduated from Frunze Military Academy (1949) and Academy of the General Staff (1959); commander of company, deputy commander battalion, regiment, commander regiment (1941–1945); commander of a regiment (1951–1954); commander of a division (1954–1959); staff and command positions (until 1967); commander of the Belorussian Military District (1967–1976). General of the Army (1976). Candidate member of Central Committee (1971–1976). Member of Central Committee (since 1976). Hero of the Soviet Union (1945). Hero of Socialist Labor (1982).

19. *Petr Georgiyevich Lushev.* Born 1923. Russian. Commander of the Moscow Military District (since 1980). Career: Graduated from the Military Academy of Armored Forces (1954) and the Academy of the General Staff (1966); in Great Patriotic War, took part in defense of Leningrad; commander of tank regiment, deputy commander, commander division; first deputy (1969–1971), commander of an army (1971–1973); first deputy commander in chief of Soviet Forces Germany (1973–1975); commander of Volga Military District (1975–1977); commander of Central Asian Military District (1977–1980). General of the Army (1981). Member of Central Committee (since 1981).

20. *Grigoriy Ivanovich Salmanov.* Born 1922. Russian. Commander of the Transbaykal Military District (1978–1984). Career: Graduated from Frunze Military Academy (1949) and the Academy of the General Staff (1964); in Great Patriotic War; commander regiment, chief of staff of a division (1949–1957); commander of a division (1957–1962); first deputy chief of staff, Turkestan Military District (1964–1967); special assignment (1967–1969); commander of Kiev Military District (1969–1975); deputy commander in chief of Ground Forces for Combat Training (1975–1978). General of the Army (1979). Candidate member of Central Committee (1971–1976). Member of Central Committee (since 1976).

21. *Sergey Fedorovich Akhromeyev.* Born 1923. Russian. First deputy chief of the General Staff (since 1979). Career: Graduated from Military Academy of Armored Forces (1952) and Academy of the General Staff (1967); in Great Patriotic War, battalion commander; chief of staff, commander tank regiment, deputy commander, chief of staff division, commander division (1946–1964); chief of staff, first deputy commander, commander of an army (1964–1972); chief of staff and first deputy commander of the Far Eastern Military District (1972–1974); head of

a main directorate and deputy chief of the General Staff (1974–1979). Marshal of the Soviet Union (1983). Candidate member of Central Committee (1981–1983). Member of Central Committee (since June 1983). Hero of the Soviet Union (1982). Lenin prize winner.

22. *Anatoliy Ivanovich Gribkov.* Born 1919. Russian. First deputy chief of the General Staff and chief of staff of Warsaw Pact Forces (since 1976). Career: Graduated from Academy of the General Staff (1951); in Great Patriotic War, served as an officer of the General Staff; in General Staff after war; chief of section of staff of a military district (1952–1956); chief of a directorate and deputy chief of staff of several military districts (1956–1960); deputy chief, chief of a directorate, deputy chief of a main directorate of the General Staff; commander of an army in Transcaucasus Military District (1965–1968); first deputy commander (1968–1973), commander of Leningrad Military District (1973–1976). General of the Army (1976). Candidate member of Central Committee (1976–1981). Member of Central Committee (since 1981).

Notes

1. *Krasnaya Zvezda,* 9 May 1976. See also *Sovetskaya Voyennaya Entsiklopediya* [Soviet Military Encyclopedia] (Moscow: Voyenizdat, 1976–1980), Vol. 1, p. 588.

2. The *Voyennyy Entsiklopedicheskiy Slovar'* [Military Encyclopedic Dictionary] (Moscow: Voyenizdat, 1983), p. 100, for the first time asserts that L. I. Brezhnev was chairman of the Council of Defense since 1964. However the *Yezhegodnik* of the *Bol'shoy Sovetskoy Entsiklopedii* for 1981, p. 569, had used the year 1977 as the date he became chairman of the Defense Council *of the USSR.* The addition of the words "of the USSR" may explain this discrepancy.

3. V. D. Sokolovskiy, *Soviet Military Strategy,* 3d ed., Harriet F. Scott, ed. (New York: Crane, Russak & Co., 1975), p. 361. See also Harriet Fast Scott and William F. Scott, *The Soviet Control Structure: Capabilities for Wartime Survival* (New York: Crane, Russak & Co., 1983), for more details on this subject.

4. N. Vishnyakov and F. Arkhipov, *Ustroystvo Vooruzhennykh Sil SSSR* [Organization of the Armed Forces of the USSR] (Moscow: State Publishing House, 1930), p. 101.

5. *Bol'shaya Sovetskaya Entsiklopediya* [The Great Soviet Encyclopedia], 3d ed. (Moscow: Soviet Encyclopedia Publishing House, 1971), Vol. 5, p. 248. See also *Sovetskiye Vooruzhennyye Sily* [Soviet Armed Forces] (Moscow: Voyenizdat, 1978), pp. 195–196.

6. M. V. Zakharov, ed., *50 Let Vooruzkennykh Sil USSR* [50 Years of the Armed Forces of the USSR] (Moscow: Voyenizdat, 1968), p. 256.

7. *Krasnaya Zvezda,* 5 May 1975. See also *Sovetskaya Voyennaya Entsiklopediya,* Vol. 2, p. 621.

8. *Krasnaya Zvezda,* 11 February 1973.

9. *Constitution (Fundamental Law) of the Union of Soviet Socialist Republics* (Moscow: Novosti Press Agency, 1977), pp. 88–89.

10. D. F. Ustinov, "Immortal Feat," *Pravda,* 9 May 1983. See also *Sovetskoye Administrativnoye Pravo* [Soviet Administrative Law] (Moscow: Yuridicheskaya Literatura, 1981), p. 375, which states "The Council of Defense USSR . . . [is] headed by the chairman of the Presidium of the Supreme Soviet USSR."

11. A. A. Yepishev, ed., *KPSS i Voyennoye Stroitel'stvo* [CPSU and Military Structuring] (Moscow: Voyenizdat, 1982), p. 53. See also K. U. Chernenko and N. I. Savinkin, eds., *KPSS o Vooruzhennykh Silakh Sovetskovo Soyuza* [The CPSU of the Armed Forces of the Soviet Union] (Moscow: Voyenizdat, 1969), p. 278.

12. *Sovetskaya Voyennaya Entsiklopediya,* Vol. 4, p. 235; A. A. Yepishev, *KPSS i Voyennoye Stroitel'stvo,* p. 155; *Voyennyy Entsiklopedicheskiy Slovar',* pp. 195, 340; S. S. Maksimov, *Osnovy Sovetskogo Voyennogo Zakonodatel'stva* [Fundamentals of the Soviet Military Legislation] (Moscow: Voyenizdat, 1978), p. 53.

13. Sokolovskiy, *Soviet Military Strategy,* 3d ed., p. 361; S. N. Kozlov, *Spravochnik Ofitsera* [Officer's Handbook] (Moscow: Voyenizdat, 1971), p. 128.

14. Yepishev, *KPSS,* pp. 138–145.

15. Ibid., pp. 136–137, 145–146. This is a very good discussion of *kollegial'nost'* and what it entails.

16. *Bol'shaya Sovetskaya Entsiklopediya,* Vol. 5, p. 248. See also A. A. Yepishev, *KPSS,* p. 146; G. K. Zhukov, *Vospominaniya i Razmyshleniya* [Reminiscences and Reflections], Vol. 1, 2d ed. (Moscow: Novosti, 1974), pp. 128, 202, 209, 217, 236–237. Zhukov said that at "an enlarged meeting of the Main [the official translation calls it "Supreme"] Military Council [in 1940] . . . participants in the Finnish war and the army top echelon officers were present" (p. 202). He also stated that "at the end of September 1940 the General Staff notified us that a conference of the top echelons of Army Command had been scheduled [in late December]. . . . It was attended by the commanding officers of districts and armies, members of military councils and chiefs of staff of districts and armies, commanding officers of all military academies, professors and doctors of military science, inspectors of all arms, chiefs of central departments and ranking officers of the General Staff." Members of the Politburo also were present (pp. 204–205). This indicates that both "enlarged" meetings of the Main Military Council and also extraordinary meetings of the top echelons of the "high command" can be held.

17. Zakharov, *50 Let,* p. 267. See also S. M. Shtemenko, *General'nyye Shtab v Gody Voyny* [General Staff in the Years of the War] (Moscow: Voyenizdat, 1968), p. 29. Shtemenko states that "a board of permanent advisers to Stavka was also set up. Its members included B. M. Shaposhnikov, K. A. Meretskov, N. F. Vatutin, N. N. Voronov, A. I. Mikoyan, N. A. Voznesenskiy, A. A. Zhdanov and others."

18. Sokolovskiy, *Soviet Military Strategy,* 3d ed., p. 356.

19. Zakharov, *50 Let,* p. 269.

20. Sokolovskiy, *Soviet Military Strategy,* 3d ed., p. 375.

21. Ibid.

22. Zhukov, *Vospominaniya,* p. 324.

23. Sokolovskiy, *Soviet Military Strategy,* 3d ed., p. 357.

24. *Sovetskaya Voyennaya Entsiklopediya,* Vol. 2, p. 274. See also *Sovetskiye Vooruzhennyye Sily,* pp. 389–390. The Higher Military Council was a collegial organ under the Ministry of the Armed Forces. Its participants consisted of Politburo members, Central Committee members, and military leaders.

25. Yu. P. Petrov, *Stroitel'stvo Politorganov, Partiynykh i Komsomol'skikh Organizatsiy Armii i Flota* [The Structuring of Political Organs, Party and Komsomol Organizations of the Army and Navy] (Moscow: Voyenizdat, 1969), p. 391; *Sovetskaya Voyennaya Entsiklopediya,* Vol. 2, p. 566. See also *Voyennyy Entsiklopedicheskiy Slovar',* p. 195, which indicates that the Higher Military Council was formed in 1946 but abolished in 1950 when the Main Military Councils were formed. However, in *Sovetskiye Vooruzhennyye Sily,* p. 390, it is stated that "the highest government agency of leadership of all the Armed Forces was the Higher Military Council, created in March 1950 under the *Council of Ministers, USSR*" (emphasis added). It was moved from the ministry level to the Council of Ministers. Shtemenko (*General'nyy Shtab,* Vol. 2, p. 500) states that Stalin was the chairman of the Higher Military Council after the war and that he, Shtemenko, was its secretary. Shtemenko from 1948 to 1952 was chief of the General Staff. Yu. P. Petrov, *Partiynoye Stroitel'stvo v Sovetskoy Armii i Flote 1918–1961* [Party Structuring in the Soviet Army and Navy 1918–1961] (Moscow: Voyenizdat, 1964), p. 462, indicates that Marshal Zhukov tried (and presumably failed) to abolish the Higher Military Council (*Vysshiy Voyennyy Sovet*), "membership of which included members and candidate members of the Presidium of the Central Committee, military and political leaders of the army and navy." These were some of the charges that caused his ouster in 1957. For a discussion of the role of the Main Military Council today as an agency of collective leadership, see A. S. Zheltov, ed., *V. I. Lenin i Sovetskiye Vooruzhennyye Sily* [V. I. Lenin and the Soviet Armed Forces], 3d ed. (Moscow: Voyenizdat, 1980), p. 184. This is the first volume of the Officer's Library Series for the 1980s.

26. Zhukov, *Vospominaniya,* p. 329.

27. Sokolovskiy, *Soviet Military Strategy,* 3d ed., p. 359.

28. Ibid., p. 361.

29. Kozlov, *Officer's Handbook,* p. 127.

30. Sokolovskiy, *Soviet Military Strategy,* 3d ed., p. 361.

31. The best available books about the Soviet General Staff are by S. M. Shtemenko, *General'nyy Shtab v Gody Voyny* [The General Staff in the Years of the War], 2 vols. (Moscow: Voyenizdat, 1968–1973). Volume 1 has been published in English as S. M. Shtemenko, *The Soviet General Staff at War* (Moscow: Progress Publishers, 1970). The set was republished as two volumes in 1981 by Voyenizdat under the same title. The first volume of this set was revised by Shtemenko shortly before his death, resulting in two new chapters and additional material throughout.

32. *Sovetskaya Voyennaya Entsiklopediya,* Vol. 2, pp. 398, 511.

33. Vishnyakov and Arkhipov, *Ustroystvo,* p. 102. See also Berkhin, *Voyennaya Reforma,* p. 157.

34. *Sovetskaya Voyennaya Entsiklopediya,* Vol. 2, p. 512.

35. Zhukov, *Vospominaniya,* p. 230. See also Kulikov, *Akademiya General'novo Shtaba,* p. 44.

36. Shtemenko, *General'nyy Shtab,* Vol. 1, p. 113.

37. Shtemenko, *The Soviet General Staff at War* (English translation), p. 140.

38. Shtemenko, *General'nyy Shtab,* Vol. 1, p. 113.

39. Ibid., Vol. 2, p. 7.

40. Ibid., Vol. 1, p. 123.

41. The services of the Armed Forces are responsible for planning at the level of operational art.

42. Shtemenko, *General'nyy Shtab,* Vol. 1, p. 128.

43. Maksimov, *Osnovy Sovetskogo,* p. 53; A. G. Gornyy, ed., *Osnovy Pravovykh Znaniy* [The Fundamentals of Legal Knowledge] (Moscow: Voyenizdat, 1973), p. 88.

44. A. G. Gornyy, ed., *Spravochnik po Zakonodatel'stvu Dlya Ofitserov Sovetskoy Armii i Flota* [Handbook on Legislation for Officers of the Soviet Army and Navy] (Moscow: Voyenizdat, 1970), p. 184.

45. *Sovetskaya Voyennaya Entsiklopediya,* Vol. 2, p. 513. For those readers interested in Soviet civil defense, the Military Encyclopedia notes that the General Staff has responsibilities for "Civil Defense USSR," meaning both a military and a civilian defense function.

46. Ibid.

47. *Military Thought* is restricted in circulation, although occasionally it is mentioned in the Soviet press. Current issues normally are not available to Western researchers. Issues through 1973 have been declassified in the United States.

48. *Sovetskaya Voyennaya Entsiklopediya,* Vol. 2, p. 513.

49. Ibid., Vol. 1, p. 444.

50. V. V. Druzhinin and D. S. Kontorov, *Ideya, Algoritm, Resheniye* [Concept, Algorithm, Decision] (Moscow: Voyenizdat, 1972). This book has been translated into English and published in the Soviet Military Thought series by the U.S. Government Printing Office, Washington, D.C.

51. Druzhinin and Kontorov, *Ideya, Algoritm, Resheniye,* p. 8. For a philosophical discussion of the impact of cybernetics, see N. D. Tabunov and V. A. Bokarev, eds, *Marksistsko-Leninskaya Filosofiya i Metodologicheskiye Problemy Voyennoy Teorii i Praktiki* [Marxist-Leninist Philosophy and Methodological Problems of Military Theory and Practice] (Moscow: Voyenizdat, 1982), pp. 87–102; 386–401.

52. See "Events of the Day" section, under the heading "Volga Military District," *Krasnaya Zvezda,* 4 November 1966.

53. N. V. Ogarkov, *Vsegda v Gotovnosti k Zashchite Otechestva* [Always in Readiness to Defend the Fatherland] (Moscow: Voyenizdat, 1982), p. 37.

54. M. P. Skirdo, *Narod, Armiya, Polkovodets* [The People, the Army, and the Commander] (Moscow: Voyenizdat, 1970), p. 121. For an English translation, see W. F. Scott, ed., *Selected Soviet Military Writings, 1970–1975* (Washington, D.C.: Government Printing Office, 1977), p. 161.

55. Skirdo, *Narod, Armiya, Polkovodets,* pp. 146–147; Scott, *Selected Soviet Military Writings,* p. 148.

56. *Pravda,* 13 October 1967.

57. A. Rychkov, "CPSU on Vigilance and Combat Readiness of Troops and Forces of the Fleet at the Contemporary Stage," *Kommunist Vooruzhennykh Sil* 19 (1983), p. 73.

58. Petrov, *Stroitel'stvo,* p. 444.

59. Yu. Krinov, "We Meet the Election as a Holiday," *Krasnaya Zvezda,* 28 May 1974.

60. *Krasnaya Zvezda,* 20 June 1961.

5

The Soviet Military Services

Basic Structure

The current structure of the Soviet Armed Forces has slowly evolved since the end of World War II. In 1945 the Soviet Union possessed only the three conventional services—Ground Forces, Air Forces, and Navy. The Ground Forces and Air Forces were subordinate to the People's Commissariat of Defense, while the Navy had its own higher structure. In February 1946 the People's Commissariat of Defense and the Navy were combined into the People's Commissariat of the Armed Forces, which a month later became the Ministry of the Armed Forces.[1] A fourth service, Troops of National Air Defense (PVO), was formed in 1948.[2]

Two years later, a few months before the beginning of the Korean War, the Ministry of the Armed Forces was divided again into two ministries: the War Ministry, consisting of the Ground Forces, Air Forces, and Troops of National Air Defense; and the Navy Ministry. Just after Stalin died, in March 1953, these two ministries were again combined into the current Ministry of Defense.[3]

The 1950s were a time of great change in the Soviet Armed Forces. In this period occurred "the greatest military technical revolution in the history of mankind, which was the main cause and basic source of the revolution in military affairs."[4] One direct result was the formation of a fifth service in 1959, the Strategic Rocket Forces.[5] Soviet spokesmen correctly assert that the organization of the Soviet Armed Forces is different from that of the armed forces of any other nation:

> In the majority of states the armed forces consist of three services: Ground troops (forces, army), air force and naval forces (navy). The services of the Armed Forces of the USSR are: Strategic Rocket Forces, Ground Forces, Troops of Air Defense, Air Forces and Navy.[6]

There are other differences as well. In 1983 the Soviet defense organization was described as follows:

The Armed Forces of the USSR are divided into services: Strategic Rocket Forces (RVSN), Ground Forces (SV), Troops of Air Defense (Voyska PVO), Air Forces (VVS) and Navy (VMF) *and also includes the Rear Services of the Armed Forces (Tyl VS), staffs and troops of Civil Defense (GO)*. . . . Border Guards and Internal Troops are also part of the Armed Forces USSR.[7] (emphasis added)

The five services fall directly under the control of the Ministry of Defense, as do the Troops of the Tyl and the Troops of Civil Defense. Border Troops, however, are under the Committee of State Security of the USSR (KGB), and the Internal Troops come under the Ministry of Internal Affairs (MVD).

Still other differences exist: Construction and Billeting Troops, Troops of the Tyl, and Troops of Civil Defense, each headed by a deputy minister of defense, are not part of any one service. There also are various categories of "special troops," such as engineer, chemical, signal, railroad, and road troops, which provide support for all of the armed services and at times may be organically assigned.

This organization is shown in Chart 10.

It is impossible to make exact organizational comparisons between the armed forces of the Soviet Union and those of the United States. For example, the United States Air Force is approximately the equivalent of the Soviet Air Forces, the Strategic Rocket Forces, and the interceptor aircraft units, plus some radar units, of the Troops of Air Defense. The United States Army is roughly equivalent to the Soviet Ground Forces and the nonflying element of the Troops of Air Defense, plus a number of the special troops controlled by the Ministry of Defense in the Soviet Union. The United States Navy, with its nuclear submarines, antisubmarine units, Marines, air units, and surface ships, roughly equates to the Soviet Navy. The Soviet Navy, however, has assigned to it large formations of land-based bomber aircraft, which are used for various naval tasks, including sea surveillance.

Soviet airborne forces are in a special category, not rating as a major service but apparently assigned directly under the Ministry of Defense. Although closely associated with the Ground Forces, they are identified as a "detached (separate) branch of service."[8]

Postwar ministers of defense (commissars of defense, ministers of the armed forces, ministers of war) have been:

I. V. Stalin (until March 1947)
N. A. Bulganin (1947–1949, 1953–1955)
A. M. Vasilevskiy (1949–1953)
G. K. Zhukov (1955–October 1957)

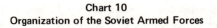

Chart 10
Organization of the Soviet Armed Forces

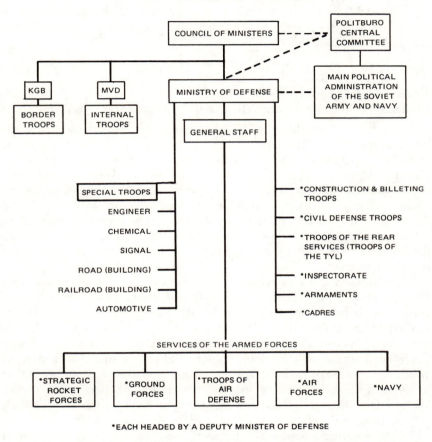

R. Ya. Malinovskiy (1957–March 1967)
A. A. Grechko (1967–April 1976)
D. F. Ustinov (since 1976)

There are no United States equivalents to either the Border Guards of the KGB or the troops of the MVD. These forces are armed with tanks, armored personnel carriers, and light infantry weapons. The many skirmishes with the Chinese along the Sino-Soviet border have involved Border Guards, not the troops of the Ministry of Defense.

Often Western misconceptions of Soviet military power stem from a failure to understand the Soviet military structure. This chapter will examine each of the Soviet services in some detail. Subsequent chapters will examine the operational structure and supporting services of the Soviet Armed Forces.

The Strategic Rocket Forces
(Raketnyye Voyska Strategicheskovo Naznacheniya—RVSN)

At the end of World War II Stalin made great efforts to obtain the secret weapons that the German High Command used in the final months of combat, particularly the V-2 ballistic rocket. Peenemunde, the German rocket test site, fell into the Soviet occupied zone. Weapons, buildings, and associated equipment from the site were moved to the Soviet Union. Thousands of German scientists and technicians also were transferred directly to the Soviet Union to set up the initial rocket plants and to instruct Soviet scientists and technicians on the state of German rocket development. For years they remained there, constructing the first Soviet rocket complexes.

The United States competed with the Soviet Union in obtaining both German rockets and rocket scientists. However, in 1949, Dr. Vannevar Bush, the highly respected scientific adviser to the president of the United States during World War II and afterward, stated in his widely read book, *Modern Arms and Free Men,* that the ballistic missile might never be practical as a nuclear weapons delivery system.[9] The payload would be too small and the cost too high, and the accuracy would be insufficient to destroy specific targets. The combined effect of Dr. Bush's analysis and sharply reduced military budgets brought the U.S. ballistic missile program virtually to a standstill in the early 1950s.

Like the United States, the Soviet Union concentrated on bomber aircraft production in the early 1950s. However, production of the Bison, the primary Soviet long-range bomber, never reached the figure of twenty-five per month that Western analysts estimated as the Soviet production capacity for this aircraft. It now appears that the reason was a Soviet decision to place primary reliance on missiles instead of manned aircraft as the means of nuclear delivery. As explained in later years,

An example of such a bold scientific strategy might be the military-technical policy of the Central Committee of the CPSU and the Soviet government. That policy allowed our country, which had concentrated efforts on creating a means of delivery which was new in principle—the rocket, to overtake the USA, which in that period had concentrated its efforts on the development of intercontinental bombers as the sole (in their opinion at the time) means of delivering nuclear charges.[10]

The Strategic Rocket Forces have been assisted in the development of their boosters by the attention given by the Party leadership to the Soviet space program. Reliability of missiles has been improved as a result of the many space launchings.

Soldiers of the Rocket Troops . . . are proud of our remarkable victories in space, of the fact that in these victories there is the contribution of the rocketeers who have made the launches of the space rockets. "A serious test of the training of the crews of Rocket Troops," observed the commander in chief of the Strategic Rocket Troops at the time, "was the launch of the ballistic rocket with the sputnikship Vostok."
. . . The successes of the USSR in space reflect like a mirror successes in the development of sciences and technology and in strengthening the capability of our Motherland. The powerful rockets, with the help of which our cosmonauts made their unprecedented cosmic flights around the earth, can lift off and deliver nuclear bombs to any point in the world.[11]

The first rocket troops in the Soviet Union were formed from guard units in 1946 and assigned as part of the artillery reserves of the Supreme High Command. As the head of the Main Artillery Directorate (1948–1950), Chief Marshal of Artillery M. I. Nedelin was closely associated with the new units. From 1952 to 1953 and from 1955 until his death in 1960 he was deputy minister of defense for armaments. His additional appointment in December 1959 as the first commander in chief of the Strategic Rocket Troops simply indicated another duty.

In October 1960 Nedelin and a large group of Soviet officers were at the largest of the Soviet missile test ranges, Tura Tam, to watch the launch of the new booster. The missile blew up on the launch pad, and Nedelin, along with perhaps 300 other officers and key scientists, was killed. His death was attributed by the Soviet news media to an aircraft accident. His replacement as commander in chief, Strategic Rocket Forces, was Marshal of the Soviet Union K. S. Moskalenko, commander of the Moscow Military District at the time.

In April 1962, while preparing for his Cuban adventure, Khrushchev selected Marshal of the Soviet Union S. S. Biryuzov, then commander in chief of the Troops of National Air Defense to replace Moskalenko as head of the Strategic Rocket Forces. In March 1963 Biryuzov was moved up to become chief of the General Staff, and Marshal of the Soviet Union N. I. Krylov, previously commander of the Moscow Military District, was assigned as his replacement. Krylov remained in this position until his death in February 1972. General of the Army V. F. Tolubko

Chart 11
Members of the Military Council of Command and Staff
of the Strategic Rocket Forces USSR (1 May 1984)

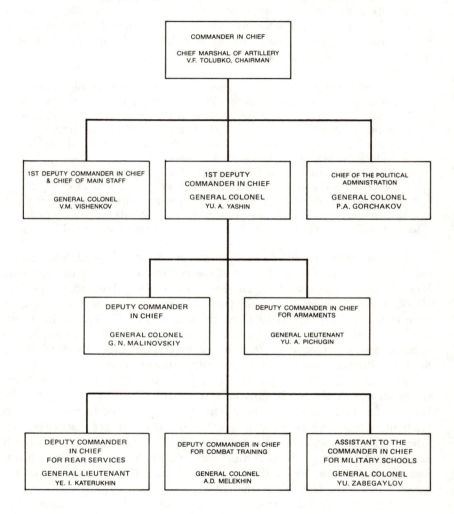

was moved from the position of commander, Far Eastern Military District, to take over the Strategic Rocket Forces. Tolubko was not a newcomer to this field, having served as Krylov's deputy in the mid-1960s.

The top leadership of the Strategic Rocket Forces, as of 1 May 1984, is shown on Chart 11. The commanders in chief of the Strategic Rocket Forces from 1959 to the present are as follows:

Chief Marshal of Artillery	M. I. Nedelin	1959–1960
Marshal of the Soviet Union	K. S. Moskalenko	1960–1962
Marshal of the Soviet Union	S. S. Biryuzov	1962–1963
Marshal of the Soviet Union	N. I. Krylov	1963–1972
Chief Marshal of Artillery	V. F. Tolubko	1972–

Secrecy and Concealment

Since the Strategic Rocket Forces were formed, they always have been referred to as the "primary service," and the commander in chief takes precedence over the commanders in chief of the other four services. The Strategic Rocket Forces "are the youngest and most formidable service of the Armed Forces, and compose the basis of the defensive might of our Motherland and are troops of instant combat readiness."[12]

Although this force is widely publicized in the Soviet news media, seldom has so much been written about a subject and so little actually said or revealed to the outside world. Once each year the Party hierarchy authorizes the parade of certain missiles through Red Square to be viewed by foreign diplomats, military attaches, foreign newsmen, and selected Soviet citizens. Whenever photographs of Soviet missiles appear in the press they generally are those taken during the 7 November parade.[13] Security with respect to the Strategic Rocket Forces is such that even the identification of the personnel of this service is kept very secret, except for a few members of its senior staff. Both officers and enlisted personnel wear insignia that is identical to that worn by the rocket troops and artillery branch of the Ground Forces, and/or by the surface-to-air missile elements of the Troops of Air Defense.

Personnel of the Strategic Rocket Troops represent the elite of the Soviet services. Future officer recruits must be endorsed by the local military commissariat before being assigned to a Strategic Rocket Forces school, a screening process not required by the other services.

All Soviet land-based missiles with ranges exceeding 1,000 kilometers are assigned to the Strategic Rocket Forces.[14] Missiles with ranges of less than 1,000 kilometers are assigned to the rocket troops and artillery branch of the Ground Forces. Many of the missiles assigned to the Strategic Rocket Forces, however, are not intercontinental in range. The purpose of the medium- and intermediate-range missiles would be to deliver nuclear strikes against Western Europe, the Middle East, and China.

The exact number of Strategic Rocket Forces missiles is not known. During arms control negotiations, such as SALT, INF, and START, almost all data on Soviet weapons systems are provided by the Western participants. The Soviets seldom reveal the designations they have given to their own missiles. Since arms control agreements are based on data

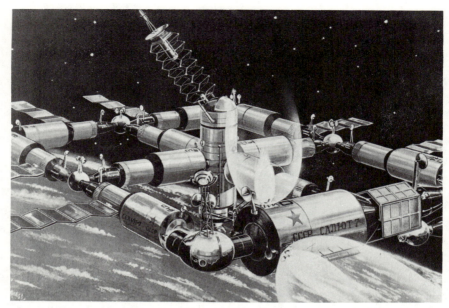

The Soviets have announced plans to have a large, permanently manned space station orbiting the earth in the 1990s. This station, which would serve military purposes, could appear as shown in this artist's depiction.

A 152 mm self-propelled Howitzer.

obtained by "national technical means of inspection," presumably meaning satellite photography, and without on-site inspections of any type, Soviet reports indicate the advantage that this procedure provides them.

> In our press it has been noted that we place our rocket equipment so that double and triple duplication are ensured. The territory of our country is huge, and we are capable of dispersing rocket equipment and concealing it well. We create such a system that if some means intended for striking a counterblow are taken out of commission it is always possible to place into operation duplicative equipment and to strike the target from reserve positions.[15]

Both the Soviet press and TV coverage show how rocket units are concealed so that any chance observer would never suspect that intercontinental ballistic rockets are placed in a given area. Books that normally one would consider authoritative and fairly responsible, at least factually, continue the same theme. For example, *Spravochnik Ofitsera* (The Officer's Handbook), published in 1971 in the Officer's Library series, states: "It is easy to disperse and camouflage them [ICBMs] on the terrain. Large launch areas are not necessary for their launch. They also can be mounted on mobile launchers."[16]

Tasks of the Strategic Rocket Forces

Soviet military doctrine and strategy stress the importance of the initial strike in war and the necessity of "frustrating" the nuclear strike of the opponent. When it became apparent to the Soviet leadership in the late 1960s that their antiballistic missile system would be unable to stop an attack of missiles armed with multiple independent reentry warheads, consideration was given to having the Strategic Rocket Forces assist the Troops of National Air Defense. As Soviet spokesmen stated:

> Therefore, we recognize the necessity of strengthening the troops of PVO, directed at the repulsing of the strikes of the enemy, the destruction of the means of his attack in flight, at barring them to the great administrative-political centers, economic regions and objectives of the country, the groups of rocket troops, aviation and navies, the regions of formations of the reserves and other objectives. In accomplishing this task the Strategic Rocket Forces will render significant help to the Troops of National PVO.[17]

How the Strategic Rocket Forces might "render significant help" to the Troops of Air Defense is never explained. Here is another typical statement in the same vein:

Strategic Rocket Forces are the basis of the defense might of the Soviet army and navy. They most completely contain the achievements of the contemporary scientific-technical revolution. Rocket complexes with ICBMs and MRBMs, equipped with automatic systems, can deliver on target, with great exactness, nuclear warheads of enormous destructive force.

Strategic Rocket Forces are designated for performing strategic tasks in nuclear war. They are the main and decisive means of achieving the goals of war since they can solve in the shortest period of time the tasks of demolishing the military economic potential of an aggressor, of destroying his strategic means of nuclear missile attack, and of crushing the main [military] groupings.[18]

According to Chief of the General Staff Marshal Ogarkov:

The chief component of [our] power in present-day conditions are the strategic nuclear forces, which serve as the basic factor deterring the aggressor and which have the capability, in case the aggressor unleashes a war with the use of nuclear weapons against the Soviet Union and the other countries of the socialist community, of immediately carrying out a crushing retaliatory strike. Launches of modern land and sea-based ballistic missiles is automated. Their performance characteristics permit delivery of strikes on enemy targets located practically anywhere in the world and with a sufficiently high degree of accuracy.[19]

The rigid centralization of control by the Soviet Supreme High Command already has been discussed. During World War II, orders had to go from the High Command to the front commanders for final execution. With strategic nuclear missiles the High Command now has a means of taking positive strategic action, resulting in major changes in the conduct of war:

The basic qualities of the Strategic Rocket Forces are: enormous destructive power; high combat readiness and exactness of delivery of nuclear rocket strikes on enemy targets; practically unlimited range of action; the capability of carrying out strikes simultaneously on many strategic objectives, successfully overcoming actions of air and ABM defense, and performing the given mission in the shortest period of time; the possibility of wide maneuver with nuclear rocket strikes; the independence of combat use from weather conditions of time of year or of the day.[20]

Negotiation with the United States on limitations of strategic nuclear weapons deployments has affected the Strategic Rocket Forces very little, if at all. New, improved missiles appear on a regularly programmed basis. To make identification by satellite observation more difficult, increased emphasis is being given to mobile launchers. Of particular interest in the mid-1980s is the SS-X-24 and the SS-X-25, both of which could either be deployed in silos or used as mobile missiles.

Although the Soviet High Command now has placed a considerable portion of its strategic nuclear weaponry aboard submarines, the Strategic Rocket Forces are likely to remain the primary Soviet service. A technological breakthrough may make it possible for an enemy to track submarines at sea and to destroy them with an initial strike. It is less likely that mobile missiles, scattered throughout the Soviet Union, could ever be identified and simultaneously attacked by an enemy power.

The Ground Forces (Sukhoputnyye Voyska—SV)

Traditionally, until the advent of the nuclear bomb and the intercontinental ballistic missile, the Ground Forces were the most important of the Soviet services. With the perfection of a weapon that could directly strike the United States, leader of the "imperialist" bloc, the Ground Forces moved to second place behind the Strategic Rocket Forces. Some lost prestige was restored when nuclear weapons were reduced in size and made available in such quantities that they could be used tactically on the battlefield. After this,

> The basic task of the Ground Forces, which are equipped with operational-tactical and tactical nuclear rocket weapons, is the destruction of means of nuclear attack and other enemy targets and the crushing of his surviving groupings. New in principle in their actions is the use in full measure of the results of nuclear strikes for swift accomplishment of the mission assigned them. The main role in achieving the goals of operations is given to operational-tactical rocket troops and aviation, and also tank, motorized rifle and airborne troops.[21]

In his booklet *Always in Readiness to Defend the Fatherland,* written in 1982 with the resolutions of the Twenty-sixth Party Congress in mind, Chief of the General Staff Marshal Ogarkov stated:

> The Ground Forces, the most numerous and, in essence, the basic service of our Armed Forces, are constantly being developed. Their firepower now is composed of rocket artillery of tactical and operational-tactical designation, which can destroy targets at a distance of from dozens to hundreds of kilometers.[22]

Since the mid-1970s many changes have taken place in the organization of the Soviet Ground Forces, and their present structure is not altogether clear.[23] In 1979, for example, the Ground Forces were described in

Soviet textbooks as consisting of the following branches of service: motorized rifle troops, tank troops, rocket troops and artillery, and troops of air defense of the Ground Forces.[24] A 1983 publication stated that the Ground Forces are composed of motorized rifle troops, tank troops, airborne troops, rocket troops and artillery, troops of troop air defense (service branches), army aviation, and also units and subunits of special troops.[25] This organization, as of 1 May 1984, is shown in Chart 12. As will be seen, troop air defense and army aviation may not be organic to the Ground Forces.

Twice since the end of World War II the Ground Forces have been without a designated commander in chief and staff. The first period, 1950 to 1955, probably was associated in some manner with the Korean War. The second, 1964 to 1967, may have been linked with the ouster of Khrushchev. Postwar commanders in chief of the Ground Forces[26] follow:

Marshal of the Soviet Union	G. K. Zhukov	Mar–Jun	1946
Marshal of the Soviet Union	I. S. Konev	Jul	1946–1950
	(None designated)	Mar	1950–1955
Marshal of the Soviet Union	I. S. Konev	Mar	1955–1956
Marshal of the Soviet Union	R. Ya. Malinovskiy	Mar	1956–1957
Marshal of the Soviet Union	A. A. Grechko	Nov	1957–1960
Marshal of the Soviet Union	V. I. Chuykov	Apr	1960–1964
	(None designated)	Jun	1964–1967
General of the Army	I. G. Pavlovskiy	Nov	1967–1980
Marshal of the Soviet Union	V. I. Petrov	Dec	1980–

The basic combat branches of the Ground Forces will be examined separately.

Motorized Rifle Troops (Motostrelkovyye Voyska)

Motorized rifle troops, a designation that came into being in 1963, "have replaced the traditional foot soldier"[27] as the most numerous branch of the Soviet Ground Forces. These troops now number over 125 divisions. Their equipment is simple, relatively easy to maintain, and highly effective. Much of it has been tested in combat in Afghanistan, the Middle East, and Southeast Asia. Workmanship, where necessary, is excellent, and in some items, including combat vehicles for the troops, both Soviet weapons technology and design surpass those of the West.[28]

Motorized rifle troops consist of motorized rifle divisions, regiments, and battalions. The divisions and regiments have tank, rocket, artillery, and surface-to-air missiles units and subunits. Special troops and rear services are also organically assigned to them.

Chart 12

Members of the Military Council of Command and Staff of the Ground Forces (1 May 1984)

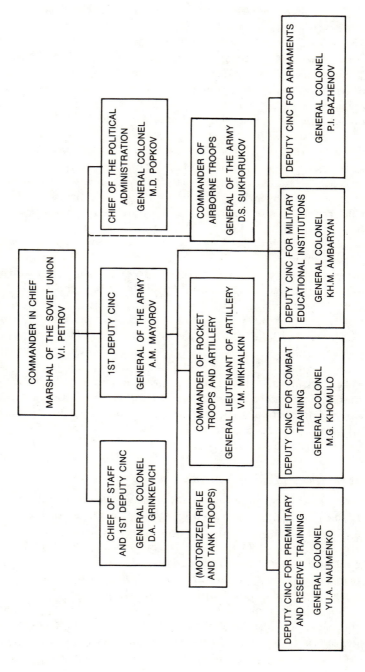

COMMANDER IN CHIEF
MARSHAL OF THE SOVIET UNION
V.I. PETROV

CHIEF OF THE POLITICAL ADMINISTRATION
GENERAL COLONEL M.D. POPKOV

COMMANDER OF AIRBORNE TROOPS
GENERAL OF THE ARMY D.S. SUKHORUKOV

DEPUTY CINC FOR ARMAMENTS
GENERAL COLONEL P.I. BAZHENOV

1ST DEPUTY CINC
GENERAL OF THE ARMY A.M. MAYOROV

CHIEF OF STAFF AND 1ST DEPUTY CINC
GENERAL COLONEL D.A. GRINKEVICH

COMMANDER OF ROCKET TROOPS AND ARTILLERY
GENERAL LIEUTENANT OF ARTILLERY V.M. MIKHALKIN

(MOTORIZED RIFLE AND TANK TROOPS)

DEPUTY CINC FOR MILITARY EDUCATIONAL INSTITUTIONS
GENERAL COLONEL KH.M. AMBARYAN

DEPUTY CINC FOR COMBAT TRAINING
GENERAL COLONEL M.G. KHOMULO

DEPUTY CINC FOR PREMILITARY AND RESERVE TRAINING
GENERAL COLONEL YU.A. NAUMENKO

Soviet planners anticipate that nuclear weapons may be introduced into a war at any time. Accordingly, Soviet ground equipment is designed for use in a chemical-biological-nuclear environment. Troops are routinely issued protective clothing, medication, and dosimeters as basic equipment. Tanks, armored personnel carriers, and other vehicles intended for use on the battlefield are designed with sealed chambers for the crews, who are able to fire their weapons while traversing areas where chemical, nuclear, or biological weapons are employed.

Soviet strategists consider that entire divisions might be completely destroyed in the event of a nuclear war. If nuclear weapons are employed, contingency mobilization plans therefore call for divisions or regiments to be replaced as units, rather than for replacement of individual casualties. If there is a conventional phase in a future war, the number of motorized rifle troops would be increased immediately upon the outbreak of hostilities, with further mobilization providing additional manpower as losses were suffered. In this case individual replacements might be used.[29]

Soviet practices do not provide motorized rifle units with sufficient motor transport organically assigned to meet their wartime needs. Instead, as demonstrated in the 1968 invasion of Czechoslovakia, trucks and other equipment are drawn as needed from the Soviet economy. All Soviet private and state-owned vehicles are registered for mobilization purposes with the military commissariat. Certain of them must pass periodic inspections, certifying their fitness for immediate mobilization. Drivers, who are in the reserve forces, also are assigned to specific units. When required, vehicles and reserve drivers simply are called up and move immediately into action. During the invasion of Czechoslovakia, for example, some drivers were taken directly from their civilian tasks without even being given time to visit their homes before going to their units.

Tank Troops (Tankovyye Voyska)

Soviet writers state that "the primary strike force of the Ground Force is the tank troops."[30] In 1983, it was estimated that there were about fifty tank divisions. Soviet tankists still enjoy some of the mystique acquired during World War II. Soviet history of that war, although constantly being rewritten, credits the massive tank armies with the primary responsibility for the successful ejection of enemy troops from Soviet soil and pursuit into German territory.

Introduction of the nuclear weapon did not lessen Soviet regard for this weapons system. As previously noted, Soviet tanks provide some degree of protection against chemical, nuclear, and biological weapons and can cross areas contaminated by nuclear fallout or chemical agents.

Smoke and artillery preparation would be used to lessen the effectiveness of enemy antitank precision-guided weapons.[31]

The Soviet leadership has made careful studies of the vulnerability of their tanks in the 1973 Middle East conflict. The findings are probably reflected in a number of the comments about tanks and antitank defenses added by Marshal Grechko in the second (1975) edition of his book, *The Armed Forces of the Soviet State*. He noted that in the constant battle between defense and offense, defensive systems in land warfare had achieved certain gains, "caused primarily by the fact that the main striking forces during an offensive operation—tanks—have become more vulnerable, while their use on the battlefield has become more complex. The continuing process of improving antitank weapons has imposed grave tasks on science and technology." And further,

> The battle between armor and antitank missiles has now shifted to the scientific research laboratories, the proving grounds, and industry. . . . Obviously the traditional method of improving the survivability of tanks— by increasing the thickness of the armor—is far from being the only solution, and probably not the best one, to the existing problem.[32]

Even if a defense is found against current antitank missiles, Grechko did not consider that survivability of tanks would be ensured, since "the development of antitank guided missiles (PTURS) has essentially only begun and the possibilities of improving these powerful new weapons of antitank warfare appear to be quite significant." There are still more problems, since "the last word has not been said about antitank artillery, where possibilities for further development are far from having been totally explored."

With at least 50,000 tanks in their inventory, Soviet military leaders are watching closely for further developments within the NATO nations in precision-guided munitions or other new antitank weapons. Marshal Grechko's 1975 book indicated a realistic appraisal of the opposition that tanks now face.

Tank troops consist of tank armies, divisions, and regiments. Such units also have motorized rifle, rocket artillery, and surface-to-air missile units and subunits, as well as special troops and rear services. Motorized rifle troops and naval infantry also have tank units. Since 1970, the number of motorized rifle divisions has risen from 90 to 134, while the number of tank divisions has remained at 50.[33]

The growing tendency to increase the number of tanks in motorized rifle units and the number of motorized rifle troops in tank units is leading to a convergence of motorized rifle and tank troops. That this might already have happened can be seen by examining the Ground

Forces command. General Colonel Yu. M. Potapov became chief of Tank Troops when Chief Marshal of Armored Troops A. Kh. Babadzhanyan died in November 1977. But by the Twenty-sixth Party Congress in 1981, Potapov was chief of the Main Armored Tank Directorate, and the post of chief of Tank Troops appears to have vanished.

Rocket Troops and Artillery (Raketnyye Voyska i Artilleriya)

Rockets and artillery assigned to the Ground Forces have ranges "from several dozen to hundreds of kilometers."[34] Such weapons, when armed with nuclear warheads, are considered to be the "principal means" of defeating the enemy in Ground Forces operations. Among these are two rockets with NATO code names *FROG* and *Scud,* with ranges of 70 kilometers and 500 kilometers, respectively. Their replacements, the SS-21 for the *FROG* and the SS-23 for the *Scud,* have increased accuracies and ranges. Rockets of this type are intended to destroy enemy targets well in the enemy rear, performing certain tasks that in the U.S. forces would be accomplished by tactical aircraft.

Artillery, divided into organic artillery and artillery of the Supreme High Command Reserve, continues to play an important role in the Soviet Ground Forces. Organic artillery is included in motorized rifle regiments and in tank and airborne units and formations. Antitank guns and antitank guided missiles are part of the organically assigned artillery. Larger guns and mortars constitute the artillery of the Reserve of the Supreme High Command.

In the 1970s and the early 1980s renewed attention was given to artillery, including both antitank guns and rifled tubes. Emphasis was also placed on development of self-propelled artillery, a type of weapon that the Soviets did not have during World War II. The Soviets did have self-propelled assault guns (SAU), which were classified as tanks and used for direct fire. Development of self-propelled artillery appeared to be for the purpose of providing crew protection against chemical, biological, and nuclear weapons, as well as for increased mobility. It is also of importance that the new heavier self-propelled howitzers and mortars have both a nuclear and conventional capability.

The Soviet press has made a legend of the "Katyusha" Guards multiple-rocket launcher that was put into mass production during World War II. The truck-mounted 122-millimeter version of this launcher, with forty tubes, is a formidable weapon, performing many of the tasks that would be assigned to tubed artillery in the United States. By its very nature this weapon is relatively inaccurate, but it is inexpensive and lays down a heavy volume of fire on a given area. A 240-millimeter version of this rocket launcher also may be deployed.

Research and development, as well as testing and delivery to the troops of new rocket and artillery systems, are the responsibility of the Main Rocket and Artillery Directorate of the Ministry of Defense (GRAU). This directorate also may have responsibilities for chemical weapons. In mid-1983 General Colonel-Engineer Yu. M. Lazarev replaced Marshal of Artillery P. N. Kuleshov, who had headed GRAU since 1965.

Troops of Troop Air Defense (Voyska Voyskovoy Protovovozdushnoy Oborony)

Troop air defense of the Ground Forces was formed in 1958. It was equipped with a wide variety of air defense weapons, which were highly maneuverable and capable of good cross-country mobility. Five higher military schools prepared officers for service in this branch. A military academy for the troops of air defense of the Ground Forces opened in 1977.[35]

By 1980, all of the schools of troop air defense, as well as the troop air defense academy, were transferred to the Troops of Air Defense, one of the five major Soviet services. In late 1980 General Colonel P. G. Levchenko, who had been chief of troops of air defense of the Ground Forces, was transferred to Troops of Air Defense. He was identified in his obituary in 1982 as having also been first deputy commander in chief of Troops of Air Defense. In late 1983 his replacement, General Colonel of Artillery Yu. T. Chesnokov, a first deputy commander in chief of Troops of Air Defense, was identified as being commander of troop air defense as well.

Although the 1983 Soviet *Military Encyclopedia Dictionary* stated that the Ground Forces have troops of troop air defense, the composition of such troops and their subordination are not clear. Based on the limited information available at present, it is believed that troop air defense personnel in the Ground Forces are from the separate service, Troops of Air Defense. This assumption would be in line with the emphasis given to combined arms forces, where operational control of forces is assigned to the commander in chief of a theater of military operations.

Army Aviation (Armeyskaya Aviatsiya)

Army aviation had existed in the Red Army at the beginning of World War II. At that time, bombers, fighters, and ground support aircraft were directly subordinate to the commanders of combined arms armies. The Red Army also contained units of troop aviation and frontal aviation. The division of the resources of the Soviet Air Forces into army, troop, and frontal aviation was found to be unsuitable, and in 1942 army aviation was abolished.

Some forty years later, in the early 1980s, the expression "army aviation" is again being used in conjunction with the Ground Forces. There also is troop aviation, consisting of aviation subunits and units that form part of the combined arms (tank) formation and large formations: "In the 1980s the tasks of troop aviation are fulfilled by army aviation."[36] But exactly what is troop aviation? What is army aviation? Soviet sources are very vague on this matter.

Given the information available in 1984, it appears that certain types of combat helicopters, which fall administratively under the Soviet Air Forces, may be assigned to Ground Force large units, such as an army. It is possible that they also may be assigned to the operational control of a division commander. Whether or not fixed wing aircraft can be so assigned cannot be determined at present.

Airborne Troops (Vozdushno-Desantnyye Voyska—VDV)

Soviet airborne troops are a mini-service, with close ties to the Ground Forces but assigned as a reserve of the High Command. These troops were formed in August 1930 as part of the Air Forces.[37] By 1935 they had made massed parachute drops—years ahead of any similar capability in the United States Army. Airborne troops were separated from the Air Forces in 1946, although they have retained the Air Force uniform color.

From 1954 to 1959 and from 1961 to 1979, the airborne troops were headed by one commander—General of the Army V. F. Margelov. In April 1979, General of the Army D. S. Sukhorukhov was named commander of airborne troops. As is the case with the Strategic Rocket Forces, much has been written about the airborne troops, but very little is actually known. In the early 1980s their strength was estimated at seven to eight divisions.

Transport is provided by the Air Forces. Tanks, artillery, and other equipment capable of being dropped from aircraft have been designed specifically for airborne operations. Although at the present time Soviet transport aircraft lags behind that of NATO forces, the Soviet airborne capability nevertheless is considerable.

Soviet military texts stress the role of airborne troops in a nuclear war. Since their primary task is to seize and destroy the nuclear means of the opponent, they would be dropped in the very initial phase of the war, with the objectives of destroying missile launch pads and of capturing or destroying nuclear stockpiles.[38] As the nuclear means of an opponent would be the first target even in a nonnuclear war, it can be expected that the airborne troops would have the same basic tasks regardless of whether the conflict were to begin with conventional or nuclear weapons.

With the increased emphasis now being given to the "international duty of the Soviet Armed Forces," it also is likely that airborne troops would be used to project Soviet military power abroad. During the 1973 Middle East conflict it was rumored that the Soviet airborne troops had been placed on instant alert, ready to be moved into the Middle East if the conflict continued.

Troops of Air Defense
(Voyska Protivovozdushnoy Oborony—V PVO)

Soviet efforts since the end of World War II to provide defense against attack from aircraft, missiles, and satellites have existed on a scale considerably beyond any such efforts seriously contemplated by the United States. Troops of Air Defense (until 1981 called Troops of National Air Defense) became independent in 1948,[39] when they were taken out from under control of the commander of artillery of the Armed Forces. Although considered a service along with the Ground Forces, Air Forces, and Navy, it was headed only by a "commander" for six years. The first "commander in chief" was designated in 1954.[40] Since that time this service generally has ranked number three in precedence within the Soviet Armed Forces, following the Strategic Rocket Troops and the Ground Troops.

The Soviet investment in aerospace defense probably has exceeded that of any other two nations. The first jet aircraft produced in significant numbers (the MiG-15) was designed primarily as a PVO interceptor. By 1949 hundreds of these aircraft were in operational service and were comparable in performance to the F-86, the most advanced USAF aircraft at the time. SA-1 ground-to-air missiles were deployed in three concentric rings around Moscow by 1955, representing an equivalent investment of billions of dollars. In 1957 and 1958, hundreds of SA-2s, a missile that proved its capability in Southeast Asia throughout the 1960s, were deployed in hundreds of sites throughout the Soviet Union with a speed that astounded Western military planners. Despite the decline in numbers of manned bombers in NATO forces, the Soviet Union still maintained approximately 10,000 surface-to-air missile launchers in 1983.

Soviet efforts to provide a defense against ballistic missiles and earth satellites also have been tremendous. It is estimated that the Soviet high-energy laser program is three to five times the United States effort, and that by the late 1980s the Soviets may be able to deploy a variety of laser weapons.[41] The Kremlin has spent billions of rubles for antimissile and antispace systems in the past. It is highly unlikely that these efforts have ceased in the 1980s; the greater probability is that they have been intensified.

In 1981 great changes took place in National Air Defense. First, as noted, the name was changed to Troops of Air Defense. Second, many, if not all, of the assets of the troops of air defense of the Ground Forces, including five higher military schools and one academy, were transferred to the Troops of Air Defense. A first deputy commander in chief of Troops of Air Defense was designated commander of troops of troop air defense.

Approximately 45 percent of the aircraft in the former Troops of National Air Defense were transferred to the Air Forces, along with the Armavir Higher Military Aviation School for Pilots and the Daugavpils Higher Aviation Engineering School for Air Defense. The only flying training school left in the new Troops of Air Defense is the Stavropol' Higher Military Aviation School for Pilots and Navigators.

Chart 13 shows the basic organizational structure of the Troops of Air Defense as of 1 May 1984. Commanders of the Troops of National Air Defense have been:

Marshal of the Soviet Union	L. A. Govorov	1948–1952
General Colonel	N. N. Nagornyy	1952–1953
Chief Marshal of Aviation	K. A. Vershinin	1953–1954

Commanders in chief of the Troops of National Air Defense (Troops of Air Defense since January 1981) follow:

Marshal of the Soviet Union	L. A. Govorov	1954–1955
Marshal of the Soviet Union	S. S. Biryuzov	1955–1962
Marshal of Aviation	V. A. Sudets	1962–1966
Marshal of the Soviet Union	P. F. Batitskiy	1966–1978
Marshal of Aviation	A. I. Koldunov	1978–

Prior to the reorganization the Soviet Union had two major air defense districts, Moscow and Baku. The remainder of the nation was divided into air defense regions. Control of both air defense districts and regions was exercised directly by the commander in chief, Troops of National Air Defense.

Only the Moscow Air Defense District remains in the new structure. The Baku Air Defense District was downgraded and merged into the Transcaucasus Military District. Air Defense units previously in air defense regions are now assigned to military districts. They are headed by a commander of air defense, who is subordinate to the commander of the military district.

Chart 13

Members of the Military Council of Troops of Air Defense (1 May 1984)

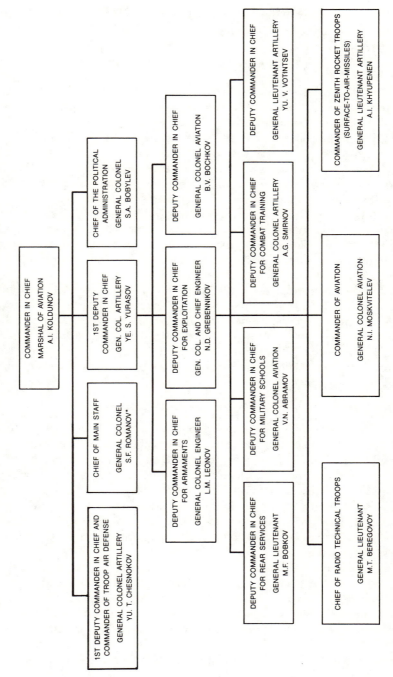

COMMANDER IN CHIEF
MARSHAL OF AVIATION
A.I. KOLDUNOV

1ST DEPUTY
COMMANDER IN CHIEF
GEN. COL. ARTILLERY
YE. S. YURASOV

1ST DEPUTY COMMANDER IN CHIEF AND COMMANDER OF TROOP AIR DEFENSE
GENERAL COLONEL ARTILLERY
YU. T. CHESNOKOV

CHIEF OF MAIN STAFF
GENERAL COLONEL
S.F. ROMANOV*

CHIEF OF THE POLITICAL ADMINISTRATION
GENERAL COLONEL
S.A. BOBYLEV

DEPUTY COMMANDER IN CHIEF
GENERAL COLONEL AVIATION
B.V. BOCHKOV

DEPUTY COMMANDER IN CHIEF FOR EXPLOITATION
GEN. COL. AND CHIEF ENGINEER
N.D. GREBENNIKOV

DEPUTY COMMANDER IN CHIEF FOR ARMAMENTS
GENERAL COLONEL ENGINEER
L.M. LEONOV

DEPUTY COMMANDER IN CHIEF FOR COMBAT TRAINING
GENERAL COLONEL ARTILLERY
A.G. SMIRNOV

DEPUTY COMMANDER IN CHIEF FOR MILITARY SCHOOLS
GENERAL COLONEL AVIATION
V.N. ABRAMOV

DEPUTY COMMANDER IN CHIEF
GENERAL LIEUTENANT ARTILLERY
YU. V. VOTINTSEV

COMMANDER OF ZENITH ROCKET TROOPS
(SURFACE-TO-AIR-MISSILES)
GENERAL LIEUTENANT ARTILLERY
A.I. KHYUPENEN

COMMANDER OF AVIATION
GENERAL COLONEL AVIATION
N.I. MOSKVITELEV

DEPUTY COMMANDER IN CHIEF FOR REAR SERVICES
GENERAL LIEUTENANT
M.F. BOBKOV

CHIEF OF RADIO TECHNICAL TROOPS
GENERAL LIEUTENANT
M.T. BEREGOVOY

*Note: Romanov died in line of duty in mid-May 1984. His replacement appears to be General Lieutenant Aviation I.M. Mal'tsev.

There are three basic components of Troops of Air Defense: aviation, radio technical troops, and zenith rocket troops.[42] Each is headed by a commander or a chief.

Aviation of Air Defense (Aviatsiya PVO—A PVO)

Among the many changes that have taken place in the Soviet air defense structure since 1979 is the type of aircraft assigned. "Aviation of air defense (*aviatsiya PVO*)" has replaced the expression "fighter aviation of air defense (*istrebitel'naya aviatsiya PVO*)," since PVO is now assigned some transport aviation and helicopters as well as fighter aircraft.

In the early 1980s, air defense aircraft *in border regions* of the USSR were merged with tactical air and now are part of the air forces of the military district in these areas. Approximately 1,000 aircraft were lost by Troops of Air Defense in this merger. In 1984 some 1,200 interceptors remained in aviation of air defense, *based in interior military districts.* With surface-to-air missiles and anti-aircraft artillery providing local air defense, these interceptors are intended to intercept incoming hostile aircraft as far from intended targets as possible.

Although approximately one-half the aircraft previously assigned to Troops of Air Defense have been transferred to the Air Forces, the sophistication of the remaining aircraft has improved. The MiG-25 *Foxhound,* with its look-down, shoot-down radar capabilities and missiles, is an improvement over the *Foxbat.* Development of Soviet interceptor aircraft probably will continue regardless of the nature of NATO's manned aircraft deployments.

Zenith Rocket Troops (Zenitnyye Raketnyye Voyska—ZRV)

The Soviet investment in surface-to-air missiles throughout the past thirty years has been in the tens of billions of rubles. One missile system overlaps another. The SA-3 was designed and deployed in the early 1960s to provide an improved defense capability against low-level attack. In the 1960s a second system was deployed. This was the SA-5, the missile associated with the Tallinn Line—a group of radars deployed across the Soviet Union. With its estimated slant range of fifty miles, this missile and associated radars were believed by a number of analysts to be intended for ABM defense.

The merger of the Ground Forces' troop air defense into the Troops of Air Defense involved the transfer of field mobile SAM systems to the new organization. It is likely that their operational control will be the responsibility of the commander of the combined arms formation to which they are assigned. Among these systems are the well-known SA-4 *Ganef* and the SA-6 *Gainful.* The SA-13 is to replace the SA-9, and the SA-11 and SA-12 may have both tactical and strategic applications.

Experience gained in the use of these weapons in the Middle East will be used to make modifications or to develop completely new systems.

Radio-Technical Troops (Radiotekhnicheskiye Voyska—RTV)

A massive deployment of radars and communication systems guide and control the aircraft and missiles of the Troops of Air Defense. The radar density is not approached by that of any other nation, except possibly some areas in the Middle East where conflicts are a daily occurrence. When new radars are produced in the Soviet Union, old radars seldom are junked; instead, they remain in place as backups to the new equipment. If one type of radar is jammed, other radars will overlay the same area.

Radars deployed in the Soviet Union are of many types, ranging from long-range early warning radars to search, target-acquisition, and missile-control radars. Considerable attention has been given to antijamming capabilities and other countermeasures.

PKO (Antispace Defense) and PRO (Antirocket Defense)

In the early 1960s the Soviets began to deploy an ABM system. As part of their carefully stage-managed performance for foreign observers, two massive ABM radars were displayed near the two main highways in the Soviet Union along which foreigners are most likely to travel. One was located along the road between Moscow and Warsaw; the other between Moscow and Helsinki. In November 1964 their first antiballistic missile, the *Galosh,* was shown in the parade on Red Square. The Kremlin wanted the United States and the rest of the world to believe they had pioneered the ABM.

Two new terms, PKO (antispace defense) and PRO (antirocket defense), began to show up in increasing frequency during the mid-1960s. They were listed as components of the Troops of National Air Defense and defined as

> PKO (antispace defense)—a component part of air defense (PVO) designated for destroying the enemy's cosmic means of fighting which are being used for military purposes (in the capacity of a carrier of nuclear weapons, for carrying out reconnaissance, and so forth) in their flight orbits. Special space ships, satellite fighters, and other flying apparatuses are the basic means of PKO.
>
> PRO (antirocket defense)—a component part of PVO, designated for detecting, intercepting, and destroying enemy ballistic rockets in the trajectory of their flight and creating jamming for them. PRO fulfills its mission with the help of antirocket and special jamming equipment.[43]

In 1966, after the agreement was made between the United States and the Soviet Union that nuclear weapons and other weapons of mass destruction would not be placed in orbit, references to antispace defense were quietly dropped. References to antirocket defense were also made less and less frequently in Soviet writings after 1968. This probably was due to the fact that the Soviet antiballistic missile system, based on then current technological development, would be ineffective against the new MIRVs, which the United States had recently tested.

The inability of the Soviet ABM to cope with MIRVs, combined with the probable success of the United States ABM, the Safeguard, probably was a major factor in the Soviet agreement to hold discussions on limitation of strategic weapons systems. A possible aim of the Soviet negotiators, which succeeded, was to get the United States to delay deployment of its own ABM until the Soviet Union could develop MIRVs, thereby making the Safeguard system obsolete. By the late 1970s Soviet weapons makers were placing MIRVs on their own missiles.

In the early 1980s there were indications that the Soviets were making major efforts with respect to both antiballistic missile and antisatellite systems. Long-range early-warning antiballistic missile radars have been built, which in 1984 were considered in the United States to be in violation of the SALT I agreement. A number of antisatellite systems have also been tested. The 1980s are certain to bring further developments in these areas.

The Air Forces (Voyenno-Vozdushnyye Sily—VVS)

As already noted, the Soviet Air Forces are not the equivalent of the United States Air Force, since strategic missiles and interceptor aircraft have been assigned to the Strategic Rocket Forces and the Troops of Air Defense, respectively.

Chart 14 identifies the general organizational structure and senior personnel as of 1 May 1984. Postwar commanders in chief of the Air Forces have been:

Marshal of Aviation	K. A. Vershinin	1946–1949
Chief Marshal of Aviation	P. F. Zhigarev	1949–1957
Chief Marshal of Aviation	K. A. Vershinin	1957–1969
Chief Marshal of Aviation	P. S. Kutakhov	1969–

The Troops of Air Defense display their antiballistic missile, the Galosh.

In the early 1980s significant changes took place in the organization of the Soviet Air Force. The position of commander of Long Range Aviation was abolished in August 1981. General Colonel of Aviation V. V. Reshetnikov, who had commanded long-range aviation since 1969, was appointed deputy commander in chief of the Air Forces instead. At the same time, at the military district level, "commanders of aviation" became "commanders of the Air Forces." Two of the three aviation schools in the old Troops of National Air Defence were transferred to the Air Force.

In 1983 Soviet writers continued to refer to three primary components of the Soviet Air Forces: long-range aviation, frontal aviation, and military transport aviation. These aircraft now are assigned either to an air army or to a military district. There is no longer a commander of long-range aviation but, as shown on Chart 14, there is a commander of military transport aviation. More details will be given later.

Soviet aircraft development since World War II has shown constant technological advances in both airframes and engines. In the 1970s, new aircraft—bombers, fighters, and transport aircraft—continued to appear.

166

Chart 14

Members of the Military Council of Command and Staff of the Air Force (1 May 1984)

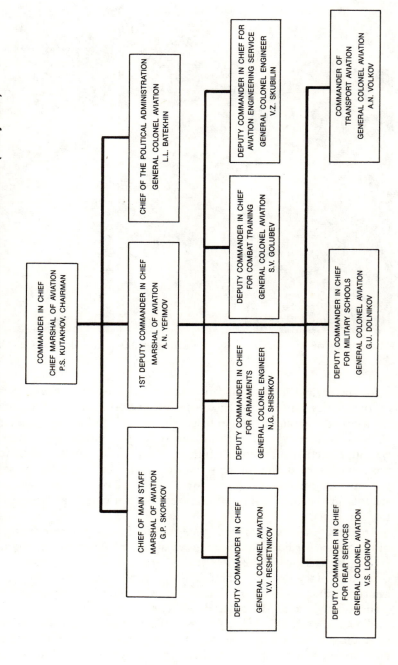

COMMANDER IN CHIEF
CHIEF MARSHAL OF AVIATION
P.S. KUTAKHOV, CHAIRMAN

CHIEF OF MAIN STAFF
MARSHAL OF AVIATION
G.P. SKORIKOV

1ST DEPUTY COMMANDER IN CHIEF
MARSHAL OF AVIATION
A.N. YEFIMOV

CHIEF OF THE POLITICAL ADMINISTRATION
GENERAL COLONEL AVIATION
L.L. BATEKHIN

DEPUTY COMMANDER IN CHIEF
FOR ARMAMENTS
GENERAL COLONEL ENGINEER
N.G. SHISHKOV

DEPUTY COMMANDER IN CHIEF
FOR COMBAT TRAINING
GENERAL COLONEL AVIATION
S.V. GOLUBEV

DEPUTY COMMANDER IN CHIEF FOR
AVIATION ENGINEERING SERVICE
GENERAL COLONEL ENGINEER
V.Z. SKUBILIN

DEPUTY COMMANDER IN CHIEF
GENERAL COLONEL AVIATION
V.V. RESHETNIKOV

DEPUTY COMMANDER IN CHIEF
FOR MILITARY SCHOOLS
GENERAL COLONEL AVIATION
G.U. DOLNIKOV

COMMANDER OF
TRANSPORT AVIATION
GENERAL COLONEL AVIATION
A.N. VOLKOV

DEPUTY COMMANDER IN CHIEF
FOR REAR SERVICES
GENERAL COLONEL AVIATION
V.S. LOGINOV

This growth and development are perhaps unmatched by any other nation in the world, including the United States. New airframes and engines are developed at fairly regular intervals; their production is unaffected by international tensions or détente.

The January 1960 speech in which Nikita Khrushchev announced the formation of rocket units and new military doctrine caused considerable speculation regarding the future of the Soviet Air Forces.

> The present level of military technique being what it is, the Air Force and the Navy have lost their former importance. These arms are being replaced and not reduced. Military aircraft is [sic] almost entirely being replaced by rockets. We have now drastically reduced, and apparently will reduce still further or even discontinue, the production of *bombers* and other obsolete aircraft.[44] (emphasis added)

It is not known whether Khrushchev really contemplated the discontinuance of the Soviet bomber forces, or if he merely overstated his position to emphasize the importance of the missile force. In any event, the Soviet Air Forces continued as a major service. To satisfy the fascination with rockets, bomber aircraft were armed with "nuclear rocket weapons" and have become long-range rocket-carrying aircraft. Fighter bombers have been developed to carry either conventional or nuclear weapons, and new models of transport aircraft have appeared. Air transport, both civilian and military, has become a major factor in supporting Soviet military actions beyond the borders of the Soviet Union.

Long-Range Aviation (Dal'nyaya Aviatsiya—DA)

In the latter part of the 1970s long-range aviation, together with certain elements of what previously had been in frontal aviation, were merged into five air armies. Although as of May 1984, all details of this organization were not clear, it appears that *Bear, Bison, Backfire, Blinder* and *Badger* bombers, together with perhaps 450 Fencer strike aircraft and over 500 tanker, reconnaissance and electronic warfare aircraft make up this new force. These air armies would provide support to theaters of military operations as required. This is a powerful air strike force, capable of carrying either nuclear or conventional weapons.[45]

Exact targeting priorities for long-range aviation are not known. Soviet publications do give listings at times, but these are not consistent. The following pattern, however, is typical: (1) bases of intercontinental rockets, (2) nuclear arsenals, (3) military naval bases, (4) air bases of strategic aviation, (5) groups of war industries that make up the military potential of the enemy, and (6) participatory actions on the ground and at sea.

A Soviet *Blackjack* long-range bomber (under development in 1984).

Destruction of the "nuclear means" of the enemy is the first task of long-range aviation, as it is for all other weapons systems with a strategic or long-range capability. The first two target priorities listed, bases of intercontinental rockets and nuclear arsenals, fall specifically within this category.

Although the Soviets have put the bulk of their intercontinental nuclear strike capability in the Strategic Rocket Forces and submarine-launched ballistic missiles, they still retain bombers that could reach targets in the United States. Some 30 *Bison* aircraft are modified to serve as tankers. This would permit the *Backfire* bomber to overfly the United States on either reconnaissance or strike missions. A new Soviet bomber, *Blackjack,* expected to enter operational service in 1986, is considerably larger than the B-1 bomber planned for the United States Air Forces.

Soviet bombers are called rocket-carriers by military spokesmen. Air-to-ground rockets permit the aircraft to launch their weapons while remaining outside the ground-to-air missile envelope. Since the rockets require only a few minutes to reach their targets if launched from aircraft near the borders of the United States, the time available for reaction to an air-to-ground rocket attack would be less than for ICBMs. Long-range aviation probably is an essential element of any Soviet intercontinental war plan.

Frontal Aviation (Frontovaya Aviatsiya—FA)

Frontal aviation in the Soviet Union is roughly equal to tactical aviation in the United States. In the reorganization of the Air Forces and the Troops of Air Defense in the late 1960s and early 1970s, as already noted, certain fighter interceptor aircraft in border areas were taken from Troops of Air Defense and reassigned to the Air Forces. In addition, over one-half of the SU-24 *Fencer* aircraft were removed from frontal aviation and assigned to the five air armies.

Helicopters are a part of frontal aviation, and are trained and administered by the Air Forces. Their operational control may be assigned to armies or to divisions.[46]

Two initial tasks of frontal aviation are to achieve air superiority and to provide air defense over the battle area or within the TVD. Other tasks are "in cooperation with the rocket troops to destroy the nuclear means of the opponent, his forces and reserves, air bases, command points, rear area and transport centers."[47]

Aircraft of frontal aviation are also assigned to the groups of Soviet forces abroad in the Warsaw Pact nations.[48] Their operational commands are somewhat similar to the unified and specified commands of the United States. Each military district commander and group of forces commander has a "commander of the air forces." Frontal aviation units also are stationed with Soviet forces in Outer Mongolia. Much of the Soviet fighting in Afghanistan has involved units of frontal aviation, seeking to destroy a population in a one-sided battle.

In a wartime situation a commander of air forces would probably come under the control of the commander in chief of a TVD. (The TVD structure will be explained in the next chapter.) Such a commander would be able to transfer aircraft from one front to another, as needed. In addition, the Soviet system of military control provides for central direction by Stavka of all available air units. A Stavka representative would have the authority to coordinate air formations in two TVDs, concentrating the forces as specified by Stavka.

In the 1960s, aircraft assigned to frontal aviation were not so versatile as their USAF counterparts. They possessed neither the range nor the payload of aircraft in the NATO forces. By the mid-1980s the situation had changed radically. *Fencer* variable-wing aircraft, similar to the USAF F-111, could cover practically all of Western Europe from Soviet bases. Advanced fighters such as the *Flanker* and *Fulcrum* are under development or in the process of deployment.

Helicopters designed specifically for support of Ground Forces were introduced in the early 1970s. By the mid-1970s the *Hind* helicopter carried more firepower than any attack helicopter in the United States

Armed Forces. The attention given to the military use of helicopters has continued into the mid-1980s.

Transport Aviation (Voyenno-Transportnaya Aviatsiya—VTA)

In the early 1930s the Soviet Air Forces gave considerable attention to transport aircraft of many types. During World War II, however, almost all available aviation resources were turned over to production of combat aircraft, with little attention given to the development of air transport. In fact, the standard transport aircraft in the early 1950s was the LI-2, identical in appearance to the famed DC-3 produced in the United States. Even as late as the 1960s these aircraft could be seen on many Soviet military airfields.[49]

Renewed attention was given to the development of transport aircraft in the postwar period when resources again became available. Some of the initial designs like the Il-14 were exact copies of Western aircraft.[50] By the early 1960s production settled primarily on the An-12, which was produced by the hundreds. A huge turboprop aircraft, the An-22 appeared in the 1960s but had serious problems and was never produced in significant numbers. The An-76, a jet transport similar to the USAF's C-141, was flown in 1971. This aircraft was entering the inventory in considerable numbers during the late 1970s. The Il-86, the Soviet Union's first wide-body jet aircraft, made its initial flight in 1976. Despite its impressive appearance, the Il-86 will not be an efficient cargo or passenger carrier unless the Soviet air leaders manage to purchase engines from abroad or improve their own engine technology.

Transport aviation also includes helicopters, which provide troop lift to the other services in addition to other special functions, such as moving equipment in areas inaccessible to surface transport means.[51]

Aeroflot, the Soviet civil air transport organization, serves as a backup to military air transport. This organization is under the Soviet Ministry of Aviation, whose chief is an active duty Air Forces officer. During the 1968 Soviet invasion of Czechoslovakia, Aeroflot personnel and aircraft carried the initial attacking forces to their landing at the Prague airport. Huge numbers of commercial aircraft may be observed by foreign tourists on the ground at major airfields, such as Kiev, Leningrad, Alma Ata, Irkutsk, Khabarovsk, and the three civilian airfields around Moscow: Sheremetyevo, Vnukovo, and Domodedovo. Maintenance of this underused aircraft capacity would bankrupt any commercial aviation company in the West. The excess of civilian passenger and cargo aircraft, with assigned crews from Aeroflot's flying personnel, serves as a military airlift reserve.

Transport aviation functions as a strategic airlift for the Ministry of Defense, which probably exercises control through the Main Air Forces staff to the deputy commander in chief, commander of Military Transport Aviation. Close coordination is maintained with the airborne troops and with those Ground Forces units transported by helicopters. For exercises and troops training, military airlift would be assigned to military district commanders or to "groups of forces" commanders by the General Staff.

According to *Soviet Military Strategy,* "The air forces can operate from the outset of war in the same composition in which they existed during peacetime, but the formation of combat and particularly transport units and rear-area airfields might by needed."[52] The Soviet Air Forces generally comply with this philosophy and maintain a high state of combat readiness. Only limited additions to the force would be required upon the outbreak of hostilities, and, as earlier mentioned, Aeroflot provides a large reservoir of transport aircraft and trained pilots to supplement regular Air Force units.

Over the years, units of the Soviet Air Forces have fought in many parts of the world. In the 1930s they provided "volunteer" pilots to Spain and to China.[53] Soviet aircraft with pilots of other nationalities also have been used in combat against aircraft made in the NATO nations. In Southeast Asia and the Middle East, the F-4 fought against the MiG-21. Even in the wars between India and Pakistan, aircraft from the Soviet Union and the United States faced each other. Regardless of the nationalities of the pilots flying these aircraft, considerable national prestige of both the Soviet Union and the United States is at stake when such confrontations occur.

The Soviet Air Forces play a major role in the Soviet manned space program. Cosmonauts are trained under Air Forces auspices and generally wear Air Forces uniforms. Close attention is given in Soviet Air Forces publications to manned space programs. It is no accident—an expression frequently used in the Soviet Union—that the official Soviet Air Forces journal is entitled *Aviation and Cosmonautics.*

The Navy (Voyenno-Morskoy Flot—VMF)

In his speech on 14 January 1960, announcing the basis of a new military doctrine, Nikita Khrushchev stated that, like the Air Forces, the Navy had lost its former significance. He then added that "the submarine fleet is acquiring great importance, whereas surface ships can no longer play the role they played in the last [war]."[54]

Traditionally, due primarily to the realities of geography, Russia has been essentially a continental power and not a major sea power. During World War II Soviet naval forces were overshadowed by huge land forces. After that war the Soviet Union's first major effort was in submarines, assigned the dual mission of attacking carrier strike forces and disrupting sea communications. Aircraft carriers, which represented the major power of the United States Navy both during and after World War II, initially received relatively little attention in the Soviet Union. Soviet Party-military spokesmen claimed that such weapons systems are too vulnerable to enemy attack, as well as too expensive to construct. This may have been deliberate disinformation, disseminated for the purpose of playing down the role of sea power while the Kremlin first concentrated on the buildup of its land-based intercontinental ballistic missile force. When these statements were being made, the Soviet naval construction already had started. By the late 1960s Soviet strategists were discussing the value of small aircraft carriers.

A 1983 Soviet publication described the Soviet Navy as follows: "The Navy of the USSR consists of the following service branches: submarines, surface ships, naval aviation, coastal rocket-artillery troops and naval infantry. . . . The main forces are submarines and aviation."[55]

In the previous year Marshal Ogarkov had stressed the same priority: "The bases of its [Navy] combat power today are nuclear-powered submarines carrying a diversified arsenal of missile and torpedo weapons, as well as missile-armed naval aviation."[56] Aircraft assigned to naval aviation are primarily land-based bombers, which could be used in antiship roles and, during peacetime, could perform long-range reconnaissance missions over naval areas.

In spreading its influence throughout the world through its projection of military power and presence, the Soviet Navy of the 1980s is one of the most powerful instruments of the Kremlin. Under the umbrella afforded by strategic nuclear forces, Soviet Naval forces have little opposition in providing support to Soviet-inspired wars of national liberation. In the harbors of Third World nations, Soviet crews, carefully trained and prepared, make port visits.[57] Local populations and leaders are impressed by Soviet technological capabilities, reflected in the ships, and by the behavior of the carefully controlled Soviet seamen.

In the event of a major war, Soviet naval forces would attempt to secure critical sea areas and strategic passages, such as the Greenland–Iceland–United Kingdom Gap, and control the Baltic Sea, the Gulf of Finland, sea passages by Denmark, and the Mediterranean. Soviet strategists note that "we must consider that up to three-fourths of all the material and personnel of the probable enemy are located across the ocean. . . . In the event of war [with NATO nations], 80 to 100 large transports should arrive daily in European ports, and 1,500 to 2,000 ships, not counting security vessels, will be enroute simultaneously." It is essential that "operations against enemy communications lines should be developed on a large scale at the very beginning of war."[58]

A typhoon-class, 25,000-ton strategic missile submarine.

The Soviet helicopter/VSTOL carrier, the *Kiev*.

Soviet naval bases and airfields for reconnaissance aircraft in Vietnam would permit Soviet ships and submarines to threaten the entire South Pacific area. Sea lanes between the United States and the nations of Eastern Asia, such as Japan and South Korea, would be difficult to maintain.

Composition of the Soviet Navy

Chart 15 indicates what is known or surmised of the command and staff of the Soviet Navy as of 1 May 1984. Postwar commanders in chief of the Navy were:

Admiral of the Fleet	N. G. Kuznetsov	1939–1947
Admiral	I. S. Yumashev	1947–1951
Admiral of the Fleet of the Soviet Union	N. G. Kuznetsov	1951–1956
Admiral of the Fleet of the Soviet Union	S. G. Gorshkov	1956–

Geography virtually dictates to the Soviet leadership that they maintain four fleets. The Northern Fleet based at Severomorsk would have difficulty supporting either the Baltic Fleet based at Baltiysk or the Black Sea Fleet based at Sevastopol. The Pacific Fleet based at Vladivostok could not easily be supported by units of any of the other three fleets. (Each fleet will be discussed in detail in the next chapter.)

Submarines. Nuclear-powered submarines with a capability to launch missiles while submerged, developed by the United States, presented new challenges to the Soviet Navy. With the help of an extensive espionage effort and the work of Soviet scientists, the Soviet Navy made rapid progress in developing its own version of this new weapon of warfare. "The creation of an oceanic nuclear submarine fleet, armed with nuclear missile weapons, marked a new qualitative jump in the development of the Soviet Armed Forces."[59] Even by the early 1980s the Soviet Union was operating over 180 nuclear-powered submarines, compared to approximately 120 in the United States Navy. At the same time the Soviets were deploying the world's largest submarine, the 25,000-ton *Typhoon,* each capable of carrying 20 ballistic missiles.

In addition to its missile-carrying submarines, the Soviet Navy also has a huge force of attack submarines, over 60 of which are nuclear powered. In this category, the *Alpha* class are believed to be the fastest submarines in the world. The Soviet Navy also had cruise missile submarines, some of which can fire, while submerged, anti-ship cruise missiles which have ranges of up to 100 kilometers. A new class of cruise missile submarines, the *Oscar,* is believed capable of launching up

Chart 15

Members of the Military Council of the Command and Staff of the Navy (1 May 1984)

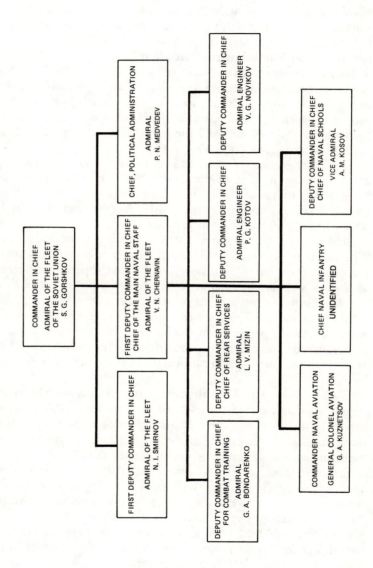

COMMANDER IN CHIEF
ADMIRAL OF THE FLEET
OF THE SOVIET UNION
S. G. GORSHKOV

FIRST DEPUTY COMMANDER IN CHIEF
ADMIRAL OF THE FLEET
N. I. SMIRNOV

FIRST DEPUTY COMMANDER IN CHIEF
CHIEF OF THE MAIN NAVAL STAFF
ADMIRAL OF THE FLEET
V. N. CHERNAVIN

CHIEF, POLITICAL ADMINISTRATION
ADMIRAL
P. N. MEDVEDEV

DEPUTY COMMANDER IN CHIEF
FOR COMBAT TRAINING
ADMIRAL
G. A. BONDARENKO

DEPUTY COMMANDER IN CHIEF
CHIEF OF REAR SERVICES
ADMIRAL
L. V. MIZIN

DEPUTY COMMANDER IN CHIEF
ADMIRAL ENGINEER
P. G. KOTOV

DEPUTY COMMANDER IN CHIEF
ADMIRAL ENGINEER
V. G. NOVIKOV

COMMANDER NAVAL AVIATION
GENERAL COLONEL AVIATION
G. A. KUZNETSOV

CHIEF NAVAL INFANTRY
UNIDENTIFIED

DEPUTY COMMANDER IN CHIEF
CHIEF OF NAVAL SCHOOLS
VICE ADMIRAL
A. M. KOSOV

to 24 antiship cruise missiles while submerged. This new missile has an estimated range of over 450 kilometers.

A few reports have filtered out to the West that the huge Soviet nuclear-powered submarine fleet is taking a heavy toll of lives. Radiation shields on Soviet submarines do not work as planned, and Soviet seamen have suffered and died as a result. This, however, has not slowed down the Soviet nuclear submarine program.

Naval Aviation.[60] Four basic missions are assigned to Soviet naval aviation: reconnaissance and surveillance, antiship strike, antisubmarine, and aviation support. In all, the Navy has approximately 1,500 aircraft, most of which are based on land. Helicopters are assigned to many Soviet ships, as well as the helicopter carriers, and VSTOL aircraft are on aircraft carriers of the *Kiev* class.

Soviet long-range reconnaissance aircraft, the *Bear* turbo-prop, flies along the eastern coast of the United States en route to its Cuban base. Similar aircraft range the Pacific, with a base in Vietnam. Shorter-range reconnaissance aircraft are the Tu-16 *Badger* and the Tu-22 *Blinder*, which has a supersonic dash capability.

Strike aircraft, with standoff cruise missiles with ranges varying from 90 to 300 kilometers, are intended primarily for attacks against carrier forces. Aircraft for this purpose include the supersonic *Backfire*, as well as *Badger* and *Blinder* bombers. In the Baltic Sea area the *Fitter* fighter-bomber might be used as naval strike aircraft as well.

Many of the naval aircraft are equipped specifically for antisubmarine warfare. These operate from Soviet land bases, flying as far out to sea as possible to track foreign submarines. Many helicopters, also used for antisubmarine purposes, are found on both Soviet cruisers and helicopter carriers.

Surface Ships. The *Kiev* aircraft carrier, commissioned in 1976, is the largest warship thus far completed in the Soviet Union. A second aircraft carrier in this same class, the *Minsk*, operates in the Pacific. It is reported that a nuclear-power carrier of about 60,000 tons, capable of supporting high-performance aircraft, is under construction.

Other elements of the Soviet surface fleet also are modern in design and expanding. Following the trend in other Soviet services, most of the armaments are rockets, both surface-to-air and surface-to-surface. The *Kirov*, a nuclear-powered battle cruiser and command ship, has a displacement of 25,000 tons and is the largest surface craft, other than aircraft carriers, built since World War II. Of particular interest in the Soviet Navy of the 1980s are its amphibious ships, such as the 13,000-ton amphibious assault ship, the *Ivan Rogov*.[61] This vessel has two helicopter decks and can also carry three air-cushion landing craft. Its 550-men complement of naval infantry, with 30 armored personnel carriers and ten tanks, gives the Soviet Navy a considerable power projection capability in Third World nations.

The Naval Infantry.[62] In the mid-1960s the Soviet leadership revived naval infantry (or marines, as they are called in the United States and Great Britain). During World War II Soviet naval infantrymen had numbered approximately 300,000. This force fought primarily as infantry, and the units were disbanded after the war. Current personnel strength is somewhere between 14,000 and 50,000. Marine units are assigned to each of the four fleets. The presence of these troops is significant, especially in view of the deployment of amphibious ships such as the *Ivan Rogov* and the emphasis in Soviet military writings on the *external* role of the Soviet Armed Forces.

Merchant Marine and Fishing Fleets. Two major components of the total Soviet maritime forces are the merchant marine and its fishing fleets, which have grown to major proportions since the end of World War II. The Soviet merchant marine fleet is a major factor in international trade. The fleet has forty "roll-on/roll-off ships,"[63] making it possible for tanks and other military vehicles to be loaded and transported to foreign nations without detection by national means of inspection (i.e., satellite surveillance). The merchant fleet provides logistic support to Soviet naval units operating in various parts of the world.

It is difficult to determine whether the collection of intelligence is the primary or secondary function of the fishing fleet. Soviet "fishing vessels" are stationed outside a number of major United States ports and are extremely active during the launching of space vehicles and ballistic missiles.

Soviet naval concepts are different in many respects from those of the United States Navy. Each of the two navies has an offensive nuclear role, and each is vitally concerned with antisubmarine warfare. On the other hand, the classic concept of "command of the sea" held by British and United States strategic planners has not in the past been of the same concern to the Soviet Navy, primarily because the Soviet Union is a continental power. Rather, Soviet strategists have thought in terms of "disrupting" the sea communications of their opponents.

There are indications, however, that Soviet views on the need for secure sea communications may be changing. As a major industrial power with a need to strengthen its worldwide economic position, the USSR will increase the use of its merchant marine. At some time in the future, the nation may need to import oil and other materials, including foodstuffs. As the self-proclaimed leader of the Communist world, the Soviet Union will increase attempts to project influence. Its military presence in noncontiguous areas already is considerable, and it will likely continue to grow. Despite the difficulties imposed by geography, the

Soviet leadership sees its Navy as one of the primary means in attaining the ultimate major goals of the Kremlin.

*   *   *

The reorganization of the Soviet Armed Forces, which began in the late 1970s, may not have run its full course by 1984. Since the beginning of the 1980s Marshal Ogarkov and other Soviet writers have referred to Soviet *strategic nuclear forces,* without specific mention of the Strategic Rocket Forces. Emphasis is being given to combined arms warfare in theaters of military operations. In many respects, ground, air, and air defense units have lost their separate identities. It is possible that within the next few years there will be a restructuring of the current five Soviet services.

The more complex operational structure of the Soviet services will be discussed in Chapter 6.

Notes

1. *Sovetskiye Vooruzhennyye Sily* [Soviet Armed Forces] (Moscow: Voyenizdat, 1978), p. 389.

2. Ibid., p. 395.

3. Ibid., p. 391.

4. M. M. Kir'yan, ed., *Voyenno-Tekhnicheskiy Progress i Vooruzhennyye Sily SSSR* [Military Technical Progress and the Armed Forces of the USSR] (Moscow: Voyenizdat, 1982), p. 7.

5. V. F. Tolubko, "Raketnyye Voyska Strategicheskogo Naznacheniya" [Rocket Troops of Strategic Designation] *Sovetskaya Voyennaya Entsiklopediya* [Soviet Military Encyclopedia] (Moscow: Voyenizdat, 1976–1980), Vol. 7, p. 51.

6. *Voyennyy Entsiklopedicheskiy Slovar'* [Military Encyclopedic Dictionary] (Moscow: Voyenizdat, 1983), p. 129.

7. Ibid., p. 158.

8. For example, see Chart 21 in a series of charts, "Army of the Soviets," number G280170 (Moscow: Publishing House of the Central Home of the Soviet Army, 30 December 1970). See also S. N. Kozlov, ed., *Spravochnik Ofitsera* [Officer's Handbook] (Moscow: Voyenizdat, 1971), p. 134. Yu. A. Naumenko, ed., *Nachal'naya Voyennaya Podgotovka* [Beginning Military Training] (Moscow: Voyenizdat, 1982), pp. 23–24, calls them an *"otdel'nyy rod voysk."* From 1967 until 1983, both the Ground Forces and the Airborne Troops were headed by four-star generals.

9. Vannevar Bush, *Modern Arms and Free Men* (New York: Simon & Schuster, 1949), pp. 81–87. Dr. Bush's book was widely quoted in the late 1940s, and many proponents of ballistic missiles considered that Dr. Bush's book was the largest single factor responsible for the delay of the United States in producing an ICBM. See also Kir'yan, *Voyenno-Tekhnicheskiy Progress,* p. 263, which notes that "in 1948, while American 'specialists on Russia' were guessing how soon

the USSR would have the atomic bomb, Soviet scientists already had everything necessary to produce such a weapon." For the inside story on the Soviet space program, see James E. Oberg, *Red Star in Orbit* (London: Harrap, 1981).

10. V. M. Bondarenko, "Military-Technical Superiority: The Most Important Factor of the Reliable Defense of the Country," *Kommunist Vooruzhennykh Sil,* September 1966. For an English translation, see W. R. Kintner and H. F. Scott, *The Nuclear Revolution in Soviet Military Affairs* (Norman, Okla.: University of Oklahoma Press, 1968), p. 361.

11. P. T. Astashenkov, *Sovetskiye Raketnyye Voyska* [Soviet Rocket Troops] (Moscow: Voyenizdat, 1967), pp. 135, 170. The introduction to this book was written by General Colonel Tolubko, commander in chief of Strategic Rocket Troops.

12. Kozlov, *Spravochnik Ofitsera,* p. 129.

13. Many of the data published in the Soviet press about rocket technology are taken from the "foreign press." For example, see N. I. Morozov, *Ballisticheskiye Rakety Strategicheskovo Naznacheniya* [Ballistic Rockets of Strategic Designation] (Moscow: Voyenizdat, 1974).

14. P. I. Skuybeda, ed., *Tolkovyy Slovar' Voyennykh Terminov* [Explanatory Dictionary of Military Terms] (Moscow: Voyenizdat, 1966), p. 387.

15. Astashenkov, *Sovetskiye Raketnyye Voyska*, p. 65.

16. Kozlov, *Spravochnik Ofitsera,* p. 65.

17. I. Kh. Bagramyan, ed., *Istoriya Voyn i Voyennovo Iskusstva* [The History of War and Military Art] (Moscow: Voyenizdat, 1970), p. 499.

18. A. S. Zheltov, ed., *V. I. Lenin i Sovetskiye Vooruzhennyye Sily* [V. I. Lenin and the Soviet Armed Forces] (Moscow: Voyenizdat, 1980), p. 317.

19. N. V. Ogarkov, *Vsegda v Gotovnosti k Zashchite Otechestva* [Always in Readiness to Defend the Fatherland] (Moscow: Voyenizdat, 1982), p. 49.

20. *Voyennyy Entsiklopedicheskiy Slovar',* p. 622. See also Tolubko, "Raketnyye Voyska Strategicheskogo Naznacheniya" [Rocket Troops of Strategic Designation], pp. 51–54; V. F. Tolubko, *Raketnyye Voyska* [Rocket Troops] (Moscow: Znaniye, 1977).

21. *Sovetskiye Vooruzhennyye Sily,* p. 478.

22. Ogarkov, *Vsegda v Gotovnosti*, p. 49.

23. As of January 1984, there was no agreement among Western analysts regarding the composition of the Soviet Ground Forces.

24. I. G. Pavlovskiy, "Ground Forces," *Sovetskaya Voyennaya Entsiklopediya,* Vol. 7, pp. 604–608.

25. *Voyennyy Entsiklopedicheskiy Slovar',* pp. 719–720; see also N. V. Cherednichenko and V. I. Malinin, *Sovetskiye Sukhoputnyye* [Soviet Ground Forces] (Moscow: Voyenizdat, 1981).

26. I. G. Pavlovskiy, "Ground Troops," *Bol'shaya Sovetskaya Entsiklopediya* [The Great Soviet Encyclopedia], 3d ed. (Moscow: Soviet Encyclopedia Publishing House, 1971), Vol. 25, p. 104.

27. N. A. Lomov, ed., *Nauchno-Tekhnicheskiy Progress i Revolyutsiya v Voyennom Dele* [Scientific-Technical Progress and the Revolution in Military Affairs] (Moscow: Voyenizdat, 1973), p. 106.

28. For example, in the opinion of a number of Western military specialists, the BMP (Combat Machine for the Infantry) surpasses any armored personnel carrier found in the West.

29. V. D. Sokolovskiy, *Soviet Military Strategy,* 3d ed., Harriet F. Scott, ed. (New York: Crane, Russak & Co., 1975), pp. 311–312.

30. Lomov, *Nauchno-Tekhnicheskiy Progress,* p. 106.

31. Considerable credit for maintaining the high level of tanks and tank troops in the Soviet Armed Forces must go to Chief Marshal of Armored Forces, Doctor of Military Sciences and Professor, P. A. Rotmistrov. Once the doctrinal decision was made that nuclear weapons would be the decisive factor in war, Rotmistrov took the lead in demonstrating how tanks could be constructed so as to be ideally suited for survival on a nuclear battlefield. At the Malinovskiy Tank Academy in Moscow, Rotmistrov's writings have had a major influence. See P. A. Rotmistrov, *Vremya i Tanki* [Time and the Tanks] (Moscow: Voyenizdat, 1972).

32. A. A. Grechko, *Vooruzhennyye Sily Sovetskovo Gosudarstva* [The Armed Forces of the Soviet State] (Moscow: Voyenizdat, 1975), p. 197. This is an addition to the first edition of the book, which appeared in 1975, but which had been sent to print prior to October 1974. The second edition has been translated into English and published in the Soviet Military Thought series.

33. "The Military Balance 1983/84" (as compiled by The International Institute for Strategic Studies, London), *Air Force Magazine,* December 1983, p. 77.

34. Ogarkov, *Vsegda v Gotovnosti,* p. 49.

35. P. G. Levchenko, "Troops of Air Defense of the Ground Forces," *Sovetskaya Voyennaya Entsiklopediya,* Vol. 2, pp. 321–323. See also "Sikhoputnyye Voyska" [Ground Forces], *Voyennyy Entsiklopedicheskiy Slovar',* pp. 719–720.

36. "Army Aviation," *Voyenny Entsiklopedicheskiy Slovar',* pp. 43, 155, 698, 720.

37. V. F. Margelov, "Airborne Troops," *Sovetskaya Voyennaya Entsiklopediya,* Vol. 2, pp. 286–289. See also V. F. Margelov, *Vozdushno-Desantnyye Voyska* [Airborne Troops] (Moscow: Znaniye, 1977); D. S. Sukhorukhov, ed., *Sovetskiye Vozdushno-Desantnyye* [Soviet Airborne] (Moscow: Voyenizdat, 1980); I. I. Lisov and A. F. Korol'chenko, *Desantniki Atakuyut s Neba* [Paratroopers Attack from the Sky] (Moscow: Voyenizdat, 1980).

38. Kir'yan, *Voyenno-Tekhnicheskiy Progress,* p. 303. See also Yu. A. Naumenko, ed., *Nachalnaya Voyennaya Podgotovka,* p. 24.

39. P. F. Batitskiy, ed., *Voyska Protivovozdushnoy Oborony Strany* [Troops of National Air Defense] (Moscow: Voyenizdat, 1968), p. 350.

40. P. F. Batitskiy, *Voyska Protivovozdushnoy Oborony Strany* [Troops of National Air Defense] (Moscow: Znaniye, 1977), p. 41.

41. U.S., Department of Defense, *Soviet Military Power* (Washington, D. C.: Government Printing Office, 1984), p. 106.

42. "Voyska Protivovozdushnoy Oborony" [Troops of Air Defense], *Voyennyy Entsiklopedicheskiy Slovar',* p. 154; P. F. Batitskiy, "Voyska Protivovozdushnoy Oborony Strany" [Troops of National Air Defense], *Sovetskaya Voyennaya Entsiklopediya,* Vol. 2, p. 316–321.

43. P. I. Skuybeda, ed., *Tolkovyy Slovar' Voyennylch Terminov* (Moscow: Voyen-izdat, 1967), pp. 348–349, 351.

44. N. Khrushchev, "Disarmament for Durable Peace and Friendship." Address delivered at the Fourth Session of the Supreme Soviet, USSR, 14 January 1960; contained in *On Peaceful Coexistence* (Moscow: Foreign Language Publishing House, 1961), p. 146.

45. V. V. Reshetnikov, "Long Range Aviation," *Sovetskaya Voyennaya Entsiklopediya,* Vol. 3, p. 91.

46. M. N. Kozhevnikov, "Frontal Aviation," *Sovetskaya Voyennaya Entsiklopediya,* Vol. 8, p. 334.

47. Kozlov, *Spravochnik Ofitsera,* p. 137.

48. Note that military districts and groups of forces abroad assigned frontal aviation units are directly subordinate to the Ministry of Defense and not to any one of the Soviet services.

49. B. A. Pestrov, "Military Transport Aviation," *Sovetskaya Voyennaya Entsiklopediya,* Vol. 2, p. 254.

50. For basic data on aircraft, see John W. R. Taylor, "Gallery of Soviet Aerospace Weapons," *Air Force Magazine* (Soviet Aerospace Almanacs, every March since 1975).

51. For discussion of the increased attention given to helicopters in the Soviet Armed Forces, compare the 1972 issues of the Soviet Ground Force journal, *Voyennyy Vestnik,* with the 1974 or 1976 issues. Articles on helicopter and airborne operations increased from between two and five per year prior to 1973 to between twenty-four and twenty-six per year after that date.

52. Sokolovskiy, *Soviet Military Strategy,* 3d ed., p. 310.

53. See S. I. Shingarev, *"Chatos" Idut v Ataku* ["Chatos" Go Into the Attack] (Moscow: Moscow Rabochiy, 1971) on Soviet pilots in Spanish Civil War, and *V Nebe Kitaya 1937–1940* [In the Skies of China] (Moscow: Nauka, 1980) on Soviet pilots in China. A. G. Rytov, *Rytsari Pyatogo Okeana* [Knights of the Fifth Ocean] (Moscow: Voyenizdat, 1968) relates the experiences of a pilot in both Spain and China.

54. Khrushchev, "Disarmament for Durable Peace and Friendship," pp. 148–149.

55. *Voyennyy Entsiklopedicheskiy Slovar',* p. 142. The single most important book on the Soviet Navy is the work by Admiral of the Fleet of the Soviet Union S. G. Gorshkov, *Morskaya Moshch' Gosudarstva* [Seapower of a State] (Moscow: Voyenizdat, 1979), 2d ed. English editions are available.

56. Ogarkov, *Vsegda v Gotovnosti,* p. 50.

57. For a more detailed account of Soviet port visits, see Bruce W. Watson, *Red Navy at Sea* (Boulder, Colo.: Westview Press, 1982), pp. 9–19.

58. Sokolovskiy, *Soviet Military Strategy,* 3d ed., p. 366

59. Kozlov, *Spravochnik Ofitsera,* p. 139. See also *Gulbinnyy Dozor* [Deep Patrol] (Moscow: Molodaya Gvardiya, 1978), a popular account of the Soviet submarine force.

60. Figures on numbers and types of naval aircraft were compiled in January 1984 from a variety of sources. For a romanticized history of Soviet naval

aviation, see *Kril'ya Nad Okeanom* [Wings Over the Ocean] (Moscow: Molodaya Gvardiya, 1982).

61. U.S., Department of Defense, *Soviet Military Power,* p. 64.

62. For an account by a Soviet writer on the naval infantry, see Kh. Kh. Kamalov, *Morskaya Pekhota v Boyakh za Rodinu* [Naval Infantry in Battles for the Motherland] (Moscow: Voyenizdat, 1983), 2d ed.

63. Trucks, tanks, and other vehicles can be driven directly onto "roll-on/ roll-off" ships and down to lower decks, where they cannot be seen. They can be driven off in the same manner.

6

Deployment of Soviet Military Forces: TVDs, Military Districts, Fleets, Border Guards, and MVD Troops

Soviet combat forces, other than the Strategic Rocket Forces and certain elements of the Air Forces and Troops of Air Defense, are deployed primarily in sixteen military districts, four groups of forces abroad, and four fleets. Contingents of Soviet troops are located in Outer Mongolia and Afghanistan as well.

In time of war, Soviet combined arms forces would be organized into theaters of military operations (TVDs). Several TVDs might be combined into a theater of war (TV). Locations of the headquarters of the TVDs, as well as headquarters personnel, probably already have been designated.

The sixteen military districts (see Map 1) encompass geographically all of the Soviet Union. Groups of forces are maintained in East Germany, Poland, Czechoslovakia, and Hungary. Soviet naval units are divided into four fleets: Northern, Baltic, Black Sea, and Pacific. In addition, a small flotilla is maintained in the Caspian Sea. Soviet spokesmen do not acknowledge their military forces in Outer Mongolia, although their presence there is clearly visible. In 1984 the Soviet press frequently discussed the actions of the forces in Afghanistan.

Both in peace and in war, theaters of war, theaters of military operations, military districts, and groups of forces abroad are subordinate to the Soviet High Command, with orders passed through the General Staff. They are not under the control of any one of the five services. In time of peace, elements of the fleet may be directly under the control of the Navy commander in chief, as shown on Chart 16.

As previously noted, the Armed Forces of the Soviet Union also include Border Guards and Internal Troops, in addition to the tyl (rear services) and civil defense troops. In this chapter, Border Guards and Internal Troops will be discussed in the context of the operational structure of the Soviet forces. Troops of the Tyl and civil defense troops will be considered as supporting forces and examined later.

Map 1
Military Districts, Fleets, and Air Defense Districts

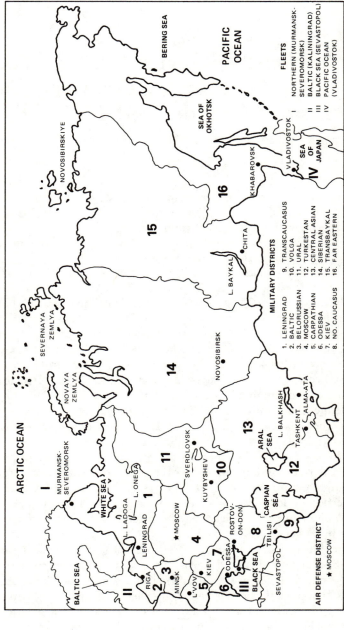

MILITARY DISTRICTS

1. LENINGRAD		9. TRANSCAUCASUS	
2. BALTIC		10. VOLGA	
3. BELORUSSIAN		11. URAL	
4. MOSCOW		12. TURKESTAN	
5. CARPATHIAN		13. CENTRAL ASIAN	
6. ODESSA		14. SIBERIAN	
7. KIEV		15. TRANSBAYKAL	
8. NO. CAUCASUS		16. FAR EASTERN	

FLEETS

I NORTHERN (MURMANSK-SEVEROMORSK)
II BALTIC (KALININGRAD)
III BLACK SEA (SEVASTOPOL)
IV PACIFIC OCEAN (VLADIVOSTOK)

THE SIXTEEN MILITARY DISTRICTS SHOWN ABOVE ARE ROUGHLY COMPARABLE TO US JOINT COMMANDS. SOVIET FRONTAL AVIATION UNITS (COMPARABLE TO US TAC AIR UNITS) ARE ASSIGNED TO THE MILITARY DISTRICTS. IN ADDITION TO THE MILITARY DISTRICTS, THERE ARE FOUR 'GROUPS OF FORCES' BASED IN THE WARSAW PACT AREA. THE PRIMARY AIR DEFENSE DISTRICT IS AT MOSCOW.

SOURCE: *AIR FORCE MAGAZINE*, MARCH 1975. COMPILED BY HARRIET FAST SCOTT.

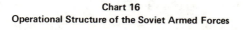

Chart 16
Operational Structure of the Soviet Armed Forces

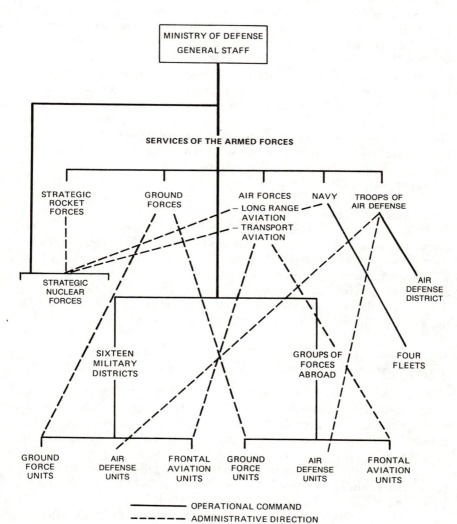

OPERATIONAL COMMAND
ADMINISTRATIVE DIRECTION

SOURCES: *SOVETSKOYE ADMINISTRATIVNOYE PRAVO* [SOVIET ADMINISTRATIVE LAW] (MOSCOW: JURIDICAL LITERATURE, 1982), P. 246; S. S. MAKSIMOV, *OSNOVY SOVETSKOGO VOYENNOGO ZAKONODATEL'STVA* [THE FUNDAMENTALS OF SOVIET MILITARY LEGISLATION] (MOSCOW: VOYENIZDAT, 1978), PP. 52–55.

Theaters of Military Operations
(Teatr Voyennykh Deystviy—TVD)

In 1979 Marshal Ogarkov, chief of the Soviet General Staff, noted that "Soviet military strategy holds that war consists of a complex system of interdependent, large-scale, simultaneous, and successive strategic operations, including operations in continental theaters of military operations."[1] Two years later he further explained: "It is not the front operation, but the larger-scale form of military operations—the strategic operation in the theater of military operations—which should be regarded as the basic operation in a possible future war."[2]

Since the end of World War II, Soviet strategists have examined carefully formations other than the front that might improve command and control. In 1968 Marshal Sokolovskiy discussed the theater of military operations: "The modern concept of the theater of military operations may include the entire territory of a belligerent or coalition, whole continents, large bodies of water, and extensive regions of the atmosphere, including space."[3]

While many Soviet writers have described the concept of TVDs, no information has been disclosed that would reveal where they might be formed. Some Western observers believe that the Soviets plan on thirteen TVDs in the event of a future war: five continental, four maritime, and four intercontinental. This, however, is speculation. On the other hand, it is certain that one organization with many characteristics of a TVD, the High Command of the Far East, has been formed.

High Command of the Far East
(Glavnoye Komandovaniye Voysk Dal'nogo Vostoka)

As shown in Chapter 1, during World War II three high commands were established in 1941: Northwest, West, and Southwest. These proved ineffective and soon were abolished. Stavka of the Supreme High Command (VGK) found it more expedient to deal with each front directly. In 1945, in preparation for joining in the war against Japan, the High Command of the Far East was established. Details for the attack had been worked out by Stavka in Moscow. The First and Second Far Eastern Fronts were formed under control of the High Command of the Far East. This organization was abolished in the summer of 1945, after the surrender of Japan.

In May 1947, when the Chinese were in the midst of their revolution, the High Command of the Far East again was formed, with the Transbaykal, Far Eastern, and Primorskaya Military Districts subordinate to it. Soviet assistance to North Korea in the early 1950s was funneled through this command. On 23 April 1953, soon after the death of Joseph Stalin, the high command was abolished.[4]

In December 1978, Leonid Brezhnev congratulated General of the Army V. I. Petrov on his new assignment, but no other details were given in the press. Western analysts determined later that Petrov, who had spent two dozen years of his career in the Far East, had been designated commander in chief of the revived post of the High Command of the Far East. This command, with its headquarters in Chita, encompasses the Transbaykal and Far Eastern districts.

Soviet writings identify this command as being headed by a commander in chief (*glavnokomanduyushchiy*), a very significant designation. The only other commanders in chief are the heads of the Warsaw Pact forces, the five Soviet services (Strategic Rocket Forces, Ground Forces, Troops of Air Defense, Air Forces, and Navy), and the Group of Soviet Forces, Germany. Heads of military districts are merely "commanders," as are the heads of the other Soviet forces in Europe.

Commanders in chief of Troops of the Far East have been:

July–October 1945	Marshal of the Soviet Union A. M. Vasilevskiy
May 1947–April 1953	Marshal of the Soviet Union R. Ya. Malinovskiy
December 1978–1980	General of the Army V. I. Petrov
December 1980–	General of the Army V. L. Govorov

Members of the Military Council of Troops of the Far East (as of 1 May 1984) are:

Commander in Chief	General of the Army V. L. Govorov (since 1980)
Chief, Political Administration	General Colonel M. I. Druzhinin (since 1979)
First Deputy Commander in Chief	General Colonel F. F. Krivda (?)
Chief of Staff	General Lieutenant Ye. A. Touzakov (?)

Military Districts

While the five services of the Soviet Armed Forces have many features in common with NATO forces, and the Soviet groups of forces abroad and fleets are organized in rather conventional patterns, it is difficult for Westerners to understand or even to ascertain the organization and role of the sixteen military districts. These organizations make it possible for the Soviet leadership to maintain military forces-in-being and reserve forces on a scale that would be impossible in Western nations.

As previously noted, all troops of the Ground Forces, except those stationed abroad, are assigned to commanders of military districts. The same is true for aircraft of frontal aviation and for troops of PVO, except for a limited number of interceptors and possible units involved with antispace and antiballistic defense.

Thus, commanders of military districts have under their direct control ground, air, and air defense units capable of waging combined arms operations. Two or more military districts could be combined to form a theater of military operations, or in some cases one military district might become a TVD. Forces in interior military districts could be moved out to form a front in a TVD, leaving behind cadres to reestablish the military district forces through mobilization of additional personnel.

In the event of a nuclear war in which communications and transportation were severely damaged or completely destroyed, military district commanders would be capable of continuing the war effort without higher direction. Their headquarters staffs are sufficiently large that they could direct all military activities within their districts.

Military district forces also support the Troops of the MVD and the KGB in the event of civil disorders. During the crop failures and the resultant food shortages throughout the USSR in 1963, for example, there was noticeable unrest among the population. In the Rostov area, regular Ground Forces units reportedly had to be called in to quell a riot, and in the process apparently a number of people were shot.[5]

The first military districts were formed in Imperial Russia in the period from 1862 to 1864, and historians of the Moscow Military District proudly trace their organization to that time. In 1918, soon after the Bolsheviks came to power, the following military districts were formed: Moscow, Yaroslavl, Orlov, White Sea, Ural, and Volga. These were primarily administrative and training organizations, charged with preparing reserves for front-line duty. Five more military districts were added in May 1918, and since then the number has varied.[6] When the Soviet Union entered World War II in 1941, there was a total of sixteen. Immediately after the war the districts were increased to thirty-three and then reduced to twenty-one in 1946. By the late 1950s they had been further reduced to fifteen. As a result of the increased tension with China and a buildup of Soviet military forces along that border, a new military district was created in 1969: the Central Asian Military District, with headquarters at Alma Ata.[7]

Military districts are geographical commands, and most military units and military installations, such as military schools, commissariats, and garrisons within the area embraced by a military district, are subordinate to its headquarters.[8] Exceptions to this subordination are units and installations of the Strategic Rocket Forces, the Moscow Air Defense District and certain other Air Defense installations, certain air armies and transport aviation components of the Air Forces, naval shore units, naval headquarters, and MVD and KBG troops and installations.

Essentially, the military districts are *training* and *housekeeping* components of the Soviet Armed Forces. In time of war, as already noted, those districts along the borders might become fronts or combined into TVDs. When the Soviet Union was invaded in 1941, the Baltic, Western, and Kiev "special" districts immediately became the Northwestern, Western, and Southwestern fronts. Two days later the Leningrad Military District became the Northern Front, and the next day the Southern Front was formed on the base of the Odessa Military District. Interior military districts formed 291 divisions and 94 brigades for the fronts between July and December 1941.

In the event of a future war those military districts in the interior of the nation would continue with training and housekeeping functions as in the past, but at a greatly accelerated pace. One of their most important tasks would be mobilization, and the machinery for this is carefully programmed. Soviet writers emphasize that "one of the most important tasks of the military districts is mobilization work."[9]

Training in the military districts is divided into many phases. First, the military district commander has certain responsibilities for *vne-voyskovaya podgotovka*—literally, "outside of troop training." This encompasses both premilitary and reserve training, as well as military training given to the population at large. The assistant commander for "outside of troop training" works with the Ministry of Education and other organizations to ensure that training standards are met both for youths going into military service and for the population as a whole.[10]

Within the Soviet Union there are 5 three-year military schools, 135 four- and five-year higher military schools, 17 military academies, and several other types of military training establishments (as of 1 May 1984). Since these schools are located within military districts, the districts' deputy commanders for military educational institutions provide certain supporting facilities. However, the overall direction of a school and its curriculum is provided by the particular service concerned, under cognizance of the General Staff.

The most important training function within the military district is the training of youths called up for their period of universal military obligation. Their total numbers run between 1.5 million and 1.8 million each year.[11] Generally, units within the military districts receive the young soldiers and provide for their training from the day they enter military service until they are discharged.

Since military districts are structured to become fronts in time of war, large-scale maneuvers may be conducted between two adjoining military districts, representing opposing military fronts. In the "Zapad-81" maneuvers, commanders of the Belorussian and Baltic military districts both took part. Units of the Baltic Fleet also participated in the two-sided exercise. In addition to senior Soviet officers, ministers of defense of many socialist countries were present.[12]

Organization of a Military District Headquarters

Some idea of the functions of a military district can be gained from an examination of a military district headquarters.[13] It should be noted that organizational charts of such staffs are never published in Soviet writings, and what is presented in Chart 17 has been compiled from a variety of sources over several years.

Orders are passed from the General Staff directly to the military council of each military district, in accordance with the Soviet principle of collective leadership.

The military council is the ruling body in the military district and is composed of the commander (chairman), his first deputy, the chief of the political administration, the chief of staff, and the local secretary of the Communist Party in the area. For example, N. N. Slyun'kov as Party secretary in Belorussia is also local Party secretary of the Military Council of the Belorussian Military District. In addition to the mandatory members of the military council, other deputy commanders in the headquarters sit on the council during discussions of matters of their functional concern or responsibility. When required, the deputy commander for combat training serves as a council member for any discussion involving his area of responsibility, and the commander of air forces (VVS) is a council member for any matter impacting upon frontal aviation.[14]

The size of the staff of a military district varies according to its size and importance. Thus internal military districts, such as the Siberian Military District with headquarters in Novosibirsk, may have fewer than five hundred people, while a more important one like Kiev will have several thousand. The commander of air forces and the senior deputy commanders and the chiefs of arms in certain military districts, especially in one of the border areas such as the Far Eastern Military District or the Central Asian Military District, may have full staffs.

By United States standards, the number of general officers assigned to the staffs of the military district headquarters is amazing. Commanders

Chart 17
Organization of a Typical Military District Headquarters

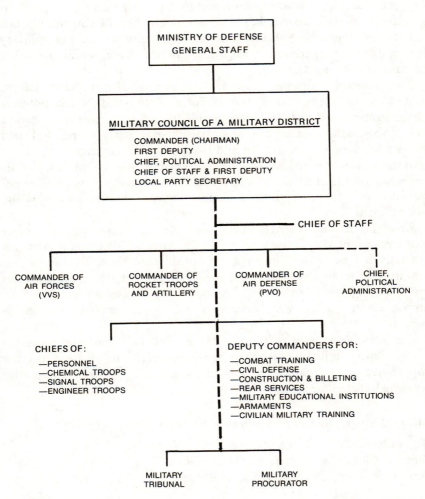

usually are general colonels (three stars), and quite a few are generals of the army (four stars). As a rule the first deputy commander is a general lieutenant (two stars), as are the chiefs of the political directorate, deputy chiefs of staff, and other senior officers, such as the chief of rocket and artillery troops. The commander of air forces often is a general colonel, but occasionally may be a general lieutenant. Many of the first deputies within the directorates are general majors (one star). Some of the larger military district headquarters may have as many as thirty-five general officers assigned, while in others there may be no more than twenty.[15] If the average number of general officers is twenty-five, then there are approximately four hundred general officers assigned to the sixteen military district headquarters alone. This of course does not include those general officers commanding units within the military districts, military garrison commanders of the larger cities, or other specialized commands.

Party control permeates the headquarters staff of a military district, as it does the entire Soviet Armed Forces. The chief of the political administration in the headquarters usually has a deputy chief for agitation and propaganda, another for organization and Party work, and still another for people's control. In addition, other directorates in the same headquarters have political sections. For example, the commander of air forces has a political department in his staff, as does the deputy commander for rear services, the deputy commander for construction and billeting, and so forth.

Since the military districts in the Soviet Union do not have any exact counterparts in the United States or in Europe, their very existence generally has been overlooked when considering the total combat capability of the Soviet Armed Forces. In actual fact, their organization and manning are major factors in the ability of the Soviet Union to survive under nuclear war conditions and to recover once the war is over.

Considerable secrecy surrounds the detailed functions and structure of the Soviet military districts. Some appreciation of their current importance can be gained by a brief look at their history and senior personnel (listed alphabetically):

Baltic Military District (Pribaltiyskiy Voyennyy Okrug—PribVO)

Hq Address: PribVO, Riga-Center, Ulitsa Merkelya, Dom 13
Officers' Club: Riga, Ulitsa Merkelya, Dom 13
Bookstore: Riga, Ulitsa Krysh'yana Barona, 11

The Baltic Military District was first formed in July 1940 when the USSR annexed the Baltic republics of Estonia, Latvia and Lithuania. During the war it became the Northwest Front, and it was reformed after the war from the Estonian, Latvian, and Lithuanian SSRs, and Kaliningrad Oblast.[16]

Members of the Military Council of the Baltic Military District (as of 1 May 1984) are:

Commander	General Lieutenant A. V. Betekhtin (since 1984)
Chief, Political Administration	General Colonel V. P. Novikov (since 1984)
First Deputy Commander	General Lieutenant A. A. Ivanov (since 1981)
Chief of Staff	General Lieutenant V. M. Kozhbakhteyev (since 1982)
Party Secretaries	A. Ye. Voss (Latvia), K. G. Vayno (Estonia)

Postwar commanders of the Baltic Military District were:

1945–1954	Marshal of the Soviet Union I. Kh. Bagramyan
1954–1958	General of the Army A. V. Gorbatov
1958–1959	General of the Army P. I. Batov
1959–1963	General of the Army I. I. Gusakovskiy
1963–1971	General of the Army G. I. Khetagurov
1971–1972	General Colonel V. L. Govorov
1972–1980	General Colonel A. M. Mayorov
1980–1984	General Colonel S. I. Postnikov*
1984–	General Lieutenant A. V. Betekhtin

Belorussian Military District (Belorusskiy Voyennyy Okrug—BVO)

Hq Address: Minsk-30, Ulitsa Krasnoarmeyskaya, Dom 3
Officers' Club: Minsk, Ulitsa Krasnoarmeyskaya, Dom 3
Bookstore: Minsk, Ulitsa Kuybysheva, Dom 10

What is now the Belorussian Military District began as the Minsk Military District, formed in November 1918. Within a short time it was renamed the Western Military District and then, in 1926, the Belorussian Military District. Its area was the scene of some of the bloodiest fighting of any district in the Soviet Union, during both the Civil War and World War II. It also has been an area for major exercises and maneuvers; the district acts as a sort of proving ground for testing the latest weaponry and tactics.

As Stalin became concerned with Hitler's growth in power in Europe, the Belorussian Military District was renamed the Belorussian Special

---

*General Postnikov was a member of the Bureau of the Central Committee of the Latvian Communist Party.

Military District (July 1938). Troops in the district were increased and provided with new equipment. In September 1939 the troops of the Belorussian Special Military District took part in the seizure of the eastern part of Poland, at which time the district became the Belorussian Front. The district headquarters was moved from Smolensk to Minsk after this, to be closer to the relocated Soviet border. On 11 July 1940 the district was renamed the Western Special Military District. Troops and equipment continued to pour into the area.

When the Germans invaded the Soviet Union in World War II, the district was transformed into the Western Front. In September 1941, when Hitler's troops occupied the territory, the front was abolished. The Belorussian Military District was reformed in October 1943, after Soviet forces cleared the Germans from the eastern part of the region. In the immediate reoccupation period, to expedite resettling and re-building, the area was divided temporarily into several districts, but consolidated again into one in February 1946. Thus, the Belorussian Military District encompasses the entire territory of the Belorussian Republic.

In the postwar era, the troops of the Belorussian Military District participated in major exercises such as Dnepr (1967), Dvina (1970), and Zapad-81. The district is the home of the Guards Motorized Rifle Rogachev Division named for the Supreme Soviet of the Belorussian SSR. The Belorussian Military District has also been commanded by some of the most famous names in Soviet military history: A. I. Kork, A. I. Yegorov, and I. P. Uborevich.[17]

Members of the Military Council of the Belorussian Military District (as of 1 May 1984) are:

Commander	General of the Army Ye. F. Ivanovskiy* (since 1980)
Chief, Political Administration	General Colonel A. V. Debalyuk (since 1970)
First Deputy Commander	General Lieutenant Tank Troops V. Osipov (since 1984)
Chief of Staff	Unidentified
Party Secretary	N. N. Slyun'kov (Belorussia)

---

*General Ivanovskiy is a member of the Bureau of the Central Committee of the Belorussian Communist Party.

Postwar commanders of the Belorussian Military District were:

1946–	Marshal of the Soviet Union S. K. Timoshenko
1946–1949	General Colonel S. G. Trofimenko
1949–1960	Marshal of the Soviet Union S. K. Timoshenko
1960–1961	General Colonel V. N. Komarov
1961–1964	General of the Army V. A. Pen'kovskiy
1964–1967	General Colonel S. S. Maryakhin
1967–1976	General of the Army I. M. Tret'yak
1976–1980	General Colonel Tanks M. M. Zaytsev
1980–	General of the Army Ye. F. Ivanovskiy

Carpathian Military District (*Prikarpatskiy Voyennyy Okrug—PrikVO*)

Hq Address: L'vov-8, Ulitsa Vatutina, Dom 12
Officers' Club: L'vov, Ulitsa Teatral'naya, Dom 22
Bookstore: L'vov, Prospekt Lenina, Dom 35; Ulitsa Belotserkovskaya, 2a

Formed in 1945 from the Fourth Ukrainian Front, this district is home of the Samaro-Ul'yanovsk, Berdichev, Zheleznaya Division. Its units have taken part in Vlatava (1966), Dnepr (1967), Neman (1968), Dvina (1970), and Karpaty (1977) exercises. They also took part in quelling the 1956 Hungarian Revolution and in invading Czechoslovakia in 1968. The area of the district encompasses Volyn, Rovno, Zhitomir, Vinnitsa, Khmel'nitskiy, Ternopol', L'vov, Ivano-Frankovsk, Chernovitsy, and Zakarpatskaya oblasts.[18]

Members of the Military Council of the Carpathian Military District (as of 1 May 1984) are:

Commander	General of the Army V. A. Belikov (since 1979)
Chief, Political Administration	General Lieutenant N. V. Goncharov (since 1984)
First Deputy Commander	General Lieutenant N. V. Kalinin (since 1983)
First Deputy Commander and Chief of Staff	General Lieutenant Tank Troops N. Grachev (since 1981)
Local Party Chief	V. F. Dobrik (L'vov)

Postwar commanders of the Carpathian Military District were:

1945–1946	Marshal of the Soviet Union A. I. Yeremenko
1946–1951	General of the Army K. N. Galitskiy

1951–1954	Marshal of the Soviet Union I. S. Konev
1955–1958	General of the Army P. I. Batov
1958–1964	General of the Army A. L. Getman
1964–1967	General of the Army P. N. Lashchenko
1967–1969	General Colonel V. Z. Bisyarin
1970–1973	General Colonel G. I. Obaturov
1973–1979	General of the Army V. I. Varennikov
1979–	General of the Army V. A. Belikov

Central Asian Military District (Sredneaziatskiy Voyennyy Okrug—SAVO)

Hq Address: Alma Ata-15, Ulitsa Auezova, Dom 125
Officers' Club: Unidentified
Bookstore: Alma Ata, Ulitsa Kirova, Dom 124

The early history of the Central Asian Military District has been discussed under the Turkestan Military District. The present Central Asian Military District, with headquarters in Alma Ata, was formed in August 1969, when tensions along the Sino-Soviet border increased. It includes Kazakh SSR, Kirgiz SSR and Tadzhik SSR.[19]

Members of the Military Council of the Central Asian Military District (as of 1 May 1984) are:

Commander	General of the Army D. T. Yazov* (since 1980)
Chief, Political Administration	General Lieutenant V. F. Arapov (since 1981)
First Deputy Commander	General Lieutenant Tank Troops N. M. Akhunov (since 1982)
Chief of Staff	Unidentified
Party Secretary	D. A. Kunayev (Kazakhstan)

Commanders of the Central Asian Military District were:

Dec 1969–1977	General of the Army N. G. Lyashchenko
Dec 1977–1980	General Colonel P. G. Lushev
Dec 1980–	General of the Army D. T. Yazov

Far Eastern Military District (Dal'nevostochnyy Voyennyy Okrug—DVO)

Hq Address: Khabarovsk-38, Ulitsa Serysheva, Dom 19
Officer's Club: Khabarovsk-38, Ulitsa Shevchenko, Dom 16

---

*General Yazov is a member of the Bureau of the Central Committee of the Kazakhstan Communist Party.

Bookstore: Khabarovsk, Ulitsa Serysheva, Dom 11, 42

The Far Eastern Military District is at the eastern extremity of Soviet territory, as far from Moscow as is Nigeria in Africa. This military district traces its origin to the East Siberian Military District, formed in 1918, which immediately became involved with the landing of U.S., Japanese, and other foreign troops in Vladivostok. These forces were sent to the area primarily in an effort to keep Russia in the war against Germany. Withdrawal of foreign troops began in the spring of 1919.

During the Civil War heavy fighting took place throughout the region. Following the defeat of Kolchak's army, the Far Eastern Republic was established in 1920, and troops formed into the People's Revolutionary Army. The People's Revolutionary Army was renamed the Special Red Banner Far Eastern Army. The Far Eastern Military District was first formed in May 1935 from the Special Red Banner Far Eastern Army. A few weeks later it was renamed the Special Red Banner Far Eastern Army, but the army functioned as a military district. The Special Red Banner Far Eastern Army became the Far Eastern Front in June 1938.

The pre–World War II history of the Far Eastern Military District is closely associated with the legendary V. K. Blyukher. In 1921 he was the minister of war of the Far Eastern Republic until it became part of the Russian Soviet Federated Socialist Republic (RSFSR) the following year. Two years later he was designated as the Soviet Union's chief military adviser to China, a position he retained until 1927. During this period he used the pseudonym General Galin and became one of Sun Yat-sen's principal advisers. From 1929 until 1938 he commanded the Special Red Banner Far Eastern Army. Blyukher's fame was such that Soviet authorities took great care to keep secret the news of his death when he was executed on Stalin's orders in 1938.

In the very last days of World War II the Soviet Union entered the war against Japan. The commander in chief of Soviet troops in that campaign was A. M. Vasilevskiy. At the end of the war three military districts in the Far East were created: The Transbaykal-Amur Military District, commanded by R. Ya. Malinovskiy; the Primorskiy Military District, commanded by K. A. Meretskov; and the Far Eastern Military District, headed by M. A. Purkayev.

In 1947 Malinovskiy was designated as commander in chief of the Troops of the Far East, with two key Soviet officers, S. S. Biryuzov and N. I. Krylov, assigned as commanders of the Primorskiy Military District and Far Eastern Military District, respectively. Within a month after the end of the Korean War, the Far Eastern Military District was reorganized to encompass what previously had been the Primorskiy Military District and the Transbaykal-Amur Military District.

Subordinate to the High Command of the Far East, the Far Eastern Military District remains one of the key Soviet defense areas. First-category (fully manned) Soviet divisions are located in the region. Geographically the Far Eastern Military District contains the Amur, Kamchatka, and Sakhalin oblasts, the Primorskaya and Khabarovsk krays and the Jewish Autonomous Oblast.[20] The commander of the military district is subordinate to the commander in chief, Troops of the Far East.

Members of the Military Council of the Far Eastern Military District (as of 1 May 1984) are:

Commander	General of the Army I. M. Tret'yak (since 1976)
Chief, Political Administration	General Lieutenant N. Kizyun (since 1984)
First Deputy Commander	General Lieutenant V. A. Vostrov (since 1983)
First Deputy Commander and Chief of Staff	General Lieutenant V. A. Patrikeyev (since 1981)
Local Party Secretary	A. K. Chernyy (Khabarovsk)

Postwar commanders of the Far Eastern Military District were:

Sep 1945	Transbaykal-Amur Military District—MSU R. Ya. Malinovskiy
	Primorskiy Military District—MSU K. A. Meretskov
	Far Eastern Military District—G/A M. A. Purkayev
May 1947	CINC Troops of the Far East—MSU R. Ya. Malinovskiy
	Primorskiy Military District—MSU S. S. Biryuzov
	Far Eastern Military District—MSU N. I. Krylov
Apr 1953–1956	Marshal of the Soviet Union R. Ya. Malinovskiy
Mar 1956–1961	General of the Army V. A. Pen'kovskiy
Aug 1961–1963	General of the Army Ya. G. Kreyzer
Dec 1963–1967	General of the Army I. G. Pavlovskiy
May 1967–1969	Marshal of Armored Troops O. A. Losik
May 1969–1972	General of the Army V. F. Tolubko

Apr 1972–1976   General of the Army V. I. Petrov
Jun 1976–   General of the Army I. M. Tret'yak

Kiev Military District (*Kiyevskiy Voyennyy Okrug—KVO*)

Hq Address: Kiev-21, Ulitsa Kirova, Dom 30/1
Officers' Club: Kiev, Ulitsa Kirova, Dom 30/1
Bookstore: Kiev, Ulitsa Krasnoarmeyskaya, Dom 43; Bul'var Lesi
   Ukrainki, 22

The Ukrainian Soviet Republic was established in December 1917, with military forces patterned after the Red Army in Soviet Russia. In March 1919, the Ukraine was divided into the Khar'kov and Kiev military districts. The Kiev Military District is of particular importance, since it encompasses some of the best agricultural lands in the Soviet Union, as well as many industrial centers.

During the period between wars this military district was commanded by a number of famous military leaders, including A. I. Yegorov, M. V. Frunze, I. E. Yakir, I. F. Fed'ko, S. K. Timoshenko, and G. K. Zhukov.

The territory of the Kiev Military District was overrun and suffered severely during the German invasion. On 10 September 1941, the district organization was disbanded, but it was reformed on 15 October 1943, as German troops were driven out. At the conclusion of World War II, a number of smaller districts were formed to expedite direct military assistance during the restoration work and resettlement of large segments of the population. Later these smaller units were reabsorbed.

In 1967 the Kiev Military District played a major role in the Dnepr military exercise. This exercise was studied closely in the United States, since it began with a nonnuclear phase and then later introduced the use of nuclear weapons. At its conclusion a major military parade was held in Kiev.

The Guards Motorized Rifle Sinel'nikovo-Budapest Red Banner, Orders of Suvorov and Bogdan Khmel'nitskiy Division named for V. I. Chapayev, is located in this military district. Additionally, many military schools are situated in the area.

The importance of the Kiev Military District, and of the Communist Party leadership in the Ukraine, can be seen from the names on the list of Kiev Military District commanders since the end of World War II. Nikita Khrushchev, first Party secretary of the Ukraine, may have helped in shaping the future military careers of the district's commanders.

The district encompasses Voroshilovgrad, Dnepropetrovsk, Donets, Kiev, Kirovograd, Poltava, Sumy, Khar'kov, Cherkassy, and Chernigov oblasts of the Ukrainian SSR.[21]

Members of the Military Council of the Kiev Military District (as of 1 May 1984) are:

Commander	General of the Army I. A. Gerasimov* (since 1975)
Chief, Political Administration	General Colonel V. S. Rodin (since 1982)
First Deputy Commander	General Lieutenant A. D. Fomin (since 1981)
First Deputy Commander and Chief of Staff	General Lieutenant A. K. Fedorov (since 1982)
Party Secretary	V. V. Shcherbitskiy (Ukraine)

Postwar commanders of the Kiev Military District were:

1945–1953	Marshal of the Soviet Union A. A. Grechko
1953–1960	Marshal of the Soviet Union V. I. Chuykov
Apr 1960–1965	Marshal of the Soviet Union P. K. Koshevoy
Jan 1965–1967	Marshal of the Soviet Union I. I. Yakubovskiy
Apr 1967–1969	Marshal of the Soviet Union V. G. Kulikov
Nov 1969–1976	General Colonel G. I. Salmanov
Aug 1976–	General of the Army I. A. Gerasimov

Leningrad Military District (*Leningradskiy Voyennyy Okrug—LVO*)

Hq Address: Leningrad, L-13, Pod'ezdnoy Per., Dom 4
Officers' Club: Leningrad, D. 28, Prospekt Liteynyy, Dom 20
Bookstore: Leningrad, Prospekt Nevskiy, 20

The Red Army officially came into being on 23 February 1918. In less than a month, on 20 March 1918, the Petrograd Military District was established, the first in the new Soviet state. Petrograd, formerly St. Petersburg, was then the capital. After Lenin's death in 1924, both the city and the military district took the name Leningrad. Among the commanders of this military district over the years have been such well-

---

*General Gerasimov is a member of the Bureau of the Central Committee of the Ukrainian Communist Party.

known Soviet military figures as B. M. Shaposhnikov, A. I. Kork, M. N. Tukhachevskiy, K. A. Meretskov, and S. K. Timoshenko.

During the 1939–1940 Winter War with Finland, the Leningrad Military District served as the primary headquarters for the combat forces. During World War II Leningrad was under siege for more than 900 days; the German blockade that was established in September 1941 was not completely broken until 27 January 1944.

In 1970, troops of the Leningrad Military District took part in the troop maneuvers Dvina, Okean, and Sever.

It may be of interest to note that G. V. Romanov, formerly the first secretary of the Party in Leningrad, became a Politburo member in 1976 and a member of the Secretariat in 1983. Born in 1923, he is one of the youngest members of the Soviet ruling hierarchy. If he was impressed by any specific member of the military council while serving on it, in all probability that individual will be in line for future promotions.

The area of the Leningrad Military District encompasses Leningrad, Murmansk, Arkhangel'sk, Vologda, Pskov, and Novgorod oblasts, as well as the Karelian Autonomous SSR.[22]

Members of the Military Council of the Leningrad Military District (since 1 May 1984) are:

Commander	General Colonel B. V. Snetkov (since 1981)
Chief, Political Administration	General Lieutenant V. S. Nechayev (since 1982)
First Deputy Commander	General Lieutenant V. N. Lobov (since 1981)
First Deputy Commander and Chief of Staff	Unidentified
Local Party Secretary	L. N. Zaykov (Leningrad)

Postwar commanders of the Leningrad Military District were:

1945–1946	Marshal of the Soviet Union L. A. Govorov
1946–1949	General Colonel D. N. Gusev
1949–1953	General of the Army A. A. Luchinskiy
1953–1957	Marshal of the Soviet Union M. V. Zakharov
1957–1960	Marshal of the Soviet Union N. I. Krylov
1960–1965	General of the Army M. I. Kazakov
Oct 1965–1967	Marshal of the Soviet Union S. L. Sokolov
Jun 1967–1972	General of the Army I. Ye. Shavrov

Feb 1973–1976   General of the Army A. I. Gribkov
Oct 1976–1981   General Colonel M. I. Sorokin
Dec 1981–   General Colonel B. V. Snetkov

The Moscow Military District (*Moskovskiy Voyennyy Okrug—MVO*)

Hq Address: Moscow, A-252, Chapayevskiy Per., Dom 14
Officers' Club: Moscow, E-250, Ulitsa Krasnokazarmennaya, Dom 1/1
Bookstore: Moscow, Danilovskaya Naberezhnaya, Dom 4-a; House of
  Military Books: Ulitsa Sadovaya-Spasskaya, Dom 3

Lenin moved the capital of Soviet Russia from Petrograd to Moscow in March 1918. In May of that year the Moscow Military District was reorganized and given as one of its primary tasks that of guarding the Party's headquarters in the Kremlin.

Since the Moscow Military District literally surrounds the power center of the Soviet Union, over the years it has been commanded by some of the most famous Soviet generals and marshals. Among them have been K. Ye. Voroshilov, B. M. Shaposhnikov, S. M. Budennyy, and, in postwar years, Marshals of the Soviet Union K. A. Meretskov, K. S. Moskalenko, and N. I. Krylov.

Because of its location the Moscow Military District is charged with functions of a type not found elsewhere. For example, this district is primarily responsible for the military hardware parades through Red Square each year. Even when Moscow was under attack in 1941, the traditional November military parade was held. Certain other military districts hold military parades on 7 November, but their parades do not compare with the spectacle in Red Square. Before 1970 these parades were held in May and November. Since then, the military part of the May Day Parade has been dropped, and only on the seventh of November do the missiles, tanks, and other equipment roll through Red Square and then on by the U.S. Embassy on the Sadovoye Koltso to make sure that sufficient details can be observed to impress Washington.

Two of the most famous Soviet divisions—the Guards Taman', Red Banner, Order of Suvorov, Motorized Rifle Division named for M. I. Kalinin and the Guards Kantemirov, Order of Lenin, Red Banner, Tank Division—are located in the Moscow Military District. Foreign military visitors from both socialist and capitalist nations are frequently given a carefully staged visit to the Taman' Division.

Members of the Military Council of the Moscow Military District (as of 1 May 1984) are:

Commander	General of the Army P. G. Lushev (since 1980)
Chief, Political Administration	General Colonel I. P. Repin (since 1982)
First Deputy Commander	General Lieutenant B. Plotin (since 1984)
First Deputy Commander and Chief of Staff	Unidentified
Party Secretary	V. I. Konotop (Moscow)

The Moscow Military District has changed its borders several times over the years. At present, it encompasses the city of Moscow and Belgorod, Bryansk, Vladimir, Voronezh, Gor'kyy, Ivanovo, Kalinin, Kaluga, Kostroma, Kursk, Lipetsk, Moscow, Orel, Ryazan, Smolensk, Tambov, Tula, and Yaroslavl' oblasts.[23]

Postwar commanders of the Moscow Military District were:

1941–1947	General Colonel P. A. Artem'yev
1947–1949	Marshal of the Soviet Union K. A. Meretskov
1949–1953	General Colonel P. A. Artem'yev
1953–1960	Marshal of the Soviet Union K. S. Moskalenko
Oct 1960–1963	Marshal of the Soviet Union N. I. Krylov
Apr 1963–1968	General of the Army A. P. Beloborodov
Jun 1968–1972	General of the Army Ye. F. Ivanovskiy
Jul 1972–1980	General of the Army V. L. Govorov
1980–	General of the Army P. G. Lushev

North Caucasus Military District (Severo-Kavkazskiy Voyennyy Okrug—SKVO)

Hq Address: Rostov-on-the-Don-18, Ulitsa Tekucheva, Dom 135
Officers' Club: Rostov-on-the-Don, Prospekt Budennovskiy, Dom 59
Bookstore: Rostov-on-the-Don, Prospekt Budennovskiy, Dom 76

The North Caucasus Military District was formed in 1918. The territory of the district was almost entirely occupied by German troops in World War II. Abolished in 1942, it thereby became part of the Transcaucasus Front. In June 1943, as enemy troops retreated, it was reformed. Several military districts were formed from it at the end of the war—notably, the Kuban, Don and Stavropol'—but by 1953, all were combined into the North Caucasus Military District. Covered by the district are Krasnodar and Stavropol' krays; Dagestan, Kabardino-Balkar, Kalmyk, Severo-Osetin, and Checheno-Ingush Autonomous SSRs; and Astrakhan, Volgograd, and Rostov oblasts.[24]

Members of the Military Council of the North Caucasus Military District (as of 1 May 1984) are:

Commander	General Colonel V. K. Meretskov (since 1980)
Chief, Political Administration	General Major Ye. Aunapu (since 1984)
First Deputy Commander	General Lieutenant L. S. Shustko (since 1984)
Chief of Staff	General Lieutenant G. A. Andresyan (since 1983)
Local Party Secretary	I. A. Bondarenko (Rostov)

Postwar commanders of the North Caucasus Military District were:

1946–1948	General Colonel P. A. Belov
1948–1949	General Colonel V. Z. Romanovskiy
1949–1953	General Colonel F. G. Trofimenko
1953–	General Colonel N. P. Pukhov
1953–1958	Marshal of the Soviet Union A. I. Yeremenko
1958–1968	General of the Army I. A. Pliyev
1968–1970	General Colonel A. T. Altunin
1970–1976	General Colonel D. I. Litovtsev
1976–1979	General Colonel V. A. Belikov
1979–1980	General Colonel S. I. Postnikov
1980–	General Colonel V. K. Meretskov

Odessa Military District (Odesskiy Voyennyy Okrug—OdVO)

Hq Address: Odessa-30, Ulitsa Pirogovskaya, Dom 11
Officers' Club: Odessa A-12, Ulitsa Pirogovskaya, Dom 7/9
Bookstore: Odessa, Deribasovskaya, Dom 13; Ulitsa Perekopskoy Divizii Dom 16/6

First formed in 1919, the Odessa Military District was the site of active fighting during the Civil War. After four months, however, it was disbanded. It was not until 1939, after Moldavia was annexed by the Soviet Union, that the Odessa Military District again came into being. The area suffered acutely at the beginning of the German invasion, and in September 1941 it was again disbanded. In March 1944, it came to life once more. Since 1956, the district has encompassed Moldavian SSR, and Odessa, Nikolayev, Kherson, Zaporozh'ye, and Crimean oblasts of the Ukrainian SSR.[25]

Members of the Military Council of the Odessa Military District (as of 1 May 1984) are:

Commander	General Colonel A. S. Yelagin (since 1982)
Chief, Political Administration	General Lieutenant V. Plekhanov (since 1983)
First Deputy Commander	General Lieutenant A. N. Zaytsev (since 1981)
Chief of Staff	Unidentified
Local Party Secretary	N. K. Kirichenko (Odessa)

Postwar commanders of the Odessa Military District were:

1946–1948	Marshal of the Soviet Union G. K. Zhukov
1948–1951	General Colonel N. P. Pukhov
1951–1954	General Colonel K. N. Galitskiy
1954–1959	General of the Army A. I. Radziyevskiy
1959–1967	Chief Marshal Armored Troops A. Kh. Babadzhanyan
1967–1968	General Colonel M. V. Lugovtsev
1968–1974	General Colonel A. G. Shurupov
1974–1982	General Colonel I. M. Voloshin
1982–	General Colonel A. S. Yelagin

Siberian Military District (*Sibirskiy Voyennyy Okrug—SibVO*)

Hq Address: Novosibirsk-91, Prospekt Krasnyy, Dom 63
Officers' Club: Novosibirsk, Prospekt Krasnyy, Dom 65
Bookstore: Novosibirsk, Prospekt Krasnyy, Dom 61; Ulitsa Gogolya, 4

Started as the Omsk Military District in 1919, it soon became the Western Siberian Military District. In 1924, it was named the Siberian Military District. The Twenty-fourth Army, formed in the district, assisted in the battles of Moscow, Stalingrad, Kursk, and beyond. In 1945, it was again named the Western Siberian Military District, as part of its area was given to the newly formed Eastern Siberian Military District. Restored in 1953, it was renamed the Siberian Military District in 1956. The district now encompasses Altay and Krasnoyarsk krays; Kemerovo, Novosibirsk, Omsk, Tomsk, Tyumen oblasts; and Tuvin Autonomous SSR.[26]

Members of the Military Council of the Siberian Military District (as of 1 May 1984) are:

Commander	General Colonel N. I. Popov (since 1981)
Chief, Political Administration	General Lieutenant V. G. Samoylenko (since 1982)
First Deputy Commander	General Lieutenant I. P. Volkhonskiy (since 1980)
First Deputy Commander and Chief of Staff	General Lieutenant Yu. Petrov (since 1984)
Local Party Secretary	A. P. Filatov (Novosibirsk)

Postwar commanders of the Siberian Military District were:

(West Siberian)

1946–1953	Marshal of the Soviet Union A. I. Yeremenko
1953–1957	General Colonel N. P. Pukhov

(Siberian)

1957–1960	Marshal of the Soviet Union P. K. Koshevoy
1960–1964	General Colonel G. V. Baklanov
1964–1968	General of the Army S. P. Ivanov
1968–1969	General of the Army V. F. Tolubko
1969–1979	General Colonel M. G. Khomulo
1979–1981	General Colonel B. V. Snetkov
1981–	General Colonel N. I. Popov

Transbaykal Military District (*Zabaykal'skiy Voyennyy Okrug—ZabVO*)

Hq Address: Chita-Center, Ulitsa Lenina, Dom 86
Officers' Club: Chita-2, Ulitsa Lenina, Dom 86
Bookstore: Chita, Ulitsa Lenina, Dom 111-a

The Transbaykal Military District was formed in 1935 on the base of the Transbaykal Group of the Special Red Banner Far Eastern Army (see Far Eastern Military District for further details). The troops of the Transbaykal Military District went to the aid of Mongolian forces in 1939 and took part in the battle of Khal'khan Gol. At the beginning of the war, the district became the Transbaykal front. After the war, this front became the Transbaykal-Amur Military District; it was renamed the Transbaykal Military District in 1947.

Along with the Far Eastern Military District, the Transbaykal Military District is part of the High Command of the Far East, established in the late 1970s.

Chita and Irkutsk oblasts and Buryat-Mongolian and Yakutsk Autonomous SSRs have been part of the Transbaykal Military District since 1953.[27]

Members of the Military Council of the Transbaykal Military District (as of 1 May 1984) are:

Commander	General Colonel S. I. Postnikov (since 1984)
Chief, Political Administration	General Lieutenant V. M. Lomov (since 1980)
First Deputy Commander	General Lieutenant P. Lidyayev (since 1983)
Chief of Staff	General Colonel V. N. Verevkin-Rakhal'skiy (since 1981)
Local Party Secretaries	M. I. Matafonov (Chita), V. Sitnikov (Irkutsk)

Postwar commanders of the Transbaykal Military District were:

1947–1951	General Colonel K. A. Koroteyev
1951–1953	General Colonel D. N. Gusev
1953–1956	General Colonel Ye. G. Trotsenko
1956–1958	General of the Army D. D. Lelyushenko
1958–1960	General of the Army Ya. G. Kreyzer
1960–1966	General Colonel D. F. Alekseyev
1966–1979	General of the Army P. A. Belik
1979–1984	General of the Army G. I. Salmanov
1984–	General Colonel S. I. Postnikov

Transcaucasus Military District (*Zakavkazskiy Voyennyy Okrug—ZakVO*)

Hq Address: Tbilisi-4, Ulitsa Dzneladze, Dom 46
Officers' Club: Tbilisi, Prospekt Rustaveli, Dom 16
Bookstore: Tbilisi, Pl. Lenina, Dom 4

The Transcaucasus Military District encompasses the three Soviet republics of Azerbaydzhan, Armenia, and Georgia. These three republics are successors to the independent Transcaucasus Republic, which was formed in 1917, immediately following the Russian Revolution. In 1921 the Eleventh Army conquered the Transcaucasus area, which was then broken into its present structure. For its successes, this army was renamed the Caucasus Red Banner Army.

Later, this army again was used in controlling local populations, in putting down uprisings in Georgia in 1924, and in Azerbaydzhan in the early 1930s, when the peasants revolted against forced collectivization.

In June 1935 the Transcaucasus Military District was formed from the area occupied by the Eleventh Army. Immediately after World War II, during the period of territorial restoration and relocation of those groups displaced by the war, the area was divided into the Tbilisi and Baku military districts. In May 1946 the area was reestablished as one military district with headquarters in Tbilisi.[28]

Some of the most famous figures of the early Bolshevik revolution served with the Red Army in the Transcaucasus area in the early 1920s, including M. N. Tukhachevskiy, Sergo Ordzhonikidze, and S. M. Kirov. Other equally famous leaders served as early military district commanders, among them A. I. Yegorov, A. I. Kork, and I. F. Fed'ko. Most of the early commanders suffered the same fate—death by order of Stalin.

Members of the Military Council of the Transcaucasus Military District (as of 1 May 1984) are:

Commander	General Colonel V. M. Arkhipov* (since 1983)
Chief, Political Administration	General Lieutenant A. I. Shirinkin (since 1980)
First Deputy Commander	General Lieutenant M. M. Sotskov (since 1983)
Chief of Staff	General Colonel V. K. Kirilyuk (since 1979)
Party Secretary	E. A. Shevardnadze (Georgia)

Postwar commanders of the Transcaucasus Military District were:

1946–1947	General of the Army I. I. Maslennikov
1947–1949	Marshal of the Soviet Union F. I. Tolbukhin (died 1949)
1950–1954	General of the Army A. I. Antonov
1954–1957	General of the Army I. I. Fedyuninskiy

---

*Arkhipov's predecessor was a member of the Bureau of the Central Committee of the Georgian Communist Party. Arkhipov will soon take his place.

Oct 1957–1958	Marshal of the Soviet Union K. K. Rokossovskiy
Jan 1958–1961	General of the Army K. N. Galitskiy
May 1961–1968	General of the Army A. T. Stuchenko
1968–1971	General of the Army S. K. Kurkotkin
Oct 1971–1978	General Colonel P. V. Mel'nikov
Feb 1978–1983	General Colonel O. F. Kulishev
1983–	General Colonel V. M. Arkhipov

Turkestan Military District (Turkestan Voyennyy Okrug—TurkVO)

Hq Address: TurkVO, Tashkent-5, Ulitsa Oktyabr'skoy Revolyutsii, Dom 28
Officers' Club: Tashkent, Ulitsa Engel'sa, Dom 13
Bookstore: Tashkent-77, Shosse Lunacharskovo, Dom 61

Until 1969, the Turkestan Military District encompassed the five central Asian republics. Most of the area is desert and steppes, with great mountainous areas in the south and southeast. During the Civil War there were many battles in the area of the Turkestan Autonomous Soviet Socialist Republic, as it was called at the time. In 1919 M. V. Frunze, at the age of 35, gained fame as commander of the Turkestan front. By 1930 the area was divided into the Central Asian Military District (Uzbek, Tadzhik, Turkmen, and Kirgiz SSRs) and the Military Commissariat of Kazakh ASSR located in Alma Ata, which included Kazakh ASSR and Kara-Kalpak Autonomous Oblast.

World War II brought great changes to central Asia. Three hundred factories were evacuated to the Uzbek Republic alone. Many military schools were set up temporarily in the area. In September 1941 Soviet troops from central Asia and the Transcaucasus Military District moved into Teheran to protect the southern flanks of the Soviet Union. (After the end of World War II the U.S. and British governments had to pressure Stalin into removing his troops.)

In the immediate postwar period, the Turkestan Military District took in the territories of Turkmen, Uzbek, Tadzhik, and Kirgiz SSRs. Subsequently, Kazakh SSR was added. Border incidents continually erupted during the late 1960s along the area facing China, and so in August 1969 the Central Asian Military District, with headquarters in Alma Ata, was reformed. The Turkestan Military District, now comprising the Uzbek and Turkmen SSRs, continues to have its headquarters in Tashkent.[29]

Members of the Military Council of the Turkestan Military District (as of 1 May 1984) are:

Commander	General of the Army Yu. P. Maksimov* (since 1978)
Chief, Political Administration	General Lieutenant N. A. Moiseyev (since 1982)
First Deputy Commander	General Lieutenant Yu. V. Tukharinov (since 1979)
Chief of Staff	General Lieutenant G. F. Krivosheyev (since 1981)
Party Secretary**	M. G. Gapurov (Turkmen), I. B. Usmankhodzhayev (Uzbek)

Postwar commanders of the Turkestan Military District were:

1945–1952	General of the Army I. Ye. Petrov
1952–1953	General Lieutenant A. I. Radziyevskiy
1953–1957	General of the Army A. A. Luchinskiy
1957–1965	General of the Army I. I. Fedyuninskiy
1965–1969	General Colonel N. G. Lyashchenko
1969–1978	General Colonel S. Ye. Belonozhko
1978–	General Colonel Yu. P. Maksimov

Ural Military District (*Ural'skiy Voyennyy Okrug—UrVO*)

Hq Address: Sverdlovsk, K-75, Ulitsa Pervomayskaya, Dom 27
Officers' Club: Sverdlovsk, Ulitsa Pervomayskaya, Dom 27
Bookstore: Sverdlovsk, Ulitsa Lenina 101

The Ural Military District was created by a decree signed on 4 May 1918 by V. I. Lenin. After the Civil War, with the introduction of territorial militia, the Ural Military District was abolished. It was formed again in 1935.

In the late 1930s this military district was a major supply and training base for supporting Soviet fighting in the Far East. During World War II it served the same function with respect to Soviet troops fighting the invading Germans.

The most famous of the postwar district commanders was Marshal of the Soviet Union G. K. Zhukov. Between 1948 and 1953 Zhukov

---

*General Maksimov is a member of the Bureau of the Central Committee of the Uzbekistan Communist Party.
**First Secretary of the Uzbekistan Communist Party Sh. R. Rashidov died in October 1983. Rashidov was a candidate member of the Politburo of the CPSU.

was "exiled" in the Urals, largely because of his popularity both in the Soviet Union and in the West.

On May Day in 1960, troops of the Ural Military District made history by shooting down the U.S. U-2 aircraft piloted by Gary Powers. According to a book on the history of the Ural Military District, this event made such an impression on the youth of that area that several thousand Komsomol members asked to join the Communist Party at the time of the 1962 Cuban missile crisis, and many volunteered to go to Cuba to fight "U.S. imperialism."[30]

Sverdlovsk, where the Ural Military District headquarters is located, is a "closed" city, and foreigners are forbidden to visit it. The district includes Komi and Udmurt Autonomous SSRs and Kirov, Kurgan, Perm', Sverdlovsk, and Chelyabinsk oblasts.

Members of the Military Council of the Ural Military District (as of 1 May 1984) are:

Commander	General Colonel I. A. Gashkov (since 1984)
Chief, Political Administration	General Lieutenant V. A. Sharygin (since 1982)
First Deputy Commander	General Lieutenant I. Chelombeyev (since 1984)
Chief of Staff	General Lieutenant Ye. A. Kuznetsov (since 1978)
Local Party Secretary	B. N. Yel'tsin (Sverdlovsk)

Postwar commanders of the Ural Military District were:

Feb 1945–1948	General Colonel F. I. Kuznetsov
Feb 1948–1953	Marshal of the Soviet Union G. K. Zhukov
May 1953–1956	General of the Army M. I. Kazakov
1956–1958	General of the Army N. I. Krylov
1958–1960	General Colonel D. D. Lelyushenko
1960–1961	General Colonel Ya. G. Kreyzer
1961–1965	General Colonel I. V. Tutarinov
Oct 1965–1970	General Lieutenant A. A. Yegorovskiy
May 1970–1980	General Lieutenant N. K. Sil'chenko
May 1980–1983	General Colonel M. A. Tyagunov
Jan 1984–	General Colonel I. A. Gashkov

Volga Military District (*Privolzhskiy Voyennyy Okrug—PriVO*)

Hq Address: Kuybyshev, Ulitsa Chapayevskaya, 180
Officers' Club: Kuybyshev, Ulitsa Rabochaya, Dom 7
Bookstore: Kuybyshev, Ulitsa Kuybyshevskaya, 91

Formed in 1918, this district experienced fierce fighting on its territory during the Civil War. Later, such leading military figures as V. K. Blyukher, V. V. Kuybyshev, M. N. Tukhachevskiy, M. V. Frunze, and V. I. Chapayev helped form the district. After the Civil War, it was the base from which both the Kronstadt Uprising and the Basmachi revolt (1921) were crushed (1921–early 1930s). During World War II, Kuybyshev served as the alternate capital when Moscow was under attack in 1941. One hundred and forty-five higher and secondary military schools were evacuated to the Volga Military District as western areas were occupied. Today, Kuybyshev, Orenburg, Saratov, Ul'yanovsk, and Penza oblasts, and Tatar, Bashkir, Mary, Mordvinian and Chuvash Autonomous SSRs make up the Volga Military District.[31]

Members of the Military Council of the Volga Military District (as of 1 May 1984) are:

Commander	General Colonel A. Ya. Ryakhov (since 1981)
Chief, Political Administration	General Lieutenant G. A. Gromov (since 1982)
First Deputy Commander	General Lieutenant M. Polishchuk (since 1981)
Chief of Staff	General Lieutenant V. Zhdanov (since 1983)
Local Party Secretary	Ye. F. Murav'yev (Kuybyshev)

Postwar commanders of the Volga Military District were:

1946–1950	General Colonel V. A. Yushkevich
1950–1953	General Lieutenant G. N. Perekrestov
1953–1957	General Colonel V. I. Kuznetsov
1957–1960	General Colonel V. N. Komarov
1960–1961	General Colonel A. T. Stuchenko
1961–1963	General of the Army I. G. Pavlovskiy
1963–1965	General of the Army N. G. Lyashchenko
1965–1968	Marshal of the Soviet Union N. V. Ogarkov
1968–1971	General Colonel A. M. Parshikov
1971–1975	General Colonel Yu. A. Naumenko

1975–1977	General Colonel P. G. Lushev
1977–1981	General Colonel V. N. Konchits
1981–	General Colonel A. Ya. Ryakhov

Groups of Forces Abroad

Soviet "groups of forces abroad" are part of the Warsaw Pact forces. They maintain a military presence to ensure that the Communist-led nations of Eastern Europe remain in the Soviet orbit and also are a forward military force opposing NATO.

Of the estimated thirty-one Soviet divisions in Eastern Europe, two tank divisions are believed to be in Poland (the Northern Group of Forces), two tank divisions and two motorized rifle divisions in Hungary (Southern Group of Forces), and two tank and three motorized rifle divisions in Czechoslovakia (Central Group of Forces). The remaining twenty divisions are in the Soviet Group of Forces, Germany, ten of which are tank, nine motorized rifle, and one artillery. These forces provide an offensive capability that is unequaled in any other Eastern European sector. Air support for Eastern Europe is provided by four tactical air armies, containing a total of approximately 2,000 aircraft.[32]

Only the Soviet Group of Forces, Germany, will be discussed in detail. Soviet sources provide but limited data on the forces located in the other nations of Eastern Europe. Some understanding of the origins and nature of the Warsaw Pact is an essential prerequisite to analyzing the total Soviet Armed Forces structure.

Origins and Nature of the Warsaw Pact

The presence of Soviet forces in Eastern Europe is a direct outgrowth of World War II. The nations overrun by the Red Army were forced to accept Soviet rule, and in the 1940s the Kremlin established puppet Communist regimes in all of the Eastern European nations. During this period (as described in the Orwellian language of Soviet pronouncements), "agreements of friendship, cooperation, and mutual aid"[33] were signed with Albania, Czechoslovakia, Poland, Rumania, Hungary, and Bulgaria. Troops remained after the war in the last four nations, as well as in East Germany. Only Yugoslavia—which had contributed substantially to its own liberation—retained a measure of autonomy and in 1947 asserted its independence.

After Stalin's death in 1953, Eastern Europe became restive. In June of that year major strikes occurred in Czechoslovakia, with Czech and U.S. flags being flown in Prague. Some rioting took place, but it was controlled by Czech police. Rioting was more serious in East Germany, and local police were overwhelmed. Soviet occupation forces declared martial law, and tank crews fired into crowds. Several hundred East Germans were killed then and over a hundred later executed. Feelings of the local population were such that General V. I. Chuykov, then commander in chief of Soviet forces in East Germany, was withdrawn after the uprising was quelled; he was replaced by General A. A. Grechko.

The Warsaw Pact, or Pact of Mutual Assistance and Unified Command, was signed in May 1955.[34] This formal organization did not actually change any existing situation, since bilateral agreements previously signed between Moscow and individual countries already had established the basis for a Soviet military presence and control over their armed forces. An organizational structure for the Warsaw Pact forces, modeled after NATO, was established for formal display. A senior body, the Political Consultative Committee (PKK), was formed,[35] on which each member nation is represented. A Soviet marshal was designated to lead the "unified military forces," a practice still followed.

After Nikita Khrushchev related Stalin's crimes in a secret speech to the Twentieth Party Congress in February 1956, doubts about the validity and capability of the Soviet Union's top Party leadership began to spread throughout Eastern Europe. During the same period Chou En-lai was traveling in the area, calling for other nations to heed the example that China had set—to follow one of the many roads to socialism—"to let a hundred flowers bloom."

In June 1956, Poland appeared to be taking the lead in resisting the controls imposed by the Soviet Union. In particular, many leading Poles resented the fact that the Polish Armed Forces had been commanded since 1949 by Marshal of the Soviet Union K. K. Rokossovskiy (although he was given the rank of marshal of Poland), who spoke Polish only with a heavy accent. Although Rokossovskiy was of Polish origin, he was raised in Russia, joined the Red Guard in 1917, and thereafter served the Red Army. As unrest continued in the country, it was rumored that Rokossovskiy had made preparations to take control of the government and had drawn up a list of names of those to be arrested.[36] Under the leadership of A. Gomulka, the Polish Communist Party came to an agreement with Moscow. Polish leaders were given a somewhat greater voice in the management of their own affairs, and Rokossovskiy and his senior staff of "Polish-Russian" generals left the country.

In Hungary the situation was more serious. On 23 October 1956, a major uprising began. Soviet tanks and armored cars moved in and joined in battle against Hungarian civilians. Initially the Soviets had to withdraw, but they returned in force. Despite their bravery, Hungarian fighters could not stand against Soviet armor. A new government was formed, and for a brief period the rebellion appeared to have quieted. However, the newly formed government still wanted freedom and rights that Moscow was unwilling to grant. Soviet military forces again were used to oust this government and to create a puppet nation completely dominated by the Soviet Union. Approximately 3,000 Hungarians were killed, most of them by Soviet troops.[37]

The continuing need for a Soviet military presence in Eastern Europe was demonstrated again in 1968. Party leaders in Czechoslovakia sought to gain freedoms for that nation, which in theory they already possessed. Under the cover of maneuvers in which Polish, East German, and other Warsaw Pact forces, except Rumania, participated, Soviet troops moved into Prague in much the same manner as they had operated in Budapest in the previous decade. Against the massive military forces deployed, the Czech people recognized that resistance was useless.

Labor unrest flared in Poland in the summer of 1980. An independent labor union, Solidarity, was approved in November 1980. Shortages and a declining economy led to the declaration of martial law in December 1981. Solidarity was outlawed in 1982 as Poland continued to be a rigid police state. Conditions eased somewhat in 1983 when martial law was lifted. Many of the provisions of martial law, however, remain in disguised forms.

Despite the underlying hostility of the majority of people in Eastern European nations under Soviet control, the non-Soviet forces of the Warsaw Pact could be effective in the event of a conflict with NATO. Eastern European troops, including most of the senior officers, are trained in the Soviet Union, and weapons are standardized with those of the Soviet forces. Additionally, "experienced professor-instructor staffs from Soviet military academies are being sent [to the Pact nations], and mutual exchanges of delegations of military academies and schools are being conducted."[38]

The Structure of the Warsaw Pact

The Political Consultative Committee (PKK) theoretically heads the Warsaw Pact structure. It "works out questions of international relations which affect Pact members, examines problems connected with strengthening their defense capability and fulfilling their obligations in joint defense."[39] In 1969 a Committee of Ministers of Defense was formed to develop agreed recommendations and proposals.[40] The Military Council of the United Armed Forces of the Warsaw Pact meets in various cities and appears to serve protocol rather than any substantive purpose. A Technical Committee is concerned with standardization of weapons and equipment.

Warsaw Pact forces have conducted exercises and maneuvers, of which the following have been publicized:[41]

Burya	Oct 1961	Major operational command-staff exercise (GDR, Poland, Czech., western USSR)
		Exercise leader: A. A. Grechko (USSR)
Quartet	Sep 1963	Maneuver (GDR, Poland, USSR, Czech.); in GDR
		Maneuver leader: G. Goffman (GDR)
October Storm	Oct 1965	Exercise (GDR, Poland, USSR, Czech.); in GDR
Vltava	Sep 1966	Exercise (Hungary, USSR, Czech.); in Czechoslovakia
Manevr	June 1967	Exercise (Hungary, USSR, Czech.); in Hungary and Czechoslovakia
Rodopy	Aug 1967	Exercise (Bulgaria, Rumania, USSR); in Bulgaria and Black Sea (troops and fleets)
		Exercise leader: D. Dzhurov (Bulgaria)
Shumava	June 1968	Command-staff exercise (GDR, Poland, USSR, Czech., Hungary)
		Exercise leader: I. I. Yakubovskiy (USSR)
Neman	Jul–Aug 1968	Exercise (GDR, Poland, USSR)
		Ended with invasion of Czechoslovakia
Vesna-69	Apr 1969	Exercise (GDR, Poland, USSR, Czech.)
Oder-Neisse	Sep 1969	Exercise (GDR, Poland, USSR, Czech.); in Poland
		Exercise leader: V. Yaruzel'skiy (Poland)

Brothers in Arms	Oct 1970	Exercise (Staff and troops of ground forces, air forces, and navies of all Warsaw Pact countries); in GDR Exercise leader: G. Goffman (GDR)
Visla-El'ba-71	July 1971	Rear services exercise (GDR, Poland, USSR)
Opal-71	Aug 1971	Exercise (Hungary, USSR, Czech.); in Hungary and Czechoslovakia
Shchit-72	Sep 1972	Exercise (Hungary, GDR, Poland, USSR, Czech.); in Czechoslovakia
Leto-74	June 1974	Exercise (Poland, Soviet troops in Poland)
Shchit-76	Sep 1976	Exercise (Warsaw Pact Forces); in Poland Exercise leader: V. Yaruzel'skiy (Poland)
Soyuz-77	Mar 1977	Exercise (Hungary, USSR, Czech.); in Hungary and Czechoslovakia
Druzhba-79	Feb 1979	Exercise (USSR, Czech.); in Czechoslovakia
Shchit-79	May 1979	Exercise (Bulgaria, Hungary, USSR, Czech.; Romania, staff only); in Hungary Exercise leader: L. Tsinege (Hungary)
Brothers in Arms	Sep 1980	Exercise (GDR, Bulgaria, Hungary, Poland, USSR, Czech.) Exercise leader: G. Goffman (GDR)
Soyuz-81	Mar 1981	Exercise (Poland, GDR, USSR, Czech.) Exercise leader: V. G. Kulikov (USSR)
Shchit-82	Sep 1982	Exercise (in Bulgaria) Exercise leader: D. Dzhurov (Bulgaria)

The following Warsaw Pact air defense exercises have also been publicized:

Zenith-69	1969	Exercise leader: P. F. Batitskiy (USSR)
Zenith-70	1970	Exercise leader: P. F. Batitskiy (USSR)
PVO Exercise	1973	Exercise leader: P. F. Batitskiy (USSR)
PVO Exercise	1974	Exercise leader: P. F. Batitskiy (USSR)
PVO Exercises to 1979	1979	Exercise leaders: not given

Warsaw Pact naval exercises included:

Sever	July 1968	Exercise (USSR, Poland, GDR)
Black Sea Exercise	1972	Operational-tactical exercise
Baltic Sea Exercise	1974	Operational-tactical exercise

The Staff of the United Armed Forces (OVS) of the Warsaw Pact has its headquarters in Moscow. All commanders in chief of the Warsaw Pact forces have been Soviet marshals, and the chief of staff, also a Soviet officer, wears a second hat as first deputy chief of the Soviet General Staff. United Armed Forces of the Warsaw Pact are composed of "troop formations and units, control agencies and rear services, ground, air and naval forces, and air defense troops."[42] This organization is shown in Chart 18.

In addition to the formal Warsaw Pact structure, the Soviet Ministry of Defense has Soviet "representatives" to the armed forces of each of the Warsaw Pact nations. In time of war these officers could become "representatives" of Stavka and directly pass orders from the Kremlin. (See Chart 19.)

The following have served as commanders in chief of the Warsaw Pact Forces:

Marshal of the Soviet Union I. S. Konev	1955-Jun 1960
Marshal of the Soviet Union A. A. Grechko	Jun 1960-Jul 1967
Marshal of the Soviet Union I. I. Yakubovskiy	Jul 1967-Dec 1976
Marshal of the Soviet Union V. G. Kulikov	Dec 1976-

Chart 18
United Armed Forces of the Warsaw Pact

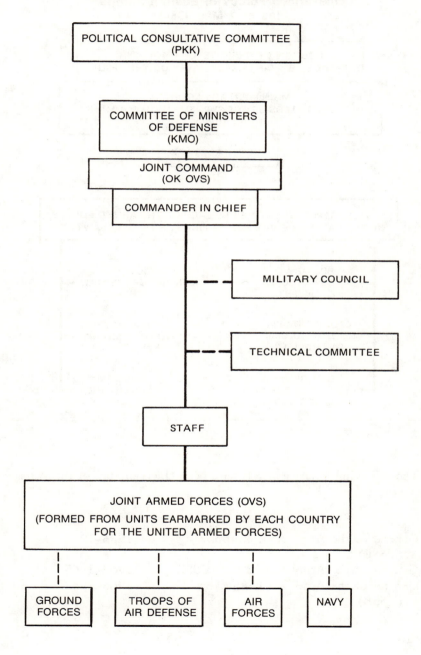

Chart 19
Possible Wartime Control Structure Over
the Armed Forces of Eastern Europe
(as of 1 May 1984)

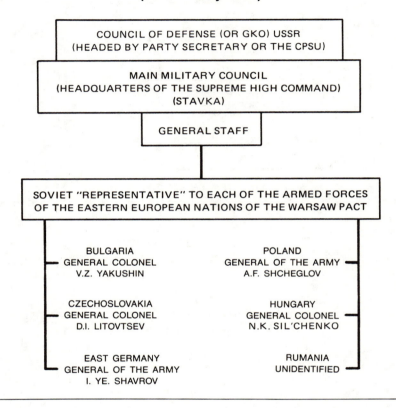

The following Soviet generals have been chiefs of staff of the Warsaw Pact Forces:

General of the Army A. I. Antonov (USSR)	1955–1962
General of the Army P. I. Batov (USSR)	1962–1965
General of the Army M. I. Kazakov (USSR)	1965–1968

General of the Army S. M. Shtemenko*   1968–1976
    (USSR)
General of the Army A. I. Gribkov   1976–
    (USSR)

Group of Soviet Forces, Germany (Gruppa Sovetskikh Voysk v Germanii—GSVG)

One indication of the importance of the Group of Soviet Forces, Germany,[43] is the fact that it is headed by a commander in chief (*glavnokomandyushchiy*), the same designation given to the heads of the Warsaw Pact, the five services, and the High Command of the Far East. Another indication is that approximately thirty people of the very top hierarchy of the Soviet military structure, as already noted, are members or candidate members of the Central Committee. The commander in chief of the Group of Soviet Forces, Germany, is a member of this very select group.

The famed Marshal G. K. Zhukov was the first commander in chief of the Soviet forces in Germany. He also was the Soviet high commissioner, chief of the Soviet Military Administration, and member of the Control Commission. His replacement in 1946 was Marshal V. D. Sokolovskiy, who became famous in later years as the editor of *Military Strategy*.

In March 1954, the "occupation" function of the Soviet troops in Germany theoretically was dropped. The following year, with the creation of the Warsaw Pact, an agreement was signed with the German Democratic Republic defining the status of Soviet troops. East German forces were formally assigned to the pact in 1958.[44]

As previously noted, the Soviets used troops and tanks against East German citizens during the riots of 1953 following the death of Stalin. Trouble was expected again in 1961 when the Berlin Wall was erected. At that time Marshal I. I. Yakubovskiy, then a general of the army, was temporarily replaced as a commander in chief by Marshal of the Soviet Union I. S. Konev, a leading World War II hero. When the crisis subsided, Yakubovskiy again assumed command.

The post of commander in chief of the Group of Soviet Forces, Germany, always has served as a stepping-stone to the highest Ministry of Defense positions. Zhukov and Grechko became ministers of defense; Sokolovskiy, Zakharov, and Kulikov became chiefs of the General Staff; Konev, Grechko, and Yakubovskiy became commanders in chief of the Warsaw Pact forces; and Zhukov, Konev, Grechko, and Chuykov became

---

*Assigned as chief of staff in preparation for the Soviet invasion of Czechoslovakia.

commanders in chief of the Soviet Ground Troops. The tradition of transferring the commander of the Kiev Military District to Germany (or vice versa) was broken in 1971, when General Kurkotkin was transferred to Germany from the Transcaucasus Military District.

Members of the Military Council of Group of Soviet Forces, Germany (as of 1 May 1984), are:

Commander in Chief	General of the Army M. M. Zaytsev (since 1980)
Chief, Political Administration	General Colonel A. D. Lizichev (since 1982)
First Deputy Commander in Chief	General Colonel V. M. Gordiyenko (since 1979)
First Deputy Commander in Chief and Chief of Staff	General Colonel I. V. Sviridov (since 1981)
Soviet Ambassador	V. I. Kochemasov

Commanders in chief, Group of Soviet Forces, Germany, were:

1946–1946	Marshal of the Soviet Union G. K. Zhukov
1946–1949	Marshal of the Soviet Union V. D. Sokolovskiy
1949–1953	Marshal of the Soviet Union V. I. Chuykov
1953–1957	Marshal of the Soviet Union A. A. Grechko
1957–1960	Marshal of the Soviet Union M. V. Zakharov
1960–1961	Marshal of the Soviet Union I. I. Yakubovskiy
1961–1962	Marshal of the Soviet Union I. S. Konev
1962–1965	Marshal of the Soviet Union I. I. Yakubovskiy
1965–1969	Marshal of the Soviet Union P. K. Koshevoy
1969–1971	Marshal of the Soviet Union V. G. Kulikov
1971–1972	General of the Army S. K. Kurkotkin
1972–1980	General of the Army Ye. F. Ivanovskiy
1980–	General of the Army M. M. Zaytsev

Central Group of Forces (*Tsentral'naya Gruppa Voysk—TsGV*)

The Central Group of Forces serves as the Soviet occupation troops of Czechoslovakia. They are an outgrowth of the 1968 Soviet invasion. They have a strength of five divisions, two of which are tank divisions. As with Soviet forces in other parts of Eastern Europe, the troops are confined to specific areas and are hated by the majority of the local populations.[45]

Members of the Military Council of Central Group of Forces (as of 1 May 1984) are:

Commander	General Colonel G. G. Borisov (since 1981)
Chief, Political Administration	General Lieutenant N. S. Kovalenko (since 1983)
First Deputy Commander	General Lieutenant S. Bokov (since 1982)
Chief of Staff	General Lieutenant V. Pankratov (since 1983)
Soviet Ambassador	A. P. Botvin

Past commanders of Central Group of Forces (Czechoslovakia) were:

1968–1972	General Lieutenant A. M. Mayorov
1972–1976	General Colonel I. I. Tenishchev
1976–1979	General Colonel D. S. Sukhorukov
1979–1981	General Colonel D. T. Yazov
1981–	General Colonel G. G. Borisov

Northern Group of Forces (Severnaya Gruppa Voysk—SGV)

The Northern Group of Forces, located in Poland, consists of two tank divisions.[46]

Members of the Military Council of Northern Group of Forces (as of 1 May 1984) are:

Commander	General Colonel Yu. F. Zarudin (since 1978)
Chief, Political Administration	General Lieutenant N. A. Lushnichenko (since 1979)
First Deputy Commander	General Lieutenant G. S. Klusov (since 1976)
First Deputy Commander and Chief of Staff	General Lieutenant A. N. Kapochkin (since 1983)
Soviet Ambassador	A. N. Aksenov

Past commanders of Northern Group of Forces (Poland) were:

1945–1949	Marshal of the Soviet Union K. K. Rokossovskiy
1949–1950	General Colonel K. P. Trubnikov
1950–1952	General Lieutenant A. I. Radziyevskiy
1952–1955	General Lieutenant M. P. Konstantinov
1955–1958	General of the Army K. N. Galitskiy
1958–1963	General Colonel G. I. Khetagurov

1963–1964	General Colonel S. S. Maryakhin
1964	General Lieutenant A. P. Rudakov
1964–1967	General Colonel G. V. Baklanov
1967–1968	General Colonel I. N. Shkadov
1968–1973	General Colonel M. T. Tankayev
1973–1975	General Colonel I. A. Gerasimov
1975–1978	General Colonel O. F. Kulishev
1978–	General Colonel Yu. F. Zarudin

Southern Group of Forces (Yuzhnaya Gruppa Voysk—YuGV)

The Southern Group of Forces is located in Hungary and consists of two tank divisions and two motorized rifle divisions. A primary purpose of its presence in Hungary is to remind the population of Soviet military power, which would be used to crush any revolt.[47]

Members of the Military Council of Southern Group of Forces (as of 1 May 1984) are:

Commander	General Colonel K. A. Kochetkov (since 1982)
Chief, Political Administration	General Lieutenant N. D. Shevkun (since 1980)
First Deputy Commander	General Lieutenant S. K. Nurmagambetov (since 1981)
First Deputy Commander and Chief of Staff	General Lieutenant V. Kolesov (since 1983)
Soviet Ambassador	V. N. Bazovskiy

Past commanders of Southern Group of Forces (Hungary) were:

1956–1960	General of the Army M. I. Kazakov
1960–1962	General of the Army P. I. Batov
1962–1969	General Colonel K. V. Provalov
1969–1975	General Colonel B. P. Ivanov
1975–1979	General Colonel F. F. Krivda
1979–1982	General Colonel V. I. Sivenok
1982–	General Colonel K. A. Kochetkov

The Fleets

Western interest in the Soviet Navy has increased measurably since the early 1970s, when the Kremlin intensified its efforts to project its military power and military presence into the Middle East and Third

Chart 20
Combat Structure of the Soviet Navy
(as of 1 May 1984)

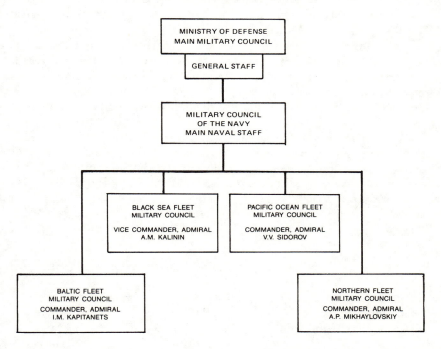

World areas, and Soviet nuclear-powered submarines appeared on station in the world oceans. This naval force is formed into four fleets, as shown in Chart 20.

Baltic Fleet (*Baltiyskiy Flot—BF*)

This is the oldest of the Russian fleets, dating from 1702 and the founding of St. Petersburg. The Baltic Fleet has played a major role in Soviet history, beginning with the revolt of sailors on board the cruiser *Aurora,* one of the highlights of the revolution. This cruiser, docked in Leningrad, serves today as a memorial and as a floating museum.

Soviet historians write less about the naval garrison at Kronstadt that revolted in March 1921 against the excesses of Soviet rule. Leon Trotsky and M. N. Tukhachevskiy led an attack across the ice and subdued the 14,000 sailors who supported the Kronstadt uprising, a few of whom survived. Contemporary writers speak of this as a *chistka* ("purging") that rid the fleet of "bad elements."

In June 1941 Germany's attack caught the Baltic Fleet by surprise. After a battle at the Soviet base in Tallinn, 200 ships of various types managed to reach Kronstadt, which guards the approach to Leningrad from the Baltic Sea. For most of the remainder of the war the Baltic Fleet was bottled up in the harbor at Leningrad.

In July and August 1940, the Soviet Union had annexed the Baltic republics and acquired East Prussia with the defeat of Germany. Headquarters of the Baltic Fleet was moved to Baltiysk in Kaliningrad Oblast, formerly in East Prussia. The fleet was divided in two units in 1946—the Fourth Fleet and the Eighth Fleet—and reunited in a major reorganization in 1956.

In the mid-1980s the Baltic Fleet was the smallest of the Soviet fleets, with a strength of approximately 34 submarines, 47 major combatant ships, and 270 aircraft. Leningrad remains a major shipbuilding port, and most of the naval schools are located there. Riga and Tallinn also are important bases.[48]

Members of the Military Council of the Baltic Fleet (as of 1 May 1984) are:

Commander	Admiral I. M. Kapitanets (since 1981)
Chief, Political Administration	Vice Admiral I. F. Alikov (since 1980)
First Deputy Commander	Not identified
Chief of Staff	Vice Admiral K. Makarov (since 1983)
Local Party Secretary	N. S. Konovalov (Kaliningrad)

Postwar commanders of the Baltic Fleet were:

Fourth Fleet

(1939)–1946	Admiral V. F. Tributs
1946–1947	Admiral G. I. Levchenko
1947–1952	Admiral V. A. Andreyev
1952–1956	Admiral A. G. Golovko

Eighth Fleet

1946–1947	Admiral V. F. Tributs
1947–1950	Admiral F. V. Zozulya
1950–1954	Admiral N. M. Kharlamov
1954–1956	Admiral V. A. Kasatonov

Baltic Fleet

1956–1956	Admiral A. G. Golovko
1956–1959	Admiral N. M. Kharlamov
1959–1967	Admiral A. Ye. Orel
1967–1976	Admiral V. V. Mikhaylin
1976–1978	Vice Admiral A. M. Kosov
1978–1981	Vice Admiral V. V. Sidorov
1981–	Admiral I. M. Kapitanets

Black Sea Fleet (*Chernomorskiy Flot—ChF*)

This fleet dates from May 1783, when the Crimea was annexed from Turkey. The Black Sea Fleet, although restricted by the narrow exit at Istanbul, has played a major role in both Russian and Soviet history. It controls the major warm water ports of the nation—Odessa, Sevastopol, Novorossiysk, Tuapse, Poti, and Batumi. (The Crimea is at the same latitude as the state of Maine.)

In Soviet history and legend, the mutiny in 1905 of the men of the imperial battleship *Potemkin* remains a major event. However, during the 1917 October Revolution, sailors of the Black Sea Fleet were slow to join the Bolshevik forces, until persuaded by delegations of sailors from the Baltic Sea Fleet. By April 1918, most of the fleet was bottled up in Novorossiysk, and many of the ships were sunk deliberately rather than being surrendered to the Germans. In December 1918, French and British ships entered the Black Sea and occupied Odessa, Nikolayev, Novorossiysk, Batumi, Sevastopol, and other ports. They were joined briefly by eight ships of the United States Navy. In 1920 White Russian forces evacuated many of their troops from Black Sea ports, and on 15 November of that year the Red Army took Sevastopol.

At the beginning of World War II the Black Sea Fleet consisted of 1 battleship, 6 cruisers, 47 submarines, and 636 aircraft. The German attack took the fleet by surprise, and by 4 July 1942 German forces occupied the two major ports of Odessa and Sevastopol. Most of the sailors of the fleet fought as infantrymen, helping to defend the approaches to the Caucasus. The Germans started withdrawing in 1944, and on 4 November 1944 the Black Sea Fleet returned to Sevastopol. In February 1945, only a few miles from Sevastopol, leaders of the Soviet Union, the United States, and Great Britain met at Yalta.[49]

In the mid-1980s the Black Sea Fleet, together with the Caspian Sea Flotilla, numbered approximately 26 submarines, 76 major combatant ships, and about 385 aircraft. Its primary task is to show the

Soviet flag in the Mediterranean, in an attempt to counter the presence of the United States Sixth Fleet in the area.

Members of the Military Council of the Black Sea Fleet (as of 1 May 1984) are:

Commander	Vice Admiral A. M. Kalinin (since 1983)
Chief, Political Administration	Vice Admiral R. N. Likhvonin (since 1981)
First Deputy Commander	Unidentified
Chief of Staff	Vice Admiral N. G. Klitnyy (since 1981)
Local Party Secretary	V. S. Makarenko (Crimea)

Postwar commanders of the Black Sea Fleet were:

(1944)–1948	Admiral F. S. Oktyabr'skiy
Nov 1948–1951	Admiral N. Ye. Basistyy
Aug 1951–1955	Admiral/Fleet/Soviet Union S. G. Gorshkov
Jul 1955–1955	Vice Admiral V. A. Parkhomenko
Dec 1955–1962	Admiral/Fleet V. A. Kasatonov
Jul 1962–1968	Admiral S. Ye. Chursin
Dec 1968–1974	Admiral V. S. Sysoyev
Mar 1974–1983	Admiral N. I. Khovrin
July 1983–	Vice Admiral A. M. Kalinin

Northern Fleet (Severnyy Flot—SF)

"The Soviet Union is a great naval power." Thus begins a Soviet book, *Severnyy Flot* [Northern Fleet]. "Two-thirds of the borders of the state are washed by seas or oceans; of them twelve thousand kilometers are on the Arctic Ocean and serve as the home waters of the Northern Fleet."[50]

Construction of a port at Murmansk was started in 1915 during World War I. After the outbreak of the Russian Revolution, with Russian troops withdrawing from the war with Germany, the Allies landed marines at Arkhangelsk and Murmansk to protect Allied supplies. This occupation lasted until 1920. The Northern Fleet was formed in 1932, and the "SevMorPut" (Northern Seaway) was established as a summer route following the northern coast from the White Sea to the Bering Straits. A group of four ships and two submarines from the Baltic Fleet in 1933 traveled through the new White Sea Canal to form the Northern Military Flotilla, the nucleus of the

Northern Fleet. A major reorganization of the fleet took place in 1937.

During World War II—as in World War I—Murmansk and Arkhangelsk became the chief ports for receiving goods from the United States and Britain. British and U.S. seamen paid a heavy price, running the gauntlet of German submarines with their convoys to reach these ports. The Northern Fleet could offer little protection.

In the postwar period the Northern Fleet has become the most important element of the Soviet Navy. The Black Sea Fleet must pass through the Bosporus to enter the Mediterranean and through the Straits of Gibraltar to enter the Atlantic Ocean. The Baltic Fleet must pass through the Danish Sounds, the Kattegat, and the Skagerrak to reach the North Sea and then through the English Channel or Norwegian Sea to get to the Atlantic. The Pacific Fleet also is hemmed in by Japan, and the Japanese islands form a half-moon around Vladivostok. It is only through the Barents Sea that the Soviet Navy can enter a major ocean without high risk of detection. For this reason as many as 181 submarines may be assigned to the fleet, of which 46 may carry ballistic missiles. These vessels can move under ice and therefore are not confined to ports during periods when surface ships cannot move. An additional 76 major surface combatant ships, and about 385 aircraft may be assigned. Headquarters is in Severomorsk.

Members of the Military Council of the Northern Fleet (as of 1 May 1984) are:

Commander	Admiral A. P. Mikhaylovskiy (since 1982)
Chief, Political Administration	Vice Admiral N. V. Usenko (since 1980)
First Deputy Commander	Vice Admiral V. S. Kruglyakov (since 1976)
Chief of Staff	Vice Admiral V. K. Korobov (since 1980)
Local Party Secretary	V. N. Ptitsyn (Murmansk)

Postwar commanders of the Northern Fleet were:

(1940)–1946	Admiral A. G. Golovko
Aug 1946–1952	Admiral V. I. Platonov
Apr 1952–1962	Admiral A. T. Chabanenko
Feb 1962–1964	Admiral of the Fleet V. A. Kasatonov
Jun 1964–1972	Admiral of the Fleet S. M. Lobov
May 1972–1977	Admiral of the Fleet G. M. Yegorov

| July 1977–1982 | Admiral V. N. Chernavin |
| Jan 1982– | Admiral A. P. Mikhaylovskiy |

Pacific Ocean Fleet (Tikhookeanskiy Flot—TOF)

In 1724 a Russian expedition reached the Kamchatka peninsula and began exploring the area. To provide a base for Russian activities in the western hemisphere, a special Russian-American Company was formed in 1784. Fort Novo-Arkhangelsk in Alaska was built in 1804, and the following year a warship was sent from St. Petersburg to provide protection for the settlement. Fort Ross, near San Francisco, was established in 1812. By 1854 Petropavlovsk-Kamchatka had become the primary Russian port on the Pacific Ocean. Vladivostok was founded on 2 July 1860 and by 1871 had become the main Russian naval base in the area.

During the Russo-Japanese War the Pacific Fleet was blockaded. By the terms of the Treaty of Portmouth of 5 September 1905 ending the war with Japan, Russia lost Port Arthur and Southern Sakhalin.

Following the formation of the Far Eastern Republic, under Communist rule, the Pacific Fleet became the Fleet of the Far Eastern Republic. On 21 April 1932, it was redesignated the Pacific Ocean Fleet. In 1938 a flotilla of this fleet at Lake Khasan took part in actions against the Japanese. Like the Baltic Fleet, the Pacific Ocean Fleet was divided in two—the Fifth and the Seventh Fleets—shortly after World War II, in which it did not participate. The two fleets were reunited in 1953.[51]

A rapid expansion of the Pacific Ocean Fleet has taken place in the postwar years. It is the second largest of the four fleets, consisting of approximately 128 submarines (of which 26 may be nuclear), 89 major surface combat ships, and about 420 aircraft. In the 1970s Soviet authors began to refer to their nation as a "Pacific power" rather than as an "Asian power," the expression previously used.

Tragedy struck the Pacific Ocean Fleet in 1981. As delegates were on their way to attend the Twenty-sixth Party Congress, their plane crashed near Leningrad. According to western reports, as many as seventy military men, including a score of admirals and generals, were killed in the crash. Soviet newspapers carried the obituaries of the commander, Admiral Emil Spiridonov, the political officer, and the commander of the fleet's air wing. Admiral Sidorov, commander of the Baltic Fleet, was named as Spiridonov's replacement.

Members of the Military Council of the Pacific Ocean Fleet (as of 1 May 1984) are:

Commander	Admiral V. V. Sidorov (since 1981)
Chief, Political Administration	Vice Admiral N. P. D'yakonskiy (since 1981)
First Deputy Commander	Vice Admiral N. Ya. Yasakov (since 1979)
Chief of Staff	Vice Admiral G. Khvatov (since 1984)
Local Party Secretary	V. P. Lomakin (Primorskiy Kray)

Postwar commanders of the Pacific Fleet were:

| (1939)-1947 | Admiral I. S. Yumashev |

Fifth Fleet
1947–1950	Vice Admiral A. S. Frolov
1950–1951	Admiral/Fleet/Soviet Union N. G. Kuznetsov
1951–1953	Admiral Yu. A. Panteleyev

Seventh Fleet
| 1947–1950 | Admiral I. I. Baykov |
| 1951–1953 | Vice Admiral G. N. Kholostyakov |

Pacific Ocean Fleet
Jan 1953–1956	Admiral Yu. A. Panteleyev
Jan 1956–1958	Vice Admiral V. A. Chekurov
Feb 1958–1962	Admiral V. A. Fokin
Jun 1962–1969	Admiral N. N. Amel'ko
Oct 1969–1974	Admiral/Fleet N. I. Smirnov
Nov 1974–1979	Admiral V. P. Maslov
1979–1981	Admiral E. N. Spiridonov
Mar 1981–	Admiral V. V. Sidorov

Flotillas

In addition to the four main fleets, since the establishment of the Soviet state, nearly three dozen flotillas of the Soviet fleet have operated on rivers, seas, and lakes, in the USSR and abroad, chiefly in support of military actions during war. The Azov, Amu-Darya, Amur, Aral, Astrakhan-Caspian, Baykal, White Sea, Volga, Volga-Kama, Volga-Caspian, Vol'sk, Volga-Il'men, Dnepr, Don-Azov, Don, Dunai, Yenesey, West-Dvina, Il'men, Caspian, Kura, Ladoga, Onezh, Pinsk, Pripyatsk, Saymin, North Dvina, North Pacific Ocean, Seliger-Volga, Siberian,

Syr-Darya, Tempyuk, Ural, Ust-Dnepr, Arctic, and Chuda flotillas have existed at one time or another. At the present time only the Caspian Flotilla, with headquarters in Baku, is active.

Caspian Flotilla (Kaspiyskaya Flotiliya)

Members of the Military Council of the Caspian Flotilla[52] (as of 1 May 1984) are:

Commander	Vice Admiral G. G. Kasumbekov (since 1977)
Chief, Political Section	Rear Admiral V. P. Nekrasov (since 1981)
Chief of Staff	Rear Admiral V. Tolkachev (since 1981)

Leningrad Naval Base (Leningradskaya Voyenno-Morskaya Baza—LVMB)

Leningrad is the largest naval base in the Soviet Union. Because so many naval personnel and schools are located in Leningrad, it has its own structure:[53]

Commander	Admiral V. A. Samoylov (since 1982)
Chief, Political Section	Rear Admiral A. I. Korniyenko (since 1982)

Air Defense

The Troops of *National* Air Defense had two primary air defense districts: Baku and Moscow. As already noted, Baku Air Defense District was abolished in 1980. Since the reorganization, other Troops of Air Defense have been part of military districts, where they come under the command of Air Defense of the district. Moscow Air Defense District remains to guard the capital.

Moscow Air Defense District (Moskovskiy Okrug PVO—MOPVO)

Protecting Moscow, the center of the power structure of the Communist Party, is one of the most vital tasks of the Troops of Air Defense. Here are concentrated not only interceptors and surface-to-air missiles to protect against a manned aircraft attack, but also antiballistic missile defenses. SALT I and subsequent agreements have given the Soviet Union and the United States the right to deploy ABMs in one location. The Soviets chose to provide ABM protection to Moscow. The total area covered by the Moscow Air Defense District is not known.[54]

Members of the Military Council of the Moscow Air Defense District (as of 1 May 1984) are:

Commander	General Colonel Aviation A. U. Konstantinov (since 1980)
Chief, Political Administration	General Lieutenant Aviation V. A. Ponomarev (since 1975)
First Deputy Commander	General Lieutenant Artillery V. P. Vinogradov (since 1973)
Chief of Staff	General Colonel Artillery Yu. A. Gor'kov (since 1983)
Party Secretary	V. V. Grishin (Moscow)

Commanders of the Moscow Air Defense District were:

Aug 1954–Mar 1965	Marshal of the Soviet Union P. F. Batitskiy
Mar 1965–July 1966	Vacant
July 1966–1970	General Colonel V. V. Okunev
1970–1975	General Colonel Aviation A. I. Koldunov
1975–1980	General Colonel Aviation B. V. Bochkov
1980–	General Colonel Aviation A. U. Konstantinov

Baku Air Defense District (Bakinskiy Okrug PVO—BOPVO)

The Baku Air Defense District was formed in 1954 from the Baku Air Defense Region. At that time the Baku area was the major source of oil for the entire Soviet Union. The area remains of strategic importance, protecting the USSR's southern flank. In 1980, as part of the reorganization of Troops of Air Defense, it was downgraded and merged into the Transcaucasus Military District.

Postwar commanders of the Baku Air Defense District were:

1954–1956	Chief Marshal of Aviation K. A. Vershinin
1956–1959	General of the Army V. D. Ivanov
1959–1966	General of the Army A. F. Shcheglov

1966–1973	General Colonel F. A. Olifirov
Jun 1973–1980	General Colonel Aviation A. U. Konstantinov

Troops of the KGB and MVD

Troops of the KGB (Committee of State Security) and the MVD (Ministry of Internal Affairs) are part of the Soviet Armed Forces, although they are not subordinate to the Ministry of Defense. Certain of the troops are organized in much the same manner as Ministry of Defense forces, from whom they receive considerable support. Manpower for both KGB and MVD forces is provided through the system of universal military service, with the length of military obligations corresponding to that of personnel assigned to units under the Ministry of Defense. Arms and other equipment are standardized with those used by other Soviet forces.

Over the years the organizations that now are the KGB and MVD have undergone many changes and had several names (see Chart 21). The NKVD (People's Commissariat of Internal Affairs) was created in 1917. Another agency, the Cheka (All-Russian Extraordinary Commission for Combating Counterrevolution and Sabotage), was formed on 27 January 1918. Some of its functions overlapped those of the NKVD. The Cheka's first chief was Felix E. Dzerzhinskiy, who became notorious for institutionalizing terror as a deliberate Party policy. In 1922 the Cheka was renamed the GPU (State Political Administration) and subordinated to the NKVD.

Later that year the GPU was detached from the NKVD, subordinated to the Council of People's Commissariats, and renamed the OGPU (Unified State Political Administration) as part of the conversion of the Federation of Soviet Republics into the USSR in December. The infamous "Iron Felix" Dzerzhinskiy remained head of the dreaded OGPU until his death in 1926. Dzerzhinskiy's successor was V. R.

Chart 21
The Changing Organization of the KGB and MVD

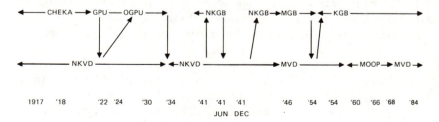

Menzhinskiy, who at his death in 1934 was succeeded by G. G. Yagoda. At that time the NKVD, which had been abolished in 1930, was reestablished, and Yagoda was placed as its head. The OGPU was absorbed into the new organization.

The NKVD of the 1930s controlled the regular police, Border Guards, Internal Troops, concentration and labor camps, most of the transportation system, and a number of economic enterprises. It was responsible for the deaths of millions of Soviet citizens—men, women, and children. The grey world of the Gulag, where human beings were treated in a manner comparable to the worst recorded in the annals of history, has been exposed by the pen of Aleksandr Solzhenitsyn. Yagoda was executed during Stalin's purges and replaced by another individual equally infamous, N. I. Yezhov, who later also was executed. He was replaced by the equally inhumane L. P. Beria. In 1941, for a short time, the NKVD was split into the NKVD and the NKGB (People's Commissariat of State Security).

When the Soviet Union entered World War II, in June 1941, the NKGB and NKVD again were joined, only to be divided once more in December 1941. In 1946 they were designated as ministries and renamed the MVD and MGB (Ministry of State Security). Beria, head of the MGB, was elevated to membership in the Politburo and was replaced by V. S. Abakumov. General Lieutenant S. N. Kruglov was designated head of the MVD. Immediately after Stalin's death in March 1953, Beria got rid of Kruglov and A. D. Ignat'yev, who had replaced Abakumov as MGB head, and consolidated the two organizations into the MVD. Beria then took over as the head of this combined organization and may have been in the process of a major bid for power. However, within a short time he was shot under circumstances that still are unknown.[55]

Following Beria's death the MVD again was split into the KGB and MVD. In 1960 Khrushchev abolished the latter organization, which had been headed by N. P. Dudorov. Each union republic had its own MVD, even though the MVD USSR had been abolished. These local MVDs were renamed ministries for preserving the public order (MOOPs) in 1962. However, in 1966, a single agency was again created, the MOOP USSR. General Colonel N. A. Shchelokov became its chief. In November 1968, it was renamed the MVD USSR.

The previous head of the KGB, General Lieutenant I. A. Serov, was replaced in 1958 by Aleksandr Shelepin, former secretary of the Komsomols. Shelepin was elevated to the Party secretariat in 1961 and replaced by V. Ye. Semichastnyy, his successor as Komsomol secretary, who in November 1967 was succeeded in turn by Yu. V.

Andropov. In 1978, the KGB, which had been attached to the Council of Ministers, became the KGB of the USSR.

With the death of Party ideologist Mikhail Suslov in January 1982, Yuri Andropov replaced him in the Secretariat (in April 1982). V. V. Fedorchuk, chairman of the KGB of the Ukraine, replaced Andropov as KGB chief. When Brezhnev died in November 1982 and Yuri Andropov became the new General Secretary of the CPSU, Fedorchuk was moved to the MVD as minister and promoted to General of the Army. V. M. Chebrikov, formerly Andropov's first deputy, took over the chairmanship of the KGB, and in November 1983 he, too, was promoted to four-star rank. The former minister of the interior (MVD), General of the Army N. A. Shchelokov, was removed from the Central Committee and reprimanded in June 1983. After Andropov's death in February 1984, Konstantin Chernenko, the new General Secretary, indicated his intentions to continue the policy of his predecessor on weeding out corruption.

Troops of the KGB

On 28 May 1918, Lenin signed a decree to form units to guard the borders of the new state. This decree was fully implemented at the end of the Civil War when the best units were taken out of the Red Army to form the Border Guards under control of the Cheka. By 1923 Border Guard districts were formed along the entire Soviet periphery. Since 1980, there have been ten of them. Control remained under the Cheka and its successors, including the KGB of the 1980s.

When Hitler's forces invaded the Soviet Union in June 1941, the first Soviet soldier killed was a Border Guard. During the war Border Guards fought in Austria, Hungary, Yugoslavia, Czechoslovakia, Bulgaria, Rumania, and Poland, engaged primarily in cleaning up remaining resistance as the Soviet fronts moved forward.

Border Guards—not forces under control of the Ministry of Defense—have been the Soviet participants in hundreds of incidents along the Sino-Soviet border since the end of World War II. One of the most publicized of these engagements was the 1969 Battle of Damanskiy Island. Little known is the fact that on the Soviet side only Border Guards were engaged.

Border Guards are equipped with ships, tanks, armored personnel carriers, helicopters, light aircraft, and other modern weaponry. Some of the border is patrolled on horseback, and dogs are specially trained to work with the guards. Much of the border is plowed to ensure that footprints will be identifiable, and it is equipped with manned guard towers and searchlights to maintain continuous observation.[56]

Borders between the Soviet Union and its Eastern European Warsaw Pact allies are guarded and patrolled in much the same manner as the borders with Turkey, a NATO member, or tiny Finland. Equipped with heavy armament and depth charges, ships of the Border Guard flotillas are constantly patrolling coastlines.

Among the first Soviets that tourists see when arriving in the Soviet Union, and the last seen when departing, are Border Guards. These troops are present at international airports, collecting and checking passports of all who enter or leave the country. Travelers entering the country by train or auto must first be cleared at designated checkpoints by Border Guards armed with submachine guns.

According to Soviet law, the border zone is 2 kilometers wide, but in actual practice the zone is much wider. Immediately inside a border zone, as for example between Leningrad and Tallinn, automobile travelers are forbidden even to pause by the roadside, despite the fact the actual coastline may be 20 or 30 kilometers from the road.

Border Guards maintain their own schools, which appear to be comparable to counterpart schools in the Ground Forces. Young men enter these schools at ages seventeen to twenty-two, after having been selected through competitive examination. After four years of intensive work, graduates receive degrees and are commissioned as lieutenants.

Border Guards are not the only troops under KGB control. The Kremlin Guards, seen by thousands of tourists, guarding Lenin's Mausoleum in Red Square, also are part of the KGB force. These troops can easily be identified by the bright royal blue color of their lapel tabs, which are in contrast to the green lapel tabs of the Border Guards.

There are other KGB troops as well, about which little is known. KGB troops are stationed in each of the fifteen republics of the Soviet Union. They control nuclear weapons stockpiles, extremely sensitive installations, and high-level communications among Party officials and between the Ministry of Defense and major military headquarters.

Senior Border Guard officers (as of 1 May 1984) are:

Chief	General of the Army V. A. Matrosov (since 1972)
Chief of Political Administration	General Major V. S. Ivanov (since 1983)
First Deputy Chief and Chief of Staff	General Lieutenant Yu. A. Neshumov (since 1977)
Deputy Chief	Vice Admiral N. N. Dalmatov
Deputy Chief	General Major–Engineer G. Preobrazhenskiy

Commanders of Border Guard Districts (as of May 1984) are:

Baltic	General Major G. F. Moiseyenko
Central Asian	General Major G. A. Zgerskiy (Hq: Ashkhabad)
Eastern	General Major V. S. Donskov (Hq: Alma-Ata)
Far Eastern	General Lieutenant V. M. Krylovskiy (Hq: Khabarovsk)
Kamchatka (formed in 1980)	Unidentified
North Western	General Lieutenant A. G. Viktorov (Hq: Leningrad)
Pacific Ocean	General Major V. K. Gaponenko
Transbaykal	Unidentified
Transcaucasus	General Major B. Sentyurin
Western	General Lieutenant N. V. Lavrinenko

Past chiefs of the Border Guards were:

1942–1951	General Lieutenant N. P. Strakhov
1952–1972	General Colonel P. I. Zyryanov
1972–	General Colonel V. A. Matrosov

Internal Troops of the MVD

Like the KGB troops, Internal Troops of the MVD are considered a part of the Soviet Armed Forces but are not under the Ministry of Defense. Internal Troops can be distinguished by the dull brick-red tabs on their lapels, darker than the crimson red of the motorized troops of the Ground Forces. The letters VV (written in Russian) appear on their shoulders to denote that they are Internal Troops.

These troops were first formed in January 1918 and attached to the Cheka under Dzerzhinskiy. Their functions—now as then—are to protect internal installations, such as labor camps, and to perform convoy duties. During time of war they guard the rear areas, prevent sabotage, guard war prisoners, and maintain order.[57]

Internal troops are armed in much the same manner as the Border Guards, with armored personnel carriers and light weapons, but they do not appear to have aircraft. Like the Border Guards they also have their own military schools, whose graduates are commissioned as lieutenants and are awarded a higher education degree.

In September 1974 the MVD opened a military academy, corresponding roughly to a war college in the United States, to provide additional professional training for its officers.

The Soviet militia (police) and firemen also are under control of the Ministry of Internal Affairs.

The Senior MVD officer as of 1 May 1984 is:

Commander of Internal   General of the Army I. K.
  Troops   Yakovlev (since 1968)

Soviet military services, military districts, groups of forces abroad, and fleets and troops of the KGB and MVD are all backed by massive support forces and special troops. This Soviet support structure is generally copied by other nations of the Warsaw Pact. In the event of a Warsaw Pact–NATO conflict—whether short or protracted, conventional or nuclear—victory may well go to the side that has the better support capability for its armed forces. How the Soviets measure up in this regard will be shown in the next chapter.

Notes

1. N. V. Ogarkov, "Military Strategy," *Sovetskaya Voyennaya Entsiklopediya* [Soviet Military Encyclopedia] (Moscow: Voyenizdat, 1976–1980), Vol. 7, p. 564.

2. N. V. Ogarkov, "On Guard Over Peaceful Labor," *Kommunist* 10, July 1981.

3. V. D. Sokolovskiy, *Soviet Military Strategy,* Harriet F. Scott, ed. (New York: Crane, Russak & Co., 1975), 3d ed., p. 13.

4. N. P. Suntsov et al., *Krasnoznamennyy Dal'nevostochnyy* [Red Banner Far Eastern] (Moscow: Voyenizdat, 1971), pp. 220, 269, 272–275; *Voyennyy Entsiklopedicheskiy Slovar'* [Military Encyclopedic Dictionary] (Moscow Voyenizdat, 1983), p. 194; *XXVI S"yezd Kommunisticheskoy Partii Sovetskogo Soyuza: Stenograficheskiy Otchet* [Twenty-sixth Congress CPSU: Stenographic Notes] (Moscow: Politizdat, 1981), Vol. 3, pp. 332, 349.

5. This report was widely circulated in Moscow at the time. Further credence was given by the fact that travel to that area was forbidden to foreigners. See also A. I. Solzhenitsyn, *The Gulag Archipelago*, Vol. 3 (New York: Harper and Row, 1974), pp. 506–514, for a similar incident.

6. *Sovetskaya Voyennaya Entsiklopediya,* Vol. 2, p. 197.

7. Ibid., Vol. 2, p. 271.

8. *Bol'shaya Sovetskaya Entsiklopediya* [The Great Soviet Encyclopedia], 3d ed. (Moscow: Soviet Encyclopedia Publishing House, 1971), Vol. 5, p. 248.

9. *Sovetskaya Voyennaya Entsiklopediya,* Vol. 2, p. 271.

10. Ibid., Vol. 2, p. 395.

11. The number of male youths annually reaching eighteen years of age in the USSR is approximately 2,000,000. If 80 percent are called up for service each year, the annual number of inductees would be approximately 1,600,000.

12. A. I. Skryl'nik, *Zapad-81* (Moscow: Voyenizdat, 1982). See also *Krasnaya Zvezda*, 2–16 September 1981.

13. All of the military district headquarters are located in major cities, many in the capitals of the republics. Although approximately 325 of the 400 largest cities in the Soviet Union are closed to foreigners, 13 of the 16 military district headquarters are in cities that can be visited by foreign tourists. Often the headquarters buildings are in the main area of the city, on the main street.

14. A. A. Yepishev, "Military Councils," *Sovetskaya Voyennaya Entsiklopediya*, Vol. 2, pp. 272–273.

15. Military district headquarters in border regions, such as the Far Eastern Military District and the Central Asian Military District, are much more active and have more general officers than an interior one like the Siberian Military District.

16. V. A. Ofitserov, "Pribaltiyskiy Voyennyy Okrug" [Baltic Military District], *Sovetskaya Voyennaya Entsiklopediya*, Vol. 6, p. 516. See also *Boyevoy Put' i Traditsii Voinov Krasnoznamennogo Pribaltiyskogo Voyennogo Okruga* [History and Traditions of the Red Banner Baltic Military District] (Riga: Znaniye Soc, 1979).

17. I. M. Tret'yak, "Belorusskiy Voyennyy Okrug" [Belorussian Military District], *Sovetskaya Voyennaya Entsiklopediya*, Vol. 1, p. 434. See also N. V. Yakovlev, *Stranitsy Geroicheskoy Istorii* [Pages of an Heroic Story] (Minsk: Belarus', 1968); *Budni Belorusskogo Krasnoznamennogo* [Daily Life of the Belorussian Red Banner] (Minsk: Belarus', 1970); *Krasnoznamennyy Belorusskiy Voyennyy Okrug* [Red Banner Belorussian Military District] (Minsk: Belarus', 1973).

18. M. A. Tyagunov, "Prikarpatskiy Voyennyy Okrug" [Carpathian Military District], *Sovetskaya Voyennaya Ensitklopediya*, Vol. 6, p. 533. See also *Krasnoznamennyy Prikarpatskiy* [Red Banner Carpathian] (L'vov: Kamenyar, 1976); *Prisyage Rodine Verny* [True to the Oath of the Motherland] (L'vov: Kamenyar, 1977); *Krasnoznamennyy Prikarpatskiy* [Red Banner Carpathian] (Moscow: Voyenizdat, 1982).

19. "Sredneaziatskiy Voyennyy Okrug" [Central Asian Military District], *Sovetskaya Voyennaya Entsiklopediya*, Vol. 7, p. 505. See also the books listed under the Turkestan Military District; *Ty Sluzhish v Krasnoznamennom Sredneaziatskom* [You Are Serving in the Red Banner Central Asian] (Alma Ata: Kazakhstan, 1979).

20. M. I. Bezkhrebtyy and A. S. Sysoyev, "Dal'nevostochnyy Voyennyy Okrug" [Far Eastern Military District], *Sovetskaya Voyennaya Entsiklopediya,* Vol. 3, p. 84. See also *Krasnoznamennyy Dal'nevostochnyy* [Red Banner Far Eastern] (Moscow: Voyenizdat, 1971); *Krasnoznamennyy Dal'nevostochnyy* (Khabarovsk: Khabarovsk Book Publishers, 1978).

21. I. D. Yershov, "Kiyevskiy Voyennyy Okrug" [Kiev Military District], *Sovetskaya Voyennaya Entsiklopediya*, Vol. 4, p. 164. See also *Kiyevskiyy Krasnoznamennyy* [Kiev Red Banner] (Kiev: Political Admin. KVO, 1969); *Kiyevskiyy Krasnoznamennyy* (Moscow: Voyenizdat, 1974); *Krasnoznamennyy Kiyevskiy* [Red Banner Kiev] (Kiev: Politizdat Ukraine, 1979), 2d ed.

22. F. F. Viktorov, "Leningradskiy Voyennyy Okrug" [Leningrad Military District], *Sovetskaya Voyennaya Entsiklopediya*, Vol. 4, p. 614. See also *Istoriya Ordena Lenina Leningradskogo Voyennogo Okruga* [History of the Order of Lenin Leningrad Military District] (Moscow: Voyenizdat, 1974); G. Ye. Yefanov, *Nash Okrug Leningradskiy* [Our Leningrad District] (Leningrad, 1974); I. G. Inozemtsev, *Pod Krylom—Leningrad* [Under the Wind—Leningrad] (Moscow: Voyenizdat, 1978).

23. V. L. Govorov, "Moskovskiy Voyennyy Okrug" [Moscow Military District], *Sovetskaya Voyennaya Entsiklopediya*, Vol. 5, p. 421. See also *Ordena Lenina Moskovskiy Voyennyy Okrug* [Order of Lenin Moscow Military District] (Moscow: Voyenizdat, 1971); *Ordena Lenina Moskovskiy Voyennyy Okrug* (Moscow: Voyenizdat, 1977); A. M. Nedosugov, *Na Polyakh Ucheniy* [On the Fields of Exercises] (Moscow: Moskovskiy Robochiy, 1974).

24. V. A. Belikov, "Severo-Kavkazskiy Voyennyy Okrug" [North Caucasus Military District], *Sovetskaya Voyennaya Entsiklopediya*, Vol. 7, p. 305. See also *Krasnoznamennyy Severo-Kavkazskiy* [Red Banner North Caucasus] (Rostov/Don: Book Publishers, 1971); *Krasnoznamennyy Severo-Kavkazskiy* (Rostov/Don: Book Publishers, 1978), 2d ed.; G. R. Pavlov, ed., *V Orlinom Krayu* [In Eagle Territory] (Rostov/Don: Book Publishers, 1977); *Severo-Kavkaztsy v Boyakh za Rodini* [North Caucasians in Battles for the Motherland] (Moscow: Voyenizdat, 1966).

25. I. M. Voloshin, "Odesskiy Voyennyy Okrug" [Odessa Military District], *Sovetskaya Voyennaya Entsiklopediya*, Vol. 6, p. 24. See also *Odesskiy Krasnoznamennyy* [Odessa Red Banner] (Kishinev: Kartya Moldovenyaske, 1975).

26. Yu. A. Khvorost'yanov, "Sibirskiy Voyennyy Okrug" [Siberian Military District], *Sovetskaya Voyennaya Entsiklopediya*, Vol. 7, p. 337. See also *V Plameni i Slave* [In Flames and Glory] (Novosibirsk: Zap-Sib Book Publishers, 1969).

27. P. A. Belik, "Zabaykal'skiy Voyennyy Okrug" [Transbaykal Military District], *Sovetskaya Voyennaya Entsiklopediya*, Vol. 3, p. 356. See also *Zabaykal'skiy Voyennyy Okrug* [Transbaykal Military District] (Irkutsk: Vost-Sib Book Publishers, 1972); *Ty Sluzhbi Nesesh v Zabaykal'ye* [You are serving in Transbaykal] (Irkutsk: Vost-Sib Book Publishers, 1974).

28. D. A. Grinkevich, "Zakavkazskiy Voyennyy Okrug" [Transcaucasus Military District], *Sovetskaya Voyennaya Entsiklopediya*, Vol. 3, p. 396. See also *Krasnoznamennyy Zakavkazskiy Voyennyy Okrug* [Red Banner Transbaykal Military District] (Moscow: Voyenizdat, 1969); *50 Let na Strazhe Yuzhnykh Rubezhey Otchizny* [50 Years on Guard Over the Southern Borders of the Fatherland] (Tbilisi: Merani, 1971).

29. G. F. Krivosheyev, "Turkestanskiy Voyennyy Okrug" [Turkestan Military District], *Sovetskaya Voyennaya Entsiklopediya*, Vol. 8, p. 144. See also *Krasnoznamennyy Turkestanskiy* [Red Banner Turkestan] (Moscow: Voyenizdat, 1976); *60 Let na Strazhe Rodiny* [60 Years on Guard Over the Motherland] (Tashkent:

Uzbekistan, 1978); *Na Samykh Yazhnykh Rubezhakh* [On the Southernmost Borders] (Tashkent: Uzbekistan, 1978).

30. Ye. A. Kuznetsov, "Ural'skiy Voyennyy Okrug" [Ural Military District], *Sovetskaya Voyennaya Entsiklopediya*, Vol. 8, p. 210. See also *Istorii Ural'skogo Voyennogo Okruga* [History of the Ural Military District] (Moscow: Voyenizdat, 1970).

31. V. N. Verevkin-Rakhal'skiy, "Privolzhskiy Voyennyy Okrug" [Volga Military District], *Sovetskaya Voyennaya Entsiklopediya*, Vol. 6, p. 524. See also *Krasnoznamennyy Privolzhskiy* [Red Banner Volga] (Kuybyshev, 1975).

32. "The Military Balance 1983/84," as compiled by the International Institute for Strategic Studies, London, reprinted in *Air Force Magazine*, December 1983, pp. 69ff.

33. M. V. Zakharov, *50 Let Vooruzhennykh Sil SSSR* [50 Years of the Armed Forces of the USSR] (Moscow: Voyenizdat, 1968), p. 548.

34. I. I. Yakubovskiy, *Boyevoye Sodruzhestvo Bratskikh Narodov i Armiy* [Combat Community of Fraternal Peoples and Armies] (Moscow: Voyenizdat, 1975), pp. 88–89. See also *Organizatsiya Varshavskovo Dogovora, 1955–1975: Dokumenty i Materialy* [Organization of the Warsaw Pact, 1955–1975: Documents and Materials] (Moscow: Political Literature Publishing House, 1975), pp. 5–12.

35. M. G. Sobolev, ed., *Partiyno-Politicheskaya Rabota v Sovetskikh Vooruzhennykh Silakh* [Party-Political Work in the Soviet Armed Forces] (Moscow: Voyenizdat, 1974), p. 591.

36. D. J. Dallin, *Soviet Foreign Policy After Stalin* (Philadelphia: J. B. Lippincott Co., 1961), p. 358.

37. Ibid., p. 381.

38. Zakharov, *50 Let*, p. 553.

39. Sobolev, *Partiyno-Politicheskaya Rabota*, p. 591.

40. G. F. Vorontsov, *Voyennyye Koalitsii i Koalitsionnyye Voyny* [Military Coalitions and Coalition War] (Moscow: Voyenizdat, 1976), pp. 267–284. See also Sobolev, *Partiyno-Politicheskaya Rabota*, p. 591.

41. For an account of many of the Warsaw Pact exercises, see P. I. Yefimov, *Boyevoy Soyuz Bratskikh Armiy* [Fighting Union of Fraternal Armies] (Moscow: Voyenizdat, 1974), pp. 24–25. See also V. Gol'tsev, *Bol'shiye Manevry* [Great Maneuvers] (Moscow: DOSAAF Publishing House, 1974); *Varshavskiy Dogovor— Soyuz vo Imya Mira i Sotsializma* [Warsaw Pact—Union in the Name of Peace and Socialism] (Moscow: Voyenizdat, 1980), pp. 154–55, 272–293. A. A. Yepishev, *KPSS i Voyennoye Stroitel'stvo* [CPSU and the Military Buildup] (Moscow: Voyenizdat), p. 277, provides a further list of code-named exercises.

42. *Varshavskiy Dogovor*, pp. 162-168, gives a description of each one.

43. For a general account of the Group of Soviet Forces, Germany, see Ye. F. Ivanovskiy, ed., *Na Boyevom Postu: Kniga o Voinakh Gruppy Sovetskikh Voysk v Germanii* [At the Combat Post: A Book About the Soldiers in the Group of Soviet Forces, Germany] (Moscow: Voyenizdat, 1975).

44. Ye. F. Ivanovskiy, "Gruppa Sovetskikh Voysk v Germanii" [Group of Soviet Forces, Germany], *Sovetskaya Voyennaya Entsiklopediya*, Vol. 3, p. 63.

45. V. M. Kozhbakhteyev and I. N. Kulikov, "Tsentral'naya Gruppa Voysk" [Central Group of Forces], *Sovetskaya Voyennaya Entsiklopediya*, Vol. 8, p. 410.

46. R. G. Rizatdinov, "Severnaya Gruppa Voysk" [Northern Group of Forces], *Sovetskaya Voyennaya Entsiklopediya,* Vol. 7, p. 288.

47. V. N. Verevkin-Rakhal'skiy and I. N. Kulikov, "Yuzhnaya Gruppa Voysk" [Southern Group of Forces], *Sovetskaya Voyennaya Entsiklopediya,* Vol. 8, p. 628.

48. "Baltiyskiy Flot" [Baltic Fleet], *Sovetskaya Voyennaya Entsiklopediya,* Vol. 1, p. 383. See also N. Grechanyuk et al., *Baltiyskiy Flot* [Baltic Fleet] (Moscow: Voyenizdat, 1960); V. F. Tributs, *Baltiytsy Vstupayut v Boy* [Baltic Sailors Go into Battle] (Kaliningrad: Book Publishers, 1972); *Krasnoznamennyy Baltiyskiy Flot v Bitve za Leningrad* [Red Banner Baltic Fleet in the Battle for Leningrad] (Moscow: Voyenizdat, 1973); *Dvazhdy Krasnoznamennyy Baltiyskiy Flot* [Twice Red Banner Baltic Fleet] (Moscow: Voyenizdat, 1978).

49. V. S. Sysoyev, "Chernomorskiy Flot" [Black Sea Fleet], *Sovetskaya Voyennaya Entsiklopediya,* Vol. 8, p. 458. See also P. Bolgari et al., *Chernomorskiy Flot* [Black Sea Fleet] (Moscow: Voyenizdat, 1967); G. I. Vaneyev, *Chernomortsy v Velikoy Otechestvennoy Voyne* [Black Sea Sailors in the Great Patriotic War] (Moscow: Voyenizdat, 1978); *Krasnoznamennyy Chernomorskiy Flot* [Red Banner Black Sea Fleet] (Moscow: Voyenizdat, 1979).

50. V. N. Chernavin, "Severnyy Flot" [Northern Fleet], *Sovetskaya Voyennaya Entsiklopediya,* Vol. 7, p. 294. See also I. A. Kozlov and V. S. Shlomin, *Severnyy Flot* [Northern Fleet] (Moscow: Voyenizdat, 1966); V. S. Boyko, *Kryl'ya Severnogo Flota* [Wings of the Northern Fleet] (Murmansk: Book Publishers, 1976); *Krasnoznamennyy Severnyy* [Red Banner Northern] (Murmansk: 1976); I. A. Kozlov and V. S. Shlomin, *Krasnoznamennyy Severnyy Flot* [Red Banner Northern Fleet], (Moscow: Voyenizdat, 1977); *Krasnoznamennyy Severnyy* [Red Banner Northern] (Moscow: Voyenizdat, 1981), photo album.

51. A. I. Rodionov, "Tikhookeanskiy Flot" [Pacific Ocean Fleet], *Sovetskaya Voyennaya Entsiklopediya,* Vol. 8, p. 57. See also S. Ye. Zakharov et al., *Tikhookeanskiy Flot* [Pacific Ocean Fleet] (Moscow: Voyenizdat, 1966); *Krasnoznamennyy Tikhookeanskiy Flot* [Red Banner Pacific Ocean Fleet] (Moscow: Voyenizdat, 1973), 2d ed.; *My—Tikhookeantsy* [We are Pacific Ocean Sailors] (Vladivostok: Far East Book Publishers, 1977); *Krasnoznamennyy Tikhookeanskiy Flot* [Red Banner Pacific Ocean Fleet] (Moscow: Voyenizdat, 1981), 3d ed.

52. See *Kaspiyskaya Krasnoznamennaya* [Caspian Red Banner] (Makhachkala: Dagestan Book Publishers, 1974); A. A. Gritchenko, *Eto Bylo na Kaspii* [That Was on the Caspian] (Alma-Ata: Zhalyn, 1976); A. A. Makovskiy and B. M. Radchenko, *Kaspiyskaya Krasnoznamennaya* [Caspian Red Banner] (Moscow: Voyenizdat, 1982).

53. "Leningradskaya Voyenno-Morskaya Baza" [Leningrad Naval Base], *Sovetskaya Voyennaya Entsiklopediya,* Vol. 4, p. 614.

54. A. I. Koldunov, "Moskovskiy Okrug PVO" [Moscow Air Defense District], *Sovetskaya Voyennaya Entsiklopediya,* Vol. 5, p. 424. See also *Na Strazhe Neba Stolitsy* [On Guard Over the Sky of the Capital] (Moscow: Voyenizdat, 1971); A. F. Fedorov, *Aviatsiya v Bitve pod Moskvoy* [Aviation in the Battle of Moscow] (Moscow: Voyenizdat, 1971); A. U. Konstantinov, ed., *Ordena Lenina Moskovskiy Okrug PVO* [Order of Lenin Moscow Air Defense District] (Moscow: Voyenizdat, 1981).

55. G. S. Kalinin and G. V. Shevkov, eds., *Istoriya Gosudarstva i Prava SSSR* [History of State and Law USSR] (Moscow: Juridical Literature, 1981), Part 2. For one of the most reliable accounts of Beria's death, see Peter Deriabin, *Watchdogs of Terror* (New Rochelle, N.Y.: Arlington House, 1972), pp. 328–334.

56. "Pogranichnyy Okrug" [Border Guard District], *Sovetskaya Voyennaya Entsiklopediya,* Vol. 6, p. 370. See also *Pogranichnyye Voyska USSR* [Border Guards USSR] (Moscow: Nauka, 1970–1976). So far, six volumes of this history have been published covering the period 1918–1950. In addition, see *Zastava, v Ruzh'ye!* [Post, Take Guns!] (Moscow: Sov Rossiya, 1980); *Slovo o Pogranichnikakh* [Word About Border Guards] (Moscow: Sov Rossiya, 1978); *Pogranichnaya Zastava* [Border Guard Post] (Moscow: Politizdat, 1980).

57. I. K. Yakovlev, "Vnutrenniye Voyska" [Internal Troops], *Sovetskaya Voyennaya Entsiklopediya,* Vol. 2, p. 164. See also *Prikazano Zastupit'* [Ordered to Protect] (Moscow: Mol Gvardiya, 1974); I. G. Belikov, I. K. Boyko, and M. S. Logunov, *Imeni Dzerzhinskogo* [Named for Dzerzhinskiy] (Moscow: Voyenizdat, 1976).

7
Supporting Services and Special Troops

"The Military Balance 1983/84," prepared by the International Institute for Strategic Studies, London, listed the "total armed forces" for the Soviet Union as 5,050,000. The report went on to state that this number "excludes some 400,000 Border Guards, internal security, railroad, and construction troops, but includes some 1,500,000 command and general support troops not otherwise listed." "The Military Balance 1982/83" had placed the "total armed forces" at 3,705,000, but indicated in a footnote that this figure "excludes some 560,000 Border Guards, internal security, railroad and construction troops."[1]

This wide variation from one year to the next in estimates of Soviet military manpower strengths has many implications for Western military planners. Before 1975, many analysts concerned with the Soviet Armed Forces had considered only the number of personnel assigned to the five Soviet combat services—Strategic Rocket Forces, Ground Forces, Troops of National Air Defense, Air Forces, and Navy. They had failed to identify the strength of the vast support structure that backs up the combat elements of the Soviet military services. As a result of this oversight, it was generally believed by United States military authorities that Soviet planners envisaged only a short, blitzkrieg-type war, since the Soviet Union apparently lacked the support forces that would be required in order to wage a protracted conflict. The 1983/84 manpower estimate may cause even more changes in Western perceptions of Soviet military capabilities.

A major reason that the Soviet support forces had been overlooked is that their structure is so different from anything found in the West. Furthermore, a number of Soviet support services and special troops did not exist until recently in their present form. Construction and Billeting Troops, now frequently seen erecting apartment houses, offices, and other facilities in Moscow, are largely fulfilling tasks that were performed by forced labor during the long regime of Joseph Stalin.

Also, units of rail and road construction troops, now included among components of "special troops," were not formed until the late 1950s, after forced labor camps had been reduced in size. A number of senior Soviet officers who had been in charge of these labor camps were transferred to key positions in the newly established construction troops.[2] These matters are not discussed in Soviet publications and, in fact, appear to be concealed deliberately. It is not surprising that Western analysts, as a general rule, have failed to take the full number of the Soviet support troops into account.

As noted previously (see Chart 10), Troops of the Tyl (Rear Services), Construction and Billeting Troops, and Troops of Civil Defense are headed by deputy ministers of defense. The special troops—engineer, signal, chemical, railroad (construction), road (construction), and automotive—each headed by a general officer or marshal, are not assigned to a single organization. There is no single commander of special troops since each has its own chief, reporting directly to the minister of defense.

This chapter will examine the supporting services and the special troops. The largest and most complex of these is the support service designated Troops of the Tyl.

The Tyl (Rear Services)

Formation and Early History

In the Russian language, *tyl* literally means the reverse side of something, such as a coin. When applied to a military organization, tyl is the "rear" as opposed to the "front"—or support forces as opposed to combat forces. At times it is used to refer to the entire interior of a nation, and Soviet writers frequently assert that in a nuclear rocket war the distinction between the front and the tyl will be erased.[3]

A satisfactory organization of the tyl, enabling it to provide essential services to the combat fronts, has been a major problem for the Soviet leadership since the Red Army first was formed. The All-Russian Main Staff, established on 8 May 1918, had seven directorates: Command Personnel, Mobilization, Organization, Operations, Military Educational Institutions, Repair for the Army, and VOSO—Military Transport Agencies.[4] All local military administrative apparatuses were subordinate to this main staff.

Supply for the Red Army during the Civil War was difficult, since much of the military equipment that previously had been in the Russian Imperial Army had fallen into the hands of the White Russians. Newly formed Soviet military commissariats took inventories of weapons and military equipment in their areas. Norms for pay, rations, uniforms, and the like were determined. Central supply directorates were reorganized. The Main Artillery Directorate was formed in December 1917. The Central Military Technical Directorate, established in February 1918, was renamed the Main Military Engineering Directorate. On 1 June 1918 the existing supply directorates were combined into one central control organization—the Central Directorate for Supply of the Red Army (TsUS). On 2 September of the same year the Revolutionary Military Council of the Republic was established, and all military institutions were subordinated to it, including TsUS.[5] By this time all of the area controlled by the Red Army was under a complete wartime economy.

On 30 November 1918 the Council of Workers' and Peasants' Defense, with Lenin as chairman, was created as the supreme agency of government. One of the tasks of this council was to mobilize all resources of the country to supply the Red Army with food, clothing, and ammunition. Supply and support were critically short and often completely lacking. Soldiers frequently wore the uniforms of the old Russian Imperial Army, with all identifying markings ripped off. By 1920 the beginning of a tyl was in operation and providing the necessary support.[6] A major exception was in the Ukraine, where the population as a whole continued to resist Soviet rule. F. E. Dzerzhinskiy, head of the Cheka, was sent to the Ukraine with 50,000 internal troops to "liquidate" anti-Soviet bands and to protect the rear areas.[7]

As fighting died away on the various fronts, soldiers were used as a labor source, subject to being called up to fight on short notice. The Council of Workers' and Peasants' Defense accordingly was changed into the Council of Labor and Defense in March 1920. The practice of using Soviet military personnel as a labor source thus has had a long history.

At the end of the Civil War the nature of the future peacetime military forces was widely discussed. Various military reforms were introduced, including measures to improve the supply service within the Red Army.[8] A new Directorate of Supply Chiefs of the Workers' and Peasants' Red Army (RKKA), headed by I. S. Unshlikht, was assigned responsibility for the material support of the military forces, except for special supplies required by the Air Forces and Navy, which had their own supply channels and chiefs.[9] In theory, supplies in peacetime were to go from centralized warehouses out to military districts and then to units, which were charged with providing direct support to the troops. Direct levies were to be placed by Red Army commanders upon the various civilian agencies in their areas. Financial budgets of all the Red forces, including the Navy, were consolidated as time passed, and eventually a single supply system, or tyl, was formed that included both the Air Forces and the Navy. Reportedly, this reorganization of the central apparatus improved supply and at the same time permitted reduction of support personnel by 25 percent.

By 1935 the increased size of the Soviet Armed Forces made the task of the tyl more difficult. Recognizing that war with Germany or Japan was a distinct possibility, the Party leadership gave special attention to plans for mobilization both of the Armed Forces and of the economy. At this time the Soviet Union was in turmoil because of Stalin's forced collectivization of agriculture, and in many parts of the nation people were starving. Despite this widespread starvation and lack of consumer goods of all types, increases were made in the military's "untouchable reserves" (*neprikosnovennaya zapasa*), which were carefully stored and periodically renewed.[10]

In the early 1930s the organization dealing with food supply and clothing was divided into two separate agencies. In 1936 an administration for fuel supply (USG) was created. With the growth of automotive transport, a new directorate was formed in the General Staff to handle problems associated with this new transportation element. In 1938 an independent highway service organization was formed in VOSO (*voyennyye soobshcheniya*, literally, "military communications"), which to a large extent relieved the General Staff of its automotive transport responsibilities. During the mid-1930s special attention was given to improving medical services; a separate naval commissariat was formed, and still other tyl organizations were established.[11]

The first combat test of the tyl came with the fighting at Lake Khasan in 1938, followed by the battle of Khal'khan Gol in 1939. There is no evidence of serious problems in either case. But Stalin's purges in 1937 and 1938 had liquidated tens of thousands of Soviet officers, and the tyl had suffered along with the combat forces. New schools for supply and support officers were established in 1939 and 1940, and six of the existing military academies introduced courses for tyl specialists. Still, however, when war came there were many poorly qualified officers in key positions.[12]

The attack on Finland revealed major weaknesses in supply and support, particularly shortages of warm clothing. With temperatures down to −50°F, thousands of inadequately clad, poorly fed, and poorly equipped troops died needlessly.[13] Even more men died as slave laborers, forced by Stalin to build a railroad under impossible conditions to support the war effort.

The Tyl During World War II

When Hitler attacked in June 1941, the tyl was being reorganized. As is customary Soviet practice, theoretical questions first had to be worked out, and tyl theoreticians had failed to consider many problems, including that of supplying a front in time of war.[14] At this time each chief of staff at the army level had a deputy for the tyl. The fifth directorate of the General Staff—the Directorate for the Tyl and Supply— was responsible for supplying troops with artillery, engineering equipment, gas masks, communications gear, and quartermaster supplies, which included food, fodder, clothing, and boots.

General Georgiy K. Zhukov, chief of the General Staff in June 1941, was responsible for managing support equipment and supply, as well as for arranging transport and fuel. Marshal S. M. Budennyy headed another organization responsible for sanitary and veterinary services as well as material stocks. This organizational structure did not provide for overall management or control of the tyl. Centralization of rear services, according to previous Soviet planning, was to begin during the mobilization period immediately preceding the outbreak of any war. In the absence of a mobilization period, there was no alternate plan for centralizing control over rear services.[15]

Soviet planning also provided that tyl units would be assigned to divisions as they went over to a wartime footing. Therefore, when Hitler launched his surprise attack, there were no tyl units with the combat forces to provide support. Even worse, war materials were stored in warehouses in the military districts, with the greater part of the supplies in the border areas. For example, the Western Special Military District had eighteen food warehouses, Kiev—fifteen, Leningrad—twelve, Moscow—six, Volga—four. The Directorate of Food Supply of the Red Army had in reserve only a total of four central warehouses. The Administration of Fuel Supply was without any fuel reserves, and there was only one fuel depot for aviation fuel.[16] But that was not all. Most of the supplies for the entire Red Army were concentrated in the Kiev Military District. The Germans quickly overran these in the first few weeks of war, before the supplies could be distributed to Soviet troops. Prewar Soviet military theory had not considered the possibility of rapid advances by tanks supported by aircraft. In fact Soviet planning had assumed that, at the beginning of a war, Soviet forces would launch an offensive into enemy territory.

The army tyl region began 100 kilometers from the border and extended back to 250 kilometers; the front tyl region extended from this point back to 500 kilometers. The troop tyl region was at permanent military installations.[17] Troops moving from the rear to the combat zone in compliance with Stalin's order of "No retreat!" did not have transport equipment or loading and unloading facilities and could not take with them the reserves that had been accumulated for wartime use. In the first months of the war Soviet troops fought with practically no organized logistical support.

In the re-Stalinization era of the 1970s, Soviet military historians and writers of military memoirs glossed over Soviet mistakes and lack of preparedness in the early World War II period.[18] However, some idea of what actually happened during 1941 and 1942 did emerge during the de-Stalinization era of the early and middle 1960s. For example, the late Marshal A. A. Grechko, writing in 1966 during the twenty-fifth anniversary of the beginning of the Great Patriotic War, attributes the main reasons for the early Soviet reverses to Stalin's miscalculations. While the Soviets had greater numbers of tanks and aircraft, Grechko notes that only 9 percent of the Soviet tank force of 1941 were new models comparable to those of the Germans, only 20 percent of available aircraft were of modern design by contemporary standards, and the Red Army had only 30 percent of its established requirements for automatic weapons.[19]

The future Soviet minister of defense was named commander of the Thirty-fourth Cavalry Division in early July 1941 and was told he would have to take his force into combat without any heavy weapons. He succeeded finally in obtaining one 1927-model cannon. Rifles and ammunition were in very short supply. The only available antitank weapons were those that the men in his division had made themselves, such as "Molotov cocktails"—bottles filled with gasoline. It was not until October, four months after the beginning of the war and when German troops were near Rostov-on-the-Don in the North Caucasus, that Grechko's division managed to obtain twelve antitank guns.[20]

In addition to the near-total collapse of the front-line logistical system, replenishment of weapons and equipment was almost impossible, since most of the armaments industry was located in the western regions of the country. This industrialized area soon fell into German hands; many factories were overrun; the others were moved to the east as quickly as possible. Although the Soviets did accomplish remarkable feats in the relocation of their industries, considerable time still was required to get the relocated factories into operation.

Initially, overworked Soviet staff officers had little time to spend on plans to reorganize the tyl. Chiefs of the various supply services tried individually to find solutions to their all but impossible tasks. New answers had to be found. One of Stalin's initial solutions to the reverses caused in large part by inadequate equipment was to shoot many of the senior commanders and staff officers who had been forced to retreat in the face of the German attack. Another was to order counterattacks, sending Soviet troops to almost certain death or capture. A third solution, and the only one that achieved any success in providing supplies and equipment, was to reorganize the tyl completely and to staff it with the most competent individuals that could be found.

After the State Committee of Defense was established on 30 June 1941, specific responsibilities were assigned to individuals whose capabilities had been demonstrated in previous key assignments. A. I. Mikoyan was given the task of supplying the Red Army with fuel, food, and clothing. A. A. Andreyev was tasked with running the railroads. V. L. Vannikov, N. A. Voznesenskiy, A. G. Zverev, M. I. Kalinin, A. N. Kosygin, V. A. Malyshev, and N. M. Shvernik were given the task of evacuating industry and placing the nation on a wartime footing.[21]

On 28 July 1941 GKO decreed a complete reorganization of the tyl. The position of chief of the tyl was created, and a main administration of the tyl was formed, consisting of the staff of the chief of the tyl, the administration of military communications (VOSO), and the Highway Administration.[22] The Main Quartermaster Administration, the Administration of Fuel Supply, the Main Military-Sanitary Administration, and the Veterinarian Administration were made subordinate to the chief of the tyl. This reorganization took the tyl out from under the General Staff, and made the chief of the tyl a deputy people's commissar (*narkom*) of defense. This position was given to General A. V. Khrulev, with General M. V. Zakharov as his deputy. Zakharov, who later served on two occasions in the 1960s as chief of the General Staff, remained in the deputy position only from August to December 1941, but the experience made a deep impression that lasted throughout his career.

Tyl directorates were created in each front and army. The chief of the tyl of each front and each army also was made a deputy commander of the troops. An experienced, capable individual was selected as chief of the tyl of each front, and equally capable men were selected to head each of the various administrations or directorates under Khrulev.

With these changes and personnel assignments, some semblance of a supply organization was established. Transportation remained a major problem. Railroad transport managed to perform to the limit of its rolling stock and rail network. Hundreds of locomotives were provided by the United States, many of which still were in use in the eastern regions of the Soviet Union in the 1970s. Truck transport was in very short supply, and 30,000 trucks and drivers were taken from the civilian economy. Trucks were never produced in quantities sufficient to meet military needs, and eventually tens of thousands of vehicles were provided by the United States under lend-lease.[23]

In the reconstruction period following World War II, heavy demands still were placed on the tyl. There were demobilized soldiers to be relocated, thousands of German and Japanese prisoners to be guarded, and new military districts to be established. There also was the task of maintaining the huge numbers of Soviet occupation troops who were ensuring Soviet control throughout Eastern Europe.

In 1943 A. V. Khrulev was given the rank of general of the Army, and his position was redesignated as deputy minister of defense for the tyl. He retained this position until 1951, when he was replaced by General Colonel V. I. Vinogradov, who formerly had been the tyl chief of staff. In 1953 the Ministry of War and Naval Ministry were combined into a single Ministry of Defense. This helped to bring about the centralization of a number of tyl agencies. In the postwar years the tyl troops gradually were mechanized and motorized. By 1958, with the appointment of Marshal of the Soviet Union I. Kh. Bagramyan as chief of the tyl and deputy minister of defense, the organization was structured generally as it exists in the mid-1980s.

The Tyl (Rear Services) in the 1980s

By Soviet definition the present Tyl of the Armed Forces consists of

bases and warehouses with reserves of various kinds of materiel; special troops (railroad, automotive, road and pipe-laying), fleet auxilliary; airport engineers, aviation technical, medical, veterinarian and units, establishments and subunits. It may also have units and subunits of engineer and chemical troops, signal troops, air defense and guards. For convenience, the following divisions can be made: by scale and nature of mission to be peformed— strategic [central], operational, and troop tyls.[24]

Division of the tyl into center, operational, and troop is reflected in Table 5.

As indicated, there is one tyl organization, the center, that plans for and supports the Soviet Armed Forces as a whole or each individual service. At this level, direction is provided by the Ministry of Defense through the chief of the tyl or by the services. This represents the "strategic" link through the chiefs of the tyl.

Each of the services of the Armed Forces has a deputy commander in chief for the tyl who provides for its supply services.

Marshal Ogarkov, chief of the General Staff, expressed concern over tyl problems in modern war. He wrote:

It is quite natural that with the quantitative and qualitative changes which are taking place in military affairs, preparation for and conduct of complex modern operations predetermine new content for the system of

TABLE 5
Organization of the Tyl

Kind of Tyl	Category of Military Art	Troop Organization	"Links" of the Tyl
Center	Strategy	The armed forces as a whole; services of the armed forces	Tyl of the armed forces (strategic)
Operational	Operational Art	Army, Front, Fleet	Tyl of an army, front, or fleet (operational)
Troop	Tactics	Troop subunits and units	Tyl of a regiment or division (tactical or troop)

Source: A. N. Logovskiy, *Strategiya i Ekonomika* [Strategy and Economics] (Moscow: Voyenizdat, 1961), p. 192.

all types of support, especially rear services and technical. The scale of such support is in no degree comparable with operations of the last war. Today demands for materiel have increased tenfold or more. At the same time one must bear in mind that with today's weapons, troops can sustain heavy losses in combat equipment and weapons in the course of combat operations. This results in a manifold increase in volume of repair and maintenance of combat equipment and weapons, as well as a change in the nature of repair and maintenance activities. And this, in turn, requires a new, improved organization of technical support of modern operations.[25]

Troop subunits and units, that is, regiments and divisions, have tyl units assigned. Support personnel at this level are somewhat fewer than would be found in comparable U.S. organization. This is due to the fact that more of the Soviet support personnel are centrally controlled and not assigned down to division level. Total combat-to-support force ratios, however, are approximately the same in the Soviet Armed Forces as in the armed forces of the United States.[26]

The organization of the staff of the chief of the tyl of the Armed Forces in the Ministry of Defense provides an indication of the support given by tyl agencies at all levels. This structure reflects the centralized nature of the Soviet Armed Forces and the direct control exercised by the Ministry of Defense.

Staff positions and personnel assigned to the Tyl of the Soviet Armed Forces (as of 1 May 1984) are:

Chief of the Tyl of the Armed Forces USSR— Deputy Minister of Defense	Marshal of the Soviet Union S. K. Kurkotkin (since 1972)
First Deputy Chief	General Colonel P. I. Sysoyev (since 1971)
First Deputy Chief & Chief of Staff	General Colonel I. M. Golushko (since 1970) (Doctor of Military Sciences)
Deputy Chief	General Colonel N. S. Rozhkov (since 1977)
Deputy Chief	General Colonel G. T. Tarasov
Chief, Central Military Medical Administration	General Colonel of Medical Services F. I. Komarov (Doctor of Medical Sciences)
Chief, Fuel Supply Administration	General Colonel-Engineer V. V. Nikitin
Chief, Central Food Supply Administration	General Colonel I. D. Isayenko
Chief, Central Clothing Supply Administration	General Lieutenant QM F. P. Petrov
Chief, Main Administration of Trade	General Lieutenant QM Ye. I. Gol'dberg
Chief, Rear Cadres Administration	General Lieutenant V. G. Zaytsev
Chief, Railroad Troops	General Colonel Technical Troops A. M. Kryukov
Chief, Pipelaying Troops	Unidentified
Chief, Central Administration of Military Communications (VOSO)	General Colonel Technical Troops A. S. Klemin
Chief, Military Veterinarian Service	General Major Veterinarian Service O. S. Belen'kiy
Chief, Motortransport Service	General Major Technical Troops V. P. Petrov
Chief, Highway Directorate	General Major Technical Troops N. Vasil'yev

| Chief, Tourism and Excursion Administration | General Major QM A. P. Gashchuk |
| Chief, Political Section, Staff & Administrations of the Tyl | General Major V. P. Timonin |

Postwar commanders of the tyl of the Armed Forces were:

Aug 1941–1951	General of the Army A. V. Khrulev
Jan 1951–1958	General Colonel V. I. Vinogradov
Jun 1958–1968	Marshal of the Soviet Union I. Kh. Bagramyan
Apr 1968–1972	General of the Army S. S. Maryakhin
Jul 1972–	General of the Army S. K. Kurkotkin

Troop subunits and units and their equivalents also have deputy commanders for the tyl. These commanders are required each year to prepare a "housekeeping plan," centered around the winter and summer periods of training, reflecting most of the areas under the tyl of the Armed Forces except medical, transport, and trade.[27] The plan must indicate the volume or cost of work; the demands for workers and transport, material and financial means, and where they are to be obtained; the time in which the work is to be done; and the responsibility for fulfillment of the tasks outlined. Both the chief of staff of the unit and the deputy commander of the tyl sign the annual plan, which then is confirmed by the commander.

The plan is usually divided into six parts: (1) general problems of housekeeping, planning, and control; (2) requirements for fuel supply; (3) requirements for food supply; (4) requirements for clothing supply; (5) measures for quarters exploitation service; and (6) other measures or requirements.[28]

General tasks of the annual plan include raising the combat readiness of the supply service; preparing tyl units for field exercises; supporting the troops' arrival at the field training center; providing for reinforcements or additions to units; preparing servicemen for their discharge into the reserves; providing support for reserve units on temporary duty; selecting candidates to be specialists in the tyl services; and ensuring adherence to the plan.

Fuel requirements include storing and dispensing POL products and also handling fire prevention measures, quality control, repair work, and related duties. Food supply requirements include preserving potatoes and vegetables, supplying centers for food preparation during exercises, making inventories, and repairing refrigerators, storehouses, vegetable sheds, scales, and kitchens. Units also are expected to raise vegetables in small gardens. Quarters exploitation service entails the building and repair of bunkhouses and common rooms, furniture repair, and related duties.

The tyl, throughout the Armed Forces, has the following functions: (1) finance, (2) medicine, (3) fuel supply, (4) military communications (VOSO), (5) food supply, (6) clothing supply, (7) main administration of trade, (8) military veterinary medicine, (9) motortransport, and (10) quarters exploitation.

The number of personnel assigned to each of the tyl components is unknown. In some components, personnel may number in the tens of thousands. Nor is much known of their organization. Like service personnel in the United States, tyl personnel may be responsible to two agencies. For example, medical personnel in a unit within a military district would be responsible to the division commander, up through to the military district commander. They would also be responsible, for specialized medical matters, to the chief of the Central Military Medical Administration.

Functions of finance,[29] medicine, fuel supply, and veterinary medicine are adequately described by their designations. A few comments on the other components may be helpful.

The Central Administration of Military Communications (transport), commonly referred to as VOSO, is responsible for planning and organizing the movement of military supplies by rail, ship, and aircraft.[30] These troops are *not* responsible for building and maintaining roads and railroads, for providing drivers and vehicles, or for maintaining vehicles. Rather they administer military transport needs, ensuring that personnel and goods are routed by the most efficient means and that whatever is transported reaches its destination. VOSO offices are located in many of the larger Soviet railway stations, and similar offices can be seen frequently in the larger airports.

At various times in the past, VOSO was placed under different agencies. General of the Army S. M. Shtemenko, former chief of staff of the Warsaw Pact Forces and first deputy chief of the General Staff, described the various positions of the VOSO:

The military transport agencies were often made subordinate to various other departments but they were never outside the control of the General Staff. At the beginning of the war VOSO was organizationally a part of the General Staff. Then they became independent for a time and their chief was the people's commissar for railways. Then this department was reallocated to the chief of rear services who simultaneously held the post of people's commissar for railways. At the end of the war the military transport agencies (VOSO) again came under the control of the General Staff. Experience had confirmed the undeniable fact that no matter who was in charge of these agencies they could not function independently of the General Staff. Since operational movements are continually taking place in wartime and the fate of operations is largely dependent on them, the General Staff must plan and control them daily, even hourly in some cases, giving the military transport agencies (VOSO) concrete instructions and maintaining a continuous check on their fulfillment.[31]

The chief, Central Food Supply Administration, is responsible not only for ensuring the procurement of food for the Armed Forces, but also for supervising a number of military *sovkhozes* ("state farms").[32] Throughout the Soviet Union, especially in Central Asia, Siberia, and the Far East, these military farms supply part of the food—vegetables, grain, and livestock—required by the Armed Forces. The number and size of these farms are regarded as a military secret.[33] Within recent years their numbers have increased, and the Armed Forces appear to be more dependent upon their output. Many of the farm workers are civilians; however, some military personnel are assigned to them.

The Clothing Supply Administration supplies uniforms, including boots, to all inducted personnel, as well as certain items to officers. During their period of compulsory military service, inducted personnel are required to wear uniforms at all times; their civilian clothing is sent to their homes or placed in storage. When the period of compulsory military service is completed, a *new* uniform is issued to each individual, who is "discharged into the reserve." He will wear this uniform when he travels home and when he is called up for refresher training. Officers may be issued bolts of cloth, which they may take to a local tailor to have their uniforms made to measure.

The Main Administration of Trade (Voyentorg) is responsible for military stores, military bookstores, and other related functions. (The nearest counterparts to the Soviet military stores in the United States are post exchanges, base exchanges, and ship stores.) Prices are the same as in civilian stores, and civilians are permitted to make purchases.[34]

The responsibility of the chief of Motortransport Service is to provide trucks, prime movers, and other vehicles used in transport. VOSO, as already noted, has responsibility for planning the movement of men and material and ensuring that cargos are properly dispatched. Drivers are provided by the automotive troops, a category of special troops that will be discussed later. The motortransport service also probably has a role in ensuring that vehicles in civilian industries are given mobilization numbers so that they can be utilized in an emergency.

The Tyl of the Armed Forces has its own schools for the training and education of its required specialists. These may serve in the tyl at any of its three levels—the Tyl of the Armed Forces; the tyl of armies, fronts, or fleets; or the tyl of the regiment or division. It is obviously difficult to determine what percentage of the total manpower of the tyl is assigned to the various services and units and what percentage provides common service to all. What is clear, however, is that the Soviet leadership has made careful provisions for the quartermaster-type support of its Armed Forces.

The Tyl of the Armed Forces is closely connected with the nation's economy. It follows the same socialist principles in planning, placing orders, supplying the troops, and using the transportation system and medical, finance, and trade services as the rest of the country. Soviet authors claim that military-technical progress has brought automated control systems to this process, streamlining its operations. Modeling is also coming into wide use in planning.[35] These claims, however, may be far from actual reality.

Railroad Troops

The railroad troops of the Ministry of Defense play an active role in building and maintaining the Soviet railroad system. This rail system is of the utmost importance, for even in the mid-1980s there is no connecting highway network between the western and eastern regions of the Soviet Union. East of the Urals, and particularly east of Lake Baykal, rail and air transport is the only link that many of the cities have with the outside world.

Before 1955 most of the new rail lines constructed during the Soviet regime were built by prison labor. Solzhenitsyn has provided a partial list of these stupendous rail lines: Kotlas-Vorkuta, Rikasikha-Molotovsk, Salekhard-Igarka (railroad of death), Lalsk-Pinyug, Karaganda-Mointy-Balkhash, Trans-Siberian second tracks, and Taishet-Lena.[36] With the release of the majority of the concentration camp inmates, another means of mobile labor had to be found. The railroad troops, in part, have fulfilled this need.

Since 1974, hundreds of miles to the north of the present Trans-Siberian Railway, thousands of railroad troops have been building the Baykal-Amur Mainline railroad (BAM) to provide a second rail link to the Pacific Coast. In other parts of the Soviet Union, far removed from any known military installation, railroad troops can be observed laying new track or doing repair work.

Railroad troops have their own insignia. Although presently one of the components of special troops, they still appear to retain close ties with VOSO (military communication). Throughout World War II, and well into the postwar years, the railroad troops were a part of the tyl under VOSO. At that time most of the railroad troops probably were prisoner laborers. Currently, officer inputs are provided in part by the Leningrad Higher Command School of Railroad Troops and Military Communication, a VOSO school under the rear services. Officers are selected to attend the Academy of the Rear Services and Transport.[37]

Railroad troops are formed into battalions and companies. Unlike a number of the other special troops, they are not organically assigned. Postwar chiefs of railroad troops were:

1945–1968	General Colonel of Technical Troops P. A. Kabanov
1968–1982	General Colonel of Technical Troops A. M. Kryukov
1983–	General Colonel of Technical Troops M. K. Makartsev

Road Troops (Construction)

Just as the railroad troops construct and maintain railroads, the road troops construct and maintain roads and bridges for motor traffic.[38] Prior to 1955 most work of this type was performed by Soviet prisoners.

Although road troops generally work on roads that have a primary military use, they also can be observed constructing new roads that appear to have little immediate military justification. This suggests that in time of peace road troops may be used as a source of mobile labor, training for their wartime role.

Officers may be obtained from civilian engineering schools. Apparently there is no academy specifically designated to provide officers in the road troops with advanced education and training. Some related courses may be offered at the Rear Services and Transport Academy in Leningrad.

General Lieutenant Engineer Troops M. G. Kokornikov was chief of the Highway Directorate of the Ministry of Defense from 1975 to 1983. He was then succeeded by General Major Technical Troops N. Vasil'yev.

Automotive Troops

Soviet military strategy postulates that in any future war railroads will be subject to intensive air and missile strikes and that major dependence will be placed on road transport. For this reason, great attention is paid to the automotive troops.[39] These consist primarily of drivers and mechanics for trucks, fuel trucks, tank trailers, refrigerator trucks, ammunition trucks, and so on. Automotive troops also maintain mobile automotive repair shops.

It is difficult to keep separate the various troops that have something to do with automotive transport. VOSO, under the tyl, has responsibility for determining how goods and personnel will be moved and for ensuring that such transport is effected. The motortransport service of the tyl provides the necessary vehicles. Road troops (construction) build and maintain roads. Lastly, the automotive troops provide the drivers to move goods as prescribed by VOSO, in vehicles provided by the motortransport service of the tyl, over roads constructed and maintained by the road troops.

Automotive troops are formed into units and subunits and are organic parts of larger units and the tyl. They may range in size from platoons to battalions and are assigned to regiments, divisions, and fronts. Officer inputs into automotive troops are provided by four higher military automotive command schools. Professional education and training of officers is provided by the Military Academy of Rear Services and Transport.

General Major Technical Troops V. P. Petrov has been chief of the Motortransport Service of the Ministry of Defense since 1975.

Construction and Billeting Troops

In the curious twilight world of the Soviet support structure, the origins of Construction and Billeting Troops remain obscure. These troops were not formed until the mid-1950s, and since then very little has been published about their training and organization. However, they are perhaps the most visible troops that one encounters in the Soviet Union, since they work on both military and civilian construction projects. *Fundamentals of Soviet Military Legislation* provides the following information:

> Starting in the 1950s, callups [for required military service] have been taking place of citizens for military construction detachments which have been designated for construction and erection work and for making prefabricated items and lumber in industrial and lumbering enterprises of the Ministry of Defense. The manpower for military construction detachments primarily comes from callups who have finished construction schools or have construction or associated specialities or experience in construction work (sanitary technicians, bulldozer operations, cable layers). The rights, obligations, and responsibilities of military builders are determined by military law, but their labor activities are regulated by labor legislation. . . . Pay for the work of military builders is according to the existing norms. The obligatory period of time working in military construction detachments counts as active military duty.[40]

Like the chief of the tyl, the chief of Construction and Billeting Troops is a deputy minister of defense. Previous deputy ministers of defense for Construction and Billeting Troops were:

1958–1963	General Colonel QM A. I. Shebunin
1963–1973	General of the Army A. N. Komarovskiy
1973–1978	Marshal of Engineer Troops A. V. Gelovani
1978–	Marshal of Engineer Troops N. F. Shestopalov

Inductees are assigned to these troops by the military commissariat when entering military service.[41] They must be capable of hard physical labor. Inductees serve for two years in Construction and Billeting Troops units, as do those assigned to other areas, and they have the same rights, obligations, and responsibilities as those in other military units.[42]

Chiefs of some of the administrations of Construction and Billeting Troops (as of 1 May 1984) are:

Chief, Main Quarters Exploitation Administration	General Colonel-Engineer A. F. Fedorov
Chief, Main Military Construction Administration	General Lieutenant-Engineer V. N. Charkin
Chief, Administrative-Management Administration	General Lieutenant-Engineer L. S. Chuvakhin

It has been hypothesized that those assigned to Construction and Billeting Troops include a large percentage of minority groups in the USSR, whose reliability might be questioned. It also is possible that many assigned to this organization may lack the mental capability to perform in units that have complex weapons systems and where personnel must be technically proficient. On the other hand, there is some evidence that an assignment in Construction and Billeting Troops is considered a privilege, since such troops receive considerable reimbursement when they work on projects for ministries other than the Ministry of Defense. Whatever the true state of affairs, it is apparent that Construction and Billeting Troops are needed as a mobile labor force, capable of being assigned under military control on short notice to perform work as required by the Party-military leadership.

Those assigned to construction and billeting units have completed the premilitary training required of all Soviet youth. Once assigned, they receive only a short period of purely military training. Like all Soviet military personnel, they receive lectures in political studies, but somewhat fewer than in the other services, branches, and components. For example, political studies are required of enlisted personnel throughout the Soviet Armed Forces as follows:

Personnel serving in military construction units assigned to:
　routine projects—(winter) once a week for three hours
　　　　　　　—(summer) once a week for two hours
　major projects—once a week for two hours
Personnel serving in all other components of the Armed Forces:
　normal duty—twice a week for two hours
　on ships—once a week for three hours[43]

The diminished emphasis on political training given to Construction and Billeting Troops leads to conjecture. Since they are not likely to be in direct contact with an enemy, they seemingly require less "military-patriotic" education. During the summer (when work can be performed outdoors and the daylight hours are long) as well as when working on major projects, these troops receive only half as much political indoctrination as regular troops, and during the winter only three-fourths as much.

Large Soviet cities such as Moscow may have a military building administration.

The Sheremet'yevo International Airport (most foreign tourists enter Moscow through this airport) and many buildings on the new Kalinin Prospect, the most modern street in the entire USSR, which begins only a block from the United States Embassy, were constructed by military builders in Moscow.[44] Almost all of the facilities built for the 1980 Olympics in Moscow were the product of the military builders. Many were brought into the Moscow area to help complete the job on time.

Numbers of building and construction troops are unknown. Estimates vary between 100,000 and 400,000. Whatever their actual numbers and amount of military training, they represent an important component of the Soviet Armed Forces, able to perform a variety of building and construction tasks on very short notice. Weapons of mass destruction have created a requirement for troops of mass construction.

Troops of Civil Defense

Only a few months after the president of the United States journeyed to Moscow to sign the SALT I agreement, in October 1972 the chief of civil defense in the Soviet Union was designated deputy minister of defense. In September 1973, the *Yezhegodnik* ("Yearbook") of the *Bolshaya Entsiklopediya* listed civil defense troops at the same level as the Strategic Rocket Forces, Ground Forces, Troops of National Air Defense, Air Forces, and Navy.[45] Relatively little information is available to the West about the size or composition of these troops, despite frequent items about and photographs of civil defense troops in military newspapers and journals, and references to individuals assigned to civil defense units.

Until 1960 civil defense in the Soviet Union was under the control of the Ministry of Internal Affairs and was known as MPVO, meaning "local air defense."[46] Then in 1960, MPVO was shifted to the Ministry of Defense.

In the summer of 1961 a number of changes took place in the Soviet defense structure, apparently due to the tensions the Soviet leadership anticipated when planning the building of the Berlin Wall. In July of that year, one month before the wall was constructed, civil defense was reorganized at the national level to become Civil Defense of the USSR still under the Ministry of Defense. Marshal Vasiliy Chuykov, commander in chief of the Ground Forces and deputy minister of defense at the time, was given the additional title and duties of chief of civil defense. He was succeeded in July 1972 by General of the Army A. T. Altunin.

The underlying concept of the new Soviet military doctrine adopted in 1961 was that "the Armed Forces, the country, and the whole Soviet people must be prepared for the eventuality of nuclear rocket war."[47] Since Khrushchev was preparing a dual challenge to the United States and to other Western nations, one in Berlin and another in Cuba the following year, civil defense became a matter of national importance. In fact it was demanded by the "revolution in military affairs" brought about by the introduction of the nuclear rocket into the Soviet Armed Forces.

In the early and mid-1960s the Soviet leadership thought that their antiballistic missile system would be able to blunt any missile attack. But multiple independent reentry warheads, developed by the United States, made the ABM system then possessed by the Soviets of little value. In an attempt to provide for maximum population survival, the importance of civil defense was reemphasized.

The Moscow Military School for Civil Defense opened in 1967. One of its three-year courses prepares officers for the mechanized units of civil defense; another prepares commanders of subunits for antiradiation and antichemical protection; a third course prepares officers as radio technicians. The first graduation took place in 1969, the initial students having been rushed through an accelerated course.[48] In 1974, the school became a four-year one and was renamed the Moscow Higher Command School of Road and Engineer Troops.

It is probable that the designation of Road and Engineer Troops is a cover; indeed, the school may continue to prepare officers for civil defense duties.

Military personnel assigned to civil defense fall into two separate categories. In the first category are those in supervisory and administrative positions associated with the "civilian" side of civil defense. These positions include a chief of staff for civil defense, usually a general major, in each of the fifteen republics of the Soviet Union; a chief of staff in the grade of colonel or lieutenant colonel in each autonomous republic, autonomous oblast, national okrug, kray, oblast, or city over 100,000 in population; a civil defense chief (military) in the 3,097 rayons or regions not part of cities and in 1,900 cities with populations of less than 100,000. When these positions and supporting staffs are considered, it is estimated that approximately 50,000 military personnel are assigned to civil defense duties in this category of civil defense.

In the second category are deputy commanders for civil defense within the headquarters of each of the sixteen military districts of the Soviet Union, with their assigned Troops of Civil Defense. The primary task of this portion of civil defense is Rescue and Urgent Disaster and Restoration Work (SNAVR). This includes locating and marking areas of contamination; localizing and extinguishing fires; giving first aid to and evacuating the injured; removing people from disaster areas; disinfecting people and decontaminating clothing, transport, equipment, and so on.[49] Such work is carried on by both troop and nonmilitary units.

An indication of the training and responsibilities of the Troops of Civil Defense may be drawn from this account:

> Rocket signals light up the dark morning sky and the woods come to life. People in military clothing spring up in the woods from camouflaged shelters and cover. With a roar of motors, tanks, armored transports, powerful trailers, and trucks crawl up to the highway. A few minutes pass and then the combat columns form up along the edge of the highway ready to march. On the trailers are bulldozers, autocranes, excavators; also fire engines and ambulances are in the column. This troop subunit is going to practice fighting a special "enemy"—fire, destruction, flooding, and other consequences of use of weapons of mass destruction by the enemy.
>
> Circumstances are not simple. City X has been hit by a nuclear strike. Hurrying to the city, they find the bridge is out. The heavy equipment must make a detour. They reach the city and are met by a wall of fire. They put out the fire and meet a crater on the road. The bulldozers make short work of it. Practices like these are everyday happenings for the Troops of Civil Defense.[50]

Fragmentary evidence of troop organization leads to the conclusion that there probably are as many as 50,000 troops assigned to civil defense in military units. This force, combined with a military force of approximately 50,000 assigned to civil defense duties outside the formal military establishment, suggests that at least 100,000 military personnel are engaged in civil defense duties of some type.

Soviet political-military leaders assert that civil defense is now a matter of strategic significance.[51] Such statements, in combination with indications of shelters, food reserves, and civil defense equipment cause considerable concern in non-Communist nations. Western leaders somewhat belatedly have awakened to the fact that, contrary to popular assumptions in the West, the Soviet leadership has not accepted the concept of assured mutual destruction and through the use of civil defense may indeed have upset the strategic balance.

Previous chiefs of civil defense, USSR, have been:

Jul 1961–1972	Marshal of the Soviet Union V. I. Chuykov
Jul 1972–	General of the Army A. T. Altunin

Special Troops

As shown in Chart 10, special troops include engineer, chemical, signal (radiotechnical), railway construction, road construction, and automotive troops. Chiefs of these troops are senior generals or marshals. However, they are not deputy ministers of defense as are the chiefs of the tyl, construction and billeting, and civil defense.

Special troops are directly subordinate to the minister of defense and are part of the services of the Armed Forces or the Tyl. Their designation is determined by their organization, arms, and equipment. Almost all of the services have Engineer Troops, Chemical Troops, Signal Troops, radiotechnical units, and topographic subunits. Some services have unique special troops—for example, the Air Forces, with their units of aviation engineering service. As already noted, automobile troops, road troops, railroad troops, pipe-laying troops, and others are part of the Rear Services.[52]

As will be described in detail later, each of the special troop branches has its own military and higher military schools, and the larger branches, such as signal, have their own academies.

Engineer Troops

Engineer troops provide engineering support "for combat operations of all the services and service branches." They "are subdivided into general (combat engineer) and special categories (which includes pontoon and bridge, assault crossing, highway, works service, camouflage, construction, and others)."[53]

Further, "according to their affiliation," engineer troops may be a component part of Ground Force units or designated for assignment "to an army, front, Supreme High Command Reserve, Navy, air, or one of the other services of the Armed Forces."[54]

An Aviation Engineering Service (IAS) provides engineering support to Air Force units, and probably to the air component of the Troops of Air Defense as well. It may be assumed that the Strategic Rocket Force and Navy have special engineer units for specific support.

Since the introduction of nuclear weapons Soviet engineer troops have been given the additional role of preparing defenses against nuclear attack.[55] Because of the requirements for dispersion of all military units, the task is complicated. In a number of topical areas engineer troops must work closely with civil defense troops in order to coordinate defensive measures against nuclear attack.

The Soviet Armed Forces take great pride in their engineers and engineering equipment, some of which is very advanced. The United States Army does not have any bridging equipment equal to Soviet truck-mounted bridge spans. The Soviet floating combination railroad and highway bridge is the only bridge of its type in any nation.

In the Soviet Ground Forces, engineer troops are assigned organically down through the regimental level, each division including an engineer battalion.

Postwar chiefs of engineer troops were:

1946–1952	Marshal of Engineer Troops M. P. Vorob'yev
1952–1965	Marshal of Engineer Troops A. I. Proshlyakov
1965–1975	Marshal of Engineer Troops V. K. Kharchenko
1975–	Marshal of Engineer Troops S. Kh. Aganov

Chemical Troops

During the 1973 Middle East war, Israeli forces captured a considerable amount of Soviet equipment used by the Arab nations. When this equipment was examined, many Westerners were amazed to find that it had been designed for an environment in which nuclear, chemical, and bacteriological weapons might be used. This design extended even to soldiers' clothing. The United States armed forces have done little to provide clothing and other equipment that would enable the individual to survive in nuclear war conditions. In contrast, Soviet soldiers must perform part of their duties wearing protective clothing, which includes gas masks. At the squadron level in the Soviet Air Forces, ground crews must practice washing aircraft to remove radioactive fallout. The Soviet political-military leadership gives serious attention to the possibility that chemical, nuclear, and bacteriological weapons will be introduced in any future conflict.

Defense against chemical, nuclear, and bacteriological weapons is the responsibility of the chemical troops. Their tasks include "radiation and chemical reconnaissance, control over radioactive irradiation of personnel, processing of troops, degasification and disinfecting of the area, and other special measures."[56] Emphasis given to these tasks is believed to be unequaled in the armed forces of any other nation.

Three higher military schools prepare officers for service in the chemical troops. Two are higher military command schools for chemical defense and the third is the higher military engineering school of chemical defense. The first two schools offer four-year courses; the third offers a five-year course. Nothing is revealed about the syllabus or size of student bodies in these schools. They are located at Kastroma, Saratov, and Tambov, in areas denied to foreigners.

After officers have served in units for a number of years, they may be selected to attend the Military Academy of Chemical Defense named for Marshal of the Soviet Union S. K. Timoshenko. This academy, located in Moscow, offers a standard three-year course.

Like the engineer troops, chemical troops are assigned throughout the five services of the Soviet Armed Forces. The greatest numbers are found in the Ground Forces, since this is not only the largest service but also the one that will be in direct contact with the enemy. It is not known if the duties of chemical troops are confined to providing protection against possible nuclear, chemical, and bacteriological attacks, or if they have responsibilities in connection with the employment of Soviet weapons of mass destruction.

Postwar chiefs of chemical troops were:

1946–1965	General Colonel Technical Troops I. F. Chukhnov
1965–1966	General Lieutenant Technical Troops N. S. Danilov
1966–1969	General Lieutenant Technical Troops I. F. Manets
1969–	General Colonel Technical Troops V. K. Pikalov

Signal Troops

In the highly centralized Soviet military structure, designed to permit the Kremlin to exercise daily and hourly control over fronts during wartime, great attention is given to military signal communications. Signal troops have the task of ensuring that communications systems are available for troop control throughout the Soviet Armed Forces and at all levels of command.[57]

At the present time much of the Soviet Union is connected by underground cable, ensuring a high degree of communications reliability in the event of war. Since the 1970s a major effort has been under way in the far eastern regions of the USSR, particularly along the Chinese border, to place all telephone lines in underground cables. Various other types of communications are employed, including point-to-point microwave, short-wave, and satellite communications, each providing backup to the other in the event that one system is jammed or destroyed. As the Soviets develop means to disrupt or to destroy the satellites of their opponents, they also realize that their own communications satellites may be neutralized.

While not neglecting sophisticated means of communications, Soviet textbooks also emphasize the need to know and to be able to employ basic means of signaling. Use of smoke, flags, hand signals, lights, and other signaling methods are taught and practiced on maneuvers.[58] Experiences of World War II, when Soviet forces were required to operate in very primitive conditions, still are remembered. Soviet writings also stress that any message transmitted by electrical means may be intercepted. Some maneuvers are conducted using only basic, nonelectronic communications.

In the event of war the civilian Ministry of Communications probably would be merged with the signal troops of the Ministry of Defense. Ties between these two organizations already are close. For example, from 1948 to 1975 the minister of communications of the USSR was General Colonel of Signal Troops N. D. Psurtsev, who, before becoming minister, was chief of communications of the General Staff. Postwar chiefs of signal troops were:

1946–1956	Marshal of Signal Troops I. T. Peresypkin
1956–1958	General Colonel of Signal Troops I. T. Bulychev
1958–1970	Marshal of Signal Troops A. I. Leonov
1970–	Marshal of Signal Troops A. I. Belov

The actual number of signal troops is unknown. However, some idea of the size of this force can be obtained simply by noting that there are twelve schools that graduate officers. Nine of these schools are classified as higher military command schools of signals, with four-year courses. Two other schools are higher military engineering schools of signals, and another is a higher military engineering school of radioelectronics. These latter schools require five years for graduation. After serving for a number of years, officers may be selected to attend the

Military Academy of Signals named for Marshal of the Soviet Union S. M. Budennyy.

Like most of the other special troops, signal troops are organically assigned throughout the Soviet Armed Forces, both within the services and at the many headquarters.

Certain very high level communications, such as those from the Ministry of Defense to military districts, groups of forces abroad, and fleets, may be under control of the KGB. There is no discussion of this, however, in Soviet military writings.

In November 1977, the Soviet press revealed that Marshal of Signal Troops A. I. Belov, chief of signal troops, was also a deputy chief of the General Staff.

Main and Central Directorates/Administrations

In addition to special troops, the Ministry of Defense has a number of main and central directorates. Although subordinated to the minister of defense or his deputies, they are closely connected to the General Staff, the Main Political Administration, the services of the Armed Forces and their staffs, the Rear Services and Civil Defense staffs, and other sections of the Ministry of Defense.

Main and central directorates organize, direct, and control their own support functions. They perform military-scientific and scientific research, test construction, apply modern methods of efficiency, do inventive work, and develop regulations for their support functions or work. Many such directorates have schools, research facilities, central bases, and depots at their disposal. Some perform the functions of giving orders to industry, supplying or repairing armaments and military equipment, and developing specifications for new kinds of equipment or improving older ones. Others construct major facilities, including housing and barracks, and supply troops with provisions. The main and central directorates include the following:

Main Directorate of Schools	General Colonel D. I. Litovtsev
Main Rocket and Artillery Directorate	General Lieutenant-Engineer Yu. M. Lazarev
Main Armored Tank Directorate	General Colonel Yu. M. Potapov
Main Directorate of Navigation and Oceanography	Admiral A.I. Rassokho
Main Trade Directorate	General Lieutenant QM Ye. I. Gol'dberg

Central Finance Directorate	General Colonel QM V. N. Dutov
Central Food Supply Directorate	(see entries under Rear Services–Tyl)
Central Clothing Supply Directorate	(see entries under Rear Services–Tyl)
Central Military Medical Directorate	(see entries under Rear Services–Tyl)
Central Directorate of Military Communications (VOSO)	(see entries under Rear Services–Tyl)

In addition to those listed are many other main and central directorates, some about which only little is known.

*   *   *

There is no reason why the Soviet Union's military structure should resemble that of the United States, since the roles of the military forces of the two nations are so different. The U.S. Army, for example, must be organized so that virtually all of its units can be transported overseas and fight, supported by a logistics tail extending back to the interior of the United States. In contrast, except possibly for its airborne troops, naval infantry, and fleet, the Soviet Armed Forces are structured to fight in areas contiguous to the Soviet Union.

Soviet planning envisages that in any major conflict all civilian transportation and communications facilities would be mobilized. Even during the Soviet invasion of Czechoslovakia in August 1968, certain categories of support troops were obtained through calling up reserve units for maneuvers. During World War II, in the Soviet advance on Berlin, frontline troops were supported logistically by any means of transport that could be found. It is anticipated that the same situation would exist in any future war.

While expecting any future war between major powers to be of short duration due to the use or threat of the use of nuclear weapons, Soviet strategists always note the possibility of a protracted war. Their supporting services and special troops are indicative of the fact that they have planned for this possibility.

Notes

1. "The Military Balance 1983/84," *Air Force Magazine*, December 1983, pp. 76, 78 (footnote 8). See December issues of *Air Force Magazine* for earlier military balances.

2. One reason that the Soviet leadership may have been so aroused over the publication of Solzhenitsyn's *The Gulag Archipelago* is that names given in the book have made it possible to relate some Gulag supervisors and chiefs to later assignments. For example, in Book 2, pp. 83–84, Solzhenitsyn describes Yakov Rapoport and an incident that occurred during the building of a canal. On page 99 he talks of "six hired murderers each of whom accounted for thirty thousand lives." Among these six were S. Ya. Zhuk and Yakov Rapoport. Rapoport became head of an institute named in honor of Zhuk. *Krasnaya Zvezda* published the obituary of General Major Engineer–Technical Services (reserve) Yakov D. Rapoport on 3 July 1962. General of the Army A. N. Komarovskiy, the second chief of the Building and Construction Troops, described in his book, *Zapiski Stroitelya* [Notes of a Builder] (Moscow: Voyenizdat, 1972), p. 82, his great respect for his former boss, S. Ya. Zhuk.

3. For example, see N. A. Sbytov, "The Revolution in Military Affairs and its Results," *Krasnaya Zvezda,* 15 February 1963. For an English translation see W. R. Kintner and H. F. Scott, *The Nuclear Revolution in Soviet Military Affairs* (Norman, Okla.: University of Oklahoma Press, 1968), pp. 23–24.

4. M. V. Zakharov, ed., *50 Let Vooruzhennykh Sil SSSR* [50 Years of the Armed Forces of the USSR] (Moscow: Voyenizdat, 1968), p. 35. See also A. N. Lagovskiy, *V. I. Lenin ob Ekonomicheskom Obespechenyy Oborony Strany* [V. I. Lenin on the Economic Support of the Defense of the Country] (Moscow: Voyenizdat, 1976), for a detailed description of this period.

5. Ibid., p. 46.

6. Ibid., p. 121.

7. Ibid., p. 125. For an account of this period by a Western author covering early development of the Red Army in general, see John Erickson, *The Soviet High Command* (London: St. Martin's Press, 1962), pp. 3–164.

8. Zakharov, *50 Let,* p. 171.

9. V. K. Vysotskiy, *Tyl Sovetskoy Armii* [Rear Services of the Soviet Army] (Moscow: Voyenizdat, 1968), pp. 57–58. This is one of the most comprehensive accounts of the development of the Soviet rear services yet published. *Tyl Vooruzhennykh Sil v Sovremennoy Voyne* [Rear Services of the Armed Forces in Modern War] (Moscow: Voyenizdat, 1975) won the Frunze Prize for outstanding military books.

10. Vysotskiy, *Tyl Sovetskoy Armii,* p. 66–67.

11. Ibid., p. 68.

12. Ibid., p. 93.

13. Ibid., p. 82.

14. Ibid., p. 88. See also P. N. Pospelov, ed., *Sovetskiy Tyl v Velikoy Otechestvennoy Voyne* [The Soviet Rear Services in the Great Patriotic War] (Moscow: Mysl' Publishing House, 1974), Vols. 1, 2. This was apparently written to show the Soviet Union's "economic victory" over Germany, and it primarily compares Soviet production with that of Germany. P. N. Pospelov was editor of *Pravda* during World War II. See also S. K. Kurkotkin, ed., *Tyl Sovetskikh Vooruzhennykh Sil v Velikoy Otechestvennoy Voyne 1941–1945 gg.* [Rear of the Soviet Armed Forces in the Great Patriotic War 1941–1945] (Moscow: Voyenizdat, 1977). This book,

by the Institute of Military History of the Ministry of Defense USSR, is one of the better works on the subject.

15. Vysotskiy, *Tyl Sovetskoy Armii*, p. 90.

16. Ibid., p. 91.

17. Ibid., p. 84.

18. P. N. Pospelov, *Istoriya Velikoy Otechestvennoy Voyny Sovetskovo Soyuza, 1941–1945* [History of the Great Fatherland War of the Soviet Union, 1941–1945] (Moscow: Voyenizdat, 1961), Vol. 1, p. 459. This six-volume history, the first volume of which appeared in 1961, was edited by the same P. N. Pospelov who was editor of *Sovetskiy Tyl v Velikoy Otechestvennoy Voyne*. In 1961 Pospelov and his contributors wrote as "de-Stalinists." In 1974, in line with Party policy, their writings follow the "re-Stalinization" theme.

19. A. A. Grechko, "25 Years Ago," *Voyenno-Istoricheskii Zhurnal* [Military History Journal], Vol. 6, June 1966, p. 9.

20. Ibid.

21. Vysotskiy, *Tyl Sovetskoy Armii*, p. 111.

22. Zakharov, *50 Let*, p. 273.

23. During World War II, 375,883 trucks were shipped from the United States to the Soviet Union under lend-lease.

24. *Voyennyy Entsiklopedicheskiy Slovar'* [Military Encyclopedic Dictionary] (Moscow: Voyenizdat, 1983), p. 758.

25. N. V. Ogarkov, *Vsegda v Gotovnosti k Zashchite Otechestva* [Always in Readiness to Defend the Fatherland] (Moscow: Voyenizdat, 1982), p. 40.

26. Philip H. Lowry and William F. Scott, *United States and Soviet Combat-to-Support Ratios* (McLean, Va.: Operations Analysis Division, General Research Corporation, July 1975).

27. I. V. Safronov, ed., *Spravochnik Ofitsera Po Voyskovomu Khozyaystvu* [Officer's Guide for Quartermasters] (Moscow: Voyenizdat, 1968), pp. 14–15. See also S. S. Maksimov, ed., *Osnovy Sovetskogo Voyennogo Zakonodatel'stva* [Fundamentals of Soviet Military Legislation] (Moscow: Voyenizdat, 1978), pp. 101–126.

28. Ibid., pp. 16–17.

29. For an interesting account of how financial matters are handled in the Soviet military structure, see M. V. Terpilovskiy, ed., *Finansovaya Sluzhba Vooruzhennykh Sil SSSR v Period Voyny* [Financial Service of the Armed Forces of the USSR in the Period of War] (Moscow: Voyenizdat, 1967).

30. S. V. Khvoshchev, ed., *Ukhodili Na Front Eshelony* [The Echelons Leave for the Front] (Moscow: Voyenizdat, 1974). This is an account of the work of VOSO during World War II.

31. S. M. Shtemenko, *The Soviet General Staff at War: 1941–1945* (Moscow: Progress Publishers, 1975), p. 129.

32. Vysotskiy, *Tyl Sovetskoy Armii*, p. 303.

33. I. Kh. Bagramyan, "The Rear Service of Our Troops," *Yest' Stat' v Stroy* [To Be in Formation] (Moscow: Young Guards Publishing House, 1967).

34. The Central Military Department Store is at Prospect Kalinin, 10, Moscow, between the United States Embassy and Red Square.

35. I. M. Golushko and N. V. Varlamov, *Osnovy Modelirovaniya i Avtomatizatsii Upravleniya Tylom* [Fundamentals of Modeling and Automation of Control of Rear Services] (Moscow: Voyenizdat, 1982).

36. A. I. Solzhenitsyn, *The Gulag Archipelago*, Parts III, IV (New York: Harper & Row, 1975), pp. 591–593.

37. A. M. Kryukov, "Zheleznodorozhnyye Voyska" [Railroad Troops], *Sovetskaya Voyennaya Entsiklopediya* [Soviet Military Encyclopedia] (Moscow: Voyenizdat, 1976–1980), Vol. 3, p. 321. See also A. S. Klemin, ed., *Eshelon za Eshelonom* [Echelon After Echelon] (Moscow: Voyenizdat, 1981).

38. V. P. Oboyanskiy, "Dorozhnyye Voyska" [Road Troops], *Sovetskaya Voyennaya Entsiklopediya*, Vol. 3, p. 251.

39. Ye. A. Bezymyannov, "Avtomobil'nyye Voyska" [Automobile Troops], *Sovetskaya Voyennaya Entsiklopediya*, Vol. 1, p. 88.

40. A. I. Lepeshkin, ed., *Osnovy Sovetskovo Voyennovo Zakonodatel'stva* [Fundamentals of Soviet Military Legislation] (Moscow: Voyenizdat, 1972), p. 58. S. S. Maksimov, *Osnovy Sovetskovo Voyennovo Zakonodatel'stva* (1978) is identical except for "Beginning in the 1950s," p. 69.

41. A. G. Gornyy, ed., *Osnovy Pravovykh Znaniy* [The Fundamentals of Legal Knowledge] (Moscow: Voyenizdat, 1973), p. 100.

42. A. G. Gornyy, ed., *Osnovy Sovetskovo Voyennovo Zakonodatel'stva* [Fundamentals of Soviet Military Legislation] (Moscow: Voyenizdat, 1966), p. 112. For a popular account of the military builder, see M. Korsunskiy, *Tovarishchi Moi, Voyennyye Stroiteli* [My Comrades, Military Builders] (Moscow: DOSAAF, 1982).

43. A. Y. Khmel, *Education of the Soviet Soldier: Party-Political Work in the Soviet Armed Forces* (Moscow: Progress Publishers, 1972), pp. 100–101.

44. A. I. Romashko, *Voyennyye Stroiteli Na Stroykakh Moskvy* [Military Builders and Construction Work in Moscow] (Moscow: Voyenizdat, 1972). Photographs show many of the buildings constructed by military personnel.

45. *Yezhegodnik, 1973, Bol'shoy Sovetskoy Entsiklopedii* [Yearbook 1973, of the Great Soviet Encyclopedia] (Moscow: Soviet Encyclopedia Publishing House, 1973), p. 68.

46. A. T. Altunin, "Mestnaya PVO" [Local Air Defense], *Sovetskaya Voyennaya Entsiklopediya*, Vol. 5, p. 253. See also A. T. Altunin, "Grazhdanskaya Oborona," ibid., Vol. 3, p. 23.

47. S. S. Lototskiy, *The Soviet Army* (Moscow: Progress Publishers, 1971), p. 333.

48. O. P. Nikolayev, "The Competition Was Strong," *Military Knowledge*, April 1968, p. 25.

49. P. T. Yegorov et al., *Grazhdanskaya Oborona* [Civil Defense] (Moscow: Higher Schools Publishing House, 1966).

50. K. G. Kotlukov, ed., *Grazhdanskaya Oborona Vchera i Sevodnya* [Civil Defense Yesterday and Today] (Moscow: Atomizdat, 1975), pp. 112–113.

51. For example, see A. A. Grechko, *Vooruzhennyye Sily Sovetskovo Gosudarstva* [Armed Forces of the Soviet State] (Moscow: Voyenizdat, 1975), p. 115. For current views on civil defense training, see Yu. A. Naumenko, *Nachal'naya*

Voyennaya Podgotovka [Beginning Military Training] (Moscow: Voyenizdat, 1982), and A. T. Altunin, ed., *Grazhdanskaya Oborona* [Civil Defense] (Moscow: Voyenizdat, 1980). The first book is for 15- to 16-year-old students, and the latter is for general preparation of the population.

52. "Spetsial'nyye Voyska" [Special Troops], *Voyennyy Entsiklopedicheskiy Slovar'* [Military Encyclopedic Dictionary] (Moscow: Voyenizdat, 1983), p. 698. For a discussion of special troops, see P. F. Rodionov, ed., *Posobiye Dlya Ofitserov Zapasa Motostrelkovykh i Tankovykh Voysk* [Textbook for Reserve Officers of Motorized Rifle and Tank Troops] (Moscow: Voyenizdat, 1973), pp. 71–111. See also S. N. Kozlov, *Spravochnik Ofitsera* [Officer's Handbook] (Moscow: Voyenizdat, 1971), pp. 133–134.

53. V. K. Kharchenko, "Inzhenernyye Voyska" [Engineer Troops], *Sovetskaya Voyennaya Entsiklopediya*, Vol. 3, p. 344; also refer to other entries such as "Engineering Support," "Engineering Psychology," etc. See also A. I. Radzi-yevskiy, *Slovar' Osnovnykh Voyennykh Terminov* [Dictionary of Basic Military Terms] (Moscow: Voyenizdat, 1965), p. 69.

54. V. Ya. Plyaskin, ed., *Inzhenernoye Obespecheniye Obshchevoyskovovo Boya* [Engineer Support in Combined Arms Battle] (Moscow: Voyenizdat, 1972).

55. Ibid., pp. 336–339.

56. V. K. Pikalov, "Khimicheskiye Voyska" [Chemical Troops], *Sovetskaya Voyennaya Entsiklopediya*, Vol. 8, p. 372.

57. A. I. Belov, "Voyska Svyazi" [Signal Troops], *Sovetskaya Voyennaya Entsiklopediya*, Vol. 2, p. 323.

58. "Glavnyye i Tsentral'nyye Upravleniya" [Main and Central Directorates], *Sovetskaya Voyennaya Entsiklopediya*, Vol. 2, p. 565.

Part 3

A NATION IN ARMS

8
The Party and
the Armed Forces

The Communist Party of the USSR came to power through the Red Guards, forerunner of the Soviet Armed Forces of today. This force was created as an instrument of the Party for seizing and keeping power. It still serves that purpose. The Party is alert to ensure that it maintains control over the Armed Forces. Top military leaders also are top Party leaders, with seats on the Central Committee.

To exercise control over the Armed Forces, the Communist Party uses a variety of means. Party-political work encompasses literally every aspect in the life and work of the Armed Forces, "rallies Soviet soldiers about the CPSU, and motivates them to steadily raise the combat power and readiness of the Armed Forces."[1]

The extent of Party control over the Soviet Armed Forces, and the methods by which this control is maintained, may seem incomprehensible to Western readers. Probably no other organization in the Soviet Union is as watched and courted by the Party leadership as the Soviet Armed Forces. Political officers, by decree of the Central Committee, are members of military councils.[2] The Main Political Administration controls the Soviet military press.[3] Komsomol (Young Communist League) cells are found in practically every military unit, and about 80 percent of the soldiers and sergeants are Komsomol members. For the Armed Forces as a whole, approximately 90 percent of officers, warrant officers and enlisted personnel are members of either the Komsomol or the Party.[4]

Additional controls of the Party over the military are exercised by the KGB's Directorate (Armed Forces Counterintelligence). KGB personnel from this directorate are assigned not only to units of the Ministry of Defense, but also to the Ministry of Internal Security (MVD) and even to the KGB Border Guards. The basic technique used for checking on both officers and enlisted men is the informant net. KGB members are assigned down to company level in the Armed Forces and report upward through their own chain of command. A close watch is maintained for any evidence of ideological deviation.

Establishment of the Military Commissar System

In large measure, the basic instrument of Party control over the Soviet military has been the military commissar[5] and his heir, the political officer of today who operates under the direction of the Main Political Administration (MPA) of the Soviet Army and Navy. As noted earlier, the military commissar system began during the Civil War. The All-Russian Bureau of Military Commissars, which was to direct the work of the military commissars and military council members throughout the entire Red Army, was formed soon after September 1918, when the Revvoyensoviet of the Republic replaced the Higher Military Council as the highest agency of military power within the country.[6]

Duties of the commissars and members of the military council were direct: they were to exercise complete control over the old czarist military specialists commanding the troops, and at the same time they were to conduct political education. Successful commissars and Revvoyensoviet members rose to rapid fame. Among these were J. V. Stalin, S. M. Kirov, M. V. Frunze, A. I. Mikoyan, G. K. Ordzhonikidze, K. Ye. Voroshilov, V. V. Kuybyshev, and I. E. Yakir.[7] During World War II, N. S. Khrushchev and L. I. Brezhnev also served in capacities that were somewhat similar.

In early 1918 Party organizations outside the Party-military structure had directed the work of the military commissars. These were local organizations that often failed to keep up with the needs of the military and did not understand problems facing military commanders. By the end of 1918, military commissars, working within the military structure, had taken control over all Party organizations in the Red Army. In a few months this was recognized by the Party leadership, and instructions were issued defining the relationship of the military commissar to Party cells within the military structure.[8]

The Party program, adopted at the Eighth Party Congress in March 1919, declared that "the Communist Party is the organizer, leader, and inspirer of the Red Army and Navy. The Red Army is the instrument of the new social order."[9] This same congress redesignated the Political Department as the Political Administration of the Revvoyensoviet of the Republic (PUR), with five basic departments: (1) agitation and information, (2) culture and education, (3) literature and publications, (4) inspectorate, and (5) administration and finance.[10] This structure was duplicated to a large extent in lower echelons. By 1920 a political department in a Red Army division had 30 men in the organization-information section, 13 in the educational section, and 83 in administration, a total of 130 men.[11] *Politruks* (political instructors) were assigned to each company, battery, and squadron to indoctrinate the soldiers daily in Party tenets. *Politruks* were under the direct control of the military commissar.

To combat illiteracy, which was prevalent within the society—and thus within the Red Army—the *politruks* were directed to establish schools. This and other work performed by commissars helped to establish in the minds of the Party hierarchy the continued need for them. With the successful conclusion of the Civil War the political bodies were made a permanent part of the Armed Forces. In January 1922, the Central Committee confirmed the positions of military commissars in the Red Army and Navy. Positions of *politruks* in companies and equivalent units were confirmed at the same time. According to Party spokesmen, the chief task of military commissars in the peacetime force would be directing Party-political work, not countersigning operational orders of commanders.[12]

In 1925, M. V. Frunze succeeded Leon Trotskiy as chairman of the Revvoyensoviet and introduced a number of reforms. One of these measures was "unity of command" (*yedinonachaliye*), abolishing the requirement for a commander's orders to be countersigned by a military commissar. The need for this change long had been recognized, but the Party leadership considered that it could not be instituted until sufficient Communist Party officers had been trained in military skills to fill positions of trust. By this time 85 percent of corps commanders and more than 40 percent of company, regimental, and division commanders were Communists. In preparing for the introduction of unity of command, officers were tested annually to determine the level of their "political knowledge." According to contemporary Soviet writers, those who failed the tests were not given more responsible positions.[13]

Unity of command was instituted by order of the Revvoyensoviet on 2 March 1925. Forty percent of corps commanders, 14 percent of division commanders, and 25 percent of regimental commanders were considered qualified to become full commanders, whose orders did not have to be signed by a political officer.[14] Three-fourths of those so approved were former military commissars, whose military credentials were considered sufficient to permit them to assume military command. It was not until 1931, six years later, that unity of command was declared to exist throughout the Red Army. This was not actually true, since many units within the Air Forces and Navy still operated under the dual system of military specialist and military commissar.[15]

With the introduction of the unified commander, Party-political work was carried out through an assistant for political units. All orders concerning Party affairs still were signed by both the commander and his political-officer assistant. In fact, there really was no unity of command; the commander had no disciplinary rights over his political assistant, nor did the commander write his effectiveness report. The company *politruk* was usually considered a "middle commander," subordinate to the battlion commander and not to the company commander. He had disciplinary powers over those who worked in his office, which the company commander did not.[16]

A major buildup in the size of the Soviet Armed Forces began in 1930. By the end of the following year, there were 200,000 Communists in uniform, increasing to 300,000 by 1932. At this stage Party members made up more than one-fourth of all military personnel.[17] This situation was short-lived; in 1933 the Party rechecked the political credentials of its members, and many lost their cards. During Stalin's major purges, from 1933 to 1938, few new members were taken into the Party. As a result, Party membership in the Armed Forces dropped to a low of 150,000 in 1935. Military councils in districts, armies, and fleets were abolished.

In 1937 Stalin's purges concentrated on the military. The resultant deaths and imprisonment of thousands of Soviet officers made it necessary to give command positions to relatively inexperienced officers, few of whom had any background in political affairs. To ensure continued Party control, military commissars once again were introduced, with *politruks* assigned down to company level.[18] Military councils were reestablished, with the local Party secretary added as a new member.

According to Soviet writers in the 1970s, the reintroduction of military commissars in 1937 did not mean the "rejection of the concept of unity of command." Rather, it was called "the incomplete form of unity of command." The commander was to be responsible for the military side, the commissar for the political.[19] This was described as a temporary measure.

By 1939 Stalin's personal control over the Party and the Armed Forces appeared to be complete. Tens of thousands of new members were brought into the Communist Party, and at the same time there was a rapid buildup in military manpower. These two factors resulted in the Party having 435,000 military members, associated with 9,468 primary Party organizations in military units.[20] A training program was under way to prepare political workers and to provide political commissars with military skills. These new military commanders and political workers, as a general rule, owed their new positions to Stalin's policies. On 12 August 1940, the principle of unity of command once again was introduced.[21] The crisis brought about by the purges had subsided.

Nevertheless, exceptions to the unity of command principle continued to exist. Stalin retained some of his military commissars to keep close watch over both the military commanders and the political situation in new areas that the Red Army occupied. These included part of Poland, into which Stalin had moved his forces to link up with Hitler's troops and, later, the Baltic republics—Estonia, Latvia, and Lithuania.[22]

Events in June 1941 shattered the confidence of the Soviet leadership. In the first few weeks of Hitler's attack there was near panic within the very top Soviet hierarchy. In many areas—particularly the Ukraine—the invading German troops were being welcomed as liberators; Soviet forces not overwhelmed were retreating rapidly; and many Soviet officers who failed to stem the German advance were shot on Stalin's orders. In the mobilization period of the early days of the war, thousands of officers were called up from the reserves. The political reliability of these men had not been tested; therefore, they were not considered qualified to handle both military and political matters. Within a month after the entry of the Soviet Union into World War II, the system of military commissars once again was introduced throughout the entire Red Army.[23]

By the fall of 1942 the German drive, in general, had been stopped, and Stalin was confident of his control over the Red Army. The officers who had survived his several purges and had achieved successes on the battlefields were assumed to be loyal to the Party. In October of that year the unity of command principle was again reinstated, but at the same time, deputy commanders for political units were designated to control Party-political work.[24]

During most of World War II over one-half of the Party members were in the Armed Forces. Manpower losses were very high, and, in order to maintain Party influence within the military, rules for becoming Party members were relaxed in late August 1941. The number of candidate members and members serving in the Armed Forces and admitted to the Party in the war years are shown in Table 6.

Komsomol organizations also played a role during World War II in maintaining Party influence in the Armed Forces. The number of Komsomol members in the Armed Forces during the war years is shown in Table 7.

Did the Communist Party members, candidate members, and Komsomols contribute significantly to restoring the shattered Soviet armies in the first months of the war and in the victories that followed? Or was the determination of the people to resist the invaders due primarily to German atrocities and to the basic patriotism of the Soviet people? Soviet writers are not permitted even to examine the latter question. A major purpose of the outpouring of writings about the Great Patriotic War is to glorify the role of the Party and the great wisdom of its leaders in saving the nation.

TABLE 6
Party Members in the Armed Forces During World War II

Year	Candidate Members Admitted	Party Members Admitted	Total Members[a]
1941 (second half)	148,870	60,699	1,234,373
1942	1,173,267	441,204	1,938,327
1943	1,432,362	837,594	2,702,566
1944	977,640	862,010	3,030,758
1945 (first half)	243,063	292,711	2,973,793

Source: Yu. P. Petrov, *Stroitel'stvo Politorganov, Partiynykh i Komsomol'skikh Organizatsiy Armii i Flota* [Construction of the Political Organs of the Party and Komsomol Organizations of the Army and Navy] (Moscow: Voyenizdat, 1968), pp. 326-339. For total membership, see A. V. Komarov, *Spravochnik Politrabotnika* [Political Worker's Guide] (Moscow: Voyenizdat, 1973), p. 138.

[a]Total candidate members and members of Party in the Armed Forces at any one time. Note that figures are not cumulative, since losses were extremely high.

TABLE 7
Komsomol Members in the Armed Forces During World War II

Year	Red Army	Navy
1 June 1941	1,726,046	not given
1 January 1942	1,568,987	172,000
1 January 1943	2,204,582	not given
1 January 1944	2,223,016	not given
1 January 1945	2,202,945	166,600
1 June 1945	2,172,245	221,000

Source: Yu. P. Petrov, *Stroitel'stvo Politorganov, Partiynykh i Komsomol'skikh Organizatsiy Armii i Flota* [Construction of the Political Organs of the Party and Komsomol Organizations of the Army and Navy] (Moscow: Voyenizdat, 1968), p. 374. A. V. Komarov, *Spravochnik Politrabotnika* [Political Worker's Guide] (Moscow: Voyenizdat, 1973), p. 151, gives different dates and figures.

Party-Political Relations in the Postwar Period

Soon after the end of the war the State Committee of Defense (GKO) was abolished, and the Politburo and Central Committee resumed a measure of their former importance, at least in theory. In reality, Stalin ruled as a dictator. Stavka of the Supreme High Command was replaced by the Higher Military Council. Ground, air, and naval forces were headed by military councils, under the commanders in chief of these services.[25]

In 1946 the Main Political Administration (MPA) of the Soviet Armed Forces was formed in the People's Commissariat of the Armed Forces (later to become the Ministry of Defense). The MPA worked as a department of the Central Committee, and it was designated the directing and controlling agency for questions of Party-political work in all the Armed Forces. Political administrations were created for each service, as well as for the groups of forces abroad, military districts, and fleets.[26]

Requirements for Party membership were tightened in the immediate postwar period, and those who already were Party members were required to study Party history and Marxism-Leninism. Division commanders and higher, and their deputies and chiefs of staff, were forced to attend twenty-four hours of lectures each year, with additional independent reading required. Officers in lower units had forty hours of required attendance at lectures. Enlisted personnel were scheduled each week for two-hour lectures on political studies.[27]

In October 1946 the Party leadership ruled that certain military Party workers would be included in the *nomenklatura* of the Central Committee. This meant that appointments to key Party positions in the Armed Forces would be directly under control of the Central Committee and outside the Ministry of Defense. Positions listed in the *nomenklatura* included the chief of the Main Political Administration, his deputies, political chiefs of administrations and leading departments, political officers who were members of military councils, and chiefs of political administrations of the services of the Armed Forces and service branches, groups of forces abroad, districts, fleets, armies, flotillas, chiefs of political departments of corps, divisions, squadrons of ships, and so on. The Central Committee assumed complete control over the assignment of political officers, down to division level.[28]

The new emphasis on Marxism-Leninism required ideological guidance. In 1947, the Lenin Military-Political Academy, which had been evacuated during the war, was reopened, with a new course length of four years. It was to be the most important center within the Soviet educational structure for "scientific-military-theoretical thought."[29] One hundred officers were taken into its postgraduate program; correspondence courses were offered; and a newspaper editorial staff faculty was opened. A network of two-year military-political schools was organized, and nine military schools prepared political officers for work in the various services.[30]

Approximately 2.5 million members and candidate Party members left the Armed Forces in the first eighteen months after the end of the war. Only about 15 percent of the Party members remained in uniform, the same percentage as in 1940. Few of the remaining enlisted personnel were either Party or Komsomol members. The Ground Forces were so short of Party workers that two-thirds of the companies had no Party organizations, and only 8 percent of the companies had Party organizations with six or more members.[31] In the prewar years there had been political workers in each company to work with enlisted personnel; in the early postwar years there were none.

In 1950, to restore Party control, deputy commanders for political units were introduced at the company level, first in groups of forces abroad and then in western military districts, the Air Forces, and training units. Military councils were formed in the services, service branches, groups of forces abroad, military districts, fleets, armies, and flotillas. Since 1947 the military councils had been only *consultative* agencies, limited to an advisory role. By the early 1950s they were designated as *collegial* agencies, with power to direct troop activities.[32] Local Party secretaries were made members of these military councils, strengthening the ties of the military with local Party officials and organizations.

Universal military service at this time started at age nineteen. As the young inductees entered the postwar Armed Forces, the role of the Komsomols increased. Initially only 15 to 20 percent of the inductees were Komsomol members, but by 1949 their numbers had increased to 40 percent. Komsomol strength in the Armed Forces then stood at 1,272,000, carried in 26,780 primary organizations. Of these, 56,000 were officers, 127,000 cadets and "other," 483,000 were sergeants, and 606,000 were of lower ranks.[33]

The Party and Marshal Zhukov

Stalin's death in March 1953 caused repercussions in Party-military relations. Party leaders, concerned that their control over the Armed Forces might be lessened, felt it essential to extend their influence and attempted to accomplish this in February 1956 by a Central Committee Resolution requiring Party workers to participate in and criticize military training. The resolution noted that a technical reequipping of the Armed Forces with modern equipment was under way and that discipline and combat training had to be improved. Time-honored means of combat had to be reexamined in light of new weapons and new concepts, and the Central Committee wanted assurance that the Armed Forces would maintain their combat capability.[34] The role of the political officer no longer would be restricted to political and morale affairs; he also had a responsibility for the combat readiness of the Armed Forces.

In February of the following year the Central Committee issued new *Instructions* to Party organizations within the Armed Forces. These *Instructions* had been discussed in the Secretariat and in the Presidium (Politburo) and were even studied by a special commission of Presidium members, among them Brezhnev and Suslov. The *Instructions* thus are formal documents, confirmed by the Central Committee, and they serve as a directive for political-military workers.[35] The first *Instructions* were issued in January 1919, and later *Instructions* followed in 1921, 1928, and 1934. While Stalin held absolute sway, no new *Instructions* were written. After the long hiatus, the February 1957 *Instructions* represented a reaffirmation of early practices. They confirm the role of the Main Political Administration, which has the rights of a department of the Central Committee, as the controlling agency for Party work in the Army and Navy. Subsequent *Instructions* were issued in 1963 and 1973.

Within the Armed Forces the primary organization for Party work was designated as the regiment or its equivalent.[36] Cells of Party members in battalions are part of the primary Party organizations within the military. Criticism and self-criticism are emphasized as vital measures for increasing Party influence. Further, and of major importance, criticisms are to be concerned with *military* as well as political matters.

The Central Committee Resolution of February 1956, combined with the 1957 special new *Instructions*, established a major Party voice in purely military matters, with a responsibility for combat training. An objection to this encroachment by Party workers upon military matters was quietly made by Marshal G. K. Zhukov, who had been appointed minister of defense in 1955, was designated an alternate member of the Presidium in 1956, and became a full member in June 1957. (Interestingly enough, Zhukov had influenced Party matters when, in June 1957, he supported Khrushchev in his struggle with Malenkov, Kaganovich, and Molotov.)

Zhukov wanted to make the professional military officer preeminent in military matters and to restrict the political officers to a minor role. His effort to achieve this was one of the reasons he was removed from office.

"Without any reason," according to his opponents, Zhukov eliminated one-third of the political agencies within the Armed Forces in May 1957.[37] The number of students enrolled in the Lenin Military-Political Academy was "drastically reduced." Party workers within the military structure were "prevented from being promoted" and their status was lowered. The position of company deputy command for political matters was eliminated. When examining the educational requirements for specific assignments within the Armed Forces, Zhukov directed that officers who were "regimental propagandists" need not be required to have "higher education" and that only one-fourth of division propagandists need have special educational requirements. This meant a major lowering of the prestige of political officers. Even more telling was Zhukov's ruling that the rank of colonel would be the highest that could be held by a political worker in the Armed Forces. This meant there would be no more political officers holding the rank of general or admiral.[38] Ties between political officers in military districts and local Party organizations gradually were broken.

Probably many of the accusations against Zhukov were not completely accurate, and possibly other individuals and other factors were involved. Whatever the actual facts—which the Soviet press has not revealed—an attempt was indeed made in 1957 to curtail significantly the role of political officers within the Soviet military structure. With the ouster of Zhukov in October, however, Party controls were swiftly reestablished. Military councils were directed to reassert Party influence throughout the Armed Forces. The Lenin Military-Political Academy was enlarged, and all courses were reinstated. For a short time, the political administrations of the services were disbanded, and all work was concentrated in the Main Political Administration, where departments for each service were created. This move was to ensure that Party controls and directives would be the same for all services. Lecture groups were formed in 1958 to teach Marxist-Leninist theory to officer personnel and to explain political matters to lower ranks. The Party hierarchy sought to ensure that its control over the Armed Forces could never again be seriously threatened.[39]

Contemporary Party-Military Structure and Activities

Party organizations within the Soviet Armed Forces in the mid-1980s retain the basic structure that was established more than half a century ago. Attempts by Trotskiy to place military professionalism above ideological work had ended in failure. Marshal Zhukov's efforts in the 1950s to achieve the same end met the same fate. The Soviet Armed Forces remain an arm of the Party, subject to its dictates. Control is ensured by a complex structure starting at the very top and extending throughout all levels (Chart 22).

Chart 22

The Structure of Political Organs in the Soviet Army and Navy

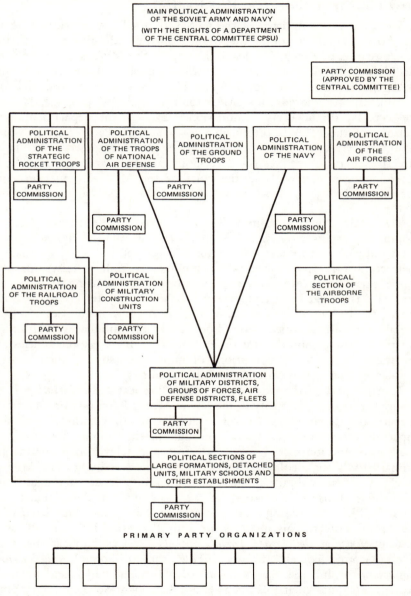

MAIN POLITICAL ADMINISTRATION OF THE SOVIET ARMY AND NAVY

(WITH THE RIGHTS OF A DEPARTMENT OF THE CENTRAL COMMITTEE CPSU)

PARTY COMMISSION (APPROVED BY THE CENTRAL COMMITTEE)

POLITICAL ADMINISTRATION OF THE STRATEGIC ROCKET TROOPS

POLITICAL ADMINISTRATION OF THE TROOPS OF NATIONAL AIR DEFENSE

POLITICAL ADMINISTRATION OF THE GROUND TROOPS

POLITICAL ADMINISTRATION OF THE NAVY

POLITICAL ADMINISTRATION OF THE AIR FORCES

PARTY COMMISSION

PARTY COMMISSION

PARTY COMMISSION

PARTY COMMISSION

PARTY COMMISSION

POLITICAL ADMINISTRATION OF THE RAILROAD TROOPS

POLITICAL ADMINISTRATION OF MILITARY CONSTRUCTION UNITS

POLITICAL SECTION OF THE AIRBORNE TROOPS

PARTY COMMISSION

PARTY COMMISSION

POLITICAL ADMINISTRATION OF MILITARY DISTRICTS, GROUPS OF FORCES, AIR DEFENSE DISTRICTS, FLEETS

PARTY COMMISSION

POLITICAL SECTIONS OF LARGE FORMATIONS, DETACHED UNITS, MILITARY SCHOOLS AND OTHER ESTABLISHMENTS

PARTY COMMISSION

PRIMARY PARTY ORGANIZATIONS

SOURCE: N. A. PETROVICHEV, ED., *PARTINOYE STROITEL'STVO* [PARTY STRUCTURE] (MOSCOW: POLITIZ-DAT, 1976), P. 218. FOR A SIMILAR CHART, SEE M. G. SOBOLEV, ED., *PARTIYNO-POLITICHESKAYA RABOTA V SOVETSKIKH VOORUZHENNYKH SILAKH* [PARTY-POLITICAL WORK IN THE SOVIET ARMED FORCES] (MOSCOW: VOYENIZDAT, 1974), P. 154.

The Main Political Administration of the Soviet Army and Navy (MPA) (*GlavPU SAiVMF*)

The Central Committee of the CPSU guides Party-political work in the Armed Forces through the Main Political Administration of the Soviet Army and Navy. The leading body in the MPA is the Bureau of the Main Political Administration, which consists of the chief of the MPA, his assistant chief for Komsomols, heads of Party-organization administrations, the administration for agitation and propaganda, and the secretary of the Party commission.[40] Each of the departments and sections of the MPA is responsible for a specific Party activity. Since 1960 the MPA has been a "collegial agency," empowered to issue directives. Basic directives on Party-political works are signed by both the minister of defense and the chief of the MPA. Instructions and decrees on day-to-day activities are issued only in the name of the chief of the MPA.

The Main Political Administration is accountable to the Central Committee for its activity. The MPA "is the channel through which the Party influences all aspects of the Armed Forces' life and activity, enhances their combat readiness, strengthens military discipline, raises the personnel's political level and boosts their morale."[41] According to its charter the MPA is charged with reporting on the overall state of the Armed Forces to the minister of defense. The MPA's responsibilities for "the overall state of the Armed Forces" put it into the military area, although its specific responsibilities are vague. Included in its responsibilities are the status of the living conditions of military personnel, their general well-being, and provisions for "cultural facilities."

A major part of the work of the Main Political Administration is to ensure the ideological purity of the Soviet Armed Forces. Political officers prepare and teach Marxist-Leninist studies to all personnel and also supervise the educational system throughout the military structure.

Newspapers, journals, books, and radio and television programs are primary tools for ideological indoctrination and training. The MPA is in charge of all military publications, including those of the Military Publishing House (Voyenizdat), as well as "other media of mass propaganda,"[42] encompassing radio and television programs associated with the Armed Forces. This includes not only Party-political journals, such as *Communist of the Armed Forces*, but also service publications, such as the Ground Forces' *Military Herald*, the Air Forces' *Aviation and Cosmonautics*, and the Navy's *Naval Selections*. The belief held by some Western analysts—that there is a semi-independent Soviet military press in which generals and admirals may express their own particular views—does not correspond to the actuality of the tight Party-military control that is exercised over all military publications.

In the shakeup within the Main Political Administration following Marshal Zhukov's ouster in 1957, General of the Army F. I. Golikov, one-time head of the GRU (Soviet military intelligence) and subsequently commandant of the Tank Academy, was made chief.[43] In 1962 he was succeeded by General of the Army A. A. Yepishev, who had served as ambassador to Rumania and Yugoslavia and earlier as deputy to the infamous Lavrenty Beria, chief of the KGB. Yepishev was still serving as chief of the MPA in 1984; thus, he has been in this key position for more than twenty years. His place in the inner circles of the Party-military hierarchy appears firmly established. Since at least the early 1960s Yepishev has ranked number four in precedence among the Soviet military leaders, with protocol placing him immediately following the commander in chief of the Warsaw Pact Forces.

The Main Political Administration of the Soviet Army and Navy remains the key organization in the Party-military structure. If the Party is to continue to exist, it must control the military. The MPA is the primary agency through which this control is exercised. Of immense importance for the future, the MPA has a major role in the military indoctrination of Soviet youth, beginning with premilitary training. This administration stands in the forefront of the "ideological war" in which the Soviet leadership asserts that there will be no détente or compromise with the West.

Military Councils

As previously discussed, the highest Party-military agency is the Council of Defense, headed by the Party general secretary. At the Ministry of Defense level is the Main Military Council, headed by the minister of defense. The military councils of the five services are next in importance.[44]

In theory, and to some degree in fact, the power and authority of the commander in chief of each Soviet military services stems from his position as chairman of the military councils. These councils, whose membership is approved by the Central Committee of the CPSU, are corporate bodies for troop control. They are established in the most important formations in the Soviet Armed Forces—in the military services, military districts, groups of forces abroad, fleets, and certain commands.[45]

Military councils consider and take action on all aspects of military life and activity and are responsible to the Central Committee, the Soviet government, the Ministry of Defense, and "military councils of higher order" for the state of and combat preparedness of the troops.[46] As collegial bodies, military councils have the power to issue directives.

The Main Political Administration, as an agency of the Central Committee, appears to have a hand in the selection of military council members. Generally, a military council includes: (1) the commander of the organization (chairman); (2) a senior member of the military political body (political worker); (3) the secretary of the local Party committee; (4) the first deputy commander; (5) a chief of staff; and (6) the commanders of aviation, tank troops, artillery, and so on, depending on the character of the military council.[47]

The commander in chief, or commander, presides over council meetings, and decisions are implemented "in accordance with his orders." Soviet writers assert that the role of the commander is not weakened or belittled by the existence of the military councils. "On the contrary, they give them strength and confidence in the correctness of the adopted decision."[48] In actual fact, however, the role of the military councils may be one of the reasons so much appears in the Soviet press extolling "unity of command." If unity of command actually existed, there would be less reason for it to continue to be an issue in Soviet writings.

In the 1950s military councils were under control of the commanders in chief of the services. In the 1960s, perhaps as an aftermath of the Zhukov affair, the service councils became the primary controlling agencies. Military orders and directives are now formally passed from military council to military council, as, for example, from the Council of Defense to the Main Military Council on to the Military Council of the Strategic Rocket Forces. Since both the deputy for political affairs and the secretary of the local Party committee are required, by directive of the Central Committee, to serve on military councils, the changed role of the councils strengthened the Party's control. Party influence is brought into the councils at two levels: through the political officer representing the Main Political Administration and through the local Party secretary representing other Party organs. With these two individuals on the councils, the Party is directly involved with day-to-day matters in the operational elements of the Soviet Armed Forces.

Although this situation may seem strange by Western standards, there does not appear to be any basic reason for, or actual evidence of, a Party-military split, with two factions competing for power. Commanders in chief of all the Soviet services, as well as key personnel within the Ministry of Defense and the commanders of major military districts, possess considerable political power themselves as members or candidate members of the Central Committee.

Party Organizations Within the Armed Forces

Each of the five services has its own chief of political administration, whose duties are specified. As noted, this individual is a member of the military council of the service. Military districts, air defense commands, and fleets have political administrations "which organize and direct Party-political work in the army and naval units, and at their military institutions and educational establishments, as well as in the Ministry of Defense units and institutions subordinated to them where Party-political work is concerned. These political bodies are headed by members of military councils who are chiefs of the political administration."[49]

Party workers operate at all levels within each service. For example, there are Party workers at both the division and regimental levels. The regimental political apparatus is basic and consists of "the deputy commander for political affairs, propagandist, and club administrator" (see Chart 23). Component elements of the regiments, battalions, and companies also have deputy commanders for political affairs, with responsibilities for Party and Komsomol functions. Soviet writers state that "the deputy commander for political affairs is subordinate to the commander of the regiments." At the same time he "is directly in charge of the personnel of the regiment and is fully responsible for the organization and state of Party-political work in the regiments."[50]

One Soviet writer describes the deputy commander for political affairs as "first and foremost a Party functionary" and also a qualified combat officer who "flies supersonic aircraft and sails in nuclear-powered submarines, drives tanks and handles a gun like a marksman, jumps with a parachute and takes part in mine clearing, is quite at home with powerful missiles, radar, and other equipment. All this enables him to fulfill his duties well."[51] An attempt is made to project the image of a political officer who is not simply an authority on political questions; rather, he is to be portrayed as the best pilot of a squadron or the best tank specialist in a tank company.

In 1967 higher military-political schools were established to prepare cadets to become political officers in the services and branches of services of the Armed Forces. These schools, which youths enter between the ages of seventeen and twenty-three, have four-year courses. Cadets who are to enter the Ground Forces as political officers study in higher military schools located in Minsk, Novosibirsk, and Sverdlovsk. A higher political-military school in Riga prepares cadets for service in the Strategic Rocket Forces. Similar schools at Leningrad, Kurgan, and Kiev prepare political officers for the Troops of Air Defense, Air Forces, and Navy, respectively. Others are located in Tallinn and Simferopol' (for construction troops), and Donetsk (for engineer and signal troops.)

Although a political officer in a company or squadron is supposed to be the equivalent of any other officer with respect to operational training, it is difficult to imagine how an officer trained in a political school of the Ground Forces could compete on equal terms with an officer graduating from a four-year higher command tank school.

The number of graduates from the various schools for preparing political officers is insufficient to meet the requirements for all political

Chart 23
Structure of the Party-Political Apparatus of a Regiment

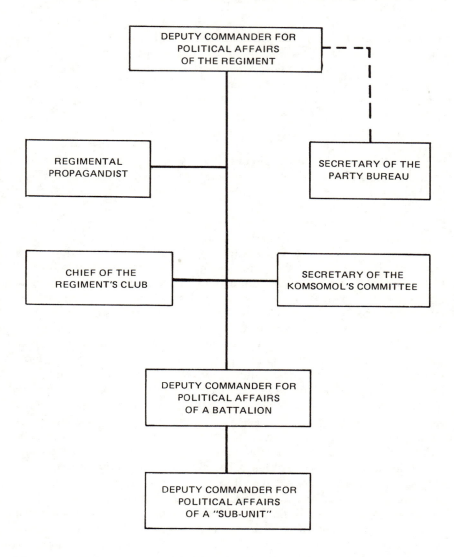

SOURCE: M. G. SOBOLEV, ED., *PARTIYNO-POLITICHESKAYA RABOTA V SOVETS-KIKH VOORUZHENNYKH SILAKH* [PARTY-POLITICAL WORK IN THE SOVIET ARMED FORCES] (MOSCOW: VOYENIZDAT, 1974), P. 161.

officer positions, particularly those of deputy commanders for political affairs at the battalion and company (or squadron) level. As a means of alleviating this shortage, an otherwise qualified officer may be encouraged to study political affairs and attend training seminars in order to be assigned as a political officer. In this way an ambitious officer can receive favorable ratings from deputy commanders for political affairs, an aid to future promotion.

In addition to a unit's plan (regiment, battalion, company) for Party-political work, political officers also have responsibilities for working both with Party and with Komsomol activities.[52] An examination of these two organizations in units of the Soviet Armed Forces may help to explain Party-military relations in greater detail.

Communist Party and Komsomol Organizations in the Armed Forces

Party organizations within the Armed Forces are described as among "the most militant detachments of the CPSU." Their activities are guided "by the CPSU Program and Rules and by the decisions of the Party congresses and conferences by the CPSU Central Committee. In their practical work they also proceed from the directives issued by the USSR minister of defense and the chief of the Main Political Administration of the Soviet Army and Navy."[53] Responsibilities of the Party organizations include directing "the personnel's efforts toward maintaining vigilance and *combat readiness at a high level*, carrying out in exemplary fashion the tasks relating to *combat training* and political education, *combat duty and military service*, and *the handling of military equipment and weapons*"[54] (emphasis added). Party organizations in the Armed Forces further are charged to ensure that "Communists play the leading role in the sphere of training and service and "influence all aspects of life and activity in the unit."[55]

The role of the Communist Party in military activities is most difficult for any Western student to understand. It seems as though the Party is interfering in matters that clearly are the responsibility of the military alone, but it must always be remembered that the majority of both officers and enlisted personnel themselves are Party members. With this in mind, the relationship becomes much more understandable.

Within the Armed Forces the party organizations "attach much importance to attracting new members." Throughout Soviet society as a whole the Party seeks to bring into its ranks the most qualified individuals in the nation. Observing inductees during their required period of military service is one method of determining the most able men for future Party membership. One of the major reasons for the system of universal military service in the USSR may be to ensure that almost all males receive a firm indoctrination in Party affairs.

In accordance with Party rules, people are admitted to Party membership on a strictly individual basis, with each applicant submitting "an application written in his own hand." Questions relating to the increase in Party membership and the education of young Communists are discussed systematically at Party meetings, which, in primary Party organizations, are held at least once a month. During such meetings Party members have the right to criticize any Party or candidate member "irrespective of the post he holds," when the training and the matter of strengthening discipline are discussed.[56]

Most enlisted personnel in the Soviet Armed Forces are within the age group for Komsomol: fourteen to twenty-eight years. (Eighteen is the minimum age for consideration as a Party member.) Considerable efforts go into persuading inductees to join the Komsomol, and relatively few can resist the pressure. Eighty percent of all enlisted personnel[57] and 20 percent of the officers are Komsomol members.[58] Most officers are either Party members or candidates for Party membership. It is possible to be both a Komsomol and a Party member at the same time, and 80 percent of secretaries of primary Komsomol organizations are members of the Communist Party.[59] The mission of the Komsomols in the Armed Forces is "to actively help the CPSU organizations implement the Party's policy and enhance combat power."[60]

Komsomol organizations (Chart 24) are established in battalions, squadrons, and similar units, as well as in military educational establishments and construction units, provided there are at least three Komsomol members in the unit. These organizations concentrate "on the task of educating class-conscious, ideologically staunch, efficient, and selfless patriots." They are credited with doing "a big, all-around job in enhancing the combat preparedness" of the units and attempt to direct the young servicemen's efforts toward "mastering the weapons of their particular service."[61]

While the basic Communist Party apparatus in the Armed Forces is at regimental level, Komsomol work concentrates at the company (or squadron) level, "which is the soldier's family and school."[62] Here "combat training and political education are organized by the commander," who is assisted by Party and Komsomol organizations. His primary assistant is his deputy for political affairs, on whom regulations place specific responsibilities.

How Party and Komsomol organizations are supposed to function is explained in a Soviet text.

Here is how Captain Rukavitsyn organizes socialist competition in his company. First, he studies the battalion's monthly plan and then familiarizes the personnel with it. Platoon commanders are squad leaders and the

Chart 24
Structure of Komsomol Organizations in a Unit

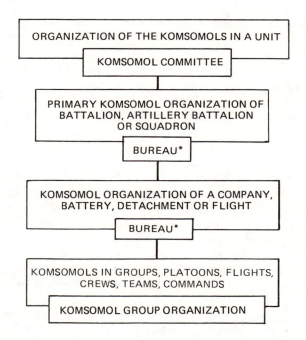

ORGANIZATION OF THE KOMSOMOLS IN A UNIT

KOMSOMOL COMMITTEE

PRIMARY KOMSOMOL ORGANIZATION OF BATTALION, ARTILLERY BATTALION OR SQUADRON

BUREAU*

KOMSOMOL ORGANIZATION OF A COMPANY, BATTERY, DETACHMENT OR FLIGHT

BUREAU*

KOMSOMOLS IN GROUPS, PLATOONS, FLIGHTS, CREWS, TEAMS, COMMANDS

KOMSOMOL GROUP ORGANIZATION

* A KOMSOMOL ORGANIZATION OF TEN OR MORE MEMBERS ELECTS SOME OF THE MEMBERS TO SERVE AS A BUREAU FOR A YEAR TO TAKE CARE OF CURRENT AFFAIRS. IF THERE ARE FEWER THAN TEN MEMBERS IN THE KOMSOMOL ORGANIZATION, ONLY A SECRETARY AND HIS DEPUTY ARE DESIGNATED.

SOURCE: M. G. SOBOLEV, ED., *PARTIYNO-POLITICHESKAYA RABOTA V SOVETSKIKH VOORUZHENNYKH SILAKH* [PARTY-POLITICAL WORK IN THE SOVIET ARMED FORCES] (MOSCOW: VOYENIZDAT, 1974), P. 198.

Communists and Komsomol members talk with each serviceman and help them decide on personal targets which should be as high as possible and at the same time realistic. The targets of the squads, platoons, and company are decided upon with due consideration of the individual commitments of the privates, sergeants, and officers.

Every practical training drill in the company is imbued with the spirit of comradely competition.

The officers of the company see to it that the squad leaders take an active part in the day-to-day organization and direction of competition. This is very important, for the sergeants are in charge of many drill exercises, are very close to the privates, and consequently are in a position constantly to influence them.

At the end of the day, summing up the results, the squad leaders give those willing to speak a chance to voice their views. The privates speak of their own shortcomings and criticize the comrades who waste training time.[63]

In a number of ways, political officers and Party and Komsomol organizations appear to perform some functions in the Soviet Armed Forces similar to those performed in the armed forces of the United States by special service officers, club officers, training officers, and commanders.

Formulation of Political-Military Ideological Indoctrination

Tens of thousands of political officers in the Soviet Armed Forces must present a specified number of hours of political instruction each week. As would be expected in the Soviet state, the content of the lectures is determined by the Party-military hierarchy. One of the means by which the work of the political instructors is directed is through articles published in *Kommunist Vooruzhennykh Sil* (Communist of the Armed Forces), the fortnightly journal of the Main Political Administration.

Each issue of the journal contains a section entitled "For Leaders of Political Study Groups." The section generally consists of a single article with detailed instructions on how the content of the article is to be taught. "The Soviet Armed Forces at the Contemporary Stage," the theme for issue number 14, July 1983, is typical. Political instructors are told:

Studies on this theme are designed to promote the mastery by students of the content of the postwar transformations of the Soviet Armed Forces, the deep realization of the necessity of further perfecting the defense capabilities of the country in contemporary conditions, the tasks of personnel in raising vigilance and combat readiness, and the reliable defense of the historic gains of socialism.

Ten hours are allocated to the study of this theme. It is advisable to assign the time as follows: 2 hours allocated to narration (lecture), 4 hours of independent preparation, 4 hours discussion.

In the narrative (lecture) examination of the following questions is recommended: (1) the transformation of the Army and Navy to peacetime conditions and their development in the first postwar years, (2) the technical equipping and the further development of the Armed Forces of the USSR, (3) the concern of the Party about the growth of military cadres, strengthening the spiritual potential of the Army and Navy and, (4) constant high combat readiness—the primary demand of the Armed Forces at the contemporary stage.[64]

Political officers are to explain that in the postwar period:

Nuclear rocket weapons became the basic fire and strike power of the Soviet Armed Forces. . . .

The means of armed combat radically changed the existing views of the role of the services of the Armed Forces and the service arms, their tasks and methods of combat utilization in contemporary war. The chief place in the system of defense of the country was occupied by the newly created Strategic Rocket Forces. . . .

Considering the Strategic Rocket Forces as the primary strike force, the Party at the same time takes into account that the security of the country, and in the event of war—victory in it will be assured by the efforts of all services of the Armed Forces and service arms.[65]

An analysis of articles published in *Kommunist Vooruzhennykh Sil* since the early 1960s will show that views presented in this journal—the official organ of the Main Political Administration of the Soviet Army and Navy—are the same as those given in other Soviet military publications. The presentations may not be identical, since officers with advanced degrees in military or naval sciences may discuss matters of doctrine and strategy somewhat differently from those having advanced degrees in philosophical sciences (for example, Marxism-Leninism). However, the essence is the same.

Those officers whose articles appear in the political studies section of *Kommunist Vooruzhennykh Sil* generally are associated with the Lenin Military-Political Academy, the senior school for political officers. Many of its faculty members are prolific writers, whose articles have been discussed in the Western press. At times officers from the General Staff, the General Staff Academy, and the Lenin Military-Political Academy may all contribute chapters to a single book. This was the case, for example, with the final book in the Officer's Library series, *Scientific-Technical Progress and the Revolution in Military Affairs*.[66]

Each year the work of the political officers in the Soviet Armed Forces is becoming more difficult. The youths called up for military service in the 1980s are better educated than were their predecessors in the 1960s. A large percentage are familiar with Western music and, to some extent, Western youth culture. Indoctrinating youth who follow Western dress styles and manners in the basic tenets of Marxism-Leninism may pose problems. The seriousness of this matter was demonstrated in 1982 when Marshal Ogarkov discussed the necessity to develop in young people a feeling of Soviet patriotism, and to teach them that "peace is not the usual state of society."[67]

Western influences and pacifism make the political officer's work even more important. One of the reasons for reducing the length of military service to two years was to make it possible for practically every Soviet male to serve in the Armed Forces and thus receive compulsory Party indoctrination. (With approximately 2 million males reaching military age each year, military service of three years would have kept nearly 6 million inductees in the Armed Forces at all times.) Party Secretary Brezhnev and other Party spokesmen have emphasized that the "ideological struggle" must be intensified and that "ideological détente" is impossible. But at the same time Soviet citizens are coming into contact with foreigners more and more each year—a price the Soviet leadership is paying in order to acquire foreign technology and to earn hard currency through tourist travel. Political officers must offset the possible influence of foreign contacts and thus have as a primary task "exposing the bankruptcy" of foreign ideas and customs.

A threat to Party control, such as that posed by Zhukov in the 1950s, now has receded. The Central Committee has a determining voice both in promotions and in assignments of officers to key positions. The Party has co-opted many of the best and most ambitious officers to serve as political officers in a part-time role. Within the Armed Forces the Party structure has been designed to ensure that political officers have a voice in every activity of their military units.

Notes

1. A. A. Grechko, *The Armed Forces of the Soviet State*, translated and published under the auspices of the United States Air Force (Washington, D.C.: Government Printing Office, 1976), p. 290. This work, in the main, is identical to *Vooruzhennykh Sily Sovetskovo Gosudarstva* [The Armed Forces of the Soviet State] (Moscow: Voyenizdat, 1975), 2d ed. Before the Soviet government would permit the book to be published in the United States, the translation had to be approved by Soviet censors. As a condition to granting permission to publish Marshal Grechko's work, Soviet censors made a number of changes in the original Soviet text.

2. Yu. P. Petrov, *Stroitel'stvo Politorganov, Partiynykh i Komsomol'skikh Organizatsiy Armii i Flota* [Construction of the Political Organs of the Party and Komsomol Organizations of the Army and Navy] (Moscow: Voyenizdat, 1968), p. 36.

3. K. U. Chernenko and N. I. Savinkin, *KPSS o Vooruzhennykh Silakh Sovetskovo Soyuza* [The CPSU on the Armed Forces of the Soviet Union] (Moscow: Voyenizdat, 1969), p. 363. For a fuller description, see M. G. Sobolev, I. S. Mareyev, *Partiyno-Politicheskaya Rabota v Sovetskoy Armii i Flota* [Party-Political Work in the Soviet Armed Forces] (Moscow: Voyenizdat, 1979), pp. 202–208.

This work is a textbook to be used in higher military command and engineer schools.

4. A. A. Yepishev, *KPSS i Voyennoye Stroitel'stvo* [The CPSU and Military Development] (Moscow: Voyenizdat, 1982), p. 225. This 90 percent figure has been a consistent one for many years. See also Mareyev, *Partiyno-Politicheskaya Rabota v Sovetskoy Armii i Voyenno-Morskom Flote* [Party-Political Work in the Soviet Army and Navy] (Moscow: Voyenizdat, 1982), p. 10. This book is part of the 1980 Officer's Library Series. For the Komsomol figure, see Yu. I. Deryugin, *Armiya i Komsomol* [The Army and the Komsomol] (Moscow: Molodaya Gvardiya, 1983), p. 20.

5. Soviet writers use the expression "military commissars" (*voyennyye kommissary*). Some western authors use the term "political commissars"; for example, see Merle Fainsod, *How Russia Is Ruled* (Cambridge, Mass.: Harvard University Press, 1967), p. 468.

6. *Sovetskaya Voyennaya Entsiklopediya* [Soviet Military Encyclopedia] (Moscow: Voyenizdat, 1976–1980), Vol. 2, p. 268.

7. Petrov, *Stroitel'stvo*, p. 36.

8. N. A. Petrovichev, ed., *Partinoye Stroitel'stvo* [Party Structure] (Moscow: Politizdat, 1976), p. 214.

9. Petrov, *Stroitel'stvo*, p. 67.

10. Ibid., p. 81.

11. Ibid., p. 82.

12. P. F. Isakov, "Politruk" [Political Instructor], *Sovetskaya Voyennaya Entsiklopediya*, Vol. 6, p. 423; V. G. Kulychev, "Voyennyy Komissar" [Military Commissar], *Sovetskaya Voyennaya Entsiklopediya*, Vol. 2, p. 268. See also Chernenko and Savinkin, *KPSS o Vooruzhennykh*, pp. 184–185.

13. Petrov, *Stroitel'stvo*, p. 158.

14. A. Y. Khmel, ed., *Education of the Soviet Soldier: Party-Political Work in the Soviet Armed Forces* (Moscow: Progress Publishers, 1972), p. 23. See also Petrov, *Stroitel'stvo*, p. 163.

15. Khmel, *Education*, p. 23.

16. Ibid.

17. Petrov, *Stroitel'stvo*, p. 224.

18. Ibid., p. 261. See also *Sovetskaya Voyennaya Entsiklopediya*, Vol. 2, p. 269.

19. Khmel, *Education*, p. 24.

20. Petrov, *Stroitel'stvo*, p. 236.

21. Ibid., p. 261.

22. Ibid.

23. Khmel, *Education*, p. 23. For details of Party work during the war, see K. V. Kraynyukov, *Partiyno-Politicheskaya Rabota v Sovetskikh Vooruzhennykh Silakh v Gody Velikoy Otechestvennoy Voyny* [Party-Political Work in the Soviet Armed Forces in the Years of the Great Patriotic War] (Moscow: Voyenizdat, 1968).

24. Petrov, *Stroitel'stvo*, p. 310.

25. Ibid., p. 391.

26. Ibid., p. 392.

27. Ibid., pp. 297–298.

28. Ibid., p. 406. See also Petrovichev, *Partinoye Stroitel'stvo*, p. 217.

29. Ibid., p. 403. See also Ye. Ye. Mal'tsev, *Akademiya Imeni V. I. Lenina* [Academy Named for V. I. Lenin] (Moscow: Voyenizdat, 1980), pp. 149–155.

30. Ibid., p. 404.

31. Ibid., p. 409.

32. Ibid., p. 414. See also A. A. Yepishev, *Mogucheye Oruzhiye Partii* [The Powerful Weapon of the Party] (Moscow: Voyenizdat, 1973), pp. 68–69.

33. Petrov, *Stroitel'stvo*, pp. 421–442.

34. Ibid., p. 426.

35. P. F. Isakov, "Instruktsiya Organizatsiyam KPSS" [Instructions to Organizations of the CPSU], *Sovetskaya Voyennaya Entsiklopediya*, Vol. 3, p. 555. See also A. A. Yepishev, *Some Aspects of Party-Political Work in the Soviet Armed Forces* (Moscow: Progress Publishers, 1973), p. 70; Petrov, *Stroitel'stvo*, p. 431.

36. Petrov, *Stroitel'stvo*, p. 431. See also Khmel, *Education*, pp. 49–54.

37. Petrov, *Stroitel'stvo*, p. 435.

38. *KPSS o Vooruzhennykh Silakh Sovetskovo Soyuza: Sbornik Dokumentov: 1917–1958* [The CPSU on the Armed Forces of the Soviet Union: Collection of Documents: 1917–1958] (Moscow: Politizdat, 1958), pp. 406–409. This work was published shortly after Zhukov was ousted. See also P. I. Yefimov, "Ties of the Army and People are Unbreakable," in V. A. Karamyshev, *Vmeste s Narodom k Velikoy Tseli* [Together with the People to the Great Goal] (Moscow: Voyenizdat, 1965), p. 45. For a Western account of Zhukov's ouster, see Fainsod, *How Russia Is Ruled*, pp. 483–486.

39. Fainsod, *How Russia Is Ruled*, pp. 486–487. See also Petrov, *Stroitel'stvo*, pp. 440–442.

40. Petrov, *Stroitel'stvo*, p. 441.

41. Khmel, *Education*, p. 37.

42. Ibid., p. 38.

43. Petrov, *Stroitel'stvo*, p. 440.

44. See ibid., pp. 441–442, which lists the duties of the military council.

45. In 1963, by a decision of the Central Committee, the railroad troops also were given authority to form a military council. See Petrov, *Stroitel'stvo*, p. 441, and Khmel, *Education*, p. 27.

46. Khmel, *Education*, p. 27.

47. Petrov, *Stroitel'stvo*, p. 444.

48. Khmel, *Education*, p. 27.

49. Ibid., p. 38.

50. Ibid., p. 50. See also Yepishev, *Some Aspects*, pp. 119–131. A comprehensive account is also given by Sobolev and Mareyev, *Partiyno-Politicheskaya Rabota*. See also *Ustav Vnutrenney Sluzhby Vooruzhennykh Sil SSSR* [Internal Service Regulations of the Armed Forces USSR], adopted on 30 July 1975, for the official duties of deputy commanders for political units.

51. Khmel, *Education*, p. 50.

52. Ibid., p. 53.

53. Ibid., pp. 55–62.

54. Ibid., p. 56.

55. Ibid.

56. Ibid., p. 62.

57. A. V. Komarov, *Spravochnik Politrabotnika* [Political Worker's Guide] (Moscow: Voyenizdat, 1973), p. 145.

58. S. Arutyunyan, "Lenin's Komsomol Reports," *Kommunist Vooruzhennykh Sil* 4, February 1976, p. 24.

59. Deryugin, *Armiya i Komsomol*, p. 104.

60. Khmel, *Education*, p. 68.

61. Ibid., p. 72.

62. Ibid., p. 76.

63. Ibid., p. 83.

64. P. Bushyev, "Soviet Armed Forces at the Contemporary Stage," *Kommunist Vooruzhennykh Sil* 14, July 1983, p. 75.

65. Ibid., p. 77.

66. N. A. Lomov, ed., *Nauchno-Teknicheskiy Progress i Revolyutsiya v Voyennom Dele* [Scientific-Technical Progress and the Revolution in Military Affairs] (Moscow: Voyenizdat, 1973). Translation by United States Air Force (Washington, D.C.: Government Printing Office, 1974), p. 2. One of the contributing authors to this work was, for example, General Major I. I. Anureyev, doctor of military sciences and professor, who chairs a department at the Academy of the General Staff.

67. N. V. Ogarkov, *Vsegda v Gotovnosti k Zashchite Otechestva* [Always in Readiness to Defend the Fatherland] (Moscow: Voyenizdat, 1982), p. 65.

9

The Soviet Military-Industrial Complex and Defense Costs

One of the Kremlin's most closely guarded secrets, kept not only from the outside world but also from the Soviet public, is the true cost of defense. There was general acceptance in the West during the early 1970s that Soviet defense costs were somewhat less than 6 percent of the gross national product (GNP). By 1976 this figure was revised upward, not by a factor of 10 or 20 percent, but by over 100 percent.[1] Some Washington analysts believe that the actual figure is much higher, and that the rate of spending on the Soviet Armed Forces in the early 1980s is between 16 and 18 percent.[2]

A number of Soviet dissidents argue that over 40 percent of the Soviet gross national product goes for military purposes. Their rationale may take into account hidden costs for which there are no counterparts in the United States. The maintenance of between 4.5 million and 5.5 million men in uniform, combined with the procurement and maintenance of the Soviet Union's strategic missiles, submarines, aircraft, tanks, armored personnel carriers, and other weaponry is only part of the Soviet military program. To this must be added paramilitary training of the population and premilitary and reserve training. Civil defense programs, hardening of both military and industrial facilities, and dispersion and duplication of industries for defense purposes are additional costs. The cost of highways and railroads constructed primarily for strategic purposes, even though they have some peacetime use, must be considered. Foreign military aid is another factor.

"Voluntary" support of the Soviet Armed Forces, extracted from workers on the basis of what is called "socialist obligations," may amount to hundreds of millions of rubles annually. The "socialist obligation" of workers in a mattress factory, for instance, may be that one mattress out of each ten produced is to go to the Armed Forces as a "voluntary" gift from the factory workers. This mattress must be made according to certain specifications and is closely inspected. Essential supplies provided to the Armed Forces through "voluntary socialist obligations" from industrial plants are never calculated in the Soviet defense budget.

The Soviet defense structure is so much different from that of the United States that comparisons between the two nations are difficult at best, and in many areas, especially in their respective military-industrial complexes, virtually impossible. Comparing defense costs is equally difficult. Soviet categories of defense expenditures cannot be "mirror-imaged" with those of the United States. Practically all defense costs in the United States are openly published; the defense budget given in the Soviet press represents only a fraction of the Kremlin's total defense spending.[3]

Many Western economists examine and compare the two basic sectors of the Soviet economy: the "A sector," which produces for military use and the "B sector," which supports the civilian economy. This technique, while useful in some areas, has limitations. General Secretary Brezhnev, in his address to the Twenty-fourth Party Congress in 1971, stated that "as much as 42 percent of [the Soviet Union's] defense industry's output is used for civilian purposes."[4] However, no figures or estimates have been given on how much of the civilian economic output is used by the military.

The Soviet defense burden is not limited to the supply of goods and productive facilities devoted to military use. Equally important are other critical resources that are most difficult to measure; the best scientists, engineers, managers, workers, machine tools, and advanced technology are drained from the civilian economy to be used for military purposes.[5] Mobilization of the best brains, plant facilities, and needed raw materials has made possible Soviet advances in space and in submarines, tanks, aircraft, and other sophisticated weaponry. At the same time, the civilian sector of the economy has been bled to support the Soviet military machine.

The nature of the Soviet military-industrial complex and the true cost of Soviet defense have defied Western analysts for decades. Some insight into how the system works can be gained from an examination of its beginning and its development.

Beginning of the Defense Industries

When the USSR officially came into being on 30 December 1922 the new nation was in difficult economic circumstances. Industrial output was at approximately 15 percent of its prewar level.[6] Most factories were without power and raw materials, and transportation was all but impossible. People were starving, with agricultural production only 65 percent of what it had been a decade earlier.

The serious economic plight of the country notwithstanding, immediate measures were taken to modernize and reequip the armed forces. Technology and management skills were needed—and both were in short supply in the new Soviet state. Peter the Great had looked to the West for assistance in building up his armed forces. The new Soviet rulers did the same.

As discussed earlier, military support first came from Germany, which was prohibited by the Treaty of Versailles from developing certain industries or even improving technology in other areas. German military and political leaders were seeking ways to rebuild military strength. As early as 1921 secret discussions were taking place between German and Soviet military specialists. Since the Treaty of Versailles specifically forbade the construction of armaments, the Germans wanted a place where they could establish aviation, tank, and chemical industries and train their military personnel, away from the prying eyes of the Allied Control Commission.[7] Soviet leaders needed internal facilities for training men to help compensate for those Russian designers and scientists who had been killed or who had fled the country. They also wanted new equipment and designs. The Lipetsk Flying School near Voronezh was specifically constructed to train German pilots. The Kazan' Armored School and the Saratov Chemical Warfare Research Institute stem also from this early Soviet-German cooperation.[8]

The other aspect of German-Soviet military cooperation was to provide staff training for Soviet officers in German military schools. This training apparently extended to the study of armaments production. Two of the most noted Soviet officers to head the military side of the armament drive in the following years, I. P. Uborevich and M. N. Tukhachevskiy, were trained in German schools.

The Soviets did not depend solely on German aid. Tanks were bought from Britain, France, and the United States, and Soviet air leaders dealt with both British and French aircraft firms. Large orders for munitions were placed with the Czech Skoda Works. (In later years, one of the reasons Stalin signed the 1939 Non-Aggression Pact with Hitler was the latter's promise that arms shipments from German-occupied Czechoslovakia would continue to meet the needs of the Soviet Armed Forces.)

A major goal of the Party leadership was to make the Soviet Union self-sufficient in the production of military equipment, but specific goals had to be identified and a plan submitted. The basic concept of military operations developed in the 1920s was that of the "deep operation" (*glubokaya operatsiya*), which would be undertaken by the combined actions of "aviation, artillery, and tanks."[9] Soviet strategists, such as Tukhachevskiy and Uborevich, had concluded that trench warfare, which had so bled Europe during World War I, was obsolete. A future war could be mobile, with success going to the side having the best maneuver capability.

A five-year plan for building up the Soviet Armed Forces was approved in principle in 1928 by both the Central Committee of the Communist Party and the Soviet government. On 17 July 1929 the Revvoyensoviet (Revolutionary Military Council) of the USSR gave orders to the staff of the Red Army to work out a five-year plan for armaments production and to submit it for approval.[10] Later in that same year the Politburo issued a document "On the State of Defense of the USSR," which recommended speeding up the plan of development. The plan was updated in June 1930 and again in January 1931. J. V. Stalin, K. Ye. Voroshilov, G. K. Ordzhonikidze, S. M. Kirov, S. V. Kosior, and A. A. Zhdanov were "the direct managers of the work on the technical reconstruction of the army."[11]

One immediate result of the Red Army's five-year plan was to create the post of chief of armaments. I. P. Uborevich, one of the Soviet Union's best military brains, was the first assigned to this post. In 1931 he was succeeded by M. N. Tukhachevskiy, an equally capable officer, who at the same time held the position of a deputy people's commissar (*narkom*) for military and naval affairs.

In accordance with the doctrine of deep operations previously formulated, the goal of the five-year plan was to give the Soviet Union superiority in the three decisive types of weaponry: aircraft, artillery, and tanks.[12] An Administration of Motorization and Mechanization of the Red Army was established. Design bureaus were set up for artillery, tank, and aircraft research and development.[13]

The Soviet armaments buildup was impressive by any standard. Results of the emphasis given to armaments production during the 1930s are obvious from the statistics shown in Table 8.

"Capitalists'" Contributions to the Development of the Soviet Economy

Buildup of the Soviet armaments industry was one of the major reasons for the Soviet drive to industrialize its entire economy. This industrialization program would have met with extreme difficulty, and might have been delayed for years, without help from the despised "capitalist nations." During the periods of the first and second five-year plans (1929–1932; 1933–1937), foreign investment and technology were eagerly sought. British technicians and French engineers, attracted to the Soviet Union by high wages, found leading industrialists from the United States making deals with the Soviet government long before the United States had established formal relations with Moscow.[14] Thirty-seven million dollars worth of equipment and machinery were shipped from the United States to the Soviet Union between 1921 and 1926.[15]

TABLE 8
Annual Output of Defense Industry

Item	For the Year 1930-31	For the Year 1938
Artillery	1,911	12,687
Rifles	174,000	1,174,000
Machine guns	40,980	74,657
Aircraft	860	5,469
Tanks	740	2,271

Source: Statistics from M. V. Zakharov, ed., *50 Let Vooruzhennykh Sil USSR* [50 Years of the Armed Forces of the USSR] (Moscow: Voyenizdat [Military Publishing House], 1968), p. 193.

Sweden, Denmark, and Austria vied with Britain, France, and the United States to contribute to the Soviet industrial buildup.

The Ford Motor Company built an automobile plant in Gorkiy in 1930. Stalingrad's famed tractor works also came from Detroit, built by John Calder, who also constructed the tractor plant in Chelyabinsk, the "biggest tractor plant in the world" at the time. Colonel Hugh Cooper, with his staff of U.S. engineers, built for the Soviet government the world's largest power plant at Dneprostroi.[16] An 85,000-horsepower turbine, also then the largest of its kind in the world, was imported from the United States. Many other industrial firms and noted engineers from the United States and Western Europe made equivalent contributions to Soviet industrial development.

Not only did the Soviets obtain plant and engineering talent from the West, but they also purchased equipment of the most advanced design. Payment was prompt and in gold. How this gold was mined from the Lena River area and the Kolyma River center is best described by Solzhenitsyn in *The Gulag Archipelago*.[17]

Soviet historians, including those who contributed to the twelve-volume *History of World War II*, completed in 1982, attempt to belittle the role of foreign contributions in completing the *first* five-year plan. They cite figures for 1932 to show that only 12.7 percent of machinery was imported.[18] In actual fact, most of the German industrial aid was provided in the 1920s. Magnitogorsk was well under way in 1929, as were seventy other large construction projects managed by foreigners, which together provided the basis for the first five-year plan (1929–1932). Ford built the automobile plant in 1930, the tractor plant at Stalingrad was in production in 1930, the dam on the Dniepr was completed by 1932. The steel centers of Sverdlovsk and Nijni Tagil, the enormous plants at Kuznetskstroi and Stalinsk, the oil refineries at Batumi, and the Ural Asbestos Works—all were started in the 1920s under the direction of U.S. and other foreign engineers. Soviets were taught how to operate the machinery. By 1932 the first five-year plan was completed ahead of time, and foreign help was being phased out. But Soviet historians and economists never cease trying to convince the Soviet people that the transformation of their country to an industrialized society was exclusively the product of the superior "socialist structure" of the Soviet state.

Impact of the Rearmament Drive upon the Red Army

The basic task of the second five-year plan for military construction was to ensure for the Soviet Armed Forces *superiority over capitalist armies*.[19] (Previously, it was merely "the enemy.") In this period the Red Army dropped the territorial system of manning and went to a cadre system. In the process the Red Army increased in size from 885,000 in 1933 to 1,513,000 on 1 January 1938.[20] Thoroughly trained military personnel were needed, able to master the more complicated equipment and in numbers adequate for the expanded military force.

With industrialization of the country, military academies were assigned the task of producing not only military specialists, but also officers qualified for the planning and production of armaments. In 1925 the Artillery Academy and the Engineer Academy were combined to make the Military-Technical Academy. By the beginning of the second five-year plan highly qualified officers were needed, not only for duty with troops, but also for assignments to industry design bureaus and scientific research institutes. Five specialized academies were founded in 1932 by drawing on personnel in the Military-Technical Academy and three civilian institutes: Artillery, Military Engineer, Military Chemical, Electrotechnical, and the Academy of Mechanization and Motorization.[21]

Many graduates of the Military-Technical Academy and the five specialized academies went to the new defense industries. Other designers, engineers, technicians, and related specialists were drawn from civilian institutions. Later, during World War II, favored designers and industrialists were awarded the rank of general (general major, general lieutenant, or general colonel) of Engineer Artillery Service, Engineer Tank Service, or Engineer Aviation Service. After World War II the three services were combined into the Engineer-Technical Service. In 1971 the designation was further simplified to general major–engineer, general lieutenant–engineer, and general colonel–engineer.

The attention given to specialization and the training and education of engineers showed results in the 1930s, as demonstrated by Soviet development and production of artillery, tanks, and aircraft.

With respect to artillery and mortars, the Military Scientific Research Committee of the Revvoyensoviet had created a fluid mechanics laboratory (GDL) in 1928. In 1931 OSOAVIAKHIM[22] formed two groups to study jet propulsion (GIRD), one in Moscow and the other in Leningrad, headed by F. A. Tsander and V. V. Razumov, respectively. In 1934, with the support of the People's Commissar of Heavy Industry, Sergo Ordzhonikidze, and the People's Commissar for Military and Naval Affairs, M. N. Tukhachevskiy, the rocket designers were combined into the Jet-Propulsion Scientific Research Institute (RNII).[23] One of their products was tested on 21 June 1941, the day before the German invasion. This weapon was the BM-13, better known as the Katyusha mortar, actually a multiple rocket launcher, which Soviet historians credit as being one of the most outstanding weapons of World War II.

V. G. Grabin (later to become general colonel of Technical Troops) headed a group that in 1936 developed the 76-millimeter divisional cannon. F. F. Petrov headed a design group that produced the 122-millimeter howitzer in 1938. At the same time, ammunition, mines, and shells were being developed by Ye. A. Verkalov, N. F. Drozdov, and P. A. Gel'vikh, who later were given the ranks of general lieutenant of Engineer Technical Service, general lieutenant of Artillery, and general major of Artillery, respectively.[24]

Best known of the early artillery engineers is the minister of defense (since 1976), Marshal of the Soviet Union D. F. Ustinov. In 1934 he completed the course at the Military-Technical Institute and began working as an engineer in the Artillery Scientific-Research Naval Institute, then as an engineer-constructor and later as director of a plant.[25] In 1941, at the age of 32, he became people's commissar of armaments, and he was promoted on 19 November 1944 to the rank of general colonel of Engineer Artillery Service. He remained in this same position until 1957 (although the title was changed to minister of armaments in 1946 and then to minister of defense industry in 1953).

The development of Soviet tanks, like artillery, started in the 1920s. "To answer the demands formulated by Soviet military doctrine," the Main Administration of Military Industry (GUVP) was directed in 1923 to create a "tracked combat machine."[26] An experimental task was finished in 1925, tested in 1927, and adopted that same year as the MS-1. In 1929 responsibility for design and production of tanks was given to the newly created Administration of Mechanization and Motorization of the RKKA, under the direction of I. A. Khalepskiy. British Vickers tanks and U.S. Christy tanks were imported for tests, comparisons, and design study. By order of the Revvoyensoviet, the T-27 "tankette" was adopted in 1931. The T-37 and T-38 tanks, both amphibious, followed in 1932 and 1936.[27]

One of the best-known tanks of World War II was the T-34, designed under the supervision of M. I. Koshkin and produced under the direction of General Majors Technical Services A. A. Morozov, N. A. Kucherenko, and others.[28] This tank was accepted officially by the Red Army in 1939. One hundred and fifteen T-34s were produced in 1940, and 1,110 in the first half of 1941, before the German attack.[29]

In June 1940, the Politburo directed that tanks should be produced at the Chelyabinsk tractor plant. In short order John Calder's Stalingrad Tractor Works also was turned to tank production, as was the Sormovskiy Shipbuilding Plant. Overall direction of tank production was given to Zh. Ya. Kotin, a 1932 graduate of the Dzerzhinskiy Military-Technical Academy who became the deputy people's commissar of tank industry.[30]

Aircraft development in the Soviet Union also started in the early 1920s. In 1922 the government awarded 35 million gold rubles to the Air Forces to plan "a minimum program of development."[31] The Volunteer Society of Friends of the Air Fleet (ODVF), formed in 1923, collected 6 million rubles in two years to build 300 military aircraft, at a time when 90 percent of Soviet aircraft were purchased from abroad.[32] German aircraft designers, engineers, and pilots established aircraft plants (such as the aircraft factory at Fili, on the banks of the Moscow River) and started a civil airline. In 1929 the aircraft production program in the first five-year plan called for the Soviet Union to free itself from dependence on foreign aircraft imports.

One facet of the relationship between the military and industry can be observed by studying the career of a famed Soviet aircraft designer, A. S. Yakovlev. He graduated from the Zhukovskiy Military Aviation (Engineering) Academy, as did many other outstanding Soviet aircraft designers. Some time after graduation he was sent to work at the Menzhinskiy Plant with D. P. Grigorovich and N. N. Polikarpov, two of the most famous Soviet aircraft designers of the 1930s. The plant belonged to the Central Construction Bureau (TsKB), which was under the technical direction of the GPU, Stalin's dreaded secret police. Both Grigorovich and Polikarpov were caught up in Stalin's purges and arrested. Still, they continued to work in a hanger that had been converted into a jail to contain them. Both were released after one of their aircraft, the I-5, was successfully flown.[33]

At the time there was only one other center for aircraft design, the Central Aerodynamic Institute (TsAGI) headed by A. N. Tupolev.[34] TsKB designed fighters, and TsAGI, as might be expected of any organization headed by Tupolev, designed bomber, transport, and passenger aircraft. Designers and engineers, in the main, came from either the Zhukovskiy Military Aviation Academy or the Moscow Aviation Institute (MAI), which had been established in 1930. Both TsKB and TsAGI worked closely with the All-Union Institute of Aviation Materials (VIAM) and the Central Institute for Aviation Motor Construction (TsIAM).[35]

During the rapid Soviet armaments buildup in the 1930s Soviet leaders had stressed quantity in setting production quotas. They were impressed with large production figures and often forgot that quality also was essential in weapons systems. Failures of Soviet aircraft sent to fight in the Spanish Civil War astounded the High Command. They awoke to the fact that one result of their massive armaments effort to surpass the "capitalist" nations of Western Europe was to provide their forces with large amounts of second-rate or obsolete equipment.

According to Yakovlev, Stalin took a personal and direct interest in solving the problem. "Early in 1939," engineers, designers, pilots, and leading aviation industrialists were summoned to the Oval Hall of the Kremlin, with Stalin, Molotov, Voroshilov, and other Party heads present. A result of the meeting was a revamping of the People's Commissariat of the Aviation Industry.[36] M. M. Kaganovich, People's Commissar of the Aviation Industry, was replaced by General Shakhurin, and Yakovlev became his deputy. Even in this capacity Yakovlev continued to design fighters.

Part of the problem in Soviet aircraft production resulted from the fact that many of the best aviation leaders were killed in Stalin's purges. Specialists were called in to head the departments of the reorganized People's Commissariat of Aviation Industry. There was a major shakeup in aviation design bureaus and research institutes. TsAGI, according to Yakovlev's account, had become a refuge for researchers working on their dissertations, some of whom had never been in an airplane or even visited an airport. Intense concentration was given to designing aircraft that would be the equivalent of those possessed by Germany. Stalin required personal reports on new aircraft under development.[37]

Armaments Production and the National Economy

In the great industrialization drive in the 1920s, overall direction was the responsibility of the Supreme Council for the National Economy (VSNKH). This council was subdivided in 1932 into the People's Commissariats for Light Industry, Heavy Industry, and Timber Industry. Concentration on military production in the second five-year plan made it necessary in 1936 to separate Defense Industry from Heavy Industry. After the Eighteenth Party Congress in 1939, and after the results of experience with Soviet military equipment in Spain were analyzed, Defense

Industry was divided into four new organizations: the People's Commissariats for Aviation Industry, Armaments, Ammunition, and Shipbuilding. Machine Building had been separated from Heavy Industry in 1937, and in 1939 it was divided into Heavy Machine Building, Medium Machine Building, and General Machine Building. In 1941 Tank Industry was formed from a component of Medium Machine Building.

It is instructive to examine briefly the state of the civilian economy and the living standards of the Soviet people as they were at the time this industrialization and massive buildup in the armaments industry were taking place in the Soviet Union. As the Soviet Armed Forces were being given guns, how did the civilian population fare with butter?

Stalin's forced collectivization, a "revolution from above," was initiated in the winter of 1929. The majority of the peasants bitterly opposed this measure, and many slaughtered their farm animals rather than place them on the collective farms. In 1928 there were approximately 60,100,000 cattle in the Soviet Union.[38] By 1934 this number was reduced to 33,500,000—a drop of almost 50 percent.[39] The number of sheep declined by almost two-thirds in the same period. In some areas the 1928 level of livestock was not restored until the mid-1950s.

Hundreds of thousands of Soviet citizens starved to death during the period. Millions more died in Stalin's forced labor camps, whose inmates were responsible for many of the major industrial achievements during the 1930s. The number of deaths of Soviet citizens resulting from Stalin's measures, taken before, during, and after World War II, approaches that of Soviet losses resulting directly from the war itself.[40]

Armaments Production During World War II

The formation of the State Committee of Defense (GKO) on 30 June 1941 marked the beginning of a process that was to turn the Soviet Union into a "single armed camp," such as had been accomplished by Lenin during the Civil War. GKO became the supreme agency of state power. Its first concern was production of armaments to replace the huge losses of the first months after the German invasion. Problems of armaments production were discussed in sessions attended by leading Party officials, industrial chiefs, and members of the Government Planning Committee (Gosplan). For example, a meeting on tank production, held on 15 July 1941, was attended by General V. A. Malyshev, people's commissar of tank industry, General D. F. Ustinov, people's commissar of armaments, I. F. Tevosyan, people's commissar of ferrous metallurgy, and N. A. Voznesenskiy, chairman of Gosplan.[41] On 28 July 1941, GKO examined the problems of supplying arms and ammunition to the front. Present were N. A. Voznesenskiy from Gosplan, General P. N. Goremykin, people's commissar of ammunition, General D. F. Ustinov, people's commissar of armaments, and General N. D. Yakovlev, chief of the Main Artillery Administration (GAU) of the Red Army.[42]

According to General A. V. Khrulev, chief of Rear Services during World War II, GKO members freely entered Stalin's study to report on projects for which they were responsible. Military leaders, people's commissars, or other industrial leaders associated with the war effort would go directly to Stalin when important questions arose. Secretaries, protocol, and daily programs were ignored when the topic was military production and procurement. Administrative matters concerning supply problems were simplified as much as possible.

During the war Gosplan formed departments for armaments, ammunition, shipbuilding, aircraft, and tank production. These departments drew up plans for producing the needed equipment, arms, and ammunition, and at the same time were given allocations of raw materials and machinery. Gosplan had its own representatives in each of the twenty-five economic regions of the country.[43]

Of the 9,971 documents issued by GKO during the war years, each of which had the force of law, two-thirds were concerned with matters involving the war economy and organizing military production.[44] GKO called upon first secretaries of oblasts and rayons, and even outstanding academicians, to act as its representatives in local areas.

In December 1942, GKO established its own Bureau of Operations to ensure that its directives were followed.[45] At about this time all strategic reserves of raw materials established in the 1930s were exhausted. The Bureau of Operations was given control over the daily work of all defense industries, railroads, and commissariats supplying new materials to defense industries. In 1944, as the Red Army moved westward, the Bureau of Operations had a primary responsibility for restoring industry to those sections that had been pillaged by the retreating Germans.[46]

The Party leadership has survived two wars—the Civil War and the Great Patriotic War—during which all resources in the territory controlled by the Party were completely mobilized. The pattern employed by Stalin during World War II closely paralleled that used by Lenin and Trotskiy during the Civil War approximately two decades earlier. Judging from what is written in the 1970s glorifying the GKO and its earlier counterpart, a similar wartime structure would come into being in the future if the need arises.

The Soviet Military-Industrial Complex of the 1980s

Secrecy

We can only conjecture as to why the Soviet Party-Military leadership makes a massive effort to keep secret from their own populace, as well as from the West, all information about their production of weapons systems and other aspects of their military programs. Extreme examples of secrecy inexplicable from the Western viewpoint are common.

Sergei Pavlovich Korolyev was the Soviet scientist-engineer credited with putting into space the world's first artificial satellite and manned space vehicle. Soviet secrecy and security around this program were such that Korolyev's name was unknown both to the Soviet public and to Western scientists until after his death.[47]

Zhores Medvedev has described the precautions taken by the KGB before any Soviet scientist is permitted to meet with a foreigner.[48] Members of the United States SALT I negotiating team have told how military members of the Soviet delegation attempted to ensure that the nonmilitary members of their own groups were not given information on Soviet armaments production.

From March through August 1971, *USA: Economics, Politics, Ideology*, the monthly journal of Dr. Georgiy Arbatov's Institute of the USA and Canada, published in Moscow, serialized a Russian translation of Dr. Herbert York's book, *Road to Oblivion*. In his book Dr. York had listed comparative Soviet-American strategic nuclear strengths. Dr. Arbatov's institute, in its translation, carefully removed all references to numbers and yields of Soviet nuclear weapons and numbers and types of Soviet delivery vehicles.

Soviet Military Industries

The Party controls defense industries through the Defense Industry Department of the Central Committee of the CPSU. Since March 1981, this department has been headed by I. F. Dmitriyev. He replaced I. D. Serbin, who had headed the department for twenty-three years.

Deputy Chairman of the Council of Ministers L. V. Smirnov heads the Military Industrial Committee (VPK), which has supervisory responsibilities for the production of military equipment. His exact authority and his relation to Dmitriyev are not known.

The Soviet military-industrial complex, as previously noted, operates in the greatest secrecy. Relationships among these industries and the relationships of the industries with the Defense Industry Department of the Central Committee and the Military Industrial Committee are not known.[49] Within this complex only one of the ministries is called Defense Industry, although at least eight other ministries are engaged in defense production, as shown in Tables 9 and 10.

There are close ties between the defense industries and the Government Planning Committee (Gosplan), Government Building Committee (Gosstroi), State Committee on Science and Technology, and the Soviet Academy of Sciences. A great deal of funding for military purposes, from tanks to new air bases, may be in the budgets of Gosplan or

TABLE 9
Defense Production Ministries (as of 1 May 1984)

Ministry	Minister	Product
Aviation Industry	I. S. Silayev	Aircraft and helicopters
Communications Equipment Industry	E. K. Pervyshin	Other communications equipment
Defense Industry	P. V. Finogenov	Conventional armaments
Electronic Industry	A. I. Shokin	Radars
General Machine Building	O. D. Baklanov	Rockets and space equipment
Machine Building	V. V. Bakhirev	Munitions
Medium Machine Building	Ye. P. Slavskiy	Military applications of nuclear energy
Radio Industry	P. S. Pleshakov	Radios
Shipbuilding Industry	I. S. Belousev	Naval products and ships

TABLE 10
Some Military-Related Ministries (as of 1 May 1984)

Ministry	Minister	Product
Assembly and Special Construction Work	B. V. Bakin	Construction
Civil Aviation	B. P. Bugayev	Assists Air Forces
Electrical Equipment Industry	A. I. Mayorets	Electrical products
Energetics (Power) Machine Building	V. M. Velichko	Power
Machine-tool and Instrument Building Industry	B. V. Bal'mont	Rocket and space instrumentation
Maritime Fleet	T. B. Guzhenko	Assists Navy
Means of Automation and Control Systems	M. S. Shkabardnya	Guidance systems
Oil Refining and Petro-chemical Industry	V. S. Fedorov	Gas and oil products
Transport and Heavy Machine Building	S. A. Afanas'yev	Prime movers, trucks

Gosstroi. One of the primary tasks of the State Committee on Science and Technology is to ensure that the defense industries acquire the latest in science and technology. This organization works closely with the KGB and GRU.[50]

The Soviet Academy of Sciences is involved in many aspects of defense. As already discussed, a number of social science research institutes are concerned with military strategy, especially in the political-military-economic areas. Other sections or departments of the Academy of Sciences are concerned with basic technology, and priority is given to research that has possible military application.

The Military Personnel and "Civilian" Ministries

Soviet general officers fill many important nonmilitary posts. General of the Army Khrulev was chief of rear services of the Red Army and the people's commissar of means of communications during World War II. After the war he served as deputy minister of industrial building materials and as deputy minister of automotive transport and highways. General Colonel of the Engineer Technical Service V. A. Malyshev successively headed the ministries of Transport, Machine Building, Shipbuilding Industry, Transport and Heavy Machine Building, and Medium Machine Building.

General Colonel of Aviation B. P. Bugayev was appointed minister of civil aviation in May 1970, replacing Marshal of Aviation Ye. F. Loginov. In November 1973 Bugayev was promoted to marshal of aviation, and in November 1977 to chief marshal of aviation. General Lieutenant–Engineer P. V. Dement'yev held the post of minister of aviation industry from 1953 until his death in 1977. General Colonel of Signal Corps N. D. Psurtsev was the minister of communications between 1948 and 1975, and General Colonel–Engineer V. M. Ryabikov was first deputy chairman of Gosplan until his death in 1974. A number of the top aircraft designers, including A. S. Yakovlev and the late Ar. I. Mikoyan and A. N. Tupolev, have held the rank of general colonel–engineers.

Many lower ranking officers work in defense industries. Soviet military regulations specify that they will be paid and supported as follows:

> By decision of the Council of Ministers USSR officers may be sent to civilian ministries and establishments for fulfilling work of a defense nature and still remain on active duty. Such officers retain all the rights, privileges, and advantages of officers who remain in the cadres of the Soviet Army and Navy. While on such duty, their pay and uniforms will be given them at the expense of the ministries and establishments in which they work.[51]

When officers are assigned to civilian ministries and establishments where their work does not require them to be on active duty, they may be transferred into the reserves. Available Soviet regulations do not specify under what conditions such a transfer might be made.

Other military personnel working in industries are the military representatives (*voyenpreds*) of the Ministry of Defense. These "officers or professional workers of the Soviet Armed Forces" are responsible for "fulfilling military orders." They are "given the right to control the quality of the products being produced." Their powers are considerable, since they

> control the maintenance of the technological process of manufacturing armaments, military equipment, and other military production and the calculation of their costs; they carry out the acceptance of finished production after conducting corresponding tests and inspection of its quality and reliability; they organize in the enterprises the study by representatives of troop units of new kinds of armaments and military equipment; they check the elimination of insufficiencies which appear in the process of acceptance and exploitation.[52]

The strict inspection of military goods by the *voyenpreds* may be primarily responsible for the generally high quality of Soviet military equipment if, as has been asserted, "the technology of the [Soviet] armaments industry does not differ basically from the technology of civil industry."[53] However, it has been argued that, by rejecting a considerable portion of the goods received, the *voyenpreds* have caused the actual price of Soviet weaponry to be far higher than that of Western nations. Goods produced for the civilian population are subject to control and quality inspection by the Department of Technical Control (OTK). The OTK will make allowances and accept shoddy goods; the *voyenpreds* will not. Should the OTK insist on the same standards as the *voyenpreds*, it "could lead to the economic collapse of the entire country."[54]

Whatever may be the true state of affairs, with respect to military and civilian standards, Soviet military equipment has won respect throughout the world. Soviet tanks, aircraft, and small-arms weaponry are rugged, well-constructed, and capable of doing the task assigned. In contrast, except for a few of the cities and special areas that foreigners are permitted to visit, the Soviet Union resembles an underdeveloped nation. There is a wide gap between the technological level of achievement encountered in the daily environment of the populace and that found in the weapons produced for the Soviet Armed Forces. And there is little perceptible spin-off of the advanced military technology into the civilian sector.

While Soviet science and technology continue to supply advanced military equipment to the Soviet Armed Forces, the gap in living standards between Soviet citizens and the people of Eastern Europe continues to widen. This probably is one of the reasons so much of the Soviet Union is closed to all foreign visitors, including those from the "fraternal socialist" countries. The Party leadership may have trouble explaining to the Soviet people why their living standards are so low when compared with those of the defeated Germans or the Poles. Rather than answering the hard questions, the Party's partial response is to import technology from the West and to seek credits for development. What worked for Lenin and Stalin might work equally well for Stalin's heirs.

Notes

1. "Military Balance, 1976/77," *Air Force Magazine*, December 1976, p. 49. For a detailed discussion of the Soviet defense budget, see W. T. Lee, "Soviet Defense Expenditures," in W. Schneider and F. P. Hoeber, eds., *Army Man and Military Budgets, Issues for Fiscal Year 1977* (New York: Crane, Russak & Co., 1976).

2. W. T. Lee, "The Shift in Soviet National Priorities to Military Forces," *Annals of the American Academy of Political Science* 457, September 1981, pp. 46–66. William Lee was one of the first U.S. economists to recognize that actual Soviet defense expenditures were much higher than the estimates reported by the U.S. government.

3. Official Soviet figures on defense spending from 1966–1983 have been between 13 billion and 19 billion rubles each year. The defense budget for 1982 was 17.05 billion rubles, or about 4.8 percent of the total Soviet government expenditures, according to Soviet data. (The ruble, whose value is artificial, has been approximately equivalent to U.S.$1.40 since 1977.) Actual Soviet defense expenditures are several times the published figure. See "Military Balance 1983/84," compiled by the International Institute for Strategic Studies. Republished in *Air Force Magazine*, December 1983, pp. 75–76.

4. Leonid Brezhnev, general secretary, CPSU, *Twenty-fourth Congress of the Communist Party of the Soviet Union, March 30–April 4, 1971* (Moscow: Novosti Press Agency Publishing House, 1971), p. 47.

5. Mikhail Agursky, a Soviet émigré, believes that the best Soviet scientists seek to stay away from defense industries, even though higher wages are paid than in comparable civilian work. See "The Soviet Military-Industrial Complex," Radio Liberty Special Report, 21 July 1976.

6. M. V. Zakharov, ed., *50 Let Vooruzhennykh Sil USSR* [50 Years of the Armed Forces of the USSR] (Moscow: Voyenizdat, 1968), p. 167.

7. John Erickson, *The Soviet High Command* (London: St. Martin's Press, 1963), p. 145.

8. Werner Keller, *Are the Russians Ten Feet Tall?* (London: Thames and Hudson), pp. 236–237. See also Erickson, *Soviet High Command*, pp. 151–153.

9. See N. V. Ogarkov, "Glubokaya Operatsiya" [Deep Operations], *Sovetskaya Voyennaya Entsiklopediya* (Moscow: Voyenizdat, 1976–1980), Vol. 2, pp. 474–478. The significance attached by Soviet strategy to operations in depth is

demonstrated by this particular entry in the Soviet Military Encyclopedia, written, or at least signed, by the chief of the General Staff.

10. A. A. Grechko, ed., *Istoriya Vtoroy Mirovoy Voyny, 1939–1945* [History of the Second World War, 1939–1945] (Moscow: Voyenizdat, 1973), Vol. 1, p. 257.

11. Ibid., p. 258.

12. Zakharov, *50 Let*, p. 197.

13. Grechko, *Istoriya*, p. 258.

14. Keller, *Are the Russians Ten Feet Tall?* pp. 226–241.

15. Ibid., p. 216.

16. Ibid., pp. 236–237.

17. A. Solzhenitsyn, *The Gulag Archipelago* (New York: Harper & Row), Vol. 2. Various mines and the drive to mine gold are discussed throughout the book.

18. Grechko, *Istoriya*, p. 222. The first five-year plan was completed ahead of time, taking only four years and three months.

19. Zakharov, *50 Let*, p. 197.

20. Ibid., p. 198.

21. *Voyenno Istoricheskii Zhurnal* [Military History Journal], October 1962, p. 109.

22. OSOAVIAKHIM, The Association for the Promotion of Defense, Aviation, and Chemical Construction, was a paramilitary organization, a forerunner of DOSAAF (Voluntary Association for Cooperation with the Army, Aviation, and the Fleet).

23. Grechko, *Istoriya*, pp. 259–260.

24. K. P. Kazakov, ed., *Artilleriya i Rakety* [Artillery and Rockets] (Moscow: Voyenizdat, 1968), p. 64.

25. "Ustinov, Dmitriy Fedorovich," *Sovetskaya Voyennaya Entsiklopediya*, Vol. 8, p. 227.

26. Ye. A. Kosyrev et al., *Tanki* [Tanks] (Moscow: DOSAAF Publishing House, 1973), p. 28.

27. Ibid., pp. 32–33.

28. P. N. Pospelov, *Sovetskiy Tyl v Velikoy Otechestvennoy Voyne* [Soviet Rear Services] (Moscow: Mysl' Publishing House, 1974), Vol. 2, pp. 110–111.

29. N. D. Kozlov and A. D. Zaitsev, *Srazhayushchayasya Partiya* [Party Fighters] (Moscow: Voyenizdat, 1975), p. 64.

30. "Kotin, Zhozef Yakovlevich," *Sovetskaya Voyennaya Entsiklopediya*, Vol. 4, p. 409.

31. Zakharov, *50 Let*, p. 181.

32. Ibid.

33. A. S. Yakovlev, *Tsel' Zhizni* [Aim of a Lifetime] (Moscow: Political Literature Publishing House, 1966), p. 96. Note that in 1972 Progress Publishers issued an English-language edition of this book. However, many changes were made, and the fact about Grigorovich and Polikarpov being under arrest was omitted.

34. A. N. Tupolev, like many other leading Soviets, was arrested in the 1930s and spent five years in prison. See William F. Scott, "An Epitaph for Russia's Aviation Giant, A. N. Tupolev," *Air Force Magazine*, March 1973, pp. 66–67.

35. For an account of Soviet design and construction bureaus, see A. A. Kobzarev, ed., *Sovetskaya Aviatsionnaya Tekhnika* [Soviet Aviation Equipment] (Moscow: Machine Building Publishing House, 1970).

36. Yakovlev, *Tsel' Zhizni*, p. 184.

37. Ibid., pp. 447–458.

38. Michael T. Florinsky, ed., *Encyclopedia of Russia and the Soviet Union* (New York: McGraw Hill Book Co., 1961), p. 85.

39. Ibid., p. 510.

40. Robert Conquest, *The Great Terror* (New York: Macmillan, 1968), pp. 532–533. Conquest states that the estimate of 20 million deaths of Soviet citizens as a result of the actions of Stalin and the Party during Stalin's rule may be much too low.

41. Pospelov, *Sovetskiy Tyl*, Vol. 1, p. 72.

42. Ibid., Vol. 1, pp. 72–73.

43. Ibid., Vol. 1, pp. 74–75.

44. Ibid., Vol. 1, p. 76.

45. Ibid., Vol. 1, p. 77.

46. Ibid., Vol. 1, pp. 77–78.

47. For an account of Korolyev's space efforts, see James E. Oberg, *Red Star in Orbit* (London: Harrap, 1981), pp. 16–90.

48. Zhores A. Medvedev, *The Medvedev Papers* (London: Macmillan, 1970). For an account of how international scientific exchanges are managed from the Soviet side, see the section entitled, "Fruitful Meetings Between Scientists of the World," pp. 116–162.

49. The Soviets do not identify their military industries as such. This particular list is the result of approximately fifteen years of research. Industries are redesignated at times. For example, Radio Industry and Electronics Industry formerly were the Radio-Electronics Industry.

50. See, for example, Oleg Penkovskiy, *The Penkovskiy Papers* (New York: Doubleday & Co., 1965), p. 174.

51. A. G. Gornyy, *Spravochnik po Zakonodatel'stvu Dlya Ofitserov Sovetskoy Armii i Flota* [Handbook on Legislation for Officers of the Soviet Army and Navy] (Moscow: Voyenizdat, 1976), p. 183.

52. V. A. Silinskiy, "Voyennyy Predstavitel" [Military Representatives], *Sovetskaya Voyennaya Entsiklopediya*, Vol. 2, p. 271.

53. Mikhail Agursky, in an interview entitled "The Soviet Military-Industrial Complex," Radio Liberty Special Report, 21 July 1976.

54. Ibid.

10

Soviet Military Manpower, Training, and Mobilization

General

The Soviet Union has had a system of universal military training for males since 1939. Students are also given premilitary training by Soviet schools and other organizations as a part of military-patriotic training.[1] Specific premilitary training requirements and regulations governing universal military service stem from the 1967 Law on Universal Military Obligation.[2]

Basically, the Soviet military manpower system is a cadre system, with a nucleus of highly qualified professionals engaged in training inductees and then discharging them into the reserves. Virtually the entire Soviet male population serves in the Armed Forces at one time or another. Conditions in military service reflect those in the nation as a whole. The same harsh authority that rules the civilian population is found in the Armed Forces as well. If food is short in the civilian sector, there also will be shortages in the military.

Since the end of World War II the size of the Soviet Armed Forces has been influenced by the number of young men available for military service. As previously discussed, the Soviet birthrate dropped significantly after 1941 and did not return to its prewar peak until the late 1940s. In 1957 the number of nineteen-year-old males, the age for call-up, was approximately 2,329,000.[3] In 1961—slightly over nineteen years after the entry of the Soviet Union in World War II—this figure dropped below 2,000,000; it reached a low of 914,000 in 1963. Graph 1 shows the population of eighteen-year-old males from 1950. The nineteen-year curve would, of course, run one year later.

It often seemed to foreigners living in the Soviet Union in the early 1960s that the entire nation was run by women. Most of the males between the ages of nineteen and twenty-two, few as they were, were serving in the Armed Forces. There also were a small number of males between the ages of forty-five and sixty-five, the ages of veterans of

321

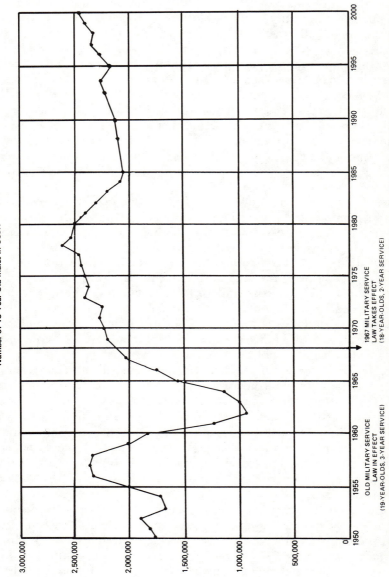

Graph 1
Number of 18-Year-Old Males in USSR

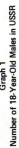

OLD MILITARY SERVICE
LAW IN EFFECT
(19-YEAR-OLDS, 3-YEAR SERVICE)

1967 MILITARY SERVICE
LAW TAKES EFFECT
(18-YEAR-OLDS, 2-YEAR SERVICE)

SOURCE: DATA FROM *NARODNOYE KHOZYAYSTVO SSSR 1922–1982* (NATIONAL ECONOMY USSR 1922–1982) (MOSCOW: FINANSY I STATISTIKA, 1982); MURRAY FESHBACH AND STEPHEN RAPAWY, "SOVIET POPULATION AND MANPOWER TRENDS AND POLICIES" IN *SOVIET ECONOMY IN A NEW PERSPECTIVE*, A COMPENDIUM OF PAPERS SUBMITTED TO THE JOINT ECONOMIC COMMITTEE, CONGRESS OF THE UNITED STATES, OCTOBER 14, 1976 (WASHINGTON, D.C.: GOVERNMENT PRINTING OFFICE, 1976), TABLE 16, P. 150; AND JOHN M. COLLINS, *AMERICAN AND SOVIET MILITARY TRENDS* (WASHINGTON, D.C.: CENTER FOR STRATEGIC AND INTERNATIONAL STUDIES, 1978), FIGURE 3, P. 49.

World War II. This severe shortage of military manpower created a strategic weakness that the Soviet leadership took great pains to conceal; there were no postwar population statistics published until 1959,[4] and these were presented in such a fashion that little was revealed.

In the mid-1950s there were approximately 5 million men in the Soviet Armed Forces. When the low birthrate of World War II began to have its impact upon the number of men available for the Armed Forces, the Party leadership considered it necessary to explain to the world why reductions in military manpower were taking place. Khrushchev publicly attributed manpower reduction in the Soviet Armed Forces to the effectiveness of the new nuclear and thermonuclear weapons, making the number of soldiers on the battlefield of little importance.[5] Soviet leaders especially tried to make this point with the Chinese,[6] who were arguing that manpower was the major component of a nation's military strength.[7]

By 1967 the number of males reaching the age of nineteen each year had almost reached the 2 million mark. At that time the period of compulsory military service was three years, except for certain naval components whose inductees were obligated to serve four years. It was apparent that with this length of service and an induction rate of approximately 80 percent of eligible youths, the size of the Soviet Armed Forces soon would exceed 6 million men, including officers and non-commissioned officers on extended duty. The solution to the problem was a new Law on Universal Military Obligation, reducing the obligation by one year for all inductees (two years for all except those naval components where the obligation now became three years).[8]

The law also reduced the call-up age from nineteen to eighteen, and deferred only full-time students. When deferred students completed "higher education," receiving institute or university degrees, they were required to serve only one year, except for those on ships, who were required to serve for eighteen months. (In 1977 this law was amended to require eighteen months for such students, except for those on ships, whose service time was increased to two years. In 1980, it was further amended to specify that school deferments applied only to schools on an approved list.)

Reducing the draft age to eighteen was probably simply the result of recognizing the facts that by that age most Soviet students have completed their basic ten years of education and that ideally military call-up should take place as soon as possible after basic schooling is completed. One of Khrushchev's "harebrained" schemes was to extend school to eleven years, requiring students to work a few days each week in factories during the last two years. When this scheme was dropped and required schooling was reduced to ten years, there often was a gap of one year between the time the student finished school and the time he became nineteen and was subject to military call-up. Moreover, the earlier the age at which obligatory military service begins, the sooner the individual can enter the civilian labor pool; through military service, men often have learned skills applicable to the civilian or defense industry. (In 1984 eleven years of schooling were reintroduced by lowering the entry age from seven to six.)

But there was another reason still for reducing the length of service. As Marshal Sokolovskiy observed in *Military Strategy*, "It is well known that the shorter the period of service in the army, the greater the number of men with military training discharged every year into the reserves."[9] And maintenance of a large reserve is the basic element of the Soviet military mobilization plan.

From the viewpoint of a professional officer, reducing the period of compulsory military service from three to two years, as specified in the 1967 military service law, decreased the effectiveness of the military force-in-being.[10] For long-term reasons, however, the Party leadership considers it more important for all Soviet males to spend some time in the Armed Forces, where they can receive intensive indoctrination in Party principles, than for fewer to stay longer. The shorter period of services makes it possible to give military training to virtually the entire male population. This provides the Party leadership with a pool of trained military manpower much larger than that in the United States or in the nations of Western Europe.

Two organizations peculiar to the Soviet Union play essential roles in the training and mobilization of the Soviet Armed Forces. The first of these is the military commissariat; the second is DOSAAF—the Volunteer Society for Cooperation with the Army, Aviation, and the Fleet.

Military Commissariats (Voyenkomaty)

Military commissariats are "agencies of local military administration,"[11] found throughout the Soviet Union. They are controlled by the General Staff of the Ministry of Defense, through the commanders of the military districts in which they are located. Their offices number in the thousands. Each of the Soviet republics has a military commissariat, headed, in most instances, by a general major, who is the military commissar of the republic. Below the republic level are autonomous republics, krays, oblasts, national districts, and autonomous oblasts (166), each of which has a military commissariat headed by a colonel, and sometimes a general major. All cities and urban regions have military commissariats, and cities large enough to be divided into regions have several. There are about 4,000 military commissariat offices at this level, each headed generally by a colonel, although occasionally higher and lower ranks will be found.

Moscow, for example, has both an oblast (district) and a city military commissariat. The city itself is divided administratively into twenty-nine rayons (regions), each with its own military commissariat (see Table 11). As another example, the military commissariat of the Republic of Lithuania is in a large, impressive building in Vilnius, the capital city, which itself has five military commissariats, one in each of the city's five regions.

According to Lenin, "Without military commissariats we would not have a Red Army."[12] There may be a great deal of truth in Lenin's statement, for the military commissariats of the 1980s provide a wide variety of functions supporting the Soviet Armed Forces, from directing beginning military training to designating pensions for retired military personnel. They work in close contact with local Party and Soviet agencies and with their direct cooperation in all matters. By law they are charged with (1) putting into effect measures pertaining to preparing for and conducting troop mobilization; (2) calculating and registering human and economic resources in the interests of the Armed Forces; (3) preparing youth for carrying out military service; (4) conducting call-ups for active military service and training assemblies; (5) carrying out other defense measures envisaged by the Law on General Military Obligation; (6) selecting and nominating candidates for military schools, training assemblies, and courses for reserve officers and also for the positions of *praporshchiki* and *michmen* (warrant officers) in troops units; and (7) examining and resolving complaints and applications of call-ups, reservists, servicemen, disabled veterans, and members of their families and families of deceased servicemen.

In addition, military commissariats (1) designate pensions for officers, warrant officers, extended-service servicemen and their families (including families of generals and admirals), and (2) cooperate in finding jobs and ensuring living space for officers released from the Armed Forces.[13]

Another task of the military commissariat is to register all guns, motorcycles, automobiles, skis, cameras, and other resources belonging to individuals that could be requisitioned for an emergency. Trucks used in industry, as well as construction and agricultural equipment, have mobilization designations for which the military commissariat also is responsible.[14]

A major function of the military commissariat offices is supervising the military training and military specialist training that Soviet male teenagers receive before they are called up for active military duty. How this is actually accomplished will be explained later in this chapter.

TABLE 11
Military Commissariat and DOSAAF Organizations in Moscow

Regional Voyenkomats	Region	Regional DOSAAF Committees
Lenskaya St. 2/21	Babushkin	Raduzhnaya St. 14
Kolodeznyy Lane 14	Kuybyshev	Kolodeznyy Lane 14
Semenovskiy Lane 21	Pervomay	5th Parkovaya St. 32
Perovskaya St. 57	Perovo	Metallurgov St. 23a
Zelenodol'skaya St. 6	Volgograd	1st Novo-Kuz'minskava St. 17
Kubanskaya St. 23	Lyublino	Yunykh Lenintsev St. 41
Old Kashiroskoye Hwy 2, Bg. 2	Krasnogvard	Khlebozavodskiy Pass. 10, Bg. 3
A N. Ostrovskovo St. 31	Sovetskiy	M. Tul'skaya St. 45
Vavilova St. 44	Cheremushkin	Vinokurova St. 12
Gr. Ochakovskaya St. 10	Gagarin	Lomonosovskiy Pros. 34
Ivana Franko St. 116	Kuntsevo	Bozhenko St. 14
Tamanskaya St. 10	Voroshilov	General Glagolev St. 2
Aerodromnaya St. 6	Tushino	Tsiolkovskovo St. 4
Alabyana St. 5	Leningrad	Alabyana St. 12, Bg. 9
Dmitrovskoye Hwy 5/1	Timiryazev	1st Dmitrovskiy Pass. 4
Goncharova St. 8/13	Kirov	Butyrskaya St. 34
Shchepkin St. 51	Dzerzhinskiy	Ol'minskovo Pass. 3
Prosvirin Lane 4	Sokol'niki	2nd Krasnosel'skiy Lane 8
Armyanskiy Lane 6	Bauman	Armyanskiy Lane 2
Gol'yanovskiya St. 7a, Bg. 4	Kalinin	Shosse Entuziastov 21
Marksistskaya St. 28/1	Zhdanov	Mel'nikova St. 12/8
1st Mashinostroyeniya 16	Proletariet	6th Kozhuknovskaya St. 4
Kadashevskaya Emb. 10	Moskvoretskiy	M. Tul'skaya St. 2/1 Bg. 26
Vavilova St. 44	Oktyabr'	Leninskiy Pros. 41
3rd Frunzenskaya St. 9	Leninskiy	Smolenskiy Blvd. 17
Studencheskaya St. 44/28	Kiev	Plotnikov Lane 20/21
Mantulinskaya St. 24	Krasnopresnenskiy	Nikolayeva St. 6
4th Lesnoy Lane 13	Frunze	Stanislovskovo St. 2
Kuznetskiy Most 6/3	Sverdlovsk	Rachmanovskiy Lane 4

Moscow Oblast Voyenkomat: 25th Oktyabrya St. 8
Moscow City Voyenkomat: 25th Oktyabrya St. 23
Commandant of the City of Moscow: Nov. Basmannaya St. 16
DOSAAF Central Committee: Volokolamskoye Shosse 33, Bg. 3
Moscow Oblast DOSAAF: Bakuninskaya St. 21
Moscow City DOSAAF: Strastnoy Blvd. 8/23

DOSAAF (Dobrovol'noye Obshchestvo Sodeystviya Armii, Aviastsii i Flotu—The Volunteer Society for Cooperation with the Army, Aviation, and the Fleet)

Even before World War II the Communist Party organized various youth groups for cooperation with military organizations and military industries. In 1951 these organizations supporting the armed services were combined into the present DOSAAF structure. DOSAAF is defined as a "popular defense-patriotic" organization whose purpose is "active cooperation for strengthening the military capability of the country and for preparing workers for the defense of the socialist fatherland."[15]

DOSAAF is headed by a general of the army, admiral of the fleet, or marshal of aviation.[16] Many active duty officers, including political officers, are assigned to it as instructors. With over 346,000 separate units, DOSAAF membership encompasses "98 million workers and students over fourteen years of age."[17] DOSAAF clubs and sport facilities are found in cities and towns throughout the entire Soviet Union. Regulations specify that a DOSAAF unit "must be" (*dolzhna byt'*) organized in each school, and that "all school children reaching fourteen years of age, teachers, and technical staffs" are expected to join.[18] Textbooks explain how these units will be formed and what will be expected of members. Millions of Soviet civilians have used DOSAAF facilities in order to "fulfill their norms" in the GTO military-sport complex. Firing with live ammunition is one of the primary requirements.

In addition to the functions already described, DOSAAF is charged under the Law on Universal Military Obligation with preparing specialists for the Armed Forces from among the seventeen-year-olds who register to be called up the following year. The Soviet Armed Forces require individuals who are trained in one or more of 500 specialties.[19] The number of specialists to be trained is established by the Council of Ministers, and the list of specialties and programs of training fall under the supervision of the Ministry of Defense.[20] An attempt is made to have those receiving specialist training obtain such training while at work or in school. Most of the training is done in DOSAAF clubs or schools and in regular professional technical schools.

The Soviet press at times shows photographs of DOSAAF schools, with faculty members identified as active duty military officers; but the names or types of courses taught, the total enrollment in these schools, and even their number are not revealed. All that is known is that every third person who is called up has received specialist training in DOSAAF facilities.

DOSAAF operates a considerable number of airfields, and DOSAAF instructors provide flight training. During the 1950s and 1960s a high percentage of famous Soviet Air Force pilots made their first solo flights while they were members of DOSAAF, before entering military service.[21] Apparently, a demonstration of flying aptitude in DOSAAF's flight program is of major help in gaining admittance to military schools offering pilot training.

There is some evidence that DOSAAF flying schools provide flight training up through jet aircraft. Individuals completing this program can, when called up for military service, proceed directly to flying units as pilots and, after a period of supervised flying within a squadron, be awarded military pilot's wings and commissions.

While DOSAAF is intended primarily for young people, it also attracts men and women of all ages. For those who like sports, the organization has a great deal to offer. Urban Soviet families live in very small apartments or may even share apartment facilities with other families. Except in a few cities, private automobiles are a rarity, as are sailboats, outboard motorboats, racing autos, and other equipment and items associated with recreation. There are no private or commercial clubs or facilities of the type that one might find in the non-Communist world. Therefore, if one wants to learn to drive an automobile, water ski, fly, hunt, parachute, be a ham radio operator, or to take part in almost any sport activity, DOSAAF often provides the only opportunity. Valentina Tereshkova, the first Soviet woman to orbit the earth, took up parachuting as a sport when she was a member of DOSAAF.

In the United States or Western Europe, the average youth entering military service is already familiar with automobiles and generally has participated in a number of sports. He also may have had some experience with mechanical or electrical equipment. Few in the West would consider the military utility of this background, and such activities are not sponsored by the government to raise the military potential of the nation's youth.

In the Soviet Union, on the other hand, both Party organizations and the minister of defense give official support to military-sport games and to hobbies that will increase the individual's potential as a soldier. Youth activities are given supervision and direction in order to make it possible for those participating in the various programs to absorb military training more quickly, to achieve proficiency in some skill that would be of value to a military organization, or to be a more skilled worker in a defense industry.

DOSAAF operates a large publishing house and issues its own daily newspaper. It also publishes a number of specialized journals, including publications for those interested in flying, parachuting, radio, and automobiles. DOSAAF annually issues "25 million copies of books, brochures, and posters," according to official statistics.[22] *Voyennyye Znaniya*, a monthly publication, is the official journal for both DOSAAF and civil defense. DOSAAF's publishing house issues a large number of civil defense pamphlets, and, as mentioned earlier, direct responsibilities are assigned to the organization for civil defense training.

DOSAAF facilities and training courses are provided at little or no cost. Training is offered to members as "chauffeurs, tractor drivers, operators, motorcyclists, electricians, radio specialists of various types, ship navigators, and others."[23] Such training is designed to improve the quality of workers entering the national economy as well as to raise the technical level of youth entering the Armed Forces.

In the United States much of the type of activity accomplished by DOSAAF would be charged to the defense budget. DOSAAF's funding, however, is never displayed in published Soviet military expenditures. Some of its funds are derived from lottery tickets sold throughout the Soviet Union. Members also pay a very small fee, but this would hardly begin to support the activities. Apparently grants are awarded by various enterprises, and some types of contributions are made by the local governments.

Any analysis of the Soviet Union's military potential, and its capability to mobilize rapidly and train its manpower for use in the Soviet Armed Forces, must consider both the military commissariat system and DOSAAF. Another factor to consider is the early military indoctrination of Soviet youth.

Military Training During the Formative Years

"Bringing up a future soldier begins, if you please, with childhood."[24] This view was expressed in one of the Soviet military journals in September 1972, in the post–SALT I period. Another view on the same theme appeared in *Red Star* the following year:

> A wise saying confirmed in the lives of many generations says it exactly— people are not born soldiers, they become soldiers. Whether in war or peacetime, military labor requires a great expenditure of effort from a person. And this is why the formation of a soldier is not easy. And it should not begin at the moment when the new recruit is enlisted into the ranks, but rather much earlier, at the time of the first signs of maturity, during the time of adolescent dreams.[25]

Militarization of German youth by Adolf Hitler in the 1930s received worldwide attention. Even the training of China's youth in the 1970s was noted by a number of Western observers. Somehow the militarization of Soviet youth throughout the last decade has gone almost unnoticed in the outside world, especially in the United States.[26]

In 1967, at about the time the Law on Universal Military Obligation was introduced, militarization of the entire Soviet population appears to have started. Exact reasons and purposes for the military emphasis still are unknown; however, some speculate that the failure of the ABM system, which made it desirable for the entire population to learn techniques for survival in the event of a nuclear strike, and fear of China and its huge population may have precipitated the new policy. Whatever the reasons, a major program to make the Soviet Union a nation trained in arms did begin in this period, with the military indoctrination of the very young starting almost in the cradle.

In the first years of the 1960s, during Nikita Khrushchev's regime, few military toys were sold in Soviet stores. Small boys at times could be seen playing partisans and Germans,[27] but this certainly was not officially encouraged. There was no attempt to arouse in the preschool child an interest in military service and the glories of combat. Soviet television programs prepared for young viewers did not emphasize violence, in contrast to the programs that children in the United States were viewing at the time. Khrushchev's efforts were commendable. Although he placed nuclear-armed missiles in Cuba, in the aftermath of that adventure he may have had a genuine concern about the dangers of a third world war. His subsequent peace efforts may have contributed to his removal from power.

A complete reversal of Khrushchev's policy occurred within a few years after his ouster. By the late 1960s, toy guns, missiles, tanks, and other military toys were prominently displayed in children's stores.[28] Children's books, with colored illustrations, showed the glorious, romantic side of military life. Full advantage was taken of "the time of adolescent dreams" to indoctrinate the youth with the power of the Soviet Armed Forces and the honor of becoming a soldier. A book featuring a twelve-year-old general was written in a manner intended to trigger the imagination of young boys who might dream of becoming generals among the partisans.[29] *We Pick Up New Rifles*, written for the preschool child, has illustrations of children being issued rifles and repelling the enemy.[30] Another book for children shows how a son follows in the footsteps of his father through service in the Red Army and ends with the note that the youthful reader, in turn, also will have an opportunity to become a soldier.[31] The Children's Literature Publishing House issued 300,000 copies of this booklet.

Socialist realism has its impact upon the subject matter and content of all Soviet publications. Only that which serves the Party's interests can be produced or published. Everything that is published in the Soviet

Reminiscent of Germans in the 1930s, Soviet youth, the Pioneers, goose-step during a changing of the guard.

Union, whether it be fiction, poetry, history, or children's books, or the contents of newspapers, pamphlets, or magazines must echo Party guidelines. Therefore, the decision to permit the publication of military-oriented books and the manufacture and sale of toy aircraft, tanks, guns, missiles, and other weapons must have been made deliberately by the Party.

Soviet teachers in the first grades of school are now directed to impress upon the young child that each must be prepared for later military activities. For example:

> Each teacher must explain to the students the policies of the Communist Party and the Soviet government concerning the *country's defense,* the requirements for and importance of *military service,* and the need to develop the moral-political qualities required by future soldiers. In essence, the work of each teacher and all training-educational work conducted at a school is directed toward training the students to fulfill their civil obligations; selfless labor in behalf of the homeland, and *a readiness and ability to defend it with gun in hand.*[32] (emphasis added)

Soviet boys and girls between eight and fifteen are expected to be members of the Pioneers, a Party-supported organization with elaborate facilities provided for the use of its members. These include Pioneer Palaces—huge buildings that can be seen in many cities—as well as various sports facilities. Most parents recognize that a child's membership in the Pioneers will be an asset to a future career and perhaps even to higher schooling.

The official Pioneer handbook *Tovarishch,* published by the Young Guard Publishing House, resembles in its general format the Boy Scout Handbook published in the United States. However, there are basic differences in content. Each edition of *Tovarishch* contains a very attractively displayed section on the Armed Forces. Colored drawings of Soviet military equipment, as well as ranks and insignia of enlisted personnel and officers, are shown. This section also gives a very clear explanation of the basic roles and missions of the five Soviet military services, as well as the Border Guards and Internal Troops.[33]

Military-Sport Games

Tovarishch goes to great lengths to explain that "you in school must prepare yourself for defense of the country, for service in the Army."[34] One method of such preparation is participation in national, competitive "military-sport games." The first of these games, Zarnitsa, was started in 1967. All-union finals of the Zarnitsa games in 1983 were held in Dnepropetrovsk. More than 15 million school children took part in them.[35]

The basic unit in Zarnitsa is the battalion, headed by a "commander, his deputy for political units with a staff of seven to nine people, and detachments of young soldiers." In each detachment there is a "commander, a political officer, commanders of sections, three to four scouts, two to three communications personnel, seven to twelve riflemen, two medical corpsmen, two cooks, and an editor for the battalion combat journal."[36]

Zarnitsa proved so successful for the Pioneers that in 1972 the Central Committee of the Komsomols organized similar games, Orlenok, for older teenagers. The Orlenok games, which have been played annually since, consist of athletic programs and premilitary exercises, including the use of small caliber guns and hand grenades.

Participation in Orlenok is intended for students—both boys and girls—in senior classes in regular schools, technical schools, and special secondary schools, and working teenagers in the sixteen- to eighteen-year-old group. Competitions, marches, tactical games, and meetings are all designed to prepare the youth for military service and to contribute to the premilitary training program. Both boys and girls learn civil defense measures.[37]

The Orlenok games are coordinated by Komsomol organizations, professional-technical education staffs, military commissariats, military units, military schools, physical culture groups and DOSAAF organizations, staffs of civil defense, and the Red Cross and Red Crescent. Games are given wide coverage on television, and the smart, well-styled uniforms of the girls are especially notable.

The Orlenok games are commanded by General Lieutenant Aviation Georgiy T. Beregovoy, a noted Soviet cosmonaut. In his directives to game leaders he has emphasized that game participants would "start taking the exercises and passing the norms of the All-Union Physical Culture Complex of GTO—Ready for Labor and Defense of the USSR."[38]

Orlenok games had over 20 million participants from 1972 through 1977, 8 million of them in 1977 alone.[39] These military-sport games help youth to master the compulsory school program of premilitary training. In one city, Krasnoyarsk, 80,000 young people participated in the 1973 games, with 14,000 reaching the finals. Final contestants went to Minsk for the last stage of the game in 1974.

The following year even greater attention was given to Orlenok. The Komsomol, Ministry of Defense, Ministry of Education, DOSAAF, chief of Civil Defense, Committee on Physical Culture and Sport, State Committee of Professional-Technical Education, and the Red Cross and Red Crescent issued a joint declaration "on the All-Union Komsomol Military Sport Games 'Orlenok.'" Again, 7 million youths had taken part in the games, but many lacked equipment. As a result, military schools and staffs of civil defense units were directed to supply the combat and technical equipment needed.[40]

In 1982, the finals of Orlenok were held in Kuybyshev. In April of that year, the games celebrated their tenth birthday. "So many million had participated in the games. And here were youth, just out of the eighth grade, who were finalists. Last year they were in the 'Zarnitsa' games. Now they are taking part in the fifth all-union finals of 'Orlenok'!"[41]

It has been argued in the United States that many Soviet youths, and their parents as well, are apathetic toward military-sport games and related military matters. There is no way in which the overall effectiveness of the program can be judged. In Moscow and Leningrad there are activities that are not sponsored by the Party in which youths can engage. However, there are few recreational activities in the more remote cities and villages. Participation in military-sport games is depicted as a glorious opportunity for adventure, and no expense is spared by Soviet authorities to make the presentation of the games as attractive as possible. Prizes are awarded, and the games end with parades and celebrations in major cities. The Orlenok games seemingly provide a means for both boys and girls to get away from home and to travel, while at the same time performing a military-patriotic duty.

Beginning Military Training

Since its formation the Soviet state has had some form of military training for its youth.[42] When the 1967 Law on Universal Military Obligation, which reduced the period of military service, was promulgated, a revised program called Beginning Military Training was made compulsory for all Soviet boys prior to their induction. This program includes instruction in basic drill, weapons familiarization, field exercises, and the fundamentals of civil defense; it also provides information about the Soviet Armed Forces. Inductees thus are ready to join units and, in the event of an emergency, could be prepared for combat duty within a few weeks. To ensure that minimum preinduction military training standards were met, the 1967 law specified:

> The Ministry of Defense of the USSR is to work out, together with the staff of Civil Defense, USSR, the Ministry of Education, USSR, the Ministry of Higher and Secondary Special Education, USSR, the State Committee of the Council of Ministers on Professional and Technical Education, the Ministry of Health, USSR, and the Central Committee of DOSAAF, a program of beginning military training (BMT) and tables of equipment; confirm the program of BMT and the TO&E (table of organization and equipment); control the quality of BMT; and establish a profile of military technical training for schools, educational institutions, and study points.[43]

Thus the Ministry of Defense has primary responsibility for beginning military training, with the assistance of DOSAAF, the various educational ministries, the staff of Civil Defense, and the Ministry of Health. After the law was passed in 1967, several years were required to establish the entire program of beginning military training, and weaknesses, such as lack of practice firing ranges in schools, probably still remained in the mid-1970s.

It was not until 1971 or 1972 that Soviet writers claimed that the beginning military training program had been introduced "in most schools," and not until the following year was it established "in all schools."[44] Other aspects of beginning military training, including military-sport games, faced similar delays in getting fully under way after institution of the 1967 law.

Beginning military training is given to both boys and girls in the ninth and tenth grades, starting at age fifteen. For working youth, beginning training is given at study points set up in DOSAAF clubs or in factories. A minimum of 140 hours of beginning military training is required. Furthermore, each male youth receives an additional 30 hours of training while attending camp during the summer, at which time he is expected to practice firing with live ammunition under realistic training conditions.[45] Girls learn the fundamentals of military training and civil defense and are trained as first-aid workers.

General management and control of beginning military training has been assigned in the Ministry of Defense to the commander in chief, Ground Forces, who also is a deputy minister of defense.[46] A department of external troop training, formed in the Ground Forces staff, coordinates the beginning military training program with the chief of Civil Defense and DOSAAF. Leadership and control are delegated to the commanders of military districts and, "on the territory of republics, krays, oblasts, and cities, it is carried out by corresponding military commissariats and also, for their part of the program, by the staff of Civil Defense."[47] Beginning military training programs in cities are managed directly by the military commissariats, which select reserve officers who become full-time members of the school staff as instructors.

For young men not in school, the law specifies that the Ministry of Defense is responsible for supplying, through DOSAAF, practice weapons, small caliber rifles, and ammunition to study points designated for beginning military study in factories, industrial enterprises, *sovkhozes,* and *kolkhozes.* Judging from pictures, study points are arranged somewhat like Lenin Rooms in military units. They are equipped with study tables and work surfaces (on which weapons can be dismantled) and are furnished with books, magazines, training aids, and posters and other decorations. As more and more young men receive a ten-year education, the study points in factories are being replaced by central study points in DOSAAF facilities.

Instruction in civil defense procedures is a significant part of the beginning military training program. The chief of civil defense is responsible for "direction and control of the teaching of civil defense to the youth through the combat training administration of civil defense," for "preparing and publishing textbooks and film strips for the civil defense section of beginning military training, and for helping schools, educational institutes, enterprises, organizations, *sovkhozes,* and *kolkhozes* teach civil defense to youth." He also is authorized to request the minister of defense to supply "means of protection and dosimeter instruments from those not needed by troops."[48]

The Call-up

Registration for call-up occurs at seventeen years of age, the year before induction. At that time a medical examination is given, and any necessary medical treatment is completed before the youth actually enters military service.

Eighteen-year-olds are called to active duty either in May/June—those who will turn 18 before 1 July—or in November/December for the rest. At these times a call-up commission is formed in each military commissariat office; it consists of a chairman, who is the military commissar, and the following members: a deputy chairman, who is a member of the executive committee of the region's soviet of workers' deputies, representatives of the regional committee of the Communist Party, the regional chief of the Komsomols, the chief or deputy chief of the militia, and a doctor.[49] The call-up commission determines the service and branch of service to which each individual will be assigned, designating men for each of the five military services, the rear services, Civil Defense, Construction and Billeting Troops, KGB troops, MVD troops, or for other special troops, such as chemical, engineering, or signal. Quotas are set by the General Staff.

Individuals assigned to military construction duty are in a somewhat different category from the others. They must be "fit for physical work," and, if possible, must have completed a course at a building school or have a specialty in a construction or building trade.

Another task of the call-up commission is to determine whether an individual will be excused from services or have his service period delayed. According to Soviet law a candidate may be excused for illness or physical unfitness, or service may be postponed in order to continue education. In 1980, stringent new regulations were introduced into the Law on Universal Military Obligation. Only students attending one of a special list of schools would be deferred. This requirement actually came into law on 1 January 1982.[50] Service also may be postponed if the candidate has two or more children, an invalid wife, a widowed or divorced mother with two or more children under eight and no other supporting children, or one or more dependent brothers or sisters who are under sixteen or are invalids who cannot be placed in a home. Men may be deferred for any of these reasons until age twenty-seven, after which they are no longer subject to induction.[51]

Few Soviet males are completely excused from military service. According to the late Marshal Grechko, "almost all" the male population undergoes military training.[52] Deferments for physical reasons are rare; if the individual can perform some useful function in civilian life he also can perform some task in the Armed Forces.

Military commissariats are a major link between the Armed Forces and the population as a whole, the funnel through which candidates must pass when entering active military service and through which they must return when they are discharged. As will be seen later, this agency also plays a key role in mobilization.

Military Training of Enlisted Personnel and Warrant Officers

In theory, the young soldier (as he is called until he takes the oath) has received sufficient premilitary training to enable him immediately to take an active part in the regiment to which he is assigned. His first few weeks in service are spent reviewing military fundamentals such as drill and handling basic weapons. Formal entry into the regiment occurs when he takes his military oath, a very ceremonial occasion.

Certain individuals, selected to become specialists on the basis of their education and training, are sent to special schools for courses that last as long as six months. Candidates for sergeant receive their six months of training in the school run by the regiment.[53] The life of the inductee is harsh, and discipline is severe. Table 12 shows a typical day in his life.

Training simulates combat conditions as closely as possible. Maneuvers by regiments and divisions take place in the spring and the fall at the end of each training period, preceding military call-up and release times. Major maneuvers, which may involve two or more military districts, or perhaps one of the groups of forces abroad, are held occasionally, on no apparent schedule. Maneuvers may be conducted to test a new type of equipment, such as the BMP, or a new concept, or even perhaps to intimidate and invade another nation, as was the case with respect to Czechoslovakia in 1968.

Different types of training are given to inductees in the various services or in individual components of the Soviet Armed Forces, such as the Border Guards or Civil Defense troops. The Strategic Rocket Forces or Air Forces may require that a large percentage of the new recruits be sent immediately to specialist school. In general the individual will be taught to perform only a specific function, with little cross-training in other skills.

Enlisted and warrant officer grades are shown in Table 13.

Every effort is made to ensure that each inductee serves his prescribed period of military service. Should he become physically incapable of performing drill or routine field duties, he is transferred to an assignment in his unit that requires a lesser degree of physical fitness. If no appropriate

TABLE 12
A Typical Day in the Life of an Inductee

0600-0609	Reveille
0610-0630	Exercise (tidying up)
0630-0650	Barracks time
0650-0720	Political information (morning inspection)
0725-0755	Breakfast
0800-1400	Training periods (six fifty-minute periods with ten-minute breaks between)
1400-1440	Dinner
1440-1510	After dinner time
1510-1530	Maintenance: personal, weapon, and equipment
1530-1830	Political education work (Monday and Thursday)
1530-1830	Equipment Maintenance (Tuesday and Friday)
1530-1830	Sports (Wednesday and Saturday)
1830-1940	Self-preparation or homework
1940-2010	Supper
2010-2040	Personal time
2040-2155	Evening walk and checkup
2200	Taps

Source: A. Yurkov, "The Order of the Day," *Military Herald,* January 1976, p. 51.

task can be found in his own unit, he will be transferred to another organization.

On entering active duty the young soldier is issued a uniform, and his civilian clothing is returned to his home or placed in storage. Shortly before his release date, he is issued a new uniform to wear back to his home. He must keep this uniform in good condition, for when he completes his active duty training his military obligations continue in the category of reserves in which he is placed.

Extended Duty Servicemen

Upon completing their required military service, soldier, sailors, sergeants, and starshinas who are military specialists of certain kinds may volunteer for extended duty, for periods of two, four, or six years, and so on each time until they turn fifty. Certain positions are designated to be filled only by extended duty servicemen, and commanders are instructed to note these positions and encourage their best men to volunteer for them. Men can also volunteer for extended service after they have completed required military service and are in the reserves,

338

TABLE 13
Soviet Grades

Type and Service	Soviet Designation	Translation[a]
Soldiers (all services)	*Ryadovoy, yefreytor*	Private, private first class
Sailors	*Matros, starshiy matros*	Seaman, senior seaman
Sergeants (all services)	*Mladshiy serzhant*	Junior sergeant
	Serzhant	Sergeant
	Starshiy serzhant	Senior sergeant
	Starshina	Sergeant major
Starhinas (Navy)	*Starshina 2nd stati*	Petty officer second class
	Starshina 1st stati	Petty officer first class
	Glavnyy starshina	Chief petty officer
	Glavnyy korabel'nyy starshina[b]	Chief ship petty officer
Warrant Officers	*Praporshchik* (all services)	Ensign
	Michman (Navy)	Midshipman
	Starshiy praporshchik[c]	Senior ensign
	Starshiy michman[c]	Senior midshipman

Source: V. Ryabov, *The Soviet Armed Forces: Yesterday and Today* (Moscow: Progress Publishers, 1976), p. 151.

Notes: Soldiers are called *ryadovoy* as soon as they are assigned to a unit. *Yefreytor* rank is given to *ryadovoys* who do their duties well and who are assigned to positions that call for *yefreytors*. *Mladshiy serzhant* is a grade given to *kursants* (cadets) who complete the program for preparing *serzhants* in the regimental school. *Serzhant* is a grade awarded to *kursants* who finish the program for preparing *serzhants* with a mark of excellent. *Starshiy serzhant* is a grade given to *serzhants* who have served six months and are assigned to a position calling for a *starshiy serzhant*.

[a]Note that these are commonly accepted translations, not equivalent grades in the U.S. armed forces.

[b]Introduced in January 1972.

[c]The senior grades for warrant officers were introduced in January 1981.

but they must do so before age thirty-five. There also are some specialist positions that are handled by four-year contracts, which can be signed at any time.[54]

Selection of candidates for extended service is determined by a permanent commission consisting of the deputy unit commander, secretary of the local Party organization, assistant to the chief of staff of the unit, unit medical officer, and secretary of the Komsomol organization. On being accepted for extended service, but not until they complete their two years of obligatory service, privates are promoted to private first class. Sergeants who are accepted are promoted to the next rank up, provided that they have had their present rank six months and that their position calls for that rank.

Warrant Officers (Praporshchiki and Michmen)

In 1971 the Ministry of Defense introduced a new rank roughly equivalent to that of warrant officer in the U.S. armed forces. These are of two kinds, with names resurrected from the time of Peter the Great: *praporshchiki*, who serve in all the services; and *michmen*, who serve in the Navy. These officers were intended to replace extended duty servicemen. Men already on extended duty were encouraged to apply for warrant officer ranks but were permitted to serve out their extended duty terms of two, four, or six years.[55] Apparently the ranks were less popular than anticipated, or there were too few qualified applicants, because, in 1973, provisions were made again for inductees to apply for extended duty.[56]

Actually, the perquisites for new warrant officers make their military careers much more attractive than those of the extended service sergeants. Their uniforms are of the same cloth and cut as those of officers, and they can take holidays at resort hotels with their families just as officers do. The law of military services permits warrant officers to take an examination to become a lieutenant after five years in rank, and after ten years they may become officers by attestation if they hold an officer's position. If they retire after ten years they become officers in the reserves. For other allowances, the warrant officers are classified the same as extended duty sergeants. They may stay on active duty to age forty-five. And last but not least, regulations make special mention of the fact that they can wear brown shoes as officers do, rather than boots.

A considerable number of one-year schools (*shkoly*) have been established for the education and training of warrant officers, but few have been specifically identified. A flying school at Saratov has been advertised as providing a two-year helicopter course for *praporshchiki*. Other training and educational institutions for warrant officers simply have been reported as "schools of technicians."

TABLE 14
Reserve Service for Soldiers and Sailors

Category	Service Over One Year (First Class)[a]	Service Less Than One Year (Second Class)[b]
First category (to age 35)	Reserve call-up four times, three months each	Reserve call-up six times, three months each (after twelve months total service, transferred to first class)
Second category (35 to 45)	Reserve call-up one to two times, two months each	
Third category (45 to 50)	Reserve call-up one time, one month	

Source: A. G. Gornyy, ed., *Spravochnik po Zakonodatel'stvu Dlya Ofitserov Sovetskoy Armii i Flota* [Handbook on Legislation for Officers of the Soviet Army and Navy] (Moscow: Voyenizdat, 1970), p. 35.

[a]This includes those who complete higher education and are required to remain on active duty only eighteen months, as well as all those who complete their normal tour of military duty.

[b]Includes those who were deferred from call-up for special hardship reasons. It should be noted that all males are in the reserves, except possibly those excused for physical reasons.

Reserve Duty and Mobilization

When Hitler attacked the Soviet Union in June 1941, the Soviet leadership reportedly was able to mobilize 5.5 million men in eight days.[57] When able-bodied men born between 1905 and 1918 (except those in central Asia and the Far East)[58] were ordered to active duty, that number swelled. With the current emphasis on reservists and mobilization procedures, the Kremlin should be able to react much more swiftly today.

According to Soviet law, inductees are placed in reserve status after active duty service and are assigned to categories depending on age. They remain subject to call-up for refresher training (as shown in Table 14) until they reach the age of fifty.

No data are released specifying the percentage of those in the reserve actually receiving refresher military training. It is believed that such training varies from republic to republic. In some cases it may be efficient and fully performed according to all regulations. In other cases it may be omitted or perfunctory at best.

Local councils of workers' deputies have a responsibility for ensuring that reservists, both officer and enlisted, attend military refresher training sessions. They act as a liaison between the military commissariats, which actually oversee the training sessions, and the factories, *kolkhozes,* and plants where the men are employed. Supporting the councils are Communist Party officials, the Komsomol, and professional trade unions, which cooperate to ensure that men are released at the appointed times, that jobs are held open for them, that they are paid while in training, and that wives and children do not suffer while the men are away from their homes.[59]

Since practically all Soviet males are in the reserves or on active military duty, a very large number of reserve officers are needed. They come from several sources: career officers who have been released from active duty; men with higher education who have completed their compulsory military service and probably have gotten commissions in reserve officer training classes while in school; "soldiers, sailors, sergeants, and *starshinas* with higher or secondary education, who have served on active duty" and returned to civilian life; "soldiers, sailors, sergeants, and *starshinas* in the reserve, who receive a higher or specialized secondary education akin to a military specialty"; and inductees in the reserve "with eight-year education, who have served on active duty, and have taken training for reserve officers and passed the established examination."[60]

Reserve officers under thirty years of age may be called up for two to three years of active duty if their specialties are required. The numbers to be called up annually are determined by the Council of Ministers.

There is no rapid "up or out" selection and promotion in the Soviet Armed Forces comparable to that in the United States; for example, a Soviet junior lieutenant can serve in that grade until he reaches the age of forty. However, there are mandatory ages for leaving active military duty and going into the reserves and mandatory retirement ages for officers from the reserve as well, as shown in Table 15.

How rapidly and how efficiently could the Soviet Union mobilize its manpower? A definitive answer to this question is impossible. Even if all facts about Soviet mobilization planning were known, which they are not, there still would be differences of interpretation. However, it is known that planning for mobilization is a direct responsibility of the General Staff and that it receives major emphasis.

With the specialized training each inductee receives during his two (or three) years of active military duty, the approximately 1.6 million young men released from the Soviet Armed Forces each year should be able to become combat-ready in a very short period of time. Many of these, if not all, should have undergone some refresher military training

TABLE 15

Mandatory Retirement Ages and Reserve Categories for Officers

	Age Limits			
	Active Duty	Reserve First Category	Reserve Second Category	Reserve Third Category
Junior lieutenant, lieutenant, and equivalent	40	40	45	50
Senior lieutenant, captain, and equivalent	40	45	50	55
Major and equivalent	45	45	50	55
Lieutenant colonel and equivalent	45	50	55	60
Colonel and equivalent	50	55	—	60
General major, general lieutenant, and equivalent	55	60	—	65
General colonel, admiral, and equivalent	60	—	—	65
Women officers	unknown	—	—	50

Source: A. G. Gornyy, ed., *Spravochnik po Zakonodatel'stvu Dlya Ofitserov Sovetskoy Armii i Flota* [Handbook on Legislation for Officers of the Soviet Army and Navy] (Moscow: Voyenizdat, 1970), p. 37.

Note: The compulsory retirement provision does not affect four- and five-star ranks. The law also provides that certain officers may be kept on active duty for an additional five years, as determined by the Council of Ministers. In January 1977, the law was amended to provide that officers may be kept on active duty for an additional five years, after the first five-year extension.

after their release from active duty service. In particular, those whose mobilizĩon assignments are in specialized technical areas will most likely have had refresher training.

In the event of a national emergency, or if the Soviet leadership desires at any time to mobilize part of the population secretly, Soviet authorities should be able to contact any or all males of military age within a very short time period. This is made possible by the system of military commissariat offices and the fact that all Soviet citizens must possess internal passports. If an individual travels from one part of the country to another and remains for more than a few days his passport must be registered with the local militia. When a worker changes jobs, he must appear within a specified number of days on the roster of the military commissariat of that location. Although the Soviet system of internal controls over its citizens may be far from perfect, the location and status of almost every adult male within a given area should be known to the local military commissariat office. Additionally, the system of military districts and military garrisons in cities can assist in ensuring that orders are carried out. Even if nuclear strikes disrupt transportation and communications, mobilization still could be effected through local agencies.

In addition to those who have completed military training, there are two other categories that increase the mobilization potential of the Soviet Union. The beginning military training program given to all male youths before induction is designed to make them able to fit directly into active combat units with some degree of effectiveness. And girls too may be expected to make a considerable contribution in some categories, for they as well as boys are required to study civil defense and to take part in military-sport games, which include instruction in some military fundamentals.

The Soviets criticize the Germans for not having planned their military manpower needs for World War II in advance and specifically for exhausting their men in the primary military age groups in the first years of the war. According to the authors of *Military Strategy*:

> The expedient distribution of manpower resources for mobilization formation and for the replacement of casualties is one of the most important problems of mobilization planning. The planning agencies should take into strict account possible manpower requirements for the entire war and not permit the calling up of eligible men of all young ages during the initial mobilization. A portion of them must be saved for replenishing the army during the war.[61]

Soviet mobilization planning, if the statements of their spokesmen are correct, would also assign a certain percentage of men in the older age groups to perform duties in rear areas.[62]

Mobilization plans for each service differ. Strategic Rocket Forces are maintained almost at full strength at all times and would be hardly affected by the initial mobilization. Troops of Air Defense are in much the same category. "The Air Forces can operate from the outset of the war in the same composition in which they existed during peacetime." Only the formation of additional military air transport units from the ranks of Aeroflot would be needed. The Navy would accomplish its mobilization "by equipping the existing ships with sufficient supplies, removing from them excess equipment and personnel with practical experience, [and] putting into service ships of the reserve that are being kept in mothballs."[63]

The Soviet leadership should be able to mobilize 2 million to 3 million men in twenty-four hours. An equivalent number again could be called up within a forty-eight-hour period, approximately doubling the regular peacetime force of between 4.5 million and 5 million men. This should give a total of between 9 million and 11 million men in uniform within two full days. Since in peacetime the Soviet Union has at least 8 million in the reserves who have had military service within a five-year period, the Soviet Armed Forces probably could reach 13 million to 14 million in less than ten days, if such numbers were required. After initial mobilization, more time would be needed to get them to combat areas.

Notes

1. A. I. Odintsov, ed., *Uchebnoye Posobiye po Nachal'noy Voyennoy Podgotovke* [Textbook for Beginning Military Training] (Moscow: Voyenizdat, 1970). This was the first edition of the official textbook used for beginning military training. After eight revisions and millions of copies, it was replaced by A. M. Popov, ed., *Nachal'naya Voyennaya Podgotovka* [Beginning Military Training] (Moscow: Voyenizdat, 1978), of which 1,300,000 copies were published. In 1983, the fifth edition was published. This is a "textbook prepared with the aim of helping teaching military affairs in general education schools, secondary specialist schools, professional-technical schools, and youth working in factories, establishments, organizations, *sovkhozes,* and *kolkhozes.*" The book itself gives a basic understanding of the Soviet Armed Forces, including staff, tactics, and organization.

2. S. M. Shtemenko, *Novyy Zakon i Voinskaya Sluzhba* [The New Law on Military Service] (Moscow: Voyenizdat, 1968).

3. Murray Feshbach, "Population," *Economic Performance and the Military Burden of the Soviet Union* (Washington, D.C.: Government Printing Office, 1970), p. 68.

4. *Chislennost' Razmeshcheniye, Vozrastnaya Struktura, Uroven' Obrasovaniya, Natsional'nyy Sostav, Yazyki i Istochniki Sredstv Sushchestvovaniya Naseleniya SSSR* [Number, Location, Age Structure, Level of Education, Nationality, Languages, and Sources of Income of the Republics of the USSR] (Moscow: Statistics, 1971).

5. Nikita S. Khrushchev, "Report Delivered at the Fourth Session of the Supreme Soviet of the USSR," 14 January 1960. For excerpts of this report that deal with military matters, see Harriet Fast Scott, *Soviet Military Doctrine: Its Continuity—1960–1970* (Menlo Park, Calif.: Stanford Research Institute, 1971), Appendix 1.

6. V. M. Bondarenko, "Military-Technical Superiority: The Most Important Factor in the Reliable Defense of the Country," *Kommunist Vooruzhennykh Sil* 17, September 1966. For an English translation, see W. R. Kintner and H. F.

Scott, *The Nuclear Revolution in Soviet Military Affairs* (Norman, Okla.: University of Oklahoma Press, 1968), p. 335.

7. Lin Piao, minister of defense, Chinese People's Republic, in a speech entitled "Long Live the Victory of the People's War," 2 September 1965. Reported in Foreign Broadcast Information Service (FBIS).

8. Shtemenko, *Novyy Zakon*.

9. V. D. Sokolovskiy, *Soviet Military Strategy*, 3d ed., Harriet Fast Scott, ed. (New York: Crane, Russak & Co., 1975), p. 309.

10. In the 1962 and 1963 editions of *Military Strategy*, Sokolovskiy warned that when the period of service is shortened, "the quality of the training and consequently the combat readiness of those discharged is correspondingly reduced." This caveat, understandably, was omitted from the 1968 edition.

11. S. M. Shtemenko, "Local Agencies of Military Control," *Krasnaya Zvezda*, 7 April 1968. See also P. I. Romanov, "Voyennyy Komissariat" [Military Commissariat], *Sovetskaya Voyennaya Entsiklopediya* [Soviet Military Encyclopedia] (Moscow: Voyenizdat, 1976–1980), Vol. 2, p. 269.

12. V. I. Lenin, *Collected Works*, 5th ed. (Moscow: Progress Publishers, 1974), Vol. 41, p. 148.

13. P. I. Romanov, "Voyennyy Komissariat," *Sovetskaya Voyennaya Entsiklopedia*, Vol. 2, p. 270.

14. Trucks and similar vehicles in the Soviet Union that have mobilization assignments are identified by a white triangle, front and rear. These vehicles are checked periodically at designated points to ensure that maintenance standards are met.

15. A. I. Pokryshkin, "DOSAAF," *Sovetskaya Voyennaya Entsiklopediya*, Vol. 3, pp. 255–257.

16. As of 1 January 1984 DOSAAF was headed by Admiral of the Fleet G. M. Yegorov. Marshal of Aviation A. I. Pokryshkin headed DOSAAF from 1971 to 1981. He succeeded General of the Army A. L. Getman.

17. *Yezhegodnik, 1982, Bolshoy Sovetskoy Entsiklopedii* [Yearbook, 1982, of the Great Soviet Encyclopedia] (Moscow: Soviet Encyclopedia Publishing House, 1982), p. 23.

18. G. B. Mizikovskiy, *Oborono-Massovaya Rabota v Shkolye* [Mass Defense Work in Schools] (Moscow: DOSAAF Publishing House, 1975), p. 18.

19. A. M. Popov, *Nachal'naya Voyennaya Podgotovka* [Beginning Military Training] (Moscow: DOSAAF, 1981), p. 48.

20. A. G. Gornyy, ed., *Spravochnik Po Zakonodatel'stvuu Dlya Ofitserov Sovetskoy Armii i Flota* [Handbook on Legislation for Officers of the Soviet Army and Navy] (Moscow: Voyenizdat, 1970), p. 27.

21. See, for example, P. Saprykin, *Shkola Yunykh Letchikov* [School for Young Pilots] (Moscow: DOSAAF Publishing House, 1975). Also see Ye. Ye. Smirov, *Khochu Letat'* [I Want to Fly] (Moscow: Voyenizdat, 1975).

22. *Yezhegodnik*, 1982, p. 23.

23. Ibid.

24. G. Bardashchuk, "Commissioned as an Officer," *Morskoy Sbornik* [Naval Collections], September 1972, p. 69.

25. N. Nikol'skiy, "They Are Becoming Soldiers," *Krasnaya Zvezda*, 22 March 1973.

26. See, for example, William E. Odom, "The 'Militarization' of Soviet Society," *Problems of Communism*, September-October 1976, p. 34.

27. Personal observation of the authors, who lived in Moscow from 1962 to 1964 and from 1970 to 1972.

28. Ibid.

29. A. Duginets, *Dvenadtsatiletniy General* [The Twelve-Year-Old General] (Moscow: Little Child's Publishing House, 1970).

30. Vladimir Mayakovskiy, *Voz'mem Vintovki Novyeya* [We Pick Up New Rifles] (Kaliningrad, USSR: Kaliningrad Truth Publishing House, 1970).

31. S. Baruzadin, *Shel Po Ulitse Soldat* [A Soldier Walks Along the Street] (Moscow: Children's Literature Publishing House, 1970).

32. O. Volodin, "Developing the Defenders of the Homeland," *Narodnoye Obrazovaniye* [Popular Education], February 1972, p. 30.

33. V. S. Khanchin, Yu. Ye. Rives, and V. I. Nikolayev, *Tovarishch* [Comrade] (Moscow: Molodaya Gvardiya, 1976), pp. 265–280.

34. Ibid., p. 272.

35. See *Krasnaya Zvezda*, 24 June 1983.

36. Ibid., pp. 272–280. See also "Zarnitsa," *Sovetskaya Voyennaya Entsiklopediya*, Vol. 3, p. 409.

37. L. A. Pesterev, "Orlenok," *Sovetskaya Voyennaya Entsiklopediya*, Vol. 6, p. 115.

38. *Krasnaya Zvezda*, 19 April 1972. See also *Krasnaya Zvezda*, 26 April 1972; and *GTO on the March* (Moscow: Physical Culture and Sport Publishers, 1975); N. G. Skachkov, *Mnogobor'ye GTO* [All-round Tournament GTO] (Moscow: DOSAAF, 1982).

39. L. A. Pesterev, "Orlenok," *Sovetskaya Voyennaya Entsiklopediya*, Vol. 6, p. 115.

40. L. Pesterev, "It Is Not a Vacation in 'Orlenok,'" *Voyennyye Znaniya* 4, April 1975.

41. N. Vasil'yev, "'Orlenok'—School of the Courageous," *Sovetskiy Voin* 20, 1982, p. 50.

42. P. A. Gusak and A. M. Rogachev, *Nachal'naya Voyennaya Podgotovka* [Beginning Military Training] (Moscow: Prosveshcheniye, 1981), p. 29, provides a chart in which the 1939 Law on Universal Military Obligation and the 1967 Law are compared.

43. Gornyy, *Spravochnik*, pp. 43–44.

44. A. I. Averin, Yu. P. Subbotin, and N. A. Yasinskiy, *Nachal'naya Voyennaya Podgotovka v Obshcheobrazovatel'noy Shkole* [Beginning Military Training in General Education Schools] (Moscow: Enlightenment Publishing House, 1973), p. 4.

45. A. N. Odintsov, *Uchebnoye Posobiye Po Nachal'noy Voyennoy Podgotovke*, [Textbook on Beginning Military Training] (Moscow: Voyenizdat, 1975), 6th ed., p. 93.

46. Gornyy, *Spravochnik*, p. 43.

47. Ibid., p. 44.

48. Ibid., p. 45.

49. A. I. Lepeshkin, *Osnovy Sovetskovo Voyennovo Zakonodatel'stva* [The Fundamentals of Soviet Military Legislation] (Moscow: Voyenizdat, 1973), p. 57.

50. "On the introduction of changes and additions into the Law USSR 'On Universal Military Obligation,'" *Vedomosti Verkhovnogo Soveta SSSR,* Decrees 1121, 1122, (no. 52), 24 December 1980, Article 5, pp. 1129, 1141.

51. Ibid., p. 1129.

52. See I. I. Yakubovskiy, *Boyevoye Sodruzhestvo Bratskikh Narodov i Armiy* [Combat Community of Fraternal Peoples and Armies] (Moscow: Voyenizdat, 1975), p. 211. Yakubovskiy quotes Marshal Grechko's statements in this example.

53. Apparently the Soviet Armed Forces maintain a number of special training battalions, as, for example, an Engineer-Sapper Training Battalion. See *Krasnaya Zvezda,* 8 September 1976, "How to Conduct the Training."

54. S. S. Maksimov, *Osnovy Sovetskogo Voyennogo Zakonodatel'stva* [Fundamentals of Soviet Military Legislation] (Moscow: Voyenizdat, 1978) pp. 90–92.

55. Order of the Presidium of the USSR Supreme Soviet: "Ensigns and Midshipmen of the USSR Armed Forces," *Vedomosti Verkhovnogo Soviet SSSR,* 24 November 1971, pp. 651–654.

56. Ibid., p. 301. See also Maksimov, *Osnovy Sovetskogo,* pp. 92–94.

57. M. V. Zakharov, ed., *50 Let Vooruzhennykh Sil SSSR* [50 Years of the Armed Forces of the USSR] (Moscow: Voyenizdat, 1968), p. 257.

58. M. M. Minasyan, *Great Patriotic War of the Soviet Union* (Moscow: Progress Publishers, 1974), p. 56.

59. V. P. Golyanov, *Rayonny, Gorodskoy Soviet i Voyenno-Patrioticheskoye Vospitaniye Naseleniya* [Regional and City Councils and Military-Patriotic Education of the Population] (Moscow: Legal Literature Publishing House, 1975), pp. 28–33.

60. Gornyy, *Spravochnik,* pp. 36–37.

61. Sokolovskiy, *Soviet Military Strategy,* 3d ed., p. 312.

62. Ibid., p. 311.

63. Ibid., p. 310.

11

Preparation, Education, and Training of Soviet Officers

Military institutions of learning (VUZ) in the Soviet Union are "designated for the training of command, political, technical engineer, and specialist cadres for the Armed Forces." They consist of "military faculties at civilian institutions, courses for training and retraining the officer corps, and also the Suvorov Military Schools and the Nakhimov Naval School."[1]

Future officers in the Soviet Armed Forces receive their military education in approximately 140 schools. A few of these are three-year military schools that give commissions and are considered secondary schools. Most are four- or five-year higher military schools. Graduates receive a degree roughly equivalent to a bachelor's degree, as well as a lieutenant's commission.

Soviet military and higher military schools resemble to some extent the three United States service academies at West Point, Annapolis, and Colorado Springs. Entry age for the Soviet schools ranges from seventeen to twenty-three, approximately the same as for the United States academies, and graduates are commissioned as lieutenants. While none of the 140 military and higher military schools in the Soviet Union is equivalent to any of the three United States academies in size or facilities, many of the Soviet schools are housed in impressive buildings with equally impressive facilities for military training.[2]

Advanced professional education and training for Soviet officers are provided primarily by seventeen "academies," which in many ways are similar to service schools, staff colleges, and war colleges in the United States. However, there are major differences. Courses at most war and staff colleges in the United States last one academic year or less. Some service school and staff college courses in the United States are measured in weeks. Soviet academies, on the other hand, offer courses that vary in length from three to five years, with the exception of the General Staff Academy, which has a two-year course.

Many of the service academies, as well as a number of higher military schools, do much more than provide professional military education for

TABLE 16.
Ranks in Major Positions at Soviet Military and Naval Schools and Academies

Commandant of an academy	General colonel, general of the army, marshal of service or branch, marshal of the Soviet Union
Heads of faculties and chairs	General lieutenant or general colonel
Senior instructor at an academy	General major
Commandant of a higher military or naval school	General lieutenant or vice admiral
Commandant of a military or naval school, deputy commandant of a higher military or naval school for scientific and study work	General major, rear admiral

Source: Data from A. G. Gornyy, *Spravochnik po Zakonodatel'stvu Dlya Ofitserov Sovetskoy Armii i Flota* (Moscow: Voyenizdat, 1970), pp. 178-182.

the Soviet officer corps. They also are military research centers, performing specialized tasks assigned them by the General Staff or by their parent service or branch. Much of the work that is contracted to "think tanks" in the United States, such as RAND or the Institute for Defense Analysis, would be accomplished in the Soviet Union by the service academies of selected higher military schools.

Military schools, academies, and other military educational institutions are located in over eighty cities throughout the Soviet Union. Students, faculties, and support personnel of these establishments may compose a force of more than one-half million men and women. Of this number, between 300 and 400 may be generals and admirals, serving as commandants and department or faculty heads.[3]

The attention given to officer education in the Soviet Armed Forces is reflected by the ranks assigned key positions in military educational institutions (as shown in Table 16).

Even though many details are not available, an examination of what is known about Soviet officer training and education provides one of the best insights into the structure of the Soviet Armed Forces, their size, missions, and possible trends for the future.

Early Development

The origins of officer education in the Soviet Union of today can be traced back to the rule of the czars of Imperial Russia. The first military schools appeared at the end of the seventeenth and the beginning of the eighteenth centuries. The Military Engineering School was established in Moscow in 1698, and the School of Mathematical and Navigational Sciences in 1701. A school for naval cadets was established in St. Petersburg in 1752, after the capital had been transferred from Moscow.

Other military educational institutions were formed at the end of the eighteenth and throughout the nineteenth centuries. The Medical and Surgeons Academy was founded in 1798, the Military Academy (later the Academy of the General Staff) in 1832, the Artillery and Engineers Academy in 1855, the Military Law Academy in 1867, the Naval Academy in 1877, and the Quartermaster Academy in 1911. All of these academies were originally located in St. Petersburg.

A network of military schools was created in the nineteenth century. Before World War I there were twenty such schools in St. Petersburg, Moscow, Kazan, Kiev, Odessa, Irkutsk, Orenburg, Tver, and elsewhere, of which eleven were infantry, three cavalry, two cossack, two artillery, one engineering, and one military topography.[4]

On 14 November 1917, one week after the October Revolution, the order was given to disband the old Russian military schools. In their place a Soviet Higher Commissar of Military Institutions of Higher Learning (VUZ) was designated to establish schools for the new regime. The first Soviet military school opened in December 1917. This was the Moscow Revolutionary Machine-Gunners' School of Commanders, now the Higher Combined Arms Command School Named for the Supreme Soviet of the Russian Soviet Federated Socialist Republic (RSFSR). The first class in the new school had 150 cadets, of whom 105 were members of the Communist Party.

By January 1918 a broad network of preparatory courses for commanders had been formed. A month later thirteen accelerated commanders' courses were started in Moscow, Petrograd, Tver, Kazan, and other cities, with an enrollment of 5,270 students. A naval school for commanders, with an initial student body of 414 sailors, was begun in Petrograd.

At the end of 1918 there were 63 military schools, with a total enrollment of 13,000 students. The number of military schools increased to 107 in 1919 and to 153 during the following year. At this time, 54,000 students were enrolled in courses lasting from four to eight months. Special recruiting campaigns were begun to increase the number of cadets. During the Civil War period, from 1918 to 1920, 40,000 Red Army officers were trained in these new military schools and in special courses.[5]

The military schools and academies had an almost impossible task. According to Soviet spokesmen, 80 to 90 percent of the total Soviet population at that time were either illiterate or semiliterate. The Soviet officer school system had to devote a great deal of time simply to providing a basic education, which in the United States and Western European nations would have been completed by every individual before even beginning officer training.

After the Civil War a network of military schools (*shkoly*) with three- and four-year courses of instruction was established. In 1922, the Red Navy was given the Naval School and the Naval Engineering School (*uchilishche*). The difference between a *shkola* and an *uchilishche* is not altogether clear, but it is known that the latter is an institution of higher learning whereas the former is not. As of 1937, military *shkoly* came to be called military *uchilishche*. Of the 75 such schools, 18 specialized in aviation, 7 in naval matters, 11 in artillery, and 9 in armored forces; the remaining 30 constituted other branches.[6]

By the mid-1930s the school system for officer preparation and education seemed well established. But then came two years of military purges, beginning in 1937. Faculties of military schools and academies were among the groups that had severe losses. The commandant of the Frunze Military Academy and many of his senior department heads and instructors were executed. Purges were equally heavy at the Naval Academy. The educational system for the Red Army, developed from a bare beginning in the previous two decades, was all but destroyed. Professors, textbooks— all were swept away in the maniacal repressions. The heaviest repressions and executions occurred in the senior ranks. What was left were young, inexperienced officers with little professional education or training. Throughout the Soviet forces so many officers were killed that students at the new Academy of the General Staff had their studies terminated so that they could help fill the gap that the purges had caused.

Dozens of new schools were formed, and existing schools increased their number of students after 1939, when Britain and France went to war with Germany. By 1941, while Britain stood alone in holding the line against Hitler, the Red Army had built up to 203 military schools, enrolling 238,000 cadets. It was too late, however, for these schools to produce the needed numbers of trained officers before Hitler attacked the Soviet Union.

After the Soviet Union was thrust into World War II, military schools and academies immediately shortened courses, and classes were graduated early. New schools also were formed. Enrollment in schools and special courses reached 534,000 cadets and officers by the end of 1941, a 38 percent increase over the previous year.[7] Another 564,000 officers were trained the following year, all of whom had entered school after the war started. Sixteen additional infantry schools and eight machine gun/ mortar schools were formed, and courses were organized in ten military districts and two inactive fleets. In 1943 military schools of the Ground

Forces turned out 161,000 junior officers, and Air Force schools graduated 16,000 flying personnel. From 1941 to 1945 Soviet military schools graduated about 2 million officers.[8]

In the words of Party spokesmen, at the end of World War II, Soviet military schools and academies were directed "to master the experience of the war." Stalin and other Party leaders wanted World War II portrayed in a manner that would best reflect on themselves. In 1946 the Frunze Military Academy opened a history faculty to prepare military historians for work in scientific research establishments and military schools. A similar faculty was established in the Academy of the General Staff in 1949.

With the formation of the Strategic Rocket Forces in December 1959 and the introduction of nuclear weapons into all Soviet services, increased attention was given to explaining military doctrine and strategy. Education and training establishments for Soviet cadets and officers have evolved gradually since that time, but they are still based on the same concept of very specialized officer training and education that was developed in Imperial Russia and continued by the Soviets in the 1920s and 1930s.

Officers for the reserves are trained in civilian universities (67 in 1982) and in certain institutes giving higher education (over 800 in 1982). The 1967 Law on Universal Military Obligation stated that those persons who had taken military courses at civilian higher or at special secondary schools could become reserve officers upon taking the established examination. They might then be called up for two or three years before the age of thirty.

As a result of this provision in the law, many students were deferred from taking military training. In 1980 the law was modified such that only those students who were attending certain specified universities and institutes were deferred. Beginning in 1982, those students in special secondary schools (4,393 schools in 1981–1982), who were enrolled in military programs for reserve officers, were deferred only if their schools were included on an approved list.[9]

Military and Higher Military Schools

Military and higher military schools are the basic sources of officers for the Soviet Armed Forces. Although there are various other ways in which one can become a regular officer, these schools produce the backbone of the Soviet officer corps.

In the United States the primary objective of the U.S. Military Academy at West Point is to produce lieutenants who are generalists—able to serve in any of the army's arms and branches. The U.S. Naval Academy and the U.S. Air Force Academy follow the same policy of generalist education. In the Soviet Union, however, the comparable schools provide specialized education and training to prepare lieutenants for duties not only in the various services but also in particular branches and specialized components of the Soviet Armed Forces.

Each branch of the Soviet Ground Forces—motorized rifle troops, tank troops, and rocket troops and artillery—has its own command and engineering schools, which provide commissioned officers for that branch. For example, tank troops have six command schools and two tank engineering schools. Troops of Air Defense have their own specialized schools for preparing officers for the surface-to-air missile branches of that service.

The annual number of graduates commissioned from each school is believed to be 250 to 500, with 300 to 350 a probable average. Since there are about 140 schools, some 50,000 lieutenants may be commissioned each year. Prior to 1958 almost all schools offered three-year courses, and graduates received a commission and a diploma. In that year the Moscow Higher Combined Arms Command School Named for the Supreme Soviet of the RSFSR, the most prestigious of the military schools, became a "higher military school" with a four-year course. Its graduates not only received commissions, but also were awarded "all-union degrees" equivalent to those awarded by civilian higher educational institutions.[10] Other military schools soon followed this pattern. To help officers cope with the increased complexity of modern weaponry and associated equipment, the trend in the 1970s has been to increase course length to five years.

By 1983 only five military schools with three-year courses remained. However, at this time an apparently pressing need for officers with special secondary education (usually three years) caused an extraordinary provision to be introduced.[11] This provision directed that special sections at higher military schools and external studies departments prepare to begin training selected students to become officers, in a three-year course. Entry into this program continues to be contingent upon the same examination as that required for the regular program. Students are housed in barracks apart from those attending the regular course.

Exact reasons for this new program have not been revealed. The transformation of almost all of the 140 military schools into "higher military schools" has diminished the number of officers who specialize as military technicians. At a time when more and more complicated military equipment is appearing, it is precisely this category of officer that is needed. An acute shortage of officers is also indicated, in spite of the increase in the number of schools in the last decade.

Age limits for entry into military and higher military schools range from seventeen to twenty-one for cadets entering from civilian life and to age twenty-three for military personnel on extended service. Warrant officers may be admitted up to age twenty-five.[12] In some schools they are permitted to enter as second-year students.

Entry into the schools is by competitive examination. Military authorities hope to have at least three candidates for each vacancy. Komsomol organizations, DOSAAF instructors, and other Party and military-affiliated organizations are urged to encourage those in their units whom they consider outstanding to prepare for the examination. By regulation, study time is made available for those on active military duty who wish to become candidates.

Advertisements used to appear in January of each year in *Red Star* and certain other Soviet military publications, listing the military and higher military schools and advising those interested how and when to apply.[13] Readily available books in military bookstores and military book sections of regular bookstores gave detailed admission requirements (including sample examinations) and listed areas of recommended study.

A major source of candidates for the military and higher military schools is the Suvorov and Nakhimov schools, which were founded in 1944 for boys orphaned by the war. In 1963 the nine Suvorov schools were turned into three-year secondary schools for boys fifteen to sixteen years of age. Entrance now is by competition, with two candidates for each vacancy. In 1969 courses were further shortened to two years, and in the 1970s a special course was offered to prepare students to take the entrance examinations for higher military schools. By the 1980s there were eight Suvorov schools in Kazan, Kalinin, Kiev, Leningrad, Minsk, Moscow, Sverdlovsk, and Ussuriysk. Every third student at the Frunze Military Academy can boast of being a Suvorov alumnus.[14]

There is only one Nakhimov School, located in Leningrad. It prepares students primarily for the Navy.[15]

The Kiev Suvorov Military School takes youths who have studied English, German, or Spanish in school, whereas the Kalinin, Minsk, Moscow, Sverdlovsk, and Ussuriysk schools require either English or German. The Leningrad Suvorov Military School requires English and the Kazan' school, English or French. The Leningrad Nakimov Naval School requires English.

Youths who wish to study military music may attend a four-year school—the Moscow Military Music School—prior to going to the Military Conductors' Faculty at the Moscow State Conservatory named for P. I. Chaykovskiy.

A candidate can apply to enter only one specified military or higher military school, and he must compete against other candidates for that school. He is not permitted to take a competitive examination at large and then apply for a school after he has successfully completed the examination or placed sufficiently high to warrant admission, although he may try again. Examinations are both written and oral, with emphasis placed on mathematics and science.[16]

The following lists show the military and higher military schools (as of 1 May 1984), broken down by service, component, and location.

Strategic Rocket Forces

Four higher military schools, each offering five-year courses, prepare cadets to become lieutenants in the Strategic Rocket Forces.[17] Selection of cadets follows the same pattern as that for cadets entering schools of the other services, with one exception. A military commissariat officer must specifically attest to the political reliability of each candidate wishing to enter Strategic Rocket Forces schools. There are four schools for training future officers of the Strategic Rocket Forces:

1. Khar'kov Higher Military Command and Engineering School named for Marshal of the Soviet Union N. I. Krylov (Khar'kovskoye VVKIU)
   Commandant: Unidentified
2. Perm' Higher Military Command and Engineering School of the Rocket Troops, named for Marshal of the Soviet Union V. I. Chuykov (Permskoye VVKIU)
   Commandant: Unidentified
3. Rostov Higher Military Command and Engineering School of the Rocket Troops, named for Chief Marshal of Artillery M. I. Nedelin (Rostovskoye VVKIU)
   Commandant: General Major P. Rybalko
4. Serpukhov Higher Military Command and Engineering School, named for Lenin's Komsomol (Serpukhovskoye VVKIU)
   Commandant: Unidentified

Two of the schools are named for previous commanders in chief of the Strategic Rocket Forces. The school at Rostov is named for the first commander in chief, who was killed in 1960 when a missile exploded on its stand prior to launch. The Khar'kov school is named for Krylov, who was commander in chief of the Strategic Rocket Forces from 1963 until shortly before his death in 1973.

Ground Forces

Courses in schools of this service generally are of four years duration, although the engineering schools' courses are five years. These schools prepare cadets to be commissioned as officers in the basic Ground Forces branches: motorized rifles, tanks, and rocket troops and artillery.

356   A Nation in Arms

There are nine combined arms* (*Obshchevoyskovoye*) schools:

1. Alma Ata Higher Combined Arms Command School, named for Marshal of the Soviet Union I. S. Konev (Alma-Atinskoye VOKU)
   Commandant: General Major A. Nekrasov
2. Baku Higher Combined Arms Command School, named for the Supreme Soviet of Azerbaydzhan (Bakinskoye VOKU)
   Commandant: General Major V. Barshatly
3. Far Eastern Higher Combined Arms Command School, named for Marshal of the Soviet Union K. K. Rokossovskiy (Dal'nevostochnoye VOKU)
   Commandant: General Major N. Ye. Baranov
4. Kiev Higher Combined Arms Command School, named for M. V. Frunze (Kievskoye VOKU)
   Commandant: General Major V. I. Lyashko
5. Leningrad Higher Combined Arms Command School, named for S. M. Kirov (Leningradskoye VOKU)
   Commandant: General Lieutenant N. Badeykin
6. Moscow Higher Combined Arms Command School, named for the Supreme Soviet of the RSFSR (Moscovkoye VOKU)
   Commandant: General Major of Tanks I. A. Magonov
7. Omsk Higher Combined Arms Command School, named for M. V. Frunze (Omskoye VOKU)
   Commandant: General Major S. Martsenyuk
8. Ordzhonikidze Higher Combined Arms Command School, named for Marshal of the Soviet Union A. I. Yeremenko (Ordzhonikid-zevskoye VOKU)
   Commandant: General Lieutenant V. A. Ul'yanov
9. Tashkent Higher Combined Arms Command School, named for V. I. Lenin (Tashkentskoye VOKU)
   Commandant: Unidentified.

There are eight tank schools:

1. Blagoveshchensk Higher Tank Command School, named for Marshal of the Soviet Union K. A. Meretskov (Blagoveshchenskoye VTKU)
   Commandant: General Major of Tanks M. Z. Luk'yanov
2. Chelyabinsk Higher Tank Command School, named for the Fiftieth Jubilee of Great October (Chelyabinskoye VTKU)
   Commandant: General Major of Tanks L. Kozhevnikov

---

*The Soviet designation of the nine "combined arms command schools" is a misnomer. Graduates of these schools serve in motorized rifles, the largest branch of the Ground Forces.

3. Kazan' Higher Tank Command School, named for the Presidium of the Supreme Soviet of the Tatar ASSR (Kazanskoye VTKU)
   Commandant: General Major of Tanks I. G. Kobyakov
4. Khar'kov Guards Higher Tank Command School, named for the Supreme Soviet of the Ukrainian SSR (Khar'kovskoye VTKU)
   Commandant: General Major of Tanks Yu. F. Kutenkov
5. Tashkent Higher Tank Command School, named for Marshal of Armored Forces P. S. Rybalko (Tashkentskoye VTKU)
   Commandant: General Major of Tanks D. Leonov
6. Ul'yanovsk Guards Higher Tank Command School, named for V. I. Lenin
   Commandant: Guards General Major of Tanks V. Korchakov
7. Kiev Higher Tank Engineering School, named for Marshal of the Soviet Union I. I. Yakubovskiy (Kievskoye VTIU) (five-year course)
   Commandant: General Lieutenant of Tanks M. F. Kolesnikov
8. Omsk Higher Tank Engineering School, named for Marshal of the Soviet Union P. K. Koshevoy (Omskoye VTIU)
   Commandant: Unidentified

Schools for training men for rocket troops and artillery are:

1. Khmel'nitskiy Higher Artillery Command School, named for Marshal of Artillery N. D. Yakovlev (Khmel'nitskoye VAKU)
   Commandant: General Major Artillery B. F. Bokov
2. Kolomna Higher Artillery Command School, named for the October Revolution (Kolomenskoye VAKU)
   Commandant: General Lieutenant Artillery A. T. Baysara
3. Leningrad Higher Artillery Command School, named for Red October (Leningradskoye VAKU)
   Commandant: General Major Artillery V. Sergiyenko
4. Odessa Higher Artillery Command School, named for M. V. Frunze (Odesskoye VAKU)
   Commandant: General Major Artillery N. Anan'yev
5. Sumy Higher Artillery Command School, named for M. V. Frunze (Sumskoye VAKU)
   Commandant: General Major Artillery A. Morozov
6. Tbilisi Higher Artillery Command School, named for Twenty-six Baku Commissars (Tbilisskoye VAKU)
   Commandant: General Major Artillery V. Shuvalov
7. Penza Higher Artillery Engineering School, named for Chief Marshal of Artillery N. N. Voronov (Penzenskoye VAIU)
   Commandant: General Major Artillery V. Zaytsev

8. Tula Higher Artillery Engineering School, named for the Tula Proletariat (Tul'skoye VAIU)
   Commandant: General Major V. Kulev
9. Saratov Higher Military Command School, named for General Major A. I. Lizyukov (Saratovskoye VVKU)
   Commandant: General Major Artillery A. S. Kobzar'
10. Kazan' Higher Military Engineering School, named for Marshal of Artillery M. N. Chistyakov (Kazanskoye VVIU)
    Commandant: General Lieutenant Artillery P. R. Nikitenko

Airborne Troops

Soviet airborne troops are not a branch of the Ground Forces, although for administrative purposes they are usually grouped with them. They are in a special category as a strategic reserve of the High Command. They also have been listed as a "mini-service." Officers are commissioned from a school at Ryazan.

1. Ryazan Higher Airborne Command School named for Lenin's Komsomol (Ryazanskoye VVDKU)
   Commandant: General Major A. Slyusar'

Troops of Air Defense

There are three components in the Air Defense Troops: surface-to-air missile troops, fighter aviation, and radio-engineering troops. Each component has its own specialized schools.

The surface-to-air missile troops schools are:

1. Dnepropetrovsk Higher Zenith Rocket Command School of Air Defense (Dnepropetrovskoye VZRKU PVO)
   Commandant: General Major Artillery Yu. Goncharenko
2. Engel's Higher Zenith Rocket Command School of Air Defense (Engel'skoye VZRKU PVO)
   Commandant: General Major Artillery V. Soldatov
3. Gor'kiy Higher Zenith Rocket Command School of Air Defense (Gor'kovskoye VZRKU PVO)
   Commandant: General Major Artillery V. Vunder
4. Ordzhonikidze Higher Zenith Rocket Command School of Air Defense, named for General of the Army I. A. Pliyev (Ordzhonikidzevskoye VZRKU PVO)
   Commandant: Unidentified

5. Yaroslavl' Higher Zenith Rocket Command School of Air Defense, named for the Sixtieth Anniversary of Great October (Yaroslavskoye VZRKU PVO)
   Commandant: General Major Artillery G. Ryleyev
6. Minsk Higher Engineering Zenith Rocket School of Air Defense (Minskoye VIZRU PVO)
   Commandant: Unidentified

In 1981, five schools for training officers for Troop Air Defense were transferred from the Ground Forces to Troops of Air Defense:

1. Leningrad Higher Zenith Rocket Command School, named for the Sixtieth Anniversary of Great October (Leningradskoye VZRKU)
   Commandant: General Major Artillery R. Todurov
2. Orenburg Higher Zenith Rocket Command School, named for G. K. Ordzhonikidze (Orenburgskoye VZRKU)
   Commandant: General Major Artillery A. Khazov
3. Poltava Higher Zenith Rocket Command School, named for General of the Army N. F. Vatutin (Poltavskoye VZRKU)
   Commandant: Unidentified
4. Kiev Higher Zenith Rocket Engineering School, named for S. M. Kirov (Kievskoye VZRIU)
   Commandant: General Major Artillery B. Parafeynikov
5. Smolensk Higher Zenith Rocket Engineering School (Smolenskoye VZRIU)
   Commandant: General Major Artillery A. Ganzhe

In 1981, two of three aviation schools moved from Troops of Air Defense to the Air Forces. Only one school was left:

1. Stavropol' Higher Military Aviation School for Pilots and Navigators (Stavropol'skoye VVAULSH)
   Commandant: General Major Aviation A. S. Ponomarenko

There are six radioelectronic schools:

1. Krasnoyarsk Higher Command School of Radioelectronics for Air Defense (Krasnoyarskoye VKURE PVO)
   Commandant: General Major S. Matveyev
2. Vil'nius Higher Command School of Radioelectronics for Air Defense (Vil'nyusskoye VKURE PVO)
   Commandant: General Major A. Dmitriyev

3. Pushkin Higher School of Radioelectronics for Air Defense (Push-kinskoye VURE PVO)
   Commandant: General Lieutenant Artillery V. Gromadin
4. Zhitomir Higher School of Radioelectronics for Air Defense, named for Lenin's Komsomol (Zhitomirskoye VURE PVO)
   Commandant: Colonel B. Bondarev
5. Cherepovets Higher Military Engineering School of Radioelectronics (Cherepovetskoye VVIURE)
   Commandant: Unidentified
6. Kiev Higher Engineering Radiotechnical School of Air Defense (Kievskoye VIRTU PVO)
   Commandant: General Major N. Polyakov

Air Forces

The Soviet Air Forces have five different types of military and higher military schools: twelve higher military aviation schools for pilots, two higher military aviation schools for navigators, seven aviation engineering schools, one signal school, and five military aviation-technical schools.[18] The aviation-technical schools are military schools, with three-year courses. The Air Forces schools for pilots are:

1. Armavir Higher Military Aviation School for Pilots (Armavirskoye VVAUL)
   Commandant: General Major Aviation N. Kryukov
2. Balashov Higher Military Aviation School for Pilots, named for Chief Marshal of Aviation A. A. Novikov (Balashovskoye VVAUL)
   Commandant: General Major Aviation V. Gorbachev
3. Barnaul Higher Military Aviation School for Pilots, named for Chief Marshal of Aviation K. A. Vershinin (Barnaul'skoye VVAUL)
   Commandant: General Major Aviation A. Goncharenko
4. Borisoglebsk Higher Military Aviation School for Pilots, named for V. P. Chkalov (Borisoglebskoye VVAUL)
   Commandant: General Major Aviation V. S. Mikhaylov
5. Chernigov Higher Military Aviation School for Pilots, named for Lenin's Komsomol (Chernigovskoye VVAUL)
   Commandant: General Major Aviation V. Garanin
6. Kacha Higher Military Aviation School for Pilots, named for A. F. Myasnikov (Kachinskoye VVAUL)
   Commandant: General Major Aviation I. Zheleznyak
7. Khar'kov Higher Military Aviation School for Pilots, named for S. I. Gritsevets (Khar'kovskoye VVAUL)
   Commandant: General Major Aviation D. Basov

8. Orenburg Higher Military Aviation School for Pilots, named for I. S. Polbin (Orenburgskoye VVAUL)
   Commandant: Colonel N. Kuchin
9. Saratov Higher Military Aviation School for Pilots (Saratovskoye VVAUL)
   Commandant: Unidentified
10. Syzran' Higher Military Aviation School for Pilots (Syzranskoye VVAUL)
    Commandant: General Major Aviation A. A. Didyk
11. Tambov Higher Military Aviation School for Pilots, named for M. M. Raskova (Tambovskoye VVAUL)
    Commandant: General Major Aviation G. N. Menyaylenko
12. Yeysk Higher Military Aviation School for Pilots, named for Cosmonaut V. M. Komarov (Yeyskoye VVAUL)
    Commandant: General Major Aviation V. Grishin

There are two Air Forces schools for navigators:

1. Chelyabinsk Higher Military Aviation School for Navigators, named for the Fiftieth Jubilee of the Komsomol (Chelyabinskoye VVAUSh)
   Commandant: Unidentified
2. Voroshilovgrad Higher Military Aviation School for Navigators, named for the Proletariat of the Donbas (Voroshilovgradskoye VVAUSh)
   Commandant: General Major Aviation Yu. M. Marchenko

All seven of the Air Forces' higher military aviation-engineer schools have five-year courses, the only higher schools in the Air Forces of this length. Three of the schools, located at Irkutsk, Tambov, and Khar'kov, jumped from three-year to five-year courses in 1976.

The aviation engineering schools are:

1. Daugavpils Higher Military Aviation Engineering School, named for Yan Fabritsius (Daugavpilsskoye VVAIU)
   Commandant: Unidentified
2. Irkutsk Higher Military Aviation Engineering School, named for the Fiftieth Jubilee of the Komsomol (Irkutskskoye VVAIU)
   Commandant: General Major Aviation A. A. Karpov
3. Kiev Higher Military Aviation Engineering School (Kievskoye VVAIU)
   Commandant: General Major–Engineer K. Chelyshev
4. Khar'kov Higher Military Aviation Engineering School (Khar'kovskoye VVAIU)
   Commandant: Colonel–Engineer G. Yakunin

5. Riga Higher Military Aviation Engineering School, named for Ya. Alksnis (Rizhskoye VVAIU)
   Commandant: General Major–Engineer N. Sukhochev
6. Tambov Higher Military Aviation Engineering School, named for F. E. Dzerzhinskiy (Tambovskoye VVAIU)
   Commandant: Unidentified
7. Voronezh Higher Military Aviation Engineering School (Voronezhskoye VVAIU)
   Commandant: General Major–Engineer O. Mylov

There is one aviation signals school:

1. Khar'kov Higher Military Aviation School of Signals, named for Lenin's Komsomols of the Ukraine (VVAUS)
   Commandant: Unidentified

Graduates of the aviation technical schools are commissioned as aviation-technical officers and awarded a diploma, not a degree. Course length is three years.

1. Achinsk Military Aviation-Technical School, named for the Sixtieth Anniversary of the Komsomol (Achinskoye VATU)
   Commandant: General Major–Engineer P. Pozdnyak
2. Kaliningrad Military Aviation-Technical School (Kaliningradskoye VATU)
   Commandant: General Major–Engineer V. Stotskiy
3. Kirov Military Aviation-Technical School (Kirovskoye VATU)
   Commandant: Unidentified
4. Perm' Military Aviation-Technical School, named for Lenin's Komsomol (Permskoye VATU)
   Commandant: Unidentified
5. Vasil'kov Military Aviation-Technical School, named for the Fiftieth Jubilee of Lenin's Komsomol (Vasil'kovskoye VATU)
   Commandant: General Major–Engineer A. Gordeyev

Navy

The Soviet Navy maintains ten higher military schools, all with five-year courses of study. Five of these schools prepare line officers for specific fleets. In addition, there are three higher naval engineering schools, one higher naval school for underwater navigation, and one higher naval school of radioelectronics.

The naval schools for line officers are:

1. Higher Naval School, named for M. V. Frunze (VVMU) (located in Leningrad; prepares its graduates for service in the Northern Fleet)
   Commandant: Vice Admiral N. K. Fedorov
2. Black Sea Higher Naval School, named for P. S. Nakhimov (Chernomorskoye VVMU) (located at Sevastopol'; the school prepares officers for the Black Sea Fleet)
   Commandant: Vice Admiral S. S. Sokolan
3. Kaliningrad Higher Naval School (Kaliningradskoye VVMU) (located in Kaliningrad; this school prepares officers for the Baltic Fleet)
   Commandant: Vice Admiral V. Pilipenko
4. Pacific Ocean Higher Naval School, named for S. O. Makarov (Tikhookeanskoye VVMU) (located in Vladivostok; prepares graduates for service in the Pacific Fleet)
   Commandant: Rear Admiral I. Karmadonov
5. Caspian Higher Naval School, named for S. M. Kirov (Kaspiyskoye VVMU) (located at Baku; prepares its graduates for service in the Caspian Sea Flotilla)
   Commandant: Vice Admiral V. Arkhipov

The schools for naval engineering are:

1. Leningrad Higher Naval Engineering School, named for V. I. Lenin (Leningradskoye VVMIU)
   Commandant: Vice Admiral–Engineer B. Lapshin
2. Sevastopol' Higher Naval Engineering School (Sevastopol'skoye VVMIU)
   Commandant: Vice Admiral–Engineer A. A. Sarkisov
3. Higher Naval Engineering School, named for F. E. Dzerzhinskiy (VVMIU) (located in Leningrad)
   Commandant: Vice Admiral N. Yegorov

The underwater navigation school is:

1. Higher Naval School of Underwater Navigation, named for Lenin's Komsomol (VVMUPP) (located in Leningrad)
   Commandant: Vice Admiral G. L. Nevolin

The naval radioelectronics school is:

1. Higher Naval School of Radioelectronics, named for A. S. Popov (VVMURE) (located in Leningrad)
   Commandant: Rear Admiral G. Avdokhin

Other Military and Higher Military Schools

In the United States officers are commissioned in a specific service: Army, Navy, Air Force, or Marines. In the Soviet Union, by contrast, between 30 and 50 percent of the officers are commissioned in branches that are apart from any single service. One of the best indications of this is to note the many military and higher military schools that commission officers to serve in branches that support the Soviet Armed Forces as a whole.

Political Administration

In 1967 nine higher military-political schools were established to prepare political officers for the Soviet Armed Forces: two for the Ground Forces; one for each of the other four services—Strategic Rocket Forces, Troops of Air Defense, Air Forces, and Navy; one school to serve both the engineer and signal troops; another school for construction troops; and a ninth, the Higher Military-Political School for the Soviet Army and Navy, to prepare officers for duty as military journalists. Graduates of the latter school serve wherever needed under the direction of the Main Political Administration.[19] Two additional schools were added in 1981.

The schools of the Main Political Administration are:

1. Donetsk Higher Military-Political School of Engineer Troops and Signal Troops (Donetskoye VVPUIViVS)
   Commandant: General Major V. Bespalov
2. Kiev Higher Naval Political School (Kievskoye VVMPU)
   Commandant: Vice Admiral N. S. Kaplanov
3. Kurgan Higher Military-Political Aviation School (Kurganskoye VVPAU)
   Commandant: General Major Aviation A. Borisov
4. Leningrad Higher Military-Political School for Air Defense (Leningradskoye VVPU PVO), named for Yu. V. Andropov
   Commandant: General Lieutenant S. S. Yevdokimov
5. L'vov Higher Military-Political School (L'vovskoye VVPU)
   Commandant: General Major O. Zolotarev
6. Minsk Higher Military-Political Combined Arms School (Minskoye VVPOU) (for Ground Forces)
   Commandant: Unidentified

7. Novosibirsk Higher Military-Political Combined Arms School, named for the Sixtieth Anniversary of Great October (Novosibirskoye VVPOU) (for Ground Forces)
Commandant: General Major B. N. Volkov

8. Riga Higher Military-Political School, named for Marshal of the Soviet Union S. S. Biryuzov (Rizhskoye VVPU) (for Strategic Rocket Forces)
Commandant: General Major V. Mikhaylov

9. Simferopol' Higher Military-Political Construction Troops School (Simferopol'skoye VVPSU)
Commandant: General Major Yu. Ya. Gudimov

10. Sverdlovsk Higher Military-Political Tank and Artillery School, named for L. I. Brezhnev (Sverdlovskoye VVPTAU) (for Ground Forces)
Commandant: General Lieutenant A. Korostylenko

11. Tallinn Higher Military-Political Construction Troops School (Tallinskoye VVPSU)
Commandant: General Major V. Gnezdilov

Rear Services

The attention given by the Soviet High Command to logistical support is reflected in the number of rear service schools.

1. Ul'yanovsk Higher Military Technical School, named for Bogdan Kheml'nitskiy (Ul'yanovskoye VVTU)
Commandant: General Major–Engineer Ye. Yakushenko
(This four- or five-year school prepares military engineers for duties associated with the use of liquid fuels in combat and auxiliary equipment and its storage and transport. Graduates of the school serve in all services of the Armed Forces.)

2. Vol'sk Higher Military School of the Rear Services, named for Lenin's Red Banner Komsomol (Vol'skoye VVUT)
Commandant: General Major N. Tolmachev
(This school prepares specialists for the services of the rear for units of all the armed forces.)

3. Gor'kiy Higher Military School of the Rear Services, named for Marshal of the Soviet Union I. Kh. Bagramyan (Gor'kovskoye VVUT)
Commandant: General Major–Engineer Yu. Kirilyuk
(This school prepares economist engineers.)

4. Leningrad Higher School of Railroad Troops and Military Communications, named for M. V. Frunze (Leningradskoye VUZhViVOSO)
Commandant: General Major Technical Troops M. Kuznetsov

5. Yaroslavl' Higher Military Finance School, named for General of the Army A. V. Khrulev (Yaroslavskoye VVFU)
   Commandant: General Major E. Rasshchupkin
6. Moscow Higher Command School of Road and Engineer Troops (Moskovskoye VKUDiIV) (formerly civil defense troops)
   Commandant: General Major V. Oboyanskiy
7. Voronezh Higher Military Aviation Engineering School (described above under Aviation Engineering)

Special Troops

Signal, engineering, chemical defense, automotive, railroad, and road building troops of the Soviet Armed Forces, referred to collectively as special troops, are organized to provide common support to all of the services and special activities of the Ministry of Defense. They are closely linked with the Ground Forces. However, graduates of special troops schools go into units that are assigned to other services as well.

The signal troops schools are:

1. Kemerovo Higher Military Command School of Signals (Kemerovskoye VVKUS)
   Commandant: General Major Signal Troops V. Timofeyev
2. Novocherkassk Higher Military Command School of Signals, named for Marshal of the Soviet Union V. D. Sokolovskiy (Novocherkasskoye VVKUS)
   Commandant: General Lieutenant Signal Troops N. D. Bykov
3. Orel Higher Military Command School of Signals, named for M. I. Kalinin (Orlovskoye VVKUS)
   Commandant: Unidentified
4. Poltava Higher Military Command School of Signals (Poltavskoye VVKUS)
   Commandant: Unidentified
5. Ryazan' Higher Military Command School of Signals, named for Marshal of the Soviet Union M. V. Zakharov (Ryazanskoye VVKUS)
   Commandant: General Major Signal Troops A. Aseyev
6. Tomsk Higher Military Command School of Signals (Tomskoye VVKUS)
   Commandant: Unidentified
7. Ul'yanovsk Higher Military Command School of Signals, named for G. K. Ordzhonikidze (Ul'yanovskoye VVKUS)
   Commandant: General Major Signal Troops N. Guzenko
8. Kiev Higher Military Engineering School of Signals, named for M. I. Kalinin (Kievskoye VVIUS)
   Commandant: General Lieutenant Signal Troops M. Pilipenko

9. Leningrad Higher Military Engineering School of Signals (Leningradskoye VVIUS)
   Commandant: Unidentified
10. Stavropol' Higher Military Engineering School of Signals, named for the Sixtieth Anniversary of the October Revolution (Stavropol'skoye VVIUS)
    Commandant: Unidentified

The schools for engineer troops are:

1. Kaliningrad Higher Engineering School of the Engineer Troops, named for A. A. Zhdanov (Kaliningradskoye VIUIV)
   Commandant: General Major Engineer Troops V. Zhigaylo
2. Kamenets-Podol'skiy Higher Military-Engineering Command School, named for Marshal of Engineer Troops V. K. Kharchenko (Kamenets-Podol'skoye VVIKU)
   Commandant: General Major Engineer Troops V. I. Yermakov
3. Tyumen' Higher Military-Engineering Command School, named for Marshal of Engineer Troops A. I. Proshlyakov (Tyumen'skoye VVIKU)
   Commandant: General Major Engineer Troops P. Sharovarov

All of the chemical defense schools are in areas that are closed to foreigners. The subject matter taught at these schools covers nuclear, chemical, and bacteriological warfare. The school at Tambov was formed in 1974. The chemical defense schools are:

1. Saratov Higher Military Engineering School of Chemical Defense (Saratovskoye VVIUKhZ)
   Commandant: Unidentified
2. Kostroma Higher Military Command School of Chemical Defense (Kostromskoye VVKUKhZ)
   Commandant: General Major Technical Troops Ye. Lebedev
3. Tambov Higher Military Command School of Chemical Defense (Tambovskoye VVKUKhZ)
   Commandant: General Major Technical Troops V. F. Shipilov

The automotive schools are:

1. Chelyabinsk Higher Military Automotive Engineering School, named for Chief Marshal of Armored Forces P. A. Rotmistrov (Chelyabinskoye VVAIU)
   Commandant: Unidentified
2. Ryazan Higher Military Automotive Engineering School (Ryazanskoye VVAIU)
   Commandant: General Lieutenant–Engineer V. Pavlov
3. Samarkand Higher Military Automotive Command School, named for the Supreme Soviet of Uzbek SSR (Samarkandskoye VVAKU)
   Commandant: General Major A. P. Red'ko
4. Ussuriy Higher Military Automotive Command School (Ussuriyskoye VVAKU)
   Commandant: General Major–Engineer N. Yerin

There is one topographical services school:

1. Leningrad Higher Military Topographical Command School, named for General of the Army A. I. Antonov (Leningradskoye VVTKU)
   Commandant: General Major Technical Troops V. D. Baranov

There are six schools for Construction and Billeting Troops:

1. Leningrad Higher Military Engineering Construction School, named for General of the Army A. N. Komarovskiy (Leningradskoye VVISU)
   Commandant: General Lieutenant–Engineer N. Vauchskiy
   (This school prepares military engineers for various construction specialties. Length of course is five years for cadets and four years for officers taking special courses.)
2. Pushkin Higher Military Engineering Construction School (Pushkinskoye VVISU)
   Commandant: Unidentified
3. Gor'kiy Higher Military Construction Command School (Gor'kovskoye VVSKU)
   Commandant: Unidentified
4. Kamyshin Higher Military Construction Command School (Kamyshinskoye VVSKU)
   Commandant: General Major–Engineer S. Petukhov
5. Tol'yatti Higher Military Construction Command School (Tol'yattinskoye VVSKU)
   Commandant: Unidentified

6. Khabarovsk Higher Military Construction School (Khabarovskoye VVSU)
   Commandant: General Major L. Lebedev

There was also a school for civil defense, the Moscow Military School of Civil Defense USSR, now called the Moscow Higher Command School of Road and Engineer Troops. (See the sixth entry under Rear Services.)

Special:
1. Krasnodar Higher Military School, named for General of the Army S. M. Shtemenko (Krasnodarskoye VVU)
   Commandant: General Lieutenant N. M. Kozlov (1975–1983)
   (The purpose of this school has not been published.)

Border Guards

As previously noted, Border Guards are part of the Soviet Armed Forces, but they do not come under the Ministry of Defense. They are a military component of the Committee of State Security (KGB). There are three four-year schools:

1. Alma-Ata Higher Border Guard Command School, named for F. E. Dzerzhinskiy
   Commandant: General Lieutenant M. K. Merkulov
2. Higher Border Guard Military-Political School, named for K. Ye. Voroshilov, Golitsyno, Moscow Oblast
   Commandant: Unidentified
3. Moscow Higher Border Guard Command School, named for Mossoviet
   Commandant: General Major KGB G. Aleynikov

Internal Troops of the MVD

Like the Border Guards of the KGB, the Internal Troops of the Ministry of Internal Security (MVD) are *not* part of the Ministry of Defense, but are part of the Soviet Armed Forces. Internal Troops have their own higher political school, as well as a school of rear services. Course length is four years, three years for warrant officers.

1. Higher Political School of the MVD (Leningrad)
   Commandant: General Major I. Orlov
2. Novosibrisk Higher Military Command School of MVD
   Commandant: Unidentified

3. Orzhonikidze Higher Military Command School of the MVD, named for S. M. Kirov
Commandant: Unidentified
4. Saratov Higher Military Command School of the MVD, named for F. E. Dzerzhinskiy
Commandant: Unidentified
5. Khar'kov Higher Military School of the Rear Services of the MVD
Commandant: Unidentified

In September 1974, the Academy of the MVD opened its doors with General Lieutenant Internal Services S. M. Krylov as the commandant. Its basic course appears to be two years. Many of the students are policemen (militia). It is not known if officers of the Internal Troops also attend the Academy of the MVD.[20]

Soviet Military Academies

At ages twenty-four to twenty-five, only a few years out of a military or higher military school, the ambitious Soviet officer must start preparing for entrance examinations[21] to one of sixteen military academies, depending upon his service and service branch. (Attendance at the senior Soviet professional school, the General Staff Academy, is not to be expected for another eight to ten years.) Senior officers and advisers recommend that lieutenants and captains spend from 2,000 to 3,000 hours studying for the examinations, which in two years amounts to over three hours of study each day, weekends and holidays included. Generally, the maximum age limits for entering the military academies are twenty-eight for officers studying engineering and thirty-two for those attending command and staff academies.

There are a number of variations to the age limits. The Dzerzhinskiy (Rocket) Academy accepts division commanders to age thirty-six, and the Gargarin Air Academy admits staff officers to age thirty-four.[22] The Academy of the General Staff, which is on a higher level than the other seventeen academies, accepts officers in their late thirties, as a general rule.

With the exception of the General Staff Academy, Soviet military academies are specialized, in much the same manner as the military and higher military schools, and all theoretically are at the same level. The Strategic Rocket Forces have their own academy; the Ground Forces have a tank academy as well as an artillery academy; and other services also have their own academies. In addition there are specialized academies for the arms and branches that are not specifically under one service, such as the Military Academy of Rear Services and Transport.

Completing the course at an academy is of major importance and will greatly influence the remainder of an officer's career. Admission is based on competitive examinations, with certain exceptions. An officer who graduated from a higher military school with a gold medal is required to pass only one examination with a "good" mark. An officer who has won good ratings for his unit may be selected for an academy if he simply passes the entrance examinations.[23] The purpose appears to be to weigh an officer's overall potential, not simply his academic ability.

Entrance examination for an academy may be attempted three times. Reserve officers who have been called up for two or three years, or who volunteer for active duty, have the same rights as regular officers to apply at the military academies.[24] Each academy prepares its own entrance examinations based on requirements as given in regulations. For example, the entrance examination to the Gagarin Air Academy covers the following five areas: Russian language and literature (written), mathematics and physics (oral), and, depending on the specialty of the individual, studies in tactics, combat equipment, bombing, training, navigation, and organization of communications of the Air Forces rear services (oral).[25]

The examining board has considerable leeway in judging the candidate's potential as an officer and can ensure that the desired balance of students is maintained among the many Soviet nationalities. All academies have officers from both Warsaw Pact and other socialist countries attending courses. Special faculties are set up for this purpose.

Courses at the academies also may be taken by correspondence, with an age limit of forty for senior officers (thirty-five for junior officers) applying. The regular entrance examination is required before permission is given to take the course. Once accepted, an officer receives all the benefits of an academy education, while continuing his regular military duties. Regulations specify that he will be freed of after-hour duties in order to have time for study and will be given time off to prepare for examinations.

Once an officer has successfully completed work at an academy, he is assigned under a special *nomenklatura*, or list, of positions[26] that can be filled only by officers who are graduates of military or naval academies or their equivalents. In general, *nomenklatura* lists are subject to approval by the Communist Party before final appointments are made. This ensures that only politically reliable officers are appointed to key positions. The basic list of positions is prepared by the Ministry of Defense. Academy graduates receive directed duty assignments "in their specialty by means of probationary training in troop units or ships, or at industrial enterprises, repair plants, arsenals, clinics, and so forth."[27]

Military academies, a few higher military schools that have special faculties for officers, and certain other higher educational institutions provide advanced schooling, described in Russian as "higher military education." Without this education an officer cannot expect to reach senior levels. Marshal Grechko, writing in 1975, said that a higher military education is possessed by "almost 100 percent of brigade commanders and higher, more than 90 percent of regimental commanders, and 100 percent of commanders of first and second rank ships."[28]

Persons receiving a higher military education with a "command profile" study social sciences, operational art and general tactics, tactics of service branches and special troops, the history of war, military art, and other subjects. Technical training also is included and consists of "the study of the tactical and technical properties of armaments and combat equipment, its structure, combat use, exploitation, and so on." Also included are "the study of weapons of mass destruction of the armies of capitalist states, and means of protection from them, parade drill, physical training, and foreign languages."[29]

Higher military-political education (that is, the Lenin Military-Political Academy) stresses military pedagogy and military psychology, organization of Party-political work among the troops, and the social sciences. A part of the curriculum is given to operations and tactics, foreign languages, and weapons of mass destruction.

Individuals receiving specialized higher military education, in medicine, finance, music, or physical culture, for example, study social sciences, general science, general engineering, and academic disciplines in their specialty. The latter must correspond in content to that given in civilian institutions of higher learning.[30] In addition, students must study operations, tactics, and other military subjects related to their particular field.

As a rule, higher military education courses run for three or four years. Special engineering courses may be five years. The shortest course, and at the highest military level, is the two-year course of the General Staff Academy.

The Soviet concept of higher military education, the special *nomenklatura* of positions that can be filled only by academy graduates, and the directed duty assignments suggest that an officer who does not attend a military academy, or its equivalent, is not likely to achieve the higher ranks. Professional officer education in the Soviet Armed Forces, especially that provided by the academies, is on a different scale from that in the United States armed forces. This will be seen more clearly as the military academies, with their three- to five-year courses (the exception being the two-year course of the General Staff Academy) and extensive research facilities, are individually examined. Academies will be grouped by service.

The Military Academy Named for F. E. Dzerzhinskiy

The Dzerzhinskiy Military Academy, sometimes referred to as the Rocket Academy, is located at Kitayskiy Proyezd 9/5 in Moscow, within a block of the huge Rossiya Hotel off Red Square. Based on the czarist Mikhaylovskiy Artillery School, founded in 1820, the academy opened in Leningrad in February 1918 and was called the Artillery Academy of the RKKA. In the 1950s emphasis at the academy was changed from artillery to missiles, and in 1938 the academy was moved to its present location in Moscow.

There is little information available on the curriculum. According to the Soviet Military Encyclopedia,

> the fundamental changes in the technical equipping of the Armed Forces and methods of armed struggle, and also the latest achievements of science and technology (especially in the realm of radiotechnology, cybernetics, calculators, automatic control processes) deeply influenced the content not only of special military disciplines but the whole general science and general technical and political training of the students.[31]

As at most Soviet academies, "the course of instruction includes social sciences, military, general science and special military disciplines."[32] Scientific research also is carried on at the academy. There are two major faculties, command and engineering—the latter, apparently, undergraduate. Very little is written about the faculty members of the academy; nor is it admitted that most of the student body is from the rocket forces.

Marshal of Artillery G. F. Odintsov was commandant of the academy from 1954 to 1969, a period of fifteen years. He was succeeded by General Colonel F. P. Tonkikh. General Tonkikh, a doctor of military sciences as well as a professor, was editor of *The Fundamentals of Scientific Organization of Labor in Military Schools,* published in 1974.

The Military Academy Named for M. V. Frunze

The Frunze Military Academy is highest in prestige among the sixteen academies at its official level. It is located in Moscow, on Proyezd Devich'yevo Polya, Dom 4, near the Novodevichiy Monastery. Originally called the General Staff Academy of the RKKA, in 1921 its name was changed to the Military Academy. In the early 1930s, higher academic courses were added to the academy, as advanced courses for those who had graduated earlier. These higher academic courses became the basis for the Academy of the General Staff, which opened in 1936.[33] After the establishment of the Academy of the General Staff, studies at the

Frunze Academy concentrated on preparing officers for combined arms warfare. Officers attending its three-year course are primarily from the Ground Forces, with some representation from other services, mostly Air Forces and Troops of Air Defense. The majority of the students entering the academy are captains, less than thirty years old. Many will have been promoted to major by the completion of the course. Officers from the various socialist nations are also represented on the student body.

Within the academy are "chairs of operational-tactical disciplines, Marxism-Leninism, history of the CPSU and Party-political work, history of war and military art, foreign languages, and other subjects and scientific research sections."[34] The library has about 2 million volumes. Most students are graduates of the higher military schools of the various services, especially of the Ground Forces, and have had some experience as unit commanders. The academy "is one of the research centers for Soviet military science." It also provides either full-time postgraduate programs or research programs for students on active duty to study such subjects as general tactics, operational art, staff duties and "history of wars and military art," leading to candidate or doctor's degrees.

Faculty members produce theoretical and historical military works, manuals, textbooks, books, and brochures. Between 1970 and 1982, more than twenty-five books were published by Voyenizdat. Among them were A. A. Sidorenko's *Nastupleniye* [The Offensive] (1970); V. Ye. Savkin's *Osnovnyye Printsipy Operativnogo Iskusstva i Taktiki* [The Basic Principles of Operational Art and Tactics] (1972); the five-book series *Taktika v Boyevykh Primerakh* [Tactics in Combat Examples] (1974 and 1976); *Upravleniye Voyskami v Nastuplenii* [Troop Control in the Offensive] (1981); and F. D. Sverdlov's *Takticheskiy Manevr* [Tactical Maneuver] (1982).[35]

Many of the faculty members have advanced degrees as candidates, or doctors, of military, historical, or technical sciences, and may spend a great part of their military careers as professors. For example, Professor and Doctor of Military Sciences General Lieutenant V. G. Reznichenko joined the Frunze faculty at least as early as 1965 and until 1975–1976 headed the Department of Tactics.[36] Later, he was made deputy commandant for scientific work and was still serving in that capacity in the 1980s. Commandants may serve equally lengthy tours. General of the Army P. A. Kurochkin served in this capacity from 1954 to 1968. His replacement, General of the Army A. T. Stuchenko, suffered a severe illness and was succeeded in 1969 by General of the Army A. I. Radziyevskiy. General Colonel P. V. Mel'nikov succeeded him in 1978. General of the Army G. I. Obaturov, a gold medalist when he graduated from the Academy of the General Staff, became the next head of Frunze Military Academy in 1982.

There probably are twenty-five to fifty general officers serving on the staff and faculty of the Frunze Military Academy—numbers that greatly exceed those at any comparable institution in the United States. An examination of the books and articles published by the Frunze faculty, the three-year course length, and research facilities demonstrates the attention given by the Soviets to professional education and training. The closest equivalent to the Frunze Academy in the United States is probably the Army Command and General Staff School at Fort Leavenworth, Kansas.

The Military Academy of Armored Forces Named for Marshal of the Soviet Union R. Ya. Malinovskiy

This academy, commonly called the Malinovskiy Tank Academy, is located in Moscow, at Krasnokursantskiy Proyezd, 3/5. It was formed in 1932 as the Stalin Military Academy of Mechanization and Motorization of the RKKA. Its establishment "was one of the most important measures of the CPSU for strengthening the Soviet Armed Forces in the prewar years, and was connected with the creation of the tank industry and the rapid development of armored tank and mechanized troops."[37] In 1954 it was formally designated the Military Academy of the Armored Forces.

In the postwar years, "scientists of the Military Academy take part in working out the most important problems of development of equipment, the theory of combat utilization, support, and organization of tank troops."[38] Faculty members have produced many textbooks and theoretical writings, including *Tanks and Tank Troops* (2nd ed., 1980), *Tank Navigation Systems* (1978), and *Construction and Combat Use of Soviet Tank Troops in the Great Patriotic War* (1979). Many faculty members have received citations and medals for their work in military science and technology. Considerable attention is given in classrooms and in textbooks to the role of the tank in a nuclear environment.

The academy buildings are impressive and the student body appears to be well over 2,000 in number. Since 1969 the academy has been headed by Marshal of the Armored Forces O. A. Losik.

The Military Artillery Academy Named for M. I. Kalinin

Formed in 1953 when it was split from the Dzerzhinskiy Military Academy, the Kalinin Military Artillery Academy is at 22 Komsomol Street, Leningrad. Its faculties teach both basic and correspondence courses, and there are chairs of social, operational-tactical, special, and general science disciplines, and scientific research laboratories. "The basic content of the study process is the deep study of Marxism-Leninism, new means of armed combat, and the operational use of rocket troops and artillery."[39]

This academy is primarily for the rocket and artillery troops of the Ground Forces. Among the concerns of the faculty are combat utilization of rocket and artillery weapons, methods of training for directing fire, and problems of automation for control of rocket and artillery troops. The academy also has responsibilities for writing military regulations and manuals.

This is a large school, with sixty doctors of science on its faculty. Commandants of the academy have been Chief Marshal of Artillery N. N. Voronov (1953–1958), General Colonel of Artillery V. S. Korobchenko (1958–1969), General Colonel of Artillery P. F. Slipchenko (1969–1983), and General Colonel of Artillery A. I. Matveyev (since 1983).

The Military Command Academy of Air Defense Named for Marshal of the Soviet Union G. K. Zhukov

The Zhukov Military Command Academy of Air Defense is designated for training command personnel and "also is a scientific center for working out problems of operational art and tactics and questions of perfecting the control of the Troops of Air Defense."[40] Formed in 1956, it is on Zhigarev Street in Kalinin, overlooking the river. Some of its buildings are impressive. They could provide classrooms for well over 2,000 students.

Military science work at the academy is directed toward "raising the scientific level of direction, perfecting combat readiness, and also toward working out the most effective methods of using surface-to-air missile troops and jet fighter aviation." Faculty members assist in working out "projected basic rules and regulations . . . and also working out recommendations for building a modern air defense." They also are concerned with the preparation of manuals and textbooks, as well as the development of armaments, organization, and "actual problems of development of tactics, operational art, and modern control of Air Defense Troops."

Various types of the combat equipment of air defense troops are available for instructional purposes at the academy, and "in the study process technical means of teaching and electronic computer equipment are widely used."[41] Many doctors of science serve on the faculty.

Marshal of Aviation G. V. Zimin headed the academy from 1966 to 1982. General Colonel Artillery Yu. Boshnyak succeeded him in March 1982.

*The Military Engineering Radiotechnical Academy of Air Defense
Named for Marshal of the Soviet Union L. A. Govorov*

The Military Engineering Radiotechnical Academy of Air Defense is
on Dzerzhinskiy Square in Khar'kov. Formerly, it was called the Artillery
Radiotechnical Academy of the Soviet Army; its present designation dates
only from 1968.

Work at the academy is

directed toward preparing military engineers . . . with technical knowledge
to exploit military equipment and use it in complicated combat conditions.
. . . In the study process, the computer center, electronic modelling
equipment, simulated training apparatus, specialized classes, and laboratories
equipped with modern technical means of instruction are widely used.[42]

Faculty members engage in basic research. They also publish mono-
graphs, such as *Standarization in Computer Equipment* (1976) and *Integrated Logic Circuits and Junctions* (1975).

Although not revealed in Soviet publications, training is given not
only to personnel responsible for the early warning radars that blanket
the Soviet Union, but also to officers in charge of the huge missile
warning radars that can be glimpsed on the roads from Moscow to the
west.

As at most Soviet military academies, commandants at the Engineering
Radiotechnical Academy of Air Defense serve for long periods of time.
Between 1955 and 1973 the commandant was Marshal of Artillery Yu.
P. Bazhanov. His successor was General Colonel of Aviation N. V.
Kubarev. In 1981, General Lieutenant of Artillery V. Strel'nikov replaced
him.

*The Military Academy of Troop Air Defense
Named for Marshal of the Soviet Union A. M. Vasilevskiy*

The newest of the military academies is the Vasilevskiy Military Academy
of Troop Air Defense, which opened in September 1977 as the Military
Academy of Air Defense of the Ground Forces. Prior to 1977, it was
a branch of the Kalinin Military Artillery Academy.[43] It was renamed
in 1980 as part of the reorganization of air defense. The academy is
located in Kiev at Vozdukhoflotskiy Prospekt, 28.

The new academy prepares command and engineer cadres for troop
air defense. It is also a scientific center for elaboration of problems of
operational art and tactics and for development of troop air defense.
The commandant of the academy is General Colonel of Artillery A. I.
Kozhevnikov.

The Military Air Academy Named for Yu. A. Gagarin

The Gagarin Military Air Academy prepares "command cadres of various aviation specialties and is a scientific center for working out problems of operational art of the Air Forces and tactics of the branches and types of aviation."[44] It is located in the town of Monino only a few miles northeast of Moscow, in an area closed to foreigners.

Formed as an offshoot of the Zhukovskiy Air Engineering Academy in 1940, the Military Air Academy is concerned primarily with operational air matters. Instruction is carried out by two basic faculties, which have four command/staff specialties and one navigator specialty. "There are courses for retraining and for raising the qualifications of aviation commanders and political workers and also postgraduate work."[45] During attendance at the academy, pilots and navigators "periodically get practice flights on modern combat aircraft, including helicopters, and also systematically use different kinds of training machines for improving flying habits."[46] The stress on flying is reflected in the fact that "more than 70 percent of academy graduates are distinguished pilots of the USSR and distinguished navigators of the USSR."[47]

Many of the faculty members are doctors of science. The library of the academy "has more than 500,000 books, chiefly on the theory and history of the use of air forces."[48]

Between 1956 and 1968 the air academy was headed by Marshal of Aviation S. A. Krasovskiy. His successor was Marshal of Aviation S. I. Rudenko, who retired in 1973 and was replaced by Marshal of Aviation N. M. Skomorokhov. Marshal Skomorokhov graduated from the Academy of the General Staff with a gold medal, holds the degree of doctor of military science, and as a wartime ace twice earned the Hero of the Soviet Union award.

The Military Air Engineering Academy
Named for Professor N. Ye. Zhukovskiy

The Zhukovskiy Military Air Engineering Academy is not only an institution of higher learning for training military aviation engineers, but also "a scientific center for working out problems in the areas of aviation technology, its technical exploitation, and combat utilization."[49] This academy is located on Leningrad Prospekt, Moscow, almost immediately across the street from Central Airfield. Some of the offices are in a very picturesque prerevolutionary palace. Certain courses at this academy are of five years duration.

From 1923 to 1940 the academy trained both engineers and pilots for the Air Forces. The latter training was taken over, in great part, by the Military Air Academy at Monino. In the post–World War II period

most of the Soviet Air Force leaders and the chief aircraft designers were
graduates of the Zhukovskiy Academy, including Chief Marshals of
Aviation K. A. Vershinin and P. F. Zhigarev, and aircraft designers S.
V. Il'yushin, A. I. Mikoyan, A. S. Yakovlev, V. F. Bolkhovitinov, and A.
N. Rafaelyants. The late Minister of Aviation Industries, General P. V.
Dement'yev, also was an alumnus.

The academy offers both full-time and correspondence postgraduate
work. Its facilities include "a large number of study and scientific research
laboratories, a major research aerodynamic base with complexes of
subsonic and supersonic aerodynamic tunnels, a unique laboratory base
for researching turbojet engines, compressors, turbines and other elements
of aviation power plants, a practice air base"[50] and other laboratories.
"There is an experimental training factory for carrying out practice in
production with students and preparing research and scientific installations and demonstration machinery."[51] Over 1 million books are in
the academy's library.

The Air Engineering Academy is closely associated with the Academy
of Sciences, and a number of academicians are on the faculty. Commandant
of the Academy from 1949 to 1969 was General Colonel of Engineer
Technical Services V. I. Volkov. He was succeeded by General Lieutenant–
Engineer N. M. Fedayev, who was in turn succeeded by General Colonel–
Engineer V. V. Filippov in 1973.

The Naval Academy Named for Marshal of the Soviet Union A. A. Grechko

The Grechko Naval Academy "trains command and engineer cadres
of the Navy and is a scientific center for working out problems of naval
art, ship construction, armaments, questions of construction, training
and utilization of the forces and means of the Navy in military actions
at sea."[52] Its impressive building can be seen at 17 Admiral Ushakov
Embankment, Leningrad.

In 1945 the engineer-technical faculty of the academy was made into
an independent Naval Academy of Shipbuilding and Armaments. A
decision was made in 1960 that the separate training of officers was
inadvisable. "Officers of the command profile needed a deeper engineering
and technical knowledge and engineers needed a knowledge of operational
art and tactics,"[53] according to the current commandant. As a result the
two academies were combined again into the Naval Academy.

Many noted scientists have served on the academy's faculty, including
A. I. Berg, P. F. Papkovich, and M. I. Yanovskiy. A number of these
have gone on to create "advanced scientific schools of thought which
have become the basis for developing new kinds of naval weapons and
combat equipment."[54] Many doctors of naval science, as well as doctors
in other academic disciplines, are on the faculty.

The importance of the Naval Academy in preparing officers for the expanded Soviet naval role has increased significantly in the 1970s.

From 1957 to 1960 the academy was headed by Admiral V. A. Andreyev. He was succeeded by Admiral Yu. A. Panteleyev, who earlier had headed the academy from 1948 to 1951. In 1967 Panteleyev was succeeded by Admiral A. Ye. Orel, who was followed by Admiral V. S. Sysoyev in 1974. In 1982, Admiral V. N. Ponikarovskiy became commandant of the academy.

The Military-Political Academy Named for V. I. Lenin

The Lenin Military-Political Academy "is a higher military-political institution of learning, designated for training leading Party-political workers and military pedagogues from officers of the Soviet Armed Forces."[55] It also is "a center of scientific research work in the field of social sciences and military discipline."[56] Located at Sadovaya 14 in Moscow, it is on the same "ring road" as the United States embassy.

In the 1956-1957 school year the Military-Political Academy began "to train instructors in the social sciences for higher military institutions of learning and military jurists."[57] Training of military jurists was halted in 1974. Correspondence and resident academic courses are available. They provide advanced training for political officers and instructors in the social sciences at military schools.

The term *social sciences* has had a somewhat different meaning in the Soviet Union from that common in Western nations. Included as social science studies are "the history of the CPSU, the history of international Communism, workers' and national-liberation movements, Marxist-Leninist philosophy, political economy, and scientific communism."[58] Students must "deeply study the theory and practice of Party construction in the Soviet Armed Forces; modern forms, methods, and means of organization and conduct of propagandistic, mass agitation work; and military and esthetic education for subunits, units, and ships."[59]

In order that graduates understand military matters, students "study the organization and structure of troop units, the methods of combat utilization of the various services of the Armed Forces and service branches in modern war, and also the latest means of armed combat— rockets, artillery, tanks, antiaircraft [weapons], gunnery, engineering, and others."[60]

The Lenin Military-Political Academy is perhaps best known in the West through the books and articles written by its faculty members. Among its most influential books have been *V. I. Lenin and the Soviet Armed Forces* (awarded the 1968 Frunze Prize), *The CPSU and the Building of the Soviet Armed Forces, Marxism-Leninism on War and the Army, Methodological Problems of Military Theory and Practice,* and *The*

Philosophical Inheritance of V. I. Lenin and Problems of Contemporary War.[61] In a somewhat different area, other works published by the academy include *Military Pedagogics, Essays on the Psychology of Personality of the Soviet Soldier*, and *Problems of Psychology in the Military Collective.*

A major task of the staff and faculty of the Lenin Military-Political Academy is to contribute articles to *Kommunist Vooruzhennykh Sil* [Communist of the Armed Forces], advising political instructors what and how to teach during their required periods.

From 1959 to 1971 the academy was headed by General Colonel A. S. Zheltov. He was succeeded by General of the Army Ye. Ye. Mal'tsev, who died in March 1981. General Colonel G. V. Sredin, first deputy chief of the Main Political Administration at the time, was named to replace him.

The Military Academy of the Rear Services and Transport

The Military Academy of Rear Services and Transport is located at 8 Admiral Makarov Embankment in Leningrad. It dates from 1800, when an Institute for Road Engineers was opened in St. Petersburg. The present academy was formed in June 1956, as a result of combining the Military Academy of Rear Services and Supply and the Military Transport Academy. "In the faculties and academic courses, command and engineer cadres are trained for all the basic specialties of the Rear Services of the Armed Forces."[62]

Faculty members have published such books as *The Rear Services of the Soviet Army* (1968), *Warriors of the Steel Rails* (1969), and *Fundamentals of Modelling and Automation of Control of the Rear* (1982). Among the key staff members have been Doctors of Science, Professors A. A. Antonov, I. A. Vazhentsev, K. I. Vostokov, I. M. Zhernosek, A. A. Kalert, and M. P. Milovskiy. General Colonel K. N. Abramov heads the academy.

The Military Medical Academy Named for S. M. Kirov

The Kirov Military Medical Academy trains military physicians for the Soviet Armed Forces and also is a scientific center of theoretical and clinical military medicine. It is located at 6 Lebedev Street, Leningrad, within easy walking distance of Intourist's Leningradskaya Hotel. Like many other Soviet academies, it was founded during Czar Paul's regime, in 1798. But "real flowering of studies and scientific work in the Military Medical Academy came after the October Revolution," according to one of its commandants.[63]

In 1956 the Naval Medical Academy was consolidated with the Military Medical Academy. The academy trains doctors for all services of the

Armed Forces and has about sixty *kafedras** (departments) and clinics, scientific research laboratories, and "the necessary field, clinical and material technical bases."[64] It is closely linked with the Academy of Medical Sciences.

Faculty members of the academy have achieved successes "in the field of anesthesiology and reanimation, the healing of thermal burns, chest surgery, endocrinology, traumatology, and medical cybernetics."[65] Members of several departments have used their skills in basic research in oxygen starvation and organic changes resulting from it.[66] Considerable experimental work is performed in its laboratories, especially with dogs.

Between 1953 and 1968 the academy was headed by General Colonel of Medical Service P. P. Goncharov. He was succeeded by General Lieutenant of Medical Service N. G. Ivanov.

The Military Academy of Chemical Defense Named for Marshal of the Soviet Union S. K. Timoshenko

The Timoshenko Military Academy of Chemical Defense is in Moscow, at Brigadirskiy Pereulok 13. It was formed in 1932 when the military chemical section of the chemistry faculty of the Military Technical Academy of the RKKA was combined with the Second Moscow Chemical Technology Institute.

Students at the Chemical Defense Academy "study social, *special* and military disciplines, *undergo training in specially equipped camps*, do practice work with the troops, and acquire habits in organizing Party-political work" (emphasis added). Students are concerned with chemical, nuclear, and biological warfare, and "instructors and scientists take an active part in improving and creating new means of protecting troops from weapons of mass destruction."[67]

The work of the Chemical Defense Academy is not limited to direct support of the Armed Forces. "A great deal of the theoretical research of the scientists of the Military Academy has not only defense significance but also significance for the national economy." What this significance might be is never explained. It is, however, of interest that

> connected with the Military Academy are the scientific and pedagogical activities of Academicians of the Academy of Sciences USSR E. G. Britske, S. I. Vol'fkovich, M. M. Dubinin, I. L. Knunyants, I. N. Kondrat'yev, and A. F. Fokin and corresponding members of the Academy of Sciences USSR N. A. Izgaryshev, B. V. Nekrasov, K. V. Chumtov, Academician of

---

*A *kafedra* is the basic scientific or educational unit of an institution of higher learning, headed, as a rule, by a professor who is a doctor of sciences.

the Latvian Academy of Sciences L. I. Lepin, and others. Eleven scientists of the Military Academy have been awarded titles of Laureates of the Lenin Prize and State Prizes of the USSR.[68]

When one considers that the Chemical Defense Academy is concerned with chemical, nuclear, and biological warfare, the number of noted Soviet scientists from the Academy of Sciences associated with the military academy is not surprising. Soviet tanks, armored personnel carriers, and other equipment, as previously noted, are designed for chemical-radiation-bacteriological warfare conditions.

General Colonel of Technical Troops D. V. Gorbovskiy commanded the Chemical Defense Academy between 1960 and 1972. His successor was General Colonel of Technical Troops V. V. Myasnikov.

The Military Engineer Academy Named for V. V. Kuybyshev

The Kuybyshev Military Engineering Academy is "for training military engineers; a scientific center for working out problems of military engineering art, topographic and geodesic support, major construction and construction for troops."[69] It is located at Pokrovskiy Boulevard 11, Moscow.

History of the academy begins with establishment of the Main Engineering School in St. Petersburg in 1819. In 1855 it was redesignated the Nikolayevsky Engineering Academy. After the October Revolution it became the Military Engineering Academy of the RKKA. Following numerous reorganizations it became the Kuybyshev Military Engineering Academy in 1932.

After World War II the academy focused on the training of military engineers in their specialties and on the "broad development of scientific research work," including a great deal of work with computers. The academy produces manuals, guides, and textbooks for military engineering students and for topographic and geodesic studies. Faculty members also work with "methods of calculating protection for buildings from modern [that is, nuclear] weapons, the theory of dynamic calculations of the effects of earthquakes on dams, and methods and instruments for improving the accuracy of geodetic measurement."[70]

A considerable amount of basic and applied research apparently is performed at the academy, indicated by the fact that a number of the faculty members have been awarded the Lenin Prize, others the State Prize of the USSR, and still others the title of Hero of Socialist Labor. Many have been identified as distinguished persons of science and technology of the Russian Soviet Federated Socialist Republic (RSFSR) and distinguished inventors of the RSFSR.

The best known graduate of the Kuybyshev Military Engineering Academy is Marshal of the Soviet Union N. V. Ogarkov, designated chief of the General Staff in 1977. In 1978 he was the second ranking officer in the Soviet Armed Forces, standing next to the minister of defense, Marshal of the Soviet Union D. F. Ustinov. Previously, the two or three top positions had gone to officers who were graduates of a "command"-type academy, such as Frunze or the Malinovskiy Tank Academy. Marshal Ogarkov, in common with practically all senior Soviet officers, is also a graduate of the Academy of the General Staff.

A more rapid turnover of commandants has occurred in the Engineering Academy than in most of the other academies. General Colonel of Engineer Troops V. L. Avseyenko headed the academy from 1969 to 1974 and was succeeded by General Lieutenant of Engineer Troops S. Kh. Aganov, who in 1975 was succeeded in turn by General Lieutenant of Engineer Troops V. Ye. Uporov. In 1980, General Colonel of Engineer Troops Ye. S. Kolibernov became commandant.

The Military Academy of Signals
Named for Marshal of the Soviet Union S. M. Budennyy

The Budennyy Military Academy of Signals is located at 3 Tikhoretskiy Prospekt in Leningrad. Founded in 1919, it was reorganized as the Military Electrotechnical Academy in 1921. In 1952 it was divided into the Military Academy of Signals (Command) and the Military Engineering Academy of Signals. In 1957 the two academies were recombined.

The present Signals Academy has both "command and engineer faculties and a faculty for correspondence courses, a training range, scientific research and study laboratories, and also a library of some 900,000 books." For practical exercises, "a modern field training base has been set up, permitting the effective conduct of studies on exploiting communications equipment in conditions as close to combat as possible."[71]

Graduates of the Signals Academy include scientists "who have made great contributions in the development of communications."[72] Apparently, considerable scientific research work is conducted by faculty members.

General Colonel of Signal Troops A. A. Frolov headed the academy for fourteen years, from 1961 to 1975. His successor was General Colonel of Signal Troops A. P. Borisov. He in turn was replaced by General Colonel of Signal Troops N. G. Popov in 1979.

The Military Academy of the General Staff
of the Armed Forces of the USSR Named for K. Ye. Voroshilov

The Voroshilov Military Academy of the General Staff, founded in 1936, is located at Khol'zunova Pereulok, Dom 14, in Moscow, a short walk from the Frunze Military Academy. A number of its first graduates achieved fame as Soviet commanders in both World War II and the postwar period. Among these were M. V. Zakharov, I. Kh. Bagramyan, A. I. Antonov, A. M. Vasilevskiy, P. A. Kurochkin, A. I. Gastilovich, and K. F. Skorobogatkin. The first class was graduated early, since the students were needed to help fill the officer ranks that had been emptied as a result of Stalin's purges. (As already noted, the officers in the first graduating class, in large measure, owed their rapid rise in ranks to the vacancies created when Stalin had the majority of his senior officers killed.)

After short courses had been provided to thousands of officers during World War II, in 1946 the academy's name was changed, and the course was set at two years. Following Stalin's death, special attention in the curriculum in the 1950s was given to the impact of nuclear weapons upon warfare. A major organizational change occurred in 1958, when the postwar Higher Military Academy named for K. Ye. Voroshilov again became the Military Academy of the General Staff of the Armed Forces of the USSR, and the academy was given the assignment of "preparing cadres for working in the central apparatus of the Ministry of Defense and the General Staff, in large formations and formations of all services of the Armed Forces."[73] In this new role, "primary attention was directed toward working out the most important problems of contemporary military art in combat employing both nuclear weapons and conventional means of destruction."[74]

Students are admitted to the Academy of the General Staff in the grade of lieutenant colonel, colonel, and general major (one star). Faculty members and students conduct research that in the United States would be performed by the various study and analysis groups in the Pentagon and by contract research organizations.

Many senior officers from socialist countries are graduates of the General Staff Academy. In 1983 these included all ministers of defense of Warsaw Pact countries, as well as of North Vietnam and other nations.

The faculty of the Academy of the General Staff, working in conjunction with the General Staff, played a major role in the development of the new Soviet military doctrine announced by Nikita Khrushchev in 1960. General Lieutenant A. I. Gastilovich, deputy commandant of the Academy for Scientific Studies at the time, was the author of the lead article in the famed *Special Collection*, "The Theory of Military Art Needs Review."[75] (As previously noted, Oleg Penkovskiy transmitted this group of papers to the West in the early 1960s.)

The new military doctrine developed during the late 1950s demanded a corresponding military strategy. Marshal Sokolovskiy's *Military Strategy*, published in 1962, which reflected the new doctrine, provided an unclassified explanation of the Soviet concept of modern warfare. Faculty members of the General Staff Academy were among the major contributors to this book. The new strategy, in turn, required a reexamination of operational art, and a new textbook on this subject was published in the latter part of 1964. "Over the course of ten years," according to V. G. Kulikov, "it was widely used for the operational training not only of generals and officers of the Soviet Army, but also for the armies of fraternal socialist countries."[76] Although this statement indicates that it has been replaced, what has replaced it is not known. Nothing is known about its contents other than that it was written by Generals I. S. Glebov, P. K. Altukhov, V. I. Vol'khin, B. M. Golovchiner, A. M. Krylov, B. G. Plashchin, and P. G. Yanovskiy and Colonels S. F. Begunov and D. K. Slepenkov. A number of the contributors to the textbook were awarded the Frunze Prizes in 1966.[77]

In 1975, preparation of a new textbook on military strategy was completed. This book contained "new views on the nature and methods of waging war, and also of strategic actions of the services of the Armed Forces."[78] General of the Army I. Ye. Shavrov was its editor, with General Lieutenant V. N. Karpov, head of the chair of strategy, heading the group of authors. The authors included Generals A. K. Zaporozhchenko, K. K. Belokonov, V. V. Solov'yev, Ye. D. Grebish, and Colonels N. N. Kuznetsov and I. F. Yermachenko. The book was published in the closed press, and its contents thus remain a mystery.

In the early part of the 1970s some faculty members of the Academy of the General Staff moved to the staffs of the newly created Institute of the USA and the revitalized Institute of World Economy and International Relations. In the beginning, these social science research institutes needed a few military strategists to round out their staffs, since some of their tasks involved problems of a military nature. General Colonel N. A. Lomov, until March 1969 head of the chair of strategy and a professor at the academy, became a consultant at Dr. Georgiy Arbatov's Institute of the USA. Colonel V. V. Larionov, previously mentioned as a contributor to *Military Strategy*, headed a section at the same institute and then in the mid-1970s returned to the Academy of the General Staff to the chair of the history of wars and military art. General Lieutenant M. A. Milshtein, a former faculty member of the General Staff Academy specializing in the armed forces of NATO nations, moved over to head a political-military section at the Institute of the USA and Canada (the name was changed in 1974) and became a spokesman for Soviet views on arms control. However, ties between the research institutes under the Academy of Sciences and the Academy of the General Staff are no longer close.

Between fifty and seventy-five generals and admirals are assigned to the academy in various capacities. Most of the faculty members have advanced degrees in military science, and they contribute to books and textbooks on military science. The impact of the academy's work is felt throughout the Soviet Armed Forces.

Since the war, the academy has been headed by Marshal of the Soviet Union M. V. Zakharov (1945–1949, 1963–1964); General of the Army V. V. Kurasov (1949–1956, 1961–1963); Marshal of the Soviet Union I. Kh. Bagramyan (1956–1958); General of the Army G. K. Malandin (1958–1961); General of the Army V. D. Ivanov (1965–1968); General of the Army S. P. Ivanov (1968–1973); General of the Army I. Ye. Shavrov (1973–1979); and General of the Army M. M. Kozlov (since 1979).

Other Soviet Military Institutions of Higher Learning

In addition to the military academies, the Ministry of Defense has a number of institutes and special shorter courses for officers.

The Military Engineering Institute Named for A. F. Mozhayskiy

The Mozhayskiy Military Engineering Institute "is a higher military institution of learning of the Soviet Armed Forces," which trains military engineers in various subjects and also is a research center for working on various technical problems.[79] It was founded in March 1941 as the Leningrad Military Air Academy, preparing military engineers for the Air Forces. After the war it broadened its profile and began training military mechanical engineers, electrical engineers, constructors, meteorologists and radioelectronic specialists. It is known for work on jet engines, automatic control, and radar. Until 1974, it was called the Mozhayskiy Military Engineering Academy. It is located in Leningrad. The course length is five years.

Details about the present role of the institute are not known. It may be associated with space programs or with new technologies. General Lieutenant N. I. Bereznyak headed the institute from 1973 to 1981. General Colonel A. I. Kholopov succeeded him.

The Military Institute of Physical Culture

The Military Institute of Physical Culture, originally founded in 1918 as the Military Main Gymnastic Fencing School, is located in Leningrad. It is a higher military institution, "designated for training officer specialists for physical culture and sport."[80] In all probability its faculty is concerned not only with the physical training of men in military service, but also with military-sport games and beginning military training. The institute is headed by General Major M. V. Gres'kov.

The Military Institute

The Military Institute is "a higher military institution of learning of the Soviet Armed Forces, designated for training military translator-reviewers, instructors in foreign languages, political workers with a knowledge of foreign languages, and officer lawyers."[81] The original institute was formed in 1942 from the Moscow State Pedagogical Institute of Foreign Languages and the Moscow Institute of Oriental Studies. The institute was disbanded in 1956 but reopened in 1963 on Volochayevskaya Street, 3/4. Prior to 1974 it was called the Military Institute of Foreign Languages. In 1974, at the time the name was changed, the "military jurisprudence faculty of the Lenin Military-Political Academy was transferred to the Military Institute."

The language side of the Military Institute probably is closely concerned with military intelligence (GRU). Sociopolitical, philological, and military subjects are studied at the institute in conjunction with language training, with the usual emphasis given to Marxist-Leninist teachings. The institute was headed by General Colonel I. S. Katyshkin from 1973 to 1979. General Colonel M. T. Tankayev replaced him in 1979.

Courses for Officers

In addition to the military academies, there are a variety of courses and classes for officers at all levels. These are in fact educational institutions that offer briefer and more specialized instruction. The most famous courses are the *Vystrel* Higher Officers' Courses, named for Marshal of the Soviet Union B. M. Shaposhnikov. There are also the Central Artillery Officers' Courses Named for Marshal of Artillery V. I. Kazakov, located in Leningrad; Higher Central Officers' Courses of Civil Defense; the Central Advanced Courses for Political Officers; Central Radiotechnical Officers' Courses of Troops of Air Defense; Higher Courses for Air Forces Officers; and Higher Special Officers' Classes sponsored by the Navy. Little is known about most of these courses. They seem to be a year or less in length. Several of the courses will be examined in greater detail.

First Higher Officers' Courses Vystrel *Named for Marshal of the Soviet Union B. M. Shaposhnikov.* This institution is located in Solnechnogorsk, near Moscow, on the main highway between Moscow and Leningrad. The courses are designed to provide additional training to the command and political staff of the Ground Forces and to instructors in military schools. The courses of instruction are less than a year in length.[82]

Vystrel means "the shot," and, appropriately, studies are concerned primarily with firing various types of weapons. The school sometimes is known as the field academy, and officer students spend 65 percent of their time in the field, on proving grounds, firing ranges, and in armored maneuver areas.[83] Special emphasis is given to exercises under nuclear war conditions. In the postwar period the courses were combined with the Central Armored Officers' courses, which considerably broadened their scope.

Vystrel courses are designed for officers at the battalion and regimental levels in the areas of tactics, gunnery, and fire preparation. In the training area are tactical battlefields, tank target ranges with automatic feedback, water areas where firing from amphibious tanks can be conducted, and antitank and anti-antitank laboratories, engineering and chemical grounds, anti-aircraft ranges, and grenade launching complexes.

Since 1969 *Vystrel* has been commanded by General Colonel of Tank Troops D. A. Dragunskiy.

Sixth Higher Special Officers' Classes of the Navy. The "Higher Special Officers' Classes compose an institution of learning of the Navy of the USSR, designated for [advanced] training of commanders of ships, their deputies, for political units and flagman specialists."[84] These classes are conducted in a permanent building in Leningrad. They are divided into three areas of advanced training: command, political, and engineer. Each of the classes lasts nearly one year.

Central Artillery Officers' Courses Named for Marshal of Artillery V. I. Kazakov. This institution celebrated its 100th birthday in 1983.[85] During the Civil War, the courses were able to prepare thousands of artillerymen in a very short time for the Ground Forces. Called "the field academy for artillerymen," it devotes more than 60 percent of study time to work in the field. Officers from socialist countries are trained in the courses as well. General Lieutenant of Artillery A. M. Sapozhnikov has headed the courses since 1974.

Central Advanced Courses for the Political Staff. This institution is headed by General Major M. Krechetov. Its classrooms are equipped with the latest technical advances in the art of instruction—tape recorders, slide projectors, and remote-control panels.[86] Little is known about the course of instruction.

Higher Border Guard Command Courses of the KGB USSR. In November 1983, the Higher Border Guard Command Courses of the KGB celebrated their sixtieth anniversary. The institution was first called the Higher Border Guard School and then the Military Institute of the KGB-MVD, but it is not clear when the present name came into use. Students study Marxism-Leninism, tactics, and the operational art of border guards and other subjects. General Lieutenant N. I. Makarov is the head of the courses at their sixty-year mark.

Other Officer Education. Officers in the Veterinarian Service go to the Moscow Veterinarian Academy for advanced officers' training courses.

Similarly, officers in the finance service may attend the special faculty at the Moscow Finance Institute. Medical officers receive refresher training at the military medical faculties of several medical institutes.[87] The musical directors' faculty at the Moscow State Conservatory prepares musicians in a five-year course.[88]

Nearly all of the seventeen military academies offer academic courses for their graduates. The Academy of the General Staff, which had dropped the higher academic courses in 1959, reestablished them in 1968. These courses originated at the Academy of the General Staff in 1946 with a nine-month program. Students were generals and promising senior officers who had risen to high rank during the war but lacked theoretical background. Among the first students to attend the courses in 1968 were Generals of the Army V. G. Kulikov, V. F. Tolubko, S. K. Kurkotkin, I. Ye. Shavrov, P. A. Belik, Ye. F. Ivanovskiy, and N. G. Lyashchenko, and General Colonels A. I. Gribkov, V. I. Varennikov, I. I. Tenishchev, and N. K. Sil'chenko. The lecture cycle included the nature of future war, the military doctrines of the main capitalist states, and actions of the services in strategic operations.

Graduate Education

As in the United States armed forces, Soviet officers are provided opportunities to obtain graduate degrees in many fields: history, engineering, geography, philosophy, and others. In addition, officers may obtain graduate degrees in military science to the doctoral level. (The United States Navy has operated a postgraduate school in Monterey, California, for decades and recently the U.S. Army Command and General Staff College at Fort Leavenworth, Kansas, has started offering a master's degree in military science.)

Work toward a graduate degree can be accomplished both by full-time study and by correspondence.[89] The General Staff decides which schools and scientific research institutes can offer advanced degrees. All military academies and certain military schools also provide graduate courses, among the latter being Kiev Aviation Engineering Military School, the Riga Higher Military Aviation Engineering School, and the Penza Higher Artillery Engineering School. These schools have special departments where officers do graduate work.

Officers also can apply to civilian educational institutions for graduate work. Those assigned as full-time students must not be over thirty-five, except for certain "operational-tactical" and political specialties for which the age limit is thirty-eight. Officers taking graduate correspondence courses must be under forty when beginning their work.

Since the early 1970s a special graduate program for generals, admirals, and other senior officers has been instituted; it is handled differently from the normal graduate programs. This select group of officers knows in advance what their dissertation theme will be, has collected the material needed for research, and has a program planned and approved. A school on a special list will offer advice and periodically check up on the work of the individual. The dissertation will be formally defended in the same school.

*   *   *

Soviet secrecy is such that even a close, detailed examination of officer preparation and subsequent professional education of Soviet officers leaves many gaps. Nevertheless, sufficient information is available to demonstrate that this training and education is impressive by any standards.

It can be argued that the extreme specialization of Soviet military and higher military schools, as well as most of the academies, produces officers with narrow professional backgrounds, unable to adapt to changing weapons systems and methods of warfare. On the other hand, the Soviet system would appear to turn out officers capable of handling immediate assignments as training officers in units. Since a primary task of the Soviet Ground Forces, as well as components of the other services, is to train the two-year inductees, this fact should be taken into account when considering the Soviet system.

Notes

1. K. V. Provorov and A. P. Porokhin, "Military Institutions of Learning," *Sovetskaya Voyennaya Entsiklopediya* [Soviet Military Encyclopedia] (Moscow: Voyenizdat, 1976–1980), Vol. 2, p. 255.

2. For photographs of a number of military and higher military schools, see I. A. Kamkov and V. A. Konoplyanik, *Voyennyye Akademii i Uchilishcha* [Military Academies and Schools] (Moscow: Voyenizdat, 1974); and *Sovetskaya Voyennaya Entsiklopediya*, Vol. 2.

3. Approximately 140 general officers and admirals head the military and higher military schools. More than 200 are assigned to the academies.

4. *Bol'shaya Sovetskaya Entsiklopediya* [The Great Soviet Encyclopedia], 3d ed. (Moscow: Soviet Encyclopedia Publishing House, 1970–1979), Vol. 5, p. 239.

5. A. Iovlev, "The Establishment and Development of Military Institutions of Higher Learning (VUZ) of the Red Army, 1918–1920," *Voyenno Istoricheskii Zhurnal* [Military History Journal], September 1974, p. 87. See also A. M. Iovlev, *Deyatel'nost' KPSS po Podgotovke Voyennykh Kadrov* [Actions of the CPSU for Training Military Cadres] (Moscow: Voyenizdat, 1976), pp. 9–69, for the 1918–1920 period.

6. Iovlev, *Deyatel'nost' KPSS*, p. 108.

7. M. V. Zakharov, ed., *50 Let Vooruzhennykh Sil USSR* [50 Years of the Armed Forces of the USSR] (Moscow: Voyenizdat, 1968), p. 272. See also Iovlev, *Deyatel'nost' KPSS*, pp. 140–190, for the wartime period.

8. Ibid., p. 459.

9. *Zakon SSSR o Vseobshchey Voinskoy Obyazannosti* [Law of the USSR on Universal Military Obligation] (adopted by the Supreme Soviet USSR 17 December 1980) (Moscow: Voyenizdat, 1981), p. 16.

10. Ye. I. Ivanovskiy, ed., *Ordena Lenina Moskovskiy Voyennyy Okrug* [History of the Order of Lenin Moscow Military Districts] (Moscow: Voyenizdat, 1971), p. 331. See also *Sovetskaya Voyennaya Entsiklopediya*, Vol. 2, p. 438.

11. *Krasnaya Zvezda,* 12 October 1983.

12. Kamkov and Konoplyanik, *Voyennyye Akademii,* p. 46.

13. Comprehensive lists were not published in *Krasnaya Zvezda* in 1982 or 1983.

14. O. V. Zinchenko, *My—Suvorovtsy* [We Are Suvorovites] (Moscow: Voyenizdat, 1974), p. 5. See also P. A. Buchenkov, *Suvorovskoye Voyennoye* [Suvorov Military (Schools)] (Moscow: Voyenizdat, 1981).

15. A. G. Gornyy, ed., *Spravochnik po Zakonodatel'stvu Dlya Ofitserov Sovetskoy Armii i Flota* [Handbook on Legislation for Officers of the Soviet Army and Navy] (Moscow: Voyenizdat, 1976), p. 237.

16. For sample examinations, see Kamkov and Konoplyanik, *Voyennyye Akademii.* Examinations in mathematics appear to be on the level that would be expected of an individual entering West Point, Colorado Springs, or Annapolis.

17. Names, locations, and details on military schools and academies have been obtained over the years from numerous Soviet sources, primarily newspapers, military journals, and books. None of the higher military schools is specifically identified as training officers for the Strategic Rocket Forces. Identification has been made by noting the name of the school and from other information.

18. For a general discussion of Soviet Air Forces schools, see V. M. Afanas'yev, "Higher Military Aviation Schools," *Sovetskaya Voyennaya Entsiklopediya*, Vol. 2, p. 435.

19. N. I. Gusev, "Higher Military-Political Schools," *Sovetskaya Voyennaya Entsiklopediya*, Vol. 2, p. 435.

20. The *Voyennyy Entsiklopedicheskiy Slovar'* [Military Encyclopedic Dictionary] (Moscow: Voyenizdat, 1983), p. 24, states that "the Academy of the MVD USSR is a scientific center for training leading cadres for agencies of internal affairs and researching problems of socialist law and order."

21. Kamkov and Konoplyanik, *Voyennyye Akademii,* p. 61.

22. Gornyy, *Spravochnik,* p. 191.

23. S. N. Kozlov, ed., *Spravochnik Ofitsera* [Officer's Handbook] (Moscow: Voyenizdat, 1971), p. 210.

24. Ibid., p. 211. See also Gornyy, *Spravochnik,* p. 200.

25. Gornyy, *Spravochnik,* p. 205.

26. Ibid., pp. 182, 184.

27. *Bol'shaya Sovetskaya Entsiklopediya*, Vol. 5, p. 224.

28. A. A. Grechko, *Vooruzhennyye Sily Sovetskovo Gosudarstva* [Armed Forces of the Soviet State] (Moscow: Voyenizdat, 1975), p. 238.

29. *Bol'shaya Sovetskaya Entsiklopediya,* Vol. 5, p. 224. Further information can be found in P. A. Kurochkin, ed., *Osnovy Metodiki Voyenno-Nauchnogo Issledovaniya* [Fundamentals of Methods of Military Science Research] (Moscow: Voyenizdat, 1969), which is a second edition of *Metodika Voyenno-Nauchnogo Issledovaniya* [Methods of Military Science Research] (Moscow: Voyenizdat, 1959), by General Major Pyotr Grigorenko, exiled Soviet civil rights activist, while he was head of the Scientific Research Branch at Frunze Military Academy; F. P. Tonkikh, ed., *Osnovy Nauchnoy Organizatsii Truda v Voyenno-Uchebnykh Zavedeniyakh* [Fundamentals of Scientific Organization of Labor in Military Schools] (Moscow: Voyenizdat, 1974); I. N. Shkadov, ed., *Voprosy Obucheniya i Vospitaniya v Voyenno-Uchebnykh Zavedeniyakh* [Questions of Training and Education in Military Schools] (Moscow: Voyenizdat, 1976); and, A. A. Zolotarev and B. F. Fedorov, *Tekhnicheskiye Sredstva Obucheniya v VVUZakh* [Technical Means of Training in Higher Military Schools] (Moscow: Voyenizdat, 1976).

30. Kamkov and Konoplyanik, *Voyennyye Akademii,* pp. 15–16.

31. F. P. Tonkikh, "The Military Academy named for F. E. Dzerzhinskiy," *Sovetskaya Voyennaya Entsiklopediya*, Vol. 2, p. 177.

32. Ibid.

33. For a general discussion of the Frunze Academy, see *Akademiya Imeni M. V. Frunze* [The Frunze Military Academy] (Moscow: Voyenizdat, 1980), 2d ed. The second edition is an improvement over the 1973 edition but still has limited information.

34. A. I. Radziyevskiy, "The Military Academy named for M. V. Frunze," *Sovetskaya Voyennaya Entsiklopediya*, Vol. 2, p. 175. This article by Radziyevskiy in the Military Encyclopedia is more informative than his entire book on the same subject. Apparently, the editors were authorized to permit publication of much more data for the encyclopedia than previously had been permitted in books.

35. See *Akademiya Imeni M. V. Frunze*, pp. 213, 244–247.

36. General Lieutenant V. G. Reznichenko was the editor of *Tactics,* published by Voyenizdat in 1966 as one of the Officer's Library series. In 1977 Reznichenko, still at Frunze, conducted a group of students from the academy on a visit to Great Britain.

37. O. A. Losik, "The Military Academy of Armored Forces," *Sovetskaya Voyennaya Entsiklopediya*, Vol. 2, p. 171.

38. Ibid., p. 172.

39. P. F. Slipchenko, "The Military Artillery Academy," *Sovetskaya Voyennaya Entsiklopediya*, Vol. 2, p. 180.

40. G. V. Zimin, "The Military Command Academy of Air Defense," *Sovetskaya Voyennaya Entsiklopediya*, Vol. 2, p. 183.

41. Ibid.

42. Yu. P. Bazhanov, "The Military Engineering Radiotechnical Academy of Air Defense," *Sovetskaya Voyennaya Entsiklopediya*, Vol. 2, p. 182.

43. N. V. Ogarkov, ed., *Voyennyy Entsiklopedicheskiy Slovar'*, p. 145.

44. N. M. Skomorokhov, "The Military Air Academy named for Yu. A. Gagarin," *Sovetskaya Voyennaya Entsiklopediya*, Vol. 2, p. 199.

45. Ibid.
46. Ibid.
47. Ibid.
48. Ibid., p. 200.
49. A. V. Shtoda, "The Military Air Engineering Academy," *Sovetskaya Voyennaya Entsiklopediya*, Vol. 2, p. 200.
50. Ibid.
51. Ibid., p. 201.
52. V. S. Sysoyev, "The Naval Academy," *Sovetskaya Voyennaya Entsiklopediya*, Vol. 2, p. 230.
53. Ibid.
54. Ibid., p. 231.
55. Ye. Ye. Mal'tsev, "The Military-Political Academy," *Sovetskaya Voyennaya Entsiklopediya*, Vol. 2, p. 246. For more information on the academy, see *Akademiya Imeni V. I. Lenina* [Academy Named for V. I. Lenin] (Moscow: Voyenizdat, 1980).
56. Ibid.
57. Ibid.
58. Ibid., p. 247.
59. Ibid.
60. Ibid.
61. This list of books is from the *Sovetskaya Voyennaya Entsiklopediya*, p. 248. Their basic theme is nuclear war.
62. K. N. Abramov, "The Military Academy of Rear Services and Transport," *Sovetskaya Voyennaya Entsiklopediya*, Vol. 2, p. 179.
63. N. G. Ivanov, "The Military Medical Academy," *Sovetskaya Voyennaya Entsiklopediya*, Vol. 2, p. 225.
64. Ibid.
65. Ibid.
66. Ibid., p. 226.
67. V. V. Myasnikov, "The Military Academy of Chemical Defense," *Sovetskaya Voyennaya Entsiklopediya*, Vol. 2, p. 179.
68. Ibid.
69. S. Kh. Aganov, "The Military Engineer Academy Named for V. V. Kuybyshev," *Sovetskaya Voyennaya Entsiklopediya*, Vol. 2, p. 220.
70. Ibid.
71. A. A. Frolov, "The Military Academy of Signals," *Sovetskaya Voyennaya Entsiklopediya,* Vol. 2, p. 178.
72. Ibid.
73. I. Ye. Shavrov, "The Military Academy of the General Staff," *Sovetskaya Voyennaya Entsiklopediya*, Vol. 2, p. 173.
74. Ibid.
75. Oleg Penkovskiy, *The Penkovskiy Papers* (New York: Doubleday & Co., 1965), p. 251.
76. V. G. Kulikov, ed., *Akademiya General'novo Shtaba* [Academy of the General Staff] (Moscow: Voyenizdat, 1976), p. 161.

77. Harriet Fast Scott, *Soviet Military Doctrine: Its Formulation and Dissemination* (Menlo Park, Calif.: Stanford Research Institute, 1971), p. 95. In the Frunze Prize competition for that year, these officers were awarded certificates, but with no mention of the type of work they had produced.

78. Kulikov, *Akademiya General'novo*, p. 205.

79. D. A. Medvedev, "The Military Engineer Institute," *Sovetskaya Voyennaya Entsiklopediya*, Vol. 2, p. 267.

80. A. P. Tikhomirov, "The Military Institute of Physical Culture," *Sovetskaya Voyennaya Entsiklopediya*, Vol. 2, p. 267.

81. I. S. Katyshkin, "The Military Institute," *Sovetskaya Voyennaya Entsiklopediya*, Vol. 2, p. 267.

82. D. A. Dragunskiy, "Vystrel," *Sovetskaya Voyennaya Entsiklopediya*, Vol. 2, p. 432. See also D. A. Dragunskiy, ed., *Polevaya Akademiya* [Field Academy] (Moscow: Voyenizdat, 1982).

83. G. Golofast, "The Vystrel Course—at 50 Years," *Voyenno-Istoricheskii Zhurnal* 3, March 1969, p. 113. See also Ya. Kreyzer, "The Vystrel Course at 50 Years," *Voyennyy Vestnik* 3, March 1969, pp. 15–21.

84. A. I. Petelin, "Higher Special Officers' Classes," *Sovetskaya Voyennaya Entsiklopediya*, Vol. 2, p. 439.

85. O. Makovey, "Central Artillery," *Voyennyy Vestnik* 7 (1983), pp. 69–71. This article was written in celebration of the centenary of the Courses and contains several pictures.

86. M. Krechetov and V. Deribas, "Methodological Study Complex," *Voyennyy Vestnik* 3 (1982), pp. 52–54.

87. M. Ye. Yastrebov, "Military Medical Faculties," *Sovetskaya Voyennaya Entsiklopediya*, Vol. 2, p. 228.

88. N. M. Nazarov, "Military Conductor Faculty," *Sovetskaya Voyennaya Entsiklopediya*, Vol. 2, p. 209.

89. For a more complete description of graduate work, see Kamkov and Konoplyanik, *Voyennyye Akademii*, pp. 192–206. Also refer to interview with General Lieutenant A. Mironov, chief of a section of the Main Directorate of Cadres of the Ministry of Defense, entitled "Those Wanting to Enter the Postgraduate Program," *Krasnaya Zvezda*, 18 November 1983.

12
Weighing the Balance

The Role of Doctrine

There is no single measure of a nation's military capability. As so well demonstrated in the Soviet invasion of Afghanistan in 1979, sophisticated weaponry does not guarantee military success. While the number of men under arms and mobilization capability are major factors in evaluating military power, these too can be offset by other less tangible considerations. Among these are the quality of military leadership, the professional competence of the officer corps, and the technical skill of the troops. Other equally significant factors are the national technical and scientific capability, industrial production potential, the government's effectiveness and stability, and, finally, that great imponderable, the national will.

A nation's military potential may never be realized without a clearly understood military doctrine or national military policy. The Soviet Armed Forces are guided by a doctrine that was developed in the 1950s and first announced in 1960, over two years before the Cuban missile confrontation of 1962. Although additions were made to this doctrine in 1967 and 1974, its basic concept is that the Soviet Armed Forces, the people, and the entire nation must be prepared for the eventuality of a nuclear rocket war.

"The nuclear age demands above all a clarification of doctrine," said Henry Kissinger.[1] With respect to weapons systems, "only a doctrine which defines the purpose of these weapons and the kind of war in which they are to be employed permits a rational choice." But even further, "strategic doctrine transcends the problem of selecting weapons systems. It is the mode of survival of society." This statement appears to describe the basic concept of Soviet military doctrine, as presented through Soviet writings. However, these views were developed in the United States in the mid-1950s at a conference chaired by Gordon Dean and reported by Henry Kissinger in *Nuclear Weapons and Foreign Policy*. Marshal Ogarkov's 1982 statement of doctrine and its purpose[2] is a reaffirmation in principle of what had been considered in the United States more than two decades earlier. Perhaps this is no accident, since *Nuclear Weapons and Foreign Policy* was translated into Russian and closely studied in the Soviet Union at the very time the new Soviet doctrine was being formulated. The warning of the need for doctrine seemingly was heeded in Moscow, but not in Washington.

Based on the guidelines established in their doctrine, the Soviet military leadership developed a military strategy. If there is any doubt about this strategy having been followed or of its impact, it is necessary only to read Marshal Sokolovskiy's *Military Strategy* and to check the type of military forces and weapons systems described in 1962 with the posture of the Soviet Armed Forces decades later. This book was available in Moscow bookstores two months before the Cuban missile crisis and confirmed much of the data contained in the *Special Collection* that had been provided earlier to London and Washington by Oleg Penkovskiy. Soviet plans to achieve strategic nuclear superiority were laid long before the nuclear confrontation of October 1962.

Soviet military doctrine and strategy are discussed at length in dozens of Soviet books and in hundreds of articles. Their principles are reflected in regulations, textbooks, and even in books written for children. Political officers are charged with explaining military doctrine and strategy in their lectures, which all members of the Soviet Armed Forces must attend. In order to pass examinations for selection to attend higher professional schooling, Soviet officers must be familiar with doctrinal and strategic concepts. As Soviet five-year economic plans provide guidelines for the economic development of the nation, military doctrine and strategy provide guidelines for the Armed Forces, including selection and production of weapons systems. This makes it possible for Soviet weapons systems to be procured on the basis of long-range planning and not subject to annual budget reviews or to temporary changes in international affairs.

Soviet strategists are perhaps without contemporary equal in providing theoretical insights into the nature of war and its specific aspects. It would be difficult to find any book written in the past two decades by an officer in the United States armed forces that matches the level of Marshal Sokolovskiy's *Military Strategy*, Marshal Ogarkov's *Always in Readiness to Defend the Fatherland*, or General Kir'yan's *Military Technical Progress and the Armed Forces of the USSR*. At the same time, it must not be forgotten that Soviet theoreticians can express the need for advanced computer systems, but must purchase even relatively unsophisticated computers from abroad. Theory in the Soviet Union is ahead of actual capability. In the military area it is intended to be so.

Command Structure and Control

Organization of the Soviet Armed Forces and their concepts of command and control often appear to be at variance with practices in the United States armed forces. There are basic differences, but also a number of similarities.

The Soviet system of command and control reflects extreme centralization, with unquestioned control by the top Party-military structure. Stalin's system of control during World War II when he was concurrently chairman of the State Committee of Defense (GKO), supreme commander in chief of the Armed Forces, and general secretary of the Communist Party is described in Soviet texts as an ideal organizational structure for any future war.

In a nuclear-scared world it is unlikely that the situation that gave the United States military leadership during World War II considerable freedom in command can again prevail. During the Korean War, to an ever-increasing degree, direct control over combat forces was exercised from Washington. At the time of the Cuban missile crisis in 1962, civilian leaders in the Department of Defense often bypassed the Pentagon's military chiefs when passing orders to military forces. This centralized direction from Washington increased during the war in Southeast Asia, when the White House sometimes gave direct approval for air strikes. With the possibility that a nation might be severely damaged within a few hours by a nuclear attack, close control over combat forces by the top political leadership is likely to continue.

Most of the Kremlin's leaders have been at the center of power for over a decade, a situation that will continue to exist even after Chernenko leaves the stage. These men have survived power struggles of many types and have dealt with a variety of complex issues at the national and international levels. Since the Armed Forces are so much a part of Soviet life, the Soviets do not feel the suspicion of the military that has been fundamental in the United States since before the Revolutionary War.

In the event of an international crisis that might lead to military action, the Soviet leadership would be composed of men with years of experience in their positions. In contrast, the top political leadership in Washington changes every four to eight years. Each new administration is influenced to some degree by young, idealistic workers from the winning party, who may be totally inexperienced in foreign affairs. Advisers on foreign affairs, with excellent theoretical backgrounds but without actual experience in international affairs or any knowledge of weapons systems or military matters, frequently are drawn from universities. Even toward the end of a four-year tour in the White House, the president and most of his staff are amateurs when compared to their counterparts in the Kremlin.

Both Moscow and Washington are groping for an optimum organizational structure for military forces. With the new weapons systems now deployed, division of forces into armies, navies, and air forces sometimes loses its traditional significance. Ballistic missiles can be launched from mobile platforms, silos, submarines, and aircraft. Soviet strategic nuclear forces are divided among the Strategic Rocket Forces, Navy, and Air Forces. Centralized control over these forces is provided by the General Staff.

In the Pentagon the civilian element of the Department of Defense has taken over many of the responsibilities and much of the authority that previously had been exercised by officers of the armed forces. To some degree this control results from the failure of the three individual services—Army, Navy, and Air Force—to agree on common goals. It might be well for the United States military forces, in the national interest as well as their own, to study the Soviet General Staff concept.

With respect to an interior military structure, the United States does not require the division of the nation into military districts with huge staffs like those in the Soviet Union. United States military and naval districts serve only an administrative function. In the USSR, however, the Party leaders still use military forces to control the population. As a spinoff, this system does provide a capability for internal controls that would be of great significance in the event of a nuclear war. Within a few hours a number of military districts could be combined to form a theater of military operations. The machinery already is in place.[3]

The Soviet system of logistical support for its Armed Forces and the designation of various categories of "special troops" are logical developments. In previous wars the Soviets depended on huge armies, fighting on or in areas contiguous to Soviet territory. Since lines of communication were relatively short, civilian workers could be mobilized on short notice to serve as support troops. There was little need for the political leader to maintain the greater part of the armed forces as self-contained combat units, ready for rapid deployment to overseas theaters. Trucks and their drivers could be employed in a Kiev industrial plant with mobilization assignments to report to a specific military unit in event of an emergency. Although this system still is adequate for the bulk of the Soviet forces, it obviously is inadequate for any forces that might be needed for the rapid projection of military power beyond Soviet frontiers.

In contrast, the United States armed forces require an integrated logistical structure, ready to move out with combat units to overseas theaters. While combat-to-support ratios between the Soviet and United States forces are interesting to compare, they have little meaning unless the total Soviet support structure and the type of wars that the Soviet Union is most likely to wage are taken into account.

Manpower and Leadership

The growing militarization of the Soviet Union should be of concern both to the non-Communist world and the People's Republic of China. Even if absolutely nothing were known about Soviet weaponry, the emphasis given to military affairs in the Soviet Union should be enough to make other nations apprehensive.

One dangerous aspect of the growing Soviet militarization is the increasing percentage of national resources allocated for military purposes. It has been estimated that if past trends continue, in 1985 between 17 and 20 percent of the Soviet gross national product will be diverted to the Soviet Armed Forces. Allocation of resources on this scale has already built up these forces to a strength greatly in excess of what conceivably might be needed for defensive purposes. A justification for these forces, as stated by Party-military spokesmen, is to prevent the "imperialists" from unleashing a world nuclear war. Since a local war might develop into world nuclear war, the Soviet Armed Forces also must be maintained on a scale sufficient to prevent "local" wars from taking place. This helps to provide an ideological justification for the projection of military power.

Concentration on armaments at the expense of improving living standards for the people may create an unstable situation within the Soviet social structure, which essentially is a feudal-like society. As did the feudal chieftains of old, the Party demands that the people labor on its behalf, and in return it provides a minimum of food, clothing, shelter, and, at times, entertainment. It is the Party's responsibility to protect the nation from foreign enemies, which is the rationale for continuing the dictatorship. Because of the military burden, as well as the general failure of the Soviet economic system, the difference in living standards between the Soviet people and the peoples of both Eastern and Western Europe continues to widen. As the Soviet people become aware of this gap, the Party leaders may feel compelled to embark on military conquests to prove the need for maintaining such massive military forces.

Another dangerous situation in the Soviet Union is the militarization of the young, which begins at a very early age. The preschool child is exposed to military indoctrination through picture books. The Soviet system seeks to exploit the fact that what a child is taught during its formative years inevitably will have a lasting impact upon beliefs carried over into adulthood. It is important to note that the military indoctrination of the preschool child did not begin until the mid-1960s, after the ouster of Nikita Khrushchev. Military-sport games, paramilitary organizations for social contact, and continual glorification of war in printed matter and on radio and television should make for a military-minded nation. From childhood through the teens, Soviet youths receive recognition and rewards for participation in paramilitary activities.

The continuation of universal military service in the Soviet Union should be of major interest to the United States and to other NATO nations. In the United States the cost of an all-volunteer military force continues to increase, forcing a cutback in military manpower. Neither the U.S. veterans of the Southeast Asian war nor those leaving the volunteer forces are being given refresher military training. Total reserve forces in the United States, including the National Guard, are less than 1 million. Should a major war occur, requiring millions of men, months would be needed for the United States to mobilize and train such a force. In contrast, the Soviet military service discharges between 1.5 and 1.8 million men into the reserves each year, giving that nation a capability to mobilize millions of men with recent military service in only a few days. The Soviet system of reserve training, while probably deficient in many respects, does help ensure that many of those mobilized in an emergency would be prepared immediately to perform combat duties.

It sometimes is argued that two years, the period of required service in most of the Soviet Armed Forces, is insufficient time to train a soldier to handle complex military equipment. But it should be remembered that the inductee has already had preparatory training in which basic knowledge of the Armed Forces and the basic weapons is provided. Moreover, much of the complex equipment is handled by well-trained junior officers, who have spent four to five years in a specialized military school, and by the career warrant officers whose rank was created in 1971 to induce technically qualified personnel to remain in military service. Inductees working under these men must inevitably be well guided.

Opportunities in recent years—in Southeast Asia, the Middle East, and Afghanistan—to observe modern Soviet weapons in action and to examine some that have been captured reveal that, complex though they are, they generally are less sophisticated and easier to operate than similar ones used by the United States. North Vietnamese crews quickly mastered the SA-2, the primary surface-to-air missile provided by the Soviets. And Egyptian soldiers did well with the Soviet equipment they had in 1973. It is unlikely that in either case there was time for more instruction than the Soviets' own men could be expected to have.

The effectiveness of a military force largely is dependent upon its officer corps. During the Finnish War in 1940 and in the first twelve to eighteen months of Soviet fighting in World War II, Soviet officers generally were inferior to those of their opponents. Although Soviet historians since the late 1960s have been engaged in rewriting World War II history to cover up the mistakes of the Soviet leadership in that war, enough was revealed during Khrushchev's de-Stalinization period to show many of the shortcomings. By the end of the war those Soviet officers in senior command positions had been tested by years of combat experience and generally were very capable.

Officer procurement, training, and education in the Soviet Union are much different from that found in the United States. The approximately 140 military schools that offer four- or five-year courses to cadets provide training that is much more specialized than that given by their nearest counterparts in the United States at West Point, Annapolis, and Colorado Springs. This same specialization continues in the professional schooling given to officers. With the exception of the General Staff Academy, and to a lesser extent the Frunze Military Academy, institutions for Soviet officer professional training focus on single components of the military service.

How would Soviet officers perform in a major war? Can the extreme specialization of Soviet military schools produce officers capable of operating capably on today's complex battlefield? Can multimillion-men armies be effectively controlled by a relatively small group of highly qualified senior officers in the General Staff, if the remainder of the officer corps are primarily specialists?

Soviet spokesmen continually express the need for officers to develop initiative, while at the same time initiative is discouraged and penalized by the system. In a carefully preplanned attack against an opponent, Soviet officers probably would perform satisfactorily. They also could be expected to fight effectively, and with all possible means, against any force invading Soviet territory. But outside the Soviet Union, in a fluid situation with communications to higher headquarters disrupted, most Soviet officers probably would be at a loss. Whether the years of one-sided Soviet fighting in Afghanistan have improved the combat performance of Soviet officers cannot be determined.

A Matter of Perception

The Soviet Party-military leadership has structured its military forces to accomplish four strategic tasks: the strategic nuclear offense, warfare in land theaters, strategic defense, and operations in naval theaters. These

tasks are outlined in Soviet military writings and demonstrated in the
organization and buildup of the Armed Forces.

First priority has been given to the development of forces for strategic
nuclear offense and strategic defense. The doctrinal decision was made
in the 1950s that the nuclear-rocket weapon would be decisive in any
future war, and priorities for weapon systems were allocated accordingly.
At the time of the Cuban missile crisis in 1962, Europe and the Middle
East were targeted by Soviet medium-range missiles. A rapid deployment
of ballistic missiles targeted on other areas followed in the 1960s and
was later supplemented by the world's largest nuclear submarine force
and by long-range aviation.

Concurrent with the attention given to the strategic nuclear offense,
an accelerated buildup of strategic defense forces began. Billions of
rubles went into surface-to-air missile systems for defense against manned
aircraft. Huge resources were invested in antiballistic missile systems,
which became obsolete when the United States deployed missiles with
multiple independent reentry warheads. This setback was met in part
by attempts to develop a first-strike capability and by participation in
international negotiations on arms control, which sought to delay the
United States from deploying its own antiballistic missile system. It is
prudent to assume that the Soviet Union has a massive effort under
way, utilizing both land-based and space-based weapons, in hopes of
solving its strategic defense problem.

Civil defense in the Soviet Union is considered an important component
of strategic defense. When the Soviet antiballistic missile system was
negated by MIRV warheads, civil defense received renewed attention.
Under the overall direction of the Ministry of Defense, this program
now has been assigned tens of thousands of individuals, both military
and civilian. Although dozens of Soviet general officers have been identified
with civil defense programs and details of training are published in
newspapers, journals, and books, the Soviet civil defense program for
some reason is regarded with skepticism by many Washington policy-
makers. Many of those who work closely with the strategic nuclear forces
in the United States feel that any civil defense effort on the part of the
Soviet leadership is a waste of time, since no protection is possible from
an all-out nuclear attack. At the other extreme, some discount published
data and assert that the Soviets have accepted the concept of mutually
assured destruction and hence would not attempt a civil defense program.

Whether or not Soviet civil defense would be effective in an all-out
strike launched by the United States is a matter of opinion. On the
other hand, any civil defense effort probably would be worthwhile in
the event of selected nuclear strikes, by, for example, less than 100
warheads. Additionally, the Soviet Union is faced with the possibility

of nuclear attack not only from the United States, but also from Great Britain, France, or China. Against a secondary nuclear power, the Soviet civil defense program might be sufficient to prevent lasting damage to the nation. In view of the growing proliferation of nuclear weapons, it would appear that a civil defense program is necessary for any nation.

After the Soviet strategic nuclear offense and strategic defense programs had gotten under way, the second strategic task, theater warfare, received attention. The buildup of theater forces became apparent in the late 1960s, with the deployment of additional Soviet divisions along the Sino-Soviet border. Once these forces had reached a predetermined level, a Soviet buildup in Eastern Europe followed. These forces include both ground and air armies, equipped with conventional and nuclear weapons.

It is difficult for NATO leaders, including those in the United States, to face up to the reality of these Soviet forces. When the United States enjoyed unquestioned strategic nuclear superiority, an attack by Soviet forces against Western Europe might have evoked strategic nuclear action by the United States. But against the superiority of the Soviet Union in numbers of missiles and warhead yield, the United States strategic nuclear deterrent becomes less credible.

Once the strategic nuclear forces of the United States were countered, and superiority in theater forces was achieved in Europe and along the Sino-Soviet border, the Soviet Union was in a position to develop forces capable of projecting military power. Doctrinal justification for this move was explained by Marshal Grechko in 1974, and subsequent Soviet moves have testified to the beginning of its implementation. The most likely direction for Soviet moves in power projection will continue to be the Middle East and Africa, primarily for the purpose of controlling oil output and deliveries.

It should not be forgotten that Soviet ballistic missiles and space spectaculars in the late 1950s astounded and frightened the West. The West may again be in for surprises by Soviet moves in space, including the use of antiballistic missile and antisatellite weapons or manned military space platforms.

This analysis of Soviet military doctrine and strategy, combined with an examination of Soviet military forces and military manpower, results in one conclusive fact. The Soviet Party-military leadership seeks overwhelming military strength for the accomplishments of four strategic tasks—strategic nuclear attack, theater warfare, strategic defense, and naval operations. How, when, and where this strength might be used will depend upon the vulnerabilities the Soviet leadership perceives both in the "imperialist" world and in China.

Notes

1. Henry A. Kissinger, *Nuclear Weapons and Foreign Policy* (New York: Harper & Row, 1957), p. 403.

2. N. V. Ogarkov, *Vsegda v Gotovnosti k Zashchite Otechestva* [Always in Readiness to Defend the Fatherland] (Moscow: Voyenizdat, 1982), p. 53.

3. See Harriet Fast Scott and William F. Scott, *The Soviet Control Structure: Capabilities for Wartime Survival* (New York: Crane, Russak & Co., National Strategy Information Center, 1983).

Appendixes

APPENDIX A
WOMEN IN THE SOVIET ARMED FORCES

Some 800,000 Soviet women served in the Soviet Armed Forces during World War II. Eighty-six of them were awarded the highest decoration of the Soviet government—Hero of the Soviet Union. The women served as snipers, pilots, communications specialists, machine gunners, tank drivers, on air crews, and in the medical service.

Valentina Tereshkova was the first woman to make a space flight (June 1963). Svetlana Savitskaya, daughter of a Soviet marshal of aviation and a test pilot of military aircraft with eight world records, became the second woman in space (August 1982). Sally Ride was the first U.S. woman to make a space flight (in 1983).

The first law related to women in the Armed Forces was enacted in 1925. The present law, adopted in 1967, establishes the role of women in service today. Women nineteen to forty years old who have medical or other special training may be put on the military rolls in peacetime and called up for practice assemblies. They may also volunteer for active duty. In wartime, they might be called into the Armed Forces to carry out auxiliary and special duties.

Women who volunteer as soldiers, sailors, sergeants, or petty officers must be between nineteen and thirty, have at least an eighth-grade education, and be unmarried and without children. They may volunteer for two, four, or six years and continue to serve until age fifty. The Ministry of Defense establishes the positions to be filled by women. They have the same rights as extended-duty servicemen and may wear civilian clothing off duty. When released into the Reserves, women go into the second category (enlisted personnel) until they are forty years old.

Women also serve as officers, although very little mention of them can be found in the press. Many women are teachers at higher military schools and military academies, especially in departments of foreign languages and mathematics. Women officers who are put on the military rolls serve in officer reserves of the third order until age fifty. They may be called up for a two-month practice assembly one time and, as with all reservists, for ten-day inspection assemblies.

The exact number of women in the Soviet Armed Forces is not known. Some sources suggest a minimum of 10,000. Along with all boys, girls in ninth grade take beginning military training, with an emphasis on first aid work. Women also are very active in DOSAAF, the paramilitary sports society. Sponsored by this organization, Valentina Zakoretskaya set a world record when she made her 6,000th parachute jump.

Whatever might be the number of Soviet women in the Armed Forces at the present time, in time of need there are few military jobs Soviet women could not fill.

APPENDIX B
SOVIET MILITARY RANKS

TABLE B1
Comparative Military Ranks—U.S. and USSR

United States		Soviet Union	
(none)	Admiral of the Fleet	Generalissimus of the Soviet Union[a]	
General of the Army		Marshal of the Soviet Union	Admiral of the Fleet of the Soviet Union
(none)		Chief Marshal of Aviation, Armored Forces, Artillery	
General	Admiral	General of the Army, Marshal of Aviation, Marshal of Armored Forces, Artillery, Engineers, Signals, etc.	Admiral of the Fleet
Lieutenant General	Vice Admiral	General Colonel, General Colonel Aviation, General Colonel Armored Forces,[b] Engineers, Justice, General Colonel Engineer, etc.	Admiral, Admiral-Engineer[b]
Major General	Rear Admiral (Upper Half)	General Lieutenant, General Lieutenant Aviation, Armored Forces, Artillery, Engineers, General Lieutenant-Engineer, etc.	Vice Admiral Vice Admiral-Engineer

Brigadier General	Rear Admiral (Lower Half)	General Major, General Major Aviation, General Major Armored Forces, Artillery, Engineers, Signals, Supply, Technical Troops, General Major–Engineer, etc.	Rear Admiral Rear Admiral-Engineer
Colonel	Captain	Colonel (Polkovnik)	Captain 1st Rank
Lieutenant Colonel	Commander	Lieutenant Colonel (Podpolkovnik)	Captain 2d Rank
Major	Lieutenant Commander	Major	Captain 3d Rank
Captain	Lieutenant	Captain	Captain-Lieutenant
1st Lieutenant	Lieutenant (Jr. Grade)	Senior Lieutenant	Senior Lieutenant
2d Lieutenant	Ensign	Lieutenant	Lieutenant
(none)	(none)	Junior Lieutenant	Junior Lieutenant

Source: Compiled by Harriet Fast Scott. Originally published in *Air Force Magazine.*

[a] Stalin is the only man who has held this rank. Awarded June 1945.

[b] *Krasnaya Zvezda* (June 12, 1984) carried the following announcement: "For the purposes of further improvement of the systems of military ranks, the Presidium of the Supreme Soviet, USSR, has introduced a number of changes into the military ranks of officers. The word engineer will be omitted from military ranks and also words indicating that the serviceman belongs to different support services (*sluzhba*)—with the exception of officers with the military rank of medical service and justice. Words indicating belonging to a service branch, will be used only for the following military ranks: marshal of artillery, marshal of engineer troops, marshal of signal troops, chief marshal of artillery, and also the military ranks of those individuals who earlier were given the military rank of marshal of armored forces."

TABLE B2
Rank and Corresponding Position for Nonflying Personnel[a]

Rank	Position
Junior Lieutenant	Platoon commander
Lieutenant	
Senior Lieutenant	
Senior Lieutenant	Deputy company or battery commander
Captain	Company or battery commander
Major	Deputy battalion commander
Lieutenant Colonel	Battalion commander; deputy regimental commander; chief of regimental staff
Colonel	Regimental commander; deputy division commander; chief of division staff
General Major	Division commander, deputy corps commander; chief of corps staff
General Lieutenant	Corps commander; chief of army staff; chief of political department of army
General Colonel	Army commander
General Colonel	Commanding officer of a military district
General of the Army	
Marshal of the Soviet Union	

Source: Compiled by Harriet Fast Scott. Originally published in *Air Force Magazine.*

[a]Does not apply to Navy personnel.

TABLE B3

Rank and Corresponding Position for Flying Personnel[a]

	Flying Personnel (except long-range)	Long-Range Aviation (depending on type of aircraft)
Lieutenant or Senior Lieutenant	Pilot	
Senior Lieutenant	Senior pilot	Senior Lieutenant or Captain — Pilot
Captain	Flight commander	Captain or Major — Aircraft commander
Major	Squadron commander	
Lieutenant Colonel	Deputy commander or chief of staff of an air regiment	Major or Lieutenant Colonel — Commander of a detachment; deputy squadron commander

TABLE B3 (continued)

Flying Personnel (except long-range)		Long-Range Aviation (depending on type of aircraft)	
Colonel	Commander of an air regiment; deputy commander or chief of staff of an air division	Lieutenant Colonel or Colonel	Squadron commander; deputy commander of an air regiment
Colonel or General Major of Aviation	Commander of an air division; deputy commander of an air corps	Colonel or General Major of Aviation	Commander of an air regiment
General Lieutenant of Aviation	Commander of an air corps; commander of military district aviation	General Major of Aviation or General Lieutenant of Aviation	Commander of an air division
General Colonel of Aviation	Commander of an air army; commander of fleet aviation		

Source: Compiled by Harriet Fast Scott. Originally published in *Air Force Magazine.*

[a] Applies to flying personnel in Air Forces, Troops of Air Defense, and Navy.

TABLE B4
Tour Length in Posts[a]

Nonflying Personnel		Flying Personnel	
Platoon commander	3 years	Pilot and Senior Pilot	3 years
		Flight commander	3 years
Deputy company or battery commander	3 years	Deputy squadron commander	2 years
Company or battery commander	4 years	Squadron commander	4 years
Deputy battalion commander	3 years		
Battalion commander	4 years		
Deputy regimental commander; chief of regimental staff	3 years	Deputy air regiment commander	2 years
Regimental commander	5 years	Air regiment commander	5 years

Source: Compiled by Harriet Fast Scott. Originally published in *Air Force Magazine.*

[a]Applies to Strategic Rocket Forces, Ground Forces, Troops of Air Defense, Air Forces, and flying component of Navy.

TABLE B5
Time in Grade

Rank	Nonflying Personnel	Flying Personnel
Junior Lieutenant	2 years	1 year
Lieutenant[a]	3 years[a]	2 years
Senior Lieutenant	3 years	2 years
Captain	4 years	3 years
Major	4 years	3 years
Lieutenant Colonel	5 years	4 years
Colonel	no set time	no set time

Source: Compiled by Harriet Fast Scott. Originally published in *Air Force Magazine.*

[a]Those who graduate from four-year military schools start as lieutenants and serve only two years in this grade. Graduates of five-year military schools serve only one year in grade.

APPENDIX C
MILITARY OFFICERS ELECTED TO THE
SUPREME SOVIET USSR ON 4 MARCH 1984

Ministry of Defense

Ustinov, D. F.	Minister of Defense
Ogarkov, N. V.	1st Deputy Minister of Defense, Chief of the General Staff
Kulikov, V. G.	1st Deputy Minister of Defense, CinC Warsaw Pact Forces
Sokolov, S. L.	1st Deputy Minister of Defense
Yepishev, A. A.	Chief, Main Political Administration
Tolubko, V. F.	Deputy Minister of Defense, CinC Strategic Rocket Forces
Petrov, V. I.	Deputy Minister of Defense, CinC Ground Forces
Koldunov, A. I.	Deputy Minister of Defense, CinC Troops of Air Defense
Kutakhov, P. S.	Deputy Minister of Defense, CinC Air Forces
Gorshkov, S. G.	Deputy Minister of Defense, CinC Navy
Moskalenko, K. S.	Deputy Minister of Defense, Inspector General
Kurkotkin, S. K.	Deputy Minister of Defense, Chief of Rear Services
Altinin, A. T.	Deputy Minister of Defense, Chief of Civil Defense USSR
Shabanov, V. M.	Deputy Minister of Defense for Armaments
Shestopalov, N. F.	Deputy Minister of Defense for Construction and Billeting Troops
Shkadov, I. N.	Deputy Minister of Defense for Cadres

Military Districts

Betekhtin, A. V.	Commander Baltic Military District
Ivanovskiy, Ye. F.	Commander Belorussian Military District

Belikov, V. A.	Commander Carpathian Military District
Yazov, D. T.	Commander Central Asian Military District
Tret'yak, I. M.	Commander Far Eastern Military District
Gerasimov, I. A.	Commander Kiev Military District
Snetkov, B. V.	Commander Leningrad Military District
Lushev, P. G.	Commander Moscow Military District
Meretskov, V. K.	Commander North Caucasus Military District
Yelagin, A. S.	Commander Odessa Military District
Popov, N. I.	Commander Siberian Military District
Postnikov, S. I.	Commander Transbaykal Military District
Arkhipov, V. M.	Commander Transcaucasus Military District
Maksimov, Yu. P.	Commander Turkestan Military District
Gashkov, I. A.	Commander Ural Military District
Ryakhov, A. Ya.	Commander Volga Military District

High Command
Govorov, V. L.	Commander in Chief Troops of the Far East

Groups Abroad
Zaytsev, M. M.	Commander in Chief Soviet Forces Germany
Zarudin, Yu. F.	Commander Northern Group of Forces
Borisov, G. G.	Commander Central Group of Forces
Kochetkov, K. A.	Commander Southern Group of Forces

Fleets
Kapitanets, I. M.	Commander Baltic Fleet
Kalinin, A. M.	Commander Black Sea Fleet

Mikhaylovskiy, A. P.   Commander Northern Fleet

Sidorov, V. V.   Commander Pacific Fleet

Air Defense District

Konstantinov, A. U.   Commander Moscow Air Defense District

Other

Akhromeyev, S. F.   1st Deputy Chief of the General Staff

Gribkov, A. I.   1st Deputy Chief of the General Staff, Chief of Staff Warsaw Pact

Yashin, Yu. A.   1st Deputy CinC Strategic Rocket Forces

Mayorov, A. M.   1st Deputy CinC Ground Forces

Yefimov, A. N.   1st Deputy CinC Air Forces

Smirnov, N. I.   1st Deputy CinC Navy

Chernavin, V. N.   1st Deputy CinC Navy, Chief of the Main Naval Staff

Political

Sorokin, A. I.   1st Deputy Chief of Main Political Administration

Gorchakov, P. A.   Chief Political Administration of Strategic Rocket Forces

Popkov, M. D.   Chief Political Administration of Ground Forces

Lizichev, A. D.   Chief Political Administration Soviet Forces Germany

Miscellaneous

Yegorov, G. M.   Chairman of DOSAAF

Ivashutin, P. I.   Deputy Chief of General Staff; head of GRU

Popov, L. I.   Cosmonaut

Selected Bibliography

This study of the Soviet Armed Forces is based essentially on material obtained from Soviet newspapers, journals, and books. The agencies responsible for the publication of the newspapers and journals are listed after the titles.

Newspapers

Izvestia. Council of Ministers.
Krasnaya Zvezda (Red Star). Ministry of Defense.
Pravda. Central Committee of the CPSU.
Sovietskiy Patriot (Soviet Patriot). DOSAAF

Journals

Aviatsiya i Kosmonavtika (Aviation and Cosmonautics). Soviet Air Forces.
Kommunist Vooruzhennykh Sil (Communist of the Armed Forces). Main Political Administration of the Soviet Army and Navy.
Mirovaya Ekonomika i Mezhdunarodnoye Otnosheniya (World Economy and International Relations). Institute of World Economy and International Relations, Academy of Sciences.
Morskoi Sbornik (Naval Collections). Soviet Navy.
Sovietskiy Voin (Soviet Soldier). Main Political Administration of the Soviet Army and Navy.
SSHA (USA). Institute of the USA and Canada, Academy of Sciences.
Teknika i Vooruzheniye (Equipment and Armaments). Ministry of Defense.
Tyl i Snabzheniye Sovietskikh Vooruzhennykh Sil (The Rear and Supply of the Soviet Armed Forces). Ministry of Defense.
Vestnik Protivovozdushnoi Oborony (Herald of the PVO). Troops of PVO.
Voyennaya Mysl' (Military Thought). General Staff, Ministry of Defense.
Voyenniy Vestnik (Military Herald). Ground Forces (combined arms).
Voyenno-Istoricheskii Zhurnal (Military History Journal). Ministry of Defense.
Voyennye Znaniye (Military Knowledge). DOSAAF and Civil Defense.
Znamenosets (Banner Carrier). Ministry of Defense.

Books

Aboltin, V. Ya. *Sovremennyye Problemy Razoruzheniya*. Moscow: Mysl' Publishing House, 1970.

Accoce, Pierre, and Pierre Quet. *A Man Called Lucy: 1939–1945*. New York: Coward, McCann, & Geoghegan, 1967.

Altunin, A. T., ed. *Grazhdanskaya Oborona*. Moscow: Voyenizdat, 1980.

Arbatov, G. A., ed. *Global'naya Strategiya SSHA v Usloviyakh Nauchno-Tekhnicheskoy Revolyutsii*. Moscow: Mysl', 1979.

Astashenkov, P. T. *Sovetskiye Raketnyye Voyska*. Moscow: Voyenizdat, 1967.

Averin, A. I., Yu. P. Subbotin, and N. A. Yasinskiy. *Nachal'naya Voyennaya Podgotovka v Obshcheobrazovatel'noy Shkole*. Moscow: Enlightenment Publishing House, 1973.

Azovtsev, N. N. *V. I. Lenin i Sovetskaya Voyennaya Nauka*, 2d ed. Moscow: Nauka Publishing House, 1982.

Babadzhanyan, A. Kh. *Tanki i Tankovyye Voyska*, 2d ed. Moscow: Voyenizdat, 1980.

Babakov, A. A., ed. *Spravochnik Propagandista i Agitatora Armii i Flota*. Moscow: Voyenizdat, 1973.

Bagramyan, I. Kh., ed. *Istoriya Voyn i Voyennovo Iskusstva*. Moscow: Voyenizdat, 1970.

———. *Tak Nachinalas' Voyna*. Moscow: Voyenizdat, 1971.

Baruzadin, S. *Shel Po Ulitse Soldat*. Moscow: Children's Literature Publishing House, 1970.

Batitskiy, P. F. *Voyska Protivovozdushnoy Oborony Strany*. Moscow: Znaniye, 1968.

———. *Voyska Protivovozdushnoy Oborony Strany,* 2d ed. Moscow: Znaniye, 1977.

Baz', I. S., et al. *O Sovetskoy Voyennoy Nauke*. Moscow: Voyenizdat, 1964.

Belikov, M. A., et al. *Uchebnoye Posobiye Po Nachal'noy Voyennoy Podgotovke*. Moscow: Voyenizdat, 1975.

Belikov, I. G., et al. *Imeni Dzerzhinskogo*. Moscow: Voyenizdat, 1976.

Belousov, N. A. *Pedagogicheskiye Osnovy Podgotovki Molodeshi k Voyennoy Slushbe*. Moscow: DOSAAF, 1979.

Berkhin, I. B. *Voyennaya Reforma v SSSR—1924–1925*. Moscow: Voyenizdat, 1958.

Bolgari, P. *Chernomorskiy Flot: Istoricheskiy Ocherk*. Moscow: Voyenizdat, 1967.

Bol'shaya Sovetskaya Entsiklopediya, 3d ed. Moscow: Soviet Encyclopedia Publishing House, 1970–1979, in thirty volumes.

Breshkarev, N. A. *V Pomoshch Doprizyvniku*. Moscow: Voyenizdat, 1967.

Bublik, L. A. *Partiyno-Politicheskaya Rabota v Sovetskoy Armii i Voyenno-Morskom Flote*. Moscow: Voyenizdat, 1982.

Buchenkov, P. A. *Suvorovskoye Voyennoye*. Moscow: Voyenizdat, 1981.

Bush, Vannevar. *Modern Arms and Free Men*. New York: Simon & Schuster, 1949.

Buyskikh, B. N., ed. *Istoriya Krasnoznamennovo Kievskovo Voyennovo Okruga: 1919–1972*. Moscow: Voyenizdat, 1974.

Cherednichenko, N. V., and Malinin, V. I. *Sovetskiye Sukhoputnyye*. Moscow: Voyenizdat, 1981.

Chernenko, K. U., and N. I. Savinkin. *KPSS o Vooruzhennykh Silakh Sovetskovo Soyuza*. Moscow: Voyenizdat, 1969.

Chirkin, P., ed. *Granitsa Na Zamke*. Moscow: Young Guards Publishing House, 1969.

Chislennost' Razmeshcheniye, Vozrastnaya Struktura, Uroven' Obrazovaniya, Natsional'nyy Sostav, Yazyki i Istochniki Sredstv Sushchestvovaniya Naseleniya SSSR. Moscow: Statistics, 1971.

Chuykov, V. I. *Grazhdanskaya Oborona v Raketno-Yadernoy Voyne*. Moscow: Atomizdat, 1969.

Clausewitz, Carl von. *On War*, edited and translated by Michael Howard and Peter Paret. Princeton, N.J.: Princeton University Press, 1976.

Conquest, Robert. *The Great Terror*. New York: Macmillan, 1968.

Constitution (Fundamental Law) of the Union of Soviet Socialist Republics. Moscow: Novosti Press Agency, 1977.

Dallin, David J. *From Purge to Coexistence*. Chicago: Henry Regnery, 1964.

———. *Soviet Foreign Policy After Stalin*. Philadelphia: L. B. Lippincott, 1961.

Davies, Joseph E. *Mission to Moscow*. New York: Simon & Schuster, 1941.

Deputaty Verkhovnovo Soveta SSSR. Moscow: Political Literature Publishing House, 1966, 1970, 1974.

Derevyanko, P. M., ed. *Problemy Revolyutsii v Voyennom Dele*. Moscow: Voyenizdat, 1965.

Deriabin, Peter. *Watchdogs of Terror*. New Rochelle, N.Y.: Arlington House, 1972.

Deryugin, Yu. I. *Armiya i Komsomol*. Moscow: Molodaya Gvardiya, 1983.

Dinerstein, H. S. *War and the Soviet Union*. New York: Praeger Publishers, 1962.

Douglass, Joseph D., Jr., and Amoretta M. Hoeber. *Selected Readings from Military Thought 1963–1973*, Vol. 5. Washington, D.C.: Government Printing Office, 1982. In two parts.

Dragunskiy, D. A., ed. *Polevaya Akademiya*. Moscow: Voyenizdat, 1982.

Druzhinin, V. V., et al. *Ideya, Algoritm, Resheniye*. Moscow: Voyenizdat, 1972.

Duginets, A. *Dvenadtsatiletniy General*. Moscow: Little Child's Publishing House, 1970.

Dushen'kin, V. *Ot Soldata Do Marshala*. Moscow: Politizdat, 1966.

XXVI S"yezd Kommunisticheskoy Partii Sovetskogo Soyuza: Stenograficheskiy Otchet. Moscow: Politizdat, 1981.

Dvazhdy Krasnoznamennyy Baltiyskiy Flot. Moscow: Voyenizdat, 1978.

Erickson, John. *The Soviet High Command*. London: St. Martin's Press, 1962.

Fainsod, Merle. *How Russia Is Ruled*. Cambridge, Mass.: Harvard University Press, 1967.

Fedorov, A. F. *Aviatsiya v Bitve pod Moskvoy*. Moscow: Voyenizdat, 1971.

Fedorov, G. A. *Marksizm-Leninism o Voyne i Armii*. Moscow: Voyenizdat, 1962.

Florinsky, Michael T., ed. *Encyclopedia of Russia and the Soviet Union*. New York: McGraw-Hill Book Co., 1961.

Frunze, M. V. *Selected Works*. Moscow: Voyenizdat, 1965.

Gaponenko, V. K. *Granitsa Rozhdayet Geroyev*. Moscow: DOSAAF Publishing House, 1976.

Gareyev, M. A. *Takticheskiye Ucheniya i Manevry*. Moscow: Voyenizdat, 1977.

Garthoff, Raymond L. *Soviet Militry Doctrine*. Glencoe, Ill.: Free Press, 1953.

_____ . *Soviet Military Policy*. New York: Praeger Publishers, 1966.

Gavrinkov, F. K. *Obshchevoinskiye Ustavy*. Moscow: DOSAAF Publishing House, 1969.

Glubinnyy Dozor. Moscow: Molodaya Gvardiya, 1978.

Gol'tsev, V. *Bol'shiye Manevry*. Moscow: DOSAAF Publishing House, 1974.

Golushko, I. M., and N. V. Barlamov. *Osnovy Modelirovaniya i Avtomatizatsii Upravleniya Tylom*. Moscow: Voyenizdat, 1982.

Golyanov, V. P. *Rayonny, Gorodskov Sovyet i Voyenno-Patrioticheskoye Vospitaniye Naseleniya*. Moscow: Legal Literature Publishing House, 1975.

Gornyy, A. G. *Osnovy Pravovykh Znaniy*. Moscow: Voyenizdat, 1973.

_____ . *Osnovy Sovetskovo Voyennovo Zakonodatel'stva*. Moscow: Voyenizdat, 1966.

_____ . *Spravochnik Po Zakonodatel'stvu Dlya Ofitserov Sovetskoy Armii i Flota*. Moscow: Voyenizdat, 1970.

Gorshkov, S. G. *Morskaya Moshch Gosudarstva*. Moscow: Voyenizdat, 1976 (2d ed., 1979).

Grechanyuk, N., ed. *Baltiyskiy Flot*. Moscow: Voyenizdat, 1976.

Grechko, A. A., ed. *Istoriya Vtoroy Mirovoy Voyny, 1939–1945*. Moscow: Voyenizdat, 1973.

_____ . *Na Strazhe Mira i Stroitel'stva Kommunizma*. Moscow: Voyenizdat, 1971.

_____ . *Vooruzhennyye Sily Sovetskovo Gosudarstva*. Moscow: Voyenizdat, 1st ed., 1974; 2d ed., 1975. *The Armed Forces of the Soviet State*, edited translation published under the auspices of the United States Air Force (Washington, D.C.: Government Printing Office, 1976).

_____ . *Yadernyy Vek i Voyna*. Moscow: Izvestia Publishing House, 1965.

Grekov, V. A., and A. T. Kuz'min, eds. *Manevry "Dvina."* Minsk: Beiarus Publishing House, 1970.

Gribkov, A. I., ed. *Istoriya Ordena Lenina Leningradskovo Voyennovo Okruga*. Moscow: Voyenizdat, 1974.

Grigorenko, P. G. *The Grigorenko Papers*. Boulder, Colo.: Westview Press, 1976.

_____ . *Memoirs*. New York and London: W. W. Norton & Co., 1982.

Grishanov, V. M., ed. *Voyna, Okean, Chelovek*. Moscow: Voyenizdat, 1980.

Grushevoy, K. S. *Dorogoy Podviga Narodnoye: Manevry "Dvina."* Moscow: Publishing House of the Political Directorate of the Moscow Military District, 1970.

Gusak, P. A., and A. M. Rogachev. *Nachal'naya Voyennaya Podgotovka*. Moscow: Prosveshcheniye, 1981.

Il'in, S. K. *Moral'nyy Faktor v Sovremennykh Voynakh*. Moscow: Voyenizdat, 1980.

_____ . *Problemy Voinskogo Vospitaniya*. Moscow: Voyenizdat, 1979.

Inozemtsev, I. G. *Pod Krylom—Leningrad*. Moscow: Voyenizdat, 1978.

Iovlev, A. M. *Deyatel'nost' KPSS po Podgotovke Voyennykh Kadrov*. Moscow: Voyenizdat, 1976.

Istoriya Ordena Lenina Leningradskogo Voyennogo Okruga. Moscow: Voyenizdat, 1974.

Istoriya Ural'skogo Voyennogo Okruga. Moscow: Voyenizdat, 1970.

Ivanovskiy, Ye. F., ed. *Na Boyevom Postu: Kniga of Voinakh Gruppy Sovetskikh Voysk v Germanii*. Moscow: Voyenizdat, 1975.

———, ed. *Ordena Lenina Moskovskiy Voyennyy Okrug*. Moscow: Voyenizdat, 1971.

Joint Economic Committee of the Congress of the United States. *Economic Performance and the Military Burden of the Soviet Union*. Washington, D.C.: Government Printing Office, 1970.

Kadishev, A. B. *Voprosy Strategii i Operativnovo Iskusstva v Sovetskikh Voyennykh Trudakh, 1917–1940*. Moscow: Voyenizdat, 1965.

Kalinin, G. S., and G. V. Shevkov. *Istoriya Gosudarstva i Prava SSSR*. Moscow: Juridical Literature, 1981.

Kamalov, Kh. Kh. *Morskaya Pekhota v Boyakh za Rodinu*. Moscow: Voyenizdat, 1983.

Kamkov, I. A., and V. M. Konoplyanik. *Voyennyye Akademii i Uchilishcha*. Moscow: Voyenizdat, 1972.

Karamyshev, V. A. *Vmeste s Narodom k Velikoy Tseli*. Moscow: Voyenizdat, 1965.

Katyshkin, I. S., ed. *Krasnoznamennyy Zakavkazskiy: Ocherko Istorii Krasnoznamennovo Zakavkazskovo Voyennovo Okruga*. Moscow: Voyenizdat, 1969.

Kazakov, K. P., ed. *Artilleriya i Rakety*. Moscow: Voyenizdat, 1968.

Keller, Werner. *Are the Russians Ten Feet Tall?* London: Thames and Hudson, 1961.

Khanchin, V. S., Yu. Ye. Rives, and V. I. Nikolayev. *Tovarishch*. Moscow: Molodaya Gvardiya, 1976.

Khmel, A. Y. *Education of the Soviet Soldier: Party-Political Work in the Soviet Armed Forces*. Moscow: Progress Publishers, 1972.

Khrushchev, N. S. *On Peaceful Coexistence*. Moscow: Foreign Languages Publishing House, 1961.

Khvoshchev, S. V., ed. *Ukhodili Na Front Eshelony*. Moscow: Voyenizdat, 1974.

Kintner, W. R., and Harriet Fast Scott. *The Nuclear Revolution in Soviet Military Affairs*. Norman, Okla.: University of Oklahoma Press, 1968.

Kir'yan, M. M. *Voyenno-Tekhnicheskiy Progress i Vooruzhennyye Sily SSSR*. Moscow: Voyenizdat, 1982.

Kissinger, Henry A. *Nuclear Weapons and Foreign Policy*. New York: Harper & Row, 1957.

Kiyevskiy Krasnoznamennyy. Kiev: Political Administration KVO, 1969.

Kiyevskiy Krasnoznamennyy, 2d ed. Moscow: Voyenizdat, 1974.

Klemin, A. S., ed. *Eshelon za Eshelonom*. Moscow: Voyenizdat, 1981.

Kobzarev, A. A., ed. *Sovetskaya Aviatsionnaya Tekhnika*. Moscow: Machine Building Publishing House, 1970.

Komarov, A. V. *Spravochnik Politrabotnika*. Moscow: Voyenizdat, 1973.

Komarovskiy, A. N. *Zapiski Stroitelya*. Moscow: Voyenizdat, 1972.

Konstantinov, A. U. *Ordena Lenina Moskovskiy Okrug PVO*. Moscow: Voyenizdat, 1981.

Korsunskiy, M. *Tovarishchi Moi, Voyennyye Stroiteli*. Moscow: DOSAAF, 1982.

Kosyrev, E. A., et al. *Tanki*. Moscow: DOSAAF Publishing House, 1973.

Kotlukov, K. G., ed. *Grazhdanskaya Oborona Vchera i Sevodnya*. Moscow: Atomizdat, 1975.

Kovalev, V. N. *Sotsialisticheskiy Voinskiy Kollektiv*. Moscow: Voyenizdat, 1980.

Kozlov, I. A., ed. *Krasnoznamennyy Severnyy Flot*. Moscow: Voyenizdat, 1977.

Kozlov, N. D., and A. D. Zaitsev. *Srazhayushchayasya Partiya*. Moscow: Voyenizdat, 1975.

Kozlov, S. N., et al., ed. *O Sovetskoy Voyennoy Nauke*. Moscow: Voyenizdat, 1964.

Krasnoznamennyy Baltiyskiy Flot v Bitve za Leningrad. Moscow: Voyenizdat, 1973.

Krasnoznamennyy Belorusskiy Voyennyy Okrug. Minsk: Belorus', 1973.

Krasnoznamennyy Chernomorskiy Flot. Moscow: Voyenizdat, 1979.

Krasnoznamennyy Dal'nevostochnyy. Khabarovsk: Khabarovsk Book Publishers, 1978.

Krasnoznamennyy Kiyevskiy, 2d ed. Kiev: Politdat Ukraine, 1979.

Krasnoznamennyy Prikarpatskiy. Moscow: Voyenizdat, 1982.

Krasnoznamennyy Severnyy [Photo album]. Moscow: Voyenizdat, 1981.

Krasnoznamennyy Tikookeanskiy Flot. Moscow: Voyenizdat, 1973, 1981.

Krasnoznamennyy Turkestanskiy. Moscow: Voyenizdat, 1976.

Krasnoznamennyy Zakavkazskiy Voyennyy Okrug. Moscow: Voyenizdat, 1969.

Kraynyukov, K. V., *Spravochnik Ofitsera*. Moscow: Voyenizdat, 1971.

_____ . *Partiyno-Politicheskaya Rabota v Sovetskikh Vooruzhennykh Silakh v Gody Velikoy Otechestvennoy Voyny*. Moscow: Voyenizdat, 1968.

Kril'ya Nad Okean. Moscow: Molodaya Gvardiya, 1982.

Kulikov, V. G., ed. *Akademiya General'novo Shtaba*. Moscow: Voyenizdat, 1976.

Kulikov, V. G. *Kollektivnaya Zashchita Sotsializma*. Moscow: Voyenizdat, 1982.

_____ . *Kievskiy Krasnoznamennyy: Kratkiy Ocherk Istorii Krasnoznamennovo Kievskovo Voyennova Okruga 1919–1969*. Kiev: Publication House of the Political Directorate of the Kiev Military District, 1969.

Kulish, V. M., ed. *Voyennaya Sila i Mezhdunarodnyye Otnosheniya*. Moscow: International Relations Publishing House, 1972.

_____ . *Vtoroi Front*. Moscow: Voyenizdat, 1960.

Kurakin, V. D. *Krasnoznamennyy Turkestanskiy*. Moscow: Voyenizdat, 1976.

Kurochkin, P. A., ed. *Osnovy Metodiki Voyenno-Nauchnogo Issledovaniya*. Moscow: Voyenizdat, 1969.

Kurkotkin, S. K., ed. *Tyl Sovetskikh Vooruzhennykh Sil v Velikoy Otechestvennoy Voyne 1941–1945 gg*. Moscow: Voyenizdat, 1977.

Lagovskiy, A. N. *V. I. Lenin ob Ekonomicheskom Obespechenii Oborony Strany*. Moscow: Voyenizdat, 1976.

_____ . *Strategiya i Ekonomika*. Moscow: Voyenizdat, 1961.

Latukhin, A. N. *Protivotankovoye Vooruzheniye*. Moscow: Voyenizdat, 1974.

Lee, W. T. "Soviet Defense Expenditures," in W. Schneider and F. P. Hoeber, eds., *Army, Man and Military Budgets, Issues for Fiscal Year 1977*. New York: Crane, Russak & Co., 1976.

_____ . "Soviet Defense Expenditures in the Twenty Five-Year Plans." *Osteurop Wirtschaft* (Summer 1977).

Lenin, V. I. *Collected Works*, 5th ed. Moscow: Progress Publishers, 1974.

Lepeshkin, A. I., ed. *Osnovy Sovetskovo Voyennovo Zakonodatel'stva*. Moscow: Voyenizdat, 1972.

Lisov, I. I. *Desantniki*. Moscow: Voyenizdat, 1968.

Lisov, I. I., and A. F. Korol'chenko. *Desantniki Atakuyut s Neba*. Moscow: Voyenizdat, 1980.

Lomov, N. A., ed. *Nauchno-Teknicheskiy Progress i Revolyutsiya v Voyennom Dele*. Moscow: Voyenizdat, 1973.

Lototskiy, S. S. *The Soviet Army*. Moscow: Progress Publishers, 1971.

Lowry, Philip H., and William F. Scott. *United States and Soviet Combat-to-Support Ratios*. McLean, Va.: General Research Corporation, July 1975.

Makovskiy, A. A., and B. M. Radchenko. *Kaspiyskaya Krasnoznamennaya*. Moscow: Voyenizdat, 1982.

Maksimov, S. S. *Osnovy Sovetskogo Voyennogo Zakonodatel'stva*. Moscow: Voyenizdat, 1978.

Mal'tsev, Ye. Ye. *Akademiya Imeni V. I. Lenina*. Moscow: Voyenizdat, 1980.

Malinovskiy, R. Ya. *Bditel'no Stoyat' Na Strazhe Mira*. Moscow: Voyenizdat, 1972.

Marchenko, A. T., and D. N. Sharinkov. *60 Tysyach Pogranichnykh Kilometrov*. Moscow: Voyenizdat, 1972.

Mareyev, I. S. *Partiyno-Politicheskaya Rabota v Sovetskoy Armii i Flotye: Uchebnoye Posobiye Dyla Vysshikh Komandnykh i Inzhenernykh Voyennykh Uchilishch*. Moscow: Voyenizdat, 1972.

Margelov, V. F. *Vozdushno-Desantnyye Voyska*. Moscow: Znaniye, 1977.

———. *Sovetskiye Vozdushno-Desantnyye*. Moscow: Voyenizdat, 1980.

Mayakovskiy, Vladimir. *Voz'mem Vintovki Novyeya*. Kaliningrad, USSR: Kaliningrad Truth Publishing House, 1973.

Medvedev, Roy A. *Let History Judge: The Origins and Consequence of Stalinism*. New York: Alfred A. Knopf, 1972.

Medvedev, Zhores A. *The Medvedev Papers*. London: Macmillan, 1970.

Milovidov, A. S. *Filosofskoye Naslediye V. I. Lenin i Problemy Sovremennoy Voyny*. Moscow: Voyenizdat, 1972.

Minasyan, M. M. *Great Patriotic War of the Soviet Union*. Moscow: Progress Publishers, 1974.

Mizikovskiy, G. B. *Oborono-Massovaya Rabota v Shkolye*. Moscow: DOSAAF Publishing House, 1975.

Morozov, N. I. *Ballisticheskiye Rakety Strategicheskovo Naznacheniya*. Moscow: Voyenizdat, 1974.

Naumenko, Yu. A., ed. *Nachal'naya Voyennaya Podgotovka,* 4th ed., rewritten. Moscow: Voyenizdat, 1982.

Nedosugov, A. M. *Na Polyakh Ucheniy*. Moscow, 1974.

Nekrich, A. M. *June 22, 1941*, translated by Vladimir Petrov and published as *"June 22, 1941"—Soviet Historians and the German Invasion*. Columbia, S.C.: University of South Carolina Press, 1968.

Newhouse, John. *Cold Dawn: The Story of SALT*. New York: Holt, Rinehart and Winston, 1973.

Nikitin, N. R. et. al. *V. I. Lenin i Sovetskiye Vooruzhennyye Sily*. Moscow: Voyenizdat, 1980.

Oberg, James E. *Red Star in Orbit*, London: Harrap, 1981.

Odintsov, A. I., ed. *Uchebnoye Posobiye po Nachal'noy Voyennoy Podgotovke*. Moscow: Voyenizdat, 1970, 1971, 1972, 1973, 1974, 1975, 1976, 1977.

Ordena Lenina Moskovskiy Voyennyy Okrug. Moscow: Voyenizdat, 1977.

Ogarkov, N. V. *Vsegda v Gotovnosti k Zashchite Otechestva*. Moscow: Voyenizdat, 1982.

Organizatsiya Varshavskovo Dogovora: 1955–1975. Moscow: Politizdat, 1975.

Pankratov, N. R. *V. I. Lenin i Sovetskiye Vooruzhennyye Sily*. Moscow: Voyenizdat, 1967.

———, ed. *Voyenno-Boyevaya Rabota Partii Bol'shevikov, 1903–1917*. Moscow: Voyenizdat, 1973.

Partiyno-Politicheskaya Rabota v Sovetskoy Armii i Voyenno-Morskom Flote. Moscow: Voyenizdat, 1982.

Pavlov, G. R., ed. *V Orlinom Krayu*. Rostov/Don: Book Publishers, 1977.

Penkovskiy, Oleg. *The Penkovskiy Papers*. New York: Doubleday & Co., 1965.

Peresada, S. A. *Zenitnyye Raketnyye Kompleksy*. Moscow: Voyenizdat, 1973.

Petrov, Yu. P. *Partiynoye Stroitel'stvo v Sovetskoy Armii i Flote 1918–1961*. Moscow: Voyenizdat, 1964.

———. *Stroitel'stvo Politorganov, Partiynykh i Komsomol'skikh Organizatsiy Armii i Flota*. Moscow: Voyenizdat, 1968.

Petrovichev, N. A., ed. *Partiynoye Stroitel'stvo*. Moscow: Politizdat, 1976.

Plotnikov, V. A., and B. V. Shipov. *Zalpy Gvardeyskikh "Katush."* Moscow: DOSAAF Publishing House, 1975.

Plyaskin, V. Ya., ed. *Inzhenernoye Obespecheniye Obshchevoyskovovo Boya*. Moscow: Voyenizdat, 1972.

Pobezhimov, I. F. *Osnovy Sovetskovo Voyennovo Zakonodatel'stva*. Moscow: Voyenizdat, 1962.

Pogranichnaya Zastava. Moscow: Politizdat, 1980.

Pogranichnyye Voyska USSR. Moscow: Nauka, 1970–1976.

Popov, A. M., ed. *Nachal'naya Voyennaya Podgotovka*. Moscow: Voyenizdat, 1978, 1979, 1980, 1981.

———. *Nachal'naya Voyennaya Podgotovka*. Moscow: DOSAAF, 1980.

Pospelov, P. N., ed. *Istoriya Velikoy Otechestvennoy Voyny Sovetskovo Soyuza, 1941–1945*. Six volumes. Moscow: Voyenizdat, 1961.

———. *Sovetskiy Tyl v Velikoy Otechestvennoy Voyne*. Moscow: Mysl' Publishing House, 1974.

———. *Velikaya Otechestvennaya Voyna Sovetskovo Soyuza: Kratkaya Istoriya*. Moscow: Voyenizdat, 1965.

Prikazano Zastupit'. Moscow: Young Guards Publishing House, 1974.

Prisyage Rodine Verny. L'vov: Kamenyar, 1977.

50 Let na Strazhe Yuzhnykh Rubezhey Otchizny. Tbilisi: Merani, 1971.

Radziyevskiy, A. I., ed. *Akademiya Imeni M. V. Frunze*. Moscow: Voyenizdat, 1972.

———, ed. *Slovar' Osnovnykh Voyennykh Terminov*. Moscow: Voyenizdat, 1965.

Reznichenko, V. G., ed. *Taktika*. Moscow: Voyenizdat, 1966.

Rodionov, P. F., ed. *Posobiye Dlya Ofitserov Zapasa Motostrelkovykh i Tankovykh Voysk*. Moscow: Voyenizdat, 1973.

Romashko, A. I. *Voyennyye Stroiteli Na Stroykakh Moskvy*. Moscow: Voyenizdat, 1972.

Rotmistrov, P. A. *Vremya i Tanki*. Moscow: Voyenizdat, 1972.

Ryabov, V. *The Soviet Armed Forces: Yesterday and Today*. Moscow: Progress Publishers, 1976.

Rytov, A. G. *Rytsari Pyatovo Okeana*. Moscow: Voyenizdat, 1968.

Safronov, I. V., ed. *Spravochnik Ofitsera Po Voyskovomu Khozyaystvu*. Moscow: Voyenizdat, 1968.

Saprykin, P. *Shkola Yunykh Letchikov*. Moscow: DOSAAF Publishing House, 1975.

Savkin, V. Ye. *Osnovnyye Printsipy Operativnoye Iskusstva i Taktiki*. Moscow: Voyenizdat, 1972.

Schneider, W., and F. P. Hoeber, eds. *Army, Man and Military Budgets*. New York: Crane, Russak & Co., 1976.

Scott, Harriet Fast. *Soviet Military Doctrine: Its Continuity—1960–1970*. Menlo Park, Calif.: Stanford Research Institute, 1971.

———. "Soviet Think Tanks—IMEMO & IUSA—and Strategy," mimeographed. Rosslyn, Va.: Strategic Studies Center, Stanford Research Institute, May 1974.

———. *Soviet Military Doctrine: Its Formulation and Dissemination*. Menlo Park, Calif.: Stanford Research Institute, 1971.

Scott, Harriet F., and William F. Scott. *The Soviet Art of War*. Boulder, Colo.: Westview Press, 1982.

———. *The Soviet Control Structure: Capabilities for Wartime Survival*. New York: Crane, Russak & Co., 1983.

Scott, William F., ed. *Selected Soviet Military Writings, 1970–1975: A Soviet View*. Washington, D.C.: Government Printing Office, 1977.

———. *Soviet Sources of Military Doctrine and Strategy*. New York: Crane, Russak & Co., 1975.

Semeyko, L. S. *Predvideniye Komandira v Boyu*. Moscow: Voyenizdat, 1966.

Serebryannikov, V. V. *Osnovy Marksistsko-Leninskovo Ucheniya o Voyne i Armii*. Moscow: Voyenizdat, 1982.

Seregeyenko, B. I. *Sovetskaya Morskaya Pekhota*. Moscow: DOSAAF Publishing House, 1971.

Severo-Kavkaztsy v Boyakh za Rodinu. Moscow: Voyenizdat, 1966.

Shavrov, I. Ye. *Lokal'nyye Voyny*. Moscow: Voyenizdat, 1981.

———, ed. *Methodologiya Voyenno-Nauchnogo Poznaniya*. Moscow: Voyenizdat, 1977.

Shingarev, S. I. *"Chatos" Idut v Ataku*. Moscow: Moscow Rabochiy, 1971.

Shkadov, I. N., ed. *Voprosy Obucheniya i Vospitaniya v Voyenno-Uchebnykh Zavedeniyakh*. Moscow, Voyenizdat, 1976.

Shtemenko, S. M. *General'nyy Shtab v Gody Voyny*. Two volumes. Moscow: Voyenizdat, 1968, 1973.

———. *Novyy Zakon i Voinskaya Sluzhba*. Moscow: Voyenizdat, 1968.

———. *The Soviet General Staff at War: 1941–1945*. Moscow: Progress Publishers, 1975.

Sidorenko, A. A. *Nastupleniye*. Moscow: Voyenizdat, 1970.

Skachkov, N. G. *Mnogobor'ye GTO*. Moscow: DOSAAF, 1982.

Skirdo, M. P. *Narod, Armiya, Polkovodets*. Moscow: Voyenizdat, 1970.

Skryl'nik, A. I. *"Zapad-81."* Moscow: Voyenizdat, 1982.

Skuybeda, P. I., ed. *Tolkovyy Slovar' Voyennykh Terminov*. Moscow: Voyenizdat, 1966.

Slovo o Pogranichnikakh. Moscow: Sov Rossiya, 1980.

Smirnov, M. V., and I. S. Baz'. *O Sovetskoy Voyennoy Nauke*. Moscow: Voyenizdat, 1960.

Sobolev, M. G., ed. *Partiyno-Politicheskaya Rabota v Sovetskikh Vooruzhennykh Silakh*. Moscow: Voyenizdat, 1974.

Sokolov, S. L. *Leninskiy Stil' v Rabote Voyennykh Kadrov*. Moscow: Voyenizdat, 1983.

Sokolovskiy, V. D. *Soviet Military Strategy*, 3d ed. Edited, with analysis and commentary, by Harriet Fast Scott. New York: Crane, Russak & Co., 1975.

Solzhenitsyn, A. *The Gulag Archipelago*. New York: Harper & Row, 1975.

Sorokin, A. I., ed. *Partiyno-Politicheskaya Rabota v Sovetskikh Vooruzhennykh Silakh*. Moscow: Voyenizdat, 1979.

Sovetskoye Administrativnoye Pravo. Moscow: Yuridicheskaya Literatura, 1981.

Sovetskaya Voyennaya Entsiklopediya. Moscow: Voyenizdat, 1976–1980 (published in 8 volumes).

Soviet Military Power. Washington, D.C.: Government Printing Office, 1981, 1984.

Sredin, G. V., et al. *Chelovek v Sovremennoy Voyne*. Moscow: Voyenizdat, 1981.

Stalin, I. V. *O Velikoy Otechestvennoy Voyne Sovetskogo Soyuze*. Moscow: Gospolitizdat, 1952.

Strokov, A. A., ed. *Istoriya Voyennovo Iskusstva*. Moscow: Voyenizdat, 1966.

———. *V. I. Lenin o Voyne i Voyennom Iskusstve*. Moscow: Nauka Publishing House, 1971.

Sukhorukov, D. S., ed. *Sovetskiye Vozdushno-Desantnyye*. Moscow: Voyenizdat, 1980.

Suntsov, N. P., ed. *Krasnoznamennyy Dal'nevostochnyy: Istoriya Krasnoznamennovo Dal'nevostochnovo Voyennovo Okruga*. Moscow: Voyenizdat, 1971.

Surinov, B. T. *Boyevoye Primeneniye Raket Sukhoputnykh Voysk*. Moscow: Voyenizdat, 1979.

Sushko, N. Ya., and S. A. Tyushkevich. *Marksizm-Leninizm o Voyne i Armii*, 4th ed. Moscow: Voyenizdat, 1965.

Sverdlov, F. D. *Takticheskiy Manevr*. Moscow: Voyenizdat, 1982.

Tabunov, N. D., and V. A. Bokarev. *Marksistsko-Leninskaya Filosofiya i Metodologicheskiye Problemy Voyennoy Teorii i Praktiki*. Moscow: Voyenizdat, 1982.

Terpilovskiy, M. V., ed. *Finansovaya Sluzhba Vooruzhennykh Sil SSSR v Period Voyny*. Moscow: Voyenizdat, 1967.

Tolubko, V. F. *Raketnyye Voyska*. Moscow: Znaniye, 1977.

Tonkikh, F. P., ed. *Osnovy Nauchnoy Organizatsii Truda v Voyenno-Uchebnykh Zavedeniyakh*. Moscow: Voyenizdat, 1974.

Ty Sluzhush v Krasnoznamennom Sredneaziatskom. Alma Ata: Kazakhstan, 1979.

Trifonenkov, P. I. *Ob Osnovnykh Zakonkakh Khoda i Iskhoda Sovremennoy Voyny*. Moscow: Voyenizdat, 1962.

Tyl Vooruzhennykh Sil v Sovremennoy Voyne. Moscow: Voyenizdat, 1975.

Tyushkevich, S. A., ed. *Filosofiya i Voyennaya Istoriya*. Moscow: Nauka, 1979.

───── . *Marksizm-Leninizm o Voyne i Armii*, 5th ed. Moscow: Voyenizdat, 1968.

───── . *Sovetskiye Vooruzhennyye Sily*. Moscow: Voyenizdat, 1978.

"Ustav Vnutrenney Sluzhby Vooruzhennykh Sil SSSR," in *Obshchevoinskiye Ustavy Vooruzhennykh Sil SSSR*. Moscow: Voyenizdat, 1979.

Ustinov, D. F. *Sluzhim Rodinye, Dely Kommunizma*. Moscow: Voyenizdat, 1982.

Vanayev, G. I. *Chernomortsy v Velikoy Otechestvennoy Voyne*. Moscow: Voyenizdat, 1978.

Varshavskiy Dogovor—Soyuz vo Imya Mira i Sotsializma. Moscow: Voyenizdat, 1980.

Vasil'ev, B. A. *Dal'nyaya Raketonosnaya*. Moscow: DOSAAF Publishing House, 1972.

Vasilevskiy, A. M. *Delo Vsey Zhizni*. Moscow: Politizdat, 1975.

Vishnyakov, N., and F. Arkhipov. *Ustroystvo Vooruzhennykh Sil SSSR*. Moscow: State Publishing House, 1930.

Vladimirov, Leonid. *The Russian Space Bluff*. New York: Dial Press, 1973.

V Nebe Kitaya 1937–1940. Moscow: Nauka, 1980.

Volkogonov, D. A., ed. *Voyna i Armiya*. Moscow: Voyenizdat, 1977.

Vorob'yev, K. A. *Vooruzhennyye Sily Razvitovo Sotsialisticheskovo Obshchestva*. Moscow: Voyenizdat, 1980.

Voyennyy Entsiklopedicheskiy Slovar'. Moscow: Voyenizdat, 1983.

Vorontsov, G. F. *Voyennyye Koalitsii i Koalitsionnyye Voyny*. Moscow: Voyenizdat, 1976.

Vysotskiy, V. I. *Tyl Sovetskoy Armii*. Moscow: Voyenizdat, 1968.

Watson, Bruce W. *Red Navy at Sea*. Boulder, Colo.: Westview Press, 1982.

Yakovlev, Alexander. *The Aim of a Lifetime*. Moscow: Progress Publishers, 1972.

───── . *Tsel' Zhizni* [Aim of a Lifetime]. Moscow: Political Literature Publishing House, 1966.

Yakovleva, L. *Tovarishch*. Moscow: Young Guards Publishing House, 1972, 1974, 1977.

Yakubovskiy, I. I. *Boyevoye Sodruzhestvo Bratskikh Narodov i Armiy*. Moscow: Voyenizdat, 1975.

Yefimov, P. I. *Boyevoy Soyuz Bratskikh Armiy*. Moscow: Voyenizdat, 1974.

Yegorov, P. T., et al. *Grazhdanskaya Oborona*. Moscow: Higher Schools Publishing House, 1966.

Yegorov, P. Ya. *Marshal Meretskov*. Moscow: Voyenizdat, 1974.

Yegorovskiy, A. A., ed. *Istorya Ural'skovo Voyennovo Okruga*. Moscow: Voyenizdat, 1970.

Yendovitskiy, N. K. *Organizatsiya Zanyatiy po Takticheskoy Podgotovke*. Moscow: DOSAAF, 1979.

Yepishev, A. A. *Ideyam Partii Verny.* Moscow: Voyenizdat, 1981.

_____ . *Mogucheye Oruzhiye Partii.* Moscow: Voyenizdat, 1973.

_____ . *Partiya—Organizator Nashikh Pobed.* Moscow: Voyenizdat, 1976.

_____ . *Some Aspects of Party-Political Work in the Soviet Armed Forces.* Moscow: Progress Publishers, 1973.

Yepishev, A. A., ed. *KPSS I Voyennoye Stroitel'stvo.* Moscow: Voyenizdat, 1982.

Yezhegodnik Bol'shoy Sovetskoy Entsiklopedii. Moscow: Soviet Encyclopedia Publishing House. Annual.

Zakharov, M. V., ed. *50 Let Vooruzhennykh Sil SSSR.* Moscow: Voyenizdat, 1968.

Zakharov, S. Ye. *Krasnoznamenny Tikhookeanskiy Flot.* Moscow: Voyenizdat, 1973.

Zakon SSSR O Vseobshchey Voinskoy Obyazannosti. Moscow: Voyenizdat, 1974.

Zakon SSSR O Vseobshchey Voinskoy Obyazannosti, 2d ed. Moscow: Voyenizdat, 1981.

Zastava, v Ruzh'ye! Moscow: Sov Rossiya, 1980.

Zemskov, V. I. *Vidi Vooruzhennykh Sil i Roda Voysk.* Moscow: DOSAAF Publishing House, 1975.

Zheltov, A. S. *Metodologicheskiye Problemy Voyennoy Teorii i Praktiki.* Moscow: Voyenizdat, 1968.

_____ . *V. I. Lenin i Sovetskiye Vooruzhennyye Sily.* Moscow: Voyenizdat, 1967.

_____ . *V. I. Lenin i Sovetskiye Vooruzhennyye Sily.* Moscow: Voyenizdat, 1980. This book is the first volume of a new "Officer's Library" series.

Zhilin, P. A. *Ocherki Sovetskoy Voyennoy Istoriografii.* Moscow: Voyenizdat, 1974.

Zhukov, G. K. *Vospominaniya i Razmyshleniya.* Moscow: Novosti Press, 1974.

Zinchenko, O. V. *My—Suvorovtsy.* Moscow: Voyenizdat, 1974.

Zolotarev, A. A., and B. F. Fedorov. *Tekhnicheskiye Sredstva Obucheniya v VVUZakh.* Moscow: Voyenizdat, 1976.

Name Index

Subject Index

About the Book and Authors

The Armed Forces of the USSR
THIRD EDITION, REVISED AND UPDATED
Harriet Fast Scott and William F. Scott

When the first edition of *The Armed Forces of the USSR* appeared in 1979, it was reviewed as "the first real textbook on the Soviet military. . . . [It] fills the needs of students and teachers and is a boon to the analyst of Soviet affairs." An updated second edition of the work appeared in 1981, shortly after the Soviet invasion of Afghanistan, while Leonid Brezhnev was still the Communist Party's general secretary.

Since then, the top Party leadership in the Kremlin has changed significantly. The Soviet Ground Forces, Air Forces, and Air Defense Forces have undergone major reorganizations, and many new faces now are seen among the generals, marshals, and admirals. New and improved weapons have entered the arsenals of the Strategic Rocket Forces and Navy. There have been changes in the laws of war and of armed combat, both of which affect military doctrine and strategy.

This new third edition of *The Armed Forces of the USSR* has been completely revised and, using the most recent sources, shows the changes that have taken place both in the Soviet military structure and the concepts upon which it is based. It is essential reading for those interested in arms control, national security, and military affairs in general.

Harriet Fast Scott, a member of the General Advisory Committee on Arms Control and Disarmament, is a consultant on Soviet military affairs to several major research organizations. Her writings on Soviet military doctrine and strategy are internationally known. **Colonel William F. Scott** (USAF, retired), following his graduation from West Point, served in a variety of flying and staff assignments. He spent four years in the USSR, first as senior air attaché (1962–1964) and later as defense and air attaché (1970–1972). Dr. Scott is a consultant to the Arms Control and Disarmament Agency and to a number of research institutions. The Scotts maintain the largest known private library of Soviet military publications in the United States.